# JOSEPHUS

LCL 433

# JOSEPHUS

## JEWISH ANTIQUITIES

### BOOKS XVIII–XIX

WITH AN ENGLISH TRANSLATION BY

## LOUIS H. FELDMAN

HARVARD UNIVERSITY PRESS

CAMBRIDGE, MASSACHUSETTS

LONDON, ENGLAND

*First published 1965*
*Reprinted 1969, 1981, 1992, 1996*

ISBN 0-674-99477-9

*Printed in Great Britain by St Edmundsbury Press Ltd,
Bury St Edmunds, Suffolk, on acid-free paper.
Bound by Hunter & Foulis Ltd, Edinburgh, Scotland.*

# CONTENTS

For maps see the concluding volume of Josephus:
*Jewish Antiquities*, Book XX, and General Index.

# APPENDICES

# CONTENTS

# PREFATORY NOTE

THE text of this volume, as of the previous volumes of this version of Josephus, is substantially that of Niese in his *editio maior*, but with a number of changes suggested by other scholars. The manuscript tradition for the last ten books of the *Antiquities* is discussed at length by Niese in the third volume of his edition, pp. iii-lvii, and summarized briefly by Ralph Marcus in the prefatory note to the sixth volume of this series. In translating these books I have, in a number of places, adopted felicitous renderings found in the rough draft left by Dr. Thackeray. Whiston's version may contain many inaccuracies, but it often is hard to improve upon for sheer verve of style, and I have not hesitated in several places to adopt his phraseology. In composing the commentary, I have learned much, especially as to bibliography, from the notes of the late Prof. Ralph Marcus in his personal copy of Josephus, which Mrs. Marcus has been kind enough to place at my disposal.

The text, translation, and commentary of this edition were submitted to the printer in September, 1960. Scholarship after this date has elucidated several points in the commentary ; for references see my critical bibliography, *Scholarship on Philo and Josephus (1937–1962)*, published this year under the auspices of Yeshiva University.

# PREFATORY NOTE

In a number of textual matters I have received assistance from Prof. Hans Petersen and from the editors of the Loeb Library. In the translation I owe much to the suggestions of my mentor, Prof. James A. Notopoulos, and the editors. Rabbi Isaiah Molotin has elucidated several passages for me from his fund of Talmudic knowledge. Finally, in the preparation of the index,* I have been aided greatly by Nathan H. Epstein, Julian Plante, Fred Schreiber, Emanuel White, and, above all, my wife Rivkah. To all of them I am sincerely grateful.

Louis H. Feldman

13 *August* 1963

* The index, covering all the works of Josephus, has been compiled independently of those at the end of volumes I and III of this series, as well as of that of Niese in his *editio maior*, but it has been checked against all of these.

# JEWISH ANTIQUITIES

# ΙΟΥΔΑΪΚΗΣ ΑΡΧΑΙΟΛΟΓΙΑΣ

## ΒΙΒΛΙΟΝ ΙΗ

(i. 1) Κυρίνιος[1] δὲ τῶν εἰς τὴν βουλὴν συναγο-
μένων ἀνὴρ τάς τε ἄλλας ἀρχὰς ἐπιτετελεκὼς καὶ
διὰ πασῶν ὁδεύσας ὕπατος γενέσθαι τά τε ἄλλα
ἀξιώματι μέγας σὺν ὀλίγοις ἐπὶ Συρίας παρῆν, ὑπὸ
Καίσαρος δικαιοδότης τοῦ ἔθνους ἀπεσταλμένος καὶ

---

[1] Κυρήνιος AMWE Eusebius : Cyrenius ut vid. Lat.

---

[a] Publius Sulpicius Quirinius, after having been consul in
12 B.C., had distinguished himself by leading a successful expedition against the wild Homanadenses in Asia Minor near
Galatia (see Tacitus' report, *Ann.* iii. 48, of Tiberius' eulogy
at Quirinius' funeral). Luke ii. 2 says that Quirinius was
governing Syria at the time that the census took place in
which Joseph and Mary went up to Bethlehem ; and some
authorities, notably W. Ramsay (*Was Christ Born at Bethlehem : A Study in the Credibility of Luke*, 1898, pp. 229-283),
attempt to vindicate Luke by arguing that Quirinius was
governor of Syria before 4 B.C. as well as at the time (A.D. 6)
here cited by Josephus. But L. R. Taylor, " Quirinius and
the Census of Judaea," *Am. Jour. of Philol.* liv, 1953, pp.
120-133, argues convincingly that at the time of the Homana-
densian War Quirinius was more probably governor of Galatia (so also R. K. Sherk, *The Legates of Galatia (Johns
Hopkins Stud. in Hist. and Pol. Sc.*, Ser. 69, 1951, pp. 21-24,
who cites abundant bibliography). In any case, our list of
the governors of Syria for the period before the birth of Jesus,

# JEWISH ANTIQUITIES

## BOOK XVIII

(i. 1) QUIRINIUS,[a] a Roman senator who had proceeded through all the magistracies to the consulship
and a man who was extremely distinguished in other
respects, arrived [b] in Syria, dispatched by Caesar [c] to
be governor [d] of the nation and to make an assess-

Assessment of property in Judaea by Quirinius.

which seems complete, does not have the name of Quirinius ;
and Tertullian, *Adv. Marcion.* iv. 19, interestingly enough,
says that the enrolment mentioned in Luke took place under
Saturninus (see the discussion by T. Corbishley, " Quirinius
and the Census : Re-study of the Evidence," *Klio* xxix
[= Neue Folge, xi], 1936, pp. 91-92). Luke ii. 2 can be vin-
dicated only if we translate with F. M. Heichelheim (" Roman
Syria," in T. Frank, *An Economic Survey of Ancient Rome,*
iv, 1938, pp. 160-161), " This census was the first before that
under the prefectureship of Quirinius in Syria."

[b] The translation " arrived with a small retinue " is unlikely. I take σὺν ὀλίγοις with μέγας to mean " one among
few," *i.e.* " extremely."

[c] Augustus.

[d] *Legatus Augusti pro praetore.* J. A. O. Larsen, " Tituli
Asiae Minoris, II, 508," *Class. Philol.* xxxviii, 1943, pp. 188-
189, observes that the word δικαιοδότης is found only here and
in inscriptions from Lycia in the sense of " governor." He
plausibly suggests that the word was not so much a title for
a governor as an honorary appellation, much like *soter* or
*euergetes.* It would emphasize the high regard with which
the governor was held as an honest judge, the duties of the
governor (in Lycia, at least) being largely judicial.

3

2 τιμητὴς τῶν οὐσιῶν γενησόμενος, Κωπώνιός τε
αὐτῷ συγκαταπέμπεται τάγματος τῶν ἱππέων,
ἡγησόμενος Ἰουδαίων τῇ ἐπὶ πᾶσιν ἐξουσίᾳ. παρῆν
δὲ καὶ Κυρίνιος εἰς τὴν Ἰουδαίαν προσθήκην τῆς
Συρίας γενομένην ἀποτιμησόμενός τε αὐτῶν τὰς
οὐσίας καὶ ἀποδωσόμενος τὰ Ἀρχελάου χρήματα.
3 οἱ δὲ καίπερ τὸ κατ' ἀρχὰς ἐν δεινῷ φέροντες τὴν
ἐπὶ ταῖς ἀπογραφαῖς ἀκρόασιν ὑπεκατέβησαν τοῦ
μὴ[1] εἰς πλέον ἐναντιοῦσθαι πείσαντος αὐτοὺς τοῦ
ἀρχιερέως Ἰωαζάρου,[2] Βοηθοῦ δὲ οὗτος υἱὸς ἦν.
καὶ οἱ μὲν ἡττηθέντες τοῦ Ἰωαζάρου τῶν λόγων
4 ἀπετίμων τὰ χρήματα μηδὲν ἐνδοιάσαντες· Ἰούδας
δὲ Γαυλανίτης ἀνὴρ[3] ἐκ πόλεως ὄνομα Γάμαλα[4]
Σάδδωκον[5] Φαρισαῖον προσλαβόμενος ἠπείγετο ἐπὶ
ἀποστάσει, τήν τε ἀποτίμησιν οὐδὲν ἄλλο ἢ ἀντι-

---

[1] μὴ] A : om. MWE.
[2] Ιοζαρο Lat.
[3] Ἰούδας δὲ Γαυλανίτης ἀνὴρ] A : Γαυλανίτης δέ τις ἀνὴρ
Ἰούδας MWE.
[4] A : Γαμάλα MW : Γαμάλας Eus. : Γάβαλα E.
[5] Σάδδωκον A : Σάδουκον M : Σάδδουκον WE Exc. Peiresc. :
Saddocum Lat. : Σαδὼκ Zonaras : Σάδδοκον et Σάδδοχον
Eusebii codd.

---

[a] First procurator of Judaea. Cf. the parallel passage in
B.J. ii. 117, which adds that his powers included the infliction
of capital punishment. The Mishnah, Middot i. 3, mentions
a Gate of Kiponus as one of the five gates of the temple. It
has been speculated by M. Simon, in the Soncino translation
ad loc., that this gate may have been named after Coponius.
[b] See Ant. xvii. 355.

ment of their property. Coponius,[a] a man of equestrian rank, was sent along with him to rule over the
Jews with full authority. Quirinius also visited
Judaea, which had been annexed to Syria, in order to
make an assessment of the property of the Jews and
to liquidate the estate of Archelaus.[b] Although the
Jews were at first shocked to hear of the registration
of property, they gradually condescended, yielding
to the arguments of the high priest Joazar,[c] the son
of Boethus, to go no further in opposition. So those
who were convinced by him declared, without shilly-
shallying, the value of their property. But a certain
Judas,[d] a Gaulanite[e] from a city named Gamala,[f]
who had enlisted the aid of Saddok, a Pharisee, threw
himself into the cause of rebellion. They said that
the assessment carried with it a status amounting to

The revolt
inspired by
Judas the
Gaulanite
and Saddok
the
Pharisee.

[c] In *Ant.* xvii. 339, we learn that Archelaus accused Joazar
of conspiring against him, and subsequently deposed him
from the high priesthood.

[d] In the parallel passage in *B.J.* ii. 118 (see Thackeray's
note) and in *Ant.* xviii. 23, Josephus refers to Judas as the
founder of the Fourth Philosophy. In Acts v. 37 he is mentioned by Gamaliel as having incited the Jews in the days of
the census. See also *Ant.* xx. 102. J. S. Kennard, " Judas
of Galilee and His Clan," *Jewish Quart. Rev.* xxxvi, 1945-46,
pp. 281-286, plausibly identifies this Judas, with the Judas
who seized the opportunity to aspire to sovereignty in Galilee
(*B.J.* ii. 56).

[e] Gaulanitis is east of the Jordan and of the Sea of Galilee.
In *B.J.* ii. 118 Judas is called a Galilaean.

[f] A city in lower Gaulanitis on the Transjordanian side of
the Sea of Galilee (not to be confused with the city by the
same name in Upper Galilee), so called because it is situated
on a hill shaped like a camel (Hebrew *gamal*). It is near the
site of modern *Jamle*. See F.-M. Abel, *Géographie de la
Palestine*, ii, 1938, p. 325 ; and A. Schlatter, " Die hebrä-
ischen Namen bei Josephus," *Beitr. z. Ford. christl. Theol.*
xvii. 3-4, 1913, p. 35.

κρυς δουλείαν ἐπιφέρειν λέγοντες καὶ τῆς ἐλευ-
5 θερίας ἐπ' ἀντιλήψει παρακαλοῦντες τὸ ἔθνος· ὡς
παρασχὸν μὲν κατορθοῦν εἰς τὸ εὔδαιμον ἀνακει-
μένης τῆς κτήσεως,¹ σφαλεῖσιν δὲ τοῦ ταύτης περι-
όντος² ἀγαθοῦ τιμὴν καὶ κλέος ποιήσεσθαι τοῦ
μεγαλόφρονος, καὶ τὸ θεῖον οὐκ ἄλλως ἢ ἐπὶ συμπράξει τῶν βουλευμάτων εἰς τὸ κατορθοῦν συμπρο-
θυμεῖσθαι μᾶλλον, ἂν μεγάλων ἐρασταὶ³ τῇ διανοίᾳ
καθιστάμενοι μὴ ἐξαφίωνται φόνου⁴ τοῦ ἐπ' αὐτοῖς.
6 καὶ ἡδονῇ γὰρ τὴν ἀκρόασιν ὧν λέγοιεν ἐδέχοντο οἱ
ἄνθρωποι, προύκοπτεν ἐπὶ μέγα ἡ ἐπιβουλὴ⁵ τοῦ
τολμήματος,⁶ κακόν τε οὐκ ἔστιν, οὗ μὴ φυέντος ἐκ
τῶνδε τῶν ἀνδρῶν καὶ περαιτέρω τοῦ εἰπεῖν ἀνε-
7 πλήσθη τὸ ἔθνος· πολέμων τε ἐπαγωγαῖς οὐχ οἷων⁷
τε⁸ ἄπαυστον τὴν βίαν ἔχειν, καὶ ἀποστερήσεσι⁹
φίλων, οἳ καὶ ἐπελαφρύνοιεν τὸν πόνον, λῃστηρίων
τε μεγάλων ἐπιθέσεσιν καὶ διαφθοραῖς ἀνδρῶν τῶν

¹ φύσεως Exc.
² A : παριόντος MW.
³ A¹ : ἐργασταὶ ex corr. A : ἐργάται MW Exc.
⁴ codd. Exc. : πόνου Hudson.
⁵ ἐπιβολὴ E ed. pr. Exc.
⁶ προύκοπτεν . . . τολμήματος] in magnum malum seditio
illorum et audacia prorumpebat Lat.
⁷ οὐχ οἵων] Bekker : οὐχ οἷον MW : οὐ..χ' ὧν (corr. ex
οὐχ..ων) A.
⁸ τε] MW Exc. : τὸ A¹ : τε οὐκ Hudson.
⁹ Bekker : ἀποστέρησιν codd.

---

ᵃ H. St. J. Thackeray, *Selections from Josephus*, 1919, p.
73, notes that the Greek is modelled on Thucydides i. 122 :
defeat " brings nothing else than downright slavery " (ἀντι-
κρυς δουλείαν). One may add that in the next passage, §§ 5-8,
one is reminded so much of Thucydides iii. 82-84 (which has
a similar context—the analysis of the psychology of civil war)
that H. Drüner, *Untersuchungen über Josephus*, 1896, pp.
1-34, esp. p. 12, and Thackeray, *Josephus, the Man and the*

downright slavery,[a] no less, and appealed to the nation to make a bid for independence. They urged that in case of success the Jews would have laid the foundation of prosperity, while if they failed to obtain any such boon, they would win honour and renown for their lofty aim ; and that Heaven would be their zealous helper to no lesser end than the furthering of their enterprise until it succeeded—all the more if with high devotion in their hearts they stood firm and did not shrink from the bloodshed [b] that might be necessary  Since the populace, when they heard their appeals, responded gladly, the plot to strike boldly made serious progress ; and so these men sowed the seed of every kind of misery, which so afflicted the nation that words are inadequate. When wars are set afoot that are bound to rage beyond control, and when friends are done away with who might have alleviated the suffering, when raids are made by great hordes of brigands and men of the highest standing are assassinated, it is supposed to be

*Historian*, 1929, pp. 110-114, have argued that *Ant.* xvii-xix is the work not of Josephus but of an assistant who was steeped in Thucydides. But *cf.* H. Petersen, " Real and Alleged Literary Projects of Josephus," *Am. Jour. of Philol.* lxxix, 1958, p. 261 n. 5, who argues cogently against this hypothesis, noting that many Thucydidean reminiscences are found in the earlier books of the *Antiquities*, and that we can account for the greater preponderance of Thucydidean phrases in these books by assuming that Josephus was, while writing xvii-xix, making an intensive study of Thucydides (so also G. C. Richards, " The Composition of Josephus' Antiquities," *Class. Quart.* xxxiii, 1939, p. 39) to improve his own style.

[b] I have adopted the reading of the MSS., since, as can be seen from § 8, the Fourth Philosophy did not shrink from murder to attain its aims. Hudson's emendation, πόνου, gives " did not shrink from the hardship that great aims require."

πρώτων, δόξα μὲν τοῦ ὀρθουμένου τῶν κοινῶν,
8 ἔργῳ δὲ οἰκείων κερδῶν ἐλπίσιν. ἐξ ὧν στάσεις
τε ἐφύησαν δι' αὐτὰς[1] καὶ φόνος πολιτικός, ὁ μὲν
ἐμφυλίοις σφαγαῖς μανίᾳ τῶν ἀνθρώπων εἴς τε ἀλλήλους καὶ αὐτοὺς χρωμένων ἐπιθυμίᾳ τοῦ μὴ
λείπεσθαι τῶν ἀντικαθεστηκότων, ὁ δὲ τῶν πολεμίων, λιμός τε εἰς ὑστάτην ἀνακείμενος ἀναισχυντίαν,
καὶ πόλεων ἁλώσεις καὶ κατασκαφαί, μέχρι δὴ καὶ
τὸ ἱερὸν τοῦ θεοῦ ἐνείματο πυρὶ τῶν πολεμίων ἥδε
9 ἡ στάσις. οὕτως ἄρα ἡ τῶν πατρίων καίνισις[2] καὶ
μεταβολὴ μεγάλας ἔχει ῥοπὰς τοῦ ἀπολουμένου
τοῖς συνελθοῦσιν, εἴ γε καὶ Ἰούδας καὶ Σάδδωκος
τετάρτην φιλοσοφίαν ἐπείσακτον ἡμῖν ἐγείραντες
καὶ ταύτης ἐραστῶν εὐπορηθέντες πρός τε τὸ παρὸν
θορύβων τὴν πολιτείαν ἐνέπλησαν καὶ τῶν αὖθις
κακῶν κατειληφότων ῥίζας ἐφυτεύσαντο τῷ ἀσυν-
10 ήθει πρότερον φιλοσοφίας τοιᾶσδε· περὶ ἧς ὀλίγα
βούλομαι διελθεῖν, ἄλλως τε ἐπεὶ καὶ τῷ κατ' αὐτῶν[3] σπουδασθέντι τοῖς νεωτέροις ὁ φθόρος τοῖς
πράγμασι συνέτυχε.
11 (2) Ἰουδαίοις φιλοσοφίαι τρεῖς ἦσαν ἐκ τοῦ πάνυ
ἀρχαίου τῶν πατρίων, ἥ τε τῶν Ἐσσηνῶν καὶ ἡ
τῶν Σαδδουκαίων, τρίτην δὲ ἐφιλοσόφουν οἱ Φαρισαῖοι λεγόμενοι. καὶ τυγχάνει μέντοι περὶ αὐτῶν
ἡμῖν εἰρημένα ἐν τῇ δευτέρᾳ βίβλῳ τοῦ Ἰουδαϊκοῦ

[1] δι' αὐτὰς] om. E.
[2] E: κένωσις, i. marg. γρ κοίνωσις A: κενώσεις MW
Exc.: novitas Lat.
[3] αὐτὴν Holwerda.

8

the common welfare that is upheld, but the truth is
that in such cases the motive is private gain. They
sowed the seed from which sprang strife between
factions and the slaughter of fellow citizens. Some
were slain in civil strife, for these men madly had re-
course to butchery of each other and of themselves
from a longing not to be outdone by their opponents ;
others were slain by the enemy in war. Then came
famine, reserved to exhibit the last degree of shame-
lessness, followed by the storming and razing of cities
until at last the very temple of God was ravaged by
the enemy's fire through this revolt. Here is a lesson
that an innovation and reform in ancestral traditions
weighs heavily in the scale in leading to the destruction of the congregation of the people.[a]   In this case
certainly, Judas and Saddok started among us an
intrusive fourth school of philosophy ; and when they
had won an abundance of devotees, they filled the
body politic immediately with tumult, also planting
the seeds of those troubles which subsequently overtook it, all because of the novelty of this hitherto unknown philosophy that I shall now describe.   My
reason for giving this brief account of it is chiefly that
the zeal which Judas and Saddok inspired in the
younger element meant the ruin of our cause.[b]

(2) The Jews, from the most ancient times, had
three philosophies pertaining to their traditions, that
of the Essenes, that of the Sadducees, and, thirdly,
that of the group called the Pharisees. To be sure, I
have spoken about them in the second book of the

The three
ancient
Jewish
philoso-
phies.

----

[a] Or " the destruction of those who handle it."
[b] The text is difficult to construe. Prof. Petersen, in a private communication, translates : " especially since, precisely
because of the popularity accorded them, destruction has be-
fallen the succeeding generations."

πολέμου, μνησθήσομαι δ' ὅμως καὶ νῦν αὐτῶν ἐπ'
ὀλίγον.

12 (3) Οἵ τε γὰρ Φαρισαῖοι τὴν δίαιταν ἐξευτελί-
ζουσιν οὐδὲν ἐς τὸ μαλακώτερον ἐνδιδόντες, ὧν τε
ὁ λόγος κρίνας παρέδωκεν ἀγαθῶν ἕπονται τῇ ἡγεμονίᾳ περιμάχητον ἡγούμενοι τὴν φυλακὴν ὧν
ὑπαγορεύειν¹ ἠθέλησεν. τιμῆς γε τοῖς ἡλικίᾳ προ-
ήκουσιν παραχωροῦσιν οὐδ' ἐπ' ἀντιλέξει τῶν
13 εἰσηγηθέντων θράσει² ἐπαιρόμενοι.³ πράσσεσθαί τε
εἱμαρμένῃ τὰ πάντα ἀξιοῦντες οὐδὲ τοῦ ἀνθρωπείου
τὸ βουλόμενον τῆς ἐπ' αὐτοῖς⁴ ὁρμῆς ἀφαιροῦνται

¹ ἀπαγορεύειν E : προαγορεύειν ed. pr.
² θράσει] E (spatio vacuo ante θράσει relicto) : ταῦτα οἱ θράσει codd. : ταῦτα θράσει ed. pr. : ταῦτα ἢ θράσει coni. Niese.
³ οὐδ' . . . ἐπαιρόμενοι] ita ut nec contrarium quiddam
aliquando respondeant Lat.
⁴ ἐπ' αὐτοῖς] E : ἀπ' αὐτῆς codd.

ᵃ B.J. ii. 119-166. Josephus here neglects to refer to his
brief discussion of the three philosophies in Ant. xiii. 171-173.
As Marcus states ·in his note on Ant. xiii. 171, Josephus
presents the three sects in such a way as to make them more
intelligible to Greek readers. Thus he elsewhere compares
the Pharisees to Stoics (Vita 12) and the Essenes to the Pytha-
goreans (Ant. xv. 371).
ᵇ Josephus perhaps thus intends to indicate a similarity
between the Pharisees and the Stoics (cf. note on § 11), and
to present a contrast with the Sadducees, who, we are told by
the Rabbis, used silver and gold vessels all their lives—" not
because they were ostentatious [lit. " of arrogant disposition "]; but the Sadducees said, ' It is a tradition amongst the
Pharisees to afflict themselves in this world; yet in the world
to come they will have nothing.' " (Abot de-Rabbi Natan v,
trans. by J. Goldin.)
ᶜ Whiston's translation, " they follow the guidance of
reason,"· which many scholars have adopted, is probably
wrong, since, as Thackeray remarks (Selections, p. 158 n. 4),
λόγος would seem to have the same meaning here and in the

*Jewish War,*[a] but nevertheless I shall here too dwell on them for a moment.

(3) The Pharisees simplify their standard of living, making no concession to luxury.[b] They follow the guidance of that which their doctrine [c] has selected and transmitted as good, attaching the chief importance to the observance of those commandments which it has seen fit to dictate to them. They show respect and deference to their elders, nor do they rashly presume to contradict their proposals. Though they postulate that everything is brought about by fate,[d] still they do not deprive the human will of the pursuit of what is in man's power,[e] since it was God's

opening sentences (§§ 16-18) presenting the doctrines of the Sadducees and the Essenes. G. F. Moore, " Fate and Free Will in the Jewish Philosophies according to Josephus," *Harv. Theol. Rev.* xxii, 1929, p. 374, is, therefore, on dubious ground when he says that Josephus is here speaking of the reasonable living of the Pharisees and that this is one of the respects in which the reader is expected to see a similarity between them and the Stoics ( *Vita* 12).

[d] As Marcus, in his note on the parallel passage, *Ant.* xiii. 172, remarks, fate (εἱμαρμένη) is the Greek equivalent of what we should call Providence. So also G. F. Moore, *op. cit.* p. 379, who notes that for εἱμαρμένη in the definition of the Greek philosophical schools, especially the Stoic, there was no equivalent word in Hebrew—and no corresponding conception.

[e] The same point about the balance between fate and free will is made in *Ant.* xiii. 172. A similar point of view, reflecting Pharisaic belief, is found in the Talmudic sayings " Everything is foreseen, yet freedom of choice is given " (*Abot* iii. 19) and " All is in the hands of Heaven except the fear of Heaven " (*Berachot* 33 b). The same point is illustrated in the following : " The angel appointed over conception is named Lailah. He takes a seminal drop, sets it before the Holy One blessed be He, and asks, ' Sovereign of the Universe ! What is to become of this drop ? Is it to develop into a person strong or weak, wise or foolish, rich or poor ? ' But

δοκῆσαν τῷ θεῷ κρᾶσιν¹ γενέσθαι² καὶ τῷ ἐκείνης
βουλευτηρίῳ καὶ τῶν ἀνθρώπων τὸ ἐθελῆσαν³ προσ-
14 χωρεῖν μετ' ἀρετῆς ἢ κακίας. ἀθάνατόν τε ἰσχὺν
ταῖς ψυχαῖς πίστις αὐτοῖς εἶναι καὶ ὑπὸ χθονὸς δι-
καιώσεις τε καὶ τιμὰς οἷς ἀρετῆς ἢ κακίας ἐπιτήδευσις ἐν τῷ βίῳ γέγονεν, καὶ ταῖς μὲν εἱργμὸν
ἀίδιον προτίθεσθαι,⁴ ταῖς δὲ ῥᾳστώνην τοῦ ἀνα-
15 βιοῦν. καὶ δι' αὐτὰ τοῖς τε δήμοις πιθανώτατοι
τυγχάνουσιν καὶ ὁπόσα θεῖα εὐχῶν τε ἔχεται⁵ καὶ
ἱερῶν ποιήσεως ἐξηγήσει τῇ ἐκείνων τυγχάνουσιν
πρασσόμενα. εἰς τοσόνδε ἀρετῆς αὐτοῖς αἱ πόλεις
ἐμαρτύρησαν ἐπιτηδεύσει τοῦ ἐπὶ πᾶσι κρείσσονος
ἔν τε τῇ διαίτῃ τοῦ βίου καὶ λόγοις.
16 (4) Σαδδουκαίοις δὲ τὰς ψυχὰς ὁ λόγος συνα-
φανίζει τοῖς σώμασι, φυλακῇ δὲ οὐδαμῶς τινων

¹ MWE : κρίσιν A.
² δοκῆσαν. . . γενέσθαι] iudicium dei futurum esse sentiunt Lat.
³ τὸ ἐθελῆσαν] E : τῷ θελήσαντι MW : τῷ ἐθελήσαντι A : τῷ θελήσοντι coni. Niese.
⁴ Ernesti : προστίθεσθαι codd. E.
⁵ A : ἔπεται MW.

no mention is made of its becoming wicked or righteous " (*Niddah* 16 b). *Cf.* also Ecclesiasticus xv. 11-17 and Psalms of Solomon ix. 7-9.

ᵃ This difficult passage is thus translated by Thackeray (*Harv. Theol. Rev.* xxv, 1932, p. 93) : " While maintaining that all things are brought about by Fate, they yet do not deprive the human will of the impulse to do them, it having pleased God that there should be a coalition between Fate's council-chamber and such men as choose to associate with it, with virtuous or vicious intent."

good pleasure that there should be a fusion and that the will of man with his virtue and vice should be admitted to the council-chamber of fate.[a] They believe that souls have power to survive death and that there are rewards and punishments under the earth [b] for those who have led lives of virtue or vice : eternal imprisonment is the lot of evil souls, while the good souls receive an easy passage to a new life.[c] Because of these views they are, as a matter of fact, extremely influential among the townsfolk ; and all prayers [d] and sacred rites of divine worship are performed according to their exposition. This is the great tribute that the inhabitants of the cities, by practising the highest ideals both in their way of living and in their discourse, have paid to the excellence of the Pharisees.

(4) The Sadducees hold that the soul perishes along with the body. They own no observance of any sort (ii) The Sadducees.

[b] Again Josephus is using a phrase for the sake of his Greek audience. S. Baron, *A Social and Religious History of the Jews*, ii², 1952, pp. 344-345 n. 46, points, however, to *B.J.* iii. 373-375, where Josephus says that the souls of the righteous are allotted the most holy place in heaven.

[c] Thackeray, *Selections*, p. 159, gives a cross-reference to *B.J.* iii. 374 (" their souls . . . are allotted the most holy place in heaven, whence in the revolution of the ages, they return to find in chaste bodies a new habitation "), in which Josephus harangues his men on the evil of suicide. This passage in *B.J.*, says Thackeray, contains a reference to metempsychosis. But our passage, the passage in *B.J.*, and the one in *Contra Ap.* ii. 218 which Thackeray cites in his note on *B.J.* iii. 374, refer not to metempsychosis, which was not a tenet of the Pharisees, but to the belief in resurrection, which was a central doctrine of the Pharisees. *Cf.* 2 Macc. vii. 9, which employs ἀναβίωσις, the noun corresponding to the verb ἀναβιόω (the word used by Josephus in our passage) in a clear reference to resurrection.

[d] Or " vows."

μεταποίησις αὐτοῖς ἢ τῶν νόμων· πρὸς γὰρ τοὺς
διδασκάλους σοφίας, ἣν μετίασιν, ἀμφιλογεῖν ἀρε-
17 τὴν ἀριθμοῦσιν. εἰς ὀλίγους δὲ ἄνδρας οὗτος ὁ
λόγος ἀφίκετο, τοὺς μέντοι πρώτους τοῖς ἀξιώμασι,
πράσσεταί τε ἀπ᾽ αὐτῶν οὐδὲν ὡς εἰπεῖν· ὁπότε γὰρ
ἐπ᾽ ἀρχὰς παρέλθοιεν, ἀκουσίως μὲν καὶ κατ᾽ ἀνάγκας, προσχωροῦσι δ᾽ οὖν οἷς ὁ Φαρισαῖος λέγει διὰ
τὸ μὴ ἄλλως ἀνεκτοὺς γενέσθαι τοῖς πλήθεσιν.
18 (5) Ἐσσηνοῖς δὲ ἐπὶ μὲν θεῷ καταλείπειν φιλεῖ
τὰ πάντα ὁ λόγος, ἀθανατίζουσιν δὲ τὰς ψυχὰς
περιμάχητον ἡγούμενοι τοῦ δικαίου τὴν πρόσοδον.[1]

---

[1] πρόοδον coni. Post.

---

[a] The Sadducees accepted the written but not the oral Law,
whereas the Pharisees accepted both. The Sadducees, however, it should be remarked, had their own traditions, as we
can see from such passages as Mishnah, *Makkot* i. 6 ; but
these were *gezerot* (decrees) and not based on the oral Law.

[b] D. Daube, " Rabbinic Methods of Interpretation and
Hellenistic Rhetoric," *Heb. Union Coll. Ann.* xxi[i], 1949, p.
243, remarks that the Sadducees had evidently taken over
from the Hellenistic schools of philosophy the ideal of work-
ing out any problems by unfettered argument and counter-
argument. But there is no indication of any contact between
the Sadducees and the Hellenistic schools ; and, in any case,
even a cursory examination of the Talmud will reveal that the
Pharisees were no whit inferior to the Sadducees in skill of
disputation. What Josephus means when he says that the
Sadducees are very argumentative is that they, as he puts it
in *B.J.* ii. 166, " are, even among themselves, rather boorish
in their behaviour, and in their intercourse with their peers
are as rude as to aliens."

[c] *Cf.* the remark of the Sadducee to his son in the Babylonian Talmud, *Yoma* 19 b : " My son, although we are
Sadducees, we are afraid of the Pharisees." That the wives
of the Sadducees followed the Pharisaic rulings with respect
to the laws of menstruation is indicated in *Niddah* 33 b.

[d] A much fuller discussion of the Essenes is found in *B.J.*

apart from the laws [a] ; in fact, they reckon it a virtue
to dispute with the teachers of the path of wisdom
that they pursue.[b] There are but few men to whom
this doctrine has been made known, but these are
men of the highest standing. They accomplish
practically nothing, however. For whenever they
assume some office, though they submit unwillingly
and perforce, yet submit they do to the formulas of
the Pharisees, since otherwise the masses would not
tolerate them.[c]

(5) [d] The doctrine of the Essenes is wont to leave (iii) The
everything in the hands of God. They regard the Essenes.
soul as immortal and believe that they ought to
strive especially to draw near to righteousness.[e] They

ii. 120-161. Most of the points peculiar to the present exposition—the number of the Essenes, their employment in agri-
culture, their attitude toward sacrifices and slavery, their ex-
clusion from the temple—are also found in Philo, *Quod Omnis
Probus Liber Sit* 75-91, upon whom Josephus may have
drawn. *Cf.* M. Smith, " The Description of the Essenes in
Josephus and the Philosophumena," *Heb. Union Coll. Ann.*
xxix, 1958, pp. 278-279, and literature cited there.

[e] The meaning of πρόσοδον presents a problem. Whiston
renders the passage thus : " that the rewards of righteousness
are to be earnestly striven for." Thackeray, *Selections*, p.
160, also translates " rewards " and in a footnote cites the
literal meaning, " revenue." Prof. Post suggests that it may
mean " an income " of righteousness ; and one is reminded
of the list of the ten good deeds (*Shabbat* 127 a) of which,
according to Pharisaic doctrine, a man enjoys the fruits in
this world, while the stock remains for him for the world to
come. But J. Strugnell, " Flavius Josephus and the Essenes :
*Antiquities* xviii. 18-22," *Jour. of Bibl. Lit.* lxxxvii, 1958, p.
109, rightly questions such an interpretation since this motive
of conduct seems odd for Essene belief. Moreover, the meaning " returns " or " revenues " occurs mostly in the plural,
though Thucydides, of whom, as has been noted, Josephus
is fond as a model particularly in these later books, does
occasionally (ii. 97 and iii. 13) use it in the singular. The

15

19 εἰς δὲ τὸ ἱερὸν ἀναθήματα στέλλοντες θυσίας ἐπιτελοῦσιν[1] διαφορότητι ἁγνειῶν, ἃς νομίζοιεν, καὶ
δι' αὐτὸ εἰργόμενοι τοῦ κοινοῦ[2] τεμενίσματος ἐφ'
αὑτῶν τὰς θυσίας ἐπιτελοῦσιν. βέλτιστοι δὲ ἄλλως

[1] ἐπιτελοῦσι] codd. : οὐκ ἐπιτελοῦσι E : non celebrant Lat.
[2] κοινοῦ] i. marg. γρ τοῦ καινοῦ A.

singular is more commonly used in the sense of " approach "
or " admission " (cf. Psalm i. 6 : ὁδὸν δικαίων, " the way of the
righteous "). The phrase should, strictly speaking, be πρόσοδον πρὸς τὸ δίκαιον, but here, as Prof. Petersen reminds me,
the mere genitive is more easily explained, since the preposi-
tion dropped is also part of the compound noun. If Strugnell's hypothesis equating the sect of the Dead Sea Scrolls
with the Essenes is correct, the meaning " approach " is
further strengthened by the close parallels which he cites (p.
109), 1 QH vii. 14 and 1 QS iv. 21. Another possible interpretation is " the approach of the righteous one," and would
refer to the strong Messianic aspirations of the Essenes (cf. also
the crucial importance of the " Teacher of Righteousness "
in the Dead Sea sect). If we emend to πρόοδον, the meaning
would be " the advance [or " progress "] of righteousness."

[a] Though the Epitome and the Latin version have the
negative—a reading adopted by E. Schürer, Geschichte des
jüdischen Volkes im Zeitalter Jesu Christi, ii[4], 1907, p. 663
n. 50 ; E. Meyer, Ursprung und Anfänge des Christentums,
ii, 1925, p. 397 n. 4 ; and¦ M. Friedländer, Die religiösen
Bewegungen innerhalb des Judentums im Zeitalter Jesu,
1905, p. 156, among others—the manuscripts omit it. Those
who insert the negative cite Philo, Quod Omnis Probus Liber
Sit 75, who says that the Essenes " have shown themselves
especially devout in the service of God not by offering sacrifices of animals but by resolving to sanctify their minds."
As R. Marcus, " Pharisees, Essenes, and Gnostics," Jour. of
Bibl. Lit. lxxiii, 1954, p. 158, notes, this does not mean that
the Essenes disapproved of animal sacrifices ; it means merely
that this was not central in their pursuit of piety. Strugnell,
op. cit. p. 114, suggests two possible translations. The first is:
" Although the Essenes send ἀναθήματα to the temple, they
do not sacrifice [sc. " there," rather than sc. " at all "] because
of a difference about the ἁγνεῖαι that should be used." The

16

send votive offerings to the temple, but perform their sacrifices [a] employing a different ritual of purification.[b] For this reason they are barred from those precincts of the temple [c] that are frequented by all the people and perform their rites by themselves. Otherwise

alternative version, which he prefers, is the basis of my own. If the Dead Sea sect is to be identified with the Essenes, it is difficult to insert οὐκ, since, as Strugnell remarks (p. 113), the Qumrân texts and archaeological evidence suggest that sacrifice was practised, though we do not know where it took place. It is, moreover, difficult to accept J. M. Baumgarten's suggestion (" Sacrifice and Worship among the Jewish Sectarians of the Dead Sea (Qumrân) Scrolls," *Harv. Theol. Rev.* xlvi, 1953, p. 155) that the reference in our passage is to spiritualized sacrifices, since the phrase is never found elsewhere in this sense.

[b] Before sundown the Pharisees would render unclean the priest who was to burn the red heifer (Num. xix. 2 ff.) so that the Sadducees might not say that the ceremony could be performed only by those who had waited until sundown before becoming clean (*cf.* Lev. xxii. 7). Z. Frankel, " Die Essäer nach talmudischen Quellen," *Monatsschr. f. Gesch. u. Wissensch. d. Jud.* ii, 1853, p. 65, says that the Essenes must have followed the Sadducaean point of view ; hence they lacked the means of purifying themselves, since the ashes of the red heifer, mixed with water, were utilized for purifying one who had touched a corpse (Num. xix. 11-13). Since they regarded the water of purification that was in use as unclean, they had to seek other means of purification, and hence did not frequent the temple.

[c] L. Ginzberg, *Eine unbekannte jüdische Sekte*, Part 1, 1922, pp. 99-100, cites a parallel in the Zadokite sect, the adherents of which found fault with their opponents for not showing sufficient holiness in their attitude toward the holy city of Jerusalem ; their first step was to hold themselves aloof from the temple so as not to share in the defilement. S. Zeitlin, " The Essenes," *Hadoar Jubilee Vol.*, 1957 [in Hebrew], p. 49, suggests that the reason why the Essenes did not send sacrifices to the temple was that they protested against the selection of Simon the Hasmonaean as high priest (since he was not of the family of Zadok) ; but this statement

17

ἄνδρες[1] τὸν τρόπον καὶ τὸ πᾶν πονεῖν ἐπὶ γεωργίᾳ
20 τετραμμένοι. ἄξιον δ' αὐτῶν θαυμάσαι παρὰ πάντας τοὺς ἀρετῆς μεταποιουμένους τόδε διὰ τὸ[2] μηδαμῶς ὑπάρξαν Ἑλλήνων ἢ βαρβάρων τισίν, ἀλλὰ
μηδ' εἰς ὀλίγον, ἐκείνοις ἐκ παλαιοῦ συνελθὸν ἐν
τῷ[3] ἐπιτηδεύεσθαι μὴ κεκωλῦσθαι· τὰ χρήματά τε
κοινά ἐστιν αὐτοῖς,[4] ἀπολαύει δὲ οὐδὲν ὁ πλούσιος
τῶν οἰκείων μειζόνως ἢ ὁ μηδ' ὁτιοῦν κεκτημένος·
καὶ τάδε πράσσουσιν ἄνδρες ὑπὲρ τετρακισχίλιοι
21 τὸν ἀριθμὸν ὄντες. καὶ οὔτε γαμετὰς εἰσάγονται
οὔτε δούλων ἐπιτηδεύουσιν κτῆσιν, τὸ μὲν εἰς ἀδι-
κίαν φέρειν ὑπειληφότες, τὸ δὲ στάσεως ἐνδιδόναι
ποίησιν,[5] αὐτοὶ δ' ἐφ' ἑαυτῶν ζῶντες διακονίᾳ[6] τῇ
22 ἐπ' ἀλλήλοις ἐπιχρῶνται. ἀποδέκτας δὲ τῶν προσόδων χειροτονοῦντες καὶ ὁπόσα ἡ γῆ φέροι ἄνδρας
ἀγαθούς, ἱερεῖς δὲ ἐπὶ[7] ποιήσει[8] σίτου τε καὶ βρω-

---

[1] AW : om. M Lat. : ἄνδρες (= οἱ ἄνδρες) coni. Post.
[2] τόδε διὰ τὸ] A : τὸ δίκαιον MWE : γρ τὸ δίκαιον μηδαμῶς i. marg. A.
[3] ἐν τῷ] fort. spuria coni. Niese.
[4] ἐστιν αὐτοῖς] A : αὐτοῖς ἐστὶν MW : αὐτοῖς εἶναι E.
[5] πρόφασιν Naber.
[6] διακονίᾳ] E : ἐπὶ διακονίᾳ codd. : ἐπιδιακονίᾳ coni. Niese.
[7] δὲ ἐπὶ] E : διὰ MW : τε διὰ A : litt. τε διὰ π i. ras. angustius m. 2 A.
[8] E : ποίησιν codd.

---

rests on the doubtful identification of the Essenes with the
Hasidim of Maccabaean times. Our passage, however, speaks
of the Essenes as being excluded and not as excluding themselves (εἰργόμενοι is always passive and never middle in
Josephus : so R. Marcus, " Pharisees, Essenes, and Gnostics," *Jour. of Bibl. Lit.* lxxiii, 1954, p. 158, and Thackeray-
Marcus, *Lexicon to Josephus, s.v.*).
  *a* The text is difficult. Whiston translates : " It also de-
serves our admiration, how much they exceed in justice
[reading τὸ δίκαιον] all other men that addict themselves to
virtue, to such a degree as has never appeared among any

they are of the highest character, devoting themselves solely to agricultural labour. They deserve
admiration in contrast to all others who claim their
share of virtue because such qualities as theirs were
never found before among any Greek or barbarian
people, nay, not even briefly, but have been among
them in constant practice and never interrupted since
they adopted them from of old. Moreover, they hold
their possessions in common,[a] and the wealthy man
receives no more enjoyment from his property than
the man who possesses nothing. The men who practise this way of life number more than four thousand.[b]
They neither bring wives into the community nor do
they own slaves, since they believe that the latter
practice contributes to injustice and that the former
opens the way to a source of dissension.[c] Instead
they live by themselves and perform menial tasks for
one another. They elect by show of hands good men
to receive their revenues and the produce of the earth
and priests [d] to prepare bread and other food.[e] Their

other men. . . . This is shown by that institution of theirs,
which will not suffer anything to hinder them from having all
things in common."

[b] The same number is given by Philo, *Quod Omnis Probus
Liber Sit* 75.

[c] *Cf.* Proverbs xxv. 24 : " It is better to dwell in a corner
of the housetop than in a house in common with a contentious
woman." The depreciation of women is also found in the
Dead Sea Scrolls, as indicated by Strugnell, p. 110.

[d] Those who see a dual leadership in the Qumrân sect (*cf.*
Strugnell, pp. 110-111), one priestly, the other non-priestly,
may discern here a parallel, which, to be sure, depends on
adopting the reading of the Epitome (though it may perhaps
be deduced from the manuscript A).

[e] Variant " good men, priests, to receive their revenues
and the produce of the earth and to prepare bread and other
food."

μάτων.¹ ζῶσι δὲ οὐδὲν παρηλλαγμένως, ἀλλ' ὅτι
μάλιστα ἐμφέροντες² Δακῶν³ τοῖς Κτίσταις⁴ λεγο-
μένοις.⁵

23 (6) Τῇ δὲ τετάρτῃ τῶν φιλοσοφιῶν ὁ Γαλιλαῖος
Ἰούδας ἡγεμὼν κατέστη,⁶ τὰ μὲν λοιπὰ πάντα
γνώμῃ τῶν Φαρισαίων ὁμολογοῦσι,⁷ δυσνίκητος⁸
δὲ τοῦ ἐλευθέρου ἔρως ἐστὶν αὐτοῖς μόνον ἡγεμόνα
καὶ δεσπότην τὸν θεὸν ὑπειληφόσιν. θανάτων τε
ἰδέας ὑπομένειν παρηλλαγμένας ἐν ὀλίγῳ τίθενται
καὶ συγγενῶν τιμωρίας καὶ φίλων ὑπὲρ τοῦ μηδένα

¹ προχειρίζονται post βρωμάτων add. E.
² ἐμφέροντες] ἐμφερῶς E : ἐμφερεῖς ὄντες Bekker.
³ Δακῶν] i. marg. οὕτως εὗρον καὶ ἐν ἄλλοις m. 1 A : Σαδδουκαίων Dupont-Sommer : αὐτῶν Carmignac (Vetus Tes-
tamentum, vii, 1957, pp. 318-319).
⁴ Ortelius : Πολιταῖς Scaliger : πλείστοις codd.
⁵ ἄνδρας . . . λεγομένοις] sacerdotes autem optimos viros
eligunt, cibus illis simplex est, habitus insumptuosus et mundus Lat.                    ⁶ ἧς οἱ τρόφιμοι ante τὰ add. E.
⁷ codd. E : ὁμολογούσῃ Niese.
⁸ δυσνίκητος] Bekker : δυσκίνητος codd. E : inmobilem im-
mutabilemque Lat.

ᵃ " Founders." The manuscript reading, " from the so-
called majority of the Dacians," does not yield sense. Ortelius' brilliant emendation, which is here adopted, is based
upon a passage of Posidonius in Strabo vii. 296, which mentions a tribe named the Ctistae who lived without wives.
Scaliger's emendation, Πολισταῖς, adopted by Thackeray,
*Selections*, p. 160, though close to the manuscript reading,
cannot be accepted since this word is rejected by the gram-
marian Pollux and is nowhere attested in extant Greek
writings. It is true that Josephus has just said (§ 20) that
righteousness such as the Essenes possess is not to be found
among any of the Greeks or the barbarians ; but the comparison in § 22 seems to be to such aspects of their life as their
avoidance of wives and slaves and their communal sharing of
goods. A. Dupont-Sommer, " On a Passage of Josephus
Relating to the Essenes (*Antiq.* xviii. 22)," *Jour. of Sem.*

manner of life does not differ at all from that of the so-called Ctistae [a] among the Dacians, but is as close to it as could be.

(6) As for the fourth of the philosophies,[b] Judas the Galilaean [c] set himself up as leader of it. This school agrees in all other respects with the opinions of the Pharisees, except that they have a passion for liberty that is almost unconquerable, since they are convinced that God alone is their leader and master. They think little of submitting to death in unusual forms and permitting vengeance to fall on kinsmen and friends if only they may avoid calling any man

The fourth sect estab-lished by Judas the Galilaean.

*Stud.* i, 1956, pp. 361-366, suggests that the manuscript reading, πλείστοις, be kept, since he sees a parallel in the familiar designation of the members of the Qumrân community as *ha-rabim*, " the many " (the Hebrew lacks a super-lative form) ; the meaning would then be that the various Essene groups closely conformed to the Qumrân community, which served as the model for all. The Qumrân sectarians called themselves " sons of Zadok " ; and Dupont-Sommer suggests (p. 364) emending Δακῶν to Σαδὼκ, or, preferably, Σαδδουκαίων. The meaning would then be " conforming as much as possible to those of the Sadducees [to be distinguished from the classical Sadducees] who are called the Many." The corruption, however, of Σαδδουκαίων into Δακῶν is palaeo-graphically very difficult to accept.

[b] It should be noted that the identification of the Fourth Philosophy with the Zealots, which scholars so often assume, is not found in Josephus here or in the account in *B.J.* iv. 121 ff. So G. F. Moore, in *Harv. Theol. Rev.* xxii, 1929, p. 373.

[c] *Cf.* the Galilaean heretic (Mishnah, *Yadaim* iv. 8 : he is called a Sadducee, but S. Lieberman, " Light on the Cave Scrolls from Rabbinic Sources," *Proc. of the Am. Acad. for Jewish Res.* xx, 1951, pp. 401-402, rightly, as we can see from the attitude of the " Sadducee " toward the state, assumes that the word is here used in the generic sense of heretic) who protests against the Pharisaic practice of including the name of the ruler on bills of divorce.

21

24 ἄνθρωπον προσαγορεύειν δεσπότην. ἑωρακόσιν δὲ
τοῖς πολλοῖς τὸ ἀμετάλλακτον αὐτῶν τῆς ἐπὶ[1]
τοιούτοις ὑποστάσεως[2] περαιτέρω διελθεῖν παρέλι-
πον· οὐ γὰρ δέδοικα μὴ εἰς ἀπιστίαν ὑποληφθῇ τι
τῶν λεγομένων ἐπ᾿ αὐτοῖς, τοὐναντίον δὲ μὴ ἐλασ-
σόνως τοῦ ἐκείνων καταφρονήματος δεχομένου τὴν
ταλαιπωρίαν τῆς ἀλγηδόνος .ὁ λόγος ἀφηγῆται.
25 ἀνοίᾳ τε τῇ ἐντεῦθεν ἤρξατο νοσεῖν τὸ ἔθνος Γεσ-
σίου Φλώρου, ὃς ἡγεμὼν ἦν, τῇ ἐξουσίᾳ τοῦ ὑβρίζειν ἀπονοήσαντος αὐτοὺς ἀποστῆναι Ῥωμαίων.
καὶ φιλοσοφεῖται μὲν Ἰουδαίοις τοσάδε.

26 (ii. 1) Κυρίνιος δὲ τὰ Ἀρχελάου χρήματα ἀπο-
δόμενος ἤδη καὶ τῶν ἀποτιμήσεων πέρας ἐχουσῶν,
αἳ ἐγένοντο τριακοστῷ καὶ ἑβδόμῳ ἔτει μετὰ τὴν
Ἀντωνίου ἐν Ἀκτίῳ ἧτταν ὑπὸ Καίσαρος, Ἰωάζα-
ρον τὸν ἀρχιερέα κατασταστασιασθέντα ὑπὸ τῆς πληθύος ἀφελόμενος τὸ ἀξίωμα τῆς τιμῆς Ἄνανον τὸν
27 Σεθὶ[3] καθίσταται ἀρχιερέα. Ἡρώδης δὲ καὶ Φίλιππος τετραρχίαν ἑκάτερος τὴν ἑαυτοῦ παρειληφό-

---

[1] Ernesti : ὑπὸ codd. E.
[2] ἐνστάσεως E.
[3] A : Σὲς MW : Σὲθ ed. pr. : τὸν Σεθὶ om. Lat.

---

[a] Named procurator of Judaea in 64 or 65 by Nero. For
an account of his cruelty and rapacity see *B.J.* ii. 277-279
and *Ant.* xx. 252-258.

[b] Augustus'. The census can thus be dated as having
taken place in A.D. 6.

[c] 2 Sept. 31 B.C. On dating from the Battle of Actium see
*B.J.* i. 398, where Josephus dates according to Actiads, the
games at Actium that were celebrated every four years.

[d] *Cf.* § 3.

[e] High priest from A.D. 6 to 15, when he was deposed by

master. Inasmuch as most people have seen the steadfastness of their resolution amid such circumstances, I may forgo any further account. For I have no fear that anything reported of them will be considered incredible. The danger is, rather, that report may minimize the indifference with which they accept the grinding misery of pain. The folly that ensued began to afflict the nation after Gessius Florus,[a] who was governor, had by his overbearing and lawless actions provoked a desperate rebellion against the Romans. Such is the number of the schools of philosophy among the Jews.

(ii. 1) Quirinius had now liquidated the estate of Archelaus ; and by this time the registrations of property that took place in the thirty-seventh year after Caesar's [b] defeat of Antony at Actium [c] were complete. Since the high priest Joazar [d] had now been overpowered by a popular faction, Quirinius stripped him of the dignity of his office and installed Ananus [e] the son of Seth [f] as high priest. [g] Meanwhile, Herod [h] and Philip had received and were taking in

the procurator Valerius Gratus (§ 34). He is to be identified with the high priest Annas of the New Testament (Luke iii. 2 ; John xviii. 13, 24 ; Acts iv. 6) before whom Jesus was delivered for his first hearing. Five of his sons became high priests (*Ant.* xx. 198), and his son-in-law (so John xviii. 13) Joseph surnamed Caïaphas (Luke iii. 2) likewise attained this office. The family of Ananus was well known for its large size, wealth, and power (so Bab. Talmud, *Pesaḥim* 57 a ; Tosefta *Menaḥot* xiii. 18). Their greed in particular is bitterly attacked by the Rabbis (Mishnah *Keritot* i. 7), and the family's wealth appears to have been destroyed by the zealots (Jerus. *Peah* ii. 16 c and *Sifre Deut.* xiv. 22). See J. Gutmann, "Ananos," *Ency. Jud.* ii, 1928, pp. 765-766.

[f] Sethi in the Greek text.

[g] §§ 27-28 are paralleled by *B.J.* ii. 167-168.

[h] Herod Antipas.

τες καθίσταντο. καὶ Ἡρώδης Σέπφωριν τειχίσας
πρόσχημα τοῦ Γαλιλαίου παντὸς ἠγόρευεν[1] αὐτὴν
Αὐτοκρατορίδα· Βηθαραμφθᾶ[2] δέ· πόλις καὶ αὐτὴ
τυγχάνει, τείχει περιλαβὼν[3] Ἰουλιάδα ἀπὸ τοῦ αὐτο-
28 κράτορος προσαγορεύει τῆς γυναικός. Φίλιππος δὲ
Πανεάδα[4] τὴν πρὸς ταῖς πηγαῖς τοῦ Ἰορδάνου κατασκευάσας ὀνομάζει Καισάρειαν, κώμην δὲ Βηθσαϊ-
δὰ πρὸς λίμνῃ τῇ Γεννησαρίτιδι πόλεως παρασχὼν
ἀξίωμα πλήθει τε οἰκητόρων καὶ τῇ ἄλλῃ δυνάμει
Ἰουλίᾳ[5] θυγατρὶ τῇ Καίσαρος ὁμώνυμον ἐκάλεσεν.
29 (2) Κωπωνίου δὲ τὴν Ἰουδαίαν διέποντος, ὃν ἔ-
φην Κυρινίῳ συνεκπεμφθῆναι, τάδε πράσσεται. τῶν
ἀζύμων τῆς ἑορτῆς ἀγομένης, ἣν πάσχα καλοῦ-
μεν, ἐκ μέσης νυκτὸς ἐν ἔθει τοῖς ἱερεῦσιν ἦν

---

[1] ἦγεν ΑΕ : i. marg. γρ ἠγόρευεν Α : προσηγόρευεν L. Dindorf : ἤγαγεν MW : ἀνῆκεν Dindorf : appellat Lat.
[2] Βηθαραμφὰ Ε : Betharamtha Lat.
[3] περιβαλὼν Ε.
[4] ΑW : Παναιάδα Α[1]M : Paniadam Lat.
[5] MW : Ἰουλίαν ΑΕ.

---

[a] In upper Galilee, probably to be identified with modern
*Saffuriyah*. *Cf. Vita* 30 and *passim*. See Schürer ii[4]. 209-
213.

[b] "Imperial" (city), perhaps "capital" (city). Since Αὐτοκράτωρ is the Greek equivalent of Imperator, one of Augustus'
titles, the name Αὐτοκρατορίς (Latin Imperatoria) probably
honours Augustus. Otherwise, "he made it autonomous";
but see Schürer ii. 211 n. 496, who rightly remarks that the
subsequent history makes it probable that already at that
time the rest of Galilee was subordinate to it.

[c] Biblical Beth-haram (Josh. xiii. 27), east of the Jordan,

24

hand their respective tetrarchies. Herod fortified Cities built<br>by Herod<br>and Philip. Sepphoris _a_ to be the ornament of all Galilee, and called it Autocratoris._b_ He also threw a wall about another city, Betharamphtha,_c_ which he called Julias _d_ after the name of the emperor's wife. Philip too made improvements at Paneas,_e_ the city near the sources of the Jordan, and called it Caesarea._f_ He also raised the village of Bethsaïda _g_ on Lake Gennesaritis _h_ to the status of city by adding residents and strengthening the fortifications. He named it after Julia, the emperor's daughter.

(2) During the administration of Judaea by Coponius, who, as I have said, had been dispatched with Quirinius, an event occurred which I shall now describe. When the Festival of Unleavéned Bread, which we call Passover, was going on, the priests were accustomed to throw open the gates of the tem- The<br>Samaritans<br>scatter<br>human<br>bones in<br>porticoes of<br>the temple.

---

Talmudic Bethramtha, in Eusebius Bethramtha. See Schürer ii. 213-216.

_d_ On Julia (or Livia), the wife of Augustus, see _Ant._ xvi. 139. Eusebius, _Onom. Sac._ (ed. Larson and Parthey), pp. 112-113, calls the city Livias. A. H. M. Jones, _The Cities of the Eastern Roman Provinces_, 1937, p. 275, suggests that Herod originally renamed the city Livias in honour of Livia, and that later (A.D. 14), when Livia was adopted into the Julian gens, he changed its name to Julias. This remained the name in official use during the first century ; ultimately it was again replaced by Livias.

_e_ Originally the name of a cave sacred to Pan on a mountain near by.

_f_ Caesarea Philippi (Matt. xvi. 13, Mark viii. 27), modern _Banias_. _Cf._ Schürer ii. 204-208.

_g_ East of the Jordan, slightly north of the Sea of Galilee, perhaps to be identified with the Bethsaida of the New Testament. Schürer ii. 208 notes that since Julia was banished in B.C. 2, the foundation of Julias-Bethsaida must have preceded that date.

_h_ The Sea of Galilee.

30 ἀνοιγνύναι τοῦ ἱεροῦ τοὺς πυλῶνας. καὶ τότε οὖν
ἐπεὶ τὸ πρῶτον γίνεται ἡ ἄνοιξις αὐτῶν, ἄνδρες
Σαμαρεῖται κρύφα εἰς Ἱεροσόλυμα ἐλθόντες διάρριψιν ἀνθρωπείων ὀστῶν ἐν ταῖς στοαῖς καὶ διὰ
παντὸς[1] τοῦ ἱεροῦ ἤρξαντο[2*3] μὴ πρότερον ἐπὶ τοιούτοις νομίζοντες τά τε ἄλλα διὰ φυλακῆς μεί-
31 ζονος ἦγον τὸ ἱερόν.[4] καὶ Κωπώνιος μετ' οὐ πολὺ
εἰς Ῥώμην ἐπαναχωρεῖ, διάδοχος δ' αὐτῷ τῆς ἀρχῆς παραγίνεται Μᾶρκος Ἀμβίβουλος,[5] ἐφ' οὗ καὶ
Σαλώμη ἡ τοῦ βασιλέως Ἡρώδου ἀδελφὴ μεταστᾶσα Ἰουλίᾳ μὲν Ἰάμνειάν τε καταλείπει καὶ τὴν

[1] καὶ διὰ παντός] διὸ καὶ πάντας Hudson.
[2] εἴρξαντο Hudson: εἶρξαν Bekker: εἰργάσαντο coni. Post.
[3] lacunam post ἱεροῦ indicavit Niese ed. min.; post ἤρξαντο
indicavi.
[4] διάρριψιν . . . ἱερόν] et per templi cunctas porticus et per
totum phanum ossa iaciunt mortuorum; et ex illo coepit in
templo custodia maior sacerdotibus exerceri Lat.
[5] coni. Niese: Ἀμβιβοῦχος MW Zon.: Ἀμβιβοοῦχος E
(cod. Laur.): om. Lat.: Ἀμβιόνιος Casaubonus ad Baron.
p. 205, 1.

[a] The five gates of the temple mount (Mishnah *Middot* i.
3). On holidays the people remained on the temple mount
and did not enter the temple proper (*cf.* Bab. *Chagigah* 26 a).
[b] Beginning at midnight. *Cf.* Mishnah *Yoma* i. 8, which
states that on all three festivals (Passover, Pentecost, Taber-
nacles), after the first watch of the evening the priests would
begin to prepare the temple for the coming day's service. By
the cock's crow, we are told, the temple area was full of people,
though we are not told precisely when the gates of the temple
were opened. On Passover, the people were busy in their
homes eating the paschal lamb, which they had until midnight
to consume; hence it would appear that they started to gather
in the temple area after midnight.

ple *a* after midnight.*b* This time, when the gates were
first opened, some Samaritans, who had secretly entered Jerusalem, began to scatter human bones in the
porticoes and throughout the temple.*c* As a result,
the priests, although they had previously observed
no such custom, excluded everyone from the temple,
in addition to taking other measures for the greater
protection of the temple.*d* *e* Not long afterwards Coponius returned to Rome. His successor in office was
Marcus Ambivulus,*f* during whose administration
Salome, the sister of King Herod, died. To Julia *g*
she bequeathed Jamnia and its territory, together

Succession
of Roman
procurators
and of
high
priests.

*c* There appears to be a lacuna in the text.

*d* The passage, as it stands in the MSS., presents difficulties,
and a few commentators have suggested that there is a lacuna.
J. Carcopino, " Encore le rescrit impérial sur les violations
de sépulture," *Rev. hist.* clxvi, 1931, p. 90, in an effort to
bring the passage into line with *B.J.* ii. 117, reads : διάρριψιν . . . ἐν ταῖς στοαῖς ποιοῦνται καὶ διὰ παντὸς τοῦ ἱεροῦ. καὶ
τότε Ῥωμαῖοι τοὺς ὀστᾶ νεκρῶν μετακεινήσαντες [correct to μετα-
κινήσαντας ?] ἀποκτείνειν ἤρξαντο, *i.e.*, the Romans began to
condemn to death those who dispersed the bones. Carcopino
would then connect this incident with the Greek inscription, dating from the last years of Augustus or somewhat
later, found in Palestine (published by F. Cumont in *Rev.
hist.* clxiii, 1930, pp. 241-266). This inscription is an edict
against transferring buried bodies to another place, the penalty for violation being death. H. Riesenfeld, " The Resurrection in Ezekiel XXXVII and in the Dura-Europos Paintings,"
*Uppsala Univ. Arsskrift*, no. 11, 1948, pp. 36-37, noting
that the vision of Ezekiel in the valley of dry bones (chap.
xxxvii) is the assigned reading from the prophets on [the
intermediate Sabbath of] Passover, stresses the Messianic
character of the belief in resurrection and its association with
Passover.

*e* §§ 31-32 are parallel with *B.J.* ii. 167-168.

*f* Also spelled " Ambibulus," " Ambivius." Procurator
*c.* A.D. 9-12. Otherwise unknown.

*g* Livia, wife of Augustus. See above, § 27.

27

τοπαρχίαν πᾶσαν, τήν τ' ἐν τῷ πεδίῳ Φασαηλίδα
καὶ Ἀρχελαΐδα, ἔνθα φοινίκων πλείστη φύτευσις καὶ
32 καρπὸς αὐτῶν ἄριστος. διαδέχεται δὲ καὶ τοῦτον
Ἄννιος[1] Ῥοῦφος, ἐφ' οὗ δὴ καὶ τελευτᾷ Καῖσαρ,
δεύτερος μὲν Ῥωμαίων αὐτοκράτωρ γενόμενος ἑπτὰ
δὲ καὶ πεντήκοντα τῆς ἀρχῆς ἔτη, πρὸς οἷς μῆνες
ἓξ ἡμέραι δυοῖν πλείονες, τούτου δὲ αὐτῷ τοῦ χρόνου
δεκατέσσαρα ἔτη συνῆρξεν Ἀντώνιος, βιώσας ἔτη
33 ἑβδομηκονταεπτά. διαδέχεται δὲ τῷ Καίσαρι τὴν
ἡγεμονίαν Τιβέριος Νέρων γυναικὸς αὐτοῦ Ἰουλίας
υἱὸς ὤν, τρίτος ἤδη οὗτος αὐτοκράτωρ, καὶ πεμπτὸς[2] ὑπ' αὐτοῦ παρῆν Ἰουδαίοις ἔπαρχος διάδοχος
34 Ἀννίῳ Ῥούφῳ[3] Οὐαλέριος Γρᾶτος· ὃς παύσας ἱερᾶ-
σθαι[4] Ἄνανον[5] Ἰσμάηλον ἀρχιερέα ἀποφαίνει τὸν
τοῦ Φαβί,[6] καὶ τοῦτον δὲ μετ' οὐ πολὺ μεταστήσας
Ἐλεάζαρον τὸν Ἀνάνου τοῦ ἀρχιερέως υἱὸν ἀπο-
δείκνυσιν ἀρχιερέα. ἐνιαυτοῦ δὲ διαγενομένου καὶ
τόνδε παύσας Σίμωνι τῷ Καμίθου[7] τὴν ἀρχιερωσύ-
35 νην παραδίδωσιν. οὐ πλείων δὲ καὶ τῷδε ἐνιαυτοῦ
τὴν τιμὴν ἔχοντι διεγένετο χρόνος, καὶ Ἰώσηπος ὁ

---

[1] Ἀννῖσος E : Ἄννισος cod. Busb.

[2] πέμπτος M : quintus Lat.

[3] Ἀννίῳ Ῥούφῳ] A : Ἀννίου Ῥούφου MW : Ἀννίνου Ῥούφου E.

[4] ἀρχιερᾶσθαι Eus. Dem. Evang.

[5] Ἄνναν Zon. : Ἄνανον Eusebii hist. codd. plerique :
Annan Lat. (cod. A).

[6] E Eus. Hist. Eccles. : Φιαβί A : Φαβῆ M : Iabi Lat. :
Φήβα Eus. Dem. : Βιοβῆ Iosephi Hypom. (Fabricius cod.
Pseudep. Vet. Test.).

[7] Καθίμου Eus. Dem. : Καθήμου Ios. Hypom. ap. Fabric.

with Phasaëlis, which lay in the plain, and Archelaïs,[a] where palms are planted in very great numbers and the dates are of the highest quality.[b] Ambivulus' successor was Annius Rufus,[c] whose administration was marked by the death of Caesar,[d] the second emperor of the Romans, who had ruled for fifty-seven years, six months, and two days. Antony had shared authority with him for fourteen years of this period. He was seventy-seven years old when he died. Caesar's successor in authority was the third emperor, Tiberius Nero, the son of his wife Julia. He dispatched Valerius Gratus [e] to succeed Annius Rufus as procurator over the Jews. Gratus deposed Ananus from his sacred office, and proclaimed Ishmaël, the son of Phabi,[f] high priest. Not long afterwards he removed him also and appointed in his stead Eleazar, the son of the high priest Ananus.[g] A year later he deposed him also and entrusted the office of high priest to Simon, the son of Camith.[h] The last-mentioned held this position for not more than a year

---

[a] Jamnia was in Philistia along the coast, Phasaëlis and Archelaïs (cf. Ant. xvii. 340) in the Jordan valley.

[b] Pliny the Elder (Hist. Nat. xiii. 44) also mentions the fame of the dates of Archelaïs.

[c] Procurator A.D. 12–15. Otherwise unknown.

[d] Augustus, whose rule is here reckoned from the death of Julius Caesar in 44 B.C. to his own death in A.D. 14. The period of his reign as given here is about a month too long, as noted in Thackeray's note on the parallel passage, B.J. ii. 168.

[e] Procurator A.D. 15–26. Otherwise unknown.

[f] High priest A.D. 15–16 but otherwise unknown. Probably not to be identified with the Ishmael ben Phabi (Ant. xx. 179) who was appointed high priest by Agrippa II in A.D. 59.

[g] High priest A.D. 16–17. Otherwise unknown.

[h] High priest A.D. 17–18. Otherwise unknown.

Καϊάφας¹ διάδοχος ἦν αὐτῷ. καὶ Γρᾶτος μὲν ταῦτα
πράξας εἰς Ῥώμην ἐπανεχώρει ἕνδεκα ἔτη διατρίψας ἐν Ἰουδαίᾳ, Πόντιος δὲ Πιλᾶτος διάδοχος
αὐτῷ ἧκεν.

36 (3) Ἡρώδης δὲ ὁ τετράρχης, ἐπὶ μέγα γὰρ ἦν τῷ
Τιβερίῳ φιλίας προελθών,² οἰκοδομεῖται πόλιν ἐπ-
ώνυμον αὐτῷ Τιβεριάδα τοῖς κρατίστοις ἐπικτίσας
αὐτὴν τῆς Γαλιλαίας ἐπὶ λίμνῃ τῇ Γεννησαρίτιδι.³
θερμά τε οὐκ ἄπωθέν ἐστιν ἐν κώμῃ, Ἀμμαθοῦς⁴
37 ὄνομα αὐτῇ. σύγκλυδες⁵ δὲ ᾤκισαν,⁶ οὐκ ὀλίγον δὲ
καὶ τὸ Γαλιλαῖον ἦν, καὶ ὅσοι μὲν ἐκ τῆς ὑπ' αὐτῷ
γῆς ἀναγκαστοὶ καὶ πρὸς βίαν εἰς τὴν κατοικίαν
ἀγόμενοι, τινὲς δὲ καὶ τῶν ἐν τέλει. ἐδέξατο δὲ
αὐτοῖς συνοίκους καὶ τοὺς πανταχόθεν ἐπισυναγο-
μένους ἄνδρας ἀπόρους, ἔστι δ' οὓς μηδὲ σαφῶς
38 ἐλευθέρους, πολλά τε αὐτοὺς κἀπὶ πολλοῖς ἠλευ-
θέρωσεν καὶ εὐηργέτησεν ἀνάγκασμα τοῦ μὴ ἀπο-
λείπειν τὴν πόλιν ἐπιθείς, κατασκευαῖς τε οἰκήσεων

---

¹ Καϊάφας] codd. E Lat. (cf. Ant. xviii. 95 et I. Lévy, ap.
Mélanges R. Dussaud ii, 1939, p. 542) : καὶ Καϊάφας Eus.
² E : προσελθών codd. : perveniens Lat.
³ AW : Γενησαρίτιδι ME : Genesar Lat.
⁴ AM : Ἀμμαοῦς W : Ἀμαθοῦς E : Amathus Lat.
⁵ συνήλυδες L. Dindorf.
⁶ Niese : ᾤκησαν codd. E : i. marg. (ad ᾤκησαν?) ταύτην A.

---

ᵃ Son-in-law of Ananus. High priest A.D. 18–36. Luke's
mention (iii. 2) of both Annas (Ananus) and Caïaphas as
high priests has led many commentators to think that Annas
was the power behind his son-in-law. He is said to have
presided over the Sanhedrin (Matt. xxvi. 57) at the trial of
Jesus. He is also mentioned by John (xi. 49, xviii. 13, 24,
28), but not by Mark and Luke, in connexion with Jesus'
crucifixion.
ᵇ Or " withdrew," " returned."

and was succeeded by Joseph, who was called Caïaphas.[a] After these acts Gratus retired [b] to Rome, having stayed eleven years in Judaea. It was Pontius Pilate who came as his successor.[c]

(3) [d] The tetrarch Herod, inasmuch as he had gained a high place among the friends of Tiberius, had a city built, named after him Tiberias, which he established in the best region of Galilee on Lake Gennesaritis. There is a hot spring not far from it in a village called Ammathus.[e] The new settlers were a promiscuous rabble, no small contingent being Galilaean, with such as were drafted from territory subject to him and brought forcibly to the new foundation. Some of these were magistrates. Herod accepted as participants even poor men who were brought in to join the others from any and all places of origin. It was a question whether some were even free beyond cavil. These latter he often and in large bodies liberated and benefited (imposing the condition that they should not quit the city), by equipping houses at his own expense and adding new

Building of Tiberias by Herod the tetrarch.

[c] A.D. 26. R. Eisler, *The Messiah Jesus*, 1931, p. 17, rejects this date, asserting, on the basis of the Maximinian *Acta Pilati*, that the crucifixion took place in 21 and that Pilate became procurator about the year 18. This dating is successfully challenged by P. L. Hadley, " Pilate's Arrival in Judaea," *Jour. of Theol. Stud.* xxxv, 1934, pp. 56-57, who, in examining the extant procuratorial coins, notes that the coin-type that emerges in 17-18 is still supreme in 24-25, whereas the coins of the years 29-32 are of an entirely different type, thus indicating, he believes, the advent of a new procurator between 25 and 29.

[d] § 36 is parallel with *B.J.* ii. 168.

[e] Between Tiberias and Gadara. The name is probably derived from the Hebrew *ḥamath* (= warm [springs]). It is mentioned several times in the Talmud (*e.g. Moed Katan* 18 a) but is not to be confused with Emmaus in Judaea.

τέλεσι τοῖς[1] αὑτοῦ καὶ γῆς ἐπιδόσει,[2] εἰδὼς παράνομον τὸν οἰκισμὸν ὄντα καὶ ἀπὸ τοῦ Ἰουδαίοις
πατρίου διὰ τὸ ἐπὶ μνήμασιν, ἃ πολλὰ τῇδε ἦν,
ἀνῃρημένοις τὴν ἵδρυσιν τῇ Τιβεριάδι γενέσθαι·
μιαροὺς δὲ ἐπὶ ἑπτὰ ἡμέρας εἶναι τοὺς οἰκήτορας
ἀγορεύει ἡμῖν τὸ νόμιμον.

39   (4) Τελευτᾷ δὲ καὶ Φραάτης ὁ Παρθυαίων βασιλεὺς κατὰ τοῦτον τὸν χρόνον ἐπιβουλῆς αὐτῷ
γενομένης ὑπὸ Φραατάκου[3] τοῦ υἱέος κατὰ τοιαύτην
40 αἰτίαν.  Φραάτης παίδων αὐτῷ γενομένων γνησίων
Ἰταλικῆς παιδίσκης ⟨ἥρα⟩,[4] ὄνομα αὐτῇ Θεσμοῦσα.[5]
ταύτῃ ὑπὸ Ἰουλίου[6] Καίσαρος μετ᾽ ἄλλων δωρεῶν
ἀπεσταλμένη τὸ μὲν πρῶτον παλλακίδι ἐχρῆτο,
καταπλαγεὶς δὲ[7] τῷ πολλῷ τῆς εὐμορφίας προϊόντος τοῦ χρόνου καὶ παιδὸς αὐτῇ τοῦ Φραατάκου[8]

---

¹ τέλεσι τοῖς] Bekker: τελείαις τῆς codd.: ex (propriis)
opibus Lat.

² Bekker: ἀποδόσει codd. E.

³ A: Φραατάκου MW: Φραάτου cod. Busb. E: fratre cod.
Alat.

⁴ coni. Petersen.

⁵ A: Θερμοῦσα MW: Θεὰ Μοῦσα Gutschmid: Φορμοῦσα
(= Formosa) Naber: Θέλπουσα coni. Petersen.

⁶ Σεβαστοῦ Bucherius: τοῦ νέου Gutschmid.

⁷ δὲ post προιόντος ponunt Richards et Shutt (Class. Quart.
xxxi, 1937, p. 176).

⁸ τοῦ Φραατάκου] A: Φραατάκου MW: ἐκ Φραάτου E:
Fraatre Lat.: ἐκ ⟨Φραάτου⟩ Φραατάκου Nicklin (Class. Rev.
xxvii, 1913, p. 264): [ἐκ] Φραατάκου Mathieu-Herrmann.

---

ᵃ Num. xix. 11-16.

ᵇ Why does Josephus devote so much space to Parthian
affairs ? One major reason seems to be the size and importance of the Jewish community of Babylonia, which was
(§ 313) subject to the Parthians. Thus the account of the

gifts of land. For he knew that this settlement was contrary to the law and tradition of the Jews because Tiberias was built on the site of tombs that had been obliterated, of which there were many there. And our law [a] declares that such settlers are unclean for seven days.

(4) [b] In the interval occurred the death of Phraates, the king of the Parthians.[c] He was the victim of a scheme promoted by his son Phraataces, whose motive sprang from the following circumstance.[d] Phraates, who already had legitimate children, was in love with[e] a young Italian slave girl named Thesmusa,[f] who had been sent to him along with other gifts by Julius Caesar.[g] At first he treated her as a concubine, but he was so smitten by her abundant charm of face and figure that with time, after she had borne a son

Story of
Phraataces
and Thes-
musa.

dynastic troubles of the Parthians culminates in the assumption of the kingship by Artabanus III (§ 48), who plays a prominent role (§§ 325 ff.) in the story of the two daring Jewish brothers, Asinaeus and Anilaeus, who established an independent state in Babylonia.

[c] On Josephus' reliability as a source for Parthian history see N. C. Debevoise, *A Political History of Parthia*, 1938, p. xxix, who notes how often Josephus' account has been confirmed from numismatic or other written sources ; and E. Täubler, *Die Parthernachrichten bei Josephus*, 1904.

[d] *Cf.* Dio Cass. lv. 10a. 4.

[e] Something like " was living with " or " fell in love with " is required by the context, but the Greek text appears to have a lacuna.

[f] After Thesmusa became queen, her name, as the coins attest (see P. Gardner, *Parthian Coinage*, 1887, p. 46) was changed to Thea Musa. But since she is introduced not as the queen but as the royal concubine, her name would hardly be expected to bear the epithet " goddess." In § 42 the unanimous tradition of the mss. is in favour of Thesmusa, and this seems preferable here as well.

[g] Augustus.

33

γενομένου γαμετήν τε τὴν ἄνθρωπον ἀποφαίνεται
41 καὶ τιμίαν ἦγεν.¹ ἐπὶ πᾶσιν² οἷς εἴποι πιθανὴ τῷ
βασιλεῖ γεγονυῖα καὶ σπεύδουσα τῷ παιδὶ τῷ αὐτῆς
γενέσθαι τὴν Πάρθων ἡγεμονίαν ἑώρα μὴ ἄλλως
γενησομένην μὴ ἀποσκευῆς αὐτῇ μηχανηθείσης τῶν
42 γνησίων τοῦ Φραάτου παίδων. πείθει οὖν αὐτὸν
ἐκπέμπειν εἰς Ῥώμην ἐφ᾽ ὁμηρείᾳ³ τοὺς γνησίους
παῖδας. καὶ οὗτοι μέν, οὐ γὰρ ἀντειπεῖν εὔπορον
Φραάτῃ τοῖς Θεσμούσης ἐπιτάγμασιν, ἐπὶ τῆς
Ῥώμης ἐξεπέμποντο. Φραατάκης δὲ μόνος ἐπὶ
τοῖς πράγμασι τρεφόμενος δεινὸν ἡγεῖτο καὶ ἅμα
χρόνιον τοῦ πατρὸς διδόντος τὴν ἀρχὴν λαμβάνειν,
ὥστε ἐπεβούλευε τῷ πατρὶ συμπράξει τῆς μητρός,
43 ᾗ δὴ καὶ συνιέναι λόγος εἶχεν αὐτόν. καὶ δι᾽ ἀμφότερα μισηθεὶς οὐδὲν ἡσσόνως τῆς πατροκτονίας τὸ
μύσος τοῦ⁴ μητρὸς ἔρωτος⁵ τιθεμένων τῶν ὑπηκόων,
· στάσει περιελαθεὶς πρότερον ἢ φῦναι μέγας ἐξέπεσε

---

¹ ἦγεν] ἦγεν. ἡ δὲ Dindorf.
² πᾶσιν] codd. : πᾶσι δ᾽ E.
³ Gutschmid : ὁμηρείαν codd. E.
⁴ τοῦ] codd. : τοῦ τῆς E : τὸν τῆς Bekker : τοὺς Gutschmid.
⁵ ἔρωτα Bekker : ἔρωτας Gutschmid.

---

ᵃ The reading ἐκ Φραάτου is a gloss (so H. Van Herwerden,
" Commentationes Flavianae Duae," *Mnemosyne*, xxi, 1893,
p. 232). Debevoise, p. 143 n. 2, identifies Phraataces as
probably the Aphrahat the son of Aphrahat who ruled over
Seleucia and Ctesiphon of Beth Aramaya, as stated by Mar
Mari in *Acta Martyrum et Sanctorum*, ed. P. Bedjan, i, 1890,
68, § 7.
ᵇ Other reasons why Phraates dispatched his four legitimate sons to Rome were to be pledges of friendship (so
Augustus, *Res Gestae* 32 ; Vell. Pat. ii. 94 ; Suet. *Aug.* 21 ;
Tac. *Ann.* ii. 1) and to prevent his being deposed, since he
realized that no revolution could gain the backing of the

Phraataces,[a] he declared this wench to be his wedded
wife and held her in honour.  When she reached the
point where the king concurred in anything that she
proposed, she, eager to procure for her son the rule
over the Parthians but realizing that this could happen only if she could first contrive to get rid of the
legitimate children of Phraates, persuaded him to
send his legitimate children away to Rome as hostages.  And so they were sent off to Rome, inasmuch as
Phraates did not find it easy to gainsay the dictates
of Thesmusa.[b]  But Phraataces, who alone was being
groomed for the throne, considered it an unsafe as
well as a tedious proceeding to receive the throne by
his father's award.  Hence he plotted against his
father with the assistance of his mother, with whom,
indeed, according to report, he also had sexual relations.[c]  He was detested on both counts, for his subjects considered the incest with his mother no less
abominable than the murder of his father, so that
before he gathered much strength he was caught up

Parthians unless it were allied with an Arsacid (so Strabo
xvi. 748 ; Tac. *Ann.* ii. 1).

[c] Starting in A.D. 2 Thesmusa appears on Parthian coins
together with Phraataces.  Debevoise, p. 149, sees a possible
connexion between the marriage of Phraataces and Thesmusa
and other changes then taking place in Zoroastrianism,
whereby customs long confined solely to the Magi (next-of-
kin marriages was one of these) were being extended to the
people generally.  But this conjecture is doubtful since the
reaction of the Parthians to this incident is one of horror.  H.
Lewy, " The Genesis of the Faulty Persian Chronology,"
*Jour. of the Am. Orient. Soc.* lxiv, 1944, p. 211 n. 132, compares the story of the marriage of Phraataces and Thesmusa
with the account of the marriage of Darius I (a more distant
relative, to be sure, of his predecessor Cambyses) to Cambyses' sister-wife Atossa and her sister Artystone (Herodotus
iii. 88, vii. 69 and 72).

44 τῶν πραγμάτων καὶ οὕτως θνήσκει. συμφρονήσαντες δὲ οἱ γενναιότατοι Πάρθων, ὡς ἀβασιλεύτοις
μὲν ἀμήχανον πολιτεύεσθαι, δέοι δὲ βασιλεύοντος[1]
ἐκ τοῦ γένους τῶν Ἀρσακιδῶν, οὐ γὰρ ἑτέροις
ἄρχειν νόμιμον, ἀπέχρη δὲ πολλάκις καὶ μέχρι νῦν
περιυβρίσθαι τὴν βασιλείαν ἔκ τε γάμων τῆς
Ἰταλικῆς παλλακίδος καὶ γενέσεων, Ὀρώδην[2] ἐκάλουν πρεσβεύσαντες ὄντ'[3] ἄλλως μὲν ἐπίφθονον τῷ
πλήθει καὶ ὑπαίτιον καθ' ὑπερβολὰς ὠμότητος,
πάνυ γὰρ ἦν σκαιὸς καὶ δυσδιάθετος εἰς ὀργήν, ἕνα
45 δὲ τῶν ἐκ τοῦ γένους. τοῦτον μὲν δὴ συστάντες
ἀποκτείνουσιν, ὡς μὲν ἔνιοί φασιν, ἐν σπονδαῖς κα
τραπέζαις, μαχαιροφορεῖν γὰρ ἔθος ἅπασιν, ὡς δ'
ὁ πλείων κατέχει λόγος, εἰς θήραν προαγαγόντες.
46 πρεσβεύσαντες δὲ εἰς Ῥώμην ᾐτοῦντο βασιλέα τῶν
ὁμηρευόντων, καὶ πέμπεται Βονώνης προκριθεὶς
τῶν ἀδελφῶν· ἐδόκει γὰρ χωρεῖν τὴν τύχην, ἣν
αὐτῷ δύο μέγισται τῶν ὑπὸ τὸν ἥλιον ἡγεμονίαι
47 προσέφερον, ἰδία καὶ ἀλλοτρία. ταχεῖα δ' ἀνατροπὴ
τοὺς βαρβάρους ὕπεισιν ἅτε καὶ φύσει σφαλεροὺς
ὄντας πρός τε τὴν ἀναξιοπάθειαν, ἀνδραπόδῳ γὰρ
ἀλλοτρίῳ[4] ποιήσειν τὸ προστασσόμενον οὐκ ἠξίουν,[5]

[1] δέοι δὲ βασιλεύοντος] Gutschmid : οἱ δὲ τοῦ βασιλεύοντος
codd. : οἱ δὲ βασιλεύοντες ed. pr.

[2] M : Ὀρώδην, Ὁ i. ras. A : Ὀρώδην W : Ἡρώδην E Lat.

[3] ὄντ'] Dindorf : εἰς δάν A : ἢν (ἦν W) δ' ἂν MW : ἢν δ' E :
εἰς Δάας Gutschmid.

[4] ἀνδραπόδῳ γὰρ ἀλλοτρίῳ] Niese : ἀνδραπόδων γὰρ ἀλλοτρίων codd.

[5] οὐκ ἠξίουν] Hudson : ἠξίουν codd. : ἀπηξίουν Cocceji.

[a] A.D. 4. Cf. P. Gardner, Parthian Coinage, p. 46. Au-

36

in a civil war, banished from the throne, and so died.[a]
Those of the Parthians who were of the highest birth
were of one mind that no form of government but the
monarchical was manageable, and that it was necessary that the occupant of the throne should belong
to the lineage of the Arsacidae, since custom did not
permit others to rule. But they had had enough, over
and over again till now, of the upstart degradation
to which the throne had been subjected by the marriage with the Italian concubine and by her offspring.
The elders therefore sent envoys and offered the
throne to Orodes, who, though the populace had no
friendly eye for him among other reasons because he
had some responsibility for acts of extreme cruelty,
being indeed utterly gauche and viciously prone to
anger, was still a member of this family. He, however, was slain [b] by a concerted attack, according to
one version, amidst drinking and feasting,[c] for it is
customary for everyone to carry a sword at such
affairs. But according to the generally received
account, they lured him into a hunting party. When Parthian
they sent envoys to Rome and asked release of one civil war
of the hostages as their king, Vonones was chosen in Vonones
preference to his brothers and was sent. For he Artabanus.
seemed to be worthy of the lot that was conferred
upon him by the two greatest empires under the sun,
one his own, one foreign. But a speedy reversal of
sentiment began to affect the barbarians, for they are
by nature fickle, when they saw the indignity that
they must swallow ; for they would not brook obedience to one who had been a slave to a foreigner—a

gustus' *Res Gestae* 32 records the fact that Phraataces (there
called Phraates) fled as a suppliant to the Romans.
    [b] *C.* A.D. 6 (so Debevoise, p. 151).
    [c] Or " as he was making libations at table."

τὴν ὁμηρείαν ἀντὶ δουλείας ὀνομάζοντες,[1] καὶ τῆς
ἐπικλήσεως τὴν ἀδοξίαν[2]· οὐ γὰρ [ἂν][3] πολέμου
δικαίῳ δεδόσθαι τὸν βασιλεύσοντα Πάρθοις, ἀλλά, ὃ
48 τῷ παντὶ χεῖρον, εἰρήνης ὕβρει. παραχρῆμα δ᾽
ἐκάλουν Ἀρτάβανον Μηδίας βασιλεύοντα γένος
Ἀρσακίδην· πείθεται δ᾽ Ἀρτάβανος καὶ μετὰ στρατιᾶς ἔπεισιν. ὑπαντιάζει δ᾽ αὐτῷ Βονώνης· καὶ τὸ
μὲν πρῶτον συμφρονήσαντος αὐτῷ τοῦ πλήθους τῶν
Πάρθων παραταξάμενος νικᾷ, καὶ φεύγει πρὸς τοὺς
49 ὅρους τῆς Μηδίας Ἀρτάβανος. μετ᾽ οὐ πολὺ δὲ
συναγαγὼν[4] συμβάλλει τε Βονώνῃ καὶ νικᾷ, καὶ
Βονώνης εἰς Σελεύκειαν ἀφιππάζεται σὺν ὀλίγοις
τοῖς περὶ αὐτόν. Ἀρτάβανος δὲ πολὺν τῇ τροπῇ
φόνον ἐργασάμενος ὑπὲρ ἐκπλήξεως τῶν βαρβάρων
πρὸς Κτησιφῶντα μετὰ τοῦ πλήθους ἀναχωρεῖ.
50 κἀκεῖνος μὲν ἐβασίλευεν ἤδη Πάρθοις, Βονώνης δ᾽
εἰς Ἀρμενίαν διαπίπτει, καὶ κατ᾽ ἀρχὰς μὲν ἐφίετο

[1] νομίζοντες Gutschmid.
[2] πρός τε . . . ἀδοξίαν] mansuetudinem eius coeperunt
contemnere indignos putantes, ut servo subicerentur alieno;
nam obsidatum servitutem esse definiebant Lat.
[3] ἂν] spurium putat Niese : νῦν Gutschmid.
[4] συναγαγὼν] congregans etiam ipse magnas turmas exer-
citus Lat. : συναγαγὼν στρατιὰν E.

[a] Variant " regarding the position of a hostage as tantamount to servitude."
[b] Or " indignant at the disgrace of having appealed to
Rome."
[c] Tac. Ann. ii. 2 cites additional reasons for the dislike
which the Parthians bore for Vonones, namely, his lack of
interest in hunting, horses, and Parthian festivals, his use of
a litter of Greek attendants, and the ease with which he could
be approached.

term they used instead of hostage [a]—nor could they
bear the opprobrium conveyed by the epithet.[b] For,
they said, it was not by the verdict of war that he had
been granted to the Parthians as a king but, far
worse, by a peacetime offence to their dignity.[c]
Straightway they summoned to the kingship Artabanus, king of Media,[d] of the family of the Arsacidae. Artabanus consented and advanced with an
army. Vonones went to meet him ; and at first,
since the majority of the Parthians were loyal to
Vonones,[e] he was victorious in a pitched battle, and
Artabanus fled to the borders of Media. Not long
afterwards Artabanus, having gathered together his
forces, engaged and defeated Vonones, who rode off
with a small body of followers to Seleucia.[f] Artabanus, who, in order to intimidate the barbarians,
had wrought much slaughter during the rout, withdrew with the majority of his troops to Ctesiphon.[g]
Artabanus now ruled the Parthians, while Vonones
escaped to Armenia.[h] Vonones' original design was
to possess that territory, and so he sent an embassy

[d] Artabanus III, king of Atropatene (modern Azerbaijan).
W. Schur, *Orientpolitik des Kaisers Nero*, 1923, pp. 70 ff.,
on the basis of Tacitus' account, questions Josephus' accuracy
in stating that Artabanus was king of Media.

[e] Or " although the majority of the Parthians were loyal
to Artabanus."

[f] A city on the west bank of the Tigris, founded by
Seleucus Nicator, somewhat south of the modern city of
Baghdad. *Cf.* §§ 372 ff.

[g] On the Tigris near Seleucia and north-east of Babylon.
It is about sixteen miles below modern Baghdad and is the
site of modern *Táki Kesré*.

[h] Armenia was at this time without a king after having
been governed by a succession of rulers (the last of whom
was a woman, Erato), most of whom had been deposed after
brief reigns. *Cf.* Tac. *Ann.* ii. 3-4 and Aug. *Res Gestae* 27.

51 τῆς χώρας καὶ πρὸς 'Ρωμαίους ἐπρέσβευεν. ὡς δ'
αὐτῷ Τιβέριος μὲν ἀπεῖπεν πρός τε τὴν ἀνανδρίαν
καὶ τοῦ Πάρθου τὰς ἀπειλάς, ἀναπρεσβεύει[1] γὰρ δὴ
πόλεμον ἀνατεινόμενος, μηχανὴ δ' ἦν ἑτέρα[2] βασιλείας οὐδεμία, καὶ γὰρ οἱ περὶ Νιφάτην δυνατοὶ
52 τῶν 'Αρμενίων 'Αρταβάνῳ προστίθενται, παραδίδωσιν αὐτὸν Σιλανῷ τῷ τῆς Συρίας στρατηγῷ.
κἀκεῖνος μὲν κατὰ αἰδῶ τῆς ἐν 'Ρώμη κομιδῆς ἐν
Συρίᾳ παρεφυλάσσετο· τὴν δὲ 'Αρμενίαν 'Ορώδη[3]
δίδωσιν 'Αρτάβανος ἑνὶ τῶν ἑαυτοῦ παίδων.

53 (5) 'Ετελεύτησεν δὲ καὶ ὁ τῆς Κομμαγηνῆς βασιλεὺς 'Αντίοχος, διέστη δὲ τὸ πλῆθος πρὸς τοὺς
γνωρίμους καὶ πρεσβεύουσιν ἀφ' ἑκατέρου μέρους,
οἱ μὲν δυνατοὶ μεταβάλλειν τὸ σχῆμα τῆς πολιτείας
εἰς ἐπαρχίαν ἀξιοῦντες, τὸ πλῆθος δὲ βασιλεύεσθαι
54 κατὰ τὰ πάτρια. καὶ ψηφίζεται ἡ σύγκλητος Γερ-
μανικὸν πέμπειν διορθώσοντα τὰ κατὰ τὴν ἀνατολήν,

---

[1] ἀντιπρεσβεύει Gutschmid.      [2] WE : ἑτέρας AM.
[3] AM : 'Ορώδη W : Herodi Lat.

---

[a] Variant " having no means of finding another kingdom."
[b] A group of mountains in Armenia belonging to the
Masius (modern *Karadjeh-Dag*) branch of the Taurus chain,
close to modern *Tûr 'Abdîn.* *Cf.* G. Boettger, *Topographi-
sches-historisches Lexicon zu den Schriften des Flavius Josephus,* 1879, pp. 193-194. It is possible, however, that Niphates is the name of an otherwise unknown Armenian leader
and that we should translate : " Niphates with his group of
Armenian grandees."
[c] Vonones did secure the Armenian throne but abdicated
in A.D. 15 or 16. According to Tacitus, *Ann.* ii. 4, it is not
that Vonones surrendered himself, but rather that Creticus
Silanus sent for him and kept him under surveillance, allowing him to keep his royal pomp and title.

to the Romans to ask for it. But Tiberius, in view of
the man's cowardice and the menace of the Parthian
king, for the latter had in fact countered with his own
envoys and a threat of war, refused his request.
Having no alternative means to secure the throne,[a]
since the Armenian grandees who dwelt around the
Niphates [b] had joined forces with Artabanus, Vonones threw himself on the mercy of Silanus the
governor of Syria.[c] Vonones was safeguarded in
Syria in deference to his education in Rome,[d] while;
Artabanus gave Armenia to Orodes, one of his own
sons.[e]

(5) Now Antiochus, king of Commagene,[f] died;
and there arose a conflict between the masses and
the men of note. Both factions sent embassies, the
men of substance requesting reconstitution of the
state as a Roman province, while the masses supported the monarchical tradition of their ancestors.[g]
The senate voted to send Germanicus to effect
needed reforms in the East. Fortune contrived to Death of
Germani-
cus.

[d] For references to Vonones' life after this incident see Tac.
*Ann.* ii. 58 and 68 and Suet. *Tib.* 49.

[e] Some scholars (see *Prosopog. Imp. Rom.* i². 1155 [pp.
229-230] and ii. 102 [p. 439]) have conjectured that this
statement has been misplaced and that it actually refers to
A.D. 35, when Artabanus sent his son Orodes to seize Armenia. But E. Täubler, *Die Parthernachrichten bei Josephus,*
pp. 9-10, disputes this on numismatic grounds. Orodes
seems to have lasted from 15 or 16 to 18, when Germanicus,
finding that the Armenians were ready to accept Zeno of
Pontus, who had grown up among the Armenians, as their
king, crowned him under the name of Artaxias. *Cf.* Tac.
*Ann.* ii. 56, Suet. *Gaius* 1, Strabo xii. 555.

[f] On Commagene see note on *B.J.* v. 461.

[g] Tacitus, *Ann.* ii. 42, also notes the division of opinion in
Commagene, remarking that a majority desired Roman rule,
while some preferred the continued rule of their own kings.

πραγματευομένης αὐτῷ τῆς τύχης εὐκαιρίαν τοῦ
θανάτου· καὶ γὰρ γενόμενος κατὰ τὴν ἀνατολὴν καὶ
πάντα διορθώσας ἀνῃρέθη φαρμάκῳ ὑπὸ Πείσωνος,
καθὼς ἐν ἄλλοις δεδήλωται.

55 (iii. 1) Πιλᾶτος δὲ ὁ τῆς Ἰουδαίας ἡγεμὼν στρατιὰν ἐκ Καισαρείας ἀγαγὼν καὶ μεθιδρύσας χει-
μαδιοῦσαν ἐν Ἱεροσολύμοις ἐπὶ καταλύσει τῶν
νομίμων¹ τῶν Ἰουδαϊκῶν ἐφρόνησε, προτομὰς Καίσαρος, αἳ ταῖς σημαίαις² προσῆσαν, εἰσαγόμενος εἰς
τὴν πόλιν, εἰκόνων ποίησιν ἀπαγορεύοντος ἡμῖν τοῦ
56 νόμου. καὶ διὰ τοῦτο οἱ πρότερον ἡγεμόνες ταῖς

---

¹ A : νόμων MWE.
² ταῖς σημαίαις] E : τοῖς σημείοις codd. : signis militaribus
Lat.

---

ᵃ A.D. 19.

ᵇ For Germanicus' mission in the East see also Tacitus,
*Ann.* ii. 43, who notes that the senatorial decree gave Germanicus power to supersede provincial governors. The story
of Piso's hostility for Germanicus is told at length by Tacitus,
*Ann.* ii. 43 ff. Tacitus does not say directly that Piso
poisoned Germanicus, but in his typical fashion he implies
it strongly (*Ann.* ii. 69).

ᶜ §§ 55-62 are parallel with *B.J.* ii. 169-177.

ᵈ E. M. Smallwood, " Some Notes on the Jews under
Tiberius," *Latomus* xv, 1956, p. 327, suggests that Pilate's
provocative behaviour in the incidents of the emperor's
busts and the building of the aqueduct was inspired by the
anti-Jewish policy followed by Tiberius' closest adviser, Sejanus, just before his death in A.D. 31 (see Philo, *In Flacc.* 1
and *Leg. ad Gaium* 159-161).

ᵉ The likeliest date for this episode, which is the first
mentioned in the account of Pilate in both the *B.J.* and the
*Ant.*, is A.D. 26, the first year of Pilate's procuratorship.

ᶠ These must be the *signa*, which often had the embossed
likeness of the emperor upon them. C. H. Kraeling, whose
article, " The Episode of the Roman Standards at Jerusalem," *Harv. Theol. Rev.* xxxv, 1942, pp. 263-289, should

make this a fit occasion for his death [a]; for when he had reached the East and had completed his reforms, he was removed by poison for which Piso was responsible, as other writers have explained.[b]

(iii. 1) [c] Now Pilate,[d] the procurator of Judaea, when he brought his army from Caesarea and removed it to winter quarters in Jerusalem,[e] took a bold step in subversion of the Jewish practices, by introducing into the city the busts of the emperor that were attached to the military standards,[f] for our law [g] forbids the making of images.[h] It was for this reason

Pilate introduces busts of the emperor into Jerusalem but has to remove them.

be consulted for this incident, thinks that they may also be *vexilla*; but this is unlikely, since the latter did not have embossed figures, and Josephus' word, προτομάς, refers to embossed figures.

[g] Ex. xx. 4, Deut. iv. 16.

[h] What did the Jews find offensive in these images? Kraeling, *op. cit.* p. 275, thinks that the objection may have been to the religious significance of the standards of the Roman army, which were regarded as *numina* and kept in special shrines. (For examples of the veneration of the standards see A. D. Nock, " The Roman Army and the Roman Religious Year," *Harv. Theol. Rev.* xlv, 1952, p. 239.) But if so, why had the Jews not objected previously to the aniconic standards? To be sure, Philo (*Leg. ad Gaium* 299-305) does mention Jewish objections to certain aniconic votive shields set up in honour of the emperor by Pilate later in his term of office in the palace of Herod at Jerusalem. Kraeling, p. 280, suggests that the real objection may have been to the introduction of the iconic images into the Antonia (*cf. Ant.* xviii. 90-95), where it would have constituted a particularly flagrant violation of the law against images, since the worship of the emperor's image would have compromised the sanctity of the priestly garments which were stored there. But there is no indication in Josephus' account that the images were brought into the Antonia, though admittedly the Antonia, as a fortress, was in an excellent position for military control of the city; and there is similarly no basis to Kraeling's conjecture (p. 281) that the Jews demanded

43

μὴ μετὰ τοιῶνδε κόσμων σημαίαις ἐποιοῦντο εἴσοδον
τῇ πόλει. πρῶτος δὲ Πιλᾶτος ἀγνοίᾳ τῶν ἀνθρώπων διὰ τὸ νύκτωρ γενέσθαι τὴν εἴσοδον ἱδρύεται
57 τὰς εἰκόνας φέρων εἰς τὰ Ἱεροσόλυμα. οἱ δ' ἐπεὶ
ἔγνωσαν κατὰ πληθὺν παρῆσαν εἰς Καισάρειαν
ἱκετείαν ποιούμενοι ἐπὶ πολλὰς ἡμέρας ἐπὶ μετα-
θέσει τῶν εἰκόνων. καὶ μὴ συγχωροῦντος διὰ τὸ
εἰς ὕβριν Καίσαρι φέρειν, ἐπείπερ οὐκ ἐξανεχώρουν
λιπαρεῖν κατὰ ἕκτην ἡμέραν ἐν ὅπλοις ἀφανῶς ἐπι-
καθίσας τὸ στρατιωτικὸν αὐτὸς ἐπὶ τὸ βῆμα ἧκεν.
τὸ δ' ἐν τῷ σταδίῳ κατεσκεύαστο, ὅπερ[1] ἀπέκρυπτε
58 τὸν ἐφεδρεύοντα στρατόν. πάλιν δὲ τῶν Ἰουδαίων
ἱκετείᾳ χρωμένων ἀπὸ συνθήματος περιστήσας τοὺς
στρατιώτας ἠπείλει θάνατον ἐπιθήσειν ζημίαν ἐκ
τοῦ ὀξέος, εἰ μὴ παυσάμενοι θορυβεῖν ἐπὶ τὰ οἰ-
59 κεῖα ἀπίοιεν. οἱ δὲ πρηνεῖς ῥίψαντες ἑαυτοὺς καὶ
γυμνοῦντες τὰς σφαγὰς ἡδονῇ δέξασθαι[2] τὸν θάνατον ἔλεγον ἢ τολμήσειν τὴν σοφίαν παραβήσεσθαι
τῶν νόμων. καὶ Πιλᾶτος θαυμάσας τὸ ἐχυρὸν[3]
αὐτῶν ἐπὶ φυλακῇ τῶν νόμων παραχρῆμα τὰς εἰ-

---

[1] ὅπου vel οὖπερ coni. Niese.
[2] δέξεσθαι ed. pr.
[3] A : ὀχυρὸν MWE.

---

the removal not only of the iconic but also of the aniconic
objects. According to *B.J.* ii. 170, the objection is to the
violation of the Jewish law which prohibits an image from
being erected in the city of Jerusalem. There is no special
law concerning images applicable to Jerusalem ; yet the

that the previous procurators, when they entered
the city, used standards that had no such ornaments
Pilate was the first to bring the images into Jerusalem [a] and set them up, doing it without the knowledge of the people, for he entered at night. But
when the people discovered it, they went in a throng
to Caesarea and for many days entreated him to take
away the images. He refused to yield, since to do so
would be an outrage to the emperor ; however,
since they did not cease entreating him, on the sixth
day he secretly armed and placed his troops in position, while he himself came to the speaker's stand.
This had been constructed in the stadium, which provided concealment for the army [b] that lay in wait.
When the Jews again engaged in supplication, at a
pre-arranged signal he surrounded them with his
soldiers and threatened to punish them at once with
death if they did not put an end to their tumult and
return to their own places. But they, casting themselves prostrate and baring their throats, declared
that they had gladly welcomed death rather than
make bold to transgress the wise provisions of the
laws. Pilate, astonished at the strength of their
devotion to the laws, straightway removed the

Jews must have felt the violation more keenly because of the
holniess of the city. The simplest explanation is that the
Jews objected to the violation of the law against the making
of an iconic figure of a man (*cf. Abodah Zarah* 47 b). *Cf.* E.
Bevan, *Holy Images*, 1940, pp. 48-63 ; E. R. Goodenough,
*Jewish Symbols in the Greco-Roman Period*, iv, 1954, pp. 11-
24 ; and C. Roth, " An Ordinance against Images in Jerusalem, A.D. 66," *Harv. Theol. Rev.* xlix, 1956, pp. 169-177.

[a] Philo, as cited by Euseb. *Dem. Evang.* viii. 2. 123, remarks that it was in the temple that Pilate set up the standards (σημαῖαι) at night.

[b] Variant " where he had concealed the army."

κόνας ἐκ τῶν Ἱεροσολύμων ἐπανεκόμισεν εἰς Καισάρειαν.

60 (2) Ὑδάτων δὲ ἐπαγωγὴν εἰς τὰ Ἱεροσόλυμα
ἔπραξεν δαπάνῃ τῶν ἱερῶν χρημάτων ἐκλαβὼν τὴν
ἀρχὴν τοῦ ῥεύματος ὅσον ἀπὸ σταδίων διακοσίων,[1]
οἱ δ' οὐκ ἠγάπων τοῖς ἀμφὶ τὸ ὕδωρ δρωμένοις
πολλαί τε μυριάδες ἀνθρώπων συνελθόντες κατεβόων αὐτοῦ παύσασθαι τοῦ ἐπὶ τοιούτοις προθυμου-
μένου, τινὲς δὲ καὶ λοιδορίᾳ χρώμενοι ὕβριζον εἰς
61 τὸν ἄνδρα, οἷα δὴ φιλεῖ πράσσειν ὅμιλος. ὁ δὲ στο-
λῇ ἐκείνων πολὺ πλῆθος στρατιωτῶν ἀμπεχόμενον,
οἳ ἐφέροντο σκυτάλας ὑπὸ ταῖς στολαῖς, διαπέμψας
εἰς ὃ περιέλθοιεν αὐτούς, αὐτὸς ἐκέλευσεν ἀναχω-
ρεῖν. τῶν δὲ ὡρμηκότων εἰς τὸ λοιδορεῖν ἀπο-
δίδωσι τοῖς στρατιώταις ὃ προσυνέκειτο σημεῖον.
62 οἱ δὲ καὶ πολὺ μειζόνως ἤπερ ἐπέταξεν Πιλᾶτος
ἐχρῶντο πληγαῖς τούς τε θορυβοῦντας ἐν ἴσῳ καὶ
μὴ κολάζοντες. οἱ δ'[2] εἰσεφέροντο μαλακὸν οὐδέν,
ὥστε ἄοπλοι ληφθέντες ὑπ' ἀνδρῶν ἐκ παρασκευῆς
ἐπιφερομένων πολλοὶ μὲν αὐτῶν ταύτῃ καὶ ἀπέ-
θνησκον, οἱ δὲ καὶ τραυματίαι ἀνεχώρησαν. καὶ
οὕτω παύεται ἡ στάσις.

---

[1] τετρακοσίων B.J. ii. 175.
[2] οἱ δ'] aut omittendum aut οὐδ' scribendum coni. Niese.

---

[a] *Megillat Taanit* xviii reads : " On the third of Kislev
the ensigns were removed from the [temple ?] court." S.
Zeitlin, *Megillat Taanit*, 1922, p. 87, sees in this statement a
reference to Pilate's removal of the standards from Jerusalem.

[b] In the parallel passage, *B.J.* ii. 175, Josephus says that
Pilate drew upon " the sacred treasure known as *Corbonas*."

images from Jerusalem and brought them back to Caesarea.[a]

(2) He spent money from the sacred treasury [b] in the construction of an aqueduct to bring water into Jerusalem, intercepting the source of the stream at a distance of 200 furlongs.[c] The Jews did not acquiesce in the operations that this involved ; and tens of thousands of men assembled and cried out against him, bidding him relinquish his promotion of such designs. Some too even hurled insults and abuse of the sort that a throng will commonly engage in. He thereupon ordered a large number of soldiers to be dressed in Jewish garments, under which they carried clubs, and he sent them off this way and that, thus surrounding the Jews, whom he ordered to withdraw. When the Jews were in full torrent of abuse he gave his soldiers the prearranged signal. They, however, inflicted much harder blows than Pilate had ordered, punishing alike both those who were rioting and those who were not. But the Jews showed no faint-heartedness ; and so, caught unarmed,[d] as they were, by men delivering a prepared attack, many of them actually were slain on the spot, while some withdrew disabled by blows. Thus ended the uprising.

Pilate uses money belonging to the temple for an aqueduct.

Thackeray, in his note, fails to realize that *Corbonas* is the Hebrew word for sacrifices, and that the Jews were outraged because Pilate was expropriating for his own secular purposes the shekalim which had been contributed by Jews everywhere for the purchase of sacrificial animals (see Mishnah *Shekalim* iii. 2).

[c] About twenty-three miles. According to *B.J.* ii. 175, the distance was twice as great.

[d] According to Niese's conjecture, the meaning would be " punishing alike both those who were rioting and those who were not and showing no weakness towards them, so that caught unarmed. . . ."

63 (3) Γίνεται δὲ κατὰ τοῦτον τὸν χρόνον Ἰησοῦς[1]
σοφὸς ἀνήρ, εἴγε ἄνδρα αὐτὸν λέγειν χρή· ἦν γὰρ
παραδόξων ἔργων ποιητής, διδάσκαλος ἀνθρώπων

---

[1] Ἰησοῦς] Ἰησοῦς τις Eusebii Praep. codd. quidam.

---

[a] R. Eisler, The Messiah Jesus (tr. by A. H. Krappe), 1931
p. 61, in the belief that the traditional text corresponds closely
to Josephus' vocabulary and style but that Christian censors
have tampered with it, has restored the original text of §§ 63-64
as follows (the words in parentheses represent words not in the
traditional text) : Γίνεται δὲ κατὰ τοῦτον τὸν χρόνον (ἀρχὴ νέων
θορύβων) Ἰησοῦς τις σοφ(ιστὴς) ἀνήρ, εἴγε ἄνδρα λέγειν χρὴ αὐτόν,
(τὸν ἐξ ἀνθρώπων ἐξαισιώτατον, ὃν οἱ μαθηταὶ υἱὸν θεοῦ ὀνομά-
ζουσιν, τὸν οἷα οὐδέποτε ἐπεποιήκει ἄνθρωπος θαύματα ἐργασά-
μενον. . . .) ἦν γὰρ παραδόξων ἔργων διδάσκαλος, ἀνθρώπων τῶν
ἡδονῇ τἀληθῆ δεχομένων (. . . .) καὶ πολλοὺς μὲν Ἰουδαίους, πολλοὺς δὲ καὶ τοῦ Ἑλληνικοῦ ἀπηγάγετο (καὶ ὑπὸ τούτων) ὁ χριστὸς
(εἶναι ἐνομίζετο. . . .) καὶ αὐτὸν ἐνδείξει τῶν πρώτων ἀνδρῶν
παρ᾿· ἡμῖν σταυρῷ ἐπιτετιμηκότος Πιλάτου οὐκ ἐπαύσαντο (θορυβεῖν) οἱ τὸ πρῶτον ἀγαπήσαντες. φανῆ(ναι) γὰρ αὐτοῖς (ἔδοξε)
τρίτην ἡμέραν ἔχων (θανάτου) πάλιν ζῶν, τῶν θείων προφητῶν
ταῦτά τε καὶ ἄλλα μυρία περὶ αὐτοῦ θαυμάσια εἰρηκότων. εἰς ἔτι
καὶ νῦν τῶν Χριστιανῶν ἀπὸ τοῦδε ὠνομασμένων οὐκ ἐπέλιπε τὸ
φῦλον.

The following is Eisler's translation (p. 62) : " Now about
his time arose (an occasion for new disturbances) a certain
Jesus, a wizard of a man, if indeed he may be called a man
(who was the most monstrous of all men, whom his disciples
call a son of God, as having done wonders such as no man
hath ever done). . . . He was in fact a teacher of astonishing
tricks to such men as accept the abnormal with delight. . . .
And he seduced many Jews and many also of the Greek
nation, and (was regarded by them as) the Messiah. . . .
And when, on the indictment of the principal men among
us, Pilate had sentenced him to the cross, still those who
before had admired him did not cease (to rave). For it seemed
to them that having been dead for three days, he had appeared
to them alive again, as the divinely-inspired prophets had
foretold—these and ten thousand other wonderful things—
concerning him. And even now the race of those who are
called ' Messianists ' after him is not extinct."

48

(3) [a] About this time [b] there lived Jesus, a wise
man, if indeed one ought to call him a man. For he
was one who wrought surprising feats and was a

Jesus
(Testi-
monium
Flavianum)

[b] Ever since Scaliger in the sixteenth century first suspected the authenticity of this so-called *Testimonium Flavianum*, an enormous literature (for which see especially
Schürer i. 544-545 and Eisler, *op. cit.* pp. 36 ff.) has developed
concerning it. Those against its genuineness include
Schürer, Niese, Norden, Zeitlin, Lewy, and Juster. The
principal arguments for its authenticity are that it is found
in all the MSS., that it is cited by Eusebius, *Hist. Eccl.* i. 11
and *Dem. Evang.* iii. 5. 105, and that the vocabulary and
style are basically Josephan. The principal arguments
against genuineness are : (1) Josephus, as a loyal Pharisaic
Jew, could not have written that Jesus was the Messiah.
(The references to Jesus in the Slavonic Josephus can hardly
be used as evidence of Josephus' attitude towards Christianity
since the authenticity of the Slavonic version is so widely
questioned) ; (2) Origen (*Contra Celsum* i. 47 and *Comment.
in Matt.* xiii. 55) explicitly states (c. A.D. 280) that Josephus
did not believe in Jesus as the Christ. Eusebius, however, c.
A.D. 324, does have our passage : hence, ever since the
seventeenth century, when Richard Montague, bishop of
Norwich, declared the phrase " he was the Messiah " a
Christian gloss, some scholars have argued that the passage
was forged, in whole or in part, during the interval between
280 and 324, perhaps, though there is no evidence, by Eusebius himself ; (3) The passage breaks the continuity of the
narrative, which tells of a series of riots. § 65 seems to belong
directly after § 62 ; (4) There are several stylistic peculiari-
ties (*e.g.*, τῶν πρώτων ἀνδρῶν παρ' ἡμῖν is not the way that
Josephus refers to the Jews), though Thackeray and Richards
and Shutt have noted a number of Josephan idioms, such as
ἡδονῇ δέχεσθαι and τρίτην ἔχων ἡμέραν. The ingenious theory
of R. Laqueur, *Der jüdische Historiker Flavius Josephus*,
1920, pp. 274 ff., that Josephus inserted the passage to secure
the favour of the rising Christian sect at a time when he himself was under severe attack, can hardly be accepted. The
most probable view seems to be that our text represents substantially what Josephus wrote, but that some alterations
have been made by a Christian interpolator.

49

τῶν ἡδονῇ τἀληθῆ[1] δεχομένων,[2] καὶ πολλοὺς μὲν
Ἰουδαίους, πολλοὺς δὲ καὶ τοῦ Ἑλληνικοῦ ἐπηγά-
64 γετο· ὁ χριστὸς[3] οὗτος ἦν. καὶ αὐτὸν ἐνδείξει τῶν
πρώτων ἀνδρῶν παρ᾽ ἡμῖν[4] σταυρῷ ἐπιτετιμηκότος
Πιλάτου[5] οὐκ ἐπαύσαντο[6] οἱ τὸ πρῶτον ἀγαπή-
σαντες· ἐφάνη γὰρ αὐτοῖς[7] τρίτην ἔχων ἡμέραν
πάλιν ζῶν τῶν θείων προφητῶν ταῦτά τε καὶ ἄλλα
μυρία περὶ αὐτοῦ θαυμάσια[8] εἰρηκότων. εἰς ἔτι τε
νῦν τῶν Χριστιανῶν ἀπὸ τοῦδε ὠνομασμένον οὐκ
ἐπέλιπε τὸ φῦλον.

65 (4) Καὶ ὑπὸ τοὺς αὐτοὺς χρόνους ἕτερόν τι δεινὸν
ἐθορύβει τοὺς Ἰουδαίους καὶ περὶ τὸ ἱερὸν τῆς
Ἴσιδος τὸ ἐν Ῥώμῃ πράξεις αἰσχυνῶν οὐκ ἀπηλ-
λαγμέναι συντυγχάνουσιν. καὶ πρότερον τοῦ τῶν
Ἰσιακῶν τολμήματος μνήμην ποιησάμενος οὕτω
μεταβιβῶ[9] τὸν λόγον ἐπὶ τὰ ἐν τοῖς Ἰουδαίοις γε-
66 γονότα. Παυλῖνα ἦν τῶν ἐπὶ Ῥώμης προγόνων τε

[1] τἀήθη Thackeray.
[2] τῶν . . . δεχομένων] τἀληθῆ σεβομένων Eus. Dem.
[3] χριστὸς] codd. : χριστὸς λεγόμενος Richards et Shutt (Class.
Quart. xxxi, 1937, p. 176) ; cf. Ant. xx. 200.
[4] τῶν ἡμῖν] codd. : τῶν παρ᾽ ἡμῖν ἀρχόντων Eus. Dem.
[5] ante οὐκ i. marg. σεβάζειν add. m. 2 M.
[6] ἐξεπαύσαντο Eusebii Praep. codd. plurimi.
[7] αὐτοῖς] αὐτοῖς ⟨ὡς ἔλεγον⟩ vel ⟨ὡς λέγουσιν⟩ coni. Richards
et Shutt.       [8] θαυμάσια] om. Eus. Dem.
[9] Naber : μεταδιδῶ MW : μεταδίδωμι A : μεταγάγω E :
transibo Lat.

[a] Variant (Thackeray's emendation) " the unusual."
[b] Variant (Richards and Shutt's emendation in *Class.
Quart.* xxi, 1937, p. 176) " the so-called Christ."
[c] Richards and Shutt suggest that " according to their
report " has been removed by the Christian censor.
[d] Actually A.D. 19, as we see from Tac. *Ann.* ii. 85, and not
c. A.D. 30, as we should deduce from the insertion of these

teacher of such people as accept the truth [a] gladly. He won over many Jews and many of the Greeks. He was the Messiah.[b] When Pilate, upon hearing him accused by men of the highest standing amongst us, had condemned him to be crucified, those who had in the first place come to love him did not give up their affection for him. On the third day [c] he appeared to them restored to life, for the prophets of God had prophesied these and countless other marvellous things about him. And the tribe of the Christians, so called after him, has still to this day not disappeared.

(4) About this same time [d] another outrage threw the Jews into an uproar ; and simultaneously certain actions of a scandalous nature occurred in connexion with the temple of Isis at Rome. I shall first give an account of the daring deed of the followers of Isis and shall then come back to the fate of the Jews.[e] There was a lady Paulina,[f] who because of her descent

Paulina and her lover ; trick played by the priests of Isis.

incidents in the midst of the narrative of the procuratorship of Pontius Pilate. E. M. Smallwood, " Some Notes on the Jews under Tiberius," *Latomus* xv, 1956, p. 326, though rejecting Josephus' date, suggests that this date was prompted by the danger in which the Jews found themselves in the year 30 because of Sejanus' opposition to them.

[e] Both Tacitus, *Ann.* ii. 85, and Suetonius, *Tib.* 36, also couple Tiberius' actions against the Egyptian and Jewish worship.

[f] C. Pharr, " The Testimony of Josephus to Christianity," *Am. Jour. of Philol.* xlviii, 1927, p. 144, remarks that this story of Mundus and Paulina in its present literary form has been influenced by the classic story of the trick of Nectanebus II, the Egyptian king who, according to Pseudo-Callisthenes, *History of Alexander*, i. 4 ff., deceived Olympias, wife of King Philip of Macedonia, into believing that he was Zeus Ammon, and through her became the father of Alexander the Great.

ἀξιώματι τῷ τε[1] καθ᾽ ἑαυτὴν ἐπιτηδεύματι[2] ἀρετῆς
ἐπὶ μέγα προϊοῦσα τῷ ὀνόματι, δύναμίς τε αὐτῇ
χρημάτων ἦν καὶ γεγονυῖα τὴν ὄψιν εὐπρεπὴς καὶ
τῆς ὥρας ἐν ᾗ μάλιστα ἀγάλλονται αἱ γυναῖκες εἰς
τὸ σωφρονεῖν ἀνέκειτο ἡ ἐπιτήδευσις τοῦ βίου.
ἐγεγάμητο δὲ Σατορνίνῳ τῶν εἰς τὰ πάντα ἀντ-
67 ισουμένων τῷ περὶ αὐτὴν ἀξιολόγῳ.[3] ταύτης ἐρᾷ
Δέκιος Μοῦνδος τῶν τότε ἱππέων ἐν ἀξιώματι
μεγάλῳ, καὶ μείζονα οὖσαν ἁλῶναι δώροις διὰ τὸ
καὶ πεμφθέντων εἰς πλῆθος περιιδεῖν ἐξῆπτο μᾶλλον, ὥστε καὶ εἴκοσι μυριάδας δραχμῶν Ἀτθίδων[4]
68 ὑπισχνεῖτο εὐνῆς μιᾶς. καὶ μηδ᾽ ὣς ἐπικλωμένης,
οὐ φέρων τὴν ἀτυχίαν τοῦ ἔρωτος ἐνδείᾳ σιτίων
θάνατον ἐπιτιμᾶν αὑτῷ καλῶς ἔχειν ἐνόμισεν ἐπὶ
παύλῃ[5] κακοῦ τοῦ κατειληφότος. καὶ ὁ μὲν ἐπεψή-
φιζέν τε τῇ οὕτω τελευτῇ καὶ πράσσειν οὐκ ἀπηλ-
69 λάσσετο. καὶ ἦν γὰρ ὄνομα Ἴδη[6] πατρῷος ἀπελευ-
θέρα τῷ Μούνδῳ παντοίων ἴδρις κακῶν, δεινῶς
φέρουσα τοῦ νεανίσκου τῷ ψηφίσματι τοῦ θανεῖν,
οὐ γὰρ ἀφανὴς ἦν ἀπολούμενος, ἀνεγείρει τε αὐτὸν
ἀφικομένη διὰ λόγου πιθανή τε ἦν ἐλπίδων τινῶν
ὑποσχέσειν, ὡς διαπραχθησομένων ὁμιλιῶν πρὸς
70 τὴν Παυλῖναν αὐτῷ. καὶ δεχομένου τὴν ἱκετείαν
ἡδονῇ πέντε μυριάδων δεήσειν αὐτῇ μόνων ἔλεγεν

---

[1] τῷ τε] Hudson : καὶ τῷ E : τῶν codd.
[2] ἐπιτηδεύματι] E : ἐπιτηδεύοντι κόσμον codd.
[3] τῷ . . . ἀξιολόγῳ] i. marg. A : τῶν περὶ αὐτὴν ἀξιολόγων
codd. E.
[4] Ἀτθίδων] A : αὑτῇ δώσειν MW : ἀττικῶν E.
[5] Naber : Παυλίνη codd.
[6] καὶ ἦν γὰρ ὄνομα Ἴδη] καὶ ἦν γὰρ Ἰσίδη, litt. ἀρισῖ i. ras.
M : καὶ ἦν γὰρ Ἴδη W : ἦν δὲ Ἴδη E.

from noble Romans and because of her own practice
of virtue was held in high regard. She also enjoyed
the prestige of·wealth, had a comely appearance, and
was at the age at which women are most exuberant,
yet devoted her life to good conduct. She was married
to Saturninus,[a] who was fully a match for her in reputation. Decius Mundus, who ranked high among the
knights of his day, was in love with her. When he
saw that her character was too strong to succumb to
gifts, since, even when he sent them abundantly, she
scorned them, his passion was inflamed all the more,
so that he actually promised to give her 200,000 Attic
drachmas if he could share her bed a single time.
When even this failed to shake her resolution, he,
finding it intolerable not to win his suit, thought that
it would be fitting to condemn himself to death by
starvation and thus to put an end to the suffering
that had overtaken him. And so he decided upon
such a death and was actually proceeding to carry out
his resolve. Mundus, however, had a freedwoman
named Ida, expert in every kind of mischief, whom
his father had emancipated. She had no patience
with the young man's resolve to die, for it was obvious
what he intended.[b] She went to him, used argument
to rouse him, and by plausibly undertaking to find a
way, held out hope that he might succeed in enjoying
intimate relations with Paulina. When he joyfully
listened to her importunity, she informed him that
she would require no more than 50,000 drachmas to

[a] E. Groag, *Prosopog. Imp. Rom.* ii A. 1528, plausibly
conjectures that this Saturninus must be one of the two
Sentii Saturnini, Gaius (consul in A.D. 4) or his brother
Lucius.

[b] Or " he was no undistinguished person who was to
perish."

ἐπὶ ἁλώσει τῆς γυναικός. καὶ ἡ μὲν ἐπὶ τούτοις
ἀνεγείρασα τὸν νεανίσκον καὶ τὸ αἰτηθὲν λαβοῦσα
ἀργύριον οὐ τὰς αὐτὰς ὁδοὺς ἐστέλλετο τοῖς προδε-
διακονημένοις ὁρῶσα τῆς γυναικὸς τὸ μηδαμῶς
χρημάτων ἁλισκόμενον, εἰδυῖα δὲ αὐτὴν θεραπείᾳ
τῆς Ἴσιδος σφόδρα ὑπηγμένην τεχνᾶταί τι τοιόνδε.
71 τῶν ἱερέων τισὶν ἀφικομένη διὰ λόγων ἐπὶ πίστεσιν
μεγάλαις τὸ δὲ μέγιστον δόσει χρημάτων τὸ μὲν
παρὸν μυριάδων δυοῖν καὶ ἡμίσει, λαβόντος δ᾽ ἔκ-
βασιν τοῦ πράγματος ἑτέρῳ τοσῷδε, διασαφεῖ τοῦ
νεανίσκου τὸν ἔρωτα αὐτοῖς, κελεύουσα παντοίως
72 ἐπὶ τῷ ληψομένῳ τὴν ἄνθρωπον σπουδάσαι. οἱ δ᾽
ἐπὶ πληγῇ[1] τοῦ χρυσίου παραχθέντες ὑπισχνοῦντο.
καὶ αὐτῶν ὁ γεραίτατος ὡς τὴν Παυλῖναν ὠσάμενος
γενομένων εἰσόδων καταμόνας διὰ λόγων ἐλθεῖν
ἠξίου. καὶ συγχωρηθὲν πεμπτὸς ἔλεγεν ἥκειν ὑπὸ
τοῦ Ἀνούβιδος ἔρωτι αὐτῆς ἡσσημένου τοῦ θεοῦ
73 κελεύοντός τε ὡς αὐτὸν ἐλθεῖν. τῇ δὲ εὐκτὸς ὁ
λόγος ἦν καὶ ταῖς τε φίλαις ἐνεκαλλωπίζετο τῇ ἐπὶ
τοιούτοις ἀξιώσει τοῦ Ἀνούβιδος καὶ φράζει πρὸς
τὸν ἄνδρα, δεῖπνόν τε αὐτῇ καὶ εὐνὴν τοῦ Ἀνούβιδος εἰσηγγέλθαι, συνεχώρει δ᾽ ἐκεῖνος τὴν σωφρο-
74 σύνην τῆς γυναικὸς ἐξεπιστάμενος. χωρεῖ οὖν εἰς
τὸ τέμενος, καὶ δειπνήσασα, ὡς ὕπνου καιρὸς ἦν,
κλεισθεισῶν τῶν θυρῶν ὑπὸ τοῦ ἱερέως ἔνδον ἐν
τῷ νεῷ καὶ τὰ λύχνα ἐκποδὼν ἦν καὶ ὁ Μοῦνδος,
προεκέκρυπτο γὰρ τῇδε, οὐχ ἡμάρτανεν ὁμιλῶν

[1] πλήθει E.

secure the woman. These proposals encouraged the youth, and she received the sum for which she had asked. She did not, however, proceed by the same course as had previous agents, since she perceived that this woman would never succumb to bribes. But knowing that the lady was very much given to the worship of Isis, Ida devised the following stratagem. She had an interview with some of the priests and promised them every assurance, above all, a sum of money amounting to 25,000 drachmas payable at once and as much more after the success of the plot. She then explained the young man's passionate desire for the woman and urged them to bend every effort to secure her for him. The impact of the money was enough to sway them, and they agreed. The eldest of them hastened to Paulina's house and, on being admitted, requested a private talk with her. This being accorded, he said that he had been sent to her by the god Anubis *a* ; the god had fallen in love with her and bade her come to him. The message was what she would most have wished. Not only did she pride herself among her lady friends on receiving such an invitation from Anubis, but she told her husband of her summons to dine with and share the bed of Anubis. Her husband concurred, since he had no doubt of his wife's chastity. Go then she did to the temple. After supper, when it came time to sleep, the doors within the shrine were shut by the priest and the lamps were cleared away. Mundus, for he had been concealed there beforehand, was not rebuffed when he sought intercourse with her. Indeed

---

*a* After Osiris, the husband of Isis, had been killed, it was Anubis who was said to have helped Isis collect the pieces in which his body had been cut. Anubis consequently became a god of the dead.

τῶν πρὸς αὐτήν, παννύχιόν τε αὐτῷ διηκονήσατο
75 ὑπειληφυῖα θεὸν εἶναι. καὶ ἀπελθόντος πρότερον ἢ
κίνησιν ἄρξασθαι τῶν ἱερέων, οἳ τὴν ἐπιβουλὴν ᾔδε-
σαν, ἡ Παυλῖνα πρωῒ ὡς τὸν ἄνδρα ἐλθοῦσα τὴν
ἐπιφάνειαν ἐκδιηγεῖται τοῦ Ἀνούβιδος καὶ πρὸς τὰς
76 φίλας ἐνελαμπρύνετο[1] λόγοις τοῖς ἐπ᾽ αὐτῷ. οἱ δὲ
τὰ μὲν ἠπίστουν εἰς τὴν φύσιν τοῦ πράγματος
ὁρῶντες, τὰ δ᾽ ἐν θαύματι καθίσταντο οὐκ ἔχοντες,
ὡς χρὴ ἄπιστα αὐτὰ κρίνειν, ὁπότε εἴς τε τὴν
77 σωφροσύνην καὶ τὸ ἀξίωμα ἀπίδοιεν αὐτῆς. τρίτῃ
δὲ ἡμέρᾳ μετὰ τὴν πρᾶξιν ὑπαντιάσας αὐτὴν ὁ
Μοῦνδος, " Παυλῖνα," φησίν, " ἀλλά[2] μοι καὶ εἴκοσι
μυριάδας διεσώσω δυναμένη οἴκῳ προσθέσθαι τῷ
σαυτῆς διακονεῖσθαί τε ἐφ᾽ οἷς προεκαλούμην οὐκ
ἐνέλιπες. ἃ μέντοι εἰς Μοῦνδον ὑβρίζειν ἐπειρῶ,[3]
μηδέν μοι μελῆσαν τῶν ὀνομάτων, ἀλλὰ τῆς ἐκ
τοῦ πράγματος ἡδονῆς, Ἀνούβιον[4] ὄνομα ἐθέμην
78 ἐμαυτῷ."[5] καὶ ὁ μὲν ἀπῄει ταῦτα εἰπών, ἡ δὲ
εἰς ἔννοιαν τότε πρῶτον ἐλθοῦσα τοῦ τολμήματος
περιρρήγνυταί τε τὴν στολὴν καὶ τἀνδρὶ δηλώσασα
τοῦ παντὸς ἐπιβουλεύματος τὸ μέγεθος ἐδεῖτο μὴ
περιωφθῆναι βοηθείας τυγχάνειν· ὁ δὲ τῷ αὐτοκρά-
79 τορι ἐπεσήμηνε[6] τὴν πρᾶξιν. καὶ ὁ Τιβέριος μαθήσεως ἀκριβοῦς αὐτῷ γενομένης ἐξετάσει τῶν ἱερέων
ἐκείνους τε ἀνεσταύρωσεν καὶ τὴν Ἴδην ὀλέθρου
γενομένην αἰτίαν καὶ τὰ πάντα ἐφ᾽ ὕβρει συνθεῖσαν
τῆς γυναικός, τόν τε ναὸν καθεῖλεν καὶ τὸ ἄγαλμα
τῆς Ἴσιδος εἰς τὸν Θύβριν ποταμὸν ἐκέλευσεν ἐμ-

---

[1] ἀνελαμβάνετο MW.  [2] ἅμα Naber.
[3] ὑβρίζειν ἐπειρῶ] A : ὕβρει διεχρῶ MWE.
[4] Ἀνούβει coni. Niese.

it was a nightlong service that she performed for him,
assuming that he was the god. He departed before
the priests, who had been informed of the scheme,
had begun to stir. Paulina went early in the morning
to her husband and described in detail the divine
manifestation of Anubis, and before the ladies, her
friends, she put on great airs in talking about him.
Those who heard, having regard to the substance of
the matter, were incredulous ; and yet, on the other
hand, finding it impossible not to believe her when
they took into consideration her chastity and position
in society, they were reduced to marvelling. Two
days after the incident, Mundus put himself in her
way and said : " Well, Paulina, you have indeed
saved me 200,000 drachmas which you could have
added to your estate, yet you have rendered to per-
fection the service I urged you to perform. As for
your attempt to flout Mundus, I did not concern
myself about names, though I did about the pleasure
to be derived from the act, so I adopted the name of
Anubis as my own." With these words he departed.
Then she, being now aware for the first time of his
dastardly deed, rent her garment ; and when she
had disclosed to her husband the enormity of the
scheme, she begged him not to neglect to obtain
redress. He in turn brought the matter to the notice
of the emperor. When Tiberius had fully informed
himself by examining the priests, he crucified both
them and Ida, for the hellish thing was her doing and
it was she who had contrived the whole plot against
the lady's honour. Moreover, he razed the temple
and ordered the statue of Isis to be cast into the

---

⁵ MW : αὐτῷ A : αὐτῷ E.
⁶ AE : ἀπεσήμηνε coni. Niese.

80 βαλεῖν. Μοῦνδον δὲ φυγῆς ἐτίμησε, κώλυμα τοῦ μὴ
μειζόνως κολάζειν τὸ μετὰ ἔρωτος αὐτῷ ἡμαρτῆ-
σθαι τὰ ἡμαρτημένα ἡγησάμενος. καὶ τὰ μὲν περὶ
τὸ ἱερὸν τῆς Ἴσιδος τοῖς ἱερεῦσιν ὑβρισμένα τοιαῦτα
ἦν. ἐπάνειμι δὲ ἐπὶ τὴν ἀφήγησιν τῶν ἐν Ῥώμῃ
Ἰουδαίοις κατὰ τοῦτον τὸν χρόνον συντυχόντων,
ὥς μοι καὶ προαπεσήμηνεν ὁ λόγος.

81 (5) Ἦν ἀνὴρ Ἰουδαῖος, φυγὰς μὲν τῆς αὐτοῦ
κατηγορίᾳ τε[1] παραβάσεων νόμων τινῶν καὶ δέει
τιμωρίας τῆς ἐπ’ αὐτοῖς, πονηρὸς δὲ εἰς τὰ πάντα.
καὶ δὴ τότε ἐν τῇ Ῥώμῃ διαιτώμενος προσεποιεῖτο

82 μὲν ἐξηγεῖσθαι σοφίαν νόμων τῶν Μωυσέως, προσ-
ποιησάμενος δὲ τρεῖς ἄνδρας εἰς τὰ πάντα ὁμοιο-
τρόπους[2] τούτοις ἐπιφοιτήσασαν Φουλβίαν[3] τῶν ἐν
ἀξιώματι γυναικῶν καὶ νομίμοις προσεληλυθυῖαν
τοῖς Ἰουδαϊκοῖς πείθουσι πορφύραν καὶ χρυσὸν εἰς
τὸ ἐν Ἱεροσολύμοις ἱερὸν διαπέμψασθαι, καὶ λαβόντες ἐπὶ χρείας[4] τοῖς ἰδίοις ἀναλώμασιν αὐτὰ
ποιοῦνται,[5] ἐφ’ ὅπερ καὶ τὸ πρῶτον ἡ αἴτησις ἐ-

83 πράσσετο. καὶ ὁ Τιβέριος, ἀποσημαίνει γὰρ πρὸς
αὐτὸν φίλος ὢν Σατορνῖνος τῆς Φουλβίας ἀνὴρ ἐπι-
σκήψει τῆς γυναικός, κελεύει πᾶν τὸ Ἰουδαϊκὸν τῆς

[1] ed. pr.: δὲ codd.: om. E.
[2] A: ὁμοιοτέρους MW.
[3] A: Φλουβίαν MW.
[4] i. marg. γρ ἐπὶ χεῖρας A.
[5] ἐπὶ . . . αὐτὰ ποιοῦνται] ἀνάλωμα ταῦτα ἐπὶ χρείαις οἰκείαις
ποιοῦνται E: propriis usibus adsumpsere Lat.

[a] On the Jewish zeal for proselytism in Rome see, most
notably, Horace, *Sat.* i. 4. 142 ff. and Tac. *Hist.* v. 5.
[b] W. A. Heidel's fantastic suggestion (" Why Were the
Jews Banished from Italy in 19 A.D. ? ", *Am. Jour. of Philol.*

Tiber River. Mundus' sentence was exile, since
Tiberius regarded the fact that his crime had been
committed under the influence of passion as a bar to
a more severe penalty. Such were the insolent acts
of the priests in the temple of Isis. I shall now return
to the story, which I promised to tell, of what happened at the same time to the Jews in Rome.

(5) There was a certain Jew, a complete scoundrel, *Jewish em-*
who had fled his own country because he was accused *bezzlers in Rome.*
of transgressing certain laws and feared punishment *Tiberius*
on this account. Just at this time he was resident in *orders the expulsion*
Rome and played the part of an interpreter of the *of the Jews.*
Mosaic law and its wisdom. He enlisted three con-
federates not a whit better in character than himself ;
and when Fulvia, a woman of high rank who had become a Jewish proselyte,[a] began to meet with them
regularly, they urged her to send purple and gold to
the temple in Jerusalem.[b] They, however, took the
gifts and used them for their own personal expenses,
for it was this that had been their intention in asking
for gifts from the start. Saturninus,[c] the husband of
Fulvia, at the instigation of his wife, duly reported
this to Tiberius, whose friend he was, whereupon the
latter ordered the whole Jewish community to leave

xli, 1920, pp. 38-47) that Fulvia was actually invited to become a temple prostitute grows out of Tacitus' statement, in
the same chapter in which he discusses the expulsion, that
Tiberius took measures to check prostitution among women
of equestrian families ; but there was no religious prostitution
among Jews at this time.

[c] The identity in the names of the husbands of Fulvia and
Paulina (§ 66) seems to be due to mere coincidence ; but R. S.
Rogers, " Fulvia Paulina C. Sentii Saturnini," *Am. Jour. of
Philol.* liii, 1932, pp. 252-256, concludes that the same Satur-
ninus is meant and that the wife of this Saturninus was named
Fulvia Paulina.

84 'Ρώμης ἀπελθεῖν.[1] οἱ δὲ ὕπατοι τετρακισχιλίους
ἀνθρώπους[2] ἐξ αὐτῶν στρατολογήσαντες ἔπεμψαν
εἰς Σαρδὼ τὴν νῆσον, πλείστους δὲ ἐκόλασαν μὴ
θέλοντας στρατεύεσθαι διὰ φυλακὴν τῶν πατρίων
νόμων. καὶ οἱ μὲν δὴ διὰ κακίαν τεσσάρων ἀνδρῶν
ἠλαύνοντο τῆς πόλεως.

85 (iv. 1) Οὐκ ἀπήλλακτο δὲ θορύβου καὶ τὸ Σαμαρέων ἔθνος· συστρέφει γὰρ αὐτοὺς ἀνὴρ ἐν ὀλίγῳ τὸ ψεῦδος τιθέμενος κἀφ' ἡδονῇ[3] τῆς πληθύος
τεχνάζων τὰ πάντα, κελεύων ἐπὶ τὸ Γαριζεὶν ὄρος
αὐτῷ συνελθεῖν, ὃ ἁγνότατον αὐτοῖς ὀρῶν ὑπείληπται, ἰσχυρίζετό τε παραγενομένοις δείξειν τὰ
ἱερὰ σκεύη τῇδε κατορωρυγμένα Μωυσέως τῇδε
86 αὐτῶν ποιησαμένου κατάθεσιν. οἱ δὲ ἐν ὅπλοις τε

---

[1] A: ἀπελαθῆναι MWE: excedere Lat.
[2] AM: ἀνθρώπων W: ἄνδρας E.
[3] κἀφ' ἡδονῇ] Niese: καὶ ἐφ' ἡδονῇ codd.: καθ' ἡδονὴν E:
Cafedon nomine Lat.

---

[a] This expulsion is also mentioned by Suet. *Tib.* 36, Dio
Cass. lvii. 18. 5a, and Tac. *Ann.* ii. 85 (who also extends it to
the adherents of the Egyptian cult); *cf.* also Sen. *Epist.*
cviii. 22. Those who refused to leave were, according to
Suetonius (*ad loc.*), expelled and threatened with slavery if
they defied the order. Dio seems to be correct (and in line
with the story in Josephus about Fulvia the proselyte) in the
reason which he gives for the expulsion of the Jews, namely,
that the Jews were converting so many Romans to their
faith. The connexion of this incident with proselytism is
corroborated by 'he statement in Suetonius (*ad loc.*) that
those who had embraced the Egyptian and Jewish cults were
forced to burn their religious vestments and other accessories;
Suetonius is further careful to mention the proselytes as being
included in the expulsion. Tacitus likewise seems to refer to
proselytes when he speaks of those expelled as *ea supersti-
tione infecti,* " tainted with this superstition." On the whole
incident of the expulsion, particularly its legal aspects, see

Rome.[a] The consuls drafted four thousand of these
Jews for military service and sent them to the island
of Sardinia ; but they penalized a good man many of them,
who refused to serve for fear of breaking the Jewish
law.[b] And so because of the wickedness of four men
the Jews were banished from the city.

(iv. 1) The Samaritan nation too was not exempt
from disturbance. For a man who made light of
mendacity and in all his designs catered to the mob,
rallied them, bidding them go in a body with him to
Mount Gerizim, which in their belief is the most
sacred of mountains. He assured them that on their
arrival he would show them the sacred vessels which
were buried there, where Moses had deposited them.[c]

Pilate puts
down the
tumult of
the
Samaritans.

M. Radin, *The Jews among the Greeks and Romans*, 1915,
pp. 306-313.
  [b] According to Tacitus, *Ann.* ii. 85, not only the Jews but
also the adherents of the Egyptian worship were transported
to the island of Sardinia. Tacitus also mentions a total of
4000 and likewise says that they were of military age ; he
adds that they were of the class of freedmen. They were sent
to Sardinia, he remarks, to put down the brigandage of that
island. Suetonius, *Tib.* 36, says that the drafting of the Jews
into the army was only a pretext for sending them off to the
unhealthy region of Sardinia, where, it was evidently expected (so also Tac. *ad loc.*) that those expelled might die.
Sardinia's climate, however, is hardly different from that of
the Italian peninsula : the reference to its severity is indeed
puzzling, and perhaps Radin (*op. cit.* p. 312) is correct in
suggesting that the removal to Sardinia was motivated
merely by the desire to remove the proselytes from Jewish
influence.
  [c] On this incident see M. Gaster, *The Samaritans*, 1925,
pp. 90-91, who sees here a reference to the Samaritan belief
in the Restorer (the *Taheb* or *Shaheb*). The belief, based on
the promise given in their tenth commandment and on Deut.
xviii. 15 and 18, is that a prophet will come out of the tribe of
Levi, from which Moses was born, and that he will discover

61

ἦσαν πιθανὸν ἡγούμενοι τὸν λόγον, καὶ καθίσαντες
ἔν τινι κώμῃ, Τιραθανὰ¹ λέγεται, παρελάμβανον
τοὺς ἐπισυλλεγομένους ὡς μεγάλῳ πλήθει τὴν ἀνά-
87 βασιν εἰς τὸ ὄρος ποιησόμενοι. φθάνει δὲ Πιλᾶτος
τὴν ἄνοδον αὐτῶν προκαταλαβόμενος ἱππέων τε
πομπῇ καὶ ὁπλιτῶν, οἳ συμβαλόντες τοῖς ἐν τῇ
κώμῃ προσυνηθροισμένοις παρατάξεως γενομένης
τοὺς μὲν ἔκτειναν, τοὺς δ' εἰς φυγὴν τρέπονται
ζωγρίᾳ τε πολλοὺς ἦγον, ὧν τοὺς κορυφαιοτάτους
καὶ τοὺς ἐν τοῖς φυγοῦσι δυνατωτάτους ἔκτεινε
Πιλᾶτος.

88 (2) Καταστάντος δὲ τοῦ θορύβου Σαμαρέων ἡ
βουλὴ παρὰ Οὐιτέλλιον ὑπατικὸν ἴασιν ἄνδρα Συρίας
τὴν ἡγεμονίαν ἔχοντα καὶ Πιλάτου κατηγόρουν ἐπὶ
τῇ σφαγῇ τῶν ἀπολωλότων· οὐ γὰρ ἐπὶ ἀποστάσει τῶν Ῥωμαίων, ἀλλ' ἐπὶ διαφυγῇ τῆς Πιλάτου
89 ὕβρεως εἰς τὴν Τιραθανὰ παραγενέσθαι. καὶ Οὐιτέλλιος Μάρκελλον τῶν αὐτοῦ φίλων ἐκπέμψας
ἐπιμελητὴν τοῖς Ἰουδαίοις γενησόμενον Πιλᾶτον

¹ A : Τιραθανᾶ M : Τιραθαβᾶ W : Tirathua (Tirathiua cod.
A) Lat.

---

the hidden vessels of the temple. On Talmudic traditions
concerning the burial of the oil and the holy vessels of the
temple see V. Aptowitzer, *Parteipolitik der Hasmonäerzeit*,
1927, pp. 192-193 n. 2.

ᵃ J. A. Montgomery, *The Samaritans*, 1907, p. 146 n. 15,
suggests that this is probably the modern *Tire*, four miles
south-west of Shechem; but this site would seem to be too
far from Mt. Gerizim. *Duwara (Dawerta)* has also been proposed. *Cf.* F.-M. Abel, *Géographie de la Palestine*, ii, 1938,
p. 484.

ᵇ This, as can be seen from the context, was a council of
the entire Samaritan community, and not merely of the city
of Samaria. A. H. M. Jones, *The Cities of the Eastern Roman
Provinces*, 1937, p. 259, thinks that this was probably a sur-

His hearers, viewing this tale as plausible, appeared in arms. They posted themselves in a certain village named Tirathana,[a] and, as they planned to climb the mountain in a great multitude, they welcomed to their ranks the new arrivals who kept coming. But before they could ascend, Pilate blocked their projected route up the mountain with a detachment of cavalry and heavy-armed infantry, who in an encounter with the firstcomers in the village slew some in a pitched battle and put the others to flight. Many prisoners were taken, of whom Pilate put to death the principal leaders and those who were most influential among the fugitives.

(2) When the uprising had been quelled, the council[b] of the Samaritans went to Vitellius,[c] a man of consular rank who was governor of Syria, and charged Pilate with the slaughter of the victims. For, they said, it was not as rebels against the Romans but as refugees from the persecution of Pilate that they had met in Tirathana. Vitellius thereupon dispatched Marcellus,[d] one of his friends, to take charge of the administration of Judaea,[e] and ordered Pilate

*(marginal note: Vitellius, Roman governor of Syria, sends Pilate to Rome.)*

vival of one of the councils set up by Gabinius (cf. *Ant.* xiv. 90-91 and *B.J.* i. 169-170), but there is no evidence to support this suggestion.    [c] Father of the emperor Vitellius.

[d] As governor of Syria Vitellius lacked the authority to appoint procurators, a function reserved for the emperors. Hence, the appointment of Marcellus must have been to be acting procurator of Judaea. Aside from the inconclusive statement of Tacitus, *Ann.* vi. 32, that Tiberius entrusted his entire Eastern policy to Vitellius, there is no basis for the assumption of Mommsen and Dessau that Vitellius had extraordinary powers in the East similar to those held by Gaius Caesar and Germanicus. See D. Magie, *Roman Rule in Asia Minor*, ii, 1950, p. 1364 n. 39.

[e] On Tiberius' practice of allowing governors and procurators to serve long terms in office see §§ 170 ff.

# JOSEPHUS

ἐκέλευσεν ἐπὶ ῾Ρώμης ἀπιέναι πρὸς ἃ κατηγοροῖεν
οἱ Σαμαρεῖται¹ διδάξοντα τὸν αὐτοκράτορα. καὶ
Πιλᾶτος δέκα ἔτεσιν διατρίψας ἐπὶ ᾿Ιουδαίας εἰς
῾Ρώμην ἠπείγετο ταῖς Οὐιτελλίου πειθόμενος ἐντο-
λαῖς οὐκ ὂν ἀντειπεῖν. πρὶν δ᾿ ἐν² τῇ ῾Ρώμῃ ἴσχειν³
αὐτὸν φθάνει Τιβέριος μετάστας.

90    (3) Οὐιτέλλιος δὲ εἰς τὴν ᾿Ιουδαίαν ἀφικόμενος
ἐπὶ ῾Ιεροσολύμων ἀνῄει, καὶ ἦν γὰρ αὐτοῖς ἑορτὴ
πάτριος,⁴ πάσχα δὲ καλεῖται, δεχθεὶς μεγαλοπρε-
πῶς Οὐιτέλλιος τὰ τέλη τῶν ὠνουμένων καρπῶν
ἀνίησιν εἰς τὸ πᾶν τοῖς ταύτῃ κατοικοῦσιν καὶ τὴν
στολὴν τοῦ ἀρχιερέως καὶ τὸν πάντα αὐτοῦ κόσμον
συνεχώρησεν ἐν τῷ ἱερῷ κειμένην⁵ ὑπὸ τοῖς ἱερεῦσιν
ἔχειν τὴν ἐπιμέλειαν, καθότι καὶ πρότερον ἦν αὐτοῖς
9    ἐξουσία.⁶ τότε δὲ ἐν τῇ ᾿Αντωνίᾳ, φρούριον δ᾿
ἐστὶν οὕτως λεγόμενον, ἡ ἀπόθεσις αὐτῆς ἦν διὰ
τοιαύτην αἰτίαν· τῶν ἱερέων τις ῾Υρκανός, πολλῶν
δὲ ὄντων οἳ τόδε ἐκαλοῦντο τὸ ὄνομα ὁ πρῶτος,
ἐπεὶ πλησίον τῷ ἱερῷ βᾶριν κατασκευασάμενος

¹ A : ᾿Ιουδαῖοι MWE Lat.
² δ᾿ ἐν] δὲ ἢ ed. pr.
³ A : προσχεῖν MWE : veniret Lat.
⁴ A : om. MWE.
⁵ A : κείμενον MWE.
⁶ MW : ἐξουσία· A : om. E.

---

ᵃ Variant " Jews."
ᵇ Tiberius died on 16 March A.D. 37. Since, as seems
probable, Pilate began his procuratorship in 26, and since he
is here stated to have held office for ten years, it would appear
that he took a year to arrive in Rome—an improbability
since Josephus here remarks that he hurried. E. M. Smallwood, " The Date of the Dismissal of Pontius Pilate from
Judaea," *Jour. of Jewish Stud.* v, 1954, p. 12, sensibly notes
that Josephus' figure of ten years is presumably a round
number, calculated to the nearest year. She dates (p. 14)

to return to Rome to give the emperor his account of the matters with which he was charged by the Samaritans.[a] And so Pilate, after having spent ten years in Judaea, hurried to Rome in obedience to the orders of Vitellius, since he could not refuse. But before he reached Rome Tiberius had already passed away.[b]

(3) Vitellius,[c] on reaching Judaea, went up to Jerusalem, where the Jews were celebrating their traditional feast called the Passover. Having been received in magnificent fashion, Vitellius remitted to the inhabitants of the city all taxes [d] on the sale of agricultural produce and agreed that the vestments of the high priest and all his ornaments should be kept in the temple in custody of the priests, as had been their privilege before. At that time the vestments were stored in Antonia [e]—there is a stronghold of that name—for the following reason. One of the priests, Hyrcanus,[f] the first of many by that name, had constructed a large house near the temple and

Vitellius remits taxes and restores to the Jews custody of the high priest's vestments.

his departure at some time between mid-December 36 and the end of February 37.

[c] Josephus had previously (*Ant.* xv. 405) given a brief account of Vitellius' first visit to Jerusalem. He there adds that the transfer of the high priest's garments to Jewish custody was made after he had written to Tiberius on the matter. Since he there makes no mention of a festival in connexion with the visit, Smallwood, *Jour. of Jewish Stud.* v, 1954, p. 19, suggests that Vitellius' first visit, in 36–37, did not coincide with a festival, but that Vitellius' second visit (*Ant.* xviii. 123) occurred during the Passover of 37.

[d] *Cf.* the requests made to Archelaus at the beginning of his reign to remove the heavy taxes on what was publicly bought and sold (*Ant.* xvii. 205).

[e] North-west of the temple area. See *Ant.* xii. 252 note *d*.

[f] John Hyrcanus I, the Hasmonaean, succeeded his father Simon as high priest (and as *de facto* king) in 135 B.C.

ταύτῃ τὰ πολλὰ τὴν δίαιταν εἶχεν καὶ τὴν στολήν,
φύλαξ γὰρ ἦν αὐτῆς διὰ τὸ καὶ μόνῳ συγκεχωρῆ-
σθαι τοῦ ἐνδύεσθαι τὴν ἐξουσίαν, ταύτην[1] εἶχεν
ἀποκειμένην, ὁπότε εἰς τὴν πόλιν κατιὼν ἀναλαμ-
92 βάνοι[2] τὴν ἰδιωτικήν. καὶ οἵ τε υἱεῖς αὐτοῦ ταῦτα
πράσσειν ἐπετήδευσαν καὶ τέκνα ἐκείνων. Ἡρώδης
δὲ βασιλεύσας τήν τε βᾶριν ταύτην ἐν ἐπιτηδείῳ
κειμένην κατασκευάσας πολυτελῶς Ἀντωνίαν καλεῖ
ὀνόματι Ἀντωνίου φίλος ὤν, καὶ τὴν στολὴν ὥσπερ
καὶ λαμβάνει τῇδε κειμένην κατεῖχεν, πιστεύων
οὐδὲν νεωτεριεῖν ἐπ᾽ αὐτῷ τὸν λαὸν διὰ τάδε.[3]
93 ἔπρασσε δὲ ὅμοια τῷ Ἡρώδῃ καὶ ὁ ἐπικατα-
σταθεὶς αὐτῷ βασιλεὺς Ἀρχέλαος υἱὸς ὤν, οὗ[4]
Ῥωμαῖοι παραδεξάμενοι τὴν ἀρχὴν ἐκράτουν τῆς
στολῆς τοῦ ἀρχιερέως ἀποκειμένης ἐν οἴκῳ λίθοις
οἰκοδομηθέντι ὑπὸ σφραγῖδι τῶν τε ἱερέων καὶ τῶν
γαζοφυλάκων τοῦ φρουράρχου τὸ ἐφ᾽ ἡμέραν ἑκά-
94 στην λύχνον ἅπτοντος.[5] ἑπτὰ δ᾽ ἡμέραις πρὸ τῆς
ἑορτῆς ἀπεδίδοτο αὐτοῖς ὑπὸ τοῦ φρουράρχου, καὶ
ἁγνισθείσῃ[6] χρησάμενος ὁ ἀρχιερεὺς μετὰ μίαν τῆς
ἑορτῆς ἡμέραν ἀπετίθετο αὖθις εἰς τὸν οἶκον, ᾗπερ
ἔκειτο καὶ πρότερον. τοῦτο ἐπράττετο τρισὶν
95 ἑορταῖς ἑκάστου ἔτους καὶ τὴν νηστείαν.[7] Οὐιτέλλιος δὲ ἐπὶ τῷ ἡμετέρῳ πατρίῳ ποιεῖται τὴν στο-

---

[1] ταύτῃ E.
[2] κατιὼν ἀναλαμβάνοι] codd. : κατίοι, ἀναλαμβάνων Richards
et Shutt.     [3] διὰ τάδε] AE : δῆθεν δὲ MW.
[4] οὗ] codd. : αὐτοῦ παρ᾽ οὗ Eusebius.
[5] ὑπὸ σφραγῖδι . . . ἅπτοντος] sub sigillo sane pontificum
et gazofylacis habebatur, a quo cetera quoque templi orna-
menta et candelabrum quoque servabatur Lat.
[6] ἁγνισθεὶς Naber.
[7] τὴν νηστείαν] i. marg. γρ κατὰ τὴν νηστείαν A : τῇ νηστείᾳ
E : per ieiunia Lat.

lived there most of the time. As custodian of the
vestments, for to him alone was conceded the right to
put them on, he kept them laid away there, whenever
he put on his ordinary clothes in order to go down to
the city. His sons and their children also followed the
same practice. When Herod became king, he made
lavish repairs to this building, which was conveniently
situated, and, being a friend of Antony, he called it
Antonia.[a] He retained the vestments there just as
he had found them, believing that for this reason the
people would never rise in insurrection against him.
Herod's successor as king, his son Archelaus, acted
similarly. After him, when the Romans took over
the government, they retained control of the high
priest's vestments and kept them in a stone building,
where they were under the seal both of the priests
and of the custodians of the treasury and where the
warden of the guard lighted the lamp day by day.
Seven days before each festival the vestments were
delivered to the priests by the warden. After they [b]
had been purified, the high priest wore them ; then
after the first day of the festival he put them back
again in the building where they were laid away
before. This was the procedure at the three festivals
each year and on the fast day.[c] Vitellius was guided
by our law in dealing with the vestments,[d] and in-

---

[a] *Cf.* L.-H. Vincent, " L'Antonia, palais primitif d'Hé-
rode," *Revue Biblique*, lxi, 1954, pp. 87-107.

[b] Variant " he."

[c] The three festivals are Passover, Pentecost, and Taber-
nacles ; the fast day is the Day of Atonement. *Cf.* Mishnah
*Yoma* i. 1, which notes the preparations of the high priest
seven days before the Day of Atonement.

[d] Or " Vitellius put the vestments under our ancestral
charge."

λήν, ᾗ τε κείσοιτο μὴ πολυπραγμονεῖν ἐπισκήψας
τῷ φρουράρχῳ καὶ ὁπότε δέοι χρῆσθαι. καὶ ταῦτα
πράξας ἐπὶ εὐεργεσίᾳ τοῦ ἔθνους καὶ τὸν ἀρχιερέα
Ἰώσηπον τὸν Καϊάφαν[1] ἐπικαλούμενον ἀπαλλάξας
τῆς ἱερωσύνης Ἰωνάθην καθίστησιν Ἀνάνου τοῦ
ἀρχιερέως υἱόν. ἐπ᾿ Ἀντιοχείας δ᾿ αὖθις ἐποιεῖτο
τὴν ὁδόν.

96    (4) Πέμπει δὲ καὶ Τιβέριος ὡς Οὐιτέλλιον γράμματα, κελεύων αὐτῷ πράσσειν φιλίαν πρὸς Ἀρτάβανον τὸν Πάρθων βασιλέα· ἐφόβει γὰρ αὐτὸν
ἐχθρὸς ὢν καὶ Ἀρμενίαν παρεσπασμένος[2] μὴ ἐπὶ
πλέον κακουργῇ· πιστεύειν δὲ τῇ φιλίᾳ μόνως
ὁμήρων αὐτῷ διδομένων, μάλιστα δὲ τοῦ Ἀρτα-
97   βάνου υἱέος.[3] ταῦτα δὲ γράφων Τιβέριος πρὸς τὸν
Οὐιτέλλιον μεγάλαις δόσεσι χρημάτων πείθει καὶ
τὸν Ἰβήρων καὶ τὸν Ἀλβανῶν[4] βασιλέα πολεμεῖν

---

[1] Καϊάφαν] καὶ Καϊάφαν E.

[2] ἐχθρὸς . . . παρεσπασμένος] i. marg. γρ ἐχθρὸν ὄντα καὶ
ἀρμενίαν παρεσπασμένον A.

[3] τοῦ . . . υἱέος] suos filios Lat.

[4] A : Ἀλανῶν MW Exc. : Ἀλμανῶν E : Labanorum Lat.

---

[a] There are several possible reasons why the Jews protested the retention of the vestments by the Romans in
Antonia. If, as seems likely, Antonia was not part of the
temple area, the Jews would object because it is prohibited
(*Yoma* 69 a) to take the priestly vestments outside the
temple. In addition, the handling of these garments by
non-Jews would defile them (*Niddah* 34 a ; see Tosafot on
*Shabbat* 21 b) according to the rabbinic decree of A.D. 66 ;
though this incident occurred about thirty years before that
time, the decree may represent merely the crystallization of a
long-standing attitude.          [b] See above, § 35.

[c] The account of the events in Parthia which follows
should be dated in A.D. 35 according to Dio Cassius lviii. 26
and Tacitus' long narrative, *Ann.* vi. 31 ff. Josephus has

structed the warden not to meddle with the question where they were to be stored or when they should be used.[a] After he had bestowed these benefits upon the nation, he removed from his sacred office the high priest Joseph surnamed Caïaphas,[b] and appointed in his stead Jonathan, son of Ananus the high priest. Then he set out on the journey back to Antioch.

(4) Now Tiberius sent a letter to Vitellius [c] bidding him to establish friendship with Artabanus, the king of the Parthians ; for Artabanus, who was hostile to him and who had already detached Armenia,[d] inspired in him the fear that he would do further mischief. But he instructed Vitellius to put faith in a treaty of friendship only if hostages, and especially the son of Artabanus, should be given to him. Even while writing this letter to Vitellius, Tiberius offered large sums of money as an inducement to the kings both of the Iberians [e] and of the Albanians [f] to come out

*Tiberius tells Vitellius to negotiate a treaty of friendship with Artabanus king of Parthia.*

thus misplaced it in inserting it after Vitellius' first visit, which took place in 36/37. On Josephus' confusion in this matter see A. Garzetti, " La data dell' incontro all' Eufrate di Artabano III e L. Vitellio legato di Siria," in *Studi in onore di A. Calderini e R. Paribeni*, i, 1956, pp. 211-229.

[d] The chief cause of Artabanus' hostility, according to Tacitus' account, *Ann.* vi. 31-32, was apparently Tiberius' attempt to replace Artabanus with Phraates and then with Tiridates. Another factor was Artabanus' elation at his successful wars and his disdain for the aged and unwarlike Tiberius. Tacitus also mentions, *Ann.* vi. 31, Artabanus' seizure of the throne of Armenia for his son Arsaces.

[e] Iberia is part of modern Georgia, midway between the Black and Caspian Seas. There is no relation between these Iberians and the inhabitants of Spain. According to Tacitus, *Ann.* vi. 32, Tiberius, in his effort to recover Armenia, used as his instrument Mithridates, the brother of the Iberian king Pharasmanes.

[f] Albania, east of Iberia, is the modern Azerbaijan on the south-west shore of the Caspian Sea.

'Αρταβάνῳ μηδὲν ἐνδοιάσαι. οἱ δὲ αὐτοὶ μὲν ἀντ-
εῖχον, 'Αλανοὺς[1] δὲ δίοδον αὐτοῖς διδόντες διὰ τῆς
αὐτῶν καὶ τὰς θύρας τὰς Κασπίας ἀνοίξαντες ἐπ-
98 άγουσι τῷ 'Αρταβάνῳ. καὶ ἥ τε 'Αρμενία ἀφήρητο
αὖθις καὶ πλησθείσης πολέμων τῆς Παρθυαίων γῆς
οἵ τε πρῶτοι τῶν τῆδε ἐκτείνοντο ἀνδρῶν ἀνάστατά
τε ἦν αὐτοῖς τὰ πάντα καὶ τοῦ βασιλέως ὁ υἱὸς ἐκ
τουτωνὶ τῶν μαχῶν ἔπεσε[2] μετὰ πολλῶν στρατοῦ
99 μυριάδων. καὶ αὐτοῦ τὸν πατέρα 'Αρτάβανον
Οὐιτέλλιος πομπῇ χρημάτων εἴς τε συγγενεῖς καὶ
φίλους τοὺς ἐκείνου γενομένη ἐμέλλησε μὲν κτιν-
νύειν διὰ τῶν τὰ δῶρα εἰληφότων, αἰσθόμενος δὲ
τὴν ἐπιβουλὴν ὁ 'Αρτάβανος ἄφυκτον οὖσαν διὰ
τὸ ὑπὸ πολλῶν καὶ τῶν πρώτων ἀνδρῶν συντεθεῖ-
100 σαν μὴ ἀνεῖσθαι τοῦ ἐπὶ πέρας ἐλθεῖν, καὶ νομίζων
καὶ ὁπόσον αὐτῷ καθαρῶς συνειστήκει καὶ τόδε
ἤτοι ἐφθαρμένον ἐπὶ δόλῳ τὴν εὔνοιαν προσποιεῖ-

---

[1] ed. pr.: 'Αλανοὶ codd.: 'Αλμανοὶ E: Scythas Lat.: Σκύ-
θας Naber: 'Αλανοῖς coni.

[2] A: ἐπέστη MW Exc. et i. marg. A.

---

[a] According to *B.J.* vii. 244, a Scythian tribe inhabiting
the banks of the River Don and the Sea of Azov. Tacitus'
account substitutes the Sarmatae, another tribe from approximately the same area, for the Alani, and states that the
Iberians poured the Sarmatae into Armenia over the Cau-
casian pass. Naber's reading, that the Iberian and Albanian
kings granted passage to the Scythians, is an attempt to
reconcile Josephus with Tacitus ; but since the Alani were a
Scythian tribe, it seems better to keep the name of the tribe
as the Alani, in line with the manuscripts. Though Tacitus
definitely has the Iberians and Albanians joining the battle

plainly for war against Artabanus. For their own part, however, those kings held out against him, but they did bring in the Alani [a] against Artabanus by allowing them free transit through their own territory after throwing open the Caspian Gates. [b] Thus Armenia was recaptured and the land of the Parthians overwhelmed with war, in the battles of which men of the highest standing were killed, all their land ravaged, and the son of the king slain, together with many tens of thousands of soldiers. [c] Vitellius sent money to the kinsmen and friends of the elder Artabanus and would have brought about his death by those who had accepted the bribes if Artabanus had not perceived that this plot would inevitably succeed since it had been concocted by many men of the highest standing. He believed too that even those who had sincerely supported him were either now seduced and craftily pretending to be loyal or that as

with the Parthians, and though it therefore appears that their initial reluctance was overcome by the assistance of the Alani (or Sarmatae), yet the region of the Alani seems too far from the Caucasus, and hence the manuscript reading, that the Alani offered a passage to the Iberians and Albanians through the Caspian Gates, seems geographically improbable.

[b] The name given to a mountain pass or a series of passes near the Caspian Sea. *Cf. B.J.* vii. 245 note *e.* Mathieu-Herrmann, in their French translation of Josephus (*ad loc.*), remark that the reference here should be to the Albanian Gates, since the Caspian Gates, properly speaking, were too far east to be meant. Tacitus, *Ann.* vi. 33, also speaks of the Caspian route of the invasion ; and Josephus' source, having similar information, may have concluded that the invasion was by way of the Caspian Gates.

[c] Tacitus, *Ann.* vi. 35, whose account of the battle is fuller, says that Artabanus' son Orodes was wounded in the fighting. The mistaken rumour that he was slain caused the Parthians to panic and gave the victory to the coalition of Iberians, Albanians, and Sarmatae.

σθαι ἢ πείρας αὐτῷ γενομένης μετατάξεσθαι[1] πρὸς
τοὺς προαφεστηκότας, εἴς τι[2] τῶν ἄνω σατραπειῶν[3]
ἔσωζεν αὐτόν. καὶ πολλὴν μετὰ ταῦτα στρατιὰν
ἀθροίσας Δαῶν[4] τε καὶ Σακῶν καὶ πολεμήσας τοὺς
ἀνθεστηκότας κατέσχε τὴν ἀρχήν.

101   (5) Ταῦτα ἀκούσας ὁ Τιβέριος ἠξίου φιλίαν αὐτῷ
γενέσθαι πρὸς τὸν Ἀρτάβανον, ἐπεὶ δὲ κἀκεῖνος
προκληθεὶς ἄσμενος ἐδέχετο τὸν περὶ αὐτῶν[5] λόγον,
ἐπὶ τὸν Εὐφράτην παρῆσαν ὅ τε Ἀρτάβανος καὶ
102 Οὐιτέλλιος. καὶ ζεύξεως τοῦ ποταμοῦ γενομένης
κατὰ τὸ μεσαίτατον τῆς γεφύρας ἀλλήλους ὑπηντίαζον μετὰ φυλακῆς ἑκάτερος τῆς περὶ αὐτόν. καὶ
λόγων αὐτοῖς συμβατικῶν γενομένων Ἡρώδης ὁ
τετράρχης εἱστίασεν αὐτοὺς κατὰ μέσον τὸν πόρον
103 σκηνίδα ἐπισκηψάμενος[6] τῷ πόρῳ πολυτελῆ. καὶ
Ἀρτάβανος πέμπει[7] Τιβερίῳ ὅμηρον Δαρεῖον τὸν
υἱὸν μετὰ πολλῶν δώρων, ἐν οἷς καὶ ἄνδρα ἑπτά-

[1] Dindorf : μετατάξασθαι codd. Exc.
[2] εἴς τι] A : ἐπὶ MW Exc. : i. marg. γρ ἐπὶ τῶν ἄνω A.
[3] εἴς τι . . . σατραπειῶν] A : ad superiores satrapias Lat. :
pro σατραπειῶν habent στρατιῶν MW Exc., στρακῶν E.
[4] A : Δακῶν MWE Exc. : Dacorum Lat.
[5] αὐτοῦ E.
[6] η i. ras. A : ἐπισκεπασάμενος Richards et Shutt.
[7] πέμπει] A : μετ᾽ οὐ πολὺ πέμπει MWE Exc.

[a] Or " in time of trial."
[b] The Dahae are also mentioned in Pliny, Hist. Nat. vi. 19 ;
the Sacae in Herodotus vii. 9.   In the only other reference to
these two Scythian tribes in Josephus, Ant. xx. 91, they are
also coupled.   Tacitus, Ann. vi. 44, corroborates Josephus'
account by stating that Artabanus raised auxiliaries in
Scythia.
[c] According to Tacitus, Ann. vi. 36, Artabanus fled to the

soon as an attempt was made on his life [a] they would join the ranks of the rebels. He therefore fled for his life to one of the upper satrapies. Subsequently he gathered together a large army of Dahae and Sacae [b] and, by military action against his opponents, secured the throne.[c]

(5) At this news Tiberius took steps to make friends with Artabanus. When the offer was made, the Parthian was delighted to discuss the matter. He and Vitellius met on the Euphrates.[d] The river was bridged and they met in the middle of the bridge, each with his bodyguard by him. After they had arrived at the terms of an agreement, Herod the tetrarch gave a feast for them in a luxurious pavilion which he constructed in the middle of the river. Artabanus sent as a hostage to Tiberius his son Darius,[e] together with many gifts, among which he

Vitellius and Artabanus meet on the Euphrates to negotiate the treaty.

remote borders of Scythia, where he hoped for help from the Hyrcanians and Carmanians, with whom he was connected by marriage. See Tacitus, *Ann.* vi. 43-44, for a vivid portrait of Artabanus in exile in Hyrcania on the Caspian, where he lived covered with filth, in which garb he remained while gathering auxiliaries for his successful fight against Tiridates, who then occupied the Parthian throne.

[d] This parley is also mentioned by Suetonius, *Vit.* 2, who praises Vitellius' masterly diplomacy. Dio Cassius lix. 17. 5 and 27. 2-3 dates the incident in the reign of Caligula rather than in that of Tiberius, as Josephus does here. Täubler, *Die Parthernachrichten bei Josephus*, pp. 33 ff., accepts Josephus' dating, arguing that the historians who were hostile to Tiberius begrudged him this success. One cannot draw conclusions from Tacitus' omission of the incident since this may be due to his bias against Tiberius, or it may argue that the event took place in Caligula's reign, Tacitus' account of which is lost.

[e] Probably to be identified with Dareus, one of the Parthian hostages with whom Caligula rode triumphantly over the bridge of ships from Baiae to Puteoli (Suet. *Calig.* 19).

πηχυν τὸ μέγεθος Ἰουδαῖον τὸ γένος Ἐλεάζαρον[1]
104 ὄνομα· διὰ μέντοι τὸ μέγεθος Γίγας ἐκαλεῖτο. ἐπὶ
τούτοις Οὐιτέλλιος μὲν ἐπ' Ἀντιοχείας ᾔει, Ἀρτάβανος δὲ ἐπὶ τῆς Βαβυλωνίας.[2] Ἡρώδης δὲ βουλόμενος δι' αὐτοῦ πρώτου γενέσθαι πύστιν[3] Καίσαρι
τῶν ὁμήρων τῆς λήψεως ἐκπέμπει γραμματοφόρους
τὰ πάντα ἀκριβῶς γράψας εἰς ἐπιστολὴν καὶ μηδὲν
105 ὑπολιπόμενος ἐπὶ μηνύσει τῷ ὑπατικῷ. πρὸς Οὐιτελλίου δὲ ἐπιπεμφθεισῶν ἐπιστολῶν καὶ τοῦ Καίσαρος ἐπισημήναντος πρὸς αὐτόν, ὡς δῆλα αὐτῷ
γένοιτο πρότερον πύστιν[4] περὶ αὐτῶν Ἡρώδου
προτεθεικότος, ταραχθεὶς ὁ Οὐιτέλλιος μεγάλως
καὶ πεπονθέναι μειζόνως ἢ ἐπέπρακτο ὑπολαμβάνων ἄδηλον τὴν ἐπ' αὐτοῖς ἔκρυπτεν ὀργήν, μέχρι
δὴ καὶ μετῆλθε Γαΐου τὴν Ῥωμαίων[5] ἀρχὴν παρειληφότος.
106 (6) Τότε δὲ καὶ Φίλιππος, Ἡρώδου δὲ ἦν ἀδελφός, τελευτᾷ τὸν βίον εἰκοστῷ[6] μὲν ἐνιαυτῷ τῆς
Τιβερίου ἀρχῆς, ἡγησάμενος δὲ αὐτὸς ἑπτὰ καὶ
τριάκοντα[7] τῆς Τραχωνίτιδος καὶ Γαυλανίτιδος καὶ
τοῦ Βατανέων[8] ἔθνους πρὸς αὐταῖς, μέτριον δὲ ἐν
οἷς ἦρχεν παρασχὼν τὸν τρόπον καὶ ἀπράγμονα·
107 δίαιταν μὲν γὰρ τὸ πᾶν[9] ἐν γῇ τῇ ὑποτελεῖ ἐποιεῖτο,
πρόοδοι δ' ἦσαν αὐτῷ σὺν ὀλίγοις τῶν ἐπιλέκτων,
καὶ τοῦ θρόνου εἰς ὃν ἔκρινεν καθεζόμενος ἐν ταῖς
ὁδοῖς ἑπομένου, ὁπότε τις ὑπαντιάσας ἐν χρείᾳ
γένοιτο αὐτῷ ἐπιβοηθεῖν, οὐδὲν εἰς ἀναβολὰς ἀλλ'

---

[1] Lazarum Lat.       [2] Βαβυλῶνος E.
[3] E : πίστιν codd. Exc.
[4] A : πίστιν MW.
[5] A : om. MWE Lat. Exc.
[6] εἰκοστῷ] vicesimo secundo Lat., quod probat Scaliger.
[7] ἑπτὰ καὶ τριάκοντα] triginta duos (xxxv alii) Lat.

74

included a man seven cubits [a] tall, a Jew by race, named Eleazar, who on account of his size was called the Giant. These terms having been arranged, Vitellius departed for Antioch and Artabanus for Babylonia. Meanwhile, Herod, in his desire to be the first to communicate the news to the emperor that hostages had been received, wrote and dispatched by couriers so precise and complete an account that he left nothing for the proconsul to report. When Vitellius had later sent his dispatch and the emperor informed him that he knew the facts because Herod had been ahead of Vitellius in putting them at his disposal, Vitellius fell into a great fury, and took the offence to be much greater than it actually was. Yet he kept his wrath concealed until he got his revenge on the accession of Gaius as emperor of the Romans.

*Herod the tetrarch anticipates Vitellius in sending news to Tiberius.*

(6) Now it was at this time that Philip,[b] Herod's brother, died [c] in the twentieth year of Tiberius' reign and after thirty-seven years of his own rule over Trachonitis and Gaulanitis, as well as over the tribe called the Bataneans. In his conduct of the government he showed a moderate and easy-going disposition. Indeed, he spent all his time in the territory subject to him. When he went on circuit he had only a few select companions. The throne on which he sat when he gave judgement accompanied him wherever he went. And so, whenever anyone appealed to him for redress [d] along the route, at once

*Death of Philip the tetrarch. His mild character.*

---

[a] About ten and a half feet.
[b] See above, §§ 27-28.     [c] A.D. 34.
[d] Or " whenever anyone met him who was in need of his assistance."

---

[8] M : Ναβαταίου A : Βαταναίων WE : Bantanaeorum Lat.
[9] τὸ πᾶν] AW : om. M.

ἐκ τοῦ ὀξέος ἱδρύσεως τοῦ θρόνου ᾗ καὶ τύχοι γενομένης καθεζόμενος ἠκροᾶτο καὶ τιμωρίας τε ἐπε-
τίμα τοῖς ἁλοῦσι καὶ ἠφίει τοὺς ἀδίκως ἐν ἐγκλή-
108 μασι γενομένους. τελευτᾷ δ᾽ ἐν Ἰουλιάδι καὶ αὐτοῦ
κομισθέντος ἐπὶ τὸ μνημεῖον, ὃ ἔτι πρότερον ᾠκοδό-
μησεν αὐτός, ταφαὶ γίνονται πολυτελεῖς. τὴν δ᾽
ἀρχήν, οὐ γὰρ κατελίπετο παῖδας, Τιβέριος παραλαβὼν προσθήκην ἐπαρχίας ποιεῖται τῆς Σύρων,
τοὺς μέντοι φόρους ἐκέλευσε συλλεγομένους ἐν τῇ
τετραρχίᾳ τῇ ἐκείνου γενομένῃ κατατίθεσθαι.

109 (v. 1) Ἐν τούτῳ δὲ στασιάζουσιν Ἀρέτας τε ὁ
Πετραῖος βασιλεὺς καὶ Ἡρώδης διὰ τοιαύτην αἰ-
τίαν· Ἡρώδης ὁ τετράρχης γαμεῖ τὴν Ἀρέτα θυγατέρα καὶ συνῆν χρόνον ἤδη πολύν. στελλόμενος
δὲ ἐπὶ Ῥώμης κατάγεται ἐν Ἡρώδου ἀδελφοῦ
ὄντος οὐχ ὁμομητρίου· ἐκ γὰρ τῆς Σίμωνος τοῦ
110 ἀρχιερέως θυγατρὸς Ἡρώδης ἐγεγόνει. ἐρασθεὶς
δὲ Ἡρωδιάδος τῆς τούτου γυναικός, θυγάτηρ δὲ ἦν
Ἀριστοβούλου καὶ οὗτος ἀδελφὸς αὐτῶν, Ἀγρίππου δὲ ἀδελφὴ¹ τοῦ μεγάλου, τολμᾷ λόγων ἅπτεσθαι περὶ γάμου. καὶ δεξαμένης συνθῆκαι γίνονται
μετοικίσασθαι παρ᾽ αὐτόν, ὁπότε ἀπὸ Ῥώμης παραγένοιτο. ἦν δὲ ἐν ταῖς συνθήκαις ὥστε καὶ τοῦ
111 Ἀρέτα τὴν θυγατέρα ἐκβαλεῖν. καὶ ὁ μὲν εἰς τὴν
Ῥώμην ἔπλει ταῦτα συνθέμενος. ἐπεὶ δὲ ἐπανεχώρει διαπραξάμενος ἐν τῇ Ῥώμῃ ἐφ᾽ ἅπερ

¹ ἀδελφοῦ E.

---

ᵃ In *Ant.* xvi. 294 we hear that he succeeded Obodas as
king of Arabia and that his previous name was Aeneas.
ᵇ The name of Herodias' husband is given as Philip in all
the mss. of Mark vi. 17, but it is omitted in the best mss. in

76

without a moment's delay the throne was set up wherever it might be. He took his seat and gave the case a hearing. He fixed penalties for those who were convicted and released those who had been unjustly accused. He died in Julias. His body was carried to the tomb that he himself had had erected before he died and there was a costly funeral. Since he had died childless, Tiberius took over his territory and annexed it to the province of Syria. Nevertheless, he ordered that the tribute which was collected in his tetrarchy should be held on deposit.

(v. 1) In the meantime, a quarrel, whose origin I shall relate, arose between Aretas,[a] king of Petra, and Herod. The tetrarch Herod had taken the daughter of Aretas as his wife and had now been married to her for a long time. When starting out for Rome, he lodged with his half-brother Herod,[b] who was born of a different mother, namely, the daughter of Simon the high priest. Falling in love with Herodias, the wife of this half-brother—she was a daughter of their brother Aristobulus and sister to Agrippa the Great—, he brazenly broached to her the subject of marriage. She accepted and pledged herself to make the transfer to him as soon as he returned from Rome. It was stipulated that he must oust the daughter of Aretas. The agreement made, he set sail for Rome. On his return after transacting his business in Rome, his wife,

*Herod the tetrarch divorces the daughter of Aretas and marries Herodias, his half-brother's wife.*

Luke iii. 19 and in codex D and the Latin versions in Matt. xiv. 3 (in the other MSS. of Luke and Matthew it has been supplied from Mark). Josephus' authority for the name, given here and in *Ant.* xviii. 148, is accepted by most authorities, who explain the reading of Mark as being due to a confusion between the husband and the son-in-law of Herodias, who was indeed named Philip. So Thackeray, *Selections from Josephus*, pp. 191-192.

ἔσταλτο, ἡ γυνὴ πύστεως[1] αὐτῇ τῶν πρὸς τὴν
Ἡρωδιάδα συνθηκῶν γενομένης πρὶν ἔκπυστος αὐτῷ γενέσθαι τὰ πάντα ἐκμαθοῦσα κελεύει πέμπειν
αὐτὴν ἐπὶ Μαχαιροῦντος, μεθόριον δ' ἐστὶ τῆς
τε Ἀρέτα καὶ Ἡρώδου ἀρχῆς, γνώμην οὐκ ἐκφαί-
112 νουσα τὴν ἑαυτῆς.[2] καὶ ὁ Ἡρώδης ἐξέπεμψεν
μηδὲν ᾐσθῆσθαι τὴν ἄνθρωπον προσδοκῶν. ἡ δέ,
προαπεστάλκει γὰρ ἐκ πλείονος εἰς τὸν Μαχαιροῦντα τότε[3] πατρὶ αὐτῆς ὑποτελῆ,[4] πάντων εἰς
τὴν ὁδοιπορίαν ἡτοιμασμένων ὑπὸ τοῦ στρατηγοῦ
ἅμα τε[5] παρῆν καὶ ἀφωρμᾶτο εἰς τὴν Ἀραβίαν
κομιδῇ τῶν στρατηγῶν ἐκ διαδοχῆς[6] παρῆν[7] τε ὡς
τὸν πατέρα ᾗ τάχος καὶ αὐτῷ τὴν Ἡρώδου διά-
113 νοιαν ἔφραζεν. ὁ δὲ ἀρχὴν ἔχθρας ταύτην ποιη-

---

[1] A : πίστεως WE et vid. Lat.
[2] MWE : αὐτῆς A.
[3] τότε] ed. pr. : τῷ τε codd.
[4] ed. pr. : ὑποτελεῖ codd.
[5] ἅμα τε] A : Ἀρέτα MWE.
[6] χρωμένη post διαδοχῆς suppl. Richards et Shutt.
[7] προαπεστάλκει . . . παρῆν] praemiserat enim ante multum
tempus ad patrem, ut ei apud Macherunta omnia praepara-
rentur, quae itineris usus exposceret, a ductoribus Aretae sus-
cipitur Lat.

---

[a] Or " to give her an escort."
[b] For a description of this fortress, just east of the Dead
Sea, see B.J. vii. 164 ff.
[c] N. Glueck, " Explorations in the Land of Ammon,"
Bull. of the Am. Sch. of Orient. Res. lxviii, Dec. 1937, p. 15,
on the basis of an archaeological survey of the area, concludes
that Josephus is approximately correct in placing Machaerus
on the border between the territory of Aretas and that of Herod,
but that he is wrong in placing it in the territory of Aretas,
which was a few miles away.

who had got wind of his compact with Herodias, before any information reached him that she had discovered everything, asked him to send her away *a* to Machaerus,*b* which was on the boundary *c* between the territory of Aretas and that of Herod. She gave no hint, however, of her real purpose. Herod let her go, since he had no notion that the poor woman saw what was afoot. Some time earlier she herself had dispatched messengers to Machaerus, which was at that time subject to her father,*d* so that when she arrived all preparations for her journey had been made by the governor. She was thus able to start for Arabia as soon as she arrived, being passed from one governor to the next as they provided transport.*e* So she speedily reached her father and told him what Herod planned to do. Aretas made this the start of a — Aretas makes war

*d* The reading of the mss. is " and to him who was subject to her father."

*e* The Nabataean inscriptions, as noted by Jones, *Cities*, p. 292, mention officers with the titles of ἔπαρχος and στρατηγός. That the Greek words are thus transliterated into Nabataean shows that the institution was of foreign origin. Jones plausibly conjectures that the Nabataean kings, after successfully trying to organize their kingdom on the centralized Hellenistic model, gave the local sheikhs the title of " governor." There is perhaps a parallel to be drawn with the magisterial boards of στρατηγοί, usually consisting of five members, often headed by a first στρατηγός, which governed the Hellenistic cities in Asia Minor and elsewhere (see Magie, *Roman Rule*, i. 643-644). G. A. Cooke, *A Textbook of North-Semitic Inscriptions*, 1903, pp. 247-248, suggests the possibility that the two στρατηγοί mentioned in *C.I.S.* ii. 169 may have assisted the daughter of Aretas, since the fortress of Machaerus was probably in the district of one of them, *Yaʿamru* by name. Another inscription mentioning a στρατηγός found in northern Transjordan and probably referring to a village sheik is described by L. Mowry, in *Bull. of the Am. Sch. of Orient. Res.* cxxxii, Dec. 1953, pp. 34-41.

79

σάμενος περί τε ὅρων ἐν γῇ τῇ Γαβαλίτιδι,[1] καὶ
δυνάμεως ἑκατέρῳ συλλεγείσης εἰς πόλεμον καθί-
114 σταντο στρατηγοὺς ἀπεσταλκότες ἀνθ᾽ ἑαυτῶν. καὶ
μάχης γενομένης διεφθάρη πᾶς ὁ Ἡρώδου στρατὸς
προδοσίας αὐτῷ γενομένης ὑπ᾽ ἀνδρῶν φυγάδων,
οἳ ὄντες ἐκ τῆς Φιλίππου τετραρχίας Ἡρώδῃ συνε-
115 στράτευον. ταῦτα Ἡρώδης γράφει πρὸς Τιβέριον.
ὁ δὲ ὀργῇ φέρων τὴν Ἀρέτα ἐπιχείρησιν γράφει
πρὸς Οὐιτέλλιον·πόλεμον ἐξενεγκεῖν καὶ ἤτοι ζῶον
ἑλόντα ἀναγαγεῖν δεδεμένον ἢ κτεινομένου πέμπειν
τὴν κεφαλὴν ἐπ᾽ αὐτόν. καὶ Τιβέριος μὲν ταῦτα
πράσσειν ἐπέστελλεν τῷ κατὰ Συρίαν στρατηγῷ.

116 (2) Τισὶ δὲ τῶν Ἰουδαίων ἐδόκει ὀλωλέναι τὸν
Ἡρώδου στρατὸν ὑπὸ τοῦ θεοῦ καὶ μάλα δικαίως
τιννυμένου[2] κατὰ ποινὴν Ἰωάννου τοῦ ἐπικαλου-
117 μένου βαπτιστοῦ. κτείνει γὰρ δὴ τοῦτον Ἡρώδης
ἀγαθὸν[3] ἄνδρα καὶ τοῖς Ἰουδαίοις κελεύοντα ἀρετὴν
ἐπασκοῦσιν καὶ τὰ πρὸς ἀλλήλους δικαιοσύνῃ καὶ
πρὸς τὸν θεὸν εὐσεβείᾳ χρωμένοις[4] βαπτισμῷ συν-

---

[1] coni. Jones, Cities, p. 449 n. 19 : Γαμαλικῇ A : Γαμαλίτιδι
MWE : Gamalica (Gamalitica cod. A) Lat. : Γαλααδίτιδι
coni. Schürer i. 445 et n. 36 : Γαβαλικῇ vel simile coni. Niese :
post Γαμαλικῇ lacunam indicat Bekker.
[2] codd. E Eus. : τιννμένου Niese.
[3] ἄγριον Eisler (Messiah Jesus, p. 248).
[4] ⟨ἐπὶ⟩ ante βαπτισμῷ coni. Richards et Shutt.

---

[a] The manuscript reading, Gamala, seems unlikely, since
this region belonged to Philip's former tetrarchy and hence
could not have been the subject of dispute between Aretas
and Herod. Schürer's emendation, Galaaditis (Gilead), is
geographically possible but is palaeographically not as close

quarrel. There was also a dispute about boundaries on Herod<br>and defeats
in the district of Gabalis.[a] Troops were mustered on him.
each side and they were now at war, but they dispatched others as commanders instead of going themselves. In the ensuing battle, the whole army of
Herod was destroyed when some refugees, who had
come from the tetrarchy of Philip and had joined
Herod's army, played him false. Herod sent an account of these events to Tiberius. The latter was incensed to think that Aretas had begun hostilities and
wrote Vitellius to declare war and either bring Aretas
to him in chains, if he should be captured alive, or,
if he should be slain, to send him his head. Such were
the instructions of Tiberius to his governor in Syria.

(2) [b] But to some of the Jews the destruction of Herod's<br>defeat is
Herod's army seemed to be divine vengeance, and attributed
certainly a just vengeance, for his treatment of John, to his mur-<br>der of John
surnamed the Baptist. For Herod had put him to the Baptist.
death, though he was a good man [c] and had exhorted
the Jews to lead righteous lives, to practise justice towards their fellows and piety towards God, and so

to the manuscript reading as Gabala, a district south of
Moabitis in Idumaea. *Cf. Ant.* ii. 6.

[b] In general, this famous passage, §§ 116-119, on the
murder of John the Baptist has been accepted as authentic,
though Graetz in his later editions regarded it as spurious on
the grounds that Josephus would not have called John a
baptist without giving an explanation of what baptism is
and that Josephus would not have used different forms for
the word " baptism." But Josephus does not explain every
movement ; and since there was no established Greek word
for baptism he might well have used two different forms of
the word.

[c] The Slavonic Josephus, the value of which has been
justly questioned by numerous scholars, speaks of John as
ἄγριος, a wild man. Eisler, p. 248, recklessly suggests that
the Church changed ἄγριος to ἀγαθός.

ἰέναι· οὕτω γὰρ δὴ καὶ τὴν βάπτισιν ἀποδεκτὴν
αὐτῷ φανεῖσθαι μὴ ἐπί τινων ἁμαρτάδων παραιτή-
σει χρωμένων, ἀλλ' ἐφ' ἁγνείᾳ τοῦ σώματος, ἅτε
δὴ καὶ τῆς ψυχῆς δικαιοσύνῃ προεκκεκαθαρμένης.
118 καὶ τῶν ἄλλων¹ συστρεφομένων, καὶ γὰρ ἤρθησαν²
ἐπὶ πλεῖστον τῇ ἀκροάσει³ τῶν λόγων, δείσας
Ἡρώδης τὸ ἐπὶ τοσόνδε πιθανὸν αὐτοῦ τοῖς ἀνθρώποις μὴ ἐπὶ στάσει⁴ τινὶ φέροι, πάντα γὰρ ἐῴκεσαν
συμβουλῇ τῇ ἐκείνου πράξοντες, πολὺ κρεῖττον
ἡγεῖται πρίν τι νεώτερον ἐξ αὐτοῦ γενέσθαι προλα-
βὼν ἀνελεῖν τοῦ⁵ μεταβολῆς γενομένης [μὴ]⁶ εἰς
119 πράγματα ἐμπεσὼν μετανοεῖν. καὶ ὁ μὲν ὑποψίᾳ

¹ MWE : λαῶν ex corr. A : perplurima multitudo Lat. :
ἀνθρώπων coni. Niese : πολλῶν coni. Eisler (Messiah Jesus,
p. 247).
² codd. E et Eusebii codd. quidam : ἤσθησαν Eusebius.
³ ἤρθησαν . . . ἀκροάσει] συνήχθησαν πλεῖστοι ⟨ἐπὶ⟩ τῇ ἀκροάσει coni. Richards et Shutt.
⁴ MWE : ἀποστάσει A.    ⁵ τοῦ] codd. : ἢ Eus.
⁶ μὴ] om. Eus. : μᾶλλον coni. Petersen.

---

ᵃ The translation " to be united by baptism " seems unlikely, since there is no indication that John championed
group baptism.
ᵇ Josephus uses two different words for baptism in this
same passage, βαπτισμός and βάπτισις.
ᶜ The identity of these others is puzzling. Perhaps the
reference is to the unjust men. Eisler, p. 247, following the
Latin version, emends to " the masses," contending that
" the others " represents a Christian alteration introduced to
mitigate the seditious effect of John's preaching.
ᵈ Or " uplifted." Variant " overjoyed." Eisler, p. 246,
argues for the manuscript reading, " they were aroused,"
suggesting that Eusebius' " they were overjoyed," which is
also found in the Slavonic Josephus, represents a Christian
interpolation made because the Church preferred to think of
John as a religious reformer rather than as one who incited
the people to revolution. Because Schürer, i. 438 n. 2, and

doing to join in baptism.[a]  In his view this was a necessary preliminary if baptism [b] was to be acceptable to God.  They must not employ it to gain pardon for whatever sins they committed, but as a consecration of the body implying that the soul was already thoroughly cleansed by right ·behaviour.  When others [c] too joined the crowds about him, because they were aroused [d] to the highest degree by his sermons, Herod became alarmed.[e]  Eloquence that had so great an effect on mankind might lead to some form of sedition,[f] for it looked as if they would be guided by John in everything that they did.  Herod decided therefore that it would be much better to strike first and be rid of him before his work led to an uprising, than to wait for an upheaval, get involved in a difficult situation and see his mistake.  Though

Niese believed that Josephus would never have viewed with sympathy one who stirred up the people thus, they adopted Eusebius' emendation.

    [e] The Gospels do not mention this reason for Herod's alarm at John's activities.  According to Mark vi. 17-21, John was imprisoned because he questioned Herod's right to marry his sister-in-law.  And there is nothing in Josephus of the story, told in Mark vi. 22-28, that Salome asked for John's head.  But there is no necessary contradiction between Josephus and the Gospels as to the reasons why John was put to death ; the Christians chose to emphasize the moral charges that he brought against the ruler, whereas Josephus stresses the political fears that he aroused in Herod.

    [f] Variant " revolt."  Eisler, p. 248, contends that the manuscript reading, " sedition," has clearer notions of revolution than Eusebius' reading, " revolt," and that the Christians changed the manuscripts here, as they did with ἤρθησαν, to avoid connecting John with political insurrection.  But ἀπόστασις means not only a turning away from established traditions but also actual defection or revolt.  The chief argument for retaining ἤρθησαν and στάσει in the text is that they are backed by the manuscript tradition.

τῇ Ἡρώδου δέσμιος εἰς τὸν Μαχαιροῦντα πεμφθεὶς
τὸ προειρημένον φρούριον ταύτῃ κτίννυται. τοῖς[1]
δὲ Ἰουδαίοις δόξα[2] ἐπὶ τιμωρίᾳ τῇ ἐκείνου τὸν
ὄλεθρον ἐπὶ τῷ στρατεύματι γενέσθαι τοῦ θεοῦ
κακῶσαι Ἡρώδην[3] θέλοντος.

120　(3) Οὐιτέλλιος δὲ παρασκευασάμενος ὡς εἰς πόλεμον τὸν πρὸς Ἀρέταν δυσὶ τάγμασιν ὁπλιτῶν
ὅσοι τε περὶ αὐτὰ ψιλοὶ καὶ ἱππεῖς συμμαχοῦντες ἐκ
τῶν ὑπὸ Ῥωμαίοις βασιλειῶν ἀγόμενος, ἐπὶ τῆς
121 Πέτρας ἠπείγετο καὶ ἔσχε Πτολεμαΐδα. ὡρμη-
μένῳ δ' αὐτῷ διὰ τῆς Ἰουδαίων ἄγειν τὸν στρατὸν
ὑπαντιάσαντες ἄνδρες οἱ πρῶτοι παρῃτοῦντο τὴν
διὰ[4] τῆς χώρας ὁδόν· οὐ γὰρ αὐτοῖς εἶναι πάτριον
περιορᾶν εἰκόνας εἰς αὐτὴν φερομένας, πολλὰς δ'
122 εἶναι σημαίαις ἐπικειμένας. καὶ πεισθεὶς μετέβα-
λέν τε τῆς γνώμης τὸ ἐπὶ τοιούτοις προβουλεῦσαν
καὶ διὰ τοῦ μεγάλου πεδίου κελεύσας χωρεῖν τὸ
στρατόπεδον αὐτὸς μετὰ Ἡρώδου τοῦ τετράρχου
καὶ τῶν φίλων εἰς Ἱεροσόλυμα ἀνῄει θύσων τῷ θεῷ
123 ἑορτῆς πατρίου τοῖς Ἰουδαίοις ἐνεστηκυίας. εἰς ἣν
ἀπαντήσας καὶ δεχθεὶς ὑπὸ τοῦ τῶν Ἰουδαίων πλήθους ἐκπρεπῶς τρεῖς μὲν ἡμέρας ταύτῃ διατριβὴν
ποιεῖται, ἐν αἷς Ἰωνάθην τὴν ἀρχιερωσύνην[5] ἀφελό-

---

[1] τισὶ coni. Eisler (Messiah Jesus, p. 248).
[2] E : δόξαν AMW : videbatur Lat. : δόξαν παρέσχεν Holwerda : ἔδοξεν Bekker : δόξα ἦν coni. Niese.
[3] κακῶσαι Ἡρώδην] E : κακῶς Ἡρώδη codd.
[4] τὴν διὰ] E : διὰ τὴν codd.
[5] MWE : ἱερωσύνην A.

[a] For a description of Ptolemaïs, modern 'Akkâ, at the
northern end of the bay of Haifa, see B.J. ii. 188-191.

John, because of Herod's suspicions, was brought in chains to Machaerus, the stronghold that we have previously mentioned, and there put to death, yet the verdict of the Jews was that the destruction visited upon Herod's army was a vindication of John, since God saw fit to inflict such a blow on Herod.

(3) Vitellius got himself ready for war against Aretas with two legions of heavy-armed infantry and such light-armed infantry and cavalry as were attached to them as auxiliaries. Proceeding from the kingdoms that were under the Roman yoke, he pushed toward Petra and occupied Ptolemaïs.[a] Since he had started to lead his army through the land of Judaea, the Jews of the highest standing went to meet him and entreated him not to march through their land. For, they said, it was contrary to their tradition to allow images,[b] of which there were many attached to the military standards, to be brought upon their soil. Yielding to their entreaty, he abandoned his original plan and ordered his army to march through the Great Plain,[c] while he himself, together with Herod the tetrarch and his friends, went up to Jerusalem to sacrifice to God during the traditional festival which the Jews were celebrating there. When he arrived there, he was greeted with special warmth by the Jewish multitude. He spent three days there, during which he deposed Jonathan from his office as high priest and conferred it on

*The expedition of Vitellius against Aretas is arrested by news of Tiberius' death.*

[b] For a similar objection on the part of the Jews to having military standards with their attached images brought into Judaea see §§ 55-59.

[c] Usually refers to the region between Samaria and Galilee (*e.g. Ant.* v. 83) but sometimes indicates the valley of the Jordan (*e.g. B.J.* iv. 455-458). It is not clear which is meant here.

124 μενος ἐγχειρίζει τῷ ἀδελφῷ αὐτοῦ Θεοφίλῳ, τῇ
τετάρτῃ δὲ γραμμάτων αὐτῷ παραγενομένων, ἃ
ἐδήλου τὴν Τιβερίου τελευτήν, ὥρκισεν τὴν πληθὺν
ἐπ᾽ εὐνοίᾳ τῇ Γαΐου. ἀνεκάλει δὲ καὶ τὸ στράτευμα
ἐπὶ τὰ οἰκεῖα ἑκάστου χειμαδιᾶν[1] πόλεμον[2] ἐκφέρειν
οὐκέθ᾽ ὁμοίως δυνάμενος διὰ τὸ εἰς Γάιον μεταπε-
125 πτωκέναι τὰ πράγματα. ἐλέγετο δὲ καὶ τὸν Ἀρέταν οἰωνοσκοπησάμενον πρὸς τὴν ἀγγελίαν τῶν
Οὐιτελλίου στρατιωτῶν φάναι μηχανὴν οὐκ εἶναι
τῷ στρατῷ τῆς ἐπὶ Πετραίους ὁδοῦ[3]· τεθνήξεσθαι
γὰρ τῶν ἡγεμόνων ἢ τὸν πολεμεῖν κελεύσαντα ἢ
τὸν γνώμῃ τῇ ἐκείνου ὡρμημένον διακονεῖσθαι καὶ[4]
ἐφ᾽ ὃν[5] γένοιτο ἡ παρασκευὴ τοῦ στρατεύματος.
126 καὶ Οὐιτέλλιος μὲν ἐπ᾽ Ἀντιοχείας ἀνεχώρησεν.
Ἀγρίππας δὲ ὁ Ἀριστοβούλου υἱὸς ἐνιαυτῷ πρότερον ἢ τελευτῆσαι Τιβέριον ἐπὶ Ῥώμης ἄνεισι πράξων τι παρὰ τῷ αὐτοκράτορι δυνάμεώς τινος αὐτῷ
127 παραγενομένης. βούλομαι οὖν εἰπεῖν ἐπὶ μακρότε-
ρον περί τε Ἡρώδου καὶ γένους αὐτοῦ ὡς ἐγένετο,
ἅμα μὲν καὶ διὰ τὸ ἀνήκειν τῇ ἱστορίᾳ τὸν περὶ
αὐτῶν λόγον, ἅμα δὲ καὶ παράστασιν ἔχειν τοῦ
θείου, ὡς οὐδὲν ὠφελεῖ πλῆθος[6] οὐδ᾽ ἄλλη τις ἀλκὴ

---

[1] AE: χειμαδιοῦντος MW: i. marg. γρ χειμαδιοῦντας A: χειμάδια coni. Niese.
[2] χειμαδιᾶν πόλεμον] litt. νπ i. ras. ut vid. m. 2 A.
[3] Πετραίους ὁδοῦ] πέτρας | εισόδου (πέτρας ex πετραί, ει ex ο, όδου ex ὁδοῦ corr.) A : πέτρας εἰσόδου MWE : ut ad Petraeos adveniret Lat.
[4] MW: ἢ A.
[5] ἐφ᾽ ὃν] codd. : ὑφ᾽ ὃν Petersen : ὑφ᾽ οὗ coni.
[6] πληθὺς MWE.

---

[a] Tiberius died on 15 March A.D. 37.
[b] The text is doubtful, and I am deeply indebted to Prof. Hans Petersen for my interpretation. Those manuscripts that

Jonathan's brother Theophilus. On the fourth day, when he received a letter notifying him of the death of Tiberius,[a] he administered to the people an oath of loyalty to Gaius. He now recalled his army, ordering each man to go to his own home for the winter, for he was no longer empowered as before to make war abroad now that the government had fallen into Gaius' hands. It was also reported that Aretas, on consulting the flight of birds when news came of Vitellius' expedition, declared that his army could by no means enter Petra. One of the leaders would die, either the one who had given orders to make war or the one who had set forth to carry out his decision to attack the man against whom the army had in fact been mustered.[b] Vitellius accordingly withdrew to Antioch. Meanwhile, Agrippa, the son of Aristobulus, when the means [c] presented itself, had gone to Rome a year before the death of Tiberius to gain some advantage at court.[d] I will now give a fuller account of Herod and the particulars of his line, both because the tale is pertinent to my history and because it affords a proof of Divine Providence, showing how neither numbers nor any other worldly advan-

Digression on the descendants of Herod the Great.

read $\tilde{\eta}$ ἐφ' ὅν cannot be construed ; ἐφ' ὅν could mean only " against whom," and we would thus have the unlikely possibility of Aretas foretelling the possibility of his own death, an event which surely would not keep the Romans out of Petra. It is straining the Greek to translate ἐφ' ὅν as " for whose sake " and have it refer to Herod. Since $\tilde{\eta}$ and καί are easily confused in minuscule writing, Prof. Petersen suggests reading καί and having the passage predict the death of either Tiberius or Vitellius.

[c] It is not clear whether this refers to financial means or influence or to a chance opportunity.

[d] Or " to transact some business with the emperor." From the parallel passage, B.J. ii. 178, we learn that the reason for Agrippa's visit was to accuse Herod the tetrarch.

τῶν ἐν ἀνθρώποις ἐπιτετευγμένων δίχα τῶν πρὸς
128 τὸ θεῖον εὐσεβειῶν, εἴ γε ἐντὸς ἑκατὸν ἐτῶν ἐξόδου[1]
συνέβη πλὴν ὀλίγων, πολλοὶ δ' ἦσαν, διαφθαρῆναι
τοὺς Ἡρώδου ἀπογόνους· φέροι δ' ἄν τι κἀπὶ
σωφρονισμῷ τοῦ ἀνθρωπείου γένους τὸ τὴν δυσ-
129 τυχίαν αὐτῶν μαθεῖν, ἅμα δὲ καὶ τὸν Ἀγρίππαν δι-
ηγήσασθαι θαύματος ἀξιώτατον γεγενημένον, ὃς ἐκ
πάνυ ἰδιώτου καὶ παρὰ πᾶσαν δόξαν τῶν εἰδότων
αὐτὸν ἐπὶ τοσόνδε ηὐξήθη δυνάμεως. εἴρηται μὲν
οὖν μοι[2] καὶ πρότερον περὶ αὐτῶν, λεχθήσεται δὲ[3]
καὶ νῦν ἀκριβῶς.

130    (4) Ἡρώδῃ τῷ μεγάλῳ θυγατέρες ἐκ Μαριάμμης[4] τῆς Ὑρκανοῦ θυγατρὸς γίνονται δύο, Σα-
λαμψιὼ[5] μὲν ἡ ἑτέρα, ἣ γαμεῖται Φασαήλῳ τῷ
αὐτῆς ἀνεψιῷ Φασαήλου παιδὶ ὄντι τοῦ Ἡρώδου[6]
ἀδελφοῦ δεδωκότος τοῦ πατρὸς αὐτήν, Κύπρος δὲ
Ἀντιπάτρῳ καὶ αὐτὴ ἀνεψιῷ Ἡρώδου παιδὶ τῆς
131 ἀδελφῆς Σαλώμης. καὶ Φασαήλῳ μὲν ἐκ Σαλαμ-
ψιοῦς[7] γίνονται πέντε παῖδες Ἀντίπατρος Ἀλέξανδρος Ἡρώδης[8] θυγατέρες τε Ἀλεξάνδρα καὶ
Κύπρος, ἣν Ἀγρίππας γαμεῖ ὁ Ἀριστοβούλου.[9]
Ἀλεξάνδραν δὲ γαμεῖ μὲν Τίμιος[10] Κύπριος ἀνὴρ[11]
132 τῶν ἀξιολόγων, παρ' ᾧ δὴ ἄτεκνος τελευτᾷ. Κύπρῳ δ' ἐξ Ἀγρίππου μὲν ἄρρενες γίνονται δύο,

[1] ἐξόδου] δι' ὅλου vel fort. περιόδου coni. Richards et Shutt.
[2] μοι A : om. MWE.          [3] δὲ] A : δέ μοι MW.
[4] Μαριάμμης] codd. : Μαριάμης τῆς Ἀλεξάνδρου καὶ Ἀλεξ-
άνδρας E.          [5] Salome Lat. (?).
[6] Ἡρώδου] Ἡρώδου i. ras. maiore m. 1 A : Φασαήλου MW :
Herodis Lat.          [7] Salampsus Lat.
[8] Ἡρώδης Ἀλέξανδρος tr. MWE Lat.
[9] Alexandri cod. A Lat.
[10] μὲν Τίμιος] codd. : μὲν om. E : Μεντίμιος coni. Niese.
[11] Τίμιος Κύπριος ἀνὴρ] honorabilis vir Cyprus Lat.

tage can avail aught without acts of piety toward the
Divine Power. For within a century of Herod's
decease it came about that all but a few of Herod's
issue, and there were many, had perished. It may
contribute to the moral instruction of mankind to
learn what their misfortunes were. It may also be
edifying to tell the story of Agrippa, which is in the
highest degree remarkable. For from a position of
no distinction at all and to the surprise of all who
knew of him, he rose to his high and mighty exaltation. To be sure, I have spoken previously [a] about
these matters, but now I shall dwell on them in detail.

(4) [b] Herod the Great [c] had two daughters by
Mariamme the daughter of Hyrcanus. One of them,
Salampsio, was given in marriage by her father to
Phasael, her cousin, the son of Herod's brother
Phasael; the other, Cypros, also married a cousin,
Antipater, the son of Herod's sister Salome. By
Salampsio Phasael had three sons—Antipater, Alex-
ander, and Herod—and two daughters—Alexandra
and Cypros. Cypros' husband was Agrippa, the son of
Aristobulus; Alexandra's was Timius of Cyprus, a
man of some importance, in union with whom she died
childless. By Agrippa Cypros had two sons, named

[a] *Ant.* xvii. 12-22.

[b] For a stemma of Herod's family see the extensible sheet
at the end of this volume.

[c] It is worthy of note that only in this passage (§§ 130, 133,
and 136) is Herod given the title ὁ μέγας. Since this title is
not found in inscriptions, coins, or elsewhere in Josephus, H.
Ewald, *Geschichte des Volkes Israel* iv³, 1867, p. 546,
plausibly conjectures that ὁ μέγας indicates that he is merely
" the elder " (like Latin *maior*) in comparison with his sons
of that name. For ὁ μέγας as " the Elder " *cf.* Drusus the
Elder in § 143.

θυγατέρες δὲ τρεῖς Βερενίκη[1] Μαριάμμη Δρούσιλλα,
Ἀγρίππας δὲ καὶ Δροῦσος τοῖς ἄρσεσιν ὀνόματα,
133 ὧν ὁ Δροῦσος πρὶν ἡβῆσαι τελευτᾷ.[2] τῷ δὲ πατρὶ[3]
τούτων Ἀγρίππας[4] ἐτρέφετο[5] μετὰ καὶ ἑτέρων
ἀδελφῶν[6] Ἡρώδου τε καὶ Ἀριστοβούλου· καὶ
Βερενίκη[8] καὶ οἵδε παῖδες τοῦ υἱέος Ἡρώδου[9] τοῦ
μεγάλου[10]· ἡ δὲ Βερενίκη Κοστοβάρου καὶ Σαλώμης
134 παῖς τῆς Ἡρώδου ἀδελφῆς. τούτους Ἀριστόβουλος νηπίους λείπεται θνήσκων ὑπὸ τοῦ πατρὸς σὺν
Ἀλεξάνδρῳ τῷ ἀδελφῷ, καθὰ προειρήκαμεν. ἡβή-
σαντες δ' ἄγονται Ἡρώδης μὲν οὗτος ὁ τοῦ Ἀγρίππου ἀδελφός[11] Μαριάμμην θυγατέρα Ὀλυμπιάδος

---

[1] A : Βερνίκη MWE.
[2] lacunam post τελευτᾷ indicat Niese.
[3] τῷ δὲ πατρὶ] ὁ δὲ πατὴρ Hudson.
[4] Ἀγρίππας] -ας in -αι corr. A.
[5] τῷ δὲ . . . ἐτρέφετο] Agrippas autem a patre nutriebatur
Lat.       [6] μετὰ . . . ἀδελφῶν] om. Lat.
[7] Ἡρώδου τε καὶ Ἀριστοβούλου] Hudson : Ἡρώδης καὶ Ἀριστόβουλος A : Ἡρώδης τε καὶ Ἀριστόβουλος MW : Ἡρώδης
δὲ καὶ Ἀριστόβουλος E.
[8] καὶ Βερενίκη] A : καὶ Βερνίκη MW : καὶ ἀδελφὴ Ἡρωδιὰς
Ἀριστοβούλου E : ἐκ Βερνίκης Hudson.
[9] τοῦ υἱέος Ἡρώδου] E : Ἡρώδου τοῦ υἱέος codd.
[10] Ἡρώδης . . . μεγάλου] Herodes autem et Aristobulus et
Verenice etiam hi quoque filii fuerunt filii maioris Herodis
Lat.                                    [11] A : υἱὸς MW.

---

a Niese indicates that there is a lacuna at the end of this
sentence, since Josephus here shifts from listing the progeny
of Salampsio and Phasael to the brothers of the Agrippa who
married Salampsio's daughter Cypros. He thinks that
Josephus would not have given such a fragmentary account
of the family of Aristobulus, the father of Agrippa, as he here
gives. He suggests the possibility that § 138, which states
that Josephus has just listed the progeny of Phasael and
Salampsio, should come after § 132, where Josephus concludes
his listing of the direct line of Phasael and Salampsio. But

Agrippa and Drusus, and three daughters, Berenice, Mariamme, and Drusilla. Of these children Drusus died before reaching adolescence.[a] Agrippa,[b] together with his brothers Herod and Aristobulus, was raised by their father.[c] Berenice, the daughter of Costobar and of Herod's sister Salome, and these sons of Aristobulus, Herod the Great's son,[d] were raised together. These were left as infants by Aristobulus when, as I have previously related,[e] he, together with his brother Alexander, was put to death by his father. When they had reached adolescence, Herod, the brother of Agrippa, married Mariamme,

the digression in §§ 133-138 is understandable inasmuch as Josephus has just mentioned Cypros' husband Agrippa in §§ 131-132 and now wishes to discuss the latter's family. Since there is so much inbreeding and since names recur so often in the family of Herod, there is bound to be confusion, but the genealogical table at the close of this volume will, it is hoped, be of some help.

[b] From the Greek it would appear that this is the Agrippa mentioned in § 132, *i.e.* the son of Agrippa the husband of Cypros. But that Agrippa had a brother Drusus, whereas this one has brothers named Herod and Aristobulus. Hence this Agrippa must be the son of Aristobulus, the son of Herod the Great. The transition in the Greek seems too abrupt, and there is probably a lacuna ; but the meaning is clear.

[c] Aristobulus. *Cf. B.J.* i. 552, which lists his progeny.

[d] The mss. have " these sons of Herod, the son of (Herod) the Great." But apart from our having no means of knowing which of several Herods by that name would be meant, we have not had, and do not have in the sections that follow, any mention of Herod, the son of Herod the Great, until we reach § 136, when he appears to be mentioned for the first time. The transposition of the Epitome, supported also by the order of words in the Latin translation, makes perfect sense, and the reference is to the son of Herod the Great, namely Aristobulus, who is the father of Cypros' husband Agrippa.

[e] *Ant.* xvi. 394.

JOSEPHUS

τῆς Ἡρώδου βασιλέως θυγατρὸς καὶ Ἰωσήπου τοῦ
Ἰωσήπου, ἀδελφὸς δὲ οὗτος Ἡρώδου τοῦ βασιλέως·
135 ἴσχει τε ἐξ αὐτῆς υἱὸν Ἀριστόβουλον. ὁ δὲ τρίτος
τοῦ Ἀγρίππου ἀδελφὸς Ἀριστόβουλος γαμεῖ Ἰω-
τάπην Σαμψιγεράμου¹ θυγατέρα τοῦ Ἐμεσῶν βασιλέως, θυγάτηρ τε αὐτοῖς γίνεται κωφή· ὄνομα
καὶ τῇδε Ἰωτάπη. καὶ τάδε μὲν τῶν ἀρσένων
136 τέκνα. Ἡρωδιὰς δὲ αὐτῶν ἡ ἀδελφὴ γίνεται
Ἡρώδῃ Ἡρώδου τοῦ μεγάλου παιδὶ γεγονότι ἐκ
Μαριάμμης τῆς τοῦ Σίμωνος τοῦ ἀρχιερέως, καὶ
αὐτοῖς Σαλώμη γίνεται, μεθ᾽ ἧς τὰς γονὰς Ἡρωδιὰς ἐπὶ συγχύσει φρονήσασα τῶν πατρίων Ἡρώδῃ
γαμεῖται τοῦ ἀνδρὸς τῷ ὁμοπατρίῳ ἀδελφῷ δια-
στᾶσα ζῶντος.² τὴν δὲ Γαλιλαίων τετραρχίαν οὗ-
137 τος εἶχεν. ἡ δὲ θυγάτηρ αὐτῆς Σαλώμη Φιλίππῳ
γαμεῖται Ἡρώδου παιδὶ τῷ τετράρχῃ τῆς Τραχωνίτιδος, καὶ ἄπαιδος τελευτήσαντος Ἀριστόβουλος
αὐτὴν ἄγεται Ἡρώδου παῖς τοῦ Ἀγρίππου ἀδελφοῦ. παῖδες δὲ ἐγένοντο αὐτοῖς τρεῖς Ἡρώδης Ἀ-
138 γρίππας Ἀριστόβουλος. τοῦτο μὲν δὴ τὸ Φασαήλου καὶ Σαλαμψιοῦς³ ἐστι γένος. Κύπρῳ δ᾽ ἐξ
Ἀντιπάτρου θυγάτηρ γίνεται Κύπρος, καὶ αὐτὴν
Ἀλεξᾶς ὁ Ἑλκίας⁴ γαμεῖ τοῦ Ἀλεξᾶ, καὶ αὐτῆς
θυγάτηρ⁵ ἦν Κύπρος. Ἡρώδης δὲ καὶ Ἀλέξανδρος,
οὓς ἀδελφοὺς ἔφην Ἀντιπάτρου, ἄτεκνοι τελευτῶ-

¹ Lapsigerami cod. A Lat.
² ζῶντος] τοῦ προτέρου γαμέτου ζῶντος ·E.
³ MWE : Salampsus Lat.
⁴ ὁ Ἑλκίας] A : Σέλκιος MW : Selcias Lat.
⁵ τοῦ Ἀλεξᾶ . . . θυγάτηρ] Alexae vero huiusque mulieris
filia Lat.

92

the daughter of Olympias—who was herself the
daughter of King Herod—and of Joseph—who was
the son of Joseph, the brother of King Herod. By
her he had a son Aristobulus. The other brother of
Agrippa, Aristobulus, married Jotape,[a] the daughter
of Sampsigeramus [b] king of Emesa.[c] They had a
daughter also named Jotape, who was a deaf-mute.
Such were the children of the sons. Their sister
Herodias was married to Herod,[d] the son of Herod
the Great by Mariamme, daughter of Simon the high
priest. They had a daughter Salome,[e] after whose
birth Herodias, taking it into her head to flout the
way of our fathers, married Herod, her husband's
brother by the same father, who was tetrarch of
Galilee ; to do this she parted from a living husband.
Her daughter Salome was married to Philip, Herod's [f]
son and tetrarch of Trachonitis. When he died
childless, Aristobulus, the son of Agrippa's brother
Herod, married her. Three sons were born to them—
Herod, Agrippa, and Aristobulus. Such then was
the line of Phasael and Salampsio. As to Cypros,
a daughter named Cypros was born to her of Antipater ; Alexas, who was surnamed Helcias and was the
son of Alexas, married this daughter, and she in turn
had a daughter named Cypros. Herod and Alexander,
who, as I have said,[g] were the brothers of Antipater,

[a] G. Macurdy, " Iotape," *Jour. of Rom. Stud.* xxvi, 1936,
p. 40, suggests that the Median Jotape was the grandmother
both of Jotape the daughter of Sampsigeramus and of Jotape,
sister-wife of Antiochus IV of Commagene (*Ant.* xviii. 140).

[b] *Cf. Ant.* xix. 338-341.

[c] A city or region in Syria on the east bank of the Orontes.

[d] Herod (Philip), mentioned in Mark vi. 17.

[e] We thus learn the name of the daughter of Herodias
mentioned in Mark vi. 22.

[f] Herod the Great's.       [g] § 131.

139 σιν. Ἀλεξάνδρῳ δὲ τῷ Ἡρώδου παιδὶ τοῦ βασιλέως τῷ ὑπὸ τοῦ πατρὸς ἀνῃρημένῳ Ἀλέξανδρος
καὶ Τιγράνης ἐγεγόνεισαν υἱεῖς ἐκ τῆς Ἀρχελάου
τοῦ Καππαδόκων βασιλέως θυγατρός. καὶ Τιγράνης μὲν βασιλεύων Ἀρμενίας κατηγοριῶν αὐτοῦ
140 ἐπὶ Ῥώμης γενομένων ἄπαις τελευτᾷ. Ἀλεξάνδρῳ
δὲ Τιγράνης ὁμώνυμος τῷ ἀδελφῷ γίνεται παῖς καὶ
βασιλεὺς Ἀρμενίας ὑπὸ Νέρωνος ἐκπέμπεται υἱός
τε Ἀλέξανδρος αὐτῷ γίνεται. γαμεῖ δ' οὗτος Ἀν-
τιόχου τοῦ Κομμαγηνῶν βασιλέως θυγατέρα Ἰω-
τάπην, Κήτιδός¹ τε² τῆς ἐν Κιλικίᾳ Οὐεσπασιανὸς
141 αὐτὸν ἵσταται βασιλέα. καὶ τὸ μὲν Ἀλεξάνδρου
γένος εὐθὺς ἅμα τῷ φῦναι τὴν θεραπείαν ἐξέλιπε
τῶν Ἰουδαίοις ἐπιχωρίων μεταταξάμενοι πρὸς τὰ
Ἕλλησι πάτρια· ταῖς δὲ λοιπαῖς θυγατράσιν Ἡρώδου τοῦ βασιλέως ἀτέκνοις τελευτᾶν συνέπεσεν.
142 τῶν δὲ γενομένων Ἡρώδου ἀπογόνων οὓς κατέλεξα
ἔμενον³ ἐν ᾧ χρόνῳ Ἀγρίππας ὁ μέγας τὴν βασιλείαν παρέλαβεν.⁴ τούτων δέ μοι τοῦ γένους προ-
δεδηλωμένων διέξειμι λοιπόν, ὁπόσαι Ἀγρίππᾳ
τύχαι συνέλθοιεν, ὥς τε αὐτῶν διάδρασιν ποιησάμενος ἐπὶ μέγιστον ἀξιώματός τε ἅμα προκόψειεν
καὶ δυνάμεως.

143 (vi. 1) Ἡρώδου τοῦ βασιλέως ὀλίγον πρὸ τῆς

---

¹ Wilhelm : ἡσίοδος codd. : isedis (Iesidi cod. Berol.) Lat.:
Νησιάδος Harduinus : νησίδος Ernesti : Κητιδός Wilhelm.
² Κήτιδός τε] om. spatio vacuo 6 litt. relicto E.
³ κατέλεξα ἔμενον] A : κατελέξαμεν ὄντων MW : κατέλεξα με-
νόντων Bekker.
⁴ τῶν δὲ . . . παρέλαβεν] Herodis autem quam memoravi
prosapia permansit usque ad tempus quo Agrippa Maior
regnum accepit Lat.: om. E.

died childless. Alexander, King Herod's son, who had been put to death by his father, had two sons, Alexander and Tigranes, by the daughter of Archelaus king of Cappadocia. Tigranes, who was king of Armenia, died childless after charges were brought against him at Rome.[a] Alexander had a son who had the same name as his brother Tigranes [b] and who was sent forth by Nero to be king of Armenia. This Tigranes had a son Alexander, who married Jotape, the daughter of Antiochus, king of Commagene ; Vespasian appointed him king of Cetis [c] in Cilicia. The offspring of Alexander abandoned from birth the observance of the ways of the Jewish land and ranged themselves with the Greek tradition. The other daughters of King Herod, it turned out, died childless. Of the descendants of Herod, those whom I have enumerated were still alive at the time when Agrippa the Great received his royal office. Now that I have given an account of their family tree by way of preface, I shall proceed to relate all the vicissitudes that Agrippa experienced and how he eluded them and forged ahead to the highest rank and power.

(vi. 1) Shortly before the death of King Herod, Relations of Agrippa with the

[a] Tacitus mentions this prosecution in *Ann.* vi. 40.

[b] Tacitus, *Ann.* xiv. 26, likewise notes that Tigranes had been selected for the throne by Nero. He adds that Tigranes' long residence in Rome as a hostage had given him a quality of abject servility and that, as the Roman choice, he was accepted by the Armenians only because of their even greater fear of Parthian domination.

[c] The manuscript reading is corrupt. Ernesti's emendation " islet " (Elaiussa-Sebaste : see Wilhelm, *Arch. Epigr. Mitth.* 1894, p. 5), Wilhelm's " Cietis " (an allusion to the tribe of Cietae mentioned in Tac. *Ann.* vi. 41, probably to be identified with the Clitae described in Tac. *Ann.* xii. 55 as savage tribes of Cilicia), or Wilhelm's " Cetis " (adopted by Jones, *Cities*, p. 438 n. 30) are best.

τελευτῆς Ἀγρίππας ἐν Ῥώμῃ διαιτώμενος καὶ
ὁμοτροφίας καὶ συνηθείας αὐτῷ πολλῆς γενομένης
πρὸς Δροῦσον τὸν Τιβερίου τοῦ αὐτοκράτορος υἱὸν
καὶ Ἀντωνίᾳ τῇ Δρούσου τοῦ μεγάλου γυναικὶ εἰς
φιλίαν ἀφίκετο, Βερενίκης τῆς μητρὸς τιμωμένης
παρ' αὐτῇ[1] καὶ προαγωγῶν ἠξιωκυίας τὸν υἱόν.[2]

144 φύσει δὲ μέγας[3] ὢν ὁ Ἀγρίππας καὶ δωρεῖσθαι
πολυτελὴς ζώσης μὲν τῆς μητρὸς οὐκ ἐξέφαινε τῆς
ψυχῆς τὸ θέλον διαδιδράσκειν αὐτῆς ἠξιωκὼς τὴν
145 ἐπὶ τοῖς τοιούτοις γενομένην[4] ὀργήν, ἐπεὶ δὲ Βερενίκη τελευτᾷ, γενόμενος ἐπὶ τῷ αὐτοῦ τρόπῳ, τὰ
μὲν εἰς πολυτέλειαν τῆς καθ' ἡμέραν διαίτης, τὰ δ'
εἰς τῶν δωρεῶν τὸ μὴ μέτρῳ προϊέμενον ἀνάλωσε
τῶν χρημάτων, τὰ πλεῖστα δ' εἰς τοὺς Καίσαρος
ἀπελευθέρους ἐτετέλεστο ἐλπίδι πράξεως[5] τῆς αὐ-
146 τῶν, πενία τε ἐν ὀλίγῳ περὶ αὐτὸν ἦν. καὶ τοῦτο ἦν κώλυμα τῆς ἐν Ῥώμῃ διαίτης, καὶ ὁ Τιβέριος τοῖς φίλοις τοῦ υἱέος τετελευτηκότος ἀπειπὼι
φοιτᾶν εἰς ὄψιν αὐτῷ, διὰ τὸ ἀνερεθίζεσθαι πρὸς
τὸ λυπεῖσθαι μνημονεύων τοῦ παιδὸς θεωρίᾳ τῇ
ἐκείνων.

147 (2) Διὰ μὲν δὴ ταῦτα ἐπὶ τῆς Ἰουδαίας πλέων
ᾤχετο κακοπραγῶν καὶ τεταπεινωμένος ὀλέθρῳ τε
ὢν εἶχεν χρημάτων καὶ ἀπορίᾳ τοῦ ἐκτίσοντος τὰ
χρέα τοῖς δανεισταῖς πολλοῖς τε οὖσιν καὶ ἀλεωρὰν

---

[1] Α : αὐτῆς MWE.
[2] καὶ . . . υἱόν] et venerabiliter appellaret Lat.
[3] μεγαλόφρων coni. Richards et Shutt.
[4] ἂν post γενομένην add. Bekker.
[5] συμπράξεως Richards et Shutt.

---

[a] Son of Tiberius by his first wife Vipsania.

Agrippa was living in Rome. He was brought up imperial family at Rome. His extravagance. with and was on very familiar terms with Drusus,[a] the son of the emperor Tiberius. He also won to friendship Antonia,[b] the wife of Drusus the Elder,[c] for his mother Berenice ranked high among her friends and had requested her to promote the son's interest. Agrippa was naturally noble in spirit [d] and lavish in giving, but so long as his mother was alive, he kept his natural bent concealed. It seemed best not to encounter the burst of temper that anything like that would have provoked in her. But when Berenice died and he was left to his own devices, he spent some of his money on the luxuries of his daily life, some on the gifts that he lavished without restraint ; but his largest payments were made to the emperor's freedmen, whose co-operation he hoped to secure.[e] So he was soon reduced to poverty, and this was an obstacle to his living on in Rome. Moreover, Tiberius forbade the friends of his deceased son [f] to pay him visits because the sight of them stirred him to grief by recalling the memory of his son.

(2) For these reasons, therefore, Agrippa set sail Agrippa sets sail for Judaea. He contemplates suicide, but is assisted by for Judaea. He was in dire plight, humiliated by the loss of the money that he had previously possessed and by the fact that he had no one to pay what he owed to the money-lenders, who were numerous and

[b] Daughter of Mark Antony the triumvir, mother of Germanicus, and grandmother of the future emperor Caligula. *Cf.* §§ 164 ff.

[c] Younger brother of the emperor Tiberius. He distinguished himself in several campaigns against the Germans but died in 9 B.C. through a fall from his horse.

[d] Or " a born aristocrat," lit. " great by nature."

[e] Lit. " in the hope of some action on their part."

[f] Tiberius' son Drusus was poisoned by Sejanus in A.D. 23 (Tac. *Ann.* iv. 8).

οὐδ' ἡντινοῦν ἐνδιδοῦσιν, ὥστε ἀπορίᾳ τῶν ποιητέων
καὶ αἰσχύνῃ τῇ ἐπ' αὐτοῖς ὑποχωρήσας εἴς τινα
πύργον ἐν Μαλάθοις¹ τῆς Ἰδουμαίας² ἐν περινοίᾳ
148 τοῦ μεταστήσοντος αὐτὸν ἦν. αἰσθάνεται δ' αὐτοῦ
τὴν διάνοιαν Κύπρος ἡ γυνὴ παντοία τε ἦν ἀπείρ-
γουσα τῶν ἐπὶ τοιούτοις βουλευμάτων. διαπέμ-
πεται δὲ καὶ ὡς τὴν ἀδελφὴν αὐτοῦ Ἡρωδιάδα
Ἡρώδῃ τῷ τετράρχῃ συνοικοῦσαν γράμματα, δη-
λοῦσα τό τε ἐπὶ τοιούτοις τοῦ Ἀγρίππα προβουλεῦσαν καὶ τὴν ἀνάγκην, ᾗ ἐπ' αὐτὰ ἐξήγαγεν·
149 ἐκέλευέν τε συγγενῆ οὖσαν βοηθεῖν θεωροῦσαν, ὡς
αὐτὴ παντοίως ὡς³ κουφίζοι τὸν ἄνδρα καὶ ταῦτα
οὐκ ἐξ⁴ ὁμοίων ἀφορμῶν.⁵ οἱ δὲ μεταπέμψαντες
αὐτὸν οἰκητήριον ἀπέδειξαν Τιβεριάδα καί τι καὶ
ἀργύριον⁶ ὥρισαν εἰς τὴν δίαιταν, ἀγορανομίᾳ τε
150 τῆς Τιβεριάδος ἐτίμησαν. οὐ μὴν ἐπὶ πλεῖόν γε
Ἡρώδης ἐνέμεινε τοῖς δεδογμένοις, καίτοι γε οὐδ'
ὡς ἀρκοῦντα ἦν· ἐν γὰρ Τύρῳ παρὰ συνουσίαν ὑπὸ
οἴνου γενομένων αὐτοῖς λοιδοριῶν, ἀνεκτὸν οὐχ
ἡγησάμενος Ἀγρίππας⁷ τοῦ Ἡρώδου⁸ τε ἐπονει-
δίσαντος εἰς ἀπορίαν καὶ τροφῆς ἀναγκαίας μετά-
δοσιν, ὡς Φλάκκον τὸν ὑπατικὸν εἴσεισιν φίλον ἐπὶ

¹ Α : Μααλάθοις MW.
² τῆς Ἰδουμαίας] om. Lat.
³ ὡς] Α : om. MW : i. marg. γρ οὐ κουφίζοι Α.
⁴ οὐκ ἐξ] MW : ἐξ Α.
⁵ θεωροῦσαν . . . ἀφορμῶν] καὶ τὸν ἄνδρα πρὸς τοῦτο παρα-
σκευάζειν Ε.
⁶ ἀργύριον] aliquantum aeris per singulos dies Lat.
⁷ Antipater Lat.      ⁸ Antipatro Lat.

ᵃ Variant " although I am as penniless as he." After " to
help him " the Epitome adds " and to dispose her husband
to do so " and omits the next sentence.

who allowed him no chance whatever of avoiding Herod the
them. And so, in his utter helplessness and shame tetrarch
and
at his condition, he withdrew into a certain tower at Herodias.
Malatha in Idumaea, where he had his mind set on
suicide. But his wife Cypros read his thoughts and
tried any and every means to deter him from such a
resolve. Among other things, she sent a letter to his
sister Herodias, the wife of Herod the tetrarch, explaining the nature of Agrippa's plan and the dire
necessity that had driven him to such a shift. She
urged Herodias as his near relative to help him :
" You see," she said, " how I myself am doing all I
can to cheer up my husband, though my resources
are by no means equal to yours." [a] So Herodias and
her husband sent for him, assigned him Tiberias as a
dwelling place, fixed him an allowance for living expenses and raised him to the position of commissioner
of markets [b] in Tiberias. Herod did not, however,
stick to this arrangement for any great while, although
even this assistance was insufficient. For once, when
they were in each other's company in Tyre and had,
under the influence of wine, exchanged taunts, Herod
reproached him with his poverty and dependence on
charity for his daily bread—reproaches which Agrippa
found it impossible to endure. And so he resorted to
Flaccus,[c] the proconsul, who had previously been a

[b] Cf. Ant. xiv. 261. The Greek word ἀγορανόμος is also
employed a number of times in Talmudic literature ; see
the instances listed in S. Krauss, Griechische und lateinische
Lehnwörter im Talmud, Midrasch und Targum, ii, 1899, p.
11. His function was similar to that of the Roman aedile,
his chief duties being to inspect the market, to regulate the
prices and quantities of items brought into the market, and
to punish those guilty of using false weights and measures.

[c] L. Pomponius Flaccus, governor of Syria c. A.D. 32–35.
Otherwise unknown.

Ῥώμης τὰ μάλιστα αὐτῷ γεγονότα πρότερον· Συρίαν δὲ ἐν τῷ τότε διεῖπεν.

151 (3) Καὶ δεξαμένου Φλάκκου παρὰ τούτῳ διῆγεν προκατειληφότος[1] αὐτὸν ἐκεῖ Ἀριστοβούλου, ὃς ἀδελφὸς ὢν Ἀγρίππου διάφορός τ᾽ ἦν. οὐ μὴν ἐβλάπτοντο ἔχθρᾳ τῇ ἀλλήλων, ὥστε μὴ φιλίᾳ τοῦ 152 ὑπατικοῦ τὰ εἰκότα τιμὴν φέρεσθαι.[2] οὐ μὴν ὅ γε Ἀριστόβουλος ἀνίει τι τοῦ πρὸς τὸν Ἀγρίππαν δυσμενοῦς μέχρι καὶ εἰς ἔχθραν αὐτὸν Φλάκκῳ καθίστησιν, αἰτίαν τοιαύτην ἐπὶ τῇ δυσμενείᾳ παρα- 153 λαβών. Δαμασκηνοὶ Σιδωνίοις περὶ ὅρων[3] διάφο- ροι καθεστῶτες, μέλλοντος Φλάκκου περὶ τούτων ἀκροᾶσθαι μαθόντες τὸν Ἀγρίππαν ὡς παρ᾽ αὐτῷ μέγα δύναιτ᾽ ἂν ἠξίουν μερίδος τῆς αὐτῶν γενέ- 154 σθαι, ἀργύριόν τε πλεῖστον ὡμολογεῖτο αὐτῷ. καὶ ὁ μὲν πάντα ἐπὶ τῇ βοηθείᾳ τῶν Δαμασκηνῶν ὥρμητο πράσσειν. Ἀριστόβουλος δέ, οὐ γὰρ ἐλάν- θανεν αὐτὸν ἡ ὁμολογία τῶν χρημάτων, καταγο- ρεύει πρὸς τὸν Φλάκκον. καὶ βασανιζομένου τοῦ πράγματος ἐπεὶ φανερὰ ἦν, ἐξωθεῖ τὸν Ἀγρίππαν 155 φιλίας τῆς πρὸς αὐτόν. ὁ δὲ εἰς ὑστάτην περι- ωσμένος ἀπορίαν εἰς Πτολεμαΐδα παρῆν, καὶ κατὰ τὸ ἄπορον τῆς ἀλλαχόθι διαίτης γνώμην ἐποιεῖτο ἐπὶ τῆς Ἰταλίας πλεῖν. εἰργόμενος δὲ χρημάτων ἀπορίᾳ ἠξίου Μαρσύαν ὄντα αὐτοῦ ἀπελεύθερον ποριστὴν γενέσθαι τῶν ἐπὶ τοιούτοις μηχανῶν[4]

---

[1] Ε : παρακατεσχηκότος codd. : προκατεσχηκότος coni. Niese.
[2] τὰ] i. marg. γρ εἰς τὰ εἰκότα αὐτῶι τιμὴν φέρεσθαι Α.
[3] περὶ ὅρων] pro militibus (h.e. limitibus) Lat.
[4] δαπανῶν Ε.

---

[a] mss. "checked."
[b] Prof. Post translates: " They did not, however, let their
100

very close friend of his in Rome and who was then governor of Syria.

(3) He was welcomed by Flaccus and lived with him. Agrippa had been anticipated [a] there by Aristobulus, who, though his brother, was on bad terms with him. Their mutual enmity was not, however, so injurious as to prevent him from winning the honour which his friendship with the proconsul brought him in due course.[b] Nevertheless, Aristobulus did not relent in his animosity against Agrippa until he had involved him in a quarrel with Flaccus. The opportunity which he seized to display his hostility was as follows. There was a disagreement between the people of Damascus and those of Sidon on the subject of boundaries. When Flaccus was about to hear the case, the Damascenes, on learning that Agrippa would have a great influence with him, asked Agrippa to favour their cause and promised him a very large sum of money. When he had committed himself to use all means to aid the Damascenes, Aristobulus, to whom it was no secret that money had been promised, denounced him to Flaccus. When, upon investigating the matter, Flaccus found it to be clearly so, he broke off his friendship with Agrippa. Thus forced into the most dire straits, Agrippa went to Ptolemaïs, and, lacking the means to live anywhere else, he resolved to set sail for Italy. Since he was restrained from doing so for want of funds, he appealed to Marsyas, his freedman, to borrow from someone and provide

mutual hatred damage the standing that they of course enjoyed as friends of the proconsul." The French translation of Mathieu and Herrmann renders the sense thus : " Their disagreements did not go so far as to prevent their showing each other honour for appearance's sake out of friendship for the proconsul."

156 δανεισάμενον παρά τινος. καὶ ὁ Μαρσύας Πρῶτον[1]
κελεύει Βερενίκης ὄντα ἀπελεύθερον τῆς Ἀγρίππου
μητρός, διαθήκης δὲ τῆς ἐκείνης[2] δικαίῳ.[3] ὑποτε-
λοῦντα τῆς Ἀντωνίας,[4] αὐτῷ γοῦν παρασχεῖν ἐπὶ
157 γράμματι καὶ πίστει τῇ αὐτοῦ. ὁ δέ, ἐπεκάλει γὰρ
τῷ Ἀγρίππᾳ χρημάτων τινῶν ἀποστέρησιν, ἀναγ-
κάζει τὸν Μαρσύαν[5] δύο μυριάδων Ἀτθίδων συμ-
βόλαιον ποιησάμενον πεντακοσίαις καὶ δισχιλίαις[6]
ἔλασσον λαμβάνειν. συνεχώρει δ' ἐκεῖνος κατὰ τὸ
158 μὴ εἶναι ἄλλως ποιεῖν. εἰλημμένου δὲ τοῦ χρήματος[7] τούτου Ἀγρίππας εἰς Ἀνθηδόνα παραγενόμενος καὶ λαβὼν ναῦν ἐν ἀναγωγαῖς ἦν. καὶ γνοὺς
Ἐρέννιος Καπίτων ὁ τῆς Ἰαμνείας ἐπίτροπος πέμπει στρατιώτας, οἳ εἰσπράξονται αὐτὸν ἀργυρίου
τριάκοντα μυριάδας θησαυρῷ τῷ Καίσαρος ὀφειλο-
μένας ἐπὶ Ῥώμης ὑπ' αὐτοῦ, ἀνάγκας τε ἐπετίθε-
159 σαν τοῦ μενοῦντος. καὶ τότε μὲν πείσεσθαι τοῖς
κεκελευσμένοις προσποιητὸς ἦν, νυκτὸς δ' ἐπιγενο-
μένης κόψας τὰ ἀπόγεια ᾤχετο ἐπ' Ἀλεξανδρείας
πλέων. ἔνθα Ἀλεξάνδρου δεῖται τοῦ ἀλαβάρχου[8]
μυριάδας εἴκοσι δάνειον αὐτῷ δοῦναι. ὁ δ' ἐκείνῳ

---

[1] Πέτρον E : primum quendam Lat.
[2] coni. Niese : ἐκείνου codd.
[3] Bekker cum Lat. : δικαίου A : δικαίως MW.
[4] διαθήκης . . . Ἀντωνίας] sed iure testamenti eius factum dicionis Antoniae Lat. : om. E.
[5] Μαρσύαν] A : Ἀγρίππαν Μαρσύαν MW.
[6] χιλίαις E.
[7] ἀργυρίου coni. Richards et Shutt.
[8] ἀβαλάρχου E.

---

[a] About £1929 or $5400.
[b] A city, also called Agrippias or Agrippeion, on the Mediterranean coast near Gaza. It is mentioned in B.J. i. 87, Ant. xiii. 357, etc.

him with the necessary means. Marsyas thereupon bade Protos, a freedman of Agrippa's mother Berenice, who under the latter's will had become a retainer of Antonia, to provide him with the money on the written bond and security of Agrippa. Protos, however, complained that Agrippa had defrauded him of some money, and forced Marsyas to draw up a bond for 20,000 Attic drachmas [a] but to accept 2500 less. The latter yielded since he had no alternative. The money once in hand, Agrippa repaired to Anthedon,[b] where he engaged a ship and was on the point of putting out to sea. But Herennius Capito,[c] the procurator of Jamnia, learned of this and sent soldiers to exact from him the 300,000 pieces of silver [d] which he owed the Imperial treasury at Rome ; and they put constraint upon him to remain. He pretended at the time that he would obey these orders, but when night fell, he cut the mooring cables and proceeded on his voyage to Alexandria. There he begged Alexander [e] the alabarch [f] to grant him a loan of 200,000 drach-

*Agrippa obtains a loan from Alexander the alabarch.*

[c] *Cf.* Philo, *Leg. ad Gaium* 199, who speaks particularly of his hatred of the Jews. He is plausibly identified by P. Fraccaro, " C. Herennius Capito di Teate," *Athenaeum*, xviii, 1940, pp. 136-144, with the C. Herennius Capito who in an inscription is called procurator of Julia Augusta, of Tiberius, and of Gaius.

[d] Presumably drachmas. Hence about £28,929 or $81,000.

[e] Alexander Lysimachus, brother of the philosopher Philo, and father of Tiberius Julius Alexander the notorious procurator and apostate. It was he who decorated the gates of the temple with gold and silver, as we learn from *B.J.* v. 205. *Cf.* also *Ant.* xix. 276 and xx. 100.

[f] The function of the alabarch has been disputed ; Rostovtzeff and Welles suggest that the office was somehow closely connected with special taxes paid by the Jews. But Baron, *Social and Religious History of the Jews*, i. 409-410

μὲν οὐκ ἂν ἔφη παρασχεῖν, Κύπρῳ δὲ οὐκ ἠρνεῖτο
τήν τε φιλανδρίαν αὐτῆς καταπεπληγμένος καὶ τὴν
160 λοιπὴν ἅπασαν ἀρετήν. ἡ δὲ ὑπισχνεῖτο, καὶ ὁ
Ἀλέξανδρος πέντε τάλαντα αὐτοῖς ἐν τῇ Ἀλεξανδρείᾳ δοὺς τὸ λοιπὸν ἐν Δικαιαρχείᾳ γενομένοις
παρέξειν ἐπηγγέλλετο, δεδιὼς τοῦ Ἀγρίππου τὸ εἰς
τὰ ἀναλώματα ἕτοιμον. καὶ Κύπρος μὲν ἀπαλλάξ-
ασα τὸν ἄνδρα ἐπὶ τῆς Ἰταλίας πλευσούμενον αὐτὴ
μετὰ τῶν τέκνων ἐπὶ Ἰουδαίας ἀνέζευξεν.

161 (4) Ἀγρίππας δὲ εἰς Ποτιόλους παραβαλὼν ἐπιστολὴν ὡς Τιβέριον τὸν Καίσαρα γράφει διαιτώ-
μενον ἐν Καπρέαις, παρουσίαν τε τὴν αὐτοῦ δηλῶν
ἐπὶ θεραπείᾳ καὶ ὄψει τῇ ἐκείνου, καὶ ἀξιῶν ἔφεσιν
162 αὐτῷ γενέσθαι εἰς Καπρέας παραβαλεῖν. Τιβέριος
δὲ οὐδὲν ἐνδοιάσας τά τε ἄλλα αὐτῷ γράφει φιλανθρωπίᾳ χρώμενος, ἐκτείνειν τε χάριν[1] ἀποσημαίνων[2]
ἐπὶ τῷ σῶν ἐπανήκειν εἰς τὰς Καπρέας,[3] ἐπεὶ δ'
ἀφικνεῖται μηδὲν ὑφελὼν τοῦ ἐν τοῖς γράμμασι προ-
163 θύμου ἠσπάζετό τε καὶ ἐξένιζεν. τῇ δ' ἑξῆς Καίσαρι γραμμάτων αὐτῷ παρὰ Ἐρεννίου Καπίτωνος
ἀφικομένων, ὅτι Ἀγρίππας μυριάδας τριάκοντα δάνεισμα ποιήσας καὶ πρὸς τὰς καταβολὰς ἐκλιπὼν
χρόνον τὸν συγκείμενον ἀπαιτήσεως γενομένης οἷ-

---

[1] ἐκτείνειν τε χάριν] Thackeray : ἐκτίνει τε χάριν codd. : καὶ
χαίρειν E : ἔτι χαίρειν ed. pr. : ἐκτίνειν τε χάριν Cocceji : ἐκ-
τείνει τε χάριν Marcus.

[2] ⟨νοῦν⟩ post ἀποσημαίνων add. Petersen.

[3] τά τε . . . Καπρέας] clementer illi et humane rescripsit
inter alia quoque gaudere se significans illum ad se sospitem
reppedare Lat.

---

n. 16, properly notes that the office is found long after the
decline of Egyptian Jewry. The traditional explanation,

mas.[a]  Alexander refused to grant this loan to him, but he did not deny it to Cypros because he marvelled at her love of her husband and all her other good qualities.  She promised to repay it ; and so Alexander gave them five talents [b] in Alexandria and offered to hand over the rest when they arrived in Dicaearchia,[c] for he did not trust Agrippa's prodigal vein.  Cypros thereupon dispatched her husband on his voyage to Italy and herself returned with her children to Judaea.

(4) When Agrippa had reached Puteoli, he sent a letter to the emperor Tiberius, who was then living at Capri, informing him that he had come to see and pay court to him and asking for permission to land at Capri.  Tiberius without hesitation wrote him a courteous reply, expressing his particular pleasure upon his safe return to Capri.  When Agrippa arrived there, Tiberius showed no less goodwill towards him than he had indicated in his letter and made him a welcome guest.  On the following day the emperor received a letter from Herennius Capito stating that Agrippa, after borrowing 300,000 drachmas, had allowed the time stipulated for repayment to pass and that when he was asked to pay, he had gone off in

*He returns to Italy and pays court to Tiberius.*

*His further difficulties with money.*

that the alabarch was a general tax administrator and in charge of customs, seems best.

[a] About £19,286 or $54,000.

[b] A talent was the equivalent of 6000 drachmas ; hence five talents would be 30,000 drachmas (about £2893 or $8100).

[c] The Greek name for Puteoli in Campania (*cf. Vita* 16). Baron i. 409 n. 16 suggests that Alexander may have had a correspondent or even a branch office in Puteoli. But the mere existence of an apparently affluent Jewish colony there (*B.J.* ii. 104) surely does not prove Baron's point. *Cf.* A. Fuchs, " Marcus Julius Alexander," *Zion* xiii-xiv, 1948–49, pp. 10-17 [in Hebrew].

χοιτο φυγὰς ἐκ τῶν ὑπ᾽ αὐτῷ χωρίων ἄκυρον αὐτὸν
164 καθιστὰς τῆς ἐπὶ τῷ εἰσπραξομένῳ[1] ἐξουσίας, ταύτην ἀναγνοὺς τὴν ἐπιστολὴν περιαλγεῖ τε ὁ Καῖσαρ
καὶ διάκλεισιν γενέσθαι τῷ ᾽Αγρίππᾳ κελεύει εἰσόδων τῶν πρὸς αὐτὸν ἄχρι δὴ καταβολῆς τοῦ χρέους.
ὁ δὲ μηδὲν τῇ ὀργῇ τοῦ Καίσαρος καταπλαγεὶς
᾽Αντωνίας δεῖται Γερμανικοῦ μητρὸς καὶ Κλαυδίου
τοῦ ὕστερον γενομένου Καίσαρος, δάνεισμα αὐτῷ
δοθῆναι τῶν τριάκοντα μυριάδων, ὡς φιλίας μὴ
165 ἁμάρτοι τῆς πρὸς Τιβέριον. ἡ δὲ Βερενίκης τε
μνήμη τῆς μητρὸς αὐτοῦ, σφόδρα γὰρ ἀλλήλαις
ἐχρῶντο αἵδε αἱ γυναῖκες, καὶ αὐτῷ ὁμοτροφίας
πρὸς τοὺς ἀμφὶ Κλαύδιον γεγενημένης, δίδωσι τὸ
ἀργύριον, καὶ αὐτῷ ἀποτίσαντι τὸ χρέος ἀνεπικώ-
166 λυτος ἦν ἡ φιλία τοῦ Τιβερίου. αὖθις δὲ αὐτῷ
Τιβέριος ὁ Καῖσαρ συνίστησιν υἱωνὸν τὸν αὐτοῦ
κελεύων τὰ πάντα αὐτῷ ταῖς ἐξόδοις παρατυγχάνειν. ᾽Αγρίππας δὲ φιλίᾳ δεχθεὶς ὑπὸ τῆς ᾽Αντω-
νίας κατὰ θεραπείαν τρέπεται τὴν Γαΐου υἱωνοῦ τε
ὄντος αὐτῇ καὶ εὐνοίᾳ τοῦ πατρὸς[2] εἰς τὰ πρῶτα
167 τιμωμένου. καὶ γὰρ[3] ἦν ἄλλος[4] Σαμαρεὺς γένος[5]

---

[1] τῷ εἰσπραξομένῳ] Bekker : τῶν εἰσπραξομένων codd.
[2] matris Lat.     [3] γὰρ] codd. : δή τις E.
[4] om. E : Θάλλος Hudson : ἄνθρωπος Miévis (Rev. Belge de
Philol. et d᾽Hist. xiii, 1934, pp. 733 sqq.).
[5] καὶ . . . γένος] erat ibi forte quidam genere Samareus
Lat.

---

[a] Capito's.
[b] §§ 166-168 are paralleled by B.J. ii. 178-180.
[c] Tiberius Gemellus, the son of Drusus the Younger. Cf.
§§ 187 ff. and 206.
[d] The future emperor Gaius Caligula.
[e] Germanicus. For the reasons accounting for his popularity see §§ 207-209.

flight from the territory under his [a] jurisdiction, thus rendering him powerless to sue and recover the money. Upon reading this letter the emperor was hurt to the quick and ordered that Agrippa's visits should be barred until he had repaid the debt. Undismayed by the emperor's anger, Agrippa asked Antonia, the mother of Germanicus and of the future emperor Claudius, to grant him a loan of 300,000 drachmas so that he might not lose the friendship of Tiberius. Antonia, both because she still remembered Berenice his mother—for the two ladies had been deeply attached to each other—and because Agrippa had been brought up with Claudius and his circle, provided the money. When he had discharged the debt, there was no longer any obstacle to his friendship with Tiberius. [b] Subsequently the emperor Tiberius recommended his grandson [c] to Agrippa and bade him always accompany him on his excursions. When Agrippa was received as a friend by Antonia, he took to attendance upon her grandson Gaius,[d] who was held in the highest honour because of the popularity enjoyed by his father.[e] Now there was, in addition,[f] He pays

[f] The manuscript reading, ἄλλος, "another," presents difficulties in this context, and most scholars have adopted Hudson's emendation, Θάλλος, identifying the Samaritan as Thallus, perhaps, as Schürer iii. 495 would have it, the author of a universal history mentioned by Eusebius (*Chron.* ed. Schoene, i. 265) which mentions an eclipse that took place at the time of the crucifixion in the fifteenth year of Tiberius (A.D. 29). But it is possible to keep the manuscript reading in the sense of "in addition to," "besides"; *cf.* Plato, *Gorgias* 473 D, Aeschines i. 163. Or we may choose to take ἄλλος as a pronoun and translate, "Now there was another, namely a Samaritan by race (birth)," as does H. A. Rigg, "Thallus: the Samaritan?" *Harv. Theol. Rev.* xxxiv, 1941, p. 119, who well explains that "the context of this passage implies that Agrippa has raised a sum of money

107

Καίσαρος δὲ ἀπελεύθερος· παρὰ τούτου δάνεισμα
μυριάδας ἑκατὸν εὑρόμενος τῇ τε Ἀντωνίᾳ κατα-
βάλλει τὸ ὀφειληθὲν χρέος καὶ τῶν λοιπῶν τῷ
ἀναλώματι θεραπεύων τὸν Γάιον μειζόνως ἐν ἀξιώματι ἦν παρ᾽ αὐτῷ.

168 (5) Προϊούσης δὲ ἐπὶ μέγα τῷ Ἀγρίππᾳ τῆς πρὸς
Γάιον φιλίας αἰωρουμένοις ποτὲ λόγος περὶ τοῦ
Τιβερίου γίνεται, καὶ τοῦ Ἀγρίππου κατ᾽ εὐχὰς
τραπομένου, μόνω δ᾽ ἤστην, ᾗ τάχος Τιβέριον
ὑπεκστάντα τῆς ἀρχῆς Γαΐῳ παραχωρεῖν ἀξιωτέρῳ
τὰ πάντα ὄντι, τούτων ἀκροᾶται τῶν λόγων Εὔτυχος, Ἀγρίππου δ᾽ ἦν ἀπελεύθερος ἡνίοχος, καὶ
169 παραχρῆμα μὲν σιγῇ παρεδίδου. κλοπῆς δὲ
ἱματίων αὐτῷ τοῦ Ἀγρίππου ἐπικαλουμένης, καὶ
ἀκριβῶς δὲ ἐκεκλόφει, φυγὼν καὶ ληφθεὶς ἀγωγῆς
αὐτοῦ ἐπὶ Πείσωνα γενομένης, ὃς ἦν φύλαξ τῆς
πόλεως, ἐρομένου τὴν αἰτίαν τῆς φυγῆς Καίσαρί
φησιν ἀπορρήτους ἔχειν λόγους εἰπεῖν ἐπ᾽ ἀσφαλείᾳ
τῆς σωτηρίας αὐτοῦ φέροντας, ὥστε δήσας αὐτὸν
ἔστελλεν εἰς τὰς Καπρέας, καὶ Τιβέριος τῷ αὐτοῦ
τρόπῳ χρώμενος εἶχεν αὐτὸν δέσμιον, μελλητὴς[1]
εἰ καί τις ἕτερος βασιλέων ἢ τυράννων γενόμενος.
170 οὔτε γὰρ πρεσβειῶν ὑποδοχὰς ἐκ τοῦ ὀξέος ἐποιεῖτο
ἡγεμόσι τε ἢ ἐπιτρόποις ὑπ᾽ αὐτοῦ σταλεῖσιν
οὐδεμία ἦν διαδοχή, ὁπότε μὴ φθαῖεν τετελευτη-

---

[1] μελητὴς M et ut vid. Lat.

---

in one direction and now borrows another sum with which to
pay off the former from another source, viz., a certain Imperial freedman who happened to be a Samaritan."

[a] About £96,429 or $270,000.

[b] According to the parallel passage, B.J. ii. 179, it was
while entertaining Gaius at dinner that Agrippa prayed that

a certain man of Samaritan origin who was a freed-<br>
man of the emperor.  Agrippa managed to borrow<br>
a million drachmas [a] from him and repaid the money<br>
that he had borrowed from Antonia.  The rest of the<br>
money he spent in paying court to Gaius, with whom<br>
he consequently rose to higher favour.

court to<br>Gaius<br>Caligula.

(5) And so Agrippa's friendship with Gaius made
great progress.  Once, while they were riding,[b] the
conversation turned to Tiberius, and Agrippa expressed a prayer—for the two of them were alone—
that Tiberius would relinquish his office with all
speed in favour of Gaius, who was more competent in
every respect.  These words were overheard by Eutychus, a freedman of Agrippa who drove his chariot,
but for the present he kept it to himself.  When,
however, he was accused of stealing some of Agrippa's
clothes, which was precisely what he had done, he
took flight, but was caught.  Being brought before
Piso, who was prefect of the city, he was asked why
he had fled.  He replied that he had a secret message
for the emperor pertaining to his personal security.
Piso sent him in chains to Capri, where Tiberius, in
his usual way—for no king or tyrant was ever more
given to procrastination—kept him a prisoner.  For
Tiberius was in no hurry to receive embassies, nor
did he replace governors or procurators sent out by
him unless they died at their posts.[c]  Similarly he was

Tiberius'<br>dilatory<br>character.

Gaius would soon succeed as emperor through the death of
Tiberius.

[c] Tiberius' practice of leaving governors in office for an
undue length of time is also mentioned by Tacitus, *Ann.* i.
80, who cites various explanations for it—Tiberius' aversion
to having to face recurrent problems and his consequent
preference for making a single permanent decision, his
jealous desire that not too many should enjoy high positions,

κότες· ὅθεν καὶ δεσμωτῶν ἀκροάσεως ἀπερίοπτος[1]
171 ἦν. ὥστε καὶ τῶν φίλων ἐρομένων τὴν αἰτίαν τοῦ
ἐπὶ τοιούτοις ὁλκῇ χρωμένου, ἔφη τὰς μὲν πρεσβείας τρίβειν, ὅπως μὴ ἀπαλλαγῆς αὐταῖς ἐκ τοῦ
ὀξέος γενομένης ἕτεροι πρέσβεις ἐπιχειροτονηθέντες
ἐπανίοιεν ὄχλος τε αὐτῷ γίγνοιτο ἐπιδοχαῖς[2] αὐτῶν
172 καὶ πομπαῖς προσκειμένῳ.[3] τὰς δ' ἀρχὰς συγχωρεῖν τοῖς ἅπαξ εἰς αὐτὰς ὑπ' αὐτοῦ καταστᾶσιν
αἰδοῦς[4] προμηθείᾳ τῶν ὑποτελῶν· φύσει μὲν γὰρ
εἶναι πᾶσαν ἡγεμονίαν οἰκείαν τοῦ πλεονεκτεῖν·
τὰς δὲ μὴ παγίους,[5] ἀλλ' εἰς ὀλίγον καὶ ἄδηλον
ὁπότε ἀφαιρεθεῖεν[6] καὶ μειζόνως ἐξοτρύνειν ἐπὶ
173 κλοπαῖς τοὺς ἔχοντας. εἰ μὲν οὖν ἐφεστήκασιν εἰς
πλέον, αὐτοὺς ἄδην τῶν κλοπῶν ἕξειν ὑπὸ τοῦ
πολλοῦ τῶν κεκερδημένων ἀμβλυτέρως τὸ λοιπὸν
αὐταῖς χρωμένους. διαδοχῆς δ' ἐπιπαραγενομένης
ἐκ τοῦ ὀξέος μηδαμῶς ἂν ἀρκέσαι τοὺς ἄθλα τοῖς
ἄρχουσι προκειμένους ἀναστροφῆς αὐτοῖς οὐ διδο-
μένης καιρῶν, ἐν οἷς πλήρεις οἱ προειληφότες γενό-

---

[1] Ernesti ex Thucy. i. 41 : περίοπτος codd. E.
[2] Dindorf : ἐπὶ δοχαῖς MWE : ἐπὶ διαδοχαῖς A.
[3] Ernesti : προκειμένων codd. : προκειμένῳ ed. pr.
[4] αἰδίους Powell (Class. Rev. l, 1936, p. 11).
[5] E et i. marg. A : πατρίους codd.
[6] τὰς δὲ . . . ἀφαιρεθεῖεν] cum igitur non se aliquis peren-
nem in officio manere perspexerit.

---

and his practice of giving governorships to able men whom
he wished to send away from Rome lest they become his
rivals. Magie, *Roman Rule*, ii. 1363 n. 37, remarks that out
of fifty-seven men who are known to have been consuls from
A.D. 6 to 23, only eight are known to have held the proconsul-
ship of the province of Asia and only seven to have held that

negligent about hearing trials of prisoners.[a] When his friends asked him why he was so slow in such matters, he replied that he kept the embassies waiting lest, if they discharged their business at once, new ambassadors might be elected and repair to him who would cause him the bother of receiving and dismissing them. As for the official appointments, he said that he allowed any whom he had once appointed to office to remain out of consideration for the feelings of the subject-peoples.[b] For it was a law of nature that governors are prone to engage in extortion. When appointments were not permanent,[c] but were for short terms, or liable to be cancelled without notice, the spur to peculation was even greater.[d] If, on the contrary, those appointed kept their posts longer, they would be gorged with their robberies and would by the very bulk of them be more sluggish in pursuit of further gain. Let succession come rapidly, however, and those who were the destined spoil of the governors could never do enough, for there would be no intervals of relaxation in which those already glutted with their spoils might abate

of Africa during Tiberius' principate. Suetonius also (*Tib.* 41) notes Tiberius' failure to make new appointments to provincial posts.

[a] In addition to the case of Eutychus, other instances where Tiberius procrastinated unduly were those of Lampon of Alexandria (Philo, *In Flacc.* 128), who had to wait two years for his trial, and Pomponius Secundus (Dio Cass. lix. 6. 2), who waited for seven years.

[b] Variant " to remain permanently out of consideration for the subject-peoples."

[c] Variant " in the homeland."

[d] Tacitus also (*Ann.* iv. 6) mentions Tiberius' concern that the provinces not suffer from the rapacity of governors, but he does not indicate that this was the reason why Tiberius allowed governors to remain in office so long.

μένοι ὑποδιδοῖέν[1] τε[2] σπουδῆς τῆς ἐπὶ τῷ λαμβάνειν, διὰ τὸ πρὶν ἐν καιρῷ γενέσθαι μεταστῆναι.
174 παράδειγμά τε αὐτοῖς φησι τοῦτον τὸν λόγον·
τραυματίᾳ τινὶ κειμένῳ μυῖαι κατὰ πλῆθος τὰς
ὠτειλὰς περιέστασαν. καί τις τῶν παρατυχόντων
οἰκτείρας αὐτοῦ τὴν δυστυχίαν καὶ νομίσας ἀδυναμίᾳ μὴ βοηθεῖν οἷος ἦν[3] ἀποσοβεῖν αὐτὰς παρα-
175 στάς. καὶ δεομένου παύσασθαι τῶν ἐπὶ τοιοῖσδε,
ὑπολαβὼν ἤρετο τὴν αἰτίαν τοῦ ἀπρομηθοῦς εἰς τὴν
διαφυγὴν κακοῦ τοῦ ἐφεστηκότος. '' μειζόνως γὰρ
ἂν ἀδικοῖς με,'' εἶπε,'' ταύτας ἀπαγαγών. ταῖς μέν
γε ἤδη πληρωθείσαις τοῦ αἵματος οὐκέθ' ὁμοίως
ἔπειξις ὄχλον μοι παρασχεῖν, ἀλλά πη καὶ ἀνίσχου-
σιν. αἱ δ' ἀκραιφνεῖ[4] τῷ κατ' αὐτὰς λιμῷ συνελ-
θοῦσαι καὶ τετρυμένον[5] ἤδη παραλαμβάνουσαι κἂν[6]
176 ὀλέθρῳ παραδοῖεν.'' διὰ τάδε οὖν καὐτὸς ὑπὸ
πολλῶν τῶν κλοπῶν διεφθαρμένοις τοῖς ὑποτελέσιν
προμηθὴς[7] εἶναι μὴ συνεχὲς ἐξαποστέλλειν τοὺς
ἡγησομένους, οἳ ἐν τρόπῳ μυιῶν ἐκπολεμοῖεν[8]
αὐτούς, φύσει πρὸς κέρδος ὀρωρεγμένοις σύμμαχον
παραλαμβάνοντες τὴν ἐλπίδα τοῦ ταχέως ἀφαιρεθη-
177 σομένου τὴν ἐνθένδε ἡδονήν. μαρτυρήσει δέ μου
τῷ λόγῳ περὶ τῆς ἐπὶ τοιούτοις φύσεως Τιβερίου
τὸ ἔργον αὐτό· ἔτη γὰρ δύο πρὸς τοῖς εἴκοσιν αὐτο-

---

[1] ὑπενδιδοῖέν coni. Niese.
[2] A : τῆς MW : om. E : τι coni. Niese.

[3] οἷος ἦν] Post : οἷός τε ἦν MWE : οἷός τ᾽ ἦν A.
[4] A : ἀκραιφνεῖς MWE.
[5] ed. pr. : τετρυμμέναι A : τετρυμέναι MW.
[6] Niese : καὶ codd. E.

[7] E : προμηθὲς A : προμηθὴς MW.
[8] Dindorf : ἐκπολεμῶεν codd. E : ἐκπορθοῖεν Richards et
Shutt.

somewhat of their grasping avarice, since before that could happen the moment would come to depart. He told them this fable by way of illustration.[a] Once a man lay wounded, and a swarm of flies hovered about his wounds. A passer-by took pity on his evil plight and, in the belief that he did not raise a hand because he could not, was about to step up and shoo them off. The wounded man, however, begged him to think no more of doing anything about it. At this the man spoke up and asked him why he was not interested in escaping from his wretched condition. "Why," said he, "you would put me in a worse position if you drove them off. For since these flies have already had their fill of blood, they no longer feel such a pressing need to annoy me but are in some measure slack. But if others were to come with a fresh appetite, they would take over my now weakened body and that would indeed be the death of me." He too, he said, for the same reason took the precaution of not dispatching governors continually to the subject-peoples who had been brought to ruin by so many thieves ; for the governors would harry them utterly[b] like flies. Their natural appetite for plunder would be reinforced by their expectation of being speedily deprived of that pleasure. The record of Tiberius' acts will bear out my account of his humour in such matters. For during the twenty-two years that he was

[a] Cf. the fable of the fox, the flies, and the hedgehog utilized by Aesop (Fable 314) according to Aristotle (Rhet. ii. 1393 b 23—1394 a 1) when he defended a wealthy demagogue before the assembly at Samos. Aesop warns the people of Samos that if they vote to put this demagogue to death, others who are not rich will come along and empty their treasury completely.

[b] Lit. "devastate them utterly by war." Variant "plunder them."

κράτωρ γενόμενος δύο τοὺς πάντας Ἰουδαίοις ἐξέπεμψεν διοικήσοντας τὸ ἔθνος, Γρᾶτον τε καὶ
178 Πιλᾶτον, ὃς αὐτῷ διεδέξατο τὴν ἡγεμονίαν. καὶ
οὐκ ἐπὶ μὲν Ἰουδαίων τοιοῦτος ἦν, ἑτεροῖος δὲ ἐπὶ
τῶν λοιπῶν ὑπηκόων. ἀλλὰ καὶ τῶν δεσμωτῶν
τὴν ὑπερβολὴν τῆς ἀκροάσεως[1] ἀπεσήμαινεν ὑπὸ
τοῦ[2] δικαιωθεῖσι μὲν θανάτῳ κούφισιν γενέσθαι τῶν
ἐνεστηκότων κακῶν, διὰ τὸ μὴ ἐπ' ἀρετῇ[3] τῶν ἐπὶ
τοιούτοις τύχῃ συνελθεῖν, τριβομένοις δὲ ἀχθηδόνι
τῇ ἐπικειμένῃ μείζονα προσρέπειν τὴν δυστυχίαν.
179   (6) Διὰ μὲν δὴ τάδε καὶ Εὔτυχος ἀκροάσεώς τε
οὐκ ἐτύγχανε καὶ δεσμοῖς ἐνείχετο.[4] χρόνου δὲ
ἐγγενομένου Τιβέριός τε ἐκ τῶν Καπρεῶν εἰς Του-
σκουλανὸν[5] παραγίνεται ὅσον ἀπὸ σταδίων ἑκατὸν
τῆς Ῥώμης, καὶ ὁ Ἀγρίππας ἀξιοῖ τὴν Ἀντωνίαν
διαπράξασθαι γενέσθαι τῷ Εὐτύχῳ τὴν ἀκροάσιν
180 ἐφ' οἷστισι τὴν κατηγορίαν ποιοῖτο αὐτοῦ. τιμία δὲ
ἦν Ἀντωνία[6] Τιβερίῳ εἰς τὰ πάντα συγγενείας τε
ἀξιώματι, Δρούσου γὰρ ἦν ἀδελφοῦ αὐτοῦ γυνή,
καὶ ἀρετῇ τοῦ σώφρονος· νέα γὰρ χηρεύειν παρέ-
μεινεν γάμῳ τε ἀπεῖπεν τῷ πρὸς ἕτερον καίπερ τοῦ
Σεβαστοῦ κελεύοντός τινι γαμεῖσθαι, καὶ λοιδοριῶν
181 ἀπηλλαγμένον διεσώσατο αὐτῆς τὸν βίον. ἰδίᾳ τε
εὐεργέτις ἦν εἰς μέγιστα τοῦ Τιβερίου· ἐπιβουλῆς
γὰρ μεγάλης συστάσης ἐπ' αὐτὸν ὑπὸ Σηιάνου

---

[1] τὴν . . . ἀκροάσεως] examinationes se differre Lat. : aut
hic aut insequentibus aliquid deesse putat Niese.
[2] ὑπὸ τοῦ] MW : ὑπὲρ τοῦ E.
[3] κούφισιν . . . ἀρετῇ] κούφισιν ⟨μὴ⟩ γενέσθαι . . . διὰ τὸ
[μὴ] ἐπ' ἀρετῇ Richards et Shutt.

emperor he sent altogether two men, Gratus and Pilate, his successor, to govern the Jewish nation. Nor did he behave so only when he dealt with the Jews; he was no different with his other subjects. Moreover, as for his procrastination in hearing the cases of prisoners he explained that this was because an immediate hearing would alleviate the present miseries of those condemned to death, whereas they did not deserve to meet with such luck. When, however, they were kept waiting, the weight of their misfortune was rendered more severe by the vexation which was laid upon them.

(6) It was for this reason that Eutychus also failed to obtain a hearing and was held in chains. In time, when Tiberius moved [a] from Capri to Tusculum, a distance of a hundred furlongs from Rome, Agrippa besought Antonia to take steps to secure a hearing on the charges which Eutychus had brought against him. Now Antonia was highly esteemed by Tiberius both because, as the wife of his brother Drusus, she was related to him, and because she was a virtuous and chaste woman. For despite her youth she remained steadfast in her widowhood and refused to marry again although the emperor urged her to do so. She thus kept her life free from reproach. She on her own had done a very great service to Tiberius. For a great conspiracy had been formed against him

How Antonia saved Tiberius from Sejanus' plot.

[a] During the latter part of the summer of A.D. 36. See R. S. Rogers in *Class. Weekly* xxxix, 1945-46, p. 43, who notes, however, that Josephus is our only evidence for this journey to Tusculum.

---

⁴ δεσμοῖς ἐνείχετο] E : retinebatur in vinculis Lat. : τὰ δεσμὰ ἠνείχετο codd.
⁵ Τουσκουλανόν] Τουσκούλανον A : τοὺς καλάνον W : κάλανον M.
⁶ Ἀντωνία] E : αὐτῷ Ἀντωνία codd.

φίλου τε ἀνδρὸς καὶ δύναμιν ἐν τῷ τότε μεγίστην
ἔχοντος διὰ τὸ τῶν στρατευμάτων εἶναι ἡγεμονίαν
αὐτῷ, καὶ τῆς τε βουλῆς οἱ πολλοὶ καὶ τῶν ἀπελευθέρων προσέθεντο καὶ τὸ στρατιωτικὸν διέφθαρτο,
προῢκοπτέν τε ἡ ἐπιβουλὴ ἐπὶ μέγα κἂν ἐπέπρακτο
Σηϊάνῳ τὸ ἔργον μὴ τῆς Ἀντωνίας τόλμῃ χρησα-
182 μένης σοφωτέρα τῆς Σηϊάνου κακουργίας. ἐπεὶ
γὰρ μανθάνει τὰ ἐπὶ τῷ Τιβερίῳ συντεθειμένα,
γράφει πρὸς αὐτὸν τὰ πάντα ἀκριβῶς καὶ Πάλλαντι
ἐπιδοῦσα τὰ γράμματα τῷ πιστοτάτῳ τῶν δούλων
αὐτῆς ἐκπέμπει πρὸς Τιβέριον εἰς τὰς Καπρέας.
ὁ δὲ μαθὼν τόν τε Σηϊᾶνον κτείνει καὶ τοὺς συνεπι-
βούλους, τήν τε Ἀντωνίαν καὶ πρὶν ἀξιολόγως
ἄγων τιμιωτέραν τε ὑπελάμβανεν κἀπὶ τοῖς πᾶσι
183 πιθανήν. ὑπὸ δὴ ταύτης τῆς Ἀντωνίας ὁ Τιβέριος παρακαλούμενος ἐξετάσαι τὸν Εὔτυχον, " ἀλλ'
εἰ μὲν καταψεύσειε," φησὶν ὁ Τιβέριος, " [ἔτι δὲ][1]
Ἀγρίππου τὰ εἰρημένα[2] Εὔτυχος, ἀρκοῦσαν κομί-
ζεται παρ' αὐτοῦ τιμωρίαν, ἣν ἐπιτετίμηκα αὐτός·
εἰ δὲ βασανιζομένου ἀληθῆ φανείη τὰ εἰρημένα, μή-

[1] ἔτι δὲ] A : ὅτι MW et i. marg. A : om. E Lat., recte ut vid. Niesio.

[2] ἀλλ' . . . εἰρημένα] siquidem, inquit Tiberius, mendacium est adversus Agrippam quod dicitur Lat.

[a] The word ἡγεμονία must clearly refer to the prefecture of the praetorian cohorts, though D. Magie, *De Romanorum iuris publici sacrique vocabulis sollemnibus in graecum sermonem conversis*, 1905, records no parallel. If Bell's restoration is correct, there is a parallel in the *Acta Isidori* ; *cf.* H. I. Bell, " A New Fragment of the Acta Isidori," *Archiv f. Papyrusforsch.* x, 1931, p. 11.

[b] *Cf.* Dio Cassius lxv. 14. 1, who reports that Antonia once sent a secret letter to Tiberius about Sejanus through a

by his friend Sejanus, who at that time held very
great power because he was prefect of the praetorian
cohorts.[a] Most of the senators and freedmen joined
him, the army was bribed, and so the conspiracy made
great progress. Indeed, Sejanus would have succeeded had not Antonia shown greater craft in her
bold move than Sejanus did in his villainy.[b] For
when she was informed of the plot against Tiberius,
she wrote him a full and accurate account of it and,
entrusting the letter to Pallas, the most trustworthy
of her slaves, sent it to Tiberius at Capri. Tiberius,
being informed, put Sejanus and his fellow-conspira-
tors to death. As for Antonia, whom he had previously held in high regard, he now valued her even
more and put full confidence in her. Urged by this
Antonia to examine Eutychus, Tiberius said : " If,
indeed, Eutychus has made a false accusation against
Agrippa, then the punishment which I myself have
inflicted is sufficient. But if it should turn out, when
he is questioned, that what he has said is true, let

certain Caenis ; otherwise the rôle of Antonia in the Sejanus
affair is nowhere mentioned. F. B. Marsh, *The Reign of
Tiberius*, 1931, p. 304, says that Dio's statement gives no
support to the idea of a conspiracy against Tiberius ; but the
secret nature of Antonia's correspondence and the statement
of Suetonius, *Tib*. 65, that Sejanus was plotting a revolution,
corroborate Josephus' account. The statement (Suet. *Tib*. 61),
on which Marsh relies so heavily (see p. 193 n. 1), that in a
brief autobiography Tiberius asserted that he had punished
Sejanus because he had discovered the latter's hatred of the
children of Germanicus, is a shrewd attempt of the emperor
to enlist sympathy by evoking the magic name of Germanicus, who was so popular among the Romans (see §§ 207-210).
Marsh (*ibid.*) thinks that Antonia wrote Tiberius informing
him of Sejanus' plot against Germanicus' children ; but it is
more likely that she gained such high favour at the court because the letter helped save Tiberius' own life.

που κολάζειν ποθῶν τὸν ἀπελεύθερον ἐπ' αὐτὸν μᾶλ-
184 λον καλοίη τὴν δίκην." καὶ ὁ Ἀγρίππας ταῦτα
φαμένης πρὸς αὐτὸν Ἀντωνίας πολλῷ μᾶλλον ἐπέκειτο ἀξιῶν ἐξέτασιν γενέσθαι τοῦ πράγματος, καὶ
ἡ Ἀντωνία, οὐ γὰρ ἀνίει πολὺς ὢν ὁ Ἀγρίππας
ἐπὶ τοῖσδε δεῖσθαι, καιρὸν παραλαβοῦσα τοιοῦτον·
185 αἰωρεῖτο μὲν Τιβέριος ἐπὶ φορείου κείμενος, προ-
ϊόντων Γαΐου τε τοῦ ἐκείνης υἱωνοῦ καὶ Ἀγρίππα,
ἀπ' ἀρίστου δ' ἦσαν, παραπεριπατοῦσα τῷ φορείῳ
παρεκάλει καλεῖσθαί τε τὸν Εὔτυχον καὶ ἐξετάζε-
186 σθαι. ὁ δέ, " ἀλλ' ἴστων μέν, Ἀντωνία," εἶπεν, " οἱ
θεοί, ὅτι μὴ τῇ ἐμαυτοῦ γνώμῃ ἀνάγκῃ δὲ τῆς
σῆς παρακλήσεως ἐξαγόμενος πράξω τὰ πραχθησό-
μενα."[1] ταῦτα εἰπὼν κελεύει Μάκρωνα, ὃς Σηϊα-
νοῦ διάδοχος ἦν, τὸν Εὔτυχον ἀγαγεῖν. καὶ ὁ μὲν
οὐδὲν εἰς ἀναβολὰς παρῆν. Τιβέριος δ' αὐτὸν ἤρετο, τί καὶ ἔχοι λέγειν κατ' ἀνδρὸς ἐλευθερίαν αὐτῷ
187 παρεσχηκότος. ὁ δέ φησιν, " ὦ δέσποτα, αἰωροῦν-
το μὲν ἐφ' ἁμάξης Γάϊός τε οὗτος καὶ Ἀγρίππας
σὺν αὐτῷ καί σφων ἑζόμην παρὰ τοῖν ποδοῖν, λόγων δὲ πολλῶν ἀνακυκλουμένων Ἀγρίππας φησὶ
πρὸς Γάϊον· εἰ γὰρ ἀφίκοιτό ποτε ἡμέρα, ᾗ μετα-
στὰς ὁ γέρων οὗτος χειροτονοίη σε ἡγεμόνα τῆς
οἰκουμένης· οὐδὲν γὰρ ἡμῖν Τιβέριος ὁ υἱωνὸς αὐτοῦ γένοιτ' ἂν ἐμποδὼν ὑπὸ σοῦ τελευτῶν, καὶ ἥ τε
οἰκουμένη γένοιτ' ἂν μακαρία κἀγὼ πρὸ αὐτῆς."[2]
188 Τιβέριος δὲ πιστὰ ἡγησάμενος τὰ εἰρημένα καὶ

---

[1] E : πραξόμενα A : προστραττόμενα M : πρασσόμενα W : πε-
πραξόμενος L. Dindorf.
[2] πρὸ αὐτῆς] cum eo Lat.

Agrippa have a care lest perchance in his eagerness
to punish his freedman he find rather that he is calling
down justice on himself." When Antonia reported
these words to Agrippa, he began to insist even more
urgently on a thorough examination of the matter.
Since Agrippa did not abandon his insistence in
making this request, Antonia seized her opportunity,
as I shall describe. Tiberius was once reclining as he
travelled in a litter ; Gaius, her grandson, and
Agrippa were in front, having just had lunch. Antonia, who was walking beside the litter, entreated
him to summon Eutychus and to examine him. " But
let the gods be witness, Antonia," he said, " that it is
not by my own will but forced by your entreaty that
I shall do what I am about to do." With these words
he ordered Macro, who was the successor of Sejanus,[a]
to bring Eutychus. The latter arrived without delay.
Tiberius asked him just what he could say against a
man who had given him his liberty. [b] " My lord," he
said, " Gaius here and Agrippa with him were riding
in a carriage, and I was sitting at their feet. In the
course of a long and varied conversation, Agrippa
said to Gaius : ' I hope that the day will at length
arrive when this old man will leave the scene and
appoint you ruler of the world. For his grandson
Tiberius [c] would by no means stand in our way, since
you would put him to death. The world would then
know bliss and I above all.' " Tiberius did not doubt
the truth of this. Moreover, it revived an old grudge

Antonia
persuades
Tiberius to
hear the
charge
against
Agrippa.

[a] As prefect of the praetorian cohorts.
[b] §§ 187–189 are parallel with *B.J.* ii. 179–180.
[c] Note that the original conversation between Agrippa
and Gaius as reported in § 168 makes no mention of Tiberius'
grandson and of Agrippa's expectation that Gaius would put
him to death.

ἅμα μῆνιν ἀναφέρων τῷ Ἀγρίππᾳ παλαιάν, διότι
κελεύσαντος αὐτοῦ θεραπεύειν Τιβέριον υἱωνόν τε
αὐτοῦ γεγονότα καὶ Δρούσου παῖδα ὄντα, ὁ Ἀγρίππας ἀτίμως ἦγεν παρακροασάμενος[1] τὰς ἐπιστολὰς[2]
189 καὶ πᾶς ὡς τὸν Γάιον μετεκάθιζεν, " τοῦτον μὲν
δή," φησί, " Μάκρων, δῆσον." Μάκρων δὲ τὰ μὲν
οὐ σαφῶς ὄντινα προστάξειεν ἐξεπιστάμενος, τὰ δὲ
οὐκ ἂν προσδοκῶν περὶ τῷ Ἀγρίππᾳ αὐτὸν βου-
λεῦσαί[3] τι τοιοῦτον, ἐπανεῖχεν ἀκριβωσόμενος τὰ
190 εἰρημένα. ἐπεὶ δ' ὁ Καῖσαρ περιοδεύσας τὸν ἱππόδρομον λαμβάνει τὸν Ἀγρίππαν ἑστηκότα, " καὶ
μὴν δή," φησίν, " Μάκρων, τοῦτον εἶπον δεθῆναι."
τοῦ δὲ ἐπανερομένου ὄντινα, "'Ἀγρίππαν γε,"
191 εἶπεν. καὶ ὁ Ἀγρίππας τρέπεται μὲν κατὰ δεήσεις,
τοῦ τε παιδὸς ᾧ συνετέθραπτο μνημονεύων καὶ τοῦ
Τιβερίου τῆς ἐκτροφῆς, οὐ μὴν ἤνυέν γέ τι, ἀλλ'
192 ἦγον αὐτὸν ἐν πορφυρίσι δέσμιον. καὶ καῦμά τε
γὰρ σφοδρὸν ἦν[4] καὶ ὑπὸ οἴνου τοῦ ἐπὶ σιτίοις μὴ
πολλοῦ γεγονότος δίψος ἐξέκαιεν αὐτόν, καί τι καὶ
ἠγωνία[5] καὶ τὸ παρ'[6] ἀξίαν κατελάμβανεν,[7] θεασά-
μενός τινα[8] τῶν Γαΐου παίδων Θαυμαστὸν ὄνομα
193 ὕδωρ ἐν ἀγγείῳ κομίζοντα ᾔτησε πιεῖν. καὶ ὀρέ-
ξαντος προθύμως πιών, " ἀλλ' εἴπερ ἐπ' ἀγαθοῖς,"
φησίν, " ὦ παῖ, τὰ τῆσδέ σου τῆς διακονίας γέγονεν,
διαφυγῆς μοι γενομένης τῶνδε τῶν δεσμῶν οὐκ
ἂν βραδύνοιμι ἐλευθερίαν εἰσπρασσόμενός σοι παρὰ
Γαΐου, ὃς καὶ δεσμώτῃ μοι γενομένῳ διακονεῖσθαι

---

[1] A : παρακρουσάμενος MWE : contempserat Lat.
[2] A : ἐντολὰς MWE.
[3] προστάξαι E : cogitare Lat. : κελεῦσαί Naber.
[4] nam aestatis tempus extabat add. Lat. post ἦν.
[5] ἀγωνία E.
[6] A : πρὸς MW.

120

against Agrippa, who, though ordered to pay court to Tiberius, the emperor's grandson and the son of Drusus, had disrespectfully ignored his orders and had given all his attention to Gaius instead. " Well then, Macro," he said, " handcuff him." Macro, partly because he was not quite sure whom he meant and partly because he would not have expected him to plan such treatment for Agrippa, waited to get the exact intent of the order. But when the emperor had made the circuit of the racecourse and found Agrippa still standing there, " I assure you, Macro," he said, " I meant this man, when I said ' Handcuff him.' " When Macro again asked him which man, he replied, " Why, Agrippa." Agrippa then began to entreat him, reminding him that he had been brought up with his son and that he had helped bring up Tiberius. These entreaties, however, were of no avail, and they led him away a prisoner in his crimson robes. The heat was intense and, since he had not had much wine at his meal, he was parched with thirst. His feelings were divided between this distress and the shock to his self-esteem. At this moment he saw one of the slaves of Gaius, Thaumastus by name, carrying water in a jug, and asked him for a drink. The slave handed the jug to Agrippa, who, after drinking from it with a will, remarked : " Sir slave, if this service of yours turns out well, when I escape from these bonds, I will lose no time in negotiating your emancipation by Gaius, for you have, in doing me service as a prisoner, omitted

---

⁷ MW : προσελάμβανεν E : ἐλάμβανε· A.

⁸ καί τι . . . τινα] unde quoque anxius factus praeter decus atque dignitatem coepit cuncta respicere, unde posset siti reperire remedium conspiciensque quendam Lat.

καθάπερ ἐν τῷ πρότερον καθεστηκότι σχήματι τῆς
194 περὶ ἐμὲ ἀξιώσεως οὐκ ἐνέλιπες." καὶ οὐκ ἐψεύ-
σατο ταῦτα εἰπών, ἀλλὰ δὴ ἡμείψατο¹· ἐν ὑστέρῳ
γὰρ βασιλεύσας τὸν Θαυμαστὸν μειζόνως² ἐλεύ-
θερόν τε ἀφῆκε παρὰ Γαΐου Καίσαρος γεγονότος
λαβὼν καὶ τῆς οὐσίας ἐπίτροπον καθίστησι, τελευτῶν τε τῷ υἱεῖ ᾿Αγρίππᾳ καὶ Βερενίκῃ τῇ θυγατρὶ
ἐπὶ τοῖς ὁμοίοις διακονησόμενον κατέλιπεν, ἐν τιμῇ
τε ὢν ταύτῃ γηραιὸς τελευτᾷ. καὶ ταῦτα μὲν
ὕστερον.³

195    (7) ᾿Αγρίππας δὲ τότε δεθεὶς εἱστήκει πρὸ τοῦ βασιλείου πρός τινι δένδρῳ κλιθεὶς ὑπὸ ἀθυμίας μετὰ
πολλῶν οἳ ἐδέδεντο. καί τινος ὀρνέου καθίσαντος
ἐπὶ τοῦ δένδρου, ᾧ ᾿Αγρίππας προσεκέκλιτο, βουβῶνα δὲ οἱ ῾Ρωμαῖοι τὸν ὄρνιν τοῦτον καλοῦσιν, τῶν
δεσμωτῶν τις Γερμανὸς⁴ θεασάμενος ἤρετο τὸν
196 στρατιώτην, ὅστις εἴη ὁ ἐν τῇ πορφυρίδι. καὶ
μαθὼν μὲν ᾿Αγρίππαν ὄνομα αὐτῷ, ᾿Ιουδαῖον δὲ τὸ
γένος καὶ τῶν ἐκείνῃ ἀξιολογωτάτων, ἠξίωσεν τὸν
συνδεδεμένον αὐτῷ στρατιώτην πλησίον ἐλθεῖν διὰ
λόγων⁵· βούλεσθαι γάρ τινα ἀμφὶ τῶν πατρίων ἔρε-
197 σθαι αὐτόν. καὶ τυχών, ἐπεὶ πλησίον ἵσταται, δι᾽
ἑρμηνέως, "ὦ νεανία," φησίν, "καταχθεῖ μέν σε
τὸ αἰφνίδιον τῆς μεταβολῆς πολλήν τε οὕτως καὶ
ἀθρόαν ἐπαγαγὸν τὴν τύχην, ἀπιστία δέ σοι·λόγων,
οἳ ἐπὶ διαφυγῇ κακοῦ τοῦ ἐφεστηκότος διαιροῖντο

---

¹ ταῦτα . . . ἡμείψατο] A Lat.: om. MWE.
² om. E.
³ ὕστερον] ὕστερον ἐγένετο MW: postea facta sunt Lat.
⁴ Γερμανὸς] Germanus nomine Lat.
⁵ διὰ λόγων] om. E Lat.

ᵃ The horned owl.

nothing of the respect that you accorded me in my former state." He did not go back on his word, but well repaid him. For later, when he became king, he received Thaumastus from Gaius, who had become emperor, at once set him free, and appointed him steward of his estate. Moreover, when Agrippa died, he left him to his son Agrippa and his daughter Berenice to serve them in the same capacity. Thaumastus kept this position till he died in his old age. But this took place later.

(7) To return to Agrippa, there he stood in chains in front of the palace together with many other prisoners, and had leaned against a tree in his despondency. Now a certain bird, which the Romans call a " bubo," [a] alighted on the tree against which Agrippa was leaning. One of the prisoners, a German, upon seeing Agrippa, asked the soldier in charge of him the identity of the man dressed in crimson. Upon learning that his name was Agrippa, that he was a Jew by race, and that he was one of the most notable men of Judaea, he asked the soldier to whom he was handcuffed [b] to allow him to approach and converse with Agrippa, since, he said, he wished to put some questions to him about the Jewish customs. His request granted, he came and stood near Agrippa and said through an interpreter : " Young man, you are in despair at your swift reversal of fortune, which has overwhelmed you at one stroke. You will hardly credit the statement that interprets Divine Providence as designing your deliverance from your present

A German prisoner prophesies Agrippa's greatness, but marks the owl as ominous.

[b] Richards and Shutt, *Class. Quart.* xxxi, 1937, p. 176, read " table-companion " since they think that the centurion was chained not to Agrippa but to a private soldier. But since Agrippa was so important a prisoner, it is perfectly possible that the centurion was chained to him.

198 τοῦ θείου τὴν πρόνοιαν. ἴσθι γε μήν, θεοὺς τοὺς
ἐμοὶ πατρῴους καὶ τοὺς τοῖσδε ἐγχωρίους, οἳ τόνδε
ἐπρυτάνευσαν ἡμῖν τὸν σίδηρον, ἐπομνύμενος λέξω
τὰ πάντα οὔτε ἡδονῇ γλωσσάργῳ διδοὺς τὸν ἐπ'
αὐτοῖς λόγον[1] οὔτε διακενῆς εὐθυμεῖν σε ἐσπουδα-
199 κώς. αἱ γὰρ ἐπὶ τοιοῖσδε προαγορεύσεις ὑστερη-
κότος τοῦ ἀποδείξοντος ἔργου χαλεπωτέραν προστίθενται τὴν ἀχθηδόνα τοῦ μηδ' εἰ τὴν ἀρχὴν
ἀκροάσαιτο αὐτῶν. ἀλλὰ καὶ τὸ ἐμὸν κινδύνοις
παραβαλλόμενος δίκαιον ἡγησάμην σοι διασαφῆσαι
200 τὴν προαγόρευσιν τῶν θεῶν. οὐκ ἔσθ' ὅπως οὐκ
εὐθέως ἀπαλλαγή τέ σοι τῶνδε τῶν δεσμῶν παρ-
έσται καὶ πρόοδος ἐπὶ μήκιστον ἀξιώματός τε καὶ
δυνάμεως, ζηλωτός τε ἂν γένοιο πᾶσιν, οἳ νῦν δι'
οἴκτου τὰς τύχας σου λαμβάνουσιν, εὐδαίμονά τε
ἂν ποιοῖο τὴν τελευτὴν παισίν, οἷς ἔσῃ[2] τὸν ὄλβον[3]
καταλειπόμενος.[4] μνημονεύειν δέ, ὁπότε εἰσαῦθις
τὸν ὄρνιν θεάσαιο τοῦτον, πέντε ἡμέραις σοι τὴν
201 τελευτὴν ἐσομένην. ταῦτα πεπράξεται μὲν ᾗπερ[5]
ἀποσημαίνει τοῦ θεοῦ τὸ ἐξαποστεῖλαι τουτονὶ τὸν
ὄρνιν. προγνώσει τε αὐτῶν σύνεσιν τὴν παραγενο-
μένην ἀποστερεῖν σε ἄδικον ἡγησάμην, ὅπως ἐπιστάμενος ἀγαθοῦ μέλλοντος λυσιτελεῖν ἐν ὀλίγῳ
τὴν ἀχθηδόνα τοῦ παρόντος τιθοῖο. μνήμην δὲ
ποιεῖσθαι εἰς χεῖράς σου παραγενομένου τοῦ εὐδαίμονος καὶ τοῦ καθ' ἡμᾶς διαφευξομένου δυστυχίαν,

[1] οὔτε . . . λόγον] neque cupidine fallendi Lat.
[2] οἷς ἔσῃ] codd. : οἱ εἶεν E : οἱ ⟨γεγονότες⟩ εἶεν Richards et
Shutt ex Lat.
[3] MWE : βίον A.
[4] εὐδαίμονά . . . καταλειπόμενος] exitus etiam vitae in beati-

124

difficulty. Be assured, nevertheless, for I swear by
my ancestral gods and by those of this country who
have ordained these iron chains for us, that I will
tell you everything not for the pleasure of garrulity
nor yet with intent to cheer you by false hopes.
Indeed, prophecies on such matters, when the event
falls short of the prediction, produce more grievous
vexation than would be the case if a man had never
heard such a statement at all. Nevertheless, notwithstanding the dangers to which I expose myself,
it seemed to me right to set forth clearly what the
gods foretell. It cannot be but that you will forthwith find release from these chains and be advanced
to the highest point of honour and of power. You
will be envied by all those who now pity your misfortunes, and you will make an end of life that is blest
by children, to whom you will be leaving your wealth.
But remember, when you see this bird again, that
your death will follow within five days.[a] This will take
place in the manner indicated by the god's dispatching of this bird. I did not think it fair to deprive you
of the understanding which comes through foreknowledge of these things ; for I wished you to know that
you are to enjoy future blessings in order that you
might make light of your present distress. But remember, when you have this good fortune in your
hands, to help me also to gain release from the mis-

---

[a] For a long list of instances in Greek and Latin literature
of the owl as an omen of death see A. S. Pease, ed., *IV
Aeneid*, 1935, pp. 375-377, who, however, omits this passage.

---

tudine te repperiet constitutum, divitiasque plurimas omnia-
que, quae prima mortales ducunt, tuis filiis, qui tibi nati
fuerint, derelinques Lat.

[b] E et i. marg. A : εἴπερ AMW et ut vid. Lat.

202 ᾗ τανῦν σύνεσμεν.'' καὶ ὁ μὲν Γερμανὸς τοσάδε
προειπὼν εἰς τοσόνδε ὦφλεν τῷ Ἀγρίππᾳ γέλωτα,
ἐφ' ὅσον ἐν τοῖς ὕστερον κατεφάνη τεθαυμάσθαι
ἄξιος. ἡ δὲ Ἀντωνία χαλεπῶς φέρουσα τοῦ
Ἀγρίππου τὴν δυστυχίαν τὸ μὲν Τιβερίῳ περὶ
αὐτοῦ διαλέγεσθαι ἐργωδέστερον ἑώρα καὶ ἄλλως
203 ἐπ' ἀπράκτοις γενησόμενον, εὑρίσκετο δ' αὐτῷ
παρὰ τοῦ Μάκρωνος στρατιωτῶν τε μετρίων ἀνδρῶν οἳ παραφυλάξειαν αὐτὸν ἐν φροντίσιν[1] καὶ
ἑκατοντάρχου τοῦ ἐφεστηξομένου τε ἐκείνοις καὶ
συνδέτου[2] ἐσομένου, λουτρά τε καθ' ἡμέραν συγ-
κεχωρῆσθαι καὶ ἀπελευθέρων καὶ φίλων εἰσόδους
τήν τε ἄλλην ῥᾳστώνην, ἣ τῷ σώματι γένοιτ' ἄν.
204 εἰσῄεσάν τε ὡς αὐτὸν φίλος τε Σίλας καὶ τῶν
ἀπελευθέρων Μαρσύας καὶ Στοιχεὺς τροφὰς εἰσ-
κομίζοντες αἷς ἔχαιρεν καὶ δι' ἐπιμελείας πάσης
ἔχοντες, ἱμάτιά τε κομίζοντες ἐπὶ προσποιήσει πρά-
σεως ὁπότε νὺξ γένοιτο ὑπεστρώννυσαν αὐτῷ συμπράξει τῶν στρατιωτῶν Μάκρωνος προειρηκότος· καὶ
ταῦτα ἐπράσσετο ἐπὶ μῆνας ἕξ. καὶ τὰ μὲν κατὰ
Ἀγρίππαν ἐν τούτοις ἦν.
205 (8) Τιβέριος δ' ἐπανελθὼν εἰς τὰς Καπρέας ἐμα-
λακίζετο τὰ μὲν πρῶτα μετρίως, ἐπιδούσης δ' εἰς
τὸ μᾶλλον τῆς νόσου πονηρᾶς ἔχων περὶ[3] αὐτῷ τὰς
ἐλπίδας Εὔοδον, ὃς ἦν αὐτῷ τιμιώτατος τῶν ἀπελευθέρων, κελεύει τὰ τέκνα προσαγαγεῖν πρὸς
αὐτόν· χρῄζειν γὰρ ἀφικέσθαι σφίσι διὰ λόγων πρὶν
206 ἢ τελευτᾶν. ἦσαν δ' αὐτῷ παῖδες γνήσιοι μὲν
οὐκέτι· Δροῦσος γὰρ δὴ ὁ μόνος αὐτῷ γεγονὼς
ἐτύγχανεν τεθνεώς· υἱὸς δὲ τούτου κατελείπετο

---

[1] ἐν φροντίσιν] codd. : sine districtione Lat. : ἐκφρόντισιν vel
simile coni. Niese.

fortune in which we are now companions." The German who made these prophecies was as ridiculous in Agrippa's eyes then as he later turned out to be deserving of admiration. Antonia, though distressed at the misfortune of Agrippa, saw that it would be too much of an undertaking to discuss his case with Tiberius and would besides be useless. She gained from Macro the following concessions for him, that the soldiers who were to guard him and that the centurion who would be in charge of them and would also be handcuffed [a] to him should be of humane character, that he should be permitted to bathe every day and receive visits from his freedmen and friends, and that he should have other bodily comforts too. His friend Silas [b] and two of his freedmen, Marsyas [c] and Stoecheus, visited him bringing him his favourite viands and doing whatever service they could. They brought him garments that they pretended to sell, but, when night came, they made him a bed with the connivance of the soldiers, who had Macro's orders to do so. These things went on for six months. Such was the situation with regard to Agrippa.

Antonia cares for Agrippa during his imprisonment.

(8) On his return to Capri Tiberius was taken ill. The malady was at first slight, but as it grew worse and worse he began to despair of his life and bade Evodus, who ranked highest of his freedmen, to bring his children to him, for he wished to speak with them before he died. He no longer had any legitimate children, for Drusus, his only son, was of course dead. But Drusus' son Tiberius, who was surnamed Gemel-

Tiberius' illness and possible successors.

---

[a] See note b on p. 123.
[b] Later appointed by Agrippa (*Ant.* xix. 299) to be in command of his entire army.  [c] *Cf. Ant.* xviii. 155-157.

[2] συνδαίτου Richards et Shutt.  [3] A : ἐπ' MW.

# JOSEPHUS

Τιβέριος ἐπικαλούμενος Γέμελλος, Γάιός τε Γερμανικοῦ παῖς, ἀδελφοῦ υἱωνός[1] γεγονώς, νεανίας τε ἤδη καὶ παιδείαν ἐκπεπονηκὼς ἐπὶ πλεῖστον εὐνοίᾳ τε τοῦ δήμου τιμώμενος διὰ τὴν Γερμανικοῦ τοῦ

207 πατρὸς ἀρετήν· ἐπὶ μέγιστον γὰρ δὴ οὗτος προῆλθεν παρὰ τοῖς πλήθεσι τιμῆς εὐσταθείᾳ τρόπου καὶ δεξιότητι τοῦ ὁμιλεῖν ἀνεπαχθὴς ὢν καὶ τὴν ἀξίωσιν

208 κτώμενος τῷ βούλεσθαι ἴσος πᾶσιν εἶναι. ἐξ ὧν οὐ μόνον ὁ δῆμος καὶ ἡ βουλὴ μειζόνως ἦγον αὐτόν, ἀλλὰ καὶ τῶν ὑποτελῶν ἕκαστον ἐθνῶν, οἱ μὲν ὡμιληκότες ἁλισκόμενοι τῇ χάριτι τῆς ἐντεύξεως, οἱ δὲ πύστει τῆς ἐκείνων ἀφηγήσεως παραλαμβά-

209 νοντες. πένθος τε αὐτοῦ τελευτήσαντος προὐτέθη πᾶσιν οὐ θεραπείᾳ τῆς ἀρχῆς ἐπιψευδομένων τὴν συμφοράν, λύπῃ δὲ ἀληθεῖ οἰκειουμένων διὰ τὸ ἴδιον τυχεῖν ἑκάστοις τὴν μετάστασιν αὐτοῦ ὑπειληφθαι· οὕτως ἀνεπαχθῶς ὡμίλησε τοῖς ἀνθρώ-

210 ποις. ἐξ ὧν μέγα ὄφελος καὶ τῷ παιδὶ αὐτοῦ παρὰ πᾶσιν κατελέλειπτο τοῖς τε ἄλλοις καὶ μάλιστα

[1] ἀδελφοῦ υἱωνός] Richards et Shutt : ἀδελφοῦ υἱός codd. : ἀδελφιδοῦ υἱός coni.

[a] The mss. read " son," but Gaius was the son of Germanicus, who was the nephew of the emperor Tiberius.
[b] *Cf.* T. S. Jerome, " The Historical Tradition about Gaius," in *Aspects of the Study of Roman History*, 1923, p. 401, who notes that Gaius delivered the oration at Livia's funeral when he was less than seventeen (Tac. *Ann.* v. 1).
[c] On Gaius' initial popularity see Suet. *Calig.* 13-21. R. R. Rosborough, *An Epigraphic Commentary on Suetonius' Life of Gaius Caligula*, 1920, p. 22, cites a number of inscriptions from the provinces indicating Gaius' popularity with the provincials and with the army : it is significant that in many of these he is mentioned as the son of Germanicus.

lus, and Gaius, the son of Germanicus and grandson [a] of the emperor's brother, were left. Gaius was now a young man who had gained a thorough education [b] and enjoyed the great goodwill of the people thanks to the good qualities of his father Germanicus.[c] [d] For Germanicus came to be held in the very highest esteem among the masses, to whom he gave no offence inasmuch as he was always equable in temper and tactful in address. He won respect by choosing to be on an equality with everyone. Consequently, he was held in high regard not only by the people and the senate but also by all of the subject nations. Those who had enjoyed his company were captivated by his charming manners, while others were won by the reports they received from those who met him. When he died, mourning was universal, not the feigned grief of those who pay court to their rulers, but the genuine sorrow of those whose hearts are touched, inasmuch as his passing was assumed by all classes to be a personal misfortune, so agreeable was he in his social encounters.[e] From this popularity his son had inherited a great advantage with all men. The army was par-

---

[d] This flattering portrait of Germanicus is confirmed by Tacitus' long account, *Ann.* i. 33 ff., and by Suetonius' brief mention, *Calig.* 3. Both emphasize his kindheartedness and modesty and his ability to win universal respect and affection. J. P. V. D. Balsdon, *The Emperor Gaius*, 1934, p. 128, says that despite the chorus of praise which resounded throughout the empire in honour of Germanicus, the Jews alone did not share in this attitude. Josephus, he admits, is an exception, but he says that this is due to Josephus' reliance upon an unnamed Roman historian. It seems more likely that the favourable view of Germanicus is part of a general exaltation of Agrippa, his friend Antonia (mother of Germanicus), and his friend Gaius Caligula (son of Germanicus).

[e] Tacitus also emphasizes the universal grief at Germanicus' death and funeral (*Ann.* ii. 82-83, iii. 1-4).

τὸ¹ στρατιωτικὸν ἦρτο, ἀρετὴν² ἀριθμοῦντες τὸ περὶ
τῆς ἀρχῆς ἐκείνῳ περιγενησομένης, εἰ δεήσει, καὶ
τελευτᾶν.

211 (9) Ὁ δὲ Τιβέριος Εὐόδῳ πρόσταγμα ποιησάμενος κατὰ τὴν ὑστεραίαν ὑπὸ τὴν ἕω εἰσαγαγεῖν
τοὺς παῖδας εὔχεται τοῖς πατρίοις θεοῖς σημεῖόν τι
πρόφαντον αὐτῷ δεῖξαι περὶ τοῦ τὴν ἡγεμονίαν
διαδεξομένου, σπεύδων μὲν τῷ υἱεῖ τοῦ παιδὸς
αὐτὴν καταλιπεῖν, μεῖζον δὲ δόξης τε καὶ βουλήσεως
τῆς αὐτοῦ πεπιστευκὼς τοῦ θεοῦ τὸ ἐπ᾽ αὐτοῖς
212 ἀποφανούμενον. οἰώνισμα δ᾽ οὖν αὐτῷ προὔκειτο,
εἰς ἐκεῖνον ἥξειν τὴν ἡγεμονίαν, ὃς ἂν κατὰ τὴν
ἐπιοῦσαν ἀφίκοιτο πρότερος πρὸς αὐτόν. ταῦτα
διανοηθεὶς πέμπει παρὰ τοῦ υἱωνοῦ τὸν παιδαγωγὸν
κελεύων ὑπὸ πρώτην ὥραν³ ἄγειν τὸν παῖδα ὡς
αὐτόν, καταμελήσεσθαι στρατηγίας τὸν θεὸν ὑπο-
λαμβάνων· ὁ δ᾽ ἀντεψήφιζεν αὐτοῦ τὴν χειροτονίαν.
213 ὁ μὲν δὴ ταῦτ᾽ ἐνθυμησάμενος, ἐπεὶ τάχιστα ἡμέρα

---

¹ ed. pr. : τὸν A : τοῦ MW.
² gloriam Lat. : αἱρετὸν ed. pr.
³ A : ἡμέραν MWE et i. marg. A.

---

ᵃ Thackeray, in his own copy of Josephus, has a pencilled
note suggesting that Josephus here sees a parallel between
the story of Tiberius' method of choosing between his grandson and grandnephew and the account in Genesis xlviii of
Jacob's blessing of Joseph's two sons. Thackeray conjectures, consequently, that Josephus' authority was possibly a
Jew. But there is no element of augury in the Biblical story,
nor is it an account of Jacob's search for a successor : there
both sons come for and receive blessings.

ᵇ None of our sources indicates that Tiberius had really
decided on a successor, but Suetonius, Calig. 19, notes that he
was inclined towards Tiberius Gemellus. Tacitus, Ann. vi.
46, also notes Tiberius' indecision about bequeathing his
empire, and like Josephus he mentions Gaius and Tiberius

ticularly enthusiastic and counted it a point of honour
even to die, if need be, so that he might become
emperor.

(9) [a] After Tiberius had given the command to
Evodus to bring his children to him on the following
day towards dawn, he prayed to his country's gods to
show him some clear indication as to his successor as
emperor. He was eager to bequeath the government
to the son of his son,[b] but he put more faith in the
revelation of their future by the god than in his own
decision and choice. He therefore proposed by way
of augury that the empire should go to the one who
should come first to him on the following day. Having
decided on this, he sent orders to his grandson's
tutor to bring the child to him at sunrise,[c] for he did
not think that the god would pay any heed to his
manœuvre. But the verdict of the god annulled the
choice made by Tiberius. With such considerations in
mind, Tiberius, as soon as it was day, ordered Evodus

Gemellus as the two leading possibilities. (Tiberius also
thought of the later emperor Claudius, according to this passage in Tacitus, but concluded that such a choice would
make the name of the Caesars a laughing-stock.) As to
Gaius, Tacitus mentions (*ibid.*) Tiberius' prediction that he
would have all of Sulla's vices and none of his virtues.
Tiberius' fear that Gaius would succeed him is indicated in
the story that Thrasyllus the astrologer had assured Tiberius
that Gaius had no more chance of being emperor than of
riding over the Gulf of Baiae with horses (see *Ant.* xix. 5-6
for a description of the bridge which Gaius built in fulfilment
of this prophecy). Suetonius, *Tib.* 62, tells us that Tiberius
at one point intended to kill both Gaius and Tiberius Gemellus, the latter of whom he hated as having been born
from adultery. It is clear from Tacitus, *Ann.* vi. 46, that
Tiberius died without reaching a decision as to his successor.

[c] Lit. " at the first hour " or more specifically " about the
beginning of the first hour."

131

# JOSEPHUS

ἦν, κελεύει τὸν Εὔοδον εἰσκαλεῖν τῶν παίδων τὸν
παρόντα πρότερον. ἐξελθὼν δ' ἐκεῖνος καὶ τὸν
Γάιον πρὸ τοῦ δωματίου καταλαβών, ὁ γὰρ Τιβέριος οὐ παρῆν μετεώρου τῆς τροφῆς αὐτῷ γενομένης,[1] ἤδει δὲ οὐδὲν ὧν ἐβούλετο ὁ δεσπότης,
" καλεῖ σε," φησίν, " ὁ πατήρ," καὶ εἰσήγαγεν αὐτόν.
214 Τιβέριος δὲ ὡς θεᾶται Γάιον, τότε πρῶτον εἰς ἐπί-
νοιαν ἐλθὼν τοῦ θείου τῆς ἐξουσίας καὶ τὴν κατ'
αὐτὸν ἡγεμονίαν παντελῶς ἀφῃρημένην ἐπικυροῦν
οἷς ψηφίσαιτο δυνάμεως ἐκεῖθεν αὐτῷ μὴ παραγενομένης, πολλὰ δὴ κατολοφυράμενος αὐτὸν μὲν τοῦ
ἐφ' οἷς προβουλεύσειε κυροῦν ἀφῃρημένου τὸ κρά-
215 τος, Τιβέριον δὲ τὸν υἱωνόν, ὡς τῆς τε Ῥωμαίων
ἀρχῆς ὁμοῦ διαμάρτοι καὶ τῆς σωτηρίας κεχρη-
μένον διὰ τὸ ἐπ' ἄλλων κρειττόνων οὐκ ἀνεκτὸν
εἰσηγησαμένων[2] τὴν συναναστροφὴν κείσεσθαι τὴν
σωτηρίαν αὐτῷ τοῦ συγγενοῦς μὴ[3] ὠφελεῖν δυνα-
μένου, φόβῳ τε καὶ μίσει τοῦ ἐφεστηκότος χρησο-
μένου πρὸς αὐτόν, τὰ μὲν ὡς προσεδρεύοντα τῇ
ἀρχῇ, τὰ δὲ ὡς ἀντεπιβουλεύειν ὑπέρ τε τῆς σωτηρίας καὶ τῆς ἀντιλήψεως[4] τῶν πραγμάτων μὴ ἀφη-
216 σόμενον. ἦν δὲ καὶ γενεθλιαλογίᾳ Τιβέριος μάλιστα
προσκείμενος καὶ κατορθούμενα αὐτῇ[5] μειζόνως
τῶν εἰς τόδε ἀνακειμένων ἑκόντων[6] τὸν βίον ἐξηγ-
μένος.[7] Γάλβαν οὖν[8] ποτε θεασάμενος ὡς αὐτὸν

---

[1] μετεώρου . . . γενομένης] ciborum acceptione tardatus
Lat.
[2] Hudson : εἰσηγησαμένω codd. : εἰσηγησομένων Bekker :
ἡγησαμένων Marcus (cf. Ant. xviii. 150).
[3] συγγενοῦς μὴ] Bekker : μὴ συγγενοῦς codd.
[4] MW : ἀναλήψεως A.
[5] καὶ κατορθούμενα αὐτῇ] κατὰ τὰ κατορθούμενα αὐτῆς Hudson.
[6] ἑκόντως Hudson.

132

to call in whichever of the boys was the first to arrive. Evodus went out and found Gaius in front of the chamber. Tiberius was not there because his breakfast was not finished.[a] Inasmuch as Evodus did not know anything of his master's preference, he said, " Your father summons you," and brought Gaius in. When Tiberius beheld Gaius, he then for the first time had some conception of the greatness of divine power. He saw himself utterly shorn of the privilege of confirming his own choice of a successor to his imperial office, since power from on high had not been vouchsafed him. Deeply did he bewail himself in that he was rendered impotent to give valid sanction to his own preliminary decision and in that his grandson Tiberius would not only fail to obtain the Roman empire, but would have no means of escape, since his survival would depend upon others who were more powerful and who would regard it as intolerable to consort with him. His kinsmen would be unable to help him since he would be feared and hated by their master, partly because he was next in line to inherit the empire, but also because he would never cease to plot against the ruler both to secure his own survival and in order to assert his claim to govern.[b] Now Tiberius was especially addicted to the casting of horoscopes and had elicited from it accurate results on a greater scale than those who have voluntarily devoted their life to it.[c] Once, for example,

[a] Or " because he had not yet digested his food."
[b] *Cf.* the story told by Tacitus, *Ann.* vi. 46, that once Tiberius, after embracing Gemellus with a flood of tears in the presence of Gaius, predicted that Gaius would slay Gemellus.    [c] *i.e.*, who practise it as their profession.

[7] A : ἐξηγμένων MW.    [8] γοῦν Richards et Shutt.

εἰσιόντα φησὶ πρὸς τοὺς ἐπιτηδειοτάτους αὐτῷ, ὡς
παραγίνοιτο ἀνὴρ τῇ Ῥωμαίων προτιμησόμενος[1]
217 ἡγεμονίᾳ. τά τε πάντα μαντειῶν ὁπόσα ἐχόμενα
πιθανὰ ἡγούμενος ἡγεμόνων μάλιστα ἀνὴρ οὗτος
ὑπὸ τοῦ ἐπαληθεύοντος αὐτῶν ἐπὶ τοῖς πράγμασιν
218 ἐχρῆτο αὐταῖς.[2] καὶ τότε ἐν χαλεποῖς ἦν συντυχίᾳ
τοῦ γεγονότος, ὡς ἐπ' ἀπολωλότι τῷ υἱεῖ τοῦ
παιδὸς ἀχθεινῶς διατιθέμενος[3] καὶ κατάμεμψιν
αὐτοῦ ποιούμενος τοῦ κατὰ τὴν οἰώνισιν προμη-
θοῦς[4]· παρὸν γὰρ [ἂν][5] αὐτῷ λύπης ἀπηλλαγμένῳ
τελευτᾶν ἀμαθίᾳ τῶν ἐσομένων, διατρίβεσθαι[6] τῷ
προεγνωκὼς τὴν ἐσομένην δυστυχίαν τῶν φιλτάτων
219 τελευτᾶν. καίπερ δὲ συντεταραγμένος τῇ παρὰ
δόξαν τῆς ἀρχῆς εἰς οὓς οὐκ ἤθελεν περιόδῳ, ἄκων
δὲ καὶ μὴ βουλόμενος φησὶ γοῦν πρὸς τὸν Γάιον·
" ὦ παῖ, καίπερ μοι συγγενεστέρου Τιβερίου ἢ
κατὰ σὲ' ὄντος δόξῃ τε τῇ ἐμαυτοῦ καὶ τῷ ὁμο-
ψήφῳ ἐπ' αὐτῇ τῶν θεῶν σοὶ φέρων ἐγχειρίζω τὴν
220 Ῥωμαίων ἡγεμονίαν. ἀξιῶ δέ σε μηδὲν ἀμνημονεῖν ὁμιλήσαντα αὐτῇ μήτ' εὐνοίας τῆς ἐμῆς, ὃς
221 εἰς τοσόνδε ἀξιώματος καθίστημι μέγεθος, μήτε
τοῦ πρὸς Τιβέριον συγγενοῦς, ἀλλ' ἐπιστάμενον, ὡς
σύν τε τοῖς θεοῖς καὶ μετ' αὐτοὺς τοιῶνδέ σοι
κατασταίην ἀγαθῶν ποριστής, ἀμείβεσθαί μου τὸ

---

[1] προτιμησόμενος] codd. : ποτε τιμησόμενος E : προτιμηθησό-
μενος Thackeray.
[2] ἦν . . . αὐταῖς (§§ 216-217)] om. Lat.
[3] διακείμενος E : διατεθειμένος coni. Niese.
[4] τοῦ . . . προμηθοῦς] quod illud augurium postulasset ac-
cipere Lat.

when he beheld Galba coming to him he said to his very close friends that a man was arriving who would some day rise to be ruler of the Romans.[a]  He believed that everything connected with divination was trustworthy ; and because its revelations turned out to be true, he, more than any other emperor, resorted to it in handling his affairs.  Now too he was upset at the turn of events and was as much grieved as if his grandson had already died.  He berated himself for his premeditated appeal to augury ; for whereas he might have died free from sorrow if he had remained ignorant of the future, he must now die tormented by his foreknowledge of the disaster that would overtake those he most loved.  Yet, though confounded by the unlooked-for transference of the empire to one not his choice, he reluctantly and against his will spoke these words to Gaius : " My son, although Tiberius is closer akin to me than you are, by my own decision, and with the concurrence of the gods, it is to you that I convey and entrust the Roman empire. I ask you, when you grow familiar with the office, not to forget either my kindness to you in appointing you to such an exalted rank or your bond of kinship with Tiberius.  Bear in mind that it was by the help of the gods and after consulting them that I took my stand to bestow such felicity upon you.  Let my cordial gift of it inspire the same feeling in you.  At the same

Tiberius appoints Gaius his successor.

---

[a] Cf. the similar prophecies in Suetonius, Galba 4, Tacitus, Ann. vi. 20, and Dio Cassius lvii. 19. 4, and the discussion of these passages by K. Scott, " Ein Ausspruch des Tiberius an Galba," Hermes lxvii, 1932, pp. 471-473.  Tacitus' prophecy can be dated in A.D. 33, Dio's in A.D. 20.

---

⁵ ἄν] spurium indicat Niese.
⁶ A : διαφθείρεσθαι MWE et i. marg. A.
⁷ κατὰ σέ] τοῦ κατὰ σὲ coni. Niese.

135

ἐπ' αὐτοῖς πρόθυμον καὶ ἅμα Τιβερίου φροντίζειν
διὰ τὴν συγγένειαν, ἄλλως τε γινώσκειν, ὡς τεῖχός
σοι καὶ τῆς ἀρχῆς ὁμοῦ καὶ τῆς σωτηρίας περιὼν
γίνοιτο ἂν Τιβέριος, φροίμιον δὲ τοῦ δυστυχοῦς
222 μεθιστάμενος. αἵ τε γὰρ μονώσεις ἐπικίνδυνοι τοῖς
εἰς τηλικούτων πραγμάτων ὄγκον καταστᾶσιν καὶ
θεοῖς οὐκ ἀτιμώρητα ὁπόσα παρὰ δίκην πρασσόμενα ἀφανίζοι τοῦ νόμου τὸ ἑτέρως πράσσειν παρα-
223 καλοῦν.'' ταῦτα μὲν ὁ Τιβέριος ἔλεγεν, οὐ μὴν
πιθανὸς ἦν Γαΐῳ καίπερ ὑπισχνουμένῳ, ἀλλὰ καταστὰς εἰς τὴν ἀρχὴν τόν τε Τιβέριον μαντείαις
ἀναιρεῖ¹ ταῖς ἐκείνου² καυτὸς ἐπιβουλῶν ἐπ' αὐτὸν
συντεθεισῶν μετ' οὐ πολὺ τελευτᾷ.
224 (10) Τιβέριος δὲ³ τὸν⁴ Γάιον ἀποδείξας διάδοχον
τῆς ἡγεμονίας⁵ ὀλίγας ἐπιβιοὺς ἡμέρας ἔθανεν σχὼν
αὐτὸς τὴν ἀρχὴν ἡμέρας τρεῖς καὶ πέντε⁶ μῆνας
πρὸς ἐνιαυτοῖν δυοῖν καὶ εἴκοσι. Γάιος δὲ ἦν
225 αὐτοκράτωρ τέταρτος. Ῥωμαίοις δ' ἦν μὲν πύστις
τῆς Τιβερίου τελευτῆς εὐφραίνοντό τε τῷ ἀγαθῷ
τῆς ἀγγελίας, οὐ μὴν πιστεύειν γε θάρσος ἦν αὐτοῖς,
οὐ τῷ μὴ βούλεσθαι, πρὸ πολλῶν γὰρ ἂν ἐτίμησαν

---

¹ Niese : αἱρεῖται codd. : αἵρεται E : extinxit Lat. : ἀναι-
ρεῖται Cocceji : αἱρεῖ Hudson.
² ⟨μὴ πειθόμενος⟩ post ἐκείνου add. Richards et Shutt.
³ Τιβέριος δὲ] sed haec postea, tunc autem Tiberius Lat.
⁴ τὸν] MW : τόν τε Α : τότε τὸν Ε.
⁵ ⟨καὶ⟩ post ἡγεμονίας add. Petersen.
⁶ vi Lat.

---

ᵃ Thackeray, in a pencilled note in his copy of Josephus,
suggests that the author who here traces the nemesis upon
the Roman emperor is the same one who read tragic significance into the history of the house of Herod (*Ant.* xviii.
127 ff.).
ᵇ A.D. 14–37. In the parallel passage, *B.J.* ii. 180, the reign

time give thought to Tiberius too because he is your
kinsman, and above all because you see that if Tiberius remains alive he will be a wall of defence for
your empire and for your personal safety, but that if
he departs, this will be the prelude to misfortune.
Indeed, it is dangerous for those who have reached
such a pinnacle of power to be isolated ; nor will the
gods allow to go unpunished any acts that are contrary to justice and that annul the law with its injunc-
tion to the contrary." Such were the words that
Tiberius spoke ; but Gaius, though he promised to
do so, did not follow his advice. For when he was
established on the throne, he put the younger Tiberius to death, just as the old man had divined. Not
long afterwards a plot was contrived against Gaius
himself whereby he met his death.[a]

(10) After appointing Gaius as his successor to the Death of<br>Tiberius.
empire, Tiberius lived on for a few days. He then
died, having held the imperial rule for twenty-two
years, five months, and three days.[b] Gaius was the
fourth emperor.[c] When the news of Tiberius' death
reached the Romans, they rejoiced at the good
tidings.[d] Nevertheless, they had misgivings about
trusting it, not that they did not want it to be true—

is said to have lasted twenty-two years, six months and three
days, a reading with which the Latin version of our text is in
agreement. Actually, as Thackeray *ad loc.* remarks, both
statements differ slightly from the figures of Tacitus (twenty-
two years, six months, and twenty-eight days) and Dio
Cassius (twenty-two years, seven months, and seven days).

[c] Counting Julius Caesar as the first emperor.

[d] There was such joy in Rome at the news of Tiberius'
death that, according to Suetonius, *Tib.* 75, people ran about
yelling " To the Tiber with Tiberius." Others prayed to
Mother Earth and the Manes to allow him no home below
except among the damned.

χρημάτων τὸ ἐπαληθεῦσαν τῶν λόγων, δέει δὲ μὴ
ψευδοῦς τῆς ἀγγελίας γενομένης προεξαναστάντες
ἐπὶ δηλώσει τοῦ αὐτῶν χάρματος εἶτ' ἀπολλύοιντο
226 διαβολῆς αὐτῶν γενομένης· πλεῖστα γὰρ ἀνὴρ εἷς
οὗτος 'Ρωμαίων τοὺς εὐπατρίδας εἰργάσατο δεινὰ
δυσόργητος ἐπὶ πᾶσιν ὢν καὶ ἀνήκεστος εἰς τὸ
ἐργάζεσθαι καταστάς, εἰ καὶ χωρὶς λόγου τὴν
αἰτίαν ἐπανέλοιτο τοῦ μισεῖν, καὶ ἐπὶ πᾶσι μὲν οἷς
κρίνειεν¹ ἐξαγριοῦν φύσιν ἔχων, εἰς θάνατον δὲ καὶ
227 τῶν κουφοτάτων ἀνατιθεὶς τὴν ζημίαν. ὥστε
ἡδονῇ τοῦ ἐπ' αὐτῷ λόγου φέροντος² τὴν ἀκρόασιν
εἰς ὅσον ἐβούλοντο ἀπολαύσματι χρῆσθαι ἐπεκεκώ-
λυντο δείμασι κακῶν, ἃ προεωρᾶτο ψευσθεῖσι τῆς
228 ἐλπίδος.   Μαρούας δὲ τοῦ 'Αγρίππου ὁ ἀπελεύθερος πυθόμενος τοῦ Τιβερίου τὴν τελευτὴν ὠθεῖτο³
δρομαῖος τὸν 'Αγρίππαν εὐαγγελιούμενος, καὶ
καταλαβὼν ἐν ἐξόδοις ὄντα εἰς τὸ βαλανεῖον συν-
νεύσας πρὸς αὐτὸν γλώσσῃ τῇ 'Εβραίων, '' τέθνηκεν
229 ὁ λέων,'' φησίν. ὁ δὲ σύνεσίν τε τοῦ λόγου ποιησάμενος καὶ χάρματι τῷ ἐπ' αὐτῷ περιενεχθείς,
'' ἀλλά σοι τῶν ἁπάντων καὶ τῆς ἐπὶ τῷδε⁴ εὐαγ-
γελίας χάριτες ἐν ἐμοὶ παντοῖαι γίνοιντο, μόνον
230 ἀληθῆ τὰ λεγόμενα εἴη.''   καὶ ὁ ἑκατοντάρχης,
ὅσπερ τῇ φυλακῇ ἐφειστήκει τοῦ 'Αγρίππου, θεώμενος τήν τε σπουδὴν μεθ' οἵας ὁ Μαρσύας ἀφίκετο
καὶ τὸ ἐκ τῶν λόγων χάρμα τῷ 'Αγρίππᾳ συνελθόν,

¹ ex corr. A : κρίνοιεν MW.
² φέροντες ed. pr.
³ A¹E : ἔθει MW et ex corr. A.
⁴ Bekker : τῶνδε codd.

138

for they would have given much money to insure that these words should prove true—but rather because they feared that if the news turned out to be in error, they might find themselves too soon off the mark in flaunting their delight and might be reported to their own destruction.[a] Indeed, he had inflicted fearful wrongs in greater numbers on the Roman nobles than any other one man, for he was always quick to anger and relentless in action, even if his grounds for conceiving hatred of a man made no sense. It was his bent to turn savage in every case that he decided; and he inflicted the death penalty even for the slightest offences. And so, though the report that they had of his death gave them pleasure, they were prevented from enjoying it as much as they would have liked by fear of the dire consequences that they foresaw if hope played them false. But Marsyas, the freedman of Agrippa, having learned of the death of Tiberius, forced his way at top speed to announce the good news to Agrippa. Finding him on his way out to the bath, he beckoned to him and said in Hebrew, " The lion is dead." [b] Agrippa grasped his meaning and, giddy with joy at this announcement, said, " My unbounded thanks to you for your whole service and for this happy news. I only hope it is true." Now the centurion, who commanded Agrippa's guards, seeing in what a hurry Marsyas had come and how pleased Agrippa was as soon as he heard the message,

*The news comes to Agrippa.*

---

[a] Thackeray, *Selections from Josephus*, p. 82, has, for the last clause, " they would be slanderously accused and lose their lives."

[b] *Cf.* Bab. *Shabbat* 30 b, where Solomon quotes Ecclesiastes ix. 4, " A living dog is better than a dead lion," in speaking of his father David, who has just died and whose corpse is threatened by hungry dogs.

ὑποτοπήσας καίνωσίν[1] τινα γεγονέναι τῶν λόγων
231 ἤρετό σφας περὶ τοῦ λόγου τοῦ ἐφεστηκότος. οἱ
δὲ τέως μὲν παρέτρεπον, ἐγκειμένῳ δὲ ἀποσημαίνει
ὁ Ἀγρίππας, ἤδη γὰρ φίλος ἦν, μηδὲν ἐνδοιάσας.
ὁ δὲ ἐκοινοῦτό τε τὴν ἡδονὴν τοῦ λόγου διὰ τὸ εἰς
ἀγαθὰ τῷ Ἀγρίππᾳ φέρειν προυτίθει τε αὐτῷ
δεῖπνον. εὐωχουμένων δ' αὐτῶν καὶ τοῦ πότου
προϊόντος παρῆν τις λέγων ζῆν τε τὸν Τιβέριον καὶ
232 ὀλίγων ἡμερῶν ἐπανήξειν εἰς τὴν πόλιν. καὶ ὁ
ἑκατοντάρχης δεινῶς θορυβηθεὶς τῷ λόγῳ διὰ τὸ
εἰς θάνατον ἀνακείμενα πεπραχέναι δεσμώτῃ τε
καὶ ἐπ' ἀγγελίᾳ θανάτου αὐτοκράτορος συνδιῃτῆ-
σθαι μετὰ χάρματος, ἀπωθεῖταί τε τὸν Ἀγρίππαν
τοῦ κλινιδίου καί, " ἦπου," φησίν, " λήσειν με ὑπο-
νοεῖς θάνατον τοῦ αὐτοκράτορος κατεψευσμένος, ἀλλ'
οὐ κεφαλῇ τῇ σῇ τοῦτον ἀναμαξόμενος τὸν λόγον; "
233 ταῦτα εἰπὼν κελεύει δῆσαι τὸν Ἀγρίππαν λελυκὼς
πρότερον αὐτὸν φυλακήν τε ἀκριβεστέραν αὐτοῦ ἢ
πρότερον καθίσταται. καὶ νύκτα μὲν ἐκείνην ὁ
234 Ἀγρίππας ἐν τοιούτοις ἦν τοῖς κακοῖς. τῇ δὲ
ὑστεραίᾳ λόγος τε πλείων ἦν κατὰ τὴν πόλιν ἰσχυρι-
ζόμενος ἐπὶ τῇ τελευτῇ τοῦ Τιβερίου, ἐθάρρουν τε
οἱ ἄνθρωποι φανερῶς ἤδη θροεῖν[2] καί τινες καὶ
θυσίας ἐπετέλουν, ἐπιστολαί τε ἀφίκοντο παρὰ τοῦ
Γαΐου, ἡ μὲν πρὸς τὴν σύγκλητον τοῦ Τιβερίου διασαφοῦσα τὴν τελευτὴν καὶ τὴν αὐτοῦ παράληψιν

---

[1] AW : καὶ γνῶσιν M : i. marg. γρ καίνισιν A : κοίνωσιν
Ernesti.
[2] A : θρυλλεῖν M : θρυλεῖν W.

---

[a] Thackeray, *Selections*, p. 83, suggests as an alternative
translation " suspected the use of a strange language,"
namely Hebrew.
[b] Tacitus, *Ann.* vi. 50, also reports that after the first news

surmised that something novel had been said [a] and asked them about the message in question. For a time they put him off, but, when he insisted, Agrippa, being now on friendly terms with him, told him the truth without reserve. He joined in the rejoicing at the news because it was to Agrippa's advantage and treated him to a dinner. While they were feasting and the drinking was under way, someone came in and said that Tiberius was alive and would return to the city within a few days.[b] The centurion was so shockingly perturbed at this report, since the penalty set for such things as he had done was death, that is, both to have dined together with a prisoner and to have rejoiced at the news of the emperor's death, that he pushed Agrippa off the couch and said : "So you thought you would fool me with a false report of the emperor's death, and would not pay for it with your own head ? " With these words he ordered the manacles to be put on Agrippa, though he had previously taken them off, and a stricter guard to be kept than before. Such was the wretched condition of Agrippa through the night. On the following day, however, the reports of Tiberius' death were more numerous and assured in the city. The people now began to have the courage to speak of it without misgiving, and some even offered sacrifices. Two letters then arrived from Gaius : one to the senate informing that body fully of the death of Tiberius and of his own

had been received of Tiberius' death and Gaius Caligula and his supporters had started to rejoice, another message was received that Tiberius was actually recovering from his faintness and calling for food. In the ensuing panic only Macro, the prefect of the praetorian cohorts, was undaunted and simply ordered that Tiberius should be smothered under a heap of clothes.

235 τῆς ἡγεμονίας γενομένην, ἡ δὲ πρὸς Πείσωνα τὸν
φύλακα τῆς πόλεως τοῦτό τε ἀγορεύουσα, καὶ τὸν
Ἀγρίππαν ἐκέλευεν ἐκ τοῦ στρατοπέδου μεταστῆ-
σαι[1] εἰς τὴν οἰκίαν, ἐν ᾗ πρότερον ἢ δεθῆναι δίαιταν
εἶχεν. τότε ἐν θάρσει λοιπὸν ἦγεν τὰ περὶ αὐτῆς·
φυλακὴ μὲν γὰρ καὶ τήρησις ἦν, μετὰ μέντοι ἀνέ-
236 σεως τῆς εἰς τὴν δίαιταν. Γάιος δὲ ὡς ἐπὶ Ῥώμης
παρῆν ἄγων τοῦ Τιβερίου τὸ σῶμα, ταφάς τε αὐτοῦ
ποιεῖται πολυτελεῖς νόμοις τοῖς πατρίοις, Ἀγρίππαν τε αὐθημερὸν λύειν ὄντα πρόθυμον κώλυμα
Ἀντωνία ἦν οὔ τι μίσει τῷ πρὸς τὸν δεδεμένον
προμηθείᾳ δὲ τοῦ Γαΐου εὐπρεποῦς, μὴ δόξαν ἀπ-
άγοιτο ἡδονῇ δεχομένου τὴν Τιβερίου μετάστασιν[2]
ἄνδρα ὑπ' ἐκείνου δεδεμένον λύων ἐκ τοῦ ὀξέος.
237 διελθουσῶν μέντοι οὐ πολλῶν ἡμερῶν μεταπεμψά-
μενος αὐτὸν εἰς τὸν οἶκον ἀποκείρει τε αὐτὸν καὶ
μεταμφιέννυσιν, εἶτα δὲ τὸ διάδημα περιτίθησιν τῇ
κεφαλῇ καὶ βασιλέα καθίστησιν αὐτὸν τῆς Φιλίππου
τετραρχίας δωρησάμενος αὐτῷ καὶ τὴν Λυσανίου
τετραρχίαν, ἀλλάττει τε σιδηρᾷ ἁλύσει χρυσῆν ἰσό-
σταθμον. ἱππάρχην[3] δὲ ἐπὶ[4] τῆς Ἰουδαίας ἐκπέμπει
Μάρυλλον.[5]

---

[1] Niese : μεταστήσειν AME : μεταστῆσιν W.
[2] MWE (cf. Ant. xviii. 89) : τελευτὴν A : mortem Lat.
[3] ἱππάρχην] codd. : magistrum equitum Lat. : ἔπαρχον
Hudson : ὕπαρχον coni. Niese.
[4] ἐκ E.     [5] Μάριλλον M.

---

[a] Josephus' statement is confirmed by Suetonius, *Calig.*
15, who speaks of the funeral oration which Gaius delivered
weepingly before a vast crowd and of the magnificent burial
that he accorded him. Dio Cassius lix. 3. 7, however, claims
that Gaius brought in Tiberius' body at night and gave him
a hasty funeral. M. P. Charlesworth, " The Tradition about
Caligula," *Camb. Hist. Jour.* iv, 1933, p. 108, cites an entry

succession to his office, the other to Piso, the prefect of the city, containing both this statement and the order that Agrippa should be removed from the camp to the house where he had lived before his imprisonment. After that he had no hardship to fear, for though he was still guarded and watched, yet the watch on his daily activities was relaxed. After Gaius had arrived in Rome with the body of Tiberius and had given him a splendid funeral in the old Roman fashion,[a] he was eager to release Agrippa on that very day. Antonia, however, restrained him, not that she wished the prisoner any harm, but she was concerned not to let Gaius commit an impropriety. It would give the impression, if he released so quickly one who had been imprisoned by Tiberius, that he joyfully welcomed Tiberius' death. [b] Not many days thereafter, he sent for Agrippa to come to his house, and he attended to cutting his hair and changing his clothes. This done, he put a diadem on his head and appointed him king of the tetrarchy of Philip,[c] presenting him also with the tetrarchy of Lysanias.[d] Furthermore, in exchange for his iron chain, he gave him a golden one of equal weight. As commander of the cavalry [e] in Judaea he dispatched Marullus.[f]

*Gaius makes Agrippa king of Philip's tetrarchy.*

---

from the Acts of the Arval Brethren and other epigraphical evidence which refute Dio and indicate that Gaius showed full respect for Tiberius.

[b] *Cf.* the parallel passage in *B.J.* ii. 181.

[c] See above, §§ 27–28, 106–108.

[d] *Cf. Ant.* xv. 344, xix. 275, xx. 138 ; Dio Cass. lix. 8. 2.

[e] Hudson emends, but without any evidence, to ἔπαρχον, " procurator," and is followed by E. Stein, " Marullus," *R.E.* xiv, 1930, p. 2053.

[f] Otherwise unknown. E. M. Smallwood, " The Date of the Dismissal of Pontius Pilate from Judaea," *Jour. of Jewish Stud.* v, 1954, p. 14, adopts S. L. DeLaet's suggestion

238   (11) Δευτέρῳ δὲ ἔτει τῆς Γαΐου Καίσαρος ἡγεμονίας Ἀγρίππας ἠξίου συγχώρησιν αὐτῷ γενέσθαι
πλεύσαντι τήν τε ἀρχὴν καταστήσασθαι καὶ τὰ
239 ἄλλα εἰς δέον οἰκονομησαμένῳ ἐπανιέναι. καὶ συγχωροῦντος τοῦ αὐτοκράτορος παρῆν παρ' ἐλπίδας
τε ὤφθη πᾶσι βασιλεὺς πολλήν τε τῆς τύχης ἐπε-
δείκνυεν ἐπὶ τοῖς ἀνθρώποις τὴν ἐξουσίαν τοῖς θεωροῦσιν ἐκ λογισμῶν ἀπορίας τε τῆς πρότερον καὶ
τοῦ ἐν τῷ παρόντι εὐδαίμονος. καὶ οἱ μὲν ἐμακάρι-
ζον τοῦ μὴ διαμαρτίᾳ χρησαμένου τῶν ἐλπίδων, οἱ
δ' ἐν ἀπιστίᾳ περὶ τῶν γεγονότων ἦσαν.

240   (vii. 1) Ἡρωδιὰς δὲ ἡ ἀδελφὴ τοῦ Ἀγρίππου
συνοικοῦσα Ἡρώδῃ, τετράρχης δὲ οὗτος ἦν Γαλιλαίας καὶ Περαίας, φθόνῳ τἀδελφοῦ τὴν ἐξουσίαν
ἐδέχετο ὁρῶσα ἐν πολὺ μείζονι ἀξιώματι γεγενημένον ἀνδρὸς τοῦ αὐτῆς, διὰ τὸ φυγῇ μὲν ποιήσασθαι τὴν ἔξοδον διαλῦσαι τὰ χρέα μὴ δυνάμενον,
κάθοδον δὲ μετ' ἀξιώματος καὶ οὕτως πολλοῦ τοῦ
241 εὐδαίμονος. ἐλυπεῖτο οὖν καὶ βαρέως ἔφερεν τῇ
ἐπὶ τοσοῦτον αὐτοῦ μεταβολῇ, καὶ μάλιστα ὁπότε
θεάσαιτο μετὰ τῶν εἰωθότων παρασήμων τῆς βασιλείας ἐπιφοιτῶντά τε τοῖς πλήθεσιν, ἐπικρύπτε-
σθαι οὐκ ἠνείχετο τὴν δυστυχίαν τοῦ φθόνου, ἀλλὰ
τὸν ἄνδρα ἐξῆρεν κελεύουσα ἐπὶ τῆς Ῥώμης πλεῖν
242 ἐπὶ μνηστείᾳ τῶν ἴσων· οὐδὲ γὰρ ἀνεκτὸν εἶναι
σφίσι τὸ ζῆν, εἰ Ἀγρίππας Ἀριστοβούλου μὲν υἱὸς
ὢν θανεῖν ὑπὸ τοῦ πατρὸς κατεγνωσμένου,[1] πενίᾳ

---

[1] ed. pr. et ut vid. Lat. : κατεγνωσμένος codd.

("Le Successeur de Ponce-Pilate," *Antiq. Class.* viii, 1939,
pp. 418-419) that this Marullus (or Maryllus) is to be identified with the Marcellus whom Vitellius had appointed (*Ant.*

(11) In the second year of the reign of the emperor Gaius, Agrippa asked for permission to set sail and make his rule secure, as well as to get all other matters duly organized, and then to return to Rome. The emperor gave consent and he went. All were surprised to see him in his royal state. He was an object lesson in demonstrating the great power of fortune over mankind to those who beheld him and speculated on the contrast between his former distress and his present prosperity. Some thought him lucky not to have failed to attain his hopes, while others were incredulous about what had happened.

*Agrippa returns home.*

(vii. 1) ᵃ Herodias, the sister of Agrippa and wife of Herod, tetrarch of Galilee and Peraea, begrudged her brother his rise to power far above the state that her husband enjoyed. Agrippa had had to flee for lack of money to pay his debts, but now he had returned in grandeur and with such great prosperity. It was consequently painful and depressing for her to see so great a reversal in his fortunes. The spectacle of his royal visits in the customary regalia before the multitudes made her especially helpless to keep this unfortunate envy to herself. Instead she instigated her husband, urging him to embark for Rome and sue for equal status. For their life was unbearable, she said, if Agrippa, who was the son of that Aristobulus who had been condemned to death by his father, who had himself known such helpless

*Herodias eggs her husband on to seek a similar fortune.*

xviii. 89) to take charge of the administration of Judaea, and that Gaius simply gave the acting governor the official position of procurator. But in addition to going counter to the unanimous authority of the manuscripts, this suggestion disregards ἐκπέμπει, which indicates that Gaius sent him forth from Rome.

ᵃ §§ 240-255 are parallel with *B.J.* ii. 181-183.

# JOSEPHUS

δὲ ἀπόρῳ συνιών, ὡς τελέως[1] αὐτῷ ἐπικουφίζεσθαι
τἀναγκαῖα τοῦ ἐφ' ἡμέρας, φυγῇ δὲ τῶν δεδανεικό-
των τὸν πλοῦν πεποιημένος ἐπανεληλύθοι βασιλεύς,
αὐτὸς δέ γε ὢν παῖς βασιλέως καὶ τοῦ συγγενοῦς[2]
τῆς ἀρχῆς καλοῦντος αὐτὸν ἐπὶ μεταποιήσει τῶν
243 ἴσων[3] καθέζοιτο ἀγαπῶν ἐν ἰδιωτείᾳ διαβιοῦν. "ἀλλ'
εἰ καὶ πρότερόν γε, Ἡρώδη, μηδὲν ἐλύπει σε τὸ ἐν
ἐλάσσονι τιμῇ πατρὸς οὗ γέγονας εἶναι, νῦν γοῦν
ὀρέχθητι συγγενοῦς ἀξιώματος μηδὲ ὑπόμενε ἡσσᾶ-
σθαι προύχοντι τιμῆς ἀνδρὶ πλοῦτον τεθεραπευκότι
τὸν σόν, μηδὲ πενίαν ἀποφήνῃς τὴν ἐκείνου τῆς
ἡμετέρας εὐπορίας ἀρετῇ μᾶλλον χρῆσθαι δυνα-
μένην, μηδὲ δευτερεύειν ἀνεπαίσχυντον ἡγοῦ τῶν
244 χθές τε καὶ πρῴην ἐλέῳ τῷ σῷ διαβεβιωκότων. ἀλλ'
ἐπὶ τῆς Ῥώμης ἴωμεν, καὶ μήτε πόνου φειδώ τις
ἔστω μήτε ἀργυρίου δαπάνης καὶ χρυσίου, διὰ τὸ
μὴ ἐπ' οὐδαμινοῖς ἐν[4] βελτίοσιν γενέσθαι τὴν τήρη-
σιν αὐτῶν ἀναλώσεως τῆς ἐπὶ κτήσει βασιλείας
ἐσομένης."
245  (2) Ὁ δὲ τέως μὲν ἀπεμάχετο ἀγαπῶν τὴν ἡσυ-
χίαν καὶ τῆς Ῥώμης τὸν ὄχλον δι' ὑποψίας λαμβάνων ἀναδιδάσκειν τε αὐτὴν ἐπειρᾶτο, ἡ δ' ἐφ'
ὅσον ἐξαναχωροῦντα ἑώρα μειζόνως ἐπέκειτο κελεύουσα μὴ ἀνιέναι πάντα πράσσειν ἐπὶ τῇ βασιλείᾳ.
246 καὶ πέρας οὐκ ἀνῆκεν ἕως ἐξενίκησεν[5] αὐτὸν ὁμο-
γνώμονα αὐτῇ ἀκουσίως γενέσθαι διὰ τὸ μὴ εἶναι
ἄλλως ἀποφυγεῖν αὐτῆς τὸ ἐπὶ τοιούτοις ψηφισά-
μενον, παρασκευασάμενός τε ὡς ἐνῆν πολυτελῶς
καὶ φειδοῖ μηδενὸς χρώμενος ἀνήγετο ἐπὶ τῆς

---

[1] ἐλέῳ (et ut vid. ὦστ') Naber.
[2] ⟨καὶ κοινωνοῦ⟩ post συγγενοῦς add. Richards et Shutt.
[3] τοῦ συγγενοῦς . . . ἴσων] et frater eius qui tetrarchiam

146

poverty that the necessities of daily life had entirely failed him, and who had set out on his voyage to escape from his creditors, should have returned as a king, while Herod himself, the son of a king, who was called by his royal birth to claim equal treatment, should rest content to live as a commoner to the end of his life. " Even if, O Herod," she said, " you were not distressed in the past to be lower in rank than the father from whom you sprang, now at least I beg of you to move in quest of the high position that you were born to. Do not patiently admit defeat by a man outranking you, who has bent the knee to your affluence. Do not inform the world that his poverty can make better use of manly qualities than our riches. Never regard it as anything but a disgrace to play second fiddle to those who were but yesterday dependent on your bounty for survival. Come, let us go to Rome ; let us spare neither pains nor expense of silver and gold, since there is no better use for which we might hoard them than to expend them on the acquisition of a kingdom."

(2) For a while he resisted and tried to change her mind, for he was content with his tranquillity and was wary of the Roman bustle. The more, however, she saw him shying away, the more urgently she insisted, bidding him not to be remiss in seeking a throne at any cost. The upshot was that she never flagged till she carried the day and made him her unwilling partisan, for there was no way of escape once she had cast her vote on this matter. And so, supplied as lavishly as possible and sparing no expense, he

---

illam ante possederat, ut magis ei cognationis iure deberetur Lat.

<sup>4</sup> ἄν coni. Niese.     <sup>5</sup> Niese : ἐξεκίνησεν codd. E.

247 Ῥώμης ἅμα καὶ τὴν Ἡρωδιάδα ἀγόμενος. Ἀγρίππας δὲ τήν τε διάνοιαν αὐτῶν καὶ τὴν παρασκευὴν αἰσθόμενος καὶ αὐτὸς παρεσκευάζετο, ἐπεί τε ἐκπεπλευκότας ἀκούει, πέμπει καὶ αὐτὸς ἐπὶ τῆς Ῥώμης Φορτουνᾶτον αὐτοῦ τῶν ἀπελευθέρων δῶρά τε κομίζοντα τῷ αὐτοκράτορι καὶ ἐπιστολὰς κατὰ τοῦ Ἡρώδου τὰ δὲ καὶ αὐτὸν διδάξοντα ἦ¹ καιρὸς

248 τὸν Γάιον. ὁ δὲ ἐπαναχθεὶς τοῖς ἀμφὶ τὸν Ἡρώδην καὶ δεξιῷ χρησάμενος τῷ πλῷ τοσόνδε ἀπελίπετο τοῦ Ἡρώδου, ὥστε τὸν μὲν ἐντυχεῖν Γαΐῳ, ὁ δὲ ἐπικατάγεται καὶ τὰς ἐπιστολὰς ἀπεδίδου. καὶ προσέπλευσαν ἀμφότεροι Δικαιαρχείᾳ καὶ τὸν

249 Γάιον ἐν Βαΐαις λαμβάνουσιν. πολύδριον² δ᾽ ἐστὶ καὶ τοῦτο τῆς Καμπανίας ὅσον ἀπὸ σταδίων πέντε τῆς Δικαιαρχείας κείμενον, βασίλειοί τέ εἰσιν οἰκήσεις αὐτόθι πολυτελέσι κεχρημέναι κατασκευαῖς φιλοτιμηθέντος τῶν αὐτοκρατόρων ἑκάστου τοὺς προγεγονότας ὑπερβάλλεσθαι, λουτρά τε παρέχεται τὸ χωρίον θερμὰ γῆθεν αὐτόματα ἀνιέντα ἀγαθὰ ἐπί τε ἰάσει τοῖς χρωμένοις καὶ ἄλλως τῷ ἀνειμένῳ

250 τῆς διαίτης συμφέροντα. Γάιος δὲ ἅμα τε προσαγορεύων τὸν Ἡρώδην, πρῶτον δὲ αὐτῷ ἐντυγχανεν, ἅμα τε τοῦ Ἀγρίππου τὰς ἐπιστολὰς ἐπιὼν ἐπὶ κατηγορίᾳ τῇ ἐκείνου συγκειμένας, κατηγόρει δὲ αὐτοῦ ὁμολογίαν πρὸς Σηιανὸν κατὰ τῆς Τιβερίου ἀρχῆς καὶ πρὸς Ἀρτάβανον τὸν Πάρθον ἐπὶ

251 τοῦ παρόντος κατὰ τῆς Γαΐου ἀρχῆς, παράδειγμά τε ἦν αὐτῷ τοῦ λόγου μυριάσιν ἑπτὰ ὁπλιτῶν ἀρκέσουσα κατασκευὴ ἐν ταῖς Ἡρώδου ὁπλοθήκαις ἀποκειμένη, ἐκινεῖτό τε ὑπὸ τῶν εἰρημένων καὶ

¹ ἦ A : εἰ MWE.
² A : πολίδριον MWE : γρ πολίδριον ἢ πολίδιον i. marg. A.
148

set sail for Rome, accompanied by Herodias.  But Agrippa, when he learned of their plan and their preparations, made his own preparations.  And when he heard that they had set sail, he himself also dispatched Fortunatus, one of his freedmen, to Rome, charged with presents for the emperor and letters against Herod, and ready to tell his story to Gaius himself as the opportunity presented itself.  Fortunatus, putting out to sea in pursuit of Herod's party, had a favourable voyage and was so little behind Herod that while the latter had obtained an audience with Gaius, he landed and delivered his letters.  Both of them had made port at Dicaearchia and had found Gaius at Baiae.  This is a little city in Campania situated at a distance of about five furlongs *a* from Dicaearchia.  There are royal residences there lavishly furnished, for each of the emperors was ambitious to outdo his predecessors.  The locality also affords hot baths, which spring naturally from the ground and have a curative value for those who use them, not to mention their contribution to easy living in other ways.  At the very time that he was greeting Herod, whom he interviewed first, Gaius was perusing the letters of Agrippa which were composed as an indictment of him.  The letters accused Herod of conspiring with Sejanus against the government of Tiberius and of being now in league with Artabanus the Parthian against the government of Gaius.  As proof of this charge the letters stated that equipment sufficient for 70,000 heavy-armed foot-soldiers was stored in Herod's armouries.  Spurred by these

*a* Josephus has underestimated the distance, which is about three miles (or about two miles, as the crow flies, according to Mathieu-Herrmann).

ἤρετο τὸν Ἡρώδην, εἰ ἀληθὴς ὁ περὶ τῶν ὅπλων
252 λόγος. τοῦ δέ, οὐ γὰρ ἦν ἕτερα εἰπεῖν διὰ τὸ
ἀντιφθέγξασθαι τὴν ἀλήθειαν, εἰπόντος εἶναι τὰ
ὅπλα, πιστὰ ἡγούμενος εἶναι τὰ ἐπὶ τῇ ἀποστάσει
κατηγορούμενα, τὴν τετραρχίαν ἀφελόμενος αὐτὸν
προσθήκην τῇ Ἀγρίππου βασιλείᾳ ποιεῖται καὶ τὰ
χρήματα ὁμοίως τῷ Ἀγρίππᾳ δίδωσιν, αὐτὸν δὲ
φυγῇ ἀιδίῳ ἐζημίωσεν ἀποδείξας οἰκητήριον αὐτοῦ
253 Λούγδουνον πόλιν τῆς Γαλλίας.¹ Ἡρωδιάδα δὲ
μαθὼν Ἀγρίππου ἀδελφὴν οὖσαν τά τε χρήματα
ἐδίδου ὁπόσα ἐκείνη ἰδίᾳ ἦν καὶ τοῦ μὴ κοινωνεῖν
νομίσαι² τῷ ἀνδρὶ τῆς συμφορᾶς τεῖχος αὐτῇ τὸν
254 ἀδελφὸν ἔλεγεν.³ ἡ δέ, " ἀλλὰ σὺ μέν, αὐτόκρατορ,"
εἶπεν, " μεγαλοφρόνως τε καὶ ἀξιώματι τῷ σαυτοῦ
πρεπόντως τάδε λέγεις, κώλυμα δέ μοί ἐστιν χρῆ-
σθαί σου τῇ χάριτι τῆς δωρεᾶς εὔνοια ἡ πρὸς τὸν
γεγαμηκότα, οὗ κοινωνόν με τῆς εὐδαιμονίας γενομένην οὐ δίκαιον ἐγκαταλιπεῖν τὸ ἐπὶ ταῖς τύχαις
255 καθεσταμένον." ὁ δὲ ὀργῇ τοῦ μεγαλόφρονος αὐτὴν ποιησάμενος συνήλαυνεν καὶ αὐτὴν τῷ Ἡρώδῃ καὶ τὴν οὐσίαν αὐτῆς τῷ Ἀγρίππᾳ δίδωσιν.
Ἡρωδιάδι μὲν δὴ φθόνου τοῦ πρὸς τὸν ἀδελφὸν καὶ
Ἡρώδῃ γυναικείων ἀκροασαμένῳ κουφολογιῶν
256 δίκην ταύτην ἐπετίμησεν ὁ θεός. Γάιος δὲ τὸν μὲν
πρῶτον ἐνιαυτὸν καὶ τὸν ἑξῆς πάνυ μεγαλοφρόνως
ἐχρῆτο τοῖς πράγμασιν καὶ μέτριον παρέχων αὐ-

---

¹ AW : Γαλιλαίας, λ secundum ex a corr. M : Γαλατίας E.
² coni. Niese : νομίσας codd. : om. E.
³ καὶ τοῦ . . . ἔλεγεν] arbitrans in consilio viri consciam

150

words, Gaius asked Herod whether the report about the arms was true. When Herod replied that the arms were there—for it was impossible for him to deny it in face of the truth—Gaius, regarding the accusations of revolt as confirmed, relieved him of his tetrarchy and added it to the kingdom of Agrippa. He likewise gave Herod's property to Agrippa and condemned Herod to perpetual exile, assigning him as his residence Lyons, a city in Gaul.[a] When Gaius learned that Herodias was a sister of Agrippa, he offered to allow her to keep all her personal property and told her to regard her brother as the bulwark who had protected her from sharing her husband's fate. She, however, replied : " Indeed, O emperor, these are generous words and such as befit your high office, but my loyalty to my husband is a bar to my enjoyment of your kind gift, for it is not right when I have shared in his prosperity that I should abandon him when he has been brought to this pass." Gaius, angered at her proud mood, exiled her also, together with Herod, and presented her possessions to Agrippa. And so God visited this punishment on Herodias for her envy of her brother and on Herod for listening to a woman's frivolous chatter. As for Gaius, he administered the empire quite highmindedly during the first and second years of his reign.[b] By exercising moderation he made great advances in popularity

---

[a] According to the parallel passage, *B.J.* ii. 183, Herod was banished to Spain.

[b] Dio Cass. lix. 2. 6 also has the good part of Gaius' reign lasting about two years, whereas from Philo, *Leg. ad Gaium* 13, and from Suetonius, *Calig.* 37, we conclude that it lasted about a year.

---

non fuisse ; tutabatur etiam eam quod sororem Agrippae cognoverat Lat.

τὸν εἰς εὔνοιαν πολλὴν προὐχώρει παρά τε 'Ρωμαίοις
αὐτοῖς καὶ τοῖς ὑπηκόοις.[1] προϊὼν δ' ἐξίστατο τοῦ
ἀνθρωπίνως φρονεῖν ὑπὸ μεγέθους τῆς ἀρχῆς ἐκθει-
άζων ἑαυτὸν καὶ τὰ πάντα ἐπ' ἀτιμίᾳ τοῦ θείου
πολιτεύειν ἦρτο.

257 (viii. 1) Καὶ δὴ στάσεως ἐν 'Αλεξανδρείᾳ γενομένης 'Ιουδαίων τε οἳ ἐνοικοῦσι καὶ 'Ελλήνων τρεῖς
ἀφ' ἑκατέρας τῆς στάσεως πρεσβευταὶ αἱρεθέντες
παρῆσαν ὡς τὸν Γάιον. καὶ ἦν γὰρ τῶν 'Αλεξαν-
δρέων πρέσβεων εἷς 'Απίων, ὃς πολλὰ εἰς τοὺς
'Ιουδαίους ἐβλασφήμησεν ἄλλα τε λέγων καὶ ὡς
258 τῶν Καίσαρος τιμῶν περιορῷεν· πάντων γοῦν
ὁπόσοι τῇ 'Ρωμαίων ἀρχῇ ὑποτελεῖς εἶεν βωμοὺς
τῷ Γαΐῳ καὶ νεὼς ἱδρυμένων τά τε ἄλλα πᾶσιν
αὐτὸν ὥσπερ τοὺς θεοὺς δεχομένων, μόνους τούσδε
ἄδοξον ἡγεῖσθαι ἀνδριᾶσι τιμᾶν καὶ ὅρκιον αὐτοῦ

---

[1] τοῖς ὑπηκόοις] apud Graecos Lat.

---

[a] The account of the strife is given at great length in
Philo's treatise *In Flaccum*, and the story of the embassy in
Philo's *Legatio ad Gaium*. The true cause of the tension was,
it seems, the Jewish attempt to gain recognition of their
claim to Alexandrian citizenship (so H. Box, ed., *Philonis
Alexandrini In Flaccum*, 1939, pp. xxxviii ff.). The immediate occasion for the strife was the visit of Agrippa to
Alexandria in A.D. 38 after he had been crowned king by
Gaius Caligula. The Jews received him with great pomp,
but the Greeks, who recalled his previous visit to the city
when he was destitute, mocked him by dressing up an im-
becile as king and addressing him as " Marin " (Aramaic
for " our Lord "). Because they feared Caligula's displeasure,
the Greeks then demanded the erection of statues of the
emperor in every synagogue so that he could be worshipped
as a god. The Roman governor, Flaccus, sided with the
Greeks and proclaimed the Jews to be foreigners and aliens ;
and soon there was a pogrom against the Jews. The Jewish

both with the Romans themselves and with their subjects. But as time went on, he ceased to think of himself as a man and, as he imagined himself a god because of the greatness of his empire, he was moved to disregard the divine power in all his official acts.

(viii. 1) Meanwhile, there was civil strife in Alexandria between the Jewish inhabitants and the Greeks.[a] Three delegates were chosen by each of the factions and appeared before Gaius.[b] One of the Alexandrian delegates was Apion,[c] who scurrilously reviled the Jews, asserting, among other things, that they neglected to pay the honours due to the emperor. For while all the subject peoples in the Roman empire had dedicated altars and temples to Gaius and had given him the same attentions in all other respects as they did the gods, these people alone scorned to honour him with statues and to swear by

embassy was then sent to Caligula to ask him to reassert the traditional Jewish rights granted by the Ptolemies and confirmed by Augustus. On these events in Alexandria and on the embassy see further H. Willrich, " Caligula," *Klio* iii, 1903, pp. 397 ff. ; H. I. Bell, *Jews and Christians in Egypt*, 1924, pp. 10-21 ; Balsdon, *The Emperor Gaius*, pp. 125-135 ; and Box, *op. cit.* pp. xxxviii ff.

[b] It is possible to date Philo's voyage to Rome (*Leg.* 190) as having occurred in the winter of 38–39 or 39–40, probably the latter (so J. P. V. Balsdon in his full discussion of the chronology of Gaius' dealings with the Jews, in *Jour. of Roman Stud.* xxiv, 1934, pp. 19-24). But *cf.* E. M. Smallwood, " The Chronology of Gaius' Attempt to Desecrate the Temple," *Latomus* xvi, 1957, pp. 3-17, who accepts the chronological indications in Philo in preference to those of Josephus where they conflict and dates the episode some months earlier. Philo, *Leg.* 370, says that he headed an embassy of five persons, and his evidence, being firsthand, is obviously to be preferred.

[c] The notorious anti-Semite against whom Josephus wrote his *Contra Apionem*.

259 τὸ ὄνομα ποιεῖσθαι. πολλὰ δὲ καὶ χαλεπὰ Ἀπίωνος εἰρηκότος, ὑφ᾽ ὧν ἀρθῆναι[1] ἤλπιζε τὸν Γάιον
καὶ εἰκὸς ἦν, Φίλων ὁ προεστὼς τῶν Ἰουδαίων τῆς
πρεσβείας, ἀνὴρ τὰ πάντα ἔνδοξος Ἀλεξάνδρου τε
τοῦ ἀλαβάρχου ἀδελφὸς ὢν καὶ φιλοσοφίας οὐκ
ἄπειρος, οἷος[2] ἦν ἐπ᾽ ἀπολογίᾳ χωρεῖν τῶν κατ-
260 ηγορημένων. διακλείει[3] δ᾽ αὐτὸν Γάιος κελεύσας
ἐκποδὼν ἀπελθεῖν, περιοργής τε ὢν φανερὸς ἦν
ἐργασόμενός τι δεινὸν αὐτούς. ὁ δὲ Φίλων ἔξεισι
περιυβρισμένος καί φησι πρὸς τοὺς Ἰουδαίους, οἳ
περὶ αὐτὸν ἦσαν, ὡς χρὴ θαρρεῖν, Γαίου λόγῳ μὲν
αὐτοῖς ὠργισμένου, ἔργῳ δὲ ἤδη τὸν θεὸν ἀντιπαρ-
εξάγοντος.
261 (2) Γάιος δὲ ἐν δεινῷ φέρων εἰς τοσόνδε ὑπὸ
Ἰουδαίων περιῶφθαι μόνων πρεσβευτὴν ἐπὶ Συρίας ἐκπέμπει Πετρώνιον διάδοχον Οὐιτελλίῳ τῆς
ἀρχῆς, κελεύων χειρὶ πολλῇ εἰσβαλόντι εἰς τὴν
Ἰουδαίαν, εἰ μὲν ἑκόντες δέχοιντο, ἱστᾶν αὐτοῦ
ἀνδριάντα ἐν τῷ ναῷ τοῦ θεοῦ, εἰ δ᾽ ἀγνωμοσύνῃ
χρῷντο, πολέμῳ κρατήσαντα τοῦτο ποιεῖν. καὶ
262 Πετρώνιος Συρίαν παραλαβὼν ἠπείγετο διακονεῖσθαι ταῖς ἐπιστολαῖς τοῦ Καίσαρος, συμμαχίαν τε
πλείστην ὅσην ἠδύνατο ἀθροίσας καὶ τάγματα δύο

[1] ἐρεθισθῆναι coni. Richards et Shutt.
[2] τε post οἷος omisi. [3] διακλείει] ex secretario excludi Lat.

[a] The word ὅρκιος is used of a god by whom one swears. So A. G. Roos, "Lesefruchte," *Mnemosyne*, iii Series, vol. 2, 1935, pp. 237-238.
[b] Mentioned in §§ 159-160 as one who lent a large sum of money to Agrippa.
[c] V. A. Tcherikover, in the prolegomena to his *Corpus Papyrorum Judaicarum*, i, 1957, p. 67, emphasizes that Philo represented the higher and wealthier circles of the

his name.[a]   And so Apion spoke many angry words
by which he hoped that Gaius would be moved, as
might be expected.   Philo, who stood at the head of
the delegation of the Jews, a man held in the highest
honour, brother of Alexander the alabarch [b] and no
novice in philosophy, was prepared to proceed with
the defence against these accusations.[c]   But Gaius
cut him short, told him to get out of his way, and,
being exceedingly angry, made it clear that he would
visit some outrage upon them.   Philo, having thus
been treated with contumely, left the room, saying
to the Jews who accompanied him that they should
be of good courage, for Gaius' wrath was a matter of
words, but in fact he was now enlisting God against
himself.

(2) [d] Indignant at being so slighted by the Jews
alone, Gaius dispatched Petronius [e] as his legate to
Syria to succeed Vitellius in this office. His orders
were to lead a large force into Judaea and, if the Jews
consented to receive him, to set up an image of Gaius
in the temple of God.   If, however, they were obsti-
nate, he was to subdue them by force of arms and so
set it up.   Petronius took over Syria and hastened to
carry out the commands of the emperor.   Gathering
together as many auxiliaries as possible, he marched

*(marginal note:)* Petronius is sent to Judaea to erect Gaius' statue in the temple.

Jewish population in Alexandria, who sought a reconciliation
with the Roman government and with the Greeks, whereas
a strong segment of the masses of the Jews were opposed to
such a reconciliation.

[d] §§ 261-262 are parallel with *B.J.* ii. 185-187. This incident is also mentioned by Philo, *Leg.* 188 and 207-208, and
by Tacitus, *Hist.* v. 9, both of whom note that Caligula
ordered the Jews to set up his statue in the temple in Jerusalem, but that they chose to take up arms rather than to
obey him.

[e] Governor of Syria A.D. 39–42.

τῆς Ῥωμαίων δυνάμεως ἄγων ἐπὶ Πτολεμαΐδος
παρῆν αὐτόθι χειμάσων ὡς πρὸς ἔαρ τοῦ πολεμεῖν
οὐκ ἀφεξόμενος, καὶ πρὸς τὸν Γάιον ἔγραφεν περὶ
τῶν ἐπεγνωσμένων. ὁ δὲ ἐπήνει τῆς προθυμίας
αὐτὸν καὶ ἐκέλευεν μὴ ἀνιέναι πολεμεῖν δὲ μὴ πει-
263 θομένοις ἐντεταμένως. Ἰουδαίων δὲ πολλαὶ μυριάδες παρῆσαν ὡς τὸν Πετρώνιον εἰς Πτολεμαΐδα
κατὰ δεήσεις μηδὲν ἐπὶ παρανομίᾳ σφᾶς ἐπαναγ-
264 κάζειν καὶ παραβάσει τοῦ πατρίου νόμου.[1] " εἰ δέ
σοι πάντως πρόκειται τὸν ἀνδριάντα φέρειν καὶ
ἱστᾶν, ἡμᾶς αὐτοὺς πρότερον μεταχειρισάμενος
πρᾶσσε τὰ δεδογμένα· οὐδὲ γὰρ δυνάμεθα περιόντες
θεωρεῖν[2] πράγματα ἡμῖν ἀπηγορευμένα ἀξιώματί
τε τοῦ νομοθέτου καὶ προπατόρων τῶν ἡμετέρων
τῶν εἰς ἀρετὴν ἀνήκειν αὐτὰ κεχειροτονηκότων."
265 Πετρώνιος δὲ ὀργὴν[3] λαβὼν εἶπεν[4]· " ἀλλ' εἰ μὲν
αὐτοκράτωρ ὢν βουλεύμασι χρῆσθαι τοῖς ἐμαυτοῦ
τάδε πράσσειν ἐπενόουν, κἂν[5] δίκαιος ἦν ὑμῖν πρός
με οὗτος ὁ λόγος. νυνὶ δέ μοι Καίσαρος ἐπεσταλ-
κότος πᾶσα ἀνάγκη διακονεῖσθαι τοῖς ἐκείνῳ προ-
ανεψηφισμένοις διὰ τὸ εἰς ἀνηκεστοτέραν φέρειν
266 ζημίαν τὴν παρακρόασιν αὐτῶν." " ἐπεὶ τοίνυν οὕτως φρονεῖς, ὦ Πετρώνιε," φασὶν οἱ Ἰουδαῖοι, " ὡς
μὴ ἂν ἐπιστολὰς τὰς Γάιου παρελθεῖν, οὐδ' ἂν αὐτοὶ
παραβαίημεν τοῦ νόμου τὴν προαγόρευσιν θεοῦ[6]
πεισθέντες ἀρετῇ[7] καὶ προγόνων πόνοις τῶν ἡμετέ-

[1] νόμου A : om. MWE.
[2] A : συγχωρεῖν MW : ammittere Lat.
[3] ὀργὴν] codd. : ὀργῇ coni. Niese : πρὸς ὀργὴν coni. Richards et Shutt.
[4] ὀργὴν . . . εἶπεν] respondit Lat.
[5] ed. pr. : καὶ AW : om. ME.

at the head of two [a] legions of the Roman army to
Ptolemaïs, intending to spend the winter there and
towards spring to engage in war without fail. He
wrote Gaius what he had in mind to do. The latter
commended him for his zeal and bade him abate
nothing but wage war vigorously against them if
they persisted in disobedience. Meanwhile, many
tens of thousands of Jews came to Petronius at
Ptolemaïs with petitions not to use force to make
them transgress and violate their ancestral code.
" If," they said, " you propose at all costs to bring in
and set up the image, slay us first before you carry
out these resolutions. For it is not possible for us to
survive and to behold actions that are forbidden us by
the decision both of our lawgiver and of our forefathers who cast their votes enacting these measures
as moral laws." To this Petronius indignantly replied : " If I were the emperor and intended to take
this action of my own choice, you would have a right to
speak as you do. As it is, I am Caesar's emissary and
bound to carry out the decision he has already made,
since to disregard it would bring on me irretrievable
punishment." " Equal to this determination of
yours, O Petronius," replied the Jews, " not to transgress the orders of Gaius, is our determination not to
transgress the declaration of the law. We have put
our trust in the goodness of God and in the labours

*Jewish embassy to Petronius at Ptolemaïs protesting.*

---

[a] The parallel passage, *B.J.* ii. 186, says that there were
three legions. Thackeray's note *ad loc.* cites the statement of
Philo, *Leg.* 207, that Petronius came with half his army ;
since there were four legions in Syria at this time Josephus'
statement here is to be preferred.

---

6 θεοῦ] θεῷ | τε, θεῷ suppl., τε ex θυ (h.e. θεοῦ) corr. A : οὖ
MW.
7 ἀρετῇ] MW : καὶ ἀρετῇ (καὶ suppl.) A.

ρων εἰς νῦν ἀπαράβατοι μεμενηκότες, οὐδ' ἂν τολ-
μήσαιμεν ἐπὶ τοσοῦτον κακοὶ γενέσθαι, ὥστε ὁπόσα
ἐκείνῳ δόξειεν μὴ πρασσόμενα ἀγαθοῦ ῥοπὴν ἡμῖν
φέρειν αὐτοὶ παραβαίνειν ποτ' ἂν θάνατον φοβη-
267 θέντες. ὑπομενοῦμεν δὲ εἰς τύχας ἰόντες ἐπὶ φυλακῇ τε πατρίων καὶ κινδυνεύειν προθεμένοις ἐλπίδα
οὖσαν ἐξεπιστάμενοι κἂν περιγενέσθαι διά τε τοῦ
θεοῦ τὸ στησόμενον μεθ' ἡμῶν ἐπὶ τιμῇ τε τῇ
ἐκείνου τὰ δεινὰ ὑποδεχομένων καὶ τῆς τύχης τὸ
ἐπ' ἀμφότερα φιλοῦν τοῖς πράγμασι παρατυγχάνειν,
268 ἐκ δὲ τοῦ σοὶ πείθεσθαι πολλὴν μὲν λοιδορίαν τοῦ
ἀνάνδρου προσκεισομένην ὡς δι' αὐτὸ[1] παράβασιν
τοῦ νομίμου προσποιουμένοις,[2] καὶ ἅμα πολλὴν
ὀργὴν τοῦ θεοῦ, ὃς καὶ παρὰ σοὶ δικαστῇ γένοιτ'
ἂν βελτίων Γαΐου."

269 (3) Καὶ ὁ Πετρώνιος ἐκ τῶν λόγων θεασάμενος
δυσνίκητον αὐτῶν τὸ φρονοῦν καὶ μὴ ἂν ἀμαχεὶ
δύναμιν αὐτῷ γενέσθαι διακονήσασθαι Γαΐῳ τὴν
ἀνάθεσιν τοῦ ἀνδριάντος πολὺν δὲ ἔσεσθαι φόνον,
τούς τε φίλους ἀναλαβὼν καὶ θεραπείαν, ἣ περὶ
αὐτὸν ἦν, ἐπὶ Τιβεριάδος ἠπείγετο χρῄζων κατα-
270 νοῆσαι τῶν Ἰουδαίων τὰ πράγματα ὡς ἔχοι. καὶ
Ἰουδαῖοι μέγαν ἡγούμενοι τὸν ἐκ τοῦ πρὸς Ῥωμαίους πολέμου κίνδυνον, πολὺ μείζονα δὲ κρίνοντες
τὸν ἐκ τοῦ παρανομεῖν, αὖθις πολλαὶ μυριάδες
ὑπηντίαζον Πετρώνιον εἰς τὴν Τιβεριάδα γενό-
271 μενον, καὶ ἱκετείᾳ χρώμενοι μηδαμῶς εἰς ἀνάγκας
τοιαύτας αὐτοὺς καθιστᾶν μηδὲ μιαίνειν ἀνδριάντος

---

[1] δι' αὐτό] ed. pr. : δι' αὐτῶν A : δι' αὐτὸν MW : δέει αὐτῶν
Cocceji.
[2] ὡς . . . προσποιουμένοις] quod timore transgressores legis
efficimur Lat.

of our forefathers and have thus hitherto remained
innocent of transgression. Nor could we ever bring
ourselves to go so far in wickedness as by our own act
to transgress, for any fear of death, the law bidding
us abstain, where He thought it conducive to our
good to do so. In order to preserve our ancestral
code, we shall patiently endure what may be in store
for us, with the assurance that for those who are determined to take the risk there is hope even of
prevailing ; for God will stand by us if we welcome
danger for His glory. Fortune, moreover, is wont to
veer now toward one side, now toward the other in
human affairs. To obey you, on the other hand,
would bring on us the grave reproach of cowardice,
because that would be the explanation of our transgressing the law, and at the same time we should
incur God's severe wrath—and He even in your eyes
must be accounted a higher power than Gaius."

(3) ᵃ Now Petronius saw from their words that
their spirit was not easily to be put down and that it
would be impossible for him without a battle to carry
out Gaius' behest and set up his image. Indeed there
would be great slaughter. Hence he gathered up
his friends and attendants and hastened to Tiberias,
for he wished to take note of the situation of the
Jews there. The Jews, though they regarded the
risk involved in war with the Romans as great, yet
adjudged the risk of transgressing the Law to be
far greater. As before, many tens of thousands faced
Petronius on his arrival at Tiberias. They besought
him by no means to put them under such constraint
nor to pollute the city by setting up a statue. " Will

*Jewish pe-
tition to
Petronius
at Tiberias.*

---

ᵃ This account of Petronius, §§ 269-288, is parallel with
*B.J.* ii. 192-202.

ἀναθέσει τὴν πόλιν. '' πολεμήσετε ἄρα Καίσαρι,''
Πετρώνιος ἔφη, '' μήτε τὴν ἐκείνου παρασκευὴν λογιζόμενοι μήτε τὴν ὑμετέραν ἀσθένειαν; '' οἱ δ᾽,
'' οὐδαμῶς πολεμήσαιμεν,'' ἔφασαν, '' τεθνηξόμεθα
δὲ πρότερον ἢ παραβῆναι τοὺς νόμους.'' ἐπί τε τὰ
πρόσωπα κείμενοι καὶ τὰς σφαγὰς προδεικνύντες
272 ἕτοιμοι κτιννύεσθαι ἔλεγον εἶναι. καὶ ταῦτ᾽ ἐπράσσετο ἐπὶ ἡμέρας τεσσαράκοντα, καὶ τοῦ γεωργεῖν
ἀπερίοπτοι τὸ λοιπὸν ἦσαν καὶ ταῦτα τῆς ὥρας
οὔσης πρὸς σπόρῳ, πολλή τε ἦν προαίρεσις αὐτοῖς
καὶ τοῦ θνήσκειν ἐπιθυμίας πρόθεσις, ἢ τὴν ἀνάθεσιν θεάσασθαι τοῦ ἀνδριάντος.

273    (4) Ἐν τούτοις ὄντων τῶν πραγμάτων Ἀριστόβουλος ὁ Ἀγρίππου τοῦ βασιλέως ἀδελφὸς καὶ
Ἑλκίας ὁ μέγας[1] ἄλλοι τε οἱ κράτιστοι τῆσδε τῆς
οἰκίας καὶ οἱ πρῶτοι σὺν αὐτοῖς εἰσίασιν ὡς τὸν
274 Πετρώνιον παρακαλοῦντες αὐτόν, ἐπειδὴ τὴν προθυμίαν ὁρᾷ τῆς πληθύος, μηδὲν εἰς ἀπόνοιαν αὐτῆς
παρακινεῖν,[2] ἀλλὰ γράφειν πρὸς Γάιον τὸ ἀνήκεστον
αὐτῶν πρὸς τὴν ἀποδοχὴν τοῦ ἀνδριάντος, πῶς τε
ἀποστάντες τοῦ γεωργεῖν ἀντικαθέζονται, πολεμεῖν
μὲν οὐ βουλόμενοι διὰ τὸ μηδ᾽ ἂν δύνασθαι, θανεῖν
δ᾽ ἔχοντες ἡδονὴν πρὶν παραβῆναι τὰ νόμιμα αὐτοῖς,
ὥστε ἀσπόρου τῆς γῆς γενομένης λῃστεῖαι ἂν
275 φύοιντο ἀδυναμίᾳ καταβολῆς τῶν φόρων. ἴσως

---

[1] ὁ μέγας] maior Lat.
[2] μηδὲν . . . παρακινεῖν] ut bene de negotio praesenti con-
suleret neque de tantae multitudinis perditione cogitaret Lat. :
pro παρακινεῖν legit παρακαλεῖν A.

---

[a] The same words, '' Will you then go to war with Caesar?'',
are also found in the parallel account, B.J. ii. 196.

you then go to war with Caesar," *a* said Petronius,
"regardless of his resources and of your own weakness?" "On no account would we fight," they said,
"but we will die sooner than violate our laws." And
falling on their faces and baring their throats,*b* they
declared that they were ready to be slain. They continued to make these supplications for forty days.*c*
Furthermore, they neglected their fields, and that,
too, though it was time to sow the seed.*d* For they
showed astubborn determinatibn and readiness to die
rather than to see the image erected.

(4) At this juncture Aristobulus, the brother of
King Agrippa, together with Helcias the Elder *e* and
other most powerful members of this house, together
with the civic leaders, appeared before Petronius and
appealed to him, since he saw the deep feeling of the
people, not to incite them to desperation but to
write to Gaius telling how incurable was their opposition to receiving the statue and how they had left
their fields to sit protesting, and that they did not
choose war, since they could not fight a war, but
would be glad to die sooner than transgress their
customs. Let him point out that, since the land was
unsown, there would be a harvest of banditry, because
the requirement of tribute could not be met. For

*Aristobulus and other leaders join in the appeal.*

*b* *Cf.* the similar phrase in § 59 in the description of the
Jewish entreaty to Pilate.

*c* Fifty, according to the parallel account in *B.J.* ii. 200.

*d* Philo, *Leg.* 249, places this incident at the harvest time.

*e* Mentioned in *Ant.* xix. 353 as the prefect and friend of
King Agrippa. After the latter's death Helcias conspired
with Herod, the ruler of Chalcis, to put to death their enemy
Silas, Agrippa's general. He is apparently identical with
the Alexas surnamed Helcias mentioned in *Ant.* xviii. 138
as the husband of Cypros, daughter of Herod the Great's
daughter Cypros.

JOSEPHUS

γὰρ ἂν ἐπικλασθέντα τὸν Γάιον μηδὲν ὠμὸν δια-
νοηθῆναι μηδὲ ἐπ' ἀναστάσει φρονῆσαι τοῦ ἔθνους·
ἐμμένοντος δὲ τῇ τότε βουλῇ τοῦ πολεμεῖν τότε δὴ
276 καὐτὸν ἅπτεσθαι τοῦ πράγματος. καὶ οἱ μὲν ἀμφὶ
τὸν Ἀριστόβουλον ἐπὶ τούτοις τὸν Πετρώνιον παρ-
εκάλουν. Πετρώνιος δὲ τοῦτο μὲν τῶν περὶ τὸν
Ἀριστόβουλον παντοίως ἐπικειμένων διὰ τὸ ὑπὲρ
μεγάλων ποιεῖσθαι τὴν δέησιν καὶ πάσῃ μηχανῇ
277 χρησαμένων εἰς τὰς ἱκετείας, τοῦτο δὲ τῶν Ἰουδαίων θεώμενος τὴν ἀντιπαράταξιν τῆς γνώμης καὶ
δεινὸν ἡγούμενος τοσαῖσδε ἀνθρώπων μυριάσιν
μανίᾳ τῇ Γαΐου διακονούμενος ἐπαγαγὼν θάνατον
ἐν αἰτίᾳ τὸ πρὸς θεὸν σεβάσμιον ἔχειν καὶ μετὰ
πονηρᾶς τὸν μετὰ ταῦτα βίον ἐλπίδος διαιτᾶσθαι,
πολὺ κρεῖσσον ἡγεῖτο ἐπιστείλας τῷ Γαΐῳ[1] τὸ ἀνήκεστον αὐτοῦ[2] ⟨τῆς⟩ ὀργῆς[3] φέρειν[4] μὴ ἐκ τοῦ
278 ὀξέως[5] δεδιακονημένου αὐτοῦ ταῖς ἐπιστολαῖς[6]· τάχα
μὲν γὰρ καὶ πείσειν· καὶ τῇ τὸ πρῶτον μανίᾳ τῆς
γνώμης ἐπιμένοντος ἄψεσθαι[7] πολέμου τοῦ πρὸς
αὐτούς, εἰ δ' ἄρα τι καὶ κατ' αὐτοῦ τρέποι τῆς
ὀργῆς,[8] καλῶς ἔχειν τοῖς ἀρετῆς μεταποιουμένοις
ὑπὲρ τοσῆσδε ἀνθρώπων πληθύος τελευτᾶν, ἔκρινε
πιθανὸν ἡγεῖσθαι τῶν δεομένων τὸν λόγον.
279 (5) Συγκαλέσας δὲ εἰς τὴν Τιβεριάδα τοὺς Ἰουδαίους, οἱ δὲ ἀφίκοντο πολλαὶ μυριάδες, καταστὰς

[1] post Γαΐῳ lacunam indicat Dindorf.
[2] ed. pr.: αὐτῶν AE: αὐτῷ MW.
[3] ⟨τῆς⟩ ὀργῆς] Petersen: ὀργὴν codd.: ὀργῇ ed. pr.
[4] Petersen: φέροντος codd.
[5] ὀξέος Dindorf.
[6] ὀργὴν . . . ἐπιστολαῖς] om. E.
[7] Bekker: ἄψασθαι codd. E.

162

perhaps Gaius would relent and not adopt a cruel plan or have the heart to exterminate the nation. But if he remained firm in his present policy of war, let Petronius then proceed with operations. When Aristobulus and the rest appealed to Petronius along such lines, he was influenced by them, for they brought pressure to bear upon him in every way, since the question at issue was of such importance, and employed every device to make their plea effective. Furthermore, he beheld the stubborn determination of the Jews to resist and thought it a terrible thing to bring death upon so many tens of thousands of men in carrying out the mad orders of Gaius, and to hold them guilty for their reverence to God, and thus to spend the rest of his life in foreboding. He considered it far better to send a letter to Gaius and to endure the latter's inexorable wrath aroused by his not carrying out the orders at once.[a] Perhaps, moreover, he might even convince him. Nevertheless, if Gaius persisted in his original lunacy, he would undertake war against them. But if, after all, Gaius should turn some of his wrath against him, a man who made virtue his goal might well die on behalf of such a multitude of men. And so he decided to recognize the cogency of the plea of the petitioners.

(5) He now convened the Jews, who arrived in many tens of thousands, at Tiberias, stood up before

Petronius<br>decides to<br>write Gaius

---

[a] The text is very uncertain, though the meaning is clear from §§ 279-283. I have adopted Prof. Petersen's emendation. If αὐτῶν is retained, the meaning of the first part is " to send a letter to Gaius that they [the Jews] were beyond cure."

---

[8] ἐπιστείλας . . . ὀργῆς] ut scriberet Gaio et aut eius animum mitigans nihil per eum iniquum contingeret; aut si forsitan indignatione concitaretur, quod eius minime mandata compleverit et adversus eum aliquid mali decerneret Lat.

ἐπ' αὐτῶν τήν τε ἐν τῷ παρόντι στρατείαν οὐ
γνώμης ἀπέφαινε τῆς αὑτοῦ τοῦ δὲ αὐτοκράτορος
τῶν προσταγμάτων, τὴν ὀργὴν οὐδὲν εἰς ἀναβολάς,
ἀλλ' ἐκ τοῦ παραχρῆμα ἐπιφέρεσθαι τοῖς προστάγ-
μασι¹ τοῖς παρακροᾶσθαι θάρσος εἰσφερομένοις·
" ᾧ² καλῶς ἔχον ἐστὶν τόν γε τιμῆς τοσαύτης ἐπι-
τετευχότα συγχωρήσει τῇ ἐκείνου οὐδὲν ἐναντίον
280 πράσσειν· οὐ μὴν δίκαιον ἡγοῦμαι ἀσφάλειάν τε
καὶ τιμὴν τὴν ἐμαυτοῦ μὴ οὐχ ὑπὲρ τοῦ ὑμετέρου
μὴ ἀπολουμένου τοσούτων ὄντων ἀναλοῦν δια-
κονουμένων³ τῇ ἀρετῇ τοῦ νόμου, ὃν πάτριον ὄντα
περιμάχητον ἡγεῖσθε, καὶ τῇ ἐπὶ πᾶσιν ἀξιώσει καὶ
δυνάμει τοῦ θεοῦ, οὗ⁴ τὸν ναὸν οὐκ ἂν περιιδεῖν
τολμήσαιμι ὕβρει πεσεῖν τῆς τῶν ἡγεμονευόντων
281 ἐξουσίας. στέλλω δὲ ὡς Γάιον γνώμας τε τὰς
ὑμετέρας διασαφῶν καί πῃ καὶ συνηγορίᾳ χρώμενος
ὑπὲρ τοῦ καθ' ἡμᾶς παρὰ⁵ γνώμην πείσεσθαι⁶ οἷς⁷
προὔθεσθε ἀγαθοῖς.⁸ καὶ συμπράσσοι μὲν ὁ θεός,
βελτίων γὰρ ἀνθρωπίνης μηχανῆς καὶ δυνάμεως ἡ
κατ' ἐκεῖνον ἐξουσία, πρυτανεύων ὑμῖν τε τὴν τήρη-
σιν τῶν πατρίων καὶ αὐτῷ τὸ μηδὲν ἀνθρωπείαις
παρὰ γνώμην βουλεύσεσι τιμῶν τῶν εἰωθυιῶν ἁμαρ-
282 τεῖν. εἰ δ' ἐκπικρανθεὶς Γάιος εἰς ἐμὲ τρέψει τὸ

---

¹ τοῖς προστάγμασι] Thackeray : τοῖς πράγμασιν codd. om.
Bekker, Holwerda.
² ed. pr. : ὁ (i. ras. A) AMW.
³ Hudson et Cocceji : διακονούμενον codd.
⁴ Cocceji : om. codd.
⁵ παρὰ] μὴ παρὰ Holwerda.

them and explained that the present expedition was
not of his own choosing but by command of the
emperor, whose wrath would descend instantly and
without any delay upon those who assumed the
audacity to disobey his commands. " It is only right
that one upon whom such high position had been conferred by grant of the emperor should thwart him in
nothing. I do not, however," he said, " deem it
right not to hazard my own safety and position in
order to save you, who are so numerous, from perishing. You are carrying out the precepts of your law,
which as your heritage you see fit to defend, and
serving the sovereign of all, almighty God, whose
temple I should not have had the heart to see fall a
prey to the insolence of imperial authority. Rather
I am sending a dispatch to Gaius fully explaining
your determination and also in some way advocating
my own case for compliance, contrary to his decree,
with the good object which you have proposed.[a] May
God assist you, since His might is above any human
ingenuity or strength ; may He enable you to maintain and to preserve your ancestral laws without His
being deprived of His customary honours by capri-
cious human plots. If, however, Gaius is embittered
and makes me the object of his inexorable wrath, I

[a] Or (with Hudson) " advocating your cause so as not to see
you suffer for the good arguments that you proffered." Prof.
Post, reading ὑπὲρ τοῦ καθ' ὑμᾶς μὴ παρὰ γνώμην πεισομένου,
suggests " acting as your advocate to defend your refusal to
obey contrary to your judgement and your moral principles."

[6] Petersen : πεισομένην codd. : πεισομένου Cocceji : πειθο-
μένου coni. Niese.

[7] καθ' ἡμᾶς . . . οἷς] μὴ ὑμᾶς παρορᾶν πεισομένους ἐφ' οἷς
Hudson.

[8] καί πη . . . ἀγαθοῖς] quantum possum causam adiuvans
et vestrum in bono propositum Lat.

ἀνήκεστον τῆς ὀργῆς, τλήσομαι πάντα κίνδυνον καὶ
πᾶσαν ταλαιπωρίαν συνιοῦσαν τῷ σώματι καὶ τῇ
τύχῃ[1] ὑπὲρ τοῦ μὴ ὑμᾶς τοσούσδε ὄντας ἐπὶ οὕτως
283 ἀγαθαῖς ταῖς πράξεσι διολλυμένους θεωρεῖν. ἄπιτε
οὖν ἐπὶ ἔργα τὰ αὐτῶν ἕκαστοι καὶ τῇ γῇ ἐπι-
πονεῖτε. πέμψω δ' αὐτὸς ἐπὶ ῾Ρώμης καὶ τὰ
πάντα ὑπὲρ ὑμῶν δι' ἐμαυτοῦ καὶ τῶν φίλων οὐκ
ἀποτραπήσομαι διακονεῖν."

284 (6) Ταῦτα εἰπὼν καὶ διαλύσας τῶν Ἰουδαίων τὸν
σύλλογον προμηθεῖσθαι τῶν εἰς τὴν γεωργίαν ἠξίου
τοὺς ἐν τέλει καὶ καθομιλεῖν τὸν λαὸν ἐλπίσι χρη-
σταῖς. καὶ ὁ μὲν εὐθυμεῖν τὸ πλῆθος ἔσπευδεν. ὁ
θεὸς δὲ παρουσίαν[2] ἐπεδείκνυτο τὴν αὐτοῦ Πετρω-
285 νίῳ καὶ τὴν ἐπὶ τοῖς ὅλοις σύλληψιν· ἅμα τε γὰρ
ἐπαύετο τοῦ λόγου, ὃν πρὸς τοὺς Ἰουδαίους εἶπεν,
καὶ αὐτίκα ὑετὸν ἠφίει μέγαν παρ' ἐλπίδα τοῖς
ἀνθρώποις γενόμενον διὰ τὸ ἐκείνην τὴν ἡμέραν
αἴθριον ἕωθεν οὖσαν οὐδὲν ὄμβριον ἀποσημαίνειν ἐκ
τῶν περὶ τὸν οὐρανὸν καὶ τὸ πᾶν ἔτος αὐχμῷ μεγάλῳ κατεσχημένον ἐπ' ἀπογνώσει ποιεῖν τοὺς ἀνθρώπους ὕδατος τοῦ ἄνωθεν, εἰ καὶ σύννεφόν ποτε
286 θεάσαιντο τὸν οὐρανόν. ὥστε δὴ τότε πολλοῦ καὶ
παρὰ τὸ εἰωθὸς καὶ παρὰ τὸ ἑτέρῳ δόξαν ἀφιγμένου
ὕδατος τοῖς τε Ἰουδαίοις ἐλπὶς ἦν ἐπ' οὐδαμοῖς
ἀτυχήσειν Πετρώνιον ὑπὲρ αὐτῶν δεόμενον, ὅ τε
Πετρώνιος κατεπέπληκτο μειζόνως ὁρῶν ἐναργῶς
τὸν θεὸν τῶν Ἰουδαίων προμηθούμενον καὶ πολλὴν
ἀποσημήναντα τὴν ἐπιφάνειαν, ὡς μηδ' ἂν τοῖς
ἔργῳ προθεμένοις τἀναντία φρονεῖν ἰσχὺν ἀντι-

---

[1] καὶ τῇ τύχῃ] A : καὶ τῇ ψυχῇ WE : καὶ ψυχῇ M : om. Lat.
[2] E : praesentiam Lat. : παρρησίαν codd.

---

[a] Variant " soul."

will endure every form of danger and every form of
suffering that may be inflicted upon my body and my
fortune <sup>a</sup> rather than behold you who are so numerous destroyed for deeds so virtuous. Go, therefore,
each to your own occupation, and labour on the land.
I myself will send a message to Rome and will not
turn aside from doing every service in your behalf
both by myself and through my friends."

(6) With these words he dismissed the assembly of
the Jews and requested those in authority to attend
to agricultural matters and to conciliate the people
with optimistic propaganda. He thus did his best to
encourage the masses. God, on His part, showed
Petronius that He was with him <sup>b</sup> and would lend
His aid in all matters. For as soon as Petronius had
finished delivering this speech before the Jews, God
straightway sent a heavy shower <sup>c</sup> that was contrary
to general anticipation, for that day, from morning
on, had been clear and the sky had given no indication
of rain. Indeed, that entire year had been beset by
so great a drought that it caused the people to despair
of rainfall even if at any time they saw the sky over-
cast. The result was that, when much rain fell at
that moment exceptionally and unexpectedly, the
Jews were hopeful that Petronius would by no means
fail in his petition on their behalf. Petronius, on his
part, was struck with great amazement when he saw
unmistakable evidence that God's providence was
over the Jews and that He had shown His presence
so abundantly that not even those who actually proposed to take the opposite view <sup>d</sup> had any heart left

*Providential rainfall encourages the Jews.*

---

<sup>b</sup> MSS. " showed Petronius His frankness."

<sup>c</sup> The account of this shower is omitted in the parallel
passage in *B.J.* ii. 199-202.

<sup>d</sup> *i.e.* that God was *not* favourable to the Jews.

287 λέξεως καταλελεῖφθαι.¹ ὡς δὲ καὶ πρὸς τὸν Γάιον
σὺν τοῖς λοιποῖς ὁπόσα ἔγραφεν, ἐπαγωγὰ δὲ ἦν τὰ
πάντα² καὶ παντοίως παρακαλοῦντα μὴ τοσαύτας
μυριάδας ἀνθρώπων ἀπονοεῖν, ἃς εἰ κτείνοι, οὐ γὰρ
δίχα γε πολέμου παραχωρήσειν τοῦ νομίμου τῆς
θρησκείας, προσόδου τε τῆς ἀπ᾽ αὐτῶν ἀποστερεῖ-
σθαι καὶ τῷ ἀποτροπαίῳ³ τῆς ἀρᾶς ὑποτίθεσθαι τὸν
288 μέλλοντα αἰῶνα.⁴ κἄλλως θείου τοῦ προεστηκότος
αὐτῶν τὴν δύναμιν ὡς ἀκραιφνῆ ἀπέφαινεν καὶ μηδὲν ἐνδοιαστὸν ἐπὶ δυνάμει τῇ αὐτῆς ἐπιδείκνυσθαι
καταλείπουσαν. καὶ Πετρώνιος μὲν ἐν τούτοις ἦν.
289 (7) Ἀγρίππας δὲ ὁ βασιλεύς, ἐτύγχανεν γὰρ ἐπὶ
Ῥώμης διαιτώμενος, προὔκοπτε φιλίᾳ τῇ πρὸς τὸν
Γάιον μειζόνως. καί ποτε προθεὶς δεῖπνον αὐτῷ
καὶ πρόνοιαν ἔχων πάντας ὑπερβαλέσθαι τέλεσί τε
τοῖς εἰς τὸ δεῖπνον καὶ παρασκευῇ τοῦ εἰς ἡδονὴν
290 φέροντος, ὡς μὴ ὅπως ἄν τινα τῶν λοιπῶν, ἀλλὰ
μηδ᾽ αὐτὸν Γάιον πιστεύειν⁵ ποτε ἰσωθῆναι θελή-
σοντα οὐχ ὅπως ὑπερβαλέσθαι· τοσοῦτον ὁ ἀνὴρ
τῇ παρασκευῇ πάντας ὑπερῆρεν καὶ τῷ τὰ πάντα
291 Καίσαρι⁶ ἐκφροντίσας⁷ παρασχεῖν.⁸ καὶ ὁ Γάιος

¹ ante ὡς lacunam statuit Hudson : post ἔγραφεν lacunam
statuit Dindorf.
² γράμματα coni. Niese.
³ Cocceji : τροπαίῳ codd. : ἀποτροπῇ coni. Thackeray (cf.
Ant. xix. 268).
⁴ καὶ τῷ . . . αἰῶνα] memoriam etiam non bonam Romani
nominis in posteriora tempora derelinqui Lat. : καὶ τὸ Ῥωμαίων ὄνομα τῇ ἀρᾷ ὑποτίθεσθαι ⟨εἰς⟩ τὸν μέλλοντα αἰῶνα coni.
Richards et Shutt ex Lat.
⁵ A : om. MW Exc.
⁶ Καίσαρι] Hudson : Καίσαρος MW Exc. : ἢ Καίσαρος AE.
⁷ A : i. marg. γρ ἐκφορτίσας A : ἐκφροντίσαι MW Exc. : ἐκ-
φροντίσει ed. pr.
⁸ τοσοῦτον . . . παρασχεῖν] om. Lat.

to dispute the fact. He included [a] this occurrence along with the other things of which he wrote to Gaius. It was all designed to induce him and entreat him in every way not to drive so many tens of thousands of men to desperation. For if he should slay them—and they would certainly not give up their accustomed manner of worship without war—he would be deprived of their revenue and would be put under the ban of a curse for all time to come. He said, moreover, that the Divinity who was in charge of them had shown His power to be unimpaired and was quite unambiguous in displaying this power. So much for Petronius.

(7) Meanwhile King Agrippa,[b] who, as it happened, was living in Rome, advanced greatly in friendship with Gaius. Once he made a banquet for him with the intention of surpassing everyone both in the expenditure on the banquet and in provision for the pleasure of the guests. He was so successful that, to say nothing of the others, even Gaius himself despaired of equalling, much less surpassing it, if he should desire to do so. So far did this man surpass everyone in his preparations and in devising and providing everything for the emperor. Gaius thoroughly

Agrippa at Rome advances in favour with Galus.

[a] There appears to be a lacuna in this sentence, though the meaning seems clear.

[b] In Philo, *Leg.* 276-329, Agrippa is depicted as unaware of the emperor's order to Petronius, about which he learns from Caligula himself. He is taken aback by the announcement and faints. After recovering, he writes at length to the emperor urging him to follow the example of his predecessors and to show tolerance towards the Jews. There is no mention of a banquet, a setting which is reminiscent of the seventh chapter of the Book of Esther, where Esther makes a plea on behalf of her people to King Ahasuerus, who is ready to offer her half his kingdom.

ἐκθαυμάσας τήν τε διάνοιαν αὐτοῦ καὶ τὴν μεγαλο-
πρέπειαν, ὡς ἐπ' ἀρεσκείᾳ τῇ αὐτοῦ βιάζοιτο καὶ
ὑπὲρ δύναμιν τῶν χρημάτων εὐπορίᾳ χρήσασθαι,
βουλόμενός τε μιμήσασθαι τὴν Ἀγρίππου φιλο-
τιμίαν ἐφ' ἡδονῇ τῇ αὐτοῦ πρασσομένην, ἀνειμένος
ὑπὸ οἴνου καὶ τὴν διάνοιαν εἰς τὸ ἱλαρώτερον ἐκτε-
τραμμένος, φησὶν ἐν συμποσίῳ παρακαλοῦντος εἰς
292 πότον· '' Ἀγρίππα, καὶ πρότερον μέν σοι τιμὴν
συνῄδειν ᾗ ἐχρῶ τὰ πρὸς ἐμὲ καὶ πολλὴν εὔνοιαν
μετὰ κινδύνων ἀποδειχθεῖσαν, οἷς ὑπὸ Τιβερίου
περιέστης δι' αὐτήν, ἐπιλείπεις τε οὐδὲν καὶ ὑπὲρ
δύναμιν ἀρετῇ χρῆσθαι τῇ πρὸς ἡμᾶς. ὅθεν, αἰσ-
χρὸν γὰρ ἡσσᾶσθαί με ὑπὸ τῆς σῆς σπουδῆς, ἀνα-
293 λαβεῖν βούλομαι τὰ ἐλλελειμμένα πρότερον· ὀλίγον
γὰρ πᾶν ὁπόσον σοι δωρεῶν ἐχόμενον ἀπεμοιρασά-
μην. τὸ πᾶν, ὅπερ σοι ῥοπὴν ἂν προσθείη τοῦ
εὐδαίμονος, δεδιακονήσεται γάρ σοι προθυμίᾳ τε
καὶ ἰσχύι τῇ ἐμῇ.'' καὶ ὁ μὲν ταῦτα ἔλεγεν οἰόμενος γῆν τε πολλὴν[1] τῆς προσόρου[2] αἰτήσεσθαι[3] ἢ
294 καί τινων προσόδους πόλεων, ὁ δὲ καίπερ τὰ πάντα
ἐφ' οἷς αἰτῆσαι παρασκευασάμενος οὐκ ἐφανέρου
τὴν διάνοιαν, ἀλλ' ἐκ τοῦ ὀξέος ἀμείβεται τὸν
Γάιον, ὅτι μήτε πρότερον κέρδος τὸ ἀπ' αὐτοῦ
καραδοκῶν παρὰ τὰς Τιβερίου ἐπιστολὰς θερα-
πεύσειεν αὐτὸν οὔτε νῦν πράσσειν τι τῶν εἰς χάριν
295 τὴν ἐκείνου κερδῶν οἰκείων ἔν τισι λήψεσι. μεγάλα
δὲ εἶναι τὰ προδεδωρημένα καὶ περαιτέρω τοῦ θράσει χρωμένου τῶν ἐλπίδων· '' καὶ γὰρ εἰ τῆς σῆς
ἐλάττονα γέγονεν δυνάμεως, τῆς γ' ἐμοῦ τοῦ εἰλη-

---

[1] γῆν τε πολλὴν] A : τήν τε πόλιν MW Exc. : τήν τε πολλὴν E.
[2] τῆς προσόρου] E : τῆς προσόδου codd. : om. ed. pr.

admired his ingenuity and magnificence and his forcible way of employing, in order to give him pleasure,
an abundance of money even beyond his means.
Gaius therefore wished to imitate the ambitious display that Agrippa had made to please him. Hence
while he was relaxed with wine and while his mood
was unusually genial, he said during the banquet
when Agrippa invited him to drink : " Agrippa, I
have known in my heart before how highly you regarded me and how you have proved your great
loyalty even amidst the dangers with which, because
of it, you were encircled by Tiberius. And now you
never fail to show kindness to us, going even beyond
your means. Consequently, inasmuch as it would be
a stain on my honour to let you outdo me in zeal, I
wish to make amends for past deficiencies. Indeed, Gaius' offer
all the gifts that I have allotted to you are but slight to grant
in amount ; any service that can add its weight in any request.
the scale of prosperity shall be performed for you Agrippa
with all my heart and power." He spoke these words
thinking that Agrippa would ask for a large accession
of territory adjoining his own or for the revenues of
certain cities. As for Agrippa, although he was quite
ready to make his request, he did not reveal his intention. On the contrary, he at once replied to
Gaius that it was not in expectation of any benefit
from him that he had in the past paid court to him in
spite of Tiberius' orders ; nor were any of his present
activities in giving him pleasure designed as a road to
personal gain. He said that the gifts that Gaius had
already presented to him were great and went beyond
any expectations that he would dare to cherish. " For
even if they have been inferior to your capacity, they

---

³ Hudson : αἰτήσασθαι codd. E Exc.

296 φότος διανοίας τε καὶ ἀξιώσεως μείζονα.'' καὶ ὁ
Γάιος ἐκπλαγεὶς τὴν ἀρετὴν¹ αὐτοῦ πλειόνως ἐνέ-
κειτο εἰπεῖν, ὅ τι χαρίζοιτ' ἂν αὐτῷ παρασχόμενος.
ὁ δέ, '' ἐπεί περ, ὦ δέσποτα, προθυμίᾳ τῇ σῇ δωρεῶν ἄξιον ἀποφαίνεις, αἰτήσομαι τῶν μὲν εἰς ὄλβον
φερόντων οὐδὲν διὰ τὸ μεγάλως με ἐνδιαπρέπειν
297 οἷς ἤδη παρέσχες· ὅ τι δ' ἂν σοὶ δόξαν προσποιοῖ²
τοῦ εὐσεβοῦς καὶ τὸ θεῖον σύμμαχον ἐφ' οἷς θελή-
σειας παρακαλοῖ³ κἀμοὶ πρὸς εὐκλείας γένοιτο παρὰ
τοῖς πυνθανομένοις, ὡς μηθενὸς ὢν χρησαίμην ὑπὸ
τῆς σῆς ἐξουσίας ἀτυχεῖν πώποτε γνόντι⁴· ἀξιῶ
γάρ σοι τοῦ ἀνδριάντος τὴν ἀνάθεσιν, ἣν ποιήσασθαι κελεύεις Πετρώνιον εἰς τὸ Ἰουδαίων ἱερόν,
μηκέτι πράσσειν διανοεῖσθαι.''

298 (8) Καὶ ὁ μὲν καίπερ ἐπικίνδυνον τοῦτο ἡγούμενος, εἰ γὰρ μὴ πιθανὰ ἔκρινε Γάιος, οὐδὲν ἄλλο ἢ
ἐς θάνατον ἔφερεν, διὰ τὸ μεγάλα νομίζειν τε καὶ
εἶναι κύβον ἀναρριπτεῖν τὸν ἐπ' αὐτοῖς ἡγεῖτο·
299 Γάιος δὲ⁵ ἅμα τε τῇ θεραπείᾳ τοῦ Ἀγρίππου ἀνει-
λημμένος καὶ ἄλλως ἀπρεπὲς ὑπολαμβάνων ἐπὶ
τοσῶνδε μαρτύρων ψευδὴς γενέσθαι περὶ ὧν προθύμως ἐβιάζετο αἰτεῖσθαι τὸν Ἀγρίππαν μετὰ τοῦ
300 ὀξέος μεταμέλῳ χρώμενος, ἅμα δὲ καὶ τοῦ Ἀγρίππου τὴν ἀρετὴν θαυμάσας ὅτι ἐν ὀλίγῳ ⟨θέμενος⟩⁶
αὔξειν⁷ τὴν οἰκείαν ἀρχὴν ἤτοι προσόδοις χρημάτων
ἢ ἄλλῃ δυνάμει τοῦ κοινοῦ⁸ τῆς εὐθυμίας ἐπιμελοῖτο

---

¹ Α : διάνοιαν MW Exc. et i. marg. A : continentiam Lat.
² Niese : προσποιῇ codd. E Exc.
³ Niese : παρακαλῶ codd. Exc. : παρακαλῇ Bekker.
⁴ ὡς . . . γνόντι] quod nihil a te petierim ad usus pertinens
temporalium rerum Lat. : γνόντι corruptum indicat Niese.
⁵ δὲ] WE : δὲ καὶ AM.
⁶ ⟨ὅτι⟩ ἐν ὀλίγῳ ⟨θέμενος⟩] Petersen : ἐν ὀλίγῳ codd. : ὅτι ἐν

exceed my thoughts and my claims as a recipient."
Gaius, amazed at his character, insisted all the more
on his telling what he might grant to please him.
Agrippa replied : " Since, my lord, in your kindness
you declare me worthy of gifts, I shall ask for nothing that would make me richer inasmuch as I am
already extremely conspicuous because of the gifts
that you have hitherto bestowed upon me. But I
shall ask for something that will bring you a reputation for piety and will induce the Deity to help you
in everything that you wish ; and it will bring me the
renown, among those who hear of it, of never having
known failure in anything that I desired your authority to obtain for me. Well, I ask you to abandon all
further thought of erecting the statue which Petronius
has your orders to set up in the temple of the Jews."

(8) Hazardous as he considered this petition—for
if Gaius did not regard it with favour, it would bring
him certain death—yet, because he thought the issue
important, as it truly was, he chose to make the
gamble on this occasion. Gaius was bound by
Agrippa's attentions to him. Furthermore, if he repented quickly of his offer, he regarded it as unseemly
to break his word before so many witnesses, when he
had by his zealous constraint compelled Agrippa to
make his request. At the same time he admired the
character of Agrippa in that he set little store on
adding to his personal authority either by increasing
his revenue or by other privileges, but had regard to
the happiness of the commonwealth, by giving prece-

*Marginal note:* Agrippa persuades Gaius to desist from setting up the statue.

---

ὀλίγῳ Cocceji : post ὀλίγῳ lacunam indicat Ernesti, excidit
θοῖτο vel aliud : post θαυμάσας ⟨εἰ ποιοῖτο⟩ vel sim. coni.
Thackeray : ποιούμενος supplet Bekker.
   [7] ἐν ὀλίγῳ αὔξειν] quod . . . non . . . amplificare cupi-
verit Lat.         [8] κοινοῦ] MWE Exc. : κοινοῦ δὲ A.

πρεσβεύων τοὺς νόμους καὶ τὸ θεῖον, συνεχώρει καὶ
γράφει πρὸς τὸν Πετρώνιον, ἐκεῖνον τῆς τε ἀθροί-
σεως τοῦ στρατεύματος ἐπαινῶν καὶ τοῦ πρὸς
301 αὐτὸν περὶ αὐτῶν ἐπεσταλκότος· " νῦν οὖν εἰ μὲν
φθάνεις τὸν ἀνδριάντα ἑστακώς, ἑστάτω[1]· εἰ δὲ
μήπω πεποίησαι τὴν ἀνάθεσιν, μηδὲν περαιτέρω
κακοπαθεῖν, ἀλλὰ τόν τε στρατὸν διάλυε καὶ αὐτὸς
ἐφ' ἃ τὸ πρῶτόν σε ἔστειλα ἄπιθι· οὐδὲν γὰρ ἔτι
δέομαι τῆς ἀναστάσεως τοῦ ἀνδριάντος Ἀγρίππᾳ
χαριζόμενος ἀνδρὶ παρ' ἐμοὶ τιμωμένῳ μειζόνως ἢ
ὥστε με χρείᾳ τῇ ἐκείνου καὶ οἷς κελεύσειεν ἀντει-
302 πεῖν." Γάιος μὲν δὴ ταῦτα γράφει πρὸς τὸν Πετρώνιον πρότερον ἢ ἐντυχεῖν ἐπὶ ἀποστάσει καταδοξάσας αὐτοὺς[2] ἐπείγεσθαι,[3] μηδὲν γὰρ ἕτερον
ἀποσημαίνειν τὴν διάνοιαν αὐτῶν, ἀλλὰ πόλεμον
303 ἄντικρυς Ῥωμαίοις ἀπειλεῖν.[4] καὶ περιαλγήσας
ὡς ἐπὶ πείρᾳ τῆς ἡγεμονίας αὐτοῦ τετολμηκότων,
ἀνὴρ ἐπὶ πᾶσιν ἥσσων μὲν τοῦ αἰσχροῦ, κρείσσων
δὲ τοῦ βελτίστου καὶ ἐφ' οἷστισι κρίνειεν ὀργῇ
χρῆσθαι παρ' ὁντινοῦν ἐπειγόμενος παιδεύσειν αὐτῆς
οὐδ' ἡντινοῦν προστιθείς, ἀλλ' ἐφ' ἡδονῇ τιθεὶς τῇ

---

[1] ἑστάτω] μὴ ἑστάτω Clementz.

[2] καταδοξάσας αὐτοὺς] Thackeray : καταδόξας αὐτοὺς A :
αὐτοὺς κατὰ δόξας MW : διὰ τὸν ἀνδριάντα Zonaras.

[3] ἐντυχεῖν . . . ἐπείγεσθαι] ἐντυχεῖν ταῖς αὐτοῦ ἐπιστολαῖς ἐμ-
φαινούσαις ἐπὶ ἀποστασίᾳ τοὺς Ἰουδαίους κατὰ δόξας αὐτοὺς ἐπείγεσθαι E, lacuna ex coniectura expleta : lacunam post ἐντυχεῖν
indicat Niese.

[4] πρότερον . . . ἀπειλεῖν] antequam seditio maior oreretur ;
nam ita iam mentes omnium tumebant, atque talia volun-
tatum eorum indicia monstrabantur, ut si forte contrarius
nuntius adveniret parati essent apertum bellum gerere cum
Romanis Lat.

dence to religion and the law. So he yielded and
wrote to Petronius commending him for having
assembled his army and for having sent him his dispatch on the subject. " Now, therefore," he said,
" if you have already set up my statue, let it stand.[a]
If, however, you have not yet dedicated it, do not
trouble yourself further but dismiss the army and
betake yourself to those matters for which I originally
dispatched you. For I no longer require the erection
of the statue, showing favour to Agrippa in this, a
man whom I hold in too high esteem to gainsay his
request and his bidding." Gaius had written this to
Petronius before reading the latter's message from
which he wrongly concluded that the Jews were bent
on revolt [b] and that their attitude indicated no other
intent than a threat of downright war against the
Romans. Upon receiving this letter, he was in agony
at the thought that they had dared to put his authority to the test. Since he was a man who always
yielded to baseness but was strong in resisting the
claim of an ideal, one who beyond all others rushed
into a rage against anyone who came under his censure, exercising no control over it whatsoever but
considering the pleasure derived from indulging it

Petronius'
letter to
Gaius
arrives.

[a] H. Clementz, in his German translation of Josephus,
says that the meaning must be " let it not stand " since otherwise the promise of Gaius to Agrippa would not be fulfilled.
But since Agrippa had asked that Gaius abandon all *further*
thought of erecting the statue, Gaius could sophistically have
claimed that his message to Petronius was in accordance with
the promise, and that Agrippa had not requested that he
*remove* the statue.
[b] The text is doubtful. If we follow the reading of the
Epitome, the meaning would be " before reading Petronius'
letters which showed that the Jews were in thought already
bent on revolt."

ἐκείνης τὴν κρίσιν τοῦ εὐδαίμονος, γράφει πρὸς τὸν
304 Πετρώνιον· '' ἐπειδὴ δῶρα ὁπόσα σοι οἱ Ἰουδαῖοι
παρέσχον ἐν μείζονι λόγῳ τῶν ἐμῶν πεποίησαι ἐντολῶν διακονεῖσθαι τὰ πάντα ἡδονῇ τῇ ἐκείνων
ἀρθεὶς ἐπὶ παραβάσει τῶν ἐμῶν ἐντολῶν, κελεύω
σε σαυτῷ κριτὴν γενόμενον λογίσασθαι περὶ τοῦ
ποιητέου σοι ὑποστάντα¹ ὀργῇ τῇ ἐμῇ, ἐπεί τοι
παράδειγμα ποιοῖτό σε οἵ τε νῦν πάντες² καὶ ὁπόσοι ὕστεροι γένοιντ᾽ ἄν,³ μηδαμῶς ἀκυροῦν αὐτοκράτορος ἀνδρὸς ἐντολάς.''

305 (9) Ταύτην μὲν γράφει Πετρωνίῳ τὴν ἐπιστολήν,
οὐ μὴν φθάνει γε ζῶντος Πετρώνιος δεξάμενος
αὐτὴν βραδυνθέντος τοῦ πλοῦ τοῖς φέρουσιν εἰς
τοσόνδε, ὥστε Πετρωνίῳ γράμματα πρὸ αὐτῆς
ἀφικέσθαι, δι᾽ ὧν μανθάνει τὴν Γαΐου τελευτήν.
306 θεὸς γὰρ οὐκ ἄρ᾽ ἀμνημονήσειν ἔμελλε Πετρωνίῳ
κινδύνων, οὓς ἀνειλήφει ἐπὶ τῇ τῶν Ἰουδαίων
χάριτι καὶ τιμῇ τῇ αὑτοῦ, ἀλλὰ τὸν Γάιον ἀποσκευασάμενος ὀργῆς ὧν ἐπὶ σεβασμῷ τῷ αὑτοῦ
πράσσειν ἐτόλμησε, τὸν μισθὸν χρεολυτεῖν.⁴ συν-
εργεῖ⁵ τῷ Πετρωνίῳ ἥ τε Ῥώμη καὶ πᾶσα ἡ ἀρχή,
μάλιστα δ᾽ ὁπόσοι τῆς βουλῆς προύχοιεν ἀξιώματι,
διὰ τὸ εἰς ἐκείνους ἀκράτῳ τῇ ὀργῇ χρῆσθαι τὸν

---

¹ ὑποστάντι Bekker : ὑπεκστάντα coni. Niese.
² ποιοῦντό . . . πάντες] codd. : ποιοῖμι (ποιοῖμ᾽ E) ἄν σε τοῖς
τε νῦν πᾶσι E et i. marg. A.
³ ἐπεί τοι . . . γένοιτ᾽ ἄν] ut exemplum efficiare cunctis et
praesentibus et futuris Lat.
⁴ lacunam post χρεολυτεῖν indicat Niese.

his criterion of happiness, he wrote to Petronius as
follows : " Since you have held the gifts that the Gaius'
Jews have bestowed upon you in higher regard than angry letter to
my orders and have presumed to minister in every- Petronius is
thing to their pleasure in violation of my orders, I bid Gaius'
you act as your own judge and consider what course death.
it is your duty to take, since you have brought my
displeasure upon yourself. For I assure you that
you shall be cited as an example by all men now and
all that will come hereafter to point the moral that
an emperor's commands are never to be flouted." [a]

(9) Such was the letter that he wrote to Petronius.
But Petronius did not receive it while Gaius was
alive since the voyage of those who brought the message was so delayed that before it arrived Petronius
had received a letter with news of the death of Gaius.[b]
Indeed, God could never have been unmindful of the
risks that Petronius had taken in showing favour to
the Jews and honouring God. No, the removal of
Gaius in displeasure at his rashness in promoting his
own claim to worship was God's payment of the debt
to Petronius. In fact, Rome and all the empire, and
especially those of the senators who were outstanding
in merit, favoured Petronius, since Gaius had vented
his wrath against them without mercy. And so

[a] The parallel passage in *B.J.* omits the whole account of
Agrippa's intercession with Caligula and merely mentions
(ii. 203) Gaius' angry reply threatening to put Petronius to
death for his tardiness in executing his orders.
[b] Gaius died on 24 January A.D. 41. According to the
parallel passage, *B.J.* ii. 203, those who bore Gaius' letter to
Petronius were weather-bound for three months at sea and
arrived twenty-seven days after those who brought news of
Gaius' death.

---

[5] MW : συνενεργετεῖν A : συνενεργετεῖται coni. Niese.

307 Γάιον.¹ καὶ τελευτᾷ μὲν οὐ μετὰ πολὺν χρόνον ἢ
γράψαι τῷ Πετρωνίῳ τὴν ἐπὶ τῷ θανεῖν ἀνακειμένην ἐπιστολήν, τὴν δ' αἰτίαν, ἐξ ἧς τελευτᾷ, καὶ
τῆς ἐπιβουλῆς τὸν τρόπον ἀφηγήσομαι προϊόντος
308 τοῦ λόγου. Πετρωνίῳ δὲ προτέρα μὲν παρῆν ἡ
διασαφοῦσα τοῦ Γαίου τὴν τελευτὴν ἐπιστολή, μετ'
οὐ πολὺ δὲ ἡ κελεύουσα αὐτὸν τελευτᾶν αὐτόχειρα,
καὶ ἤσθη τε τῇ συντυχίᾳ τοῦ ὀλέθρου, ὃς τὸν Γάιον
309 κατέλαβεν, καὶ τοῦ θεοῦ τὴν πρόνοιαν ἐξεθαύμασεν
οὐδὲν εἰς ἀναβολὰς ἀλλ' ἐκ τοῦ ὀξέος μισθὸν αὐτῷ
τιμῆς τε τῆς εἰς τὸν ναὸν καὶ βοηθείας τῆς Ἰουδαίων σωτηρίας παρασχομένου.² καὶ Πετρωνίῳ
μὲν οὕτως μὴ ἂν τοπασθεὶς³ διεφεύχθη ῥᾳδίως ὁ
κίνδυνος τοῦ θανεῖν.

310 (ix. 1) Γίνεται δὲ καὶ περὶ τοὺς ἐν τῇ Μεσοπο-
ταμίᾳ καὶ μάλιστα τὴν Βαβυλωνίαν οἰκοῦντας
Ἰουδαίους συμφορὰ δεινὴ καὶ οὐδεμιᾶς ἧστινος
ἐλάσσων φόνος τε αὐτῶν πολὺς καὶ ὁπόσος οὐχ
ἱστορημένος πρότερον. περὶ ὧν δὴ τὰ πάντα ἐπ'
ἀκριβὲς διηγησάμενος ἐκθήσομαι καὶ τὰς αἰτίας,
311 ἀφ' ὧν αὐτοῖς τὸ πάθος συνέτυχεν. Νέαρδα⁴ τῆς
Βαβυλωνίας ἐστὶ πόλις ἄλλως τε πολυανδροῦσα καὶ

¹ ἀλλὰ . . . Γάιον] sed Gaium de medio auferens mercedem
illi dignam pro illius impietate restituit, cooperatus est autem
Petronio ; nam tanta illi dilectio comparata est tam Romae
quam in unoquoque regno, ut dei gratia super eum evidens
appareret [ut . . . appareret om. cod. A]. Romae namque
omnes senatorii ordinis et quotquot dignitatibus eminebant
tam virtutis merito quam odio Gai, quod propter crudelitatem
iniquitatemque concaeperant, circa Petronium magno favore
ferebantur Lat.
² Hudson : παρασχόμενον codd.

Gaius died not long after having written to Petronius this letter consigning him to death [a]; the cause of Gaius' death and the manner in which the plot was formulated I shall relate in the course of my work.[b] Thus Petronius first received the letter which reported clearly the death of Gaius, and, not long afterwards, the one which ordered him to take his life with his own hand. He rejoiced at the coincidence that Gaius' disaster came when it did, and marvelled at the providence of God, who swiftly and punctually had paid him his reward for showing honour to the temple and coming to the rescue of the Jews. Thus for Petronius the menace of death was easily dispelled in a manner that could hardly have been foreseen.

(ix. 1) The Jews of Mesopotamia and especially those inhabiting Babylonia now met with a terrible and unparalleled disaster and were massacred in such numbers as never before in recorded history. I shall tell the whole story in detail, setting forth also the causes that were the occasion of their misfortune. Nearda [c] is a city in Babylonia that is not only populous but also possesses a rich and extensive district,

The Jews in Babylonia. Their treasure cities. Nearda and Nisibis.

---

[a] The parallel passage, *B.J.* ii. 203, says that Gaius merely threatened to put Petronius to death.

[b] *Ant.* xix. 15-114.

[c] Not far from Sippar and near the junction of the Euphrates and the *Nahr Malka*—the " King's Canal," which made the city difficult to attack : *cf.* Bab. *Kiddushin* 70 b, *Shabbat* 108 b. It is to be identified with Nehardea, the seat, in Talmudic times, of the exilarch and of a famous academy headed by Samuel in the third century.

---

[3] οὕτως μὴ ἂν τοπασθείς] A : οὕτως μὴ ἀντοπϊσθείς M : οὕτως μὴ ἀντοπιθείς W : οὕτως μὴ αὐτῷ ὀφθείς Hudson : τρόπον μὴ προὑπτὸν coni. Richards et Shutt.

[4] Νέαρδα] Νεαρδὰ MW : Νεέρδα A : Νεερδὰ E : Neerda Lat. : Νάαρδα apud Steph. Byz. vocatur.

χώραν ἀγαθὴν καὶ πολλὴν ἔχουσα καὶ σὺν ἄλλοις
ἀγαθοῖς καὶ ἀνθρώπων ἀνάπλεων.¹ ἔστιν δὲ καὶ
πολεμίοις οὐκ εὐέμβολος περιόδῳ τε τοῦ Εὐφράτου
πᾶσαν ἐντὸς αὐτὴν ἀπολαμβάνοντος καὶ κατα-
312 σκευαῖς τειχῶν. ἔστιν δὲ καὶ Νίσιβις² πόλις κατὰ
τὸν αὐτὸν τοῦ ποταμοῦ περίρρουν, ὅθεν Ἰουδαῖοι
τῇ φύσει τῶν χωρίων πεπιστευκότες τό τε δίδραχ-
μον, ὃ τῷ θεῷ καταβάλλειν ἑκάστοις πάτριον,
ταύτῃ κατετίθεντο καὶ ὁπόσα δὲ ἄλλα ἀναθήματα,
ἐχρῶντό τε ὥσπερ ταμιείῳ ταῖσδε ταῖς πόλεσιν.
313 ἐντεῦθεν δὲ ἐπὶ Ἱεροσολύμων ἀνεπέμπετο ᾗ καιρός,
πολλαί τε ἀνθρώπων μυριάδες τὴν κομιδὴν τῶν
χρημάτων παρελάμβανον δεδιότες τὰς Παρθυαίων
ἁρπαγὰς ὑποτελούσης ἐκείνοις τῆς Βαβυλωνίας.³
314 καὶ ἦσαν γὰρ Ἀσιναῖος καὶ Ἀνιλαῖος Νεερδᾶται
μὲν τὸ γένος, ἀλλήλων δὲ ἀδελφοί. καὶ αὐτούς,
πατρὸς δ᾽ ἦσαν ὀρφανοί, ἡ μήτηρ προσέταξεν ἱσ-
τῶν⁴ μαθήσει ποιήσεως,⁵ οὐκ ὄντος ἀπρεποῦς τοῖς
ἐπιχωρίοις ὥστε τοὺς ἄνδρας ταλασιουργεῖν⁶ παρ᾽
αὐτοῖς. τούτοις ὁ τοῖς ἔργοις ἐφεστώς, καὶ γὰρ

---

¹ Hudson (ex Lat.) : ἀνάπλεως codd.
² AM : Νίσιβης (η minus clarum) W : Nesebis (Nesibis
cod. Canon.) Lat.
³ δεδιότες . . . Βαβυλωνίας] om. Lat.    ⁴ ἱστίων Naber.
⁵ ἱστῶν . . . ποιήσεως] ut navium operarentur velamina Lat.
⁶ ταλασιουργεῖν] ut . . . exerceantur operibus quae usui
marino proficiant Lat. (h.e. θαλασσουργεῖν).

---

ᵃ Apparently to be distinguished from the more famous
city in north-eastern Babylonia, since, as noted by J. Sturm,
" Nisibis," no. 3, Pauly-Wissowa, xvii¹, 1936, p. 757, Josephus' city is on an island in the Euphrates near Nearda,
whereas the other Nisibis is between the Tigris and the
Euphrates.
ᵇ The equivalent of the half shekel (Ex. xxx. 13) paid by
all Jews twenty or more years of age.

which, in addition to its other advantages, is also thickly settled. It is, moreover, not easily exposed to hostile invasion because it is entirely encompassed by a bend of the Euphrates and the construction of walls. There is also a city Nisibis *a* situated on the same bend of the river. The Jews, in consequence, trusting to the natural strength of these places, used to deposit there the two-drachm coins *b* which it is the national custom for all to contribute to the cause of God, as well as any other dedicatory offerings. Thus these cities were their bank of deposit. From there these offerings were sent to Jerusalem at the appropriate time. Many tens of thousands of Jews shared in the convoy of these monies because they feared the raids of the Parthians, to whom Babylonia was subject. Now there were two brothers, Asinaeus and Anilaeus, who were natives of Nearda. Since they had lost their father, their mother apprenticed *c* them to learn the weaving trade, for it is not considered undignified by the inhabitants of that country for men to spin wool.*d* The man in charge of their

The brothers Asinaeus and Anilaeus, being outraged, collect a robber band.

---

*c* On the normal conditions of apprenticeship in Palestine and Babylonia see S. Krauss, *Talmudische Archäologie*, ii, 1911, pp. 255-256.

*d* On weaving as a disgraceful occupation see Mishnah, *Eduyoth* i. 3, which states that there is no craft lower than that of a weaver, and Bab. *Baba Batra* 21 a, where the word used is clearly derived from γερδιός, " weaver." See, in general, Krauss, *op. cit.* i, 1910, pp. 149 and 560 notes 271-275, who quotes (p. 560 n. 273) the proverb emanating from Babylonia and given in *Abodah Zarah* 26 a : " A year's scanty earnings will alter [improve] a weaver if he be not a proud fool." F. M. Heichelheim, " Roman Syria," in T. Frank, *An Economic Survey of Ancient Rome*, iv, 1938, p. 191, notes that Borsippa and Nearda in Babylonia produced large quantities of linen and woollen goods (*cf.* Strabo xvi. 39, which he cites). The Latin version interprets our passage

ἐμεμαθήκεσαν παρ' αὐτῷ, βραδυτῆτα ἐπικαλέσας
315 τῆς ἀφίξεως ἐκόλασε πληγαῖς. οἱ δὲ ἐφ' ὕβρει τὴν
δικαίωσιν λογιζόμενοι, κατασπάσαντες τῶν ὅπλων
πολλὰ ὁπόσα ἦν ἐπὶ τῆς οἰκίας φυλασσόμενα
ᾤχοντο εἴς τι χωρίον, διάρρηξιν μὲν ποταμῶν λεγόμενον,[1] νομὰς δὲ ἀγαθὰς παρασχεῖν πεφυκὸς καὶ
χιλὸν ὁπόσοι[2] εἰς τὸν χειμῶνα ἀποτιθοῖντο. συν-
ῄεσάν τε ὡς αὐτοὺς τῶν νέων οἱ ἀπορώτατοι, καὶ
τούτους τοῖς ὅπλοις φραγνύντες στρατηγοί τε ἦσαν
καὶ τῶν κακῶν ἡγεμόνες οὐκ ἐκωλύοντο εἶναι.
316 προελθόντες γὰρ ἐπὶ τὸ ἄμαχον καὶ κατασκευά-
σαντες ἀκρόπολιν διέπεμπον πρὸς τοὺς νεμοντας
φόρον αὐτοῖς κελεύοντες καταβάλλειν τῶν βοσκημάτων, ἢ ἀρκοῦσα ἐπιτροφὴ γίνοιτ' ἄν, προστιθέντες
φιλίαν τε πειθομένοις καὶ ἄμυναν τῶν ἀλλαχόθεν
ποθὲν πολεμίων, σφαγὰς δὲ τῶν ποιμνίων ἀπειθοῦ-
317 σιν. οἱ δέ, οὐ γὰρ ἦν ἕτερα παρ' αὐτὰ ποιεῖν,
ἠκροῶντο καὶ τῶν προβάτων ἔστελλον ὁπόσα
κελευσθεῖεν, ὥστε δὴ καὶ πλείων αὐτοῖς συνελέγετο
ἰσχὺς κύριοί τε ἦσαν ἐφ' οἷς βουλεύσειαν ἐκ τοῦ
ὀξέος ἐλαύνοντες κακουργεῖν. θεραπεύειν τε αὐτοὺς
ἤρκτο[3] πᾶς προστυγχάνων, καὶ ἦσαν φοβεροὶ καὶ
τοῖς πειρασομένοις, ὥστ' ἤδη προὔκοπτε λόγος περὶ
αὐτῶν κἀπὶ τοῦ Πάρθων βασιλέως.
318    (2) Ὁ δὲ τῆς Βαβυλωνίας σατράπης μαθὼν ταῦτα
καὶ βουληθεὶς ἔτι φυομένους[4] κωλῦσαι πρίν τι μεῖζον κακὸν ἐξ αὐτῶν ἀναστῆναι, συλλέξας στρατὸν

---

[1] A : ποιούμενον MWE.
[2] ὁπόσοι] ὁπόσα τε coni. Niese.
[3] AM : ἤρητο W : ἤρτο coni. Niese.
[4] ἔτι φυομένους] Gutschmid : ἐπιφυομένους codd.

---

to mean that the two brothers were apprenticed as sail-makers

182

work, from whom they had learnt their trade, called them to task for arriving late and punished them with a whipping. Because they accounted such punishment a personal indignity they dragged down a quantity of weapons which were stored on the housetop and went off to a certain district called the " Parting of the Rivers." It was capable of providing good pasturage and green fodder in sufficient quantity to be stored for winter. Young men of the poorest class gathered about them, and these they armed. They acted as their generals and leaders in mischief without let or hindrance. When it came to the point where they were unbeatable and had built themselves a citadel, they used to issue orders to the herdsmen to pay a tribute from their flocks sufficient to support them. They, in turn, proffered friendship to those who obeyed them and a defence against all their enemies from any other quarter, threatening to destroy their flocks if they refused. The inhabitants, since they had no alternative, complied and dispatched the imposed quotas of livestock. This strengthened them even further and put them in a position to injure any that they saw fit by sudden raids. All and sundry began to defer to them, while they were a source of terror to any who thought of attacking them. Hence their fame kept increasing, even making its way to the ears of the Parthian king.[a]

(2) When the satrap of Babylonia took note of this, he chose to cut them off while they were still growing and before some greater mischief should arise through

The brothers rout a Parthian force on the Sabbath.

(whence Naber's emendation), but sails would be of linen, and ταλασιουργεῖν can refer only to the spinning of wool. Moreover, sail-making is nowhere mentioned as a separate trade in antiquity.

[a] Artabanus III. *Cf. Ant.* xviii. 48 ff.

ὅσον ἐδύνατο πλεῖστον καὶ τῶν Παρθυαίων καὶ τῶν
Βαβυλωνίων ἤλασε πρὸς αὐτούς, φθῆναι θέλων
προσβαλὼν ἐξελεῖν πρὶν ἐξάγγελτος γενέσθαι κατα-
319 σκευάζων τὸν στρατόν. περικαθίσας δὲ τὸ ἕλος
ἡσύχαζεν, καὶ κατὰ τὴν ἐπιοῦσαν, ἦν δὲ σάββατον
ἀργίας παντὸς χρήματος Ἰουδαίοις ἡμέρα, οἰόμενος
οὐ τολμήσειν ἀντιστατήσειν αὐτῷ τοὺς πολεμίους,
ἀλλὰ ἀμαχεὶ λαβὼν ἄξειν δεδεμένους, κατὰ βραχὺ
δὲ προσῄει χρῄζων αἰφνίδιον ποιεῖσθαι τὴν ἐπίπτω-
320 σιν. Ἀσιναῖος δὲ ἐτύγχανε σὺν τοῖς ἑταίροις καθεζόμενος καὶ τὰ ὅπλα παρέκειτο αὐτοῖς. " ἄνδρες,"
φησί, " χρεμετισμός μοι ἵππων προσέπεσεν οὐ φορ-
βάδων, ἀλλ᾿ οἷος γένοιτ᾿ ἀνδρῶν αὐτοῖς ἐπιβεβη-
κότων, ἐπεὶ καί τινος ἀνακρούσεως αἰσθάνομαι
χαλινῶν· δέδια, μὴ λελήθασιν ἡμᾶς οἱ πολέμιοι
περιστάντες. ἀλλά τις προΐτω[1] κατόπτης ἀπαγ-
γελίαν ἡμῖν σαφῆ τῶν ἐνεστηκότων ποιησόμενος.
321 εἴη δὲ ἐπὶ ψευδέσι μοι λελέχθαι τὰ εἰρημένα." καὶ
ὁ μὲν τάδε εἶπεν, καὶ ᾤχοντό τινες προσκοποῦντες
τὸ γινόμενον καὶ ᾗ τάχος παρελθόντες, " καὶ οὔτε
αὐτὸς ψεύδη σαφής[2] εἰκαστὴς εἶναι τῶν πρασσομένων τοῖς πολεμίοις οὔτε ἐκεῖνοι[3] πλείονος ἐπι-
322 τρέψειν ἤμελλον ἡμῖν ὑβρίειν.[4] περιειλήμμεθα δόλῳ
μηδὲν βοσκημάτων διαφέροντες· τοσῆσδε ἵππου
πλῆθος ἐπελαύνουσιν ἡμῖν ἐν ἀπορίᾳ χειρῶν κειμένοις διὰ τὸ κατείργεσθαι προαγορεύσει τῶν πα-
323 τρίων εἰς τὸ ἀργεῖν." Ἀσιναῖος δὲ οὐκ ἄρα γνώμῃ
τοῦ κατασκόπου κρίνειν ἔμελλεν ἐπὶ τοῖς ποιητέοις,

---

[1] Niese : προσίτω codd. E : procurrat Lat. : ἴτω Suidas.
[2] ψευδῆ σαφής] MW : ψευδὴς σαφής τε A : ψευδὴς σαφῆναι
ed. pr. : ψευδὴς ἔφασαν Dindorf : ψευδὴς φασὶν ex Lat. Hudson.
[3] Hudson : ἐκείνοις codd.   [4] corruptum indicat Niese.

them. He therefore mustered as large an army as he could both of Parthians and Babylonians and marched against them ; his aim was to drive his attack home and annihilate them before it was even reported that he was shaping up an army. He got his men in position about the marsh and made no move. The following day was the Sabbath, a day of rest for the Jews from all work. Assuming then that the enemy would not venture to resist him and could be seized without a battle and made prisoners, he advanced little by little, eager that his attack should be unexpected.[a] As it happened, however, Asinaeus was sitting with his companions, and their arms were lying beside them. " Men," he said, " a neighing of horses has fallen upon my ears, not like that of horses grazing but like that of horses with riders, for I also catch the jingling of bridles. I fear that the enemy have surrounded us unperceived. Let someone, therefore, go forth as a scout in order to give us a full report of what is upon us. And may my statement prove to have no foundation." No sooner were the words spoken than a few men were off to see what was going on. They returned with all speed, saying : " You were not mistaken but correctly conjectured what the enemy are doing ; and we might have known that they would not let us insult them any longer. We are caught in a trap like so many animals at pasture. There are all these horsemen approaching and our hands are tied because the commandment of our ancestral law orders us to do no work." But Asinaeus, as it appeared, was not going to let the scout's pronouncement decide for him the question of duty.

[a] *Cf.* the similar plan of Mithridates to attack Anilaeus on the Sabbath (§ 354).

# JOSEPHUS

ἀλλὰ νομιμώτερον ἡγησάμενος τοῦ ἐπ' ἀπράκτοις
τελευτῶντας εὐφραίνειν τοὺς πολεμίους τὸ ἀλκῇ[1]
δεξάμενος αὐτοὺς ὑπὲρ τῆς ἀνάγκης εἰς ἣν ἐνεπε-
πτώκει παρανομεῖν τιμωρίαν ἀπολαμβάνων,[2] εἰ δέοι,
τελευτᾶν,[3] αὐτός τε ἀναλαμβάνει τὰ ὅπλα καὶ τοῖς
σὺν αὐτῷ θάρσος ἐνεποίει τῆς ἐπὶ τὰ ὅμοια ἀρετῆς.
324 ὁμόσε ἴασι τοῖς πολεμίοις, καὶ πολλοὺς κτείναντες
αὐτῶν διὰ τὸ καταφρονοῦντας ὡς ἐπὶ τὰ ἕτοιμα
χωρεῖν εἰς φυγὴν τρέπονται τὸ λοιπόν.

325 (3) Ὁ δὲ τῶν Πάρθων βασιλεύς, ἐπεὶ ἀφίκετο
αὐτῷ ἡ ἀγγελία τῆς μάχης, ἐκπλαγεὶς τῷ τολμή-
ματι τῶν ἀδελφῶν ἐπεθύμησεν αὐτοῖς ἐλθεῖν δι'
ὄψεως καὶ λόγων, καὶ πέμπει τὸν πιστότατον τῶν
326 σωματοφυλάκων λέγοντα, ὅτι " βασιλεὺς Ἀρτάβανος καίπερ ἠδικημένος ὑφ' ὑμῶν ἐπιχειρήσεως αὐτοῦ τῇ ἀρχῇ γενομένης ἐν ἐλάσσονι τὴν καθ' αὑτὸν
ὀργὴν τῆς ὑμετέρας ἀρετῆς ποιησάμενος ἀπέστειλέν
με δεξιάς τε καὶ πίστιν δώσοντα ὑμῖν, συγχωρῶν
ἄδειάν τε καὶ ἀσυλίαν ὁδῶν, χρῄζων ἐπὶ φιλίᾳ προσ-
χωρεῖν πρὸς αὐτὸν δόλου τε καὶ ἀπάτης χωρίς,
δῶρά τε δώσειν ὑπισχνεῖται καὶ τιμήν, ἥτις ὑμῖν
πρὸς τῇ νῦν οὔσῃ ἀρετῇ μελλήσει δυνάμει τῇ
327 ἐκείνου ὠφελεῖν." Ἀσιναῖος δὲ αὐτὸς μὲν ὑπερ-
βάλλεται ὁδοὺς τὰς ἐκεῖ, τὸν ἀδελφὸν δὲ Ἀνιλαῖον
ἐκπέμπει μετὰ δώρων ὁπόσα πορίσαι ἦν. καὶ ὁ
μὲν ᾤχετο καὶ εἴσοδος αὐτῷ γίνεται παρὰ βασιλέα.
Ἀρτάβανος δὲ ἐπεὶ θεᾶται τὸν Ἀνιλαῖον καταμόνας
ἥκοντα, ἤρετο τὴν αἰτίαν τοῦ κατὰ[4] τὸν Ἀσιναῖον

---

[1] E: ἀλκῆς codd.
[2] Dindorf: ἀπολαμβάνοι codd.: ἀπολαμβάνοντας ed. pr.
186

He thought it better observance of the law, instead
of gladdening the foe by a death without anything
accomplished, to take his courage in his hands, let
the straits into which he had fallen excuse violation
of the law, and die, if he must, exacting a just vengeance. So he armed himself and emboldened his
comrades to emulate his valour. When they engaged
the foe in battle, they slaughtered them in great
numbers, since they came on contemptuously, as if
the prey were theirs for the taking, and put the re-
mainder to flight.

(3) When the news of the battle reached the ears
of the Parthian king, he was amazed at the bold ad-
venture of the brothers and longed to see and speak
with them. And so he sent the most trustworthy of
his bodyguards with this message : " King Artabanus, notwithstanding the injury you have done
him in attacking his realm, has let respect for your
feats outweigh his own resentment. He has consequently dispatched me to give you a solemn pledge.
He grants you safe conduct and an inviolate passage,
for he wants you to visit him as friends without guile
and deceit ; and he promises to give you both gifts
and an office, which, with the prestige of your present
feats, is likely to give you the benefit of authority
from him." Asinaeus, for his part, postponed any
journey there, but sent forth his brother Anilaeus
with all the gifts that he could manage. The latter
departed and was admitted to the king's presence.
When Artabanus observed that Anilaeus had come
alone, he inquired why Asinaeus had stayed behind.

*Artabanus, king of Parthia, enlists their services.*

---

³ τὸ . . . τελευτᾶν] oportere iudicat, ut non sine hostium
ultione morerentur Lat.

⁴ coni. Niese : καὶ codd. : om. E.

328 ἐφυστερηκότος. ἐπεὶ δὲ πυνθάνεται αὐτὸν δείσαντα
ἐν τῷ ἕλει ὑπομένειν, ὁ δὲ τούς τε πατρῴους θεοὺς
ἐπώμνυτο μηδὲν κακὸν δράσειν αὐτοὺς πίστει τῇ
αὐτοῦ προσκεχωρηκότας, καὶ τὴν δεξιὰν ἐδίδου,
ὅπερ μέγιστον παρὰ πᾶσιν τοῖς ἐκείνη βαρβάροις
329 παράδειγμα τοῦ θαρσεῖν γίνεται τοῖς ὁμιλοῦσιν· οὐ
γὰρ ἂν ψεύσαιτό τις δεξιῶν ὑπ' αὐτοῦ δόσεων γενομένων οὐδὲ πιστεύειν ἐνδοιάσειεν, εἰ τοιᾶσδε
ἀσφαλείας δόσις γίνοιτο παρὰ τῶν ἐν ὑποψίᾳ ἀδι-
κήσειν καθεστηκότων. καὶ Ἀρτάβανος μὲν ταῦτα
πράξας ἐκπέμπει τὸν Ἀνιλαῖον πείσοντα τὸν
330 ἀδελφὸν ἐπανελθεῖν, ἔπρασσεν δὲ ταῦτα βασιλεὺς
χρῄζων ἐνστομισμάτων¹ τῇ ἀρετῇ τῶν Ἰουδαίων
ἀδελφῶν εἰς φιλίαν κτήσασθαι τῶν ἐκείνου σατραπειῶν ἐν ἀποστάσει τε οὐσῶν καὶ διανοίᾳ τοῦ
331 ἀποστησομένου μέλλων ἐλάσειν ἐπ' αὐτούς.² ἐδε-
δίει γάρ, μὴ καὶ περιεχομένου πολέμῳ τῷ ἐκείνη
κατὰ χείρωσιν τῶν ἀφεστηκότων αὐξηθῶσιν ἐπὶ
μέγα οἱ περὶ τὸν Ἀσιναῖον καὶ τὴν Βαβυλωνίαν
ἤτοι γε συστήσονται ἐπ' ἀκροάσει τῇ αὐτῶν ἢ καὶ
τούτου γε ἀποτυχόντες τοῦ κακῶσαι μειζόνως οὐ
διαμάρτοιεν.

332 (4) Ὁ μὲν δὴ ταῦτα διανοηθεὶς ἐκπέμπει τὸν
Ἀνιλαῖον, ὁ δὲ πιθανὸς ἦν τῷ ἀδελφῷ τήν τε ἄλλην
προθυμίαν εἰσηγούμενος τοῦ βασιλέως καὶ ὅρκιον
τὸ γεγενημένον, ὥστε δὴ ἠπείγοντο ὡς τὸν Ἀρτά-
333 βανον. ὁ δὲ ἡδονῇ αὐτοὺς δέχεται παραγενομένους
ἐθαύμαζέν τε τὸν Ἀσιναῖον τοῦ ἐν ταῖς πράξεσιν
εὐψύχου, θεωρῶν παντελῶς ὄντα ὀφθῆναι βραχὺν

---

¹ ἐνστομισμάτων] codd. E Suid. : ἐνστόμισμα ed. pr. : ἐνστόμισμα τῶν Holwerda : ἐπιστόμισμα Herwerden : ἐνστόμισμά τι
Post : ante τῇ lacunam indicat Holwerda.

Informed that he had remained in the marsh because of fear, Artabanus swore by his ancestral gods that he would do no evil to them, if they visited him in reliance on his pledge. He offered him his right hand, and that is for all the barbarians of those parts the highest assurance of security in making visits. For no one would ever prove false when he had given his right hand, nor would anyone hesitate to trust one that he suspected might harm him, once he had received that assurance of safety. Having taken this step, Artabanus sent off Anilaeus to persuade his brother to return with him. The king's purpose in this was to use the prowess of the Jewish brothers as a curb to ensure the loyalty of his satrapies, for some of them were in rebellion, and some were considering whether to rebel; and he was on the point of marching against them. Hence he was afraid that while he was occupied with the war in those parts and subduing the rebels, Asinaeus would grow much stronger and would either win over Babylonia to his jurisdiction or, even if he had no such success, would unfailingly inflict still greater damage.

(4) With this calculation in mind, he dispatched Anilaeus. The latter prevailed on his brother, setting forth, among other evidences of the king's goodwill, the oath that he had taken. And so they hastened to Artabanus. He welcomed them upon their arrival and was astonished at Asinaeus' courage in action, when he observed that he was quite short in outward

Artabanus plays a double game. The brothers control Mesopotamia.

---

[2] ἔπρασσεν . . . αὐτούς] agebat autem haec imperator opus habens illis fratribus pro tutamine illius satrapiae propter quod in illa regione facile possent ab imperio suo decedere, ut antequam aliquid tale contingeret ipse illos per amicitiam occuparet Lat.

τε¹ καὶ τοῖς τὸ πρῶτον ὄψει συνελθοῦσιν ἐνδοῦναι
καταφρονήματος ἀφορμὰς ὡς οὐδενί² κρίνοιεν
αὐτόν, φησί τε πρὸς τοὺς φίλους, ὡς μείζονα ἐν
τῇ παραθέσει παρέχοιτο τὴν ψυχὴν τοῦ σώματος,
παρά τε πότον δεικνὺς τὸν Ἀσιναῖον Ἀβδαγάσῃ
τῷ αὐτοῦ στρατοπεδάρχῃ τό τε ὄνομα διασαφε³

334 καὶ τὴν πᾶσαν ἀρετήν, ᾗ χρῶτο εἰς πόλεμον. τοῦ
δὲ Ἀβδαγάσου κελεύοντος συγχώρημα αὐτῷ γενέσθαι κτείναντα αὐτὸν ἄποινα ἀπολαβεῖν ὑπὲρ ὧν
ὑβρίσειεν εἰς τὴν Παρθυαίων ἀρχήν, " ἀλλ' οὐκ ἄν,"
εἶπεν ὁ βασιλεύς, " συγχώρημα διδοίην ἐπ' ἀνδρὶ
πίστει τῇ εἰς ἐμὲ τεθαρρηκότι καὶ προσέτι δεξιάν
τε πέμψας καὶ θεῶν ὅρκοις πιθανὸς γενέσθαι

335 σπουδάσας. εἰ δὲ ἀνὴρ τυγχάνεις τὰ πολέμια
ἀγαθός, μηδὲν ἐπιορκίας χρῄζων τῆς ἐμῆς Παρθυαίων ἐκδίκει τὴν ἀρχὴν περιυβρισμένην· ἐπανα-
χωροῦντι γὰρ ἐπιθέμενος περιγίνου κράτει τῷ περὶ

336 σὲ καὶ μετ' ἀγνοίας τῆς ἐμῆς." ἕωθεν δὲ μετακα-
λέσας τὸν Ἀσιναῖον, " ὥρα σοι," φησίν, " ὦ νεανία,
χωρεῖν ἐπὶ τὰ σαυτοῦ, μὴ καὶ πλείοσιν τῶν ἐνθάδε
στρατηγῶν τὴν ὀργήν ἐρεθίσειας ἐπιχειρεῖν σου τῇ

337 σφαγῇ καὶ δίχα γνώμης τῆς ἐμῆς. παρακαταθή-
κην δέ σοι δίδωμι τὴν Βαβυλωνίαν γῆν ἀλήστευτόν
τε καὶ ἀπαθῆ κακῶν ἐσομένην ὑπὸ τῶν σῶν φρον-
τίδων. ἄξιον δέ μοι τυγχάνειν σου χρηστοῦ ἀν-
επίκλητον σοι παρασχόμενος τὴν ἐμαυτοῦ πίστιν,
οὐκ ἐπὶ κούφοις ἀλλ' ἐπὶ τοῖς εἰς σωτηρίαν ἀνακει-

338 μένοις." ταῦτα εἰπὼν καὶ δῶρα δοὺς τὸ τηνίκα⁴
ἐκπέμπει τὸν Ἀσιναῖον. ὁ δὲ εἰς τὴν οἰκείαν
παραγενόμενος φρούρια κατασκευάζει καὶ ὁπόσα

---

¹ τε] codd. : ὥστε Gutschmid.
² οὐδενί] A : οὐδὲν εἰ MW : οὐδὲν Naber.

appearance and thus gave those who got sight of him for the first time reason to disregard him and judge him of no account. Indeed the king said to his friends that Asinaeus had a soul that by comparison was greater than his body. Once, while drinking, he pointed out Asinaeus to Abdagases, who was his military chief of staff, giving his name and a full account of his prowess in war. Abdagases proposed that permission be given him to slay the man and so get revenge for his insolent treatment of the Parthian realm. "No," said the king, "I cannot grant you permission against this man who puts confidence in my pledge. Moreover, I have given him my right hand and have made a point of winning his trust by swearing by the gods. If, however, you are truly a brave man in war, you do not need any breach of my oath. Punish him yourself for his trespass against the honour of Parthia. As he is going home, attack him with your own forces and get the better of him without my knowledge." But at dawn he called for Asinaeus and said : " It is high time, young man, for you to go to your own territory, for fear of rousing the wrath of several of the generals here who may make attempts on your life even without my consent. I am granting to you the land of Babylonia as a trust to be kept free of pillage and of other abuses by your care. I deserve kindness of you since I have kept unimpeachable faith with you when no trifles were at stake, but the means of preserving your life." With these words he gave gifts to Asinaeus and sent him away at once. On reaching his own territory, Asinaeus built forts and added to the strength of any

---

³ AW : Αὐδαγάσῃ M : Abdagati Lat.
⁴ A : ὁπηνίκα MWE.

πρότερον ὠχύρου, μέγας τε ἐν ὀλίγῳ γεγόνει καὶ
οἷος[1] οὐκ ἄλλος τῶν πρότερον ἐκ τοιαύτης ἀφορμῆς
339 ἅψασθαι πραγμάτων ἐν τόλμῃ γεγονότων, Παρθυαίων τε αὐτὸν ἐθεράπευον οἱ ταύτῃ καταπεμπό-
μενοι στρατηγοί· μικρὸν γὰρ ἐδόκει καὶ τῆς κατ᾽
αὐτὸν ἧσσον ἀρετῆς ἡ ἐκ Βαβυλωνίων προϊοῦσα
τιμή. ἦν τε ἐν ἀξιώματι καὶ δυνάμει, πάντα τε
ἤδη τὰ ἐπὶ τῆς Μεσοποταμίας πρὸς αὐτὸν ἦρτο
πράγματα, προὔκοπτέν τε αὐτῶν[2] ἡ εὐδαιμονία ἐπὶ
ἔτη πεντεκαίδεκα.

340 (5) Ἀκμαζόντων δὲ αὐτοῖς τῶν ἀγαθῶν ἀρχὴ
αὐτοὺς ἐπικαταλαμβάνει κακῶν ἐκ τοιᾶσδε αἰτίας,
ἐπειδὴ τὴν ἀρετήν, ᾗ προὔκοψαν ἐπὶ μέγα δυνάμεως, ἐκτρέπουσιν εἰς ὕβριν ἐπὶ παραβάσει τῶν
πατρίων ὑπὸ ἐπιθυμιῶν καὶ ἡδονῆς. ἐμπεσόντες
τῶν Πάρθων τινί, στρατηγὸς δὲ ἀφίκετο τῶν ταύτῃ
341 χωρίων, ᾧ δὴ καὶ εἵπετο γαμετὴ τά τε ἄλλα καὶ
εἰς τὸ ἐπαινεῖσθαι προειληφυῖα πασῶν καὶ μείζονα
ῥοπὴν ἐπ᾽ αὐτῷ λαμβάνουσα θαύματι τοῦ εὐπρε-
342 ποῦς. ταύτης εἴτε ἀκοῇ τῆς εὐπρεπείας ἐκμαθὼν
εἴτε καὶ ἄλλως αὐτόπτης γενόμενος Ἀνίλαιος ὁ
τοῦ Ἀσιναίου ἀδελφὸς ἐραστής τε ἐγεγόνει καὶ
πολέμιος, τὸ μὲν ὑπὸ τοῦ μὴ ἄλλως ἐλπίζειν ἐκ-
πράσσεσθαι τὴν σύνοδον τῆς γυναικὸς μὴ τὴν ἐξουσίαν ὡς ἐπ᾽ αὐτῇ κτηθείσῃ παραλαβών, τὸ δὲ
343 ὑπὸ τοῦ δυσαντίλεκτον κρίνειν τὴν ἐπιθυμίαν. ἅμα

---

[1] Hudson : ὁπόσα codd. Lat.
[2] AM : αὐτῷ W : eius Lat.

---

[a] A.D. 20-35.
[b] Debevoise, op. cit. pp. 163-164, remarks that the virtual
independence of Anilaeus and Asinaeus well illustrates the
situation in the Parthian empire at this time. The constant

that had existed before. He had grown great in a brief time ; there was none his equal of all who had ventured from such a beginning to grasp the reins of office. The Parthian generals who were sent down through his territory courted his favour. For the honour extended to him by the Babylonians seemed petty and less than he merited. And so he enjoyed dignity and authority ; he held sway from now on over all Mesopotamia, and for fifteen years [a] the brothers' prosperity kept on increasing.[b]

(5) When their success was at its peak, their situation began to deteriorate for the following reason. Their manly qualities had raised them to the height of power ; but now they diverted these to the service of lawlessness, into which they plunged in violation of the Jewish code at the bidding of lust and self-indulgence. The trouble arose when they met a certain Parthian, who had arrived as commander in those regions. He was accompanied by his wife, whose praises were sung beyond all other women for other qualities, yet it was her marvellous beauty that gave her most effective control over him.[c] Whether Anilaeus, the brother of Asinaeus, had learned about her beauty through hearsay or else had seen her with his own eyes, he became at once her lover and her enemy. He was her foe partly because he had no hope of union with her unless he were to get her in his power as a captive, partly because he considered his lust hard to gainsay. Therefore her husband

Anilaeus' affair with a Parthian general's wife creates a scandal.

struggles for the throne had brought Parthia to the verge of anarchy. It would seem that Artabanus was forced to grant quasi-independence to large areas of his empire, and that Parthian troops and officials were helpless.

[c] Or " and her wonderful beauty inclined the scale of praise still more in her favour."

τε οὖν πολέμιος ἐπ' αὐτῆς[1] ἀνὴρ κεχειροτόνητο
κτιλίων[2] καὶ μάχης ἐπάκτου γενομένης πεσόν-
τος ἀνῃρημένου ἁλοῦσα ἐγεγάμητο τῷ ἐραστῇ. οὐ
μὴν δίχα γε μεγάλων δυστυχιῶν Ἀνιλαίῳ τε ἅμα
αὐτῷ καὶ Ἀσιναίῳ ἡ γυνὴ ἀφίκετο εἰς τὸν οἶκον
αὐτῶν, ἀλλὰ σύν τινι μεγάλῳ κακῷ διὰ τοιαύτην
344 αἰτίαν· ἐπεὶ γὰρ τἀνδρὸς τεθνηκότος αἰχμάλω-
τος ἤγετο, τὰ ἀφιδρύματα τῶν θεῶν, ἅπερ τῷ ἀνδρὶ
καὶ αὐτῇ πατρῷα ἦν, ἐπιχώριον δὲ τοῖς ἐκείνῃ
πᾶσίν ἐστιν ἐπί τε τῆς οἰκίας ἔχειν σεβάσματα
καὶ ἰοῦσιν ἐπὶ ξένης συνεπάγεσθαι, περιστέλλουσα
καὶ ταύτῃ τοῦ πατρίου τὸ ἐπ' αὐτοῖς ἔθος συν-
απήγετο, καὶ τὸ μὲν πρῶτον λεληθότως αὐτῶν
θρησκείαν ἐποιεῖτο, γαμετὴ δὲ ἀποδειχθεῖσα ἤδη
τρόπῳ τῷ αὑτῆς εἰωθότι καὶ μεθ' οἵων νομίμων
345 ἐπὶ τοῦ προτέρου ἀνδρὸς ἐθεράπευεν αὐτούς. καὶ
τῶν ἑταίρων οἱ μάλιστα τιμώμενοι παρ' αὐτοῖς τὸ
μὲν πρῶτον ἔλεγον Ἀνιλαίῳ ὡς[3] οὐδαμῶς πράσ-
σοι Ἑβραϊκὰ οὐδὲ ὁπόσα νόμοις τοῖς αὐτῶν
πρόσφορα γυναῖκα ἠγμένος ἀλλόφυλον καὶ παραβαί-
νουσαν θυσιῶν καὶ σεβασμῶν τῶν αὐτοῖς εἰωθότων
τὴν ἀκρίβειαν· ὁρᾶν οὖν, μὴ τὰ πολλὰ τῇ ἡδονῇ
τοῦ σώματος συγχωρῶν ἀπολέσειε τὴν ἀρχὴν[4] τοῦ[5]
εὐπρεποῦς καὶ τὴν εἰς νῦν ὑπὸ τοῦ θείου προελθοῦ-

---

[1] αὐτῆς] A : αὐτοῖς MW Exc. : αὐτῇ ὁ coni. Niese.
[2] κτιλίων] Κτιλίων Κιτίων W : κτιλλίων κίτίων M : κτείνων
κιτιῶν A (κιτίωνα ex corr. A, i. marg. γρ κτιλίωνα): κτίνων
Exc. : Κιτίων omisi.
[3] πρῶτον ἔλεγον Ἀνιλαίῳ ὡς] E : πρῶτον codd. : primum
(quidem) ad ipsum Anilaeum locuti sunt quia Lat. : πρῶτον
ἐπέσκηπτον ὡς ed. pr. : plura excidisse velut προσελθόντες τοῦ
Ἀνιλαίου ἀναδιδάσκειν ἐπειρῶντο τὸ εἰς τὴν γυναῖκα προπετὲς
λέγοντες ὡς putat Niese.

was at once declared an enemy and a "dead man"[a] and forced into a battle, in which he fell. After he had been slain, his widow was captured and became the wife of her passionate wooer. Nevertheless, she did not enter the family without a train of great disasters. Of one such I shall relate the occasion, affecting not only Anilaeus but Asinaeus as well. When after the death of her husband she had been taken captive, she took along the ancestral images of the gods belonging to her husband and to herself—for it is the custom among all the people in that country to have objects of worship in their house and to take them along when going abroad.[b] She too, therefore, secretly carried them off in observance of her national custom in these matters. At first she worshipped them without attracting attention, but after she had been given the status of wife, she proceeded to worship them in her accustomed manner and with the rites that she had employed during the lifetime of her former husband. At first those who ranked highest at the court of the brothers merely told Anilaeus that his actions were quite contrary to Hebraic custom and not consonant with their laws, in that he had taken a gentile wife—one who transgressed the strict rules of their accustomed sacrifices and rituals. Let him beware, then, lest by too great indulgence of fleshly lust, he should lose the authority that he had gained by seemly conduct and the dominion that hitherto had

---

[a] Here I adopt a suggestion of Professor Abraham Schalit of the Hebrew University that ἀνὴρ . . . κτιλίων represents an Aramaic phrase *gavra ktila.* See p. 389.

[b] The story is reminiscent, in some degree, of the account of Rachel and Laban's images (Gen. xxxi. 19 ff.).

---

[4] AW : ἡδονὴν M.          [5] τοῦ] ἐκ τοῦ coni. Post.

346 σαν ἐξουσίαν. ἐπεὶ δὲ οὐδὲν ἐπέραινον, ἀλλὰ καί
τινα αὐτῶν τὸν μάλιστα τιμώμενον ὅτι πλέονι
παρρησίᾳ χρήσαιτο ἀπέκτεινε, καὶ ὃς ἀποθεώ-
μενος¹ εὐνοίας τε² τῶν νόμων καὶ³ τοῦ κτείνοντος
αὐτὸν τιμωρίαν ἐπηράσατο αὐτῷ τε Ἀνιλαίῳ καὶ
Ἀσιναίῳ καὶ πᾶσιν ἑταίροις ὁμοίαν ὑπὸ τῶν ἐχ-
347 θρῶν ἐπαχθεῖσαν γενέσθαι τελευτήν, τοῖς μὲν ὡς
ἡγεμόσι παρανομιῶν γεγονόσι, τοῖς δέ, ὅτι μὴ
βοηθοῖεν αὐτῷ τοιάδε πάσχοντι διὰ τὸ ἐκδικεῖν τοῖς
νόμοις, οἱ δὲ ἐβαρύνοντο μέν, ἠνείχοντο δέ, μνημο-
νεύοντες οὐκ ἐξ ἄλλης αἰτίας ἀλλ' ἰσχύι τῇ ἐκείνων
348 τῇ εὐδαιμονίᾳ συνελθόντες. ἐπεὶ δὲ καὶ τὴν θεραπείαν ἀκροῶνται τῶν θεῶν τῶν Παρθυαίοις τιμω-
μένων, οὐκέτι ἀνεκτὸν ἡγούμενοι τοῦ Ἀνιλαίου τὸ
ὑβρίζον εἰς τοὺς νόμους ἐπὶ τὸν Ἀσιναῖον ἐλθόντες
349 καὶ πλέονες ἤδη κατεβόων τοῦ Ἀνιλαίου, φάμενοι
καλῶς ἔχειν, εἰ μὴ πρότερον κατ' αὐτὸν ἑώρα τὸ
ὠφελοῦν ἀλλὰ νῦν γοῦν ἐπιστροφὴν ποιεῖσθαι τοῦ
γεγονότος πρὶν ἢ τὴν ἁμαρτίαν ἐκείνῳ τε καὶ πᾶσι
τοῖς ἄλλοις γενέσθαι εἰς ὄλεθρον ἀνακειμένην, τόν
τε γάμον τῆς ἀνθρώπου λέγοντες οὐ μετ' αὐτῶν⁴
οὐδ' αὐτοῖς εἰωθότων τεθεῖσθαι νόμων καὶ τὴν
θρησκείαν ἣν ἐπιτηδεύοι ἡ γυνὴ ἐπ' ἀτιμώσει θεοῦ
350 τοῦ αὐτοῖς σεβασμίου πράσσεσθαι. ὁ δὲ καὐτὸς
ᾔδει μὲν τὴν ἁμαρτάδα τοῦ ἀδελφοῦ μεγάλων αἰτίαν

¹ Post (ex B.J. ii. 310 ap. Thackeray, Lexicon): . . . θεώμενος, i. marg. γρ κτεινόμενος A : κτεινόμενος MWE Exc. :
moriens Lat. : ἀποθανούμενος Petersen.
² εὐνοίας τε] εὐνοίᾳ τῇ E.

been increased by God's favour. The appeal was
fruitless. In fact, he even put to death a man of
highest rank because he had spoken too frankly. He,
fixing his mind on loyalty to the laws and on vengeance against his slayer, pronounced a curse on Anilaeus himself and Asinaeus and all their companions,
to suffer a similar end at the hands of their enemies
—the brothers because they had been the leaders
in transgressing the laws, the others because they
failed to come to his rescue when they saw how he
was treated for championing the Law. These others
were distressed at this, but did nothing about it, for
they had not forgotten that they owed their prosperity to no other instrument than the strength of
those very men. But when they further heard of
the worship of the gods that were esteemed among
the Parthians, they regarded the trampling on the
Law by Anilaeus as no longer to be borne. They
went to Asinaeus and now in greater numbers in-
veighed against Anilaeus. They said that it did not
matter if he had not previously seen for himself the
expedient course. Now, however, he must certainly
take notice of the thing that had been done before
the guilty act resulted in the ruin of himself and
everybody else. For they said that Anilaeus' marriage with this woman had taken place without
their consent and was not in accordance with the
laws which they were accustomed to follow, and
that the worship which the woman practised showed
disrespect for the God of their religion. Asinaeus, to
be sure, knew without prompting that the sin of his
brother was and would be the cause of great mis-

---

³ καὶ] om. E.
⁴ μετ' αὐτῶν] μετὰ ὑγιῶν Gutschmid.

οὖσαν κακῶν καὶ ἐσομένην, οὐ μὴν ἀπείχετό γε[1]
εὐνοίᾳ τοῦ συγγενοῦς νικώμενος καὶ συγγνώμην
νέμων ὡς ὑπὸ κρείσσονος κακοῦ τῆς ἐπιθυμίας
351 νικωμένου. ἐπεὶ δὲ πλείους τε ὁσημέραι συνεστρέφοντο καὶ πλείους ἦσαν αἱ καταβοαί, τηνικαῦτα δή
φησιν περὶ αὐτῶν πρὸς Ἀνιλαῖον τοῖς τε πρῶτον
γεγονόσιν ἐπιτιμῶν καὶ παύσασθαι τὸ λοιπὸν κελεύων τὴν ἄνθρωπον ἀποπεμψάμενον εἰς τοὺς συγ-
352 γενεῖς. ἐπράσσετο δὲ οὐδὲν ἐκ τῶν λόγων· καὶ ἡ
γυνὴ δὲ αἰσθανομένη μὲν τοῦ θροῦ τοῦ κατέχοντος
τοὺς λαοὺς δι' αὐτήν, δεδοικυῖα δὲ περὶ τοῦ Ἀνιλαίου, μὴ καί τι πάθοι ἔρωτι τῷ πρὸς αὐτήν,
φάρμακον τῷ Ἀσιναίῳ δοῦσα ἐν τοῖς σιτίοις μεθ-
ίστατο τὸν ἄνθρωπον ἀδεής τε ἦν ἐπὶ κριτῇ τῶν
περὶ αὐτὴν πραχθησομένων τῷ ἐραστῇ γενομένη.
353  (6) Ἀνιλαῖος δὲ καταμόνας ἤδη τὴν ἡγεμονίαν
παραλαβὼν ἐξάγει στρατιὰν ἐπὶ τὰς Μιθριδάτου
κώμας ἀνδρὸς πρώτου ἐν τῇ Παρθυηνῇ καὶ βασιλέως Ἀρταβάνου τὴν θυγατέρα γεγαμηκότος,
διὰ λείας τε ἦγεν αὐτάς, καὶ πολλὰ μὲν χρήματα
καὶ ἀνδράποδα εὑρίσκεται, πολλὰ δὲ πρόβατα ἄλλα
τε πολλὰ ὁπόσα ἐπὶ προσλήψει τοῦ εὐδαίμονος
354 ὠφελεῖ τοῖς ἔχουσιν. Μιθριδάτης δέ, ἐτύγχανε
γὰρ τῇδε ὤν, ἐπειδὴ ἀκούει τῶν κωμῶν τὴν ἅλωσιν
ἐν δεινῷ φέρων, ὁπότε μὴ προάρξαντος ἀδικεῖν
Ἀνιλαῖος ἄρξαιτο καὶ παρόντος τοῦ ἀξιώματος
ὑπεριδών, ἱππέας συναγαγὼν πλείστους ὅσους ἐδύνατο καὶ τῶν πλείστων τοὺς[2] ἐν ἡλικίᾳ παρῆν ὡς
προσμίξων τοῖς περὶ τὸν Ἀνιλαῖον καὶ ἔν τινι

---

[1] οὐ μὴν ἀπείχετό γε] A : οὐ μὴν ἀλλὰ καὶ ἠνείχετό γε (γε om.
E) MWE Exc. et i. marg. A : verum tamen . . . tolerabat
Lat.

fortunes. Yet he did not restrain him because he
found the ties of blood too strong and excused his
brother as mastered by his passion, a vice that he
could not resist. But when day after day they
gathered in greater and greater numbers, and their
clamours became louder and louder, then at last he
spoke about these matters to Anilaeus, rebuking him
for his former deeds and urging him to put an end to
them for the future and to send back the woman to
her kinsfolk. He accomplished nothing, however, by
these words. Furthermore, the woman, perceiving
that the people were murmuring because of her, and
fearing that Anilaeus might come to grief through
his love for her, put poison in Asinaeus' food. She
thus dispatched the man with impunity, since her
fate would be decided by her lover. _She poisons Asinaeus._

(6) Anilaeus, who had now taken over sole command, led out an army against the villages of Mithridates, a leader among the Parthians who had married
the daughter of King Artabanus. He plundered
these villages and gained there an abundance of
money, captives, and livestock, as well as much else
that adds to the prosperity of the possessors. But
when Mithridates, who happened to be there, heard
of the capture of the villages, he was indignant that
Anilaeus had without provocation taken the initiative
in doing him wrong and had disregarded his high
rank to his face. And so he gathered together all
the cavalry that he could, selected from this number
those who were in their prime, and was ready to join
battle with the forces of Anilaeus. He had camped _Anilaeus captures the Parthian Mithridates but releases him._

---

² τῶν πλείστων τοὺς] codd. : τῶν ὁπλιτῶν τοὺς coni. Niese :
τῶν πελατῶν τοὺς Holwerda : τοὺς πλείστους τῶν Richards et
Shutt ex Lat.

κώμῃ τῶν αὑτοῦ σχὼν¹ ἡσύχαζεν, ὡς τῇ ἐπιούσῃ
μαχησόμενος διὰ τὸ εἶναι σαββάτων² ἡμέραν τοῖς
355 Ἰουδαίοις ἐν ἀργίᾳ διαγομένην. Ἀνιλαῖος δὲ
ταῦτα πυθόμενος παρὰ ἀνδρὸς Σύρου ἀλλοφύλου
ἐξ ἑτέρας κώμης τά τε ἄλλα φράζοντος ἀκριβῶς
καὶ τὸ χωρίον, ἔνθα Μιθριδάτης ἤμελλεν δαίνυσθαι,
δειπνοποιησάμενος καθ᾽ ὥραν ἤλαυνε νυκτὸς ἀμα-
θέσι τῶν ποιουμένων χρήζων τοῖς Παρθυαίοις ἐπι-
356 πεσεῖν. καὶ περὶ τετάρτην φυλακὴν ἐπιπεσὼν τοὺς
μὲν ἔτι κοιμωμένους ἀναιρεῖ τοὺς δὲ εἰς φυγὴν
τρέπει, Μιθριδάτην δὲ ζωγρίᾳ λαβὼν ἦγεν ὡς αὑτὸν
ἐπὶ ὄνον γυμνὸν ἀναθέμενος, ἥπερ ἀτιμιῶν μεγίστη
357 νομίζεται παρὰ Παρθυαίοις. καταγαγὼν δὲ εἰς τὴν
ὕλην³ μετὰ τοιοῦδε ὑβρίσματος,⁴ [καὶ]⁵ κελευόντων
τῶν φίλων ἀναιρεῖν τὸν Μιθριδάτην ἀνεδίδασκεν
αὐτοὺς σπεύδων αὐτὸς ἐναντία· μὴ γὰρ καλῶς
ἔχειν ἀναιρεῖν ἄνδρα γένους τε ὄντα τοῦ πρώτου
παρὰ Παρθυαίοις καὶ ἐπιγαμίᾳ τῇ πρὸς τὸν βασιλέα
358 μειζόνως τιμώμενον· νῦν μὲν γὰρ ἀνεκτὰ εἶναι τὰ
πεπραγμένα· καὶ γὰρ εἰ περιύβρισται Μιθριδάτης,
ἀλλ᾽ οὖν σωτηρίᾳ τῆς ψυχῆς εὐεργετούμενον χά-
359 ριτος μνήσεσθαι⁶ τοῖς τὰ τοιάδε παρασχοῦσιν, πα-
θόντος δέ τι ἀνήκεστον οὐκ ἀτρεμήσειν βασιλέα μὴ
οὐ μεγάλην σφαγὴν Ἰουδαίων τῶν ἐν Βαβυλῶνι
ποιησάμενον,⁷ ὧν φείδεσθαι καλῶς ἔχειν διά τε τὴν

---

¹ Α : κατασχὼν MW.
² Niese : σάββατον codd. E.
³ εἰς τὴν ὕλην] codd. : ad locum proprium Lat. : εἰς τὸ ἕλος
coni. Richards et Shutt.
⁴ Gutschmid : ὁρίσματος codd.
⁵ suspectum om. E.
⁶ χάριτος μνήσεσθαι] Niese : χάριτος μνήσασθαι· codd. : με-
μνήσεται χάριτος E.    ⁷ ποιησόμενον E.

in one of the latter's villages, where he rested with
the intention of fighting on the following day, inasmuch as it would be the Sabbath, a day on which the
Jews abstain from work.[a] But Anilaeus learned of
this from a Syrian gentile of another village who told
him everything in detail, including the place where
Mithridates intended to dine. Anilaeus, therefore,
dined betimes and made a night march intent on
attacking the Parthians while they were unaware of
what he was doing. About the fourth watch [b] he fell
upon them, dispatching some as they slept and putting the others to flight. Mithridates he captured
alive and brought home mounted naked upon an ass,
which is considered the highest disgrace by the Parthians. When he had brought him into the forest in
this insulting way,[c] Anilaeus' friends bade him put
Mithridates to death, but he argued with them,
zealously advocating just the contrary. For, he said,
it was not a good idea to kill a man who belonged to
the first family of the Parthians and who ranked even
higher because of his marriage connexion with the
king. As it was, what they had hitherto done was
tolerable. For even though Mithridates had been
insulted wantonly, yet the granting of his life was a
favour which he would remember to the advantage of
those who had granted it. But if Mithridates should
suffer an incurable fate, the king would not rest until
he had inflicted a great slaughter on the Jews in
Babylon. It was right that they should spare these

[a] Cf. the similar plan (§ 319) of the Babylonian satrap to
attack Asinaeus and Anilaeus on the Sabbath.

[b] About 3 A.M.

[c] Gutschmid's emendation has been adopted since the
manuscript reading makes little sense and cannot mean
" with this determination."

συγγένειαν καὶ διὰ τὸ μὴ ἀναστροφὴν¹ εἶναι ἂν αὐτοῖς πταίσματός τινος γενομένου ἀπολόμενον² τὸ³
360 κατ᾽ ἐκείνους ἀκμῆς πληθύι χρώμενον. καὶ ὁ μὲν ταῦτα διανοηθεὶς καὶ φράσας ἐν τῷ συλλόγῳ πιθανὸς ἦν ἀφίεταί τε Μιθριδάτης, ἐλθόντα δὲ αὐτὸν ὠνείδιζεν ἡ γυνή, εἰ μὴ προθυμήσεται⁴ βασιλέως τε γαμβρὸς ὢν καὶ ταύτῃ συνοικῶν⁵ τιμωρηθήσεσθαι τοὺς
361 ὑβρίσαντας εἰς αὐτὸν περιορώμενος, ἀγαπῶν δὲ τὴν σωτηρίαν μετὰ αἰχμαλωσίαν ὑπὸ Ἰουδαίων ἀνδρῶν γενομένην· "καὶ νῦν ἐπανάδραμε τὴν ἀρετήν, ἢ θεοὺς ἐπόμνυμι τοὺς βασιλείους ἦ μὴν παραλυθήσεσθαι
362 τῆς πρὸς σὲ ἐπὶ γάμῳ κοινωνίας." ὁ δὲ αὖ τοῦτο μὲν τῶν ὀνειδῶν τὴν καθ᾽ ἡμέραν ἀχθηδόνα μὴ φέρων, τοῦτο δὲ τῆς γυναικὸς τὴν μεγαλοφροσύνην δεδιώς, μὴ παραλύοιτο αὐτοῦ τῶν γάμων, ἄκων μὲν καὶ μὴ βουλόμενος συνάγει δ᾽ οὖν στρατὸν ὅσον ἐδύνατο πλεῖστον καὶ ἤλαυνεν οὐκ ἀνασχετὸν ὑπολαμβάνων ἔτι καὶ αὐτὸς τὴν σωτηρίαν, εἰ Παρθυαῖος ὢν ὑπὸ Ἰουδαίου περιωθοῖτο ἀντιπολεμοῦντος.
363 (7) Ἀνιλαῖος δὲ ὡς μανθάνει προσελαύνοντα δυνάμει πολλῇ τὸν Μιθριδάτην ἄδοξον ἡγησάμενος τὸ μένειν ἐν τοῖς ἕλεσιν, ἀλλὰ μὴ φθάσας ὑπαντιάζειν τοὺς πολεμίους, εὐτυχίᾳ τε τῇ πρότερον ἐλπίζων ὅμοια πράξειν καὶ τήν τε ἀρετὴν τοῖς τολμῶσι καὶ

---

¹ ἀποστροφὴν Ernesti.
² ἀπολόμενον supplevi : ἀπόλοιτο supplet Petersen.
³ τὸ] A : τε MW : τῇ Lowthius : τό τε Liezenberg.
⁴ MWE : προμηθήσεται A : festinaret Lat.
⁵ Post : τιμωρῶν codd.

---

ᵃ The Jews of Babylon.
ᵇ The text is difficult. Prof. Post suggests : " because they would have no place of refuge in case of a defeat ; whereas these people had among them an abundance of the

Jews both because of their kinship with them and because these Jews would have no place of refuge if any disaster overtook them,[a] and those of their numbers perished who were in the prime of life.[b] When he put his thoughts before the conference in this way, he won them over, and Mithridates was released. On his return home, his wife upbraided him if, though he was the king's son-in-law and her husband,[c] he should not set his heart on vengeance, but should overlook the perpetrators of his disgrace, being content to have come off alive after being made a prisoner by Jews. " And now," she said, " recover your valour, or I swear by the royal gods that I will verily dissolve my marriage partnership with you." Mithridates, for his part, unable to endure the painful upbraiding of his wife day after day and alarmed lest her pride should lead her to sever the marriage bond with him, reluctant and unwilling though he was, nevertheless mustered the largest army that he could and set out. He himself conceived that he could no longer bear to survive if he, a Parthian, were to be driven from pillar to post in a war with a Jew.

(7) When Anilaeus learned that Mithridates was marching against him with a great force, he regarded it as inglorious to lurk in the marshes rather than anticipate the enemy in seeking an encounter. Hoping for the same good fortune as in the past and expecting that success in battle ever attends those who are

very best." Another possible translation is : " because if any disaster befell them, their [*i.e.* Babylon's Jews'] great numbers of men in the prime of life would not be available to them [*i.e.* Anilaeus' followers]."

[c] The manuscript reading " and avenging her " is difficult to understand. It cannot mean " avenging himself for her sake."

εἰωθόσιν[1] θαρρεῖν παρατυγχάνειν,[2] ἐξῆγε τὴν δύ-
364 ναμιν. πολλοί τε πρὸς τῷ οἰκείῳ στρατῷ προσ-
εγεγόνεσαν αὐτῷ καθ' ἁρπαγὴν τῶν ἀλλοτρίων
τραπησόμενοι καὶ ὄψει πᾶν[3] προεκπλήξοντες τοὺς
365 πολεμίους. προϊοῦσι δὲ αὐτοῖς εἰς σταδίους ἐνενή-
κοντα καὶ διὰ τῆς ἀνύδρου τῆς πορείας γενομένης
καὶ μεσημβρίας τά τε ἄλλα[4] περιῆν τότε[5] τὸ δίψος
καὶ Μιθριδάτης ἐπιφανεὶς προσέβαλε τεταλαιπωρη-
μένοις ἀπορίᾳ τοῦ πιεῖν καὶ δι' αὐτὸ καὶ τὴν ὥραν
366 φέρειν τὰ ὅπλα μὴ δυναμένοις. τροπή τε οὖν γίνεται τῶν περὶ τὸν Ἀνιλαῖον αἰσχρὰ διὰ τὸ ἀπηγο-
ρευκότας ἀκραιφνέσι προσφέρεσθαι καὶ φόνος πολὺς
πολλαί τε μυριάδες ἔπεσον ἀνδρῶν, Ἀνιλαῖος δὲ
καὶ ὅσον περὶ αὐτὸν ἦν συνεστηκὸς ἐπὶ τῆς ὕλης
ἐπανεχώρουν φυγῇ μεγάλην[6] νίκης τῆς ἐπ' αὐτοῖς χα-
367 ρὰν Μιθριδάτῃ παρεσχηκότες.[7] Ἀνιλαίῳ δὲ προσῄει πλῆθος ἄπορον[8] ἀνδρῶν πονηρῶν[9] ἐν ὀλίγῳ τὴν
σωτηρίαν ποιουμένων ῥαστώνης χάριτι τῆς εἰς τὸ
παρόν, ὥστε ἀντανίσωμα τὴν τούτων πρόσοδον γενέσθαι πλήθους[10] τῶν ἀπολωλότων· οὐ μὴν ὅμοιοί
368 γε ἦσαν τοῖς πεπτωκόσι διὰ τὸ ἀμελέτητον. οὐ
μὴν ἀλλὰ καὶ τούτοις[11] ἐπιφοιτᾷ ταῖς κώμαις τῶν
Βαβυλωνίων ἀνάστατά τε ἦν πάντα ταῦτα ὑπὸ τῆς
369 Ἀνιλαίου ὕβρεως. καὶ οἱ Βαβυλώνιοι καὶ οἱ ὄντες[12]

---

[1] καὶ τήν τε . . . εἰωθόσιν] litt. καὶ τήν . . . εἰ i. ras. m. 2 A :
καὶ τήν τε τόλμησιν καὶ εἰωθόσι MW.
[2] καὶ τήν . . . παρατυγχάνειν] audentibus virtutis etiam ro-
bur adcrescere Lat.
[3] A : πάλιν MW.
[4] τά τε ἄλλα] A : om. MWE.
[5] περιῆν τότε] A : τότε περιῆν τε MW : περιῆν τὸ E.
[6] Gutschmid : μεγάλη codd.
[7] Μιθριδάτῃ παρεσχηκότες] ed. pr. : Μιθριδάτου παρεσχηκότος
codd.

bold and never afraid, he led forth his forces. In addition to his own army he was joined by many who hoped to plunder other people's property and by their mere appearance to cause consternation among the enemy. When they had advanced ninety furlongs, since there was no water along their route and it was now midday, they were indeed suffering from thirst. Then Mithridates appeared and attacked them, miserably short as they were of anything to drink, and incapable of wearing armour because of thirst and the time of day. Consequently the followers of Anilaeus suffered a disgraceful rout, since they, in their exhausted condition, were engaging men who were fresh. The slaughter was great and many tens of thousands of men fell. Anilaeus and all those who were banded together about him withdrew in flight to the forest, having afforded great joy to Mithridates at his victory over them. Anilaeus was now joined by an indigent <sup>a</sup> horde of scoundrels who held their lives cheap to gain some ease for the moment. Thus the addition of these men compensated for the multitude of those who had perished. Yet, owing to lack of training, they were not of the same quality as those who had fallen. Nevertheless, even with these he ravaged the villages of the Babylonians, and everything in the region was laid waste by the violence of Anilaeus. The Babylonians and those

---

<sup>a</sup> Or " unmanageable." Hudson's emendation, based upon the Latin version, would mean " endless."

---

<sup>8</sup> ἄπηρον ed. pr. : ἄπειρον Hudson.
<sup>9</sup> πλῆθος . . . πονηρῶν] infinita multitudo hominum pessimorum Lat. : πλῆθος ἀνδρῶν πονηρῶν δι' ἀπορίαν E.
<sup>10</sup> ex corr. AE et ut vid. Lat. : πλῆθος MW.
<sup>11</sup> Lowthius : cum hac multitudine Lat. : ταύταις codd.
<sup>12</sup> καὶ οἱ ὄντες] codd. : καμόντες Gutschmid.

ἐν τῷ πολέμῳ[1] πέμπουσιν ἐς τὰ Νέαρδα πρὸς τοὺς
ἐν αὐτῇ Ἰουδαίους Ἀνιλαῖον ἐξαιτούμενοι, καὶ μὴ
δεξομένοις τὸν λόγον τοῦτον, οὐδὲ γὰρ βουλομένοις ἔκδοτον παρασχεῖν δυνηθῆναι, εἰρήνην προὐ-
καλοῦντο· οἱ δὲ καὐτοὶ χρῄζειν ἔλεγον τῶν ἐπὶ τῆς
εἰρήνης συμβάσεων καὶ πέμπουσι μετὰ τῶν Βαβυλωνίων ἄνδρας, οἳ διαλέξοιντο πρὸς τὸν Ἀνιλαῖον.
370 οἱ δὲ Βαβυλώνιοι κατοπτίας αὐτοῖς γενομένης
μαθόντες τὸ χωρίον, ἐν ᾧ ἱδρυμένος ὁ Ἀνιλαῖος ἦν,
ἐπιπεσόντες κρύφα νυκτὸς μεθύουσι καὶ καθ᾿ ὕπνον
τετραμμένοις κτείνουσιν ἀδεῶς πάντας ὅσους ἐγ-
κατέλαβον καὶ Ἀνιλαῖον αὐτόν.

371 (8) Βαβυλώνιοι δὲ ἀπαλλαγέντες τῆς Ἀνιλαίου
βαρύτητος, ἐπιστόμισμα γὰρ ἦν αὐτῶν μίσει τῷ
πρὸς τοὺς Ἰουδαίους, ἀεὶ γὰρ ὡς ἐπὶ πολὺ διάφοροι
καθεστήκεσαν αἰτίᾳ τῆς ἐναντιώσεως τῶν νόμων
καὶ ὁποτέροις παραγένοιτο θαρρεῖν πρότεροι ἀλλήλων ἥπτοντο εἰ μὴ[2] καὶ τότε οὖν ἀπολωλότων τῶν
περὶ τὸν Ἀνιλαῖον ἐπετίθεντο τοῖς Ἰουδαίοις οἱ
372 Βαβυλώνιοι. οἱ δ᾿ ἐν δεινῷ τιθέμενοι τὴν ὕβριν τὴν
ἐκ τῶν Βαβυλωνίων καὶ μήτε ἀντιτάξασθαι μάχῃ
δυνάμενοι μήτε ἀνεκτὸν ἡγούμενοι τὴν συνοικίαν
ᾤχοντο εἰς Σελεύκειαν τῶν ἐκείνῃ πόλιν ἀξιολογω-
τάτην Σελεύκου κτίσαντος αὐτὴν τοῦ Νικάτορος.[3]
οἰκοῦσιν δ᾿ αὐτὴν πολλοὶ μὲν Μακεδόνων, πλεῖστοι
δὲ Ἕλληνες, ἔστιν δὲ καὶ Σύρων οὐκ ὀλίγον τὸ

---

[1] καὶ οἱ . . . πολέμῳ] quamvis ad bellum parati Lat.
[2] εἰ μὴ] codd.: λύμης Gutschmid: ἀεὶ Herwerden.

who were engaged in this war sent envoys to the Jews in Nearda, demanding that they should deliver up Anilaeus. When the Neardaeans refused this request—for they were not in a position to deliver him up even if they had wished—the envoys invited them to make peace. The Jews replied that they themselves desired a treaty of peace, and they sent men with the Babylonians to negotiate with Anilaeus. The Babylonians, discovering through reconnaissance the place where Anilaeus and his men were quartered, fell secretly upon them at night while they were drunk and given over to sleep, and slew unmolested all those whom they had trapped, including Anilaeus himself.[a]

*Anilaeus is defeated and killed.*

(8) The Babylonians were now rid of the pressure imposed by Anilaeus, which had curbed their hatred against the Jews—for in general they always quarrelled with them because of the contrariety of their laws, and whichever party happened to feel more self-confident would initiate an attack on the other. Accordingly, now that Anilaeus and his men were no more, the Babylonians began to attack the Jews. The latter were indignant at the insolent conduct of the Babylonians, but neither were able to face them in battle nor considered it tolerable to live together with them. So off they went to Seleucia,[b] the most notable city of the region, which Seleucus Nicator[c] had founded, whose inhabitants consisted of many Macedonians, a majority of Greeks, and not a few

*The Jews migrate to Seleucia, where the Syrians and Greeks unite to slaughter them.*

---

[a] A.D. 35 or 36.     [b] On the Tigris. *Cf.* § 49.
[c] Founder of the Seleucid kingdom in Syria. He ruled from 312 to 280 B.C. The manuscript spelling is " Nicator ": the same error occurs in *Ant.* xii. 119 and xiii. 213.

---

[3] Dindorf : Νικάνορος codd. E Lat.

373 ἐμπολιτευόμενον. εἰς μὲν δὴ ταύτην καταφεύγουσιν οἱ Ἰουδαῖοι καὶ ἐπὶ μὲν πέντε ἔτη ἀπαθεῖς κακῶν ἦσαν, τῷ δὲ ἕκτῳ ἔτει μεθ' ὃ¹ πρῶτον φθορὰ ἐν Βαβυλῶνι² ἐγένετο αὐτῶν καὶ καιναὶ κτίσεις³ ἐκ τῆς πόλεως καὶ δι' αὐτὴν ἄφιξις εἰς τὴν Σελεύκειαν⁴ ἐκδέχεται μείζων αὐτοὺς συμφορὰ δι' αἰτίαν, ἣν ἀφηγήσομαι.

374 (9) Σελευκέων τοῖς Ἕλλησι πρὸς τοὺς Σύρους ὡς ἐπὶ πολὺ ἐν στάσει καὶ διχονοίᾳ ἐστὶν ὁ βίος καὶ κρατοῦσιν οἱ Ἕλληνες. τότε οὖν συνοικούντων⁵ αὐτοῖς Ἰουδαίων γενομένων ἐστασίαζον, καὶ οἱ Σύροι καθυπέρτεροι ἦσαν ὁμολογίᾳ τῇ Ἰουδαίων πρὸς αὐτοὺς φιλοκινδύνων τε ἀνδρῶν καὶ πολεμεῖν προθύμως

375 ἐντεταγμένων. καὶ οἱ Ἕλληνες περιωθούμενοι τῇ στάσει καὶ μίαν ὁρῶντες αὐτοῖς ἀφορμὴν τοῦ ἀνασώσασθαι τὸ πρότερον ἀξίωμα, εἰ δυνηθεῖεν παῦσαι ταὐτὸν λέγοντας⁶ Ἰουδαίους καὶ Σύρους, διελέγοντο ἕκαστοι πρὸς τῶν Σύρων τοὺς αὐτοῖς συνήθεις πρὸ τοῦ γεγονότας εἰρήνην τε καὶ φιλίαν ὑπισχνούμενοι.

376 οἱ δὲ ἐπείθοντο ἄσμενοι. ἐγίνοντο οὖν ἀφ' ἑκατέρων λόγοι καὶ τῶν πρώτων παρ' ἑκατέροις ἀνδρῶν πρασσόντων ἐπιδιαλλαγὰς⁷ τάχιστα ἡ σύμβασις⁸ ἐγένετο,

---

¹ μεθ' ὅ] Bekker : μετὰ τὸ codd.

² Babylonia Lat.

³ κτίσεις] MW : κτήσεις ex corr. A : αἱ κτήσεις Gutschmid : μετοικήσεις Hudson.

⁴ καὶ καιναὶ . . . Σελεύκειαν] et ruina et hoc plurimi Seleuciam magis magisque confugiunt Lat.

⁵ συνοίκων Cocceji.

⁶ ταὐτὸν λέγοντας] ed. pr. : τὸν λέγοντα codd. : ὁμονοοῦντας E.

⁷ ἐπιδιαλλαγὰς] A : ἐπὶ διαλλαγὰς MW : ἐπὶ διαλλαγαῖς coni. Post. ⁸ AW : συμβίβασις M.

Syrians holding civic rights.[a] Here then the Jews took refuge. For five years [b] they lived there unmolested, but in the sixth year after they were first despoiled in Babylon and formed new settlements upon leaving that city, and in consequence came to Seleucia, there ensued a greater misfortune, the cause of which I shall relate.

(9) At Seleucia life is marked by general strife and discord between the Greeks and the Syrians, in which the Greeks have the upper hand. Now when the Jews came to live in the city there was continued strife, and the Syrians got the upper hand by coming to terms with the Jews, who were adventurous and joined the ranks in battle with gusto. Now the Greeks, harried by this civil conflict, saw that there was only one possibility of regaining their former prestige, namely, by breaking up the alliance between Jews and Syrians. To this end various groups among the Greeks parleyed with any of the Syrians with whom they had formerly been on intimate terms, offering a promise of peace and friendship. The Syrians on their part gladly assented. Proposals were put forward by the two parties. The leading men on both sides effected a reconciliation and an agreement was very speedily reached. Once they

---

[a] During the latter part of the first century, somewhat after this period, Seleucia had 600,000 inhabitants, according to Pliny, *Hist. Nat.* vi. 122, but such figures are often exaggerated. The city prided itself on its Greek tradition, as is clear from Tacitus' statement, *Ann.* vi. 42, that the city had never lapsed into barbarism but had clung loyally to its founder Seleucus. It appears to have attracted natives of Babylon, however, since Strabo xvi. 743 remarks that it was normal to describe a man of Seleucia as a Babylonian. See E. R. Bevan, *The House of Seleucus*, i, 1902, p. 253.

[b] A.D. 35/36–40/41.

ὁμονοήσαντές τε μέγα τεκμήριον ἑκάτεροι εὐνοίας
παρ'[1] ἀλλήλοις ἠξίουν παρασχεῖν τὸ πρὸς τοὺς Ἰουδαίους ἔχθος, ἐπιπεσόντες τε αἰφνίδιον αὐτοῖς κτεί-
νουσι μυριάδας ὑπὲρ πέντε ἀνδρῶν, ἀπώλοντό τε
πάντες πλὴν εἴ τινες ἐλέῳ φίλων ἢ γειτόνων ἐπιχω-
377 ρηθὲν αὐτοῖς ἔφυγον. τούτοις δὲ ἦν εἰς Κτησιφῶντα
ἀποχώρησις πόλιν Ἑλληνίδα καὶ τῆς Σελευκείας
πλησίον κειμένην, ἔνθα χειμάζει τε ὁ βασιλεὺς κατὰ
πᾶν ἔτος καὶ πλείστη τῆς ἀποσκευῆς αὐτοῦ τῇδε
ἀποκειμένη τυγχάνει. ἀσύνετα[2] δὲ ἦν αὐτοῖς τὴν
ἵδρυσιν πεποιημένοις[3] τιμῆς[4] τῆς βασιλείας Σελευ-
378 κέων μὴ πεφροντικότων.[5] ἐφοβήθη δὲ καὶ πᾶν τὸ
τῇδε Ἰουδαίων ἔθνος[6] τούς τε Βαβυλωνίους καὶ τοὺς
Σελευκεῖς, ἐπειδὴ καὶ ὁπόσον ἦν Σύρων ἐμπολιτεῦον
τοῖς τόποις ταὐτὸν ἔλεγον τοῖς Σελευκεῦσιν ἐπὶ πο-
379 λέμῳ τῷ πρὸς τοὺς Ἰουδαίους. καὶ συνελέγησαν
ὥστε πολὺ εἴς τε τὰ Νέαρδα καὶ τὴν Νίσιβιν ὀχυ-
ρότητι τῶν πόλεων κτώμενοι τὴν ἀσφάλειαν, καὶ
ἄλλως πληθὺς ἅπασα μαχίμων ἀνδρῶν κατοικεῖται.
καὶ τὰ μὲν κατὰ Ἰουδαίους τοὺς ἐν τῇ Βαβυλωνίᾳ
κατῳκημένους τοιαῦτα ἦν.

---

[1] om. E.
[2] ἀσύνθετα Hudson : ἀνέλπιστα coni. Richards et Shutt.
[3] ἀσύνετα . . . πεποιημένοις] nulla tamen eis iam spes vi-
vendi fuerat derelicta Lat.
[4] Hudson : τιμῇ codd.
[5] μὴ πεφροντικότων] Hudson : πεφροντικότων codd.
[6] A : γένος MWE.

---

[a] Cf. Ant. xviii. 49. V. Tcherikover, Hellenistic Civilization and the Jews, 1959, p. 503 n. 74, rightly cites Strabo xvi.
743, who terms Ctesiphon " a large village " and concludes
that the Greeks did not regard it as a polis : hence Josephus

were on good terms, both parties agreed, as a great proof of mutual loyalty, to show enmity to the Jews. They fell upon them suddenly and slew more than 50,000 men. Indeed all were slain except for some who were mercifully granted the chance to flee by friends or neighbours. Those who escaped retreated to Ctesiphon,[a] a Greek city situated near Seleucia, where the king spends the winter each year and where most of his baggage is stored, as it happens. But it was without prudence that they settled there,[b] since the Seleucians had no respect for the authority of the crown.[c] All the Jewish people in this region now became terrified of both the Babylonians and the Seleucians since all the Syrians who were citizens of these places fell in line with the Seleucians and made war against the Jews their policy. Most of the Jews flocked to Nearda and Nisibis,[d] where they were safe because these cities were fortified and were furthermore populated by men who were valiant fighters every one. Such is the story of the Jewish inhabitants of Babylonia.

is wrong in calling it a Greek city. Eusebius and Jerome identify it with the Biblical Calneh (Gen. x. 10), but on insufficient evidence. On Ctesiphon as the winter residence of the Parthian kings see Strabo xvi. 743. See, in general, Boettger, *Topographisch-Historisches Lexicon*, pp. 95-96.

[b] Hudson's emendation, ἀσύνθετα, would yield the following meaning : " They could put no solid confidence in settling there." A similar meaning is given by Richards and Shutt's emendation.

[c] For seven years (c. 37–44) the Seleucians were in revolt and were actually independent of Parthian overlordship. See Tacitus, *Ann.* xi. 9, and numismatic evidence cited by Debevoise, pp. 164-165.

[d] *Cf.* §§ 311-312.

## ΒΙΒΛΙΟΝ ΙΘ

(i. 1) Γάιος δὲ οὐκ εἰς μόνους Ἰουδαίους τοὺς ἐν Ἱεροσολύμοις καὶ τοὺς ὁπόσοι τῇδε οἰκοῦσιν ἐπεδείκνυτο τῆς ὕβρεως τὴν μανίαν, ἀλλὰ διὰ πάσης

*a* T. Mommsen's theory (" Cornelius Tacitus und Cluvius Rufus," *Hermes* iv, 1870, p. 322) that Josephus' source for the long account of the conspiracy against Gaius and the accession of Claudius is the historian Cluvius Rufus has won rather general acceptance (*cf.*, *e.g.*, Groag, in Pauly-Wissowa, iv, 1901, pp. 123-125). The chief support for this theory is the conversation recorded between Cluvius and a senator named Bathybius in which Cluvius gives an apt quotation from Homer urging Bathybius to be silent (§§ 91-92). Such an anecdote, it has been said (see Mommsen, p. 320 ; accepted by R. Syme, *Tacitus*, i, 1958, p. 287), can derive only from Cluvius Rufus himself, and not verbally, but precisely from his writings. Moreover, M. P. Charlesworth, " The Tradition about Caligula," *Camb. Hist. Jour.* iv, 1933, p. 116, cites a number of examples from this section of Book XIX in which Josephus' style is more metaphorical and more highly coloured than is usual for him ; and he suggests that Josephus had before him a Latin original written in a highly rhetorical and metaphorical style, namely Cluvius Rufus. It has even been argued by A. Momigliano, " Osservazioni sulle fonti per la storia di Caligola, Claudio, Nerone," *Rend. d. Accad. d. Lincei* viii, 1932, p. 305, that Cluvius was the main source not only of Josephus but also of the two other chief extant writers on the subject of Gaius' assassination, Suetonius and Dio Cassius. But Mommsen's theory seems to rest on rather flimsy evidence. In the first place, there is no indica-

212

# BOOK XIX

(i. 1) [a] GAIUS not only exhibited the madness [b] of his insolence in relation to the Jews who dwelt in Jerusalem and throughout Judaea, but he also sent

tion that Cluvius Rufus' history covered the period of Gaius and Claudius, since the references to it in Tacitus, *Ann.* xiii. 20 and xiv. 2, and in Pliny, *Epist.* ix. 19. 5, deal with the period of Nero alone. The anecdote in §§ 91-92 might well have been recorded by another writer, perhaps Servilius Nonianus or Aufidius Bassus (see Syme, i, pp. 287-288) or, because it was so striking, might well have been transmitted orally. There is no indication that Josephus' style in Book XIX is more metaphorical than it is in large parts of the rest of the work ; and even if it is, there is no evidence that these metaphors were borrowed from Cluvius, about whose style we know almost nothing firsthand, inasmuch as his works are lost except for very slight fragments (H. Peter, *Hist. Rom. Relliq.* ii, 1906, p. 114). The rhetorical style was widely cultivated among the Romans, and Josephus might have borrowed these metaphors from another writer who worked within the same rhetorical tradition. Several reasons have been advanced for the length of this digression on Gaius' murder and Claudius' accession. But Josephus' own moralistic reasons (§ 16), coupled with his desire to glorify the Jewish king Agrippa, who played a key rôle in Claudius' accession (§§ 236 ff.), seem sufficient.

[b] *Cf.* Suetonius, who divides his biography of Gaius Caligula into two parts, Caligula the emperor and Caligula the monster (*Calig.* 22). Gaius' madness is also referred to by Philo, *Leg. ad Gaium* 34, Dio Cass. lix. 29. 1, Tac. *Ann.* xi. 3, and Sen. *De Const. Sap.* 18. 1 (cited by J. P. V. D. Balsdon, *The Emperor Gaius* (*Caligula*), 1934, p. 212).

ἐσομένην γῆς καὶ θαλάσσης ἔστελλεν αὐτήν, ὁπόση
Ῥωμαίοις ὑπακούει, μυρίων τε ἀνέπλησεν αὐτὴν
2 κακῶν ὁπόσα μὴ ἱστόρητο πρότερον. μάλιστα δὲ
ᾐσθάνετο τοῦ δεινοῦ τῶν πρασσομένων ἡ Ῥώμη κατ' οὐδὲν αὐτὴν τιμιωτέραν τῶν λοιπῶν πόλεων ἡγουμένου, ἀλλὰ τούς τε ἄλλους ἄγοντος καὶ
φέροντος καὶ μάλιστα τὴν σύγκλητον καὶ ὁπόσοι
τούτων εὐπατρίδαι καὶ προγόνων ἐπιφανείαις τι-
3 μώμενοι. μυρία τε εὑρίσκετο καὶ κατὰ τῶν ἱππέων
μὲν καλουμένων, ἀξιώματι δὲ καὶ δυνάμει χρημάτων ὅμοια τοῖς συγκλητικοῖς ὑπὸ τῆς πόλεως
ἀγομένων διὰ τὸ ἐκ τούτων εἰς τὴν βουλὴν εἶναι
κατακλήσεις· ὧν ἀτίμωσις ἦν καὶ μετανάστασις
κτεινομένων τε καὶ τὰ χρήματα συλωμένων διὰ τὸ
καὶ τὰς σφαγὰς ὡς τὸ πολὺ ἐπ' ἀφαιρέσει τῶν
4 χρημάτων αὐτοῖς συντυγχάνειν. ἐξεθείαζέν τε ἑαυτὸν καὶ τὰς τιμὰς οὐκέτ' ἀνθρωπίνως ἠξίου γίνεσθαι παρὰ τῶν ὑπηκόων αὐτῷ· εἴς τε τοῦ Διὸς
φοιτῶν τὸ ἱερόν, ὃ Καπετώλιον[1] μὲν καλοῦσιν

---

[1] ed. pr. : Καπιτώλιον (ι ante τ i. ras. A) AME : Καπειτώλιον
W.

---

[a] At first, according to Dio lix. 6. 1, Gaius showed great
deference to the senators. But later, according to Suetonius,
Calig. 26, Gaius made some of the senators run for several
miles in their togas beside his chariot and serve as waiters
when he dined. He abused the senate as having been adherents of Sejanus and as having acted as informers against
his mother and brothers (Suet. Calig. 30). See also Sen. De
Ira iii. 18. 3-19. 2 and De Ben. ii. 12. 1-2, and Dio lix. 23. 3.
[b] Cf. Suetonius, Calig. 35, who notes that Caligula deprived the noblest men of their ancient family emblems.
Thus he took away Torquatus' gold collar, Cincinnatus' lock

214

it forth to spread over every land and sea which was
subject to the Romans, and infected the empire with
countless ills, such as had never before been chronicled
in history. Rome above all felt the horror of his
actions, since he gave it no more privilege than other
cities, but harried the citizens, especially the senators [a] and those who were of the patrician class or
had special honours because of distinguished ancestors.[b] He also devised countless attacks upon the
equites,[c] as they were called. The standing and
financial influence of this group gave them equal
status with the senators in the eyes of the city because
it was from their ranks that the senate was recruited.
He deprived the equites of their privileges and expelled them from Rome or put them to death and
robbed them of their wealth ; for it was usually as a
pretext for confiscating their property that he had
them slain.[d] He would also have deified himself and
demanded from his subjects honours that were no
longer such as may be rendered to a man. When he
visited the Temple of Jupiter [e] which they call the
Capitol [f] and which is first in honour among their

of hair, and Gnaeus Pompey's surname " the great," which
the Pompeian family had long held.

[c] According to Suetonius, *Calig.* 30, Gaius asserted that
the equestrian order had incurred his displeasure because of
their excessive devotion to attending dramas and sporting
events.

[d] *Cf.* the story of how Gaius interrupted a game of dice,
went out into the courtyard, caused two rich *equites* who
passed by to be arrested, confiscated their property, and then
returned to the game boasting of his good luck (Suet. *Calig.*
41).

[e] The temple of Jupiter Optimus Maximus stood on the
Capitoline hill, so called on account of the temple.

[f] The temple of Jupiter was also called the *aedes Capito-
lina* ; see Pliny, *Hist. Nat.* xxxiii. 5. 16, 6. 19 ; xxxv. 4. 14.

τιμιώτατον δ' ἄρα αὐτοῖς ἐστιν ἱερῶν, ἀδελφὸν
5 ἐτόλμησε προσαγορεύειν τὸν Δία· καὶ τἆλλα ἔπρασσεν μανίας οὐδὲν ἀπολελειμμένα,¹ ἐπεὶ καὶ ἀπὸ
Δικαιαρχείας² τῆς πόλεως ἐν Καμπανίᾳ κειμένης
εἰς Μισηνοὺς³ ἑτέραν πόλιν ἐπιθαλάσσιον, καὶ τὴν
6 διάβασιν δεινὸν ἡγούμενος τριήρει περατοῦν, καὶ
ἄλλως ἐπιβάλλειν ἡγούμενος αὐτῷ δεσπότῃ ὄντι
τῆς θαλάσσης ταῦτα καὶ ὁποῖα καὶ παρὰ γῆς
ἀπαιτεῖν, ἀπ' ἄκρων ἐπ' ἄκρα σταδίους τριάκοντα
μέτρον τῆς θαλάσσης⁴ ζεύξας⁵ καὶ εἴσω τὸν κόλπον
ἀπολαβὼν πάντα ἤλαυνεν ἐπὶ τῇ γεφύρᾳ τὸ ἅρμα·

¹ ex Lat.: ἀπολελειμμένος codd. E.
² Dindorf: Δικαιαρχίας codd. E.
³ Hudson: Μεσηνοὺς codd. E: Mesena Lat.
⁴ ταῦτα . . . θαλάσσης] om. W.
⁵ E: om. codd.

---

[a] It was here that the consuls made their first public sacrifice, here that the senate met, here that triumphal processions
ended, and here that archives dealing with foreign relations
were kept. *Cf.* S. B. Platner and T. Ashby, *A Topographical
Dictionary of Ancient Rome*, 1929, pp. 297-302.

[b] Suetonius, *Calig.* 22, notes that Gaius would engage in
conversation with Jupiter Capitolinus, alternately whispering
and shouting angry threats. Gaius finally announced that
Jupiter had persuaded him to live with him, and so he built
a bridge connecting the imperial palace with the Capitol.
Dio lix. 4. 2 remarks that though at first he forbade anyone
to set up images of himself, he even went on to manufacture
statues himself and to order temples to be erected and sacrifices offered to himself as a god. Dio also (lix. 28. 5 ; similarly Suet. *Calig.* 22) notes that Gaius called himself Jupiter
Latiaris, *i.e.* Jupiter of Latium, and remarks (lix. 26. 5) that
he used to impersonate all the gods.

[c] Of Baiae.

[d] Roman Puteoli. See *Ant.* xviii. 160.

[e] mss. Mesèni (for other instances of the plural " Miseni "
see Pauly-Wissowa, xv², 1932, p. 2046) ; modern Miseno.
This was the chief naval base in Italy at the time.

temples,[a] he had the audacity to address Jupiter as brother.[b] His other actions too did not fall short of madness. For instance, it was insufferable, he thought, to cross the bay [c] from the city of Dicaearchia [d] in Campania to Misenum,[e] another maritime city, in a trireme. Then, too, he considered it his privilege as lord of the sea to require the same service from the sea as he received from the land. So the thirty [f] furlongs of sea from headland to headland were connected by pontoons, which cut off the whole bay, and over this bridge [g] he drove in his chariot.

[f] Twenty-six furlongs in Dio lix. 17. 1, who says that the bridge extended from Puteoli to Bauli.

[g] For a further description of this bridge see Dio lix. 17. 1-3, who notes that it had resting-places, lodging-rooms, and even running water for drinking. Gaius celebrated the dedication of the bridge by throwing some people off it. Suetonius, however, by including the building of this bridge among the acts of Caligula the emperor (*Calig.* 19) rather than of Caligula the monster indicates, as Balsdon, *op. cit.*, p. 52, points out, that the bridge was not mere irrational caprice. Suetonius gives three reasons for the building of the bridge : (1) to improve upon Xerxes' feat of bridging the much narrower Hellespont ; (2) to arouse the awe of the Germans and Britons ; and (3) to fulfil the prophecy of Thrasyllus the astrologer, who had assured Tiberius that Gaius had no more chance of becoming emperor than of riding over the Gulf of Baiae with horses. Suetonius says that he heard the last reason from his own grandfather, who asserted that it had been revealed to him by courtiers in Caligula's confidence. Seneca, *De Brev. Vitae* 18. 5-6, like Josephus, alludes to it as an instance of Gaius' madness ; for, he says, at a time when Rome had enough food for at most seven or eight days, Gaius was making bridges of boats and playing with the resources of the empire. Josephus and Seneca apparently place the episode in the last few months of Gaius' reign, while Dio lix. 17. 1-3 and Suetonius seem to put it before A.D. 39 ; but this discrepancy gives no ground for the conjecture that the whole incident may have been fabricated.

θεῷ γὰρ ὄντι τοιαύτας ποιεῖσθαι καλῶς ἔχειν τὰς
7 ὁδούς.¹ τῶν τε ἱερῶν τῶν Ἑλληνικῶν οὐδὲν ἔτι
ἀσύλητον κατέλιπεν, ὁπόσα γραφῆς ἢ γλυφῆς ἐχόμενα καὶ τὰς λοιπὰς κατασκευὰς ἀνδριάντων καὶ
ἀναθημάτων ἄγεσθαι κελεύσας παρ' αὐτόν· οὐ γὰρ
ἐν ἑτέρῳ τὰ καλὰ κεῖσθαι καλῶς ἔχειν ἢ ἐν τῷ
καλλίστῳ, τυγχάνειν δὲ τοῦτο οὖσαν τὴν Ῥωμαίων
8 πόλιν. ἐκόσμει τε τοῖς ἐνθένδε ἀγομένοις τήν τε
οἰκίαν καὶ τοὺς κήπους ὁπόσαι τε αὐτῷ καταγωγαὶ
διὰ γῆς τῆς τῶν Ἰταλῶν. ἐπεὶ καὶ τὸν Ὀλύμπιον
τιμώμενον Δία ὑπὸ τῶν Ἑλλήνων καὶ οὕτως ὠνομασμένον Ὀλύμπιον² Φειδίου τοῦ Ἀθηναίου πε-
ποιηκότος ἐτόλμησε κελεῦσαι εἰς τὴν Ῥώμην
9 μεταφέρειν. οὐ μὴν ἔπραξέν γε τῶν ἀρχιτεκτόνων
φαμένων πρὸς Μέμμιον Ῥῆγλον,³ ὃς ἐπετέτακτο τῇ
κινήσει τοῦ Διός, ἀπολεῖσθαι τοὖργον κινήσεως αὐτοῦ γενομένης. λέγεται δὲ Μέμμιον διὰ ταῦτα καὶ
σημείων μειζόνων γενομένων, ἢ ὡς ἄν τινα μὴ⁴

¹ καὶ ἄλλως . . . . ὁδούς] subicere sibi etiam hoc elementum
posse velut domino maris existenti talia volebat etiam in
fluctibus gerere, qualia solet terrae natura sustinere.  voluit
ergo, ut a litore ad litus stadia ferme trecenta in medio mari
et intra tam vastum´sinum pontem construeret, super quem
carrucis et diversis vehiculis itinera valeret efficere Lat.
² τὸν Ὀλύμπιον . . . Ὀλύμπιον] Iovem Olympium, qui
maxime apud gentiles venerabilis habetur Lat.

That way of travelling, said he, befitted his godhead. Of the Greek temples [a] he left none unpillaged, giving orders that paintings and sculptures and all other statues and dedicatory offerings with which they were furnished should be brought to him ; for it was not right, he said, that beautiful objects should stand anywhere but in the most beautiful place, and that was the city of Rome. With the spoils which he brought from Greece, he adorned his palace and gardens and all his residences throughout the land of Italy. He even dared [b] to give orders to transport to Rome the " Zeus " that was worshipped by the Greeks at Olympia and was therefore called Olympian, a work of the artist Phidias of Athens. He did not, however, carry out this intention, for the chief technicians reported to Memmius Regulus, [c] who had the assignment of moving the Zeus, that the work would be ruined if it were moved. It is said that Memmius postponed removing the statue not only

[a] Dio lix. 28. 1 reports that Gaius desired to appropriate to his own use the large and very beautiful temple that the Milesians were building for Apollo.

[b] A.D. 40. *Cf.* Dio lix. 28. 3, who says that Gaius blamed Jupiter for occupying the Capitoline hill ahead of him and consequently hastened to build another temple on the Palatine, to which he proposed to transfer the statue of Olympian Zeus after remodelling it to resemble himself. The transfer of the statue is also mentioned by Suetonius, *Calig.* 22.

[c] Publius Memmius Regulus, consul suffectus in 31 and later governor of Moesia, Macedonia, and Achaia. According to Tacitus, *Ann.* xiv. 47, when Nero was ill and his flatterers said that if anything befell him the empire would come to an end, he replied that the state still had a resource, namely, Memmius Regulus.

---

[3] ᾽Ρήγλον, ἡ in *i* corr. A : ᾽Ρηγοῦλον MW : ᾽Ρίγλον E.
[4] om. E (sed extat in Busb.).

10 πιστὰ ἡγεῖσθαι, ὑπερβαλέσθαι τὴν ἀναίρεσιν. καὶ
γράφει τάδε πρὸς τὸν Γάιον ἐπ' ἀπολογίᾳ τοῦ ἐκ-
λιπεῖν ἀδιακόνητον τὴν ἐπιστολήν, ἀπολέσθαι τε ἐκ
τούτων αὐτῷ κινδύνου γενομένου σῴζεται φθάνον-
τος ἤδη Γαΐου τελευτῆσαι.

11 (2) Εἰς τοῦτο δὲ προύβη τὸ μανικὸν αὐτῷ, ὥστε
δὴ καὶ θυγατρὸς αὐτῷ γενομένης ἀνακομίσας ἐπὶ
τὸ Καπετώλιον ἐπὶ τοῖς γόνασι κατατίθεται τοῦ
ἀγάλματος, κοινὸν αὐτῷ τε καὶ τῷ Διὶ γεγονέναι τὸ
τέκνον καὶ δύο χειροτονεῖν αὐτῆς πατέρας, ὁπότερον

12 μείζονα φάμενος ἐν μέσῳ τε καταλιμπάνειν.¹ καὶ
τάδε ἠνείχοντο πράσσοντα αὐτὸν οἱ ἄνθρωποι.
ἐπεχώρησε² δὲ καὶ τοῖς οἰκέταις κατηγορίας ποιεῖσθαι τῶν δεσποτῶν ἐφ' οἷστισιν ἐθελήσειαν ἐγκλή-
μασιν· δεινὰ γὰρ πάντα ἦν, ὁπόσα μέλλοι λέγεσθαι,³
διὰ τὸ χάριτί τε καὶ ὑπαγορεύσει τῇ ἐκείνου τὰ

13 πολλὰ γίνεσθαι, ὥστε ἤδη καὶ Κλαυδίου ἐτόλμα
ποιήσασθαι Πολυδεύκης ὁ δοῦλος κατηγορίαν, καὶ
Γάιος ἠνείχετο κατὰ πατρῴου τοῦ αὐτοῦ δίκης
θανάτου λεγομένης ἐπ' ἀκροάσει συνελθεῖν ἐλπίδι
τοῦ παραλαβεῖν δύναμιν ἀνελεῖν αὐτόν. οὐ μὴν ἐξ-

---

¹ ὁπότερον . . . καταλιμπάνειν] om. Lat.
² coni. Niese: ἐπεχείρησε codd.: i. marg. γρ ἐπέτρεψε A: mo-
litus est . . . (servos) . . . excitare Lat.     ³ A: γενέσθαι MW.

---

ᵃ Dio lix. 28. 3 reports that the ship built to transport the
statue was shattered by thunderbolts and that loud laughter
was heard whenever anyone approached as if to take hold of
the pedestal of the statue.
ᵇ The Epitome omits the μή: " that were beyond what
anyone could believe." This would indicate that Josephus
did not accept the story.
ᶜ Cf. the similar rescue of Petronius (Ant. xviii. 305), who
had similarly violated an order of Gaius, by the death of the
emperor. According to Dio lix. 28. 3, Gaius, after hearing

for this reason but because of certain portents [a] that were too serious to be discredited.[b] He sent Gaius a letter reporting these matters and explaining his failure to carry out his orders. In consequence, he risked being executed, but he was saved by the death of Gaius which intervened.[c]

(2) So far did Gaius' frenzy go, that when a daughter was born to him he actually carried her to the Capitol [d] and deposited her on the knees of the statue,[e] remarking that the child belonged to both him and Zeus and that he had appointed two fathers for her, but left open the question which of the two was the greater. Such was the behaviour that the world had to put up with. He also permitted [f] servants to bring accusations against their masters on whatever charges they pleased. Anything that was reported was bound to have serious consequences, because most of the charges were brought for his gratification or at his suggestion. Thus Polydeuces, the slave of Claudius, dared to bring an accusation against Claudius, and Gaius was tolerant enough to attend court when a capital charge was brought against his own uncle, expecting to receive authority to put him to death. He was, however, disappointed.

why the statue could not be transported, uttered threats against the statue and set up a new one of himself.

[d] The temple of Jupiter Capitolinus.

[e] According to Suetonius, *Calig.* 25, Gaius carried his daughter, Julia Drusilla, to the temples of all the goddesses before finally placing her in the lap of Minerva, whom he called upon to direct his child's growth and education. Dio lix. 28. 7 says that Gaius placed her on the knees of Jupiter, thereby hinting that she was Jupiter's child, and put her in charge of Minerva to be suckled.

[f] Niese's emendation. Variants " entrusted to," " attempted to arouse."

14 ἐγένετό γε αὐτῷ. ἀναπεπληρωκότι δὲ αὐτῷ συ-
κοφαντιῶν καὶ κακῶν πᾶσαν τὴν οἰκουμένην, ἧς
ἐπῆρχεν, καὶ πολλὴν τὴν δουλοκρατίαν ἐπηρμένου
τοῖς δεσπόταις ἐπιβουλαὶ τὰ πολλὰ ἤδη συνίσταντο,
τῶν μὲν ἐπ' ἀμύνῃ ὧν πάθοιεν ὀργὴν ποιουμένων,
τῶν δὲ πρὶν ἐμπεσόντες κακῶν τυχεῖν μεγάλων[1] τι-
15 θεμένων τὸ μεταχειρίσασθαι τὸν ἄνθρωπον.[2] ὅθεν,
ἐπειδὴ τοῖς τε ἀπάντων νόμοις καὶ τῷ ἀσφαλεῖ
μεγάλην συνήνεγκεν εὐδαιμονίας ῥοπὴν ὁ θάνατος
αὐτοῦ ἔθνει τε τῷ ἡμετέρῳ οὐδὲ εἰς ὀλίγον ἐξεγε-
γόνει μὴ οὐκ ἀπολωλέναι μὴ ταχείας αὐτῷ τελευτῆς
παραγενομένης, βούλομαι[3] δι' ἀκριβείας τὸν πάντα
16 περὶ αὐτοῦ λόγον διελθεῖν, ἄλλως τε ἐπειδὴ καὶ
πολλὴν ἔχει πίστιν τοῦ θεοῦ τῆς δυνάμεως καὶ παρα-
μυθίαν τοῖς ἐν τύχαις κειμένοις καὶ σωφρονισμὸν
τοῖς οἰομένοις ἀίδιον τὴν εὐτυχίαν, ἀλλὰ μὴ ἐπιμετα-
φέρειν[4] κακῶς ἀρετῆς αὐτῇ μὴ παραγενομένης.

17 (3) Ὁδοὺς μὲν δὴ τρεῖς ὁ θάνατος αὐτοῦ παρεσκευάζετο καὶ τούτων ἑκάστης ἄνδρες ἀγαθοὶ τὴν
ἡγεμονίαν εἶχον. Αἰμίλιός τε γὰρ Ῥῆγλος ἐκ Κορ-
δύβης τῆς ἐν Ἰβηρίᾳ γένος συνεῖχέν τινας ἢ δι'
ἐκείνων ἢ δι' αὐτοῦ πρόθυμος ὢν ἄρασθαι Γάιον.
18 ἑτέρα δὲ αὐτοῖς συνεκροτεῖτο, ἧς Χαιρέας Κάσσιος
χιλίαρχος ἡγεμὼν ἦν. Βινουκιανὸς[5] δὲ Ἄννιος[6]

[1] μέγα coni. Richards et Shutt.
[2] τῶν δὲ . . . ἄνθρωπον] ab aliis autem praevenire homines
cupientibus, cum sibi ab eis pro culpis suis aliquod supplicium
imminere sentirent Lat.
[3] βούλομαι] Hudson ex Lat.: βούλομαι δὲ codd.: βούλομαι
δὴ coni. Niese.
[4] ἐπιμεταφέρειν] AM: ἐπιφέρειν W: ἐπὶ μήκιστον φέρειν ed.
pr.: ἐπὶ μέγα φέρειν coni. Niese.
[5] [vel Βινυκιανὸς] coni. Niese (vol. iii, praef., p. xviii): Μινουκιανὸς codd.      [6] Ἄννισος Busb.: om. Lat.

As he had made all of the inhabited world over which he ruled a prey to informers and their evil work and had raised high the power of slaves over their masters, conspiracies were now commonly formed against him. Some of the conspirators were angry and sought vengeance for the wrongs they had endured, others counted on doing away with the creature before they fell foul of him and suffered disaster. Therefore, since his death not only was of great importance in the interest of all men's laws and the safeguarding of them, but our own nation was brought to the very verge of ruin and would have been destroyed but for his sudden death, I am resolved to give an exact account of everything that happened. I have another particular motive in that the story provides good evidence of God's power.[a] It will comfort those who are in unhappy circumstances, and will teach a lesson in sobriety to those who think that good fortune is eternal and do not know that it ends in catastrophe unless it goes hand in hand with virtue. *Josephus' reasons for recounting Gaius' death.*

(3) There were three schemes in preparation for his death, and each of them had good men as leaders. Aemilius Regulus of Cordova in Iberia was the centre of one ring and heartily hoped to dispose of Gaius either by the hands of his colleagues or by his own. A second ring was in process of organization to aid them, of which Cassius Chaerea the military tribune [b] was leader. Finally, Annius Vinicianus [c] was no *Three conspiracies against Gaius.*

---

[a] Cf. *Ant.* xviii. 306.

[b] According to Suetonius, *Calig.* 56, he was tribune of a cohort of the praetorian guard.

[c] There seems to be a good deal of confusion in Josephus in the name : he seems to use the name Minucianus for both Vinicianus and Marcus Vinicius. This is clear from § 102,

οὐκ ὀλίγη μοῖρα τῶν ἐπὶ τὴν τυραννίδα παρεσκευα-
19 σμένων ἦν. αἰτία δ' αὐτοῖς μίσους τοῦ πρὸς Γάιον
συνελθεῖν, Ῥήγλῳ μὲν τὸ ἐπὶ πᾶσιν ὀργίλον καὶ
μίσει χρώμενον πρὸς τὰ μετ' ἀδικίας ἐξαγόμενα·
καὶ γὰρ ἔχει τι θυμοειδὲς ἐν τῇ διανοίᾳ καὶ ἐλευ-
θέριον, ὑφ' οὗ μηδὲ στέγειν προστίθεσθαι τῶν βου-
λευμάτων· πολλοῖς γοῦν ἀνεκοινώσατο καὶ φίλοις
20 καὶ ἄλλοις δοκοῦσιν αὐτῷ δραστηρίοις. Βινουκιανὸς[1] δὲ τὰ μὲν Λεπίδου τε ἐκδικήσων,[2] φίλον γὰρ
αὐτῷ τὰ μάλιστα ὄντα τοῦτον καὶ τῶν πολιτῶν σὺν
ὀλίγοις ἀναιρεῖ Γάιος, καὶ ἄλλως φοβηθεὶς τὰ περὶ
αὐτὸν διὰ τὸ πᾶσιν ὁμοίως τὸν Γάιον ἐπὶ θάνατον
ἀνακειμένην ἐπαφιέναι τὴν ὀργὴν ἐπὶ τὴν ἐγχεί-
21 ρησιν ἦλθεν.[3] Χαιρέας[4] δὲ αἰσχύνην φέρων τὰ
ὀνείδη[5] τὰ[6] εἰς τὴν ἀνανδρίαν ὑπὸ τοῦ Γαίου προφερό-
μενα,[7] καὶ ἄλλως τὸ ἐφ' ἡμέρᾳ κινδυνεύειν φιλίᾳ καὶ
θεραπείᾳ τὴν Γαίου τελευτὴν οὐκ ἀνελεύθερον[8] ὑπο-
22 λαμβάνων.[9] οἱ δὲ καὶ πᾶσι κοινῇ προτεθῆναι τὴν

---

[1] coni. Niese (cf. § 18): Μινουκιανὸς codd.
[2] Petersen: ἐκδικία codd.     [3] Cocceji: ἐλθεῖν codd.
[4] Dindorf: Χαιρέαν codd.
[5] φέρων τὰ ὀνείδη] Dindorf: φέροντα ὀνείδη codd.
[6] Hudson: τε codd.
[7] Hudson: προφερομένου A: προσφερομένου MW.
[8] οὐκ ἀνελεύθερον] Hudson: οὐ πάντ' ἐλεύθερον codd.
[9] συνελθεῖν . . . ὑπολαμβάνων] om. E.

---

where the mss. similarly have Μινουκιανός and where (cf. Tac.
Ann. vi. 15) Vinicius must be meant (so also Niese, preface
to vol. iii, p. xviii). Here, though the mss. have Minucianus,
it appears from Dio lx. 15. 1 that Vinicianus is meant. The
latter had been accused of treason in 32 by Tiberius (Tac.
Ann. vi. 9) and was one of the Arval Brethren. He took his
own life in 42 after an unsuccessful conspiracy against Claudius (Dio lx. 15. 1 ff.).

[a] mss. Minucianus; cf. note on § 18.

slight addition to those who were enlisted against
the tyranny. The reasons for their hatred of Gaius
were as follows : Regulus was moved by general
indignation and a detestation of unjust proceedings.
For he had in him a free man's independent spirit, so
much so that he even threw his weight against keeping any of the plots a close secret. At any rate he
informed many friends of them as well as others who
won his approval as men of action. Vinicianus [a]
joined the plot partly to avenge Lepidus,[b] a special
friend of his and one of the best citizens,[c] who had
been put to death by Gaius, and partly from fear for
himself, because when Gaius gave vent to his anger,
it was a death-dealing fury that made no exceptions.
Chaerea joined because he felt disgraced by the slurs
cast on his manliness [d] by Gaius ; moreover, there
was daily peril in his intimate attendance on Gaius,
and he considered it the part of a free man to put an
end to him.[e] These three men thought that the

[b] M. Aemilius Lepidus ; cf. § 49. Seneca, Epist. 4. 7,
reports that Gaius ordered him to bare his neck for the axe
of the tribune Dexter. There is no evidence to support
Balsdon's suggestion (p. 42) that he was a cousin of Gaius,
but he did marry Gaius' sister Drusilla (Dio lix. 11. 1 and
22. 6). After the latter's death in 38, Caligula chose him as
his successor (Dio lix. 22. 7). Several writers (Suet. Calig.
24, Dio lix. 22. 6, Tac. Ann. xiv. 2) report his adultery with
Agrippina. He and Gaetulicus were involved in a conspiracy
against Gaius (Suet. Calig. 24, Claud. 9), as was Livilla,
Gaius' sister (Suet. Calig. 24), and he was put to death in 39.

[c] A less likely meaning is " along with a few other citizens."

[d] Suetonius, Calig. 56, says that Gaius persistently taunted
Chaerea, who was well along in years, for his supposed ef-
feminacy.

[e] Text emended. Variant " because he considered the
daily danger of his friendship with and attendance upon
Gaius to be a task quite unbecoming a free-born man."

ἐπὶ τῷ πράγματι σκέψιν[1] τήν τε ὕβριν θεωμένοις
καὶ ἐπιθυμοῦσιν ἀκμὴν ἐπ' ἄλλων[2] ἀκμάζουσαν
διαφυγεῖν ἀραμένοις τὸν Γάιον· ἴσως μὲν γὰρ ἂν
κατορθῶσαι, καλῶς δὲ κατορθοῦσι τηλικούτων ἀγαθῶν σχεῖν ἐπὶ σωτηρίᾳ τῆς τε πόλεως καὶ τῆς
ἡγεμονίας πονοῦσι καὶ μετὰ ὀλέθρου ἅπτεσθαι τοῦ
23 πράγματος.[3] παρὰ πάντα δὲ Χαιρέαν ἐπείγεσθαι
ὀνόματός τε ἐπιθυμίᾳ μείζονος καὶ ἄλλως ὑπὸ τοῦ
ἀδεέστερον προσιέναι τῷ Γαΐῳ διὰ τὴν χιλιαρχίαν
ῥᾳστώνης αὐτῷ κτείνειν ἐσομένης.

24 (4) Ἐν τούτῳ δ' ἱπποδρομίαι ἦσαν· καὶ σπουδά-
ζεται γὰρ Ῥωμαίοις ἥδε ἡ θεωρία δεινῶς, συνίασίν
τε προθύμως εἰς τὸν ἱππόδρομον καὶ ἐφ' οἷς χρή-
ζοιεν δέονται τῶν αὐτοκρατόρων κατὰ πλῆθος
συνελθόντες, οἱ δὲ ἀναντιλέκτους τὰς δεήσεις κρί-
25 νοντες οὐδαμῶς ἀχαριστοῦσιν. ἐκέλευον δὴ καὶ
τὸν Γάιον ἐκθύμῳ τῇ ἱκετείᾳ χρώμενοι τῶν τε τε-
λῶν ἐπανιέναι καὶ τῶν φόρων[4] ἐπικουφίζειν τι τοῦ
ἐπαχθοῦς. ὁ δ' οὐκ ἠνείχετο, καὶ πλέον τι τῇ βοῇ
χρωμένων ἄλλους ἄλλῃ διαπέμψας κελεύει τοὺς
βοῶντας λαβεῖν τε καὶ μηδὲν εἰς ἀναβολὰς ἀνελεῖν
26 προαγαγόντας. καὶ ὁ μὲν ἐκέλευε ταῦτα καὶ οἷς
προσετέτακτο ἔπρασσον, πλεῖστοί τε ἦσαν οἱ ἐπὶ τοι-

---

[1] σκέψιν] σκέψιν φασὶ E.    [2] coni. Niese: ἀλλήλων codd.
[3] οἱ δὲ . . . πράγματος] ceteri vero cupiebant super hoc
habere commune consilium videntes tantas iniurias et exemplum pravum dari cupientibus principatum, omnes ergo
ut tantis cladibus liberarentur desiderabant adversus Gaium
aliquid geri ; decere namque ad talia negotia bonos viros
accedere pro salute pietatis et imperii macula auferenda etiam
cum suo discrimine Lat.    [4] τῶν φόρων] A : om. MWE.

---

[a] Suetonius, *Calig.* 40, notes that under Caligula there
were no goods or services that were not taxed. The new tax

matter should be laid for general consideration before everyone who had been spectators of the emperor's insolence and who desired, by removing Gaius, to avoid the sharp sword that was raging against others. Perhaps they would succeed ; and a high thing it would be to achieve such good ends by their efforts, when they were ready in any case to strike for the preservation of city and empire even if it meant their own destruction. Chaerea was especially bent on action, both because he desired to win a better reputation, and because, by his freer access to Gaius as tribune, he would more easily find an opportunity to kill him.

(4) At this time occurred chariot races. This is a kind of spectator sport to which the Romans are fanatically devoted. They gather enthusiastically in the circus and there the assembled throngs make requests of the emperors according to their own pleasure. Emperors who rule that there can be no question about granting such petitions are by no means unpopular. So in this case they desperately entreated Gaius to cut down imposts and grant some relief from the burden of taxes.[a] But he had no patience with them, and when they shouted louder and louder, he dispatched agents among them in all directions with orders to arrest any who shouted, to bring them forward at once and to put them to death. The order was given and those whose duty it was carried it out. The number of those executed in such summary fashion was very

Gaius' savagery t petitioners at the chariot races.

regulations were announced orally. When the people entreated him to put them in written form, he finally agreed, but had them written in so cramped a place and in so small a script as to cause people to incur the penalties by ignorance of the law. *Cf.* also Dio lix. 28. 11.

οὔτοις ἀποθανόντες. καὶ ὁ δῆμος ἑώρα μέν, ἠνείχετο δὲ παυσάμενος τῆς βοῆς, ἐν ὀλίγῳ[1] ἕνεκα τῶν
χρημάτων ὀφθαλμοῖς ὁρῶντες τὴν ἐπὶ τοιούτοις
27 παραίτησιν εἰς θάνατον αὐτοῖς φέρουσαν. ταῦτα
Χαιρέαν ἐνήγαγε μειζόνως ἅπτεσθαί τε τῆς ἐπιβουλῆς καὶ παύειν κατὰ τῶν ἀνθρώπων ἐξηγριω-
κότα τὸν Γάιον, καὶ πολλάκις μὲν καὶ παρὰ τὰς
ἑστιάσεις ἐμέλλησεν ἐπιχειρεῖν, οὐ μὴν ἀλλ' ἐπεί-
χετο λογισμῷ, τὸ μὲν κτείνειν οὐκέτ' ἐνδοιαστὸν
κεκρικώς, τὸν δὲ καιρὸν περισκοπῶν, ὅπως μὴ εἰς
κενόν, ἀλλ' ἐπὶ καταπράξει τῶν βεβουλευμένων
ταῖς χερσὶ χρῷτο.
28 (5) Ἐστραγγεύετο[2] δὲ πολὺν ἤδη χρόνον οὐχ
ἡδονῇ φέρων Γαΐου τὴν ἀναστροφήν.[3] ἐπεὶ δὲ
αὐτὸν ἵσταται Γάιος εἰσπραξόμενον τούς τε φόρους
καὶ ὅσα ἄλλα καταβαλλόμενα εἰς τὸν Καίσαρος θη-
σαυρὸν ἐφυστερήκει τοῖς καιροῖς διὰ τὸ ἐπιδιπλασιά-
ζεσθαι τὴν δύναμιν αὐτῶν, χρόνον ἐκεῖ[4] ποιεῖται τῇ
ἐκπράξει[5] τρόπῳ τῷ αὐτοῦ χρώμενος μᾶλλον ἢ τῇ
29 Γαΐου προστάξει, διὰ τὸ φειδοῖ χρῆσθαι τὰς τύχας[6]
οἴκτῳ λαμβάνων τῶν ὑπὸ τὴν εἴσπραξιν εἰς ὀργὴν
προὐκαλεῖτο τὸν Γάιον μαλακίαν ἐπικαλοῦντα αὐτῷ
τοῦ σχολῇ συνάγεσθαι αὐτῷ τὰ χρήματα. καὶ δὴ
τά τε ἄλλα ὕβριζεν εἰς αὐτὸν καὶ ὁπότε τὸ σημεῖον
αἰτοῖ[7] τὸ τῆς ἡμέρας καθηκούσης εἰς αὐτόν, θήλεά
30 τε ἐδίδου τὰ ὀνόματα, καὶ ταῦτα αἰσχύνης ἀνάπλεα

---

[1] ἐν ὀλίγῳ] om. E.
[2] Naber : ἐστρατεύετο codd. : militabat Lat.
[3] A : συναναστροφήν MW.
[4] ἐκείνων vel ἐκεῖνος coni. Herwerden.
[5] εἰσπράξει E.        [6] τὰς τύχας] om. E.
[7] Post: αὑτῷ codd. : αἰτοῖτο coni. Niese : παρεῖχε post αὑτῷ
add. E.

large. The people, when they saw what happened, stopped their shouting and controlled themselves, for they could see with their own eyes that the request for fiscal concessions resulted quickly in their own death. This strengthened still further Chaerea's determination to embark on the plot and to put an end to Gaius and his brutal fury against mankind. Often at entertainments he had been on the point of acting, yet nevertheless refrained when he calculated his chances. He no longer had any hesitation in his resolve to kill the man, but his search for the best moment continued, since he wished not to resort to violence fruitlessly, but to ensure the success of his plans.

(5) Progress had been blocked [a] now for some time and Chaerea was disgusted with the conduct of Gaius.[b] But when Gaius appointed him to the duty of enforcing payment of any taxes or other sums that were payable to the imperial treasury and that were overdue because the rate had been doubled, he took his time about these exactions and followed his own bent rather than the instructions of Gaius. Because he was merciful out of pity for the misfortunes which the people suffered under the exactions, he incensed Gaius, who called it womanly weakness to be so slow in collecting the money. Moreover, he not only insulted Chaerea in other ways, but whenever Chaerea as officer of the day asked for the password, Gaius would give him women's words and such as had quite obscene connotations.[c] And yet, Gaius

Cassius Chaerea is appointed tax-collector and insulted by Gaius.

[a] mss. " he had been soldiering " or " he had been carrying on his campaign."

[b] Variant " Chaerea found his relations with Gaius no pleasure."

[c] Suetonius, *Calig.* 56, and Seneca, *De Const. Sap.* 18. 3,

καὶ ταῦτα ἔπρασσεν αὐτὸς οὐκ ἀπηλλαγμένος ἔν
τινων τελεταῖς μυστηρίων, ἃς αὐτὸς συνίστατο,
στολάς τε ἐνδυόμενος γυναικείους καί τινων περι-
θέσεις πλοκαμίδων ἐπινοῶν ἄλλα τε ὁπόσα ἐπι-
καταψεύσασθαι θηλύτητα τῆς ὄψεως ἔμελλεν, αὐτὸς
τὴν ἐπὶ τοιούτοις αἰσχύνην ἐτόλμα Χαιρέᾳ προσ-
31 καλεῖν. Χαιρέᾳ δὲ καὶ ὁπότε μὲν παραλαμβάνοι
τὸ σημεῖον¹ ὀργὴ² παρίστατο, μειζόνως δ' ὁπότε
παραδιδοίη, γελώμενος ὑπὸ τῶν παραλαμβανόντων,
ὥστε καὶ οἱ συγχιλίαρχοι παιδιὰν ἐποιοῦντο αὐτόν·
ὁπότε γὰρ αὐτὸς μέλλοι τὸ σημεῖον παρ' αὐτοῦ
Καίσαρος κομίζειν, προὔλεγόν τινα τῶν εἰωθότων
32 φέρειν εἰς παιδιάν. διὰ ταῦτα δὲ αὐτῷ καὶ θάρσος
παρίστατο κοινωνούς τινας παραλαμβάνειν, ὡς οὐκ
ἐπ' ὀλίγοις³ ὀργῇ χρώμενος. καὶ ἦν γὰρ Πομπή-
διος⁴ συγκλητικὸς μέν, τὰς ἀρχὰς δὲ διεληλυθὼς
σχεδὸν ἁπάσας, Ἐπικούρειος δ' ἄλλως καὶ δι' αὐτὸ
33 ἀπράγμονος ἐπιτηδευτὴς βίου. τοῦτον ἐνδείκνυσιν
Τιμίδιος ἐχθρὸς ὢν ὡς λοιδορίᾳ χρησάμενον ἀ-
πρεπεῖ κατὰ τοῦ Γαΐου μάρτυρα παραλαμβάνων
Κυιντιλίαν γυναῖκα τῶν ἐπὶ τῆς σκηνῆς ἐπιφανείᾳ

¹ τὸ σημεῖον] haec vestimenta Lat.
² Hudson : ὀργῇ codd. E.
³ A : ἀλόγοις MW : causis minoribus Lat.
⁴ Πομπή | ιος A¹ : Pompidius Lat.

remark that when Chaerea would demand the password,
Caligula would give him " Priapus " or " Venus." Dio lix.
29. 2 says that Gaius habitually called Chaerea, who was the
hardiest of men, a wench, and that he would give him such
passwords as " Love " or " Venus."
  ᵃ A similar account of the accusation of Pompedius is

himself was not free from the same taint in the rites
of certain mysteries which he had himself contrived.
He would put on women's robes and devise wigs or
other means of counterfeiting a feminine appearance.
Yet now he actually had the effrontery to invite
mockery of Chaerea on the same score. Whenever
Chaerea received the password he was furious, and
still more when he passed it on and was derided by
those who received it from him. As a result, even
his fellow tribunes made fun of him ; whenever he
was due to go to bring them the password from
Caesar, they would mention beforehand one of the
words that lent themselves to jests. As a consequence, he gained courage to seek partners in his
plot, for he had good reason to be angry. Now there
was one Pompedius,[a] of senatorial rank, who had held
nearly all the offices of state, but except for that was
an Epicurean [b] and consequently lived a life of ease.
This Pompedius was accused by his enemy Timidius
of applying opprobrious epithets to Gaius.[c] Timidius
called as a witness Quintilia, an actress who enjoyed

---

[a] found in Dio lix. 26. 4, where, however, he is called Pomponius and where Timidius is not mentioned by name but
is merely called a friend. The attempted identification of
Pompedius with the senator Pompeius Pennus (Sen. *De Ben.*
ii. 12. 1-2) has, as noted by Stein, "Timidius," in Pauly-
Wissowa, 2. Reihe, vi[1], 1936, p. 1256, little to recommend it.

[b] Epicureanism, preaching both a cosmopolitanism and
the happiness of the individual, taught its adherents to avoid
political careers so as to maintain maximum personal liberty.
See N. W. De Witt, *Epicurus and His Philosophy*, 1954, who
quotes (p. 187) Cicero's remark to Atticus the Epicurean in
44 B.C. after the assassination of Julius Caesar : " You mention Epicurus and dare to warn me μὴ πολιτεύεσθαι" [" to
keep out of politics "] (Cic. *Ad Att.* xiv. 20. 5).

[c] Dio lix. 26. 4 says that Pomponius (*i.e.* our Pompedius)
was accused of having actually plotted against Gaius.

τοῦ ὡραίου περισπούδαστον πολλοῖς τε οὖσαν καὶ
34 τῷ Πομπηδίῳ. καὶ τῆς ἀνθρώπου, ψεῦδος γὰρ ἦν,
δεινὸν ἡγουμένης μαρτυρίαν ἐπὶ θανάτῳ τοῦ ἐρα-
στοῦ παρασχεῖν, βασάνων ἔχρῃζεν ὁ Τιμίδιος, καὶ
Γάιος παρωξυμμένος κελεύει τὸν Χαιρέαν μηδὲν
εἰς ἀναβολὰς ἀλλ᾽ εὐθέως βασανίζειν τὴν Κυιντιλίαν,[1]
χρώμενος τῷ Χαιρέᾳ πρός τε τὰ φονικὰ καὶ ὁπόσα
στρεβλώσεως δέοιτο ὑπὸ τοῦ νομίζειν ὠμότερον δια-
κονήσεσθαι τὴν λοιδορίαν φεύγοντα τῆς μαλακίας.
35 Κυιντιλία δ᾽ ἐπὶ τὴν βάσανον ἀγομένη τῶν συνιστό-
ρων τινὸς ἐπιβαίνει τῷ ποδὶ ἀποσημαίνουσα θαρσεῖν καὶ μὴ τὰς βασάνους αὐτῆς δεδιέναι· διοίσειν
γὰρ μετ᾽ ἀνδραγαθίας. βασανίζει δ᾽ αὐτὴν ὠμῶς ὁ
Χαιρέας, ἄκων μέν, κατ᾽ ἀνάγκας δὲ τὰς ὑπὲρ
αὐτοῦ, καὶ μηδὲν ἐνδοῦσαν ἦγεν εἰς τὴν ὄψιν τὴν
Γαΐου διακειμένην[2] οὐκ ἐν ἡδονῇ τοῖς θεωροῦσι.
36 καὶ ὁ Γάιος παθών τι πρὸς τὴν ὄψιν τῆς Κυιντιλίας
δεινῶς ὑπὸ τῶν ἀλγηδόνων διακειμένης τοῦ τε
ἐγκλήματος ἠφίει καὶ αὐτὴν καὶ τὸν Πομπήδιον,
ἐκείνην δὲ καὶ χρημάτων δόσει τιμᾷ παραμυθίας
ἐσομένων λώβης τε ἦν ἐλελώβητο εἰς τὴν εὐπρέ-
πειαν τοῦ τ᾽[3] ἀφορήτου τῶν ἀλγηδόνων.
37 (6) Ταῦτα δεινῶς ἠνίασεν τὸν Χαιρέαν ὡς αἴτιον[4]
ἀνθρώποις καὶ ὑπὸ Γαΐου παρηγορίας ἀξίοις[5] κακῶν

---

[1] W : Κυϊντιλλίαν A : Κυιντιλίαν M : Quintillam cod. A Lat.
[2] δεδεγμένην coni. Marcus.
[3] τοῦ τ᾽] coni. Niese : τοῦ codd.
[4] ὡς αἴτιον] om. Petersen.

232

the devotion of Pompedius and many others because of her striking beauty. This poor woman, since the charge was false, was indignant at the thought of bearing witness that would be fatal to her lover. Timidius then called for torture. Gaius in a passion ordered Chaerea not to waste a moment, but to put Quintilia to torture at once. He employed Chaerea in cases of murder and any others that called for torture, because he calculated that Chaerea's performance would be more cruel since he would not want to be abused as a weakling. Quintilia, when brought in for torture, trod on the foot of one of those privy to the conspiracy as a sign that he should keep cool and have no fear of her yielding to torture, for she would hold out bravely. Chaerea, reluctantly, but forced by superior authority, tortured her cruelly, but when she showed no weakness, he brought her— she was now in a state that brought no delight to the eyes of onlookers—into the presence of Gaius. Even Gaius was affected by the sight of Quintilia, who was in a sorry state as a result of her suffering. He acquitted both her and Pompedius of the charge and conferred a gift of money [a] on her as consolation for the maltreatment that marred her beauty and for the intolerable agonies that she had undergone.

(6) These things grievously distressed Chaerea, for he had been, so far as it was in his power, a source of misery to persons who were considered even by

Chaerea plots with Clemens and Papinius.

---

[a] So also Dio lix. 26. 4. Suetonius, *Calig.* 16, reports that Gaius, to make known his encouragement of noble action, awarded 800,000 sesterces to a freedwoman—he does not give her name—who, despite the most severe torture, kept silent about her patron's guilt.

---

[5] ἀξιουμένοις Richards et Shutt.

ὅσον ἐπ᾽[1] αὐτῷ γενόμενον,[2] φησίν[3] τε πρὸς Κλή-
μεντά τε καὶ Παπίνιον, ὧν Κλήμης μὲν ἦν ἐπὶ τῶν
στρατοπέδων, Παπίνιος[4] δὲ καὶ αὐτὸς ἦν χιλιαρ-
38 χῶν, " ἀλλ᾽ ἐπὶ φυλακῇ γε, ὦ Κλήμης, τὰ πάντα
τοῦ αὐτοκράτορος ἡμῖν πράσσειν οὐκ ἐλλέλειπται·
τῶν γὰρ συνομωμοκότων αὐτοῦ κατὰ τῆς ἡγεμονίας
προνοίᾳ καὶ πόνοις τοὺς μὲν ἀπεκτείναμεν, τοὺς δὲ
ἐστρεβλώσαμεν ἐπὶ τοσοῦτον, ὡς ἐλεεινοὺς κἀκείνῳ
γενέσθαι, μετὰ πόσης τε ἀρετῆς ἡμῖν ἐξάγεται τὰ[5]
39 τῶν στρατιῶν; "[6] σιγήσαντος δὲ τοῦ Κλήμεντος
καὶ τὸ μὲν αἰσχύνη φέρειν τὰ προστασσόμενα καὶ
τῷ βλέμματι καὶ τῷ ἐρυθήματι παριστάντος, λόγῳ
δὲ αὐτοῖς τὴν μανίαν τοῦ αὐτοκράτορος προσκαλεῖν
40 ἄδικον ἡγουμένου προνοίᾳ τοῦ ἀσφαλοῦς, Χαιρέας
ἤδη θάρσει χρώμενος ἐν λόγοις ἦν κινδύνων ἀνει-
μένοις πρὸς αὐτὸν τὰ κατέχοντα δεινὰ τὴν πόλιν
καὶ τὴν ἀρχὴν ἐπεξιών, καὶ ὅτι λόγῳ μὲν εἴη Γάιος
41 ὁ τὴν ἐπὶ τοιούτοις αἰτίαν προτιθέμενος, τοῖς δὲ τἀ-
ληθὲς ἐξετάζειν πειρωμένοις, " ἐγώ τε, ὦ Κλήμης,
καὶ οὑτοσὶ ὁ Παπίνιος καὶ πρὸ ἡμῶν σύ, ταύτας

---

[1] ὑπὸ Richards et Shutt.
[2] κακῶν ὅσον ἐπ᾽ αὐτῷ γενόμενον] Hudson : ἐν αἰτίᾳ κακῶν
τὸ ὅσον ἐπ᾽ αὐτοῖς γεγενημένοις (γενομένοις W) codd. : γενόμενον E.
[3] ὡς αἴτιον . . . φησίν] quod per eum homines torquerentur,
unde quoque suam iracundiam non sustinens dixit Lat.
[4] Παπήνιον AWE : Παμπήνιον M.
[5] Richards et Shutt ex Lat. : τὸ coni. Niese : om. codd.
[6] μετὰ . . . στρατιῶν] ita nostram militiam cum nimia
severitate tractamus Lat.

---

[a] I have adopted Hudson's emendation. The MSS. yield :
" These things grievously distressed Chaerea, as if he were
guilty [of torturing] persons [considered] even by Gaius de-

Gaius to be deserving of consolation.[a]  He thus declared himself to Clemens [b] and Papinius,[c] of whom
the former was pretorian prefect and the latter was
a military tribune like himself : " Well, Clemens, we
have not failed to go to any length at least in guarding
the emperor.  Through our forethought and toil we
have slain some of the conspirators against his rule
and tortured others to the point where even he took
pity.  How great is the virtue with which we exercise
our military commands ! "  Clemens was silent, but
by his look and blush showed how ashamed he was
of the emperor's orders ; out of regard for his own
safety, however, he did not think it right to refer
openly to the emperor's madness.  Chaerea, now
plucking up courage, began to speak to him in
language unchecked by fear of consequences, recounting the horrors to which the city and the realm
were a prey.  Though nominally, said he, Gaius
bore the responsibility for such proceedings, " to
those who try to investigate the facts it is I, O
Clemens, and Papinius here and you, more than the

serving of consolation, who had been charged with evils in
so far as they were concerned."  The text suggested by Prof.
Petersen (omission of ὡς αἴτιον and change of αὐτοῖς to αὐτῷ)
would mean :  " These things grievously distressed Chaerea,
inasmuch as he was blamed by persons (whom even Gaius
considered deserving of consolation) for violence done them
in so far as they had been turned over to him."

   [b] M. Arrecinus Clemens, father-in-law of the emperor
Titus (Suet. *Tit.* 4).  Tacitus, *Hist.* iv. 68, notes that in the
year 70, Mucianus appointed Arrecinus Clemens commander
of the praetorian guard, " alleging that his father, in the reign
of Caligula, had admirably discharged the duties of that
office."

   [c] Mathieu-Herrmann suggest that this Papinius is perhaps
related to the Sextus Papinius killed by order of Caligula (*cf.*
Sen. *De Ira* iii. 18. 3).

Ῥωμαίοις τε καὶ τῷ παντὶ ἀνθρωπείῳ τὰς στρέβλας
προσφερόμενοι, οὐκ ἐπιτάγμασιν τοῖς Γαΐου δια-
42 κονούμενοι, γνώμῃ δὲ τῇ αὑτῶν, εἰ παρὸν παῦσαι
τοσαύτῃ ἤδη χρώμενον ὕβρει εἴς τε τοὺς πολίτας
καὶ τοὺς ὑπηκόους διακονούμεθα, δορυφόροι καὶ δή-
μιοι καθεστηκότες ἀντὶ στρατιωτῶν καὶ τὰ ὅπλα
ταυτὶ φέροντες οὐχ ὑπὲρ ἐλευθερίας οὐδ᾽ ἀρχῆς τῶν
Ῥωμαίων, ἀλλ᾽ ἐπὶ σωτηρίᾳ τοῦ δουλουμένου τά τε
σώματα αὐτῶν καὶ τὰ φρονήματα, μιαινόμενοι τῷ
καθ᾽ ἡμέραν αἵματι σφαγῆς καὶ βασάνου τῆς ἐκείνων, μέχρι δή τις καὶ καθ᾽ ἡμῶν διακονήσεται[1]
43 τοιαῦτα Γαΐῳ. οὐ γὰρ εὐνοίᾳ γε[2] πολιτεύσει[3] διὰ
τάδε πρὸς ἡμᾶς, δι᾽ ὑφοράσεως δὲ μᾶλλον καὶ
ἄλλως τοῦ πολλοῦ τῶν ἀπολλυμένων ἐπιδεδωκότος[4]·
οὐ γὰρ δὴ στήσεταί ποτε Γαΐῳ τὰ τῆς ὀργῆς διὰ
τὸ μὴ δίκην ἀλλ᾽ ἡδονὴν πέρας αὐτῆς τυγχάνειν·
σκοποὶ δὲ προσκεισόμεθα καὐτοί, δέον καὶ τοῖς
πᾶσιν τὸ ἀνεπιβούλευτόν τε καὶ ἐλεύθερον βεβαιοῦν
καὶ ἡμῖν κινδύνων ἀπαλλαγὰς ψηφίσασθαι.''[5]
44 (7) Κλήμης δὲ τὴν μὲν διάνοιαν τὴν Χαιρέου
φανερὸς ἦν ἐπαινῶν, σιγᾶν δ᾽ ἐκέλευε, μὴ καὶ
φοιτῶντος εἰς πλείονας τοῦ λόγου καὶ διαχεομένων
ὁπόσα κρύπτεσθαι καλῶς ἔχοι πρὶν τυχεῖν πράξαν-
τας ἐκπύστου τοῦ ἐπιβουλεύματος γενομένου κολασθεῖεν, χρόνῳ δὲ τῷ αὖθις καὶ τῇ ἀπ᾽ αὐτοῦ ἐλπίδι
παραδιδόναι τὰ πάντα ὡς παραγενησομένης τινὸς
45 αὐτοῖς ἐπικουρίας τυχαίου· αὐτὸν μὲν γὰρ ὑπὸ

---

[1] Busb. : διακονήσηται codd. E.
[2] Niese : τε AW : om. M : τι Dindorf.
[3] Niese ex Lat. : πολιτεύει codd.
[4] Thackeray : ἀποδεδωκότος codd.
[5] σκοποὶ . . . ψηφίσασθαι] tum demum etiam nos cunctis
pereuntibus coniungemur Lat.

two of us, who are applying these tortures to Romans and to humanity at large. We are not discharging Gaius' orders, but following our own policy if, when it is possible for us to stop him from treating his fellow citizens and subjects as outrageously as he is now doing, we act as his agents, occupying a post as his bodyguard and public executioners instead of doing our duty as soldiers—bearing these arms not to preserve the liberty and government of the Romans, but to save the life of one who makes them slaves in body and mind. And we pollute ourselves with shedding their blood and torturing them daily, up to the moment, mark you, when someone as Gaius' agent will do the same to us. For he will not favour us in his policy on account of these services, but will rather be governed by suspicion, especially when the number of the slain has increased. For surely Gaius will never halt in his furious course since the end he pursues is not justice but pleasure. There we shall be, set up before him as targets,[a] when we ought to be upholding the security and independence of all the people at the same time that we cast a ballot for our own rescue from a dangerous position."

(7) Clemens, it was evident, approved the resolve of Chaerea, but bade him keep silent, lest as the story spread more widely and reports got abroad of what should properly be concealed, the plot might be discovered before they succeeded in its execution, and so they would be punished. It was rather, he said, to the future and to the hope that it inspired that he preferred to entrust everything, in the belief that some stroke of luck would come to their aid.

---

[a] Or " we shall be attached to him as his spies."

γήρως ἀφῃρῆσθαι τὴν ἐπὶ τοιοῖσδε τόλμαν, " τῶν
μέντοι γε ὑπὸ σοῦ, Χαιρέα, συντεθέντων τε καὶ
ῥηθέντων ἀσφαλέστερα μὲν ἴσως ἂν ὑποθοίμην,
46 εὐπρεπέστερα δὲ πῶς ἄν τις καὶ δύναιτο; " καὶ
Κλήμης μὲν ὡς αὐτὸν ἀναλύει διὰ λογισμῶν τῶν τε
ἀκροαθέντων καὶ ὁπόσων αὐτὸς εἰρήκει περιφερόμενος. Χαιρέας δὲ δείσας ὡς Κορνήλιον Σαβῖνον
ἠπείγετο καὶ αὐτὸν μὲν χιλίαρχον ὄντα, ἀξιόλογον
δ' ἄλλως ἐξεπιστάμενος αὐτὸν καὶ τοῦ ἐλευθέρου
ἐραστὴν καὶ δι' αὐτὸ τῇ καταστάσει τῶν πραγ-
47 μάτων πολεμίως διακείμενον, χρῄζων ἐκ τοῦ ὀξέος
ἔχεσθαι τῶν ἐγνωσμένων τῆς ἐγχειρήσεως ὑπ'
αὐτοῦ καλὰ νομίσας εἶναι προσθέσθαι[1] καὶ δέει, μὴ
ὑπὸ Κλήμεντος ἐκφοίτησις γένοιτο αὐτῶν, ἄλλως
τε τὰς μελλήσεις καὶ τῶν καιρῶν τὰς ὑπερβολὰς
πρὸς τῶν ὑπερβαλλομένων τιθέμενος.

48 (8) Ἐπεὶ δὲ ἀσμένῳ καὶ τῷ Σαβίνῳ τὰ πάντα ἦν,
ἅτε καὶ αὐτῷ γνώμης μὲν οὐχ ὑστεροῦντι τῆς ἴσης,
ἀπορίᾳ δὲ πρὸς ὅντινα εἰπὼν ἀσφαλὴς εἴη τὰ πρὸς
ἐκείνους σιγῇ παραδιδόντι,[2] ἐπεί τε ἀνδρὸς ηὐπό-
ρητο οὐ μόνον στέγειν ὧν πύθοιτο προσθησομένου,
ἀλλὰ καὶ γνώμην φανεροῦντος τὴν αὐτοῦ, πολλῷ
μᾶλλον ἦρτο, καὶ μηδὲν εἰς ἀναβολὰς ἐδεῖτο τοῦ

---

[1] ὑπ' . . . προσθέσθαι] oportunum est ratus ut cum eo rem
communicaret Lat.: om. E.
[2] Bekker: παραδιδόντος codd.

---

[a] Mentioned by Suetonius, *Calig.* 58, as the tribune who,
after Chaerea had struck Gaius the first blow, stabbed the

" I myself," he said, " am debarred by age from such a venture, but while I might perhaps advise a course safer than that which you, Chaerea, have designed and told me of, how could anyone propose a more honourable one ? " And so Clemens returned home turning over in his thoughts the proposal that he had heard and his own response to it. Chaerea, for his part, hastened in trepidation to Cornelius Sabinus,[a] who was a military tribune like himself, knowing him well as a noteworthy citizen whose devotion to independence ensured his hostility to the present government. He desired to take in hand with all speed what he had decided upon ; and though he thought it good to add new names, yet he had misgivings that their plans might be brought to the ears of others by Clemens. Besides that, in his accounting, delays and postponements of the event favoured the ruling party.[b]

The conspirators are joined by Sabinus.

(8) But Sabinus rejoiced to hear the whole story. He had not failed to come to the same conclusion himself ; and it was only for lack of one to whom he might safely speak that he had committed to silence what he was ready to join them in doing. Now he had found a man who would not only join him by keeping to himself what he was told but who even declared his own mind. Sabinus was so much the more encouraged and begged Chaerea to waste no time. So

Vinicianus is also enlisted.

emperor in the breast. Both Suetonius, *Calig.* 56 and 58, and Dio lix. 29. 1 regard him and Chaerea as the two leading conspirators. Suetonius states (*Calig.* 56) that they had been implicated, though falsely, in a previous plot against Gaius and that Gaius constantly accused them to one another in an effort to set them at odds.

[b] There is here a play on words—ὑπερβολάς, " delays," lit. " excesses," and ὑπερβαλλομένων, " exceeding," " excessive."

49 Χαιρέου.[1] τρέπονταί τε ὡς Βινουκιανόν,[2] αὐτοῖς
μὲν ἐπιτηδεύσει ἀρετῆς καὶ τῷ ὁμοζήλῳ τοῦ μεγαλόφρονος συγγενῆ, Γαΐῳ δ᾽ ὕποπτον τῆς Λεπίδου
τελευτῆς, πάνυ γὰρ δὴ φίλοι ἐγένοντο Βινουκιανός[3]
τε καὶ Λέπιδος, καὶ δείματι κινδύνων[4] τῶν καθ᾽
50 αὐτόν.[5] πᾶσι γὰρ τοῖς ἐν τέλει φοβερὸς ἦν Γάιος,
ὡς ἐπ᾽ αὐτὸν ἕκαστον καὶ πρὸς οὕστινας τῇ μανίᾳ
51 χρῆσθαι μὴ ἀφησόμενος, φανεροί[6] τε ἀλλήλοις ἦσαν
τῆς ἐπὶ πράγμασιν ἀχθηδόνος, διασαφεῖν μὲν ἀλλήλοις ἄντικρυς τὴν διάνοιαν καὶ μῖσος τὸ πρὸς Γάιον
φόβῳ τε κινδύνων ἀφέμενοι ἄλλως τε αἰσθανόμενοι
τοῦ ἀλλήλων μίσους πρὸς τὸν Γάιον καὶ δι᾽ αὐτὸ
εὐνοίᾳ χρῆσθαι τὰ πρὸς ἀλλήλους μὴ ἀπηλλαγμένοι.
52 (9) Γενομένων δ᾽ αὐτοῖς ἀξιώσεων[7] ἐπείπερ συν-
έβαλον, εἰωθότες καὶ πρότερον ὁπότε συνέλθοιεν
τίμιον ἡγεῖσθαι τὸν Βινουκιανὸν[8] ὑπεροχῇ τε ἀξιώματος, γενναιότατος γὰρ ἦν τῶν πολιτῶν, καὶ τῷ
53 ἐπὶ πᾶσιν ἐπαινουμένῳ, μᾶλλον ὡς ἅπτοιτό τινος
λόγου. φθάσας[9] κἀκεῖνος[10] ἤρετο[11] Χαιρέαν,[12] ὅ τι

---

[1] ἐδεῖτο τοῦ Χαιρέου] ἐδεῖτο ποιεῖν τοῦ Χαιρέου E : ἐδεῖτο τοῦ
Χαιρέου βοηθεῖν (vel ἐπιχειρεῖν) Richards et Shutt : ἐδεῖτο Busb.
[2] coni. Niese (cf. § 18) : Μινουκιανόν codd. ; ἀπορία . . .
Βινουκιανόν] tunc quidem tacere se dixit et ad nullum de tali
re suam proferre voluntatem, si vero tempus et hominem nan-
cisceretur, tunc non solum silentium abiecturum sed etiam
suam voluntatem manifestaturum esse firmabat. sed si
aliquid viriliter inquit volumus efficere, nihil dilatione penitus
detur, his igitur dictis exinde convertuntur ad Minucianum
Lat.        [3] coni. Niese (cf. § 18) : Μινουκιανός codd.
[4] E : κινδυνεύων codd. : periclitabatur Lat.
[5] A : αὐτόν, o i. ras. M : αὐτούς E.
[6] MW : φοβεροί AE Lat. : γρ φανεροί i. marg. A.
[7] A Busb. : ἀξιώσεως MW : ἀξίων E.
[8] coni. Niese (cf. § 18) : Μινουκιανόν codd.
[9] WE : φθάσαι AM.
[10] ἐκεῖνος Petersen.        [11] E : εἴ ποτε AM : εἴπετο W.

they betook themselves to Vinicianus,[a] who was akin
to them in honest habits and in devotion to high
ideals but was viewed with misgiving by Gaius on
account of the death of Lepidus.[b] For Vinicianus
and Lepidus had been very great friends, and Vinicianus was in fear of dangers arising therefrom.[c]
Indeed, Gaius was a source of terror to all in authority,
as one who would not desist from venting his madness
upon each and all alike. They were mutually aware
of their vexation at the state of affairs ; yet, from
fear of danger, they refrained from a full and frank
statement to one another of their thoughts and their
hatred of Gaius. Yet in other ways they were aware
of one another's loathing for Gaius and had therefore
not ceased to enjoy mutually friendly relations.

(9) At their meeting there was an exchange of
courtesies. When they had previously come together,
they had been accustomed to give precedence to
Vinicianus [d] both for his higher rank, since he was the
noblest of Roman citizens, and because of his high
repute in all respects, but particularly when he took
part in a debate.[e] Vinicianus, getting the matter
started, asked Chaerea what password he had re-

---

[a] mss. (here and later in this section) Minucianus ; *cf.* note
on § 18.　　　　　　　　　　[b] *Cf.* § 20.

[c] Prof. Post suggests that the last clause, καὶ δείματι . . .
αὐτόν, may be displaced, and he would let it refer to συγγενῆ.
The meaning would then be that the three men were also
united by their fear for themselves.

[d] mss. Minucianus ; *cf.* note on § 18.

[e] Or " so that he was more likely to begin a discussion."
A variant reading introduces this clause into the next sentence thus : " Minucianus [*i.e.* Vinicianus], more in order to
begin conversation, asked Chaerea . . ."

---

[12] μᾶλλον . . . Χαιρέαν] inter principia sermonum praece-
dens ille verba facit ad Chaeream requirens Lat.

καὶ παραλάβοι σημεῖον τῆς ἡμέρας ἐκείνης· ἀοίδιμος
γὰρ διὰ τῆς πόλεως ἦν ἡ εἰς τὸν Χαιρέαν διὰ τῶν
54 σημείων τῆς δόσεως πρασσομένη ὕβρις. ὁ δὲ χάρματι τοῦ λόγου μηδὲν μελλήσας ἠμείβετο τοῦ
Βινουκιανοῦ[1] τὸ ἐπὶ τοιοῖσδε πιστεῦσαν ὁμιλίᾳ χρήσασθαι πρὸς αὐτόν, καί, " σύ μοι δίδως," εἶπεν,
" σημεῖον ἐλευθερίας, χάρις δέ σοι τοῦ ἀνεγείραντός
55 με μειζόνως ἤπερ εἴωθα ἐμαυτὸν ὁρμᾶν, οὐδέν μοι
χρεία πλειόνων ἔτι λόγων, οἵ με θαρσοῖεν, εἰ δὴ καὶ
σοὶ ταῦτα δοκεῖ, γνώμης τε τῆς αὐτῆς κοινωνοὶ καὶ
πρότερον ἢ συνελθεῖν γεγόναμεν. καὶ ἓν μὲν ὑπ-
56 έζωμαι ξίφος, ἀμφοῖν δ' ἂν ἀρκέσειεν. ὥστε ἴθι καὶ
ἔργων ἐχώμεθα, ἡγεμών τ' ἴσθι, ᾗ βούλοιο αὐτὸς
κελεύων με χωρεῖν, ᾗ καὶ προσοίσομαι,[2] ἐπικουρίᾳ
τῇ σῇ συμπράσσοντος τε πίσυνος. οὐδὲ ἀπορία σι-
δήρου τοῖς τὴν ψυχὴν εἰς τὰ ἔργα προσφερομέ-
νοις,[3] δι' ἣν καὶ ὁ σίδηρος δραστήριος εἴωθεν εἶναι.
57 ὥρμηκά τε εἰς τὴν πρᾶξιν οὐχ ὧν ἂν αὐτὸς πά-
θοιμι ἐλπίδι περιφερόμενος· οὐ γὰρ σχολὴ κινδύνους
μοι κατανοεῖν τοὺς ἐμαυτοῦ δουλώσει τε πατρίδος
ἐλευθερωτάτης ἐπαλγοῦντι τῶν νόμων τῆς ἀρετῆς
ἀφῃρημένης τούς τε πάντας ἀνθρώπους ὀλέθρου
58 διὰ Γάιον κατειληφότος. ἄξιος δ' ἂν εἴην παρὰ σοὶ
δικαστῇ πίστεως ἐπὶ τοιούτοις τυγχάνειν ὑπὸ τοῦ
ὅμοια φρονεῖν αὐτοῖς καὶ σὲ μὴ ἀπηλλάχθαι."[4]
59 (10) Βινουκιανὸς[5] δὲ τὴν ὁρμὴν τῶν λόγων θεα-

---

[1] ϲωni. Niese (cf. § 18) : Μινουκιανοῦ codd.
[2] ᾗ καὶ προσοίσομαι] AM : οἳ ϰαὶ προσοίσομαι W : ᾗ καὶ
προείσομαι E : litt. ᾗ καὶ προσοί i. ras. m. 2 A : ᾗ καὶ προσοίσομαι Busb.
[3] ᾗ καὶ . . . προσφερομένοις] quod si coepero tui operatione
solatii persequar grassatione ferri concessa mihi te confor-
tante fiducia Lat.

ceived for that day ; for the city buzzed with the insults of which Chaerea was made the victim by the passwords given him. Chaerea was delighted at his words and without further delay returned the trust that Vinicianus [a] had put in him when he took part in a conference under such conditions and said : " Your password for me is ' Liberty,' and I thank you for rousing me to greater energy than I am accustomed to display by myself ; nor do I need any further words to encourage me if you too approve this course, so that we have arrived at one joint decision even before our conference. I have one sword in my belt ; but one will suffice for both of us. So up, let us get on with the work. Do you be leader and order me to go where you choose ; and I will betake myself there,[b] relying on your support and co-operation. Nor is there any shortage of weapons when men throw their hearts into a task, for it is the heart that is wont to make a sword effective. I have thrown myself into this enterprise unmoved by any thought of what may happen to me personally. I have no leisure to scrutinize the threats to my own life. I am tormented when I see my country reduced from unequalled freedom to slavery and robbed of its excellent laws. Because Gaius lives, the human race is overtaken by disaster. It must be that I am worthy to be trusted with such a cause in your judgement, since we are of one mind and you have not renounced me."

(10) Vinicianus,[c] noting the urgency of his words,

---

[a] mss. Minucianus ; cf. note on § 18.
[b] Variant " or else I will take the lead."
[c] mss. Minucianus ; cf. note on § 18.

---

[4] ἄξιος . . . ἀπηλλάχθαι] dignus enim sum apud te iudicem fidem rerum huiusmodi, quando etiam tu sapere talia comprobaris Lat.    [5] coni. Niese (cf. § 18) : Μινουκιανός codd.

σάμενος ἠσπάζετό τε ἀσμένως καὶ προσπαρίστατο[1]
τὴν τόλμαν αὐτοῦ ἐπαινέσας τε καὶ ἀσπασάμενος
60 μετ᾽ εὐχῶν καὶ ἱκετείας ἀπελύετο.[2] καὶ ἰσχυρίζοντό
τινες ὡς βεβαίως ταῦτα[3] εἰρημένα.[4] εἰσιόντος γὰρ[5]
εἰς τὸ βουλευτήριον Χαιρέου φωνὴν[6] ἐκ τοῦ πλήθους
γενέσθαι τινὸς ἐπ᾽ ἐξορμήσει κελεύοντος περαίνειν
μὲν δὴ τὸ πρακτέον καὶ προσλαμβάνειν τὸ δαιμό-
61 νιον. καὶ τὸν Χαιρέαν τὸ μὲν πρῶτον[7] ὑπιδέσθαι,
μὴ καί τινος τῶν συνωμοτῶν προδότου γεγονότος
ἁλίσκοιτο, καὶ τέλος συνέντα ἐπὶ προτροπῇ φέρειν
πρῶτον εἴτε παραινέσει τῶν συνεγνωκότων ἀντι-
σημαίνοντός τινος, εἴτε δὴ καὶ τοῦ θεοῦ, ὃς ἐφορᾷ
62 τὰ ἀνθρώπινα, αἴροντος αὐτόν. διεληλύθει δὲ διὰ
πολλῶν τὸ ἐπιβούλευμα καὶ πάντες ἐν ὅπλοις παρῆσαν, οἱ μὲν τῶν βουλευτῶν ὄντες οἱ δὲ ἱππεῖς καὶ
ὁπόσοι τοῦ στρατιωτικοῦ συνῄδεσαν· οὐδεὶς γὰρ ἦν,
ὃς μὴ ἐν εὐδαιμονίᾳ ἂν ἠρίθμει[8] τὴν Γαΐου μετά-
63 στασιν· καὶ δι᾽ αὐτὸ πάντες ἠπείγοντο ὁποίῳ
δύναιτό τις τρόπῳ μηδὲ ἑκὼν εἶναι τῆς ἐπὶ τοιούτοις ἀρετῆς ὑστερεῖν, ἀλλ᾽ ὡς ἔχοι προθυμίας ἢ
δυνάμεως καὶ λόγοις καὶ δι᾽ ἔργων ἦρτο[9] ἐπὶ τῇ
64 τυραννοκτονίᾳ, ἐπεὶ καὶ Κάλλιστος,[10] ἀπελεύθερος
δ᾽ ἦν Γαΐου πλεῖστά τε ἀνὴρ εἷς οὗτος ἐπὶ μέγιστον
δυνάμεως ἀφίκετο καὶ οὐδὲν ἄλλο ἢ ἰσοτύραννον
εἶχε τὴν δύναμιν φόβῳ τε τῶν πάντων καὶ μεγέθει

---

[1] προσηρέθιζε E.    [2] MWE : ἀπελύοντο A : dimisit Lat.
[3] βεβαίως ταῦτα] MW : βεβαιοῦν τὰ A : βεβαιοῦσαν τὰ Herwerden.
[4] καὶ ἰσχυρίζοντό . . . τὰ εἰρημένα] quidam enim adsevera-
bant ea quae cogitabantur quodam auspicio fuisse firmata
Lat.: καὶ ἰσχυρίζοντό ⟨τι⟩ τινες ὡς βεβαιοῦν τὰ εἰρημένα Petersen : om. E. ; lacunam post εἰρημένα indicat Niese.
[5] A : δὲ MW : nam Lat. : om. E.
[6] φωνὴν] φωνὴν λέγεται E.    [7] om. E Lat.

responded warmly and further encouraged his boldness. After he had commended and embraced him,
he dismissed him with prayers and supplication.
And some have maintained that there was a confirma-
tion of their words ; for as Chaerea was entering the
senate house there came from the crowd a voice of
someone bidding him, in order to spur him on :
" Proceed therefore to carry out thy task and accept
the support of heaven." They say that Chaerea at
first suspected that one of the conspirators had turned
traitor and that he was trapped ; but in the end he
understood that the cry was in the first place meant
to encourage him, whether it was a signal of warning
from one of the conspirators or whether it was actually
the voice of God, who watches over men and their
lives, speaking to inspire courage in him. For the
secret of the plot had reached many persons and
everybody who was there had arms—members of the
senate and of the equestrian order and all soldiers
who were privy to the plot ; for there was no one
who would not have reckoned the removal of Gaius
as a blessing. For this reason all were eager, in
whatever manner was possible, not, so far as they
were concerned, to show less courage than the situation required. With the utmost zeal, with all their
strength, whether by words or by action, all were intent on the execution of the tyrant. Take the case
of Callistus.[a] He, as a freedman of Gaius, had, of all
men, reached the highest summit of power both by
the fear which he inspired in all and through the

Callistus,
Gaius'
freedman,
joins the
plot.

---

[a] Dio lix. 29. 1 also mentions him as a leading conspirator.

[8] ἂν ἠρίθμει] Niese : ἀνηρίθμει codd. : ἠρίθμει E.
[9] MW : ἦρκτο A : erant . . . praeparati Lat.
[10] συνῆν vel παρῆν post Κάλλιστος suppl. Richards et Shutt.

245

65 χρημάτων, ἅπερ ἐγένετο αὐτῷ· δωροδοκώτατος γὰρ
ἦν καὶ ὑβριστότατος παρ' ὁντινοῦν γίνεται, ἐξουσίᾳ
χρησάμενος παρὰ τὸ εἰκός· καὶ ἄλλως τε τοῦ Γαΐου
τὴν φύσιν ἐξεπιστάμενος ἀνήκεστον οὖσαν καὶ ἐφ'
οἷστισι κρίνειεν οὐδαμῶς ἀντισπάσματι χρωμένην,
αὐτῷ τε πολλὰς μὲν καὶ ἄλλας αἰτίας τοῦ κινδυνεύειν, οὐχ ἥκιστα δὲ τὸ μέγεθος τῶν χρημάτων·
66 ὥστε δὴ καὶ Κλαύδιον ἐθεράπευε κρυπτῶς μετα-
καθίζων πρὸς αὐτὸν ἐλπίδι τοῦ κἂν εἰς ἐκεῖνον ἥξειν
τὴν ἡγεμονίαν Γαΐου μεταστάντος, αὐτῷ δὲ[1] τὴν
ὑπόθεσιν[2] τῆς τιμῆς καὶ[3] τὴν ἐφ' ὁμοίοις ἰσχὺν
προκαταθέμενος[4] χάριν καὶ φιλανθρωπίας λόγον.[5]
67 ἐτόλμησεν γοῦν εἰπεῖν, ὡς κελευσθεὶς διαχρήσασθαι
φαρμάκῳ τὸν Κλαύδιον μυρίας εὕροιτο τοῦ χρήμα-
68 τος τὰς ὑπερβολάς. δοκεῖν[6] δὲ προσεποιεῖτο[7] Κάλλιστος ἐπὶ θήρᾳ τῇ Κλαυδίου τὸν λόγον τοῦτον,[8] ἐπεί
τε[9] οὔτε Γάιος ὡρμηκὼς μεταχειρίσασθαι Κλαύδιον
ἠνείχετο τῶν Καλλίστου προφάσεων οὔτε Κάλλιστος
κελευσθείς που τὴν πρᾶξιν ἀπευκτὸν[10] ὑπελάμβανεν[11]
ἢ κακουργῶν εἰς τοῦ δεσπότου τὰς ἐπιστολὰς οὐκ
69 ἂν ἐκ τοῦ παραχρῆμα τὸν μισθὸν ἐκομίζετο.[12] ἀλλὰ

---

[1] δὲ post αὐτῷ suppl. Petersen.       [2] ὑπόσχεσιν A.
[3] καὶ post τιμῆς suppl. Post.       [4] προκαταθεμένῳ Petersen.
[5] ἐλπίδι . . . λόγον] sperans quia si ei cederet principatus
deficiente Gaio honorem similem ei praeberet, eo quod illi
gratiam et verba clementiae primitus inpendisset Lat.
[6] AW : δοκεῖ ME.       [7] προσποιεῖσθαι E.
[8] δοκεῖν . . . τοῦτον] sed mihi videtur, quia fingebat haec
Callistus volens capere Claudium Lat.
[9] ἐπεί τε] i. marg. A : ἔπειτα AMW : ἐπεὶ E : nam Lat.
[10] Post : εὐκτὸν codd. : φευκτὸν Bekker.
[11] ὑπερέβαλεν Hudson.
[12] οὔτε Κάλλιστος . . . ἐκομίζετο] neque Callistus iussus op-
tabilem Gaio rem perpetrare si distulisset mandata domini
sui potuit pericula declinare Lat.

great wealth that he had amassed. His power was
no less than a tyrant's. For he was a great taker of
bribes, and most contemptuous of rights, with none
to match him. His authority had been exercised
beyond all reason. Above all, he knew that Gaius
by temperament was implacable, that he never
allowed for any counter-influence in a case that he
had once decided ; and that he was himself in danger
not only for many other reasons but particularly
because of his great wealth. In consequence, he
even paid court to Claudius, secretly going over to
his side because he expected that in the event of
Gaius' death the empire would pass to him and that
by laying up beforehand a store of favour and credit
for his kindness he would have a basis for preferment
and strength similar to that which he now enjoyed.[a]
At any rate, he went so far as to say that though he
had been ordered to dispose of Claudius by giving
him poison, he had invented countless devices for
putting it off. My view is that Callistus invented
this story to ingratiate himself with Claudius, since
Gaius, if he had been bent on killing Claudius, would
not have tolerated Callistus' excuses, nor would Callistus, if he had ever been ordered to do the deed,
have regarded it as anything to deplore,[b] nor, if he
had sinned against his master's injunctions, would he
have failed instantly to receive the wages of dis-

---

[a] The text is difficult. Prof. Petersen suggests the following translation for his emended text : " And that Claudius'
promise to honour him would assure him the continuation of
his power on the same terms, especially since he had obliged
Claudius in advance with flattery and intimations of courtesy."
[b] Text emended. Prof. Petersen suggests keeping the
manuscript reading and translates thus : " Nor would Cal-

δὴ Κλαυδίῳ μὲν ἐκ τινος θείας δυνάμεως ἦν φυγῇ
χρήσασθαι[1] μανιῶν τῶν Γαΐου, Καλλίστῳ δὲ[2] προσ-
ποιήσασθαι χάριτος κατάθεσιν μηδαμῶς ὑπ' αὐτοῦ
γενομένης.

70 (11) Τοῖς ἀμφὶ τὸν Χαιρέαν ὑπερβολαὶ τὸ καθ'
ἡμέραν ἦσαν ὀκνούντων πολλῶν. οὐ γὰρ Χαιρέας
ἑκὼν[3] εἶναι τοῦ πράσσειν ἀναβολὴν ἐποιεῖτο, πάντα

71 καιρὸν ἐπιτήδειον τῇ πράξει νομίζων. καὶ γὰρ[4] εἰς
τὸ Καπετώλιον ἀνιόντα καὶ τὰς[5] θυσίας ὑπὲρ τῆς
θυγατρὸς ἐπιτελουμένας ὑπὸ τοῦ Γαΐου παρῆν πολλάκις καιρός, καὶ ὑπὲρ τῆς βασιλικῆς ἱστάμενον καὶ
τῷ δήμῳ χρυσίου καὶ ἀργυρίου χρήματα διαρ-
ριπτοῦντα ὦσαι κατὰ κεφαλῆς, ὑψηλὸν δ' ἐστὶ τὸ
τέγος εἰς τὴν ἀγορὰν φέρον, ἐπί[6] τε τῶν μυστηρίων

72 ταῖς ποιήσεσιν ἃ συνίστατο· πάντων γὰρ αὐτὸν ἀ-
περίοπτον εἶναι προνοίᾳ τοῦ ἐν αὐτοῖς εὐπρεπῶς
ἀναστραφησομένου καὶ ἀπογνώσει τοῦ ἐν ἐπιχειρήσει τινὶ[7] γενέσθαι πιστεύειν.[8] εἰ δὲ μηδὲν τὸ κωλῦον[9]

---

[1] ἦν φυγῇ χρήσασθαι] Post : χρήσασθαι codd. : σώσασθαι ἐκ
Hudson : περιγενέσθαι ἐκ Bekker : ⟨φυγῇ⟩ χρήσασθαι Herwerden : ⟨φυγῇ ἦν⟩ χρήσασθαι Richards et Shutt.
[2] Καλλίστῳ δὲ] Petersen : Κάλλιστος codd. : Callistus autem
Lat. : Κάλλιστον δὲ Hudson.
[3] ἑκὼν] E : . . . ἑκὼν A : ἔσται ἑκὼν MW : γε ἑκὼν coni.
Niese.
[4] ⟨κτεῖναι⟩ post γὰρ suppl. Petersen.
[5] καὶ τὰς] κατὰ E.
[6] ἐπί] ἔτι E : adhuc Lat.
[7] τινὰ E.
[8] E : πιστεύοντα codd.
[9] μηδὲν τὸ κωλῦον] Petersen : μηδὲν σημεῖον Hudson : μὴ
δέοι τινα ἐπιτίμιον Post : μηδὲν τίμιον codd.

---

listus, had he received the order, have considered the deed as
248

obedience. Rather, I think that it was through some
divine intervention that Claudius enjoyed exemption
from the mad fits of Gaius; and Callistus merely
pretended to have put Claudius in his debt when he
had done nothing at all.

(11) The party of Chaerea postponed action from
day to day because many of them were cautious.[a]
For Chaerea would not of his own free will have let
a moment slip; in his eyes any opportunity for action
was good enough. Indeed he had frequent opportunities when he went up to the Capitol [b] on occasions
when Gaius offered sacrifice for his daughter's benefit.
For as Gaius stood above the palace [c] and scattered
gold and silver money among the people, Chaerea
might with a push have sent him falling headlong,
for the roof overlooking the forum is high; or again
he might have killed him at the performances of the
mysteries that Gaius had instituted. For he was
indifferent to everything else, in his concern to acquit
himself honourably in what he did and in his convic-
tion that no one would move to act. But if no divinity

something desirable." The implication is that Callistus would
have refused to carry out the order, and Gaius would have
had to look for another agent. On the other hand, it appears
from §§ 68–69 that Josephus regards the explanation alleged
by Callistus for not putting Claudius to death as hypo-
critical; and the implication is that Callistus failed to dispatch
Claudius not because of his devotion to him but because he
had never received an order from Gaius to do so. Hudson's
emendation yields the following translation : " Nor would
Callistus, if he had ever been ordered to do the deed, which
was desired by Gaius, have postponed it."

[a] Or " shrank from the deed."

[b] The temple of Jupiter Capitolinus. *Cf.* §§ 4, 11.

[c] Mathieu-Herrmann say that this is doubtless the palace
on the Palatine between the temple of Augustus and the palace
of Caligula.

ὡς[1] τῶν θεῶν Γαΐω[2] δύναμιν τοῦ θανάτου παρα-
73 τυγχάνειν, αὐτῷ δ' ἂν ἰσχὺν ἐγγενέσθαι καὶ μὴ σιδη-
ροφορουμένῳ διαχρήσασθαι τότε[3] Γάιον. οὕτως δι'
ὀργῆς[4] εἶχε τοὺς συνωμότας ὁ Χαιρέας[5] δεδιὼς τοὺς
74 καιροὺς μὴ διαρρυεῖν. οἱ δὲ ἑώρων μὲν νομίμων
τε χρήζοντα καὶ ἐπ' ἀγαθοῖς τοῖς αὑτῶν ἐπειγόμενον,
οὐ μὴν ἀλλ' ἠξίουν εἰς ὀλίγον γοῦν ὑπερβολῇ χρήσασθαι, μὴ καί πη σφάλματος τῇ ἐπιχειρήσει συν-
ελθόντος ταράξαιεν τὴν πόλιν ζητήσεων τῶν συνεγνωκότων τὴν πρᾶξιν γινομένων καὶ τοῖς αὐτοῖς[6]
μελλήσουσιν ἐπιχειρεῖν ἄπορον τὴν ἀνδραγαθίαν[7]
75 φραξαμένου Γαΐου πρὸς αὐτοὺς μειζόνως.[8] καλῶς
οὖν ἔχειν θεωριῶν ἐν τῷ Παλατίῳ ἐπιτελουμένων
ἅπτεσθαι τοῦ χρήματος· ἄγονται δὲ ἐπὶ τιμῇ τοῦ
πρώτου μεταστησαμένου τὴν ἀρχὴν τοῦ δήμου
Καίσαρος εἰς αὐτὸν μικρόν τε πρὸ τοῦ βασιλείου
καλύβης πηκτοῦ γενομένης, καὶ Ῥωμαίων τε οἱ
εὐπατρίδαι θεωροῦσιν ὁμοῦ παισὶν καὶ γυναιξὶν καὶ
76 ὁ Καῖσαρ· ῥᾳστώνην τε αὐτοῖς ἔσεσθαι πολλῶν
μυριάδων ἀνθρώπων εἰς ὀλίγον χωρίον καθειργνυ-

[1] ὡς] ὡς ἀπὸ Hudson.　　　　[2] Petersen : αὐτῷ codd.
[3] τότε] A : τόν τε MW.
[4] δι' ὀργῆς] E : ὀργῆς i. marg. A : εὐχῆς codd.
[5] οὕτως . . . Χαιρέας] tantum habuit cum coniuratis
Chaereas ardorem Lat.
[6] τοῖς αὐτοῖς] τοῖς αὖθις Holwerda : τοῖς αὐτῇ Bekker : αὐτοῖς
τοῖς coni. Thackeray.
[7] ⟨ποιήσειαν⟩ post ἀνδραγαθίαν suppl. Thackeray.
[8] καὶ τοῖς . . . μειζόνως] et insidiarum iam non valeret
utilitas in futuro Lat.

---

[a] The mss. yield little sense. Hudson's emendation would
mean " and if no sign as from the gods came to give him
power to inflict the death." Prof. Post proposes " if there
were not bound to occur some effective occasion to deal death,
whereby the gods would wreak vengeance."

prevented Gaius from meeting his death,[a] he himself,
though he should have no sword, would summon up
the strength to dispose of Gaius. So angry was Chaerea with his fellow conspirators, fearing that the
opportunities to act would slip by. They saw that
he desired only a reign of law and that his urgency
was for their benefit ; nevertheless they begged him
to postpone action at least for a while, lest, if the
plot was frustrated, they should create a commotion
in the city while search was made for any who had
been informed of the plot, and lest in the future any
who might have intended to act should find no way
open for brave deeds because Gaius would have taken
greater precautions against them. It was therefore Action planned for the Pala-tine games
best, they thought, to undertake the business on an
occasion when shows were exhibited on the Palatine.
These [b] are held in honour of that Caesar [c] who was
first to transfer authority from the people to himself ;
during their celebration a stage [d] is set up a little in
front of the palace, and the Roman patricians look
on with their children and wives, together with
Caesar himself. They would then have the opportunity, when many tens of thousands of people would

[b] The assassination took place, as Suetonius, *Calig.* 56,
says, during the Ludi Palatini, established by Livia in honour
of Augustus just after his death in A.D. 14, which started on
17 January and culminated with theatrical exhibitions on
21, 22, and 23 January (Dio lvi. 46. 5, lix. 16. 10 [probably] ;
Tac. *Ann.* i. 73). In the year in which Gaius was assassinated
Gaius added extra days to the festival (Dio lix. 29. 5). See
G. Wissowa, *Religion und Kultus der Römer*, 1912, p. 458
n. 5. Josephus would therefore appear to be incorrect when
he says (§ 77) that Gaius was murdered on the third day of the
spectacles, since this would be 23 January, whereas the
murder occurred on 24 January (Suet. *Calig.* 58).

[c] Augustus, as is clear from § 87.

[d] Lit. " hut."

μένων ὥστε εἰσιόντι τὴν ἐπιχείρησιν ποιήσασθαι
δυνάμεως τοῖς ὑπασπισταῖς, εἰ καί τινες προθυμοῖν-
το, μὴ παρατευξομένης αὐτῷ βοηθεῖν.

77 (12) Ἠνείχετο¹ δὲ Χαιρέας, καὶ τῶν θεωριῶν ἐπ-
ελθουσῶν τῇ πρώτῃ δεδογμένον ἅπτεσθαι τῆς
πράξεως ἰσχυρότερον ἦν τοῦ κατ' ἐκείνους προβεβουλευκότος τὸ τῆς τύχης συγχωροῦν ὑπερβολάς,
καὶ τὰς τρεῖς ὑπερβαλλομένοις² τὰς νομίμους ἡμέ-
ρας³ μόλις κατὰ τὴν τελευταίαν αὐτοῖς ἐπράχθη τὸ
78 ἔργον. Χαιρέας δὲ συγκαλέσας τοὺς συνωμότας,
" πολὺς μέν," εἶπεν, " καὶ ὁ παρεληλυθὼς χρόνος
ὀνειδίσαι τὸ ἔτι μέλλον⁴ ἡμῶν ἐπὶ τοῖς οὕτω βου-
λευθεῖσιν μετ' ἀρετῆς, δεινὸν δέ, εἰ καὶ μηνύματος
γενομένου διαπεσεῖται ἡ πρᾶξις καὶ Γάιος ὑβριεῖ
79 μειζόνως. ἢ οὐχ ὁρῶμεν, ὡς τῆς ἐλευθερίας ἀφαι-
ρούμεν ὁπόσας τῶν ἡμερῶν προσθήκην τῇ Γαΐου
τυραννίδι χαριζόμεθα,⁵ δέον αὐτούς τ' ἀδεεῖς τὸ
λοιπὸν εἶναι καὶ τοῖς ἄλλοις αἰτίαν τοῦ εὐδαίμονος
παρασχόντας δι' αἰῶνος τοῦ ἅπαντος τοῖς αὖθις ἐν
80 θαύματι μεγάλῳ καὶ τιμῇ⁶ καταστῆναι·" τῶν δὲ
οὔτε⁷ ἀντειπεῖν ὡς οὐ πάνυ καλῶς⁸ δυναμένων οὔτε
τὴν πρᾶξιν ἄντικρυς δεχομένων σιγῇ δὲ καταπεπλη-
γότων, " τί," φησίν, " ὦ γενναῖοι, διαμέλλομεν; ἢ
οὐχ ὁρᾶτε τὴν σήμερον τῶν θεωριῶν ἡμέραν ὑστά-
81 την οὖσαν καὶ Γάιον ἐκπλευσούμενον;" ἐπὶ γὰρ
Ἀλεξανδρείας παρεσκεύαστο πλεῖν κατὰ θεωρίαν

¹ Ε : εἴχετο codd. : expectabat Lat. : ἠπείγετο Naber.
² Ernesti : ὑπερβαλλομένου codd.
³ τὰς νομίμους ἡμέρας] Lowthius : ταῖς νομίμοις ἡμέραις codd.

be wedged into a small space, to make the attack on him as he entered, and his bodyguards would have no chance, even if any of them should desire it, of rendering him assistance.

(12) Chaerea bore with them, and it was decided to take the business in hand when the first day of the spectacles arrived. Their plan, however, was over-ruled by Fortune, who granted one reprieve after another ; and having let pass the three days pre-scribed for the spectacles, they barely accomplished the deed on the last. Chaerea then called together the conspirators and said : " The days that have gone by put us to shame for our tardy execution of so noble a resolve. It is an appalling thought that if someone informs on us, our enterprise will fall through and Gaius will be more insolent than ever. Or do we not see that every additional day that we grant to Gaius' tyranny is subtracted from the days of liberty ? It behooves us henceforth to be fearless and, when we have laid a foundation for the eternal happiness of future generations, to establish ourselves for pos-terity as objects of great admiration and honour." They could neither deny that his words were wholly right nor yet undertake to act forthwith, but stood silent in dismay. " Why," he continued, " good sirs, do we still hesitate ? Are you not aware that today is the last day of the spectacles and that Gaius' ship will soon depart ? " (For he had made preparations

Chaerea on the last da of the games en-courages his accom-plices.

---

⁴ ἔτι μέλλον] Bekker : ἐπιμέλλον AW : ἐπιμέλον M.

⁵ καὶ Γάιος . . . χαριζόμεθα] et potius Gaius nos afficiat cunctorumque auferat libertatem his diebus quos nos ty-rannidi eius adicimus Lat.

⁶ ἐν θαύματι . . . τιμῇ] A : om. MW.

⁷ Dindorf : οὐκ AE : οὐδὲ MW.

⁸ AE : καλῶν MW : καλοῖς Hudson.

τῆς Αἰγύπτου. " καλὸν δὲ ἡμῖν προέσθαι τῶν χειρῶν τὸ ὄνειδος τῇ Ῥωμαίων μεγαλαυχίᾳ πομπεῦ-
82 σον διά τε γῆς καὶ θαλάσσης; πῶς δ' οὐκ ἂν
δικαίως κρίνοιμεν[1] αὐτοὺς[2] αἰσχύνῃ τῶν γενησομέ-
νων,[3] εἴ τις αὐτὸν Αἰγύπτιος κτείνειεν τὴν ὕβριν
οὐχ ἡγησάμενος ἀνασχετὸν τοῖς ἐλευθέροις γεγονό-
83 σιν; ἐγὼ μὲν οὖν οὐκέτι εἰς πλείονα ἀνέξομαι τὰς
σκήψεις[4] ὑμῶν, χωρήσω δὲ τοῖς κινδύνοις ὁμοῦ σήμερον ἡδονῇ φέρων πᾶν ὅ τι καὶ γένοιτο ἐξ αὐτῶν,
οὐδ' ἂν ὑπερβαλλοίμην εἴπερ εἴη· τί γὰρ δὴ καὶ
γένοιτ' ἂν ἀνδρὶ φρόνημα ἔχοντι τούτου σχετλιώ-
τερον, ἕτερον Γάιον ἀναιρεῖν ἐμοῦ ζῶντος ἐμὲ τὴν
ἐπὶ τῷδε ἀρετὴν ἀφῃρημένον; "

84 (13) Καὶ ὁ μὲν ταῦτα εἰπὼν αὐτός τε ὡρμήκει
πράξων τὸ ἔργον καὶ τοῖς λοιποῖς ἐνεποίησε θάρσος
πᾶσίν τε ἦν ἔρως ἅπτεσθαι τοῦ ἐγχειρήματος μηδὲν
85 ὑπερβαλλομένοις, ἕωθέν[5] τε ἐπὶ τοῦ Παλατίου ἐώ-
θει[6] τὸ ξίφος ὑπεζωσμένος τῶν ἱππικῶν[7]· ἔθος
γὰρ δὴ τοῖς χιλιάρχοις τοῦτο ἐζωσμένοις αἰτεῖν
παρὰ τοῦ αὐτοκράτορος τὸ σημεῖον, ἦν τε ἡ ἡμέρα
καθήκουσα εἰς αὐτὸν τῆς παραλήψεως τοῦ σημείου.
86 ἄρτι τε συνῄει πληθὺς εἰς τὸ Παλάτιον ἐπὶ προκατα-

---

[1] Niese : κρίνωμεν A : κρίνομεν MW.
[2] αὐτούς] αὐτοὺς ⟨ἐνόχους⟩ Richards et Shutt ex Lat.
[3] πῶς δ' . . . γενησομένων] nam quomodo non iuste erimus
confusionis obnoxii Lat.
[4] A : σκέψεις MW : cogitationes Lat.
[5] A : εἴωθε MW.
[6] coni. Niese (vel ὠθεῖ): εἰώθει A : om. MW : γέγονε E :
εἰστήκει Petersen.

to set sail for Alexandria to inspect Egypt.[a] " Is it honourable to let slip from our hands this blot on the proud record of the Romans that he may parade in triumph over land and sea ? Should we not be justified in passing sentence against ourselves for the disgrace that would befall us if some Egyptian, finding the insolence of Gaius intolerable to freeborn men, were to slay him ? I for one will no longer put up with your pretexts, but will face the risks this very day, accepting with a glad heart whatever outcome may ensue, nor would I postpone the issue even if it were possible. For what could be more galling to a man of spirit than that some other should slay Gaius while I live on and am robbed of the high valour of the deed ? "

(13) With these words he himself set out to do the deed and had also put heart into the rest, so that they were all consumed by desire to take the enterprise in hand without delay. In the morning Chaerea made his way [b] towards the Palatine girt with the sword of an equestrian ; for it was the custom for the tribunes to be so equipped when they asked the emperor for the password, and it was his day to receive it. A crowd was already collecting on the Palatine in anticipation of the spectacle, and there

---

[a] V. M. Scramuzza, *The Emperor Claudius*, 1940, p. 51, rightly notes that since Gaius was known to be addicted to Egyptian and Oriental ways, this projected visit brought home to the senators the danger to Latin institutions, particularly since their memory of the Egyptian influence on Antony and Caesar was still fresh.

[b] mss. was accustomed."

---

[7] μηδὲν . . . ἱππικῶν] nihilque differens diluculo ad palatium multitudo equestrium armata convenit Lat. ; τῶν ἱππικῶν] A : ἱπποκομῶν MW.

λήψει θέας πολλῷ θορύβῳ καὶ ὠθισμῷ, χαρᾷ
φέροντος Γαΐου τὴν ἐπὶ τοιοῖσδε τῶν πολλῶν σπου-
δήν, παρὸ καὶ διακέκριτο οὐδὲν οὔτε τῇ συγκλήτῳ
χωρίον οὔτε τοῖς ἱππεῦσιν, φύρδην δὲ ἔζοντο καὶ
τοῖς ἀνδράσιν ὁμοῦ αἱ γυναῖκες καὶ τῷ δούλῳ ἀνα-
87 μεμιγμένον τὸ ἐλεύθερον. Γάιος δὲ προόδων αὐτῷ
γενομένων ἔθυσε τῷ Σεβαστῷ Καίσαρι, ᾧ δὴ καὶ
τὰ τῆς θεωρίας ἤγετο, καὶ πίπτοντος τῶν ἱερείων
τινὸς συνέβη αἵματι τὴν Ἀσπρήνα στολὴν ἑνὸς τῶν
συγκλητικῶν ἀνάπλεων γενέσθαι. τοῦτο Γαΐῳ
γέλωτα μὲν παρέσχεν, ἦν δ᾽ ἄρα εἰς οἰωνὸν τῷ
Ἀσπρήνᾳ φανερόν· ἐπικατασφάζεται γὰρ τῷ Γαΐῳ.
88 Γάιον δ᾽ ἱστορεῖται παρὰ φύσιν τὴν ἑαυτοῦ εὐπροσ-
ηγορώτατον γενέσθαι κατ᾽ ἐκείνην τὴν ἡμέραν καὶ
δεξιότητι χρώμενον ὁμιλίας πάνθ᾽ ὁντινοῦν ἐκπλῆ-
89 ξαι τῶν παρατυγχανόντων. μετὰ δὲ τὴν θυσίαν ἐπὶ
τὴν θεωρίαν τραπεὶς ἐκαθέζετο καὶ περὶ αὐτὸν τῶν
90 ἑταίρων οἱ ἀξιολογώτατοι. κατεσκεύαστο δὲ τὸ
θέατρον, πηκτὸν δὲ ἐγίνετο κατὰ ἕκαστον ἐνιαυτόν,
τοιόνδε τρόπον· θύρας ἔχει δύο φερούσας τὴν μὲν
εἰς αἴθριον, τὴν δ᾽ εἰς στοὰν εἰσόδοις καὶ ἀποχωρή-
σεσιν, ὅπως μὴ ταράσσοιντο οἱ ἔνδον ἀπειλημμένοι,
ἐκ δ᾽ αὐτῆς τῆς καλύβης ἐνδοτέρω διαφράγμασιν
ἑτέραν ἀπειληφυίας ἐπ᾽ ἀναστροφῇ τοῖς ἀνταγω-
91 νισταῖς καὶ ὁπόσα ἀκροάματα.[1] συγκαθημένης δὲ
τῆς πληθύος καὶ τοῦ Χαιρέου σὺν τοῖς χιλιάρχοις

was much noise and jostling.  Gaius was delighted to
see the general enthusiasm for the proceedings, and
for that reason no seats had been set apart either for
the senate or for the equites, so that the seating
was a jumble, women mixed with men and free men
with slaves.  Gaius, when his procession entered, Gaius'<br>sacrifice is<br>ominous.
sacrificed to Augustus Caesar, in whose honour the
spectacle was presented.  It happened that, as one Description<br>of the<br>games.
of the victims fell, the robe of Asprenas,[a] a man of
senatorial rank, was spattered with blood.[b]  At this
Gaius burst out laughing, but to Asprenas it turned
out to be a manifest omen, for he was struck down
over Gaius' dead body.  It is reported that on that
day Gaius was, contrary to his wont, most affable ;
and that he overwhelmed all and sundry whom he
met with his adroit sociability.  After the sacrifice he
turned to the spectacle and took his seat surrounded
by the most prominent of his companions.  The construction of the theatre, which was set up every year,
was as follows.  It had two doors, one leading to the
open air, the other into a portico with exits and
entrances, in order that those who were separately
assembled in the portico might not be troubled by
anyone passing through.  Entrances had been made
from the stage building itself, which had an inner
partition to provide a retreat for actors and all kinds
of musical performers.  The crowd being seated,
Chaerea had his place among the tribunes not far

[a] P. Nonius Asprenas, consul in 38.
[b] Suetonius, *Calig.* 57, records, without mentioning the
name of Asprenas, that Caligula himself was splashed with
blood while he was sacrificing a flamingo.

---

[1] ἐκ δ' . . . ἀκροάματα] est etiam illic et alia cella, ubi lu-
sores exerceri solent atque cantores Lat.

οὐκ ἄπωθεν τοῦ Γαΐου, δεξιὸν δὲ τοῦ θεάτρου κέρας
ὁ Καῖσαρ εἶχεν, Βαθύβιός[1] τις τῶν συγκλητικῶν
ἀνὴρ ἐστρατηγηκὼς ἤρετο Κλούιον[2] παρακαθεζό-
μενον αὐτῷ καὶ τοῦτον ὑπατικόν, εἰ δή τις αὐτῷ
νεωτέρων πραγμάτων πέρι ἀφίκοιτο πύστις, προμηθὴς γενόμενος τοῦ μὴ ἐξάκουστος εἶναι τάδε
92 λέγων. τοῦ δὲ φαμένου μηδὲν πεπύσθαι σημεῖον,[3]
" τοιγαροῦν, ὦ Κλούιε, τυραννοκτονίας ἀγὼν πρόκειται." καὶ ὁ Κλούιος, " ὦ γενναῖε," φησίν, " σίγα,
93 μή τίς τ᾽ ἄλλος Ἀχαιῶν μῦθον ἀκούσῃ." πολλῆς
δ᾽ ὀπώρας ἐπιχεομένης τοῖς θεωροῖς καὶ πολλῶν
ὀρνέων ὁπόσα τῷ σπανίῳ τίμια τοῖς κτωμένοις, ὁ
Γάιος ἡδονῇ τὰς περὶ αὐτοῖς ἐθεώρει μάχας καὶ
94 διαρπαγὰς οἰκειουμένων αὐτὰ τῶν θεωρῶν. ἔνθα
δὲ καὶ σημεῖα συμβαίνει[4] δύο γενέσθαι[5]· καὶ γὰρ
μῖμος εἰσάγεται, καθ᾽ ὃν σταυροῦται ληφθεὶς ἡγεμών, ὅ τε ὀρχηστὴς δρᾶμα εἰσάγει Κινύραν, ἐν ᾧ
αὐτός τε ἐκτείνετο καὶ ἡ θυγάτηρ Μύρρα, αἷμά τε

---

[1] codd. Busb.: Βατίβιος E: Batybius Lat.: Οὐατίνιος
Hudson.
[2] Niese: Κλούιτον codd.: Κλαύιτον E: Cluitum Lat.:
Κλούβιον Hudson.
[3] om. E: i. marg. γρ σήμερον A, quod habuit etiam Lat.
[4] Bekker: μανθάνει codd.: μανθάνω Shilleto: οὐ λανθάνει
Petersen (et γενόμενα pro γενέσθαι).
[5] ἔνθα δὲ . . . γενέσθαι] in illo siquidem spectaculo duo ei
auguria provenerunt Lat.

---

[a] The name is unknown, whether for a person of Greek or
Roman descent, as R. Hanslik, " Vatinius," no. 5, in Pauly-
Wissowa, 2. Reihe, viii[1], 1955, p. 520, remarks. But his
suggestion, that the emendation of Hudson be adopted and
that Vatinius be read, has little to recommend it since we
know of no one by this name of equestrian or senatorial rank
during this period.

from Gaius, who occupied the right wing of the theatre. Now a certain Bathybius,[a] a man of senatorial rank who had been praetor, asked Cluvius,[b] another man of consular rank who was sitting beside him, whether any news had reached him of a revolution, taking care that this remark should not be overheard. When Cluvius replied that he had perceived no indication of this, Bathybius said, "Well then, Cluvius, the programme [c] for to-day will include assassination of a tyrant." Cluvius answered, "Be silent, good sir, lest some other of the Achaeans hear the word."[d] A considerable quantity of fruit was scattered among the spectators with a number of such birds as are prized by their possessors for their rarity ; and Gaius watched with amusement as the spectators fought over them and snatched them from one another. Here there were two new portents. In the first place a mime was presented in the course of which a chieftain is caught and crucified. Moreover, the play presented by the dancer [e] was *Cinyras*,[f] in which the hero and his daughter Myrrha [g] are

[b] Cluvius must have been consul in 39 or 40, since, as Syme, *Tacitus*, i, p. 294, remarks, we know the names of the consuls for the previous years. On Cluvius as a possible source for Josephus' account of Gaius' assassination see note on § 1.

[c] Lit. "struggle" or "contest," particularly a contest for a prize at the games.

[d] A quotation from Homer's *Iliad* xiv. 90-91, except that the word τοῦτον after 'Αχαιῶν has been omitted.

[e] Mnester, according to Suetonius, *Calig.* 57.

[f] Suetonius, *Calig.* 57, remarks that this was particularly ominous since it was the same tragedy that had been performed during the games at which Philip of Macedon was assassinated.

[g] So also Ovid, *Met.* x. 312 ; her name, as given by Plutarch, *Parall.* 22, is Smyrna.

ἦν τεχνητὸν πολὺ καὶ τὸ¹ περὶ τὸν σταυρωθέντα ἐκ-
95 κεχυμένον καὶ τὸ² περὶ τὸν Κινύραν. ὁμολογεῖται δὲ καὶ τὴν ἡμέραν ἐκείνην γενέσθαι, ἐν ᾗ
Φίλιππον τὸν ᾿Αμύντου Μακεδόνων βασιλέα κτείνει
Παυσανίας εἰς τῶν ἑταίρων εἰς τὸ θέατρον εἰσιόντα.
96 Γαΐου δ' ἐνδοιάζοντος, εἴτε παραμείνειεν εἰς τέλος
τῇ θεωρίᾳ διὰ τὸ τελευταίαν εἶναι τὴν ἡμέραν εἴτε
λουτρῷ χρησάμενος καὶ σίτῳ εἶτα ἐπανίοι καθὰ
καὶ πρότερον,³ Βινουκιανὸς⁴ ὑπὲρ τοῦ Γαΐου καθεζόμενος καὶ δεδιώς, μὴ διαχυθείη⁵ τὰ τῶν καιρῶν
εἰς κενόν, ἐξαναστὰς ἐπειδὴ καὶ Χαιρέαν ἑώρα προ-
εξεληλυθότα, ἠπείγετο θαρσύνειν αὐτὸν προελθών.
97 λαμβάνεται δ' αὐτοῦ τῆς στολῆς Γάιος κατὰ φιλο-
φροσύνην δῆθεν καί, "ποῖ δή," φησίν, "ὦ μακάριε;"
καὶ ὁ μὲν αἰδοῖ δοκεῖν τοῦ Καίσαρος καθίζει, κρείσσων δ' ὁ φόβος ἦν ὀλίγον τε διαλιπὼν εἶτα διαν-
98 ίσταται. καὶ ὁ Γάιος οὐδὲν ἐμποδὼν ἦν ἐξιόντι⁶

---

¹ M : τὸν W : om. A.
² coni. : τὸν MW : τῶν A.
³ πρότερον] ed. pr. : prius Lat. : οἱ πρότερον codd.
⁴ coni. Niese (cf. § 18) : Μινουκιανὸς codd.
⁵ διαλυθείη E : efflueret Lat.
⁶ Lowthius et Hudson : ἄξιόν τι codd. : egredienti Lat.

---

ᵃ According to the legend, Myrhha, because of the wrath
of Aphrodite, fell in love with her own father. She confided
in her nurse, who told Cinyras that a neighbouring maiden
was in love with him but was too modest to approach him
openly. Thus Myrrha managed, under cover of darkness, to
have relations with her father night after night, until Cinyras
discovered that he was the father of Myrrha's unborn child.
He threatened to kill her but she managed to escape, whereupon he killed himself. According to the various versions of
the legend, Myrrha was not killed but was changed into the

killed.[a] Thus a great quantity of artificial blood was
shed, what with the crucified man and Cinyras. It is
also agreed that the day of the year was the same as
that on which Philip, the son of Amyntas and king
of the Macedonians, was slain by Pausanias, one of
his " Companions," [b] as he entered the theatre.[c]
Gaius hesitated [d] whether to wait until the end of
the spectacle, since it was the last day, or to bathe
and dine and then come back again as he had done
previously. Vinicianus,[e] who was sitting above
Gaius, fearing that the opportunity might be dissi-
pated fruitlessly, rose to leave. When he saw that
Chaerea had preceded him to the exit, he quickened
his step to reach him first and bid him be bold. Gaius,
with an air of friendly interest, plucked his robe and
said, " Where are you going, bless you ? " Vinicianus
resumed his seat, apparently as a courtesy to Caesar,
though fear was a stronger motive. Shortly after,
however, he rose to leave again. This time Gaius
did not interfere, supposing that he was leaving his

tree that bears her name. See Ovid, *Met.* x. 298-502, and
Plutarch, *Parall.* 22.

[b] The most important body of the Macedonian cavalry.
They included the king's most prominent personal friends
and advisers. It was they whom Alexander the Great usually
chose to lead in battle.

[c] The murder of Philip by Pausanias is also mentioned in
*Ant.* xi. 304. Philip was celebrating the marriage of his
daughter Cleopatra to Alexander of Epirus. This could not
have occurred on the same day on which Gaius was assassinated (24 January) since the wedding festivities took place in
the autumn. See J. G. Droysen, *Geschichte der Hellenismus*,
i², 1877, p. 98, esp. n. 3.

[d] Suetonius, *Calig.* 58, gives the reason for this hesitation.
Gaius had an upset stomach from having overeaten on the
previous day.

[e] mss. Minucianus ; *cf.* note on § 18.

δοκῶν ἐπί τινι τῶν ἀναγκαίων[1] ποιεῖσθαι τὴν ἔξοδον. Ἀσπρήνας[2] δὲ καὶ αὐτὸς παρῄνει τῷ Γαΐῳ καθὸ πρότερον ὑπεξελθόντι πρός τε λουτρῷ καὶ ἀρίστῳ γενέσθαι καὶ ἔπειτα δὲ εἰσελθεῖν, χρῄζων ἐπὶ πέρας ἀχθῆναι τὰ ἐγνωσμένα.

99 (14) Καὶ οἱ περὶ τὸν Χαιρέαν ἔτασσον[3] μὲν ἀλλήλους ᾗ καιρός τε καὶ ἐχρῆν ἕκαστον στάντα ᾗ προσταχθείη μὴ ἀπολιμπάνεσθαι ἐπιπονοῦντες. ἤχθοντο δὲ τῇ διατριβῇ καὶ τῷ μέλλεσθαι τὰ ἐν χερσίν, ἐπεὶ καὶ περὶ ἐνάτην ὥραν ἤδη τὰ τῆς ἡμέρας ἦν.

100 καὶ Χαιρέας βραδύνοντος Γαΐου πρόθυμος ἦν ἐπεισελθεῖν ἐν τῇ καθέδρᾳ προσπεσὼν μέντοι προῄδει τοῦτο σὺν πολλῷ φόνῳ τῶν τε βουλευτῶν καὶ ὁπόσοι τῶν ἱππέων παρῆσαν καίπερ δεδιὼς πρόθυμος ἦν, καλῶς ἔχειν ἡγούμενος πᾶσιν ἀσφάλειαν καὶ ἐλευθερίαν ὠνούμενος ἐν ὀλίγῳ τίθεσθαι τὰ

101 κατὰ τοὺς ἀπολουμένους. καὶ δὴ τετραμμένων εἰς τὸ θέατρον εἰσόδῳ σημαίνεται Γάιος ἐξαναστὰς καὶ θόρυβος ἦν, ἀνέστρεφον δὲ καὶ οἱ συνωμόται καὶ ἀνεωθοῦντο τὴν πληθύν, λόγῳ μὲν διὰ τὸ δυσχεραίνειν τὸν Γάιον, ἔργῳ δὲ ἐπ᾽ ἀδείας βουλόμενοι ἐν ἐρημίᾳ τῶν ἀμυνομένων καταστήσαντες αὐτὸν

102 ἅπτεσθαι τῆς σφαγῆς. προεξῄεσαν δὲ Κλαύδιος μὲν ὁ πάτρως αὐτοῦ καὶ Μᾶρκος Βινίκιος[4] ὁ τῆς

---

[1] A : ἐν αἰτίᾳ ἑκὼν MW : necessaria Lat. : ἀναντιλέκτων. ed. pr.

[2] E : Ἀμβρωνᾶς A : Ἀμπρώνας MW : Ἀσπρίνας i. marg. A Busb. : Aspronas Lat.

[3] exacuebant Lat.

[4] Niese : Μινουκιανὸς codd. E Lat. : Οὐινίκιος Hudson.

---

[a] Some mss. have Ambronas or Ampronas.

seat for a necessary purpose. Asprenas,[a] who was also in the plot, then urged Gaius to withdraw, as had been his custom, for a bath and lunch, and then to come back. His object was to see the conspirators' plans carried to fulfilment.

(14) Chaerea's party had posted one another as the occasion required. There each man was bound to stick to his assigned duty without deserting in spite of weariness. They were now impatient with the passage of time and with the postponement of the matter in hand, for it was about the ninth hour [b] of the day. Chaerea himself, since Gaius lingered on, was ready to re-enter the theatre and to attack him where he sat. He foresaw, to be sure, that this would be attended by a great carnage of the senators and of such of the equites as were present. Yet, even with that fear in mind, he was still eager to act, for he thought it a sound principle, when purchasing security and liberty for all, to allow little weight to the cost in lives. They had actually turned to enter the theatre, when the signal was given that Gaius had risen to leave. There was a din raised, and the conspirators returned to their positions and began to thrust back the crowd, saying that Gaius would take offence, though their real object was to render themselves secure, before they proceeded with the assassination, by removing any would-be defenders from his side. Claudius, his uncle, and Marcus Vinicius,[c]

[b] About 2 P.M. Suetonius, *Calig.* 58, places his death at about the seventh hour.

[c] MSS. Minucianus. But Tacitus, *Ann.* vi. 15, makes it clear that it is Marcus Vinicius to whom Gaius' sister Julia was married and who is mentioned by Seneca, *Epist.* 122. 12. *Cf.* the substitution of this same name, Minucianus, for Vinicianus in § 18 and elsewhere in this book.

ἀδελφῆς ἀνὴρ ἔτι δὲ Οὐαλέριος Ἀσιατικός,[1] οὓς
οὐδὲ βουλομένοις διακλεῖσαι δύναμις ἦν αἰδοῖ τῆς
ἀξιώσεως, εἵπετο δ᾽ αὐτὸς σὺν Παύλῳ Ἀρουντίῳ.[2]
103 ἐπεὶ δ᾽ ἐντὸς ἦν τοῦ βασιλείου, τὰς μὲν ἐπ᾽ εὐθείας
ὁδοὺς λείπει, καθ᾽ ἃς διεστήκεσαν τῶν δούλων οἱ
θεραπεύοντες αὐτὸν καὶ προῄεσαν οἱ περὶ τὸν
104 Κλαύδιον· τρέπεται δὲ κατὰ στενωπὸν ἠρεμηκότα
καὶ ἐπίτομον[3] πρὸς λουτροῖς γενησόμενος ἅμα καὶ
παῖδας οἳ ἥκεσαν ἐκ τῆς Ἀσίας κατανοήσων, πομ-
πῆς αὐτῶν ἐκεῖθεν γενομένης ἐπὶ ὕμνοις μυστηρίων
ἃ ἐπετέλει, ἔνιοι δὲ κατὰ πυρριχισμούς, οἳ ἐν τοῖς
105 θεάτροις ἔσοιντο. ὑπαντιάζει δ᾽ αὐτὸν Χαιρέας καὶ
ᾔτησεν σημεῖον. τοῦ δὲ τῶν εἰς χλεύην ἀνακειμένων εἰπόντος οὐδὲν ἐνδοιάσας λοιδορίαις τε ἐχρᾶτο
κατὰ τοῦ Γαΐου καὶ σπασάμενος τὸ ξίφος ἐπάγει
106 πληγὴν σφοδράν· οὐ μήν γε ἦν καίριος. καίτοι γέ

---

[1] Ἀσουατικὸς A : ἀνθυπατικὸς MW Busb. : ἀνθυπατινὸς E :
Asiaticus Lat.

[2] Παύλῳ Ἀρουντίῳ] ed. pr. : ταλαιπωρουντίῳ codd. : Paulo
Arruntio Lat.

[3] coni. Niese : ἐπὶ τόπον codd. : ἐπίσκοτον Bekker.

---

[a] Julia Livilla.

[b] Consul suffectus before 41 and consul ordinarius in 46.
His friendship for Gaius is also cited by Seneca, De Const.
Sap. 18. 2. His great wealth is mentioned by Dio lx. 27. 2.
According to Tacitus, Ann. xi. 1, he was one of the leaders
of the conspiracy against Gaius. Cf. also §§ 159 and 252.

[c] mss. Aruntius. The spelling of the Latin version, Arruntius, is supported by the many inscriptions of members of this
family. Paulus Arruntius, however, is otherwise unknown.

[d] Suetonius, Calig. 58, does not mention the baths ; he
says that Gaius left for lunch.

[e] Suetonius, Calig. 58, reports that along the covered
passage through which he had to pass were some boys of
noble birth from Asia who were rehearsing their parts for a
stage performance. Dio lix. 29. 6 says that the boys were of

his sister's *a* husband, and Valerius Asiaticus *b* had
preceded Gaius' exit. No one could have blocked
their egress even if he had wanted to, such was the
respect due to their dignity. The emperor himself
followed with Paulus Arruntius.*c* But when he was
inside the palace, he quitted the direct route along
both sides of which were lined those of the slaves
who were in attendance, and which Claudius and his
party had earlier taken. Instead, he turned down a
deserted alley that was a short cut to the baths,*d*
where he was going. He also wished to inspect the
boys who had come from Asia.*e* A troop of them had
been dispatched as a choir to sing in the mysteries
which he was celebrating, and some came to take
part in Pyrrhic dances *f* that were to be performed
in the theatre. Here Chaerea waylaid him and
asked for the watchword. Gaius gave him one of
his words of mockery, whereupon without wavering
Chaerea showered abuse on Gaius and drawing his
sword dealt him a severe, though not a mortal, blow.*g*

*Gaius is assassinated. The role of Chaerea.*

exalted birth and had been summoned from Greece and
Ionia to sing a hymn in Gaius' honour.

*f* Originally these were military dances, or rather orna-
mental parades, of the Spartans and Cretans. But the dances
referred to here are more like a ballet (*cf.* Apuleius, *Met.*
x. 29), usually on a mythical theme, often connected with
the worship of Bacchus.

*g* Suetonius, *Calig.* 58, gives two versions of the actual
assassination. According to one, Chaerea came up behind
Gaius as he was talking with the boys from Asia, shouted
" Do your duty," and cut him deeply in the neck with his
sword. Then Cornelius Sabinus stabbed Gaius in the breast.
According to the other version, Sabinus told certain cen-
turions who were privy to the plot to clear away the crowd.
He then asked Gaius the watchword. The emperor gave
him " Jupiter," whereupon he shouted " So be it," and split
Gaius' jawbone with his sword.

φασίν τινες προνοίᾳ τοῦ Χαιρέου γενέσθαι τοῦ μὴ
μιᾷ πληγῇ διεργάσασθαι τὸν Γάιον, ἀλλὰ τιμωρεῖ-
107 σθαι μειζόνως πλήθει τραυμάτων. οὐ μὴν ἐμοὶ
πιθανὸς οὗτος ὁ λόγος διὰ τὸ μὴ ἐπιχωρεῖν ἐν
ταῖσδε ταῖς πράξεσιν λογισμῷ χρῆσθαι τὸν φόβον,[1]
Χαιρέαν δέ, εἴπερ οὕτως ἐφρόνει, πάντων ἥγημαι
μωρίᾳ διαφέρειν ἡδονὴν τῇ ὀργῇ χαριζόμενον μᾶλλον ἢ ἐκ τοῦ ὀξέος ἀπαλλαγὴν αὐτῷ τε καὶ τοῖς
συνωμόταις κινδύνων χαριζόμενον, διὰ τὸ πολλὰς
ἂν μηχανὰς ἔτι γενέσθαι βοηθειῶν Γαΐῳ μὴ φθάντι
τὴν ψυχὴν ἀφεῖναι κἀνταῦθα Χαιρέᾳ λόγον ἂν γενέσθαι οὐ περὶ τῆς Γαΐου τιμωρίας, ἀλλὰ τῆς αὐτοῦ
108 καὶ τῶν φίλων, ὅπου γε καὶ πράξαντι καλῶς ἂν
εἶχε σιγῇ χρωμένῳ διαδιδράσκειν τὰς ὀργὰς τῶν
ἀμυνομένων, οὐχ ὅπως ἄδηλον εἰ τύχοι κατορθῶν
ἐπ' ἀλόγοις χρῄζειν αὐτόν τε ἀπολέσαι καὶ τὸν
καιρόν. καὶ τάδε μὲν εἰκάζειν[2] παρέστω τοῖς βου-
109 λομένοις ᾗ καὶ θέλοιεν. ὁ δὲ Γάιος ἀλγηδόνι τῆς
πληγῆς περιφερόμενος, μεσσηγὺς γὰρ τοῦ τε ὤμου
καὶ τοῦ τραχήλου φερόμενον τὸ ξίφος ἐπέσχεν ἡ
κλεὶς προσωτέρω χωρεῖν, οὔτε ἀνεβόησεν ὑπ' ἐκπλήξεως οὔτε ἐπεκαλέσατό τινας τῶν φίλων εἴτε
ἀπιστίᾳ εἴτε καὶ ἄλλως ἀφρονήσει, στόνῳ δὲ χρησάμενος πρὸς τῆς ἀλγηδόνος τὸ περιὸν[3] εἰς τὸ πρόσθεν

---

[1] A : φόνον MW.
[2] αὐτόν . . . εἰκάζειν] A : om. MWE.
[3] στόνῳ . . . περιὸν] sed dolorem fortiter ferens Lat.

---

[a] M. P. Charlesworth, in *Camb. Hist. Jour.* iv, 1933, p.
112, appropriately points to Suetonius, *Calig.* 30, for the
explanation as to why the story might have arisen that
Chaerea had dispatched Gaius with a multitude of blows.
There we are told that Gaius enjoyed watching a lingering
death, and so he preferred inflicting a number of small wounds.

There are some, to be sure, who assert that Chaerea intentionally avoided dispatching Gaius with a single stroke, to have a greater revenge by inflicting a number of wounds.[a] This account, however, I cannot believe ; for in such actions fear leaves no room for deliberation. If Chaerea did entertain such a thought, I consider that he would have been foolish beyond the ordinary, a man who indulged his anger instead of granting himself and his conspirators a speedy deliverance from dangers. For Gaius might have been rescued in many different ways, had he not at once expired, and in that case Chaerea would have had to reckon not on the punishment of Gaius but on his own and that of his friends. Surely, even in case of success, it would be better to say nothing and to elude the anger of any who would retaliate ; how much more foolish, then, when success was problematical, to choose irrationally to risk his life and miss the opportunity. The field is open, however, for such guesses as those who choose desire to make. Gaius, dazed by the pain of the blow, for the sword struck him between the shoulder and the neck, where the collar-bone held it from going farther, neither cried out in alarm nor called upon any of his friends.[b] Either he could not believe what had happened or else he lacked the presence of mind. Instead he groaned in extreme agony and dashed ahead to

His order " Strike so that he may feel that he is dying " became proverbial, according to Suetonius. Hence a desire for poetic justice may have led to this account of Gaius' own death.

   [b] A different version is found in Suetonius, *Calig.* 58, who says that as Gaius lay writhing on the ground, he shouted that he was still alive. Dio lix. 29. 7 says nothing of this, but reports that when he had fallen, all the men who were present stabbed him even though he was dead.

110 ἴετο φυγῇ. καὶ δεξάμενος αὐτὸν Κορνήλιος Σαβῖνος τὴν διάνοιαν ἤδη προκατειργασμένος¹ ὠθεῖ
καὶ κλιθέντα ἐπὶ γόνυ πολλοὶ περιστάντες ἀφ' ἑνὸς
ἐγκελεύσματος ἔκοπτον τοῖς ξίφεσιν, παρακελευσ-
μός τε τὰ πρὸς ἀλλήλους καὶ πρὸς ἔρις αὐτοῖς ἦν.²
τελευταῖα δὲ Ἀκύλας, ὁμολογεῖται δὲ ὑπὸ πάντων
111 πληγὴν ἐπαγαγών, μεθίστησιν αὐτὸν ἀκριβῶς. ἀνα-
θείη δ' ἄν τις τὴν πρᾶξιν Χαιρέα· καὶ γὰρ εἰ σὺν
πολλοῖς ἐπράχθη τὸ ἔργον αὐτῷ, ἀλλ' οὖν πρῶτός τε
ἐνεθυμήθη³ μέντοι αὐτὸ ὡς πραχθείη⁴ προλαβὼν⁵
112 πολὺ τῶν ἁπάντων, καὶ πρῶτος μὲν τολμηρῶς
ἐξεῖπεν τοῖς λοιποῖς, δεχομένων δὲ τὸν ἐπὶ τῷ
φόνῳ λόγον σποράδας τε ἤθροισεν καὶ τὰ πάντα
φρονίμως συγκροτήσας ἔνθα γνωμῶν εἰσηγήσεως
ἐχρῆν πολὺ κρείσσων ἐγίγνετο καὶ λόγοις καθωμί-
λησεν χρηστοῖς ὡς οὐ τολμῶντας ἠνάγκασέν τε
113 τοὺς ἅπαντας, ἐπεί τε. καιρὸς ἐλάμβανεν χειρὶ χρήσασθαι, φαίνεται κἀνταῦθα πρῶτός τε ὁρμήσας καὶ
ἁψάμενος ἀρετῇ τοῦ φόνου καὶ τοῖς ἄλλοις εὐεπί-
βατον παρασχὼν καὶ προτεθνεῶτα Γάιον, ὥστ' ἂν
δικαίως καὶ ὁπόσα τοῖς λοιποῖς εἴη πεπραγμένα τῇ
Χαιρέου γνώμῃ τε καὶ ἀρετῇ προστίθεσθαι καὶ πό-
νῳ τῶν χειρῶν.
114 (15) Καὶ Γάιος μὲν τοιούτῳ τρόπῳ χρησάμενος
τῆς τελευτῆς ὑπὸ τοῦ πολλοῦ τῶν τραυμάτων ἀπο-

¹ MW Lat.: προκατειργασμένον A.
² ἀφ' ἑνὸς . . . αὐτοῖς ἦν] singuli ad invicem gladiis et
quasi ad certamina discerpserunt Lat.
³ εἶναι post ἐνεθυμήθη om.: κτεῖναι legit Petersen: τί δεῖν
coni. Marcus.
⁴ μέντοι αὐτὸ ὡς πραχθείη] A (litt. τοι αὐτὸ ὡς πραχθείη i. ras.
m. 2): μέντοι αὐτῷ ὃς MW: τοιαῦτα ὡς πραχθείη ed. pr.: μέν,
τοιαῦτα δ' ὡς πραχθείη Petersen: μέντοι οὕτως πραχθείη coni.
Marcus.

escape. He was confronted by Cornelius Sabinus, who had his course of action already worked out. He pushed Gaius to the ground and brought him down on one knee. Here a number of assailants encircled Gaius and at a single word of encouragement struck at him with their swords, cheering one another on and competing too. Finally Aquila, and there is no dissent about this, delivered a blow that unquestionably dispatched him. But the credit for the feat must still go to Chaerea. To be sure, he had many to help him accomplish it, but at any rate he was the first to think of the means by which to achieve it, and he planned it long before anyone else.[a] Again he was the first who had the courage to speak openly of a plot to the rest. Moreover, when scattered individuals accepted the proposal of the murder, he brought them together and prudently organized the whole scheme. Thus, where initiative was called for, he proved far superior to the rest. In addition, by his noble eloquence he won them over when their courage failed them and compelled them all to act. Finally, when the time came for action, there too he was clearly the first to move and to initiate the glorious assassination, thus making Gaius, who was as good as dead already, an easy mark for the rest. The conclusion is that whatever the others may have done, all will rightly be credited to the decision and valour of Chaerea and to the labour of his hands.

(15) Such was the manner in which Gaius came to his end ; deprived of life by his numerous wounds,

---

[a] Text slightly emended, but the meaning is clear.

[5] MW ed. pr. : προὐλαβεῖν A (litt. πρου i. ras. m. 2, litt. ιν i. ras. m. 1) : προὐλαβεν Petersen.

115 ψυχθεὶς ἔκειτο. οἱ δὲ περὶ τὸν Χαιρέαν ἐπειδὴ
κατείργαστο αὐτοῖς ἤδη Γάιος, ὁδοὺς μὲν τὰς αὐτὰς[1]
ἰόντες σώζειν αὐτοὺς ἀμήχανον ἑώρων, ὄκνῳ τε τῶν
γεγονότων, οὐ γὰρ μικρὸν ἦν τὸν αὐτοκράτορα
ἀνῃρηκόσι τὸ κινδύνευμα ὑπό τε ἀνοίας τοῦ δήμου
τιμώμενον καὶ ὄντα προσφιλῆ καὶ τῶν στρατιωτῶν

116 μὴ ἀναιμωτὶ ποιησομένων τὴν ζήτησιν αὐτοῦ, ἄλλως τε στενῶν οὐσῶν τῶν ὁδῶν, καθ᾽ ἃς ἔπραξαν
τὸ ἔργον, καὶ μεγάλου πλήθους ἐμφράξαντος αὐτὰς
τῆς τε θεραπείας καὶ ὁπόσοι τῶν στρατιωτῶν ἐπὶ
φυλακῇ τοῦ αὐτοκράτορος ἐκείνην παρῆσαν τὴν

117 ἡμέραν, ὁδούς τε ἑτέρας χωροῦντες παρῆσαν εἰς
τὴν Γερμανικοῦ μὲν οἰκίαν τοῦ Γαΐου πατρός, ὃν
τότε ἀνῃρήκεσαν, συνημμένη δὲ ἐκείνη,[2] διὰ τὸ ἐν
τὸ βασίλειον ὂν ἐπ᾽ ἐποικοδομίαις[3] ἑκάστου τῶν ἐν
τῇ ἡγεμονίᾳ γεγονότων ἀσκηθὲν ἀπὸ μέρους ὀνόματι τῶν οἰκοδομησαμένων[4] ἢ καί τι τῶν μερῶν[5]
οἰκήσεις ἀρξάντων τὴν ἐπωνυμίαν παρασχέσθαι.

118 καὶ διεκπεσόμενοι ἐκ τοῦ πλήθους τὴν ἔφοδον ἐν
ἀδείᾳ τὸ παρὸν ἦσαν[6] λανθάνοντος ἀκμὴν κακοῦ τοῦ

119 τὸν αὐτοκράτορα παρειληφότος. πρώτους δὲ εἰς
τοὺς Γερμανοὺς ἡ αἴσθησις ἀφίκετο τῆς Γαΐου
τελευτῆς. δορυφόροι δ᾽ ἦσαν οὗτοι ὁμώνυμον[7] τῷ
ἔθνει ἐφ᾽[8] οὗ κατειλέχατο[9] Κελτικοῦ τάγμα παρεχό-

---

[1] τὰς αὐτὰς] Hudson : τοσαύτας codd. E : eadem Lat.
[2] συνημμένη δὲ ἐκείνη] συνημμένην δὲ ἐκείνην Bekker : συνημμένην δὲ ἐκείνῃ coni. Niese (secundum Lat.).
[3] A : οἰκοδομίαις MW : ἐποικοδομαῖς Holwerda.
[4] ed. pr. : οἰκοδομηθησομένων codd.
[5] ed. pr. : ἡμερῶν A : ἡμετέρων MW et i. marg. A.
[6] συνημμένη . . . ἦσαν] erat enim haec domus coniuncta
regalibus eo quod hi qui in eminentia constituti sunt diebus
suae potentiae in talibus habitare noscuntur. et declinantes
multitudinis invasionem esse iam videbantur in requie Lat.

there he lay. Chaerea and his companions, once they had settled their business with Gaius, saw that there was no chance of escape if they followed the route by which they had come. For one thing they had cause for alarm in what they had done, and it was no small danger that menaced the emperor's assassins. For he was held in honour and affection by the foolish mob; and the soldiers, in their search for him, would not refrain from bloodshed. Moreover, the passage-ways along which they had done the deed were narrow and blocked by a great crowd of his attendants and of such soldiers as were present for duty that day as the emperor's bodyguard. So they took another route, and came to the house of Germanicus, the father of the Gaius whom they had just now killed, which was contiguous to the palace of Gaius. For the palace, although a single edifice, had been enlarged part by part, and this occasioned the naming of the additions for members of the ruling family who completed or else started some part of the structure. Having escaped the mob without an assault, they were now free from danger, since the disaster which had overtaken the emperor was still undetected. The Germans were the first [a] to discover the death of Gaius. They were the emperor's bodyguard and bore the name of the nation from which they had been enlisted; and it was they who made

The German bodyguard avenge Gaius.

---

[a] Suetonius, *Calig.* 58, says that even before the arrival of the German bodyguards, Gaius' litter-bearers ran to help him.

---

[7] ex Lat. : ὁμώνυμοι codd.
[8] AM : ἀφ' W.
[9] κατειλέχατο] Dindorf : κατειλήχαστὸ, σ ex ν corr. A : κατείλεχαν τὸ MW.

120 μενοι τὸ αὐτῶν. θυμῷ δὲ χρῆσθαι πάτριόν ἐστιν
αὐτοῖς, ὥσπερ σπάνιον εἴ[1] τισιν ἑτέροις βαρβάρων
διὰ τὸ ἡσσόνως λογισμὸν ἐπιδέχεσθαι τῶν ποιουμένων, ῥωμαλέοι τε τοῖς σώμασι καὶ τῇ πρώτῃ
ὁρμῇ συνιόντες τοῖς πολεμίοις, οὓς ἂν νομίσωσι,[2]
121 μεγάλα κατορθοῦντες. οὗτοι οὖν πυθόμενοι τοῦ
Γαΐου τὴν σφαγὴν καὶ περιαλγήσαντες διὰ τὸ μὴ
ἀρετῇ κρίνειν ἐπὶ τοῖς ὅλοις, ἀλλὰ συμφέροντι τῷ
αὑτῶν, μάλιστα δὲ αὐτοῖς προσφιλὴς ἦν Γάιος
122 δόσεσι χρημάτων τὸ εὔνουν αὐτῷ κτώμενος, σπασά-
μενοι τὰ ξίφη, προειστήκει δ' αὐτῶν Σαβῖνος χιλι-
αρχῶν οὐ δι' ἀρετὴν καὶ γενναιότητα προγόνων,
μονομάχος γὰρ ἦν, ἰσχύι δὲ σώματος τὴν ἐπὶ τοιούτοις κτησάμενος ἀνθρώποις[3] ἀρχήν,[4] διεξῄεσαν τῆς
οἰκίας ἀνερευνώμενοι τοὺς σφαγέας τοῦ Καίσαρος.
123 Ἀσπρήναν τε κρεουργήσασιν αὐτοῖς διὰ τὸ πρώτῳ
περιπεσεῖν, οὗ τὴν στολὴν μιᾶναν τὸ αἷμα τῶν
θυμάτων, ὥς μοι λέλεκται πρότερον, οὐκ ἐπ'
ἀγαθῷ τὴν συντυχίαν ἀπεσήμαινε τοῦ γεγονότος,
δεύτερος Νωρβανὸς[5] ὑπηντίαζεν ἐν τοῖς γενναιοτά-

---

[1] σπάνιον εἴ] Hispanis aut Lat. : Ἰσπανοῖς καί Richards et
Shutt ex Lat.

[2] οὓς ἂν νομίσωσι] quibuscumque congressi Lat. : οἷς ἂν
ὁμόσ' ἴωσι Richards et Shutt ex Lat.

[3] κτησάμενος ἀνθρώποις coni. : κτησάμενος ἄθροισιν A : κτησάμενος MWE : κτησάμενος ἀνδράσιν Bekker.

[4] ed. pr. : ἀρετήν codd. : dignitatem Lat.

[5] δεύτερος Νωρβανὸς] A : βάρβαρος Ῥωμανὸς M : βάρβαρος
Νωρμανὸς W : post hunc (occurrit eis) barbarus Norbanus
Lat. : Βάλβος Νωρβανὸς Groag (ap. Pauly-Wissowa, xvii[1],
1936, p. 932).

---

[a] Not the Cornelius Sabinus who was one of the leaders
in the conspiracy to assassinate Gaius (§§ 46 ff.). This Sabinus was one of the Thracians whom Caligula put in charge

up the Celtic band. It is a national trait of theirs to
act furiously to a degree such as is rarely if ever met
with among other barbarians, for the Germans pause
less for calculation of the consequences. They are
also physically powerful and win great success in the
first onset whenever they engage any whom they consider enemies. These men, then, when they learned
of the murder of Gaius, were full of resentment,
for they did not decide issues on their merits according to the general interest, but according to their
own advantage. Gaius was especially popular with
them because of the gifts of money by which he acquired their goodwill. With swords drawn, they burst
out from the palace in search of Caesar's murderers.
They were led by Sabinus,[a] a military tribune [b] who
owed his command over such men not to the services
and nobility of his ancestors, for he was a gladiator,
but to his physical strength. Asprenas [c] was the
first whom they came upon, and that was good reason
to carve him limb from limb ; it was he whose robe
had been soiled by the blood of the victims, as I have
mentioned above, an omen which boded no good.
The second to fall in their way was Norbanus,[d] one

of his German bodyguard, according to Suetonius, *Calig.* 55·
Later, when Claudius was eager to see him killed in a gladiatorial contest, he was saved by Messalina, whose paramour
he was (Dio lx. 28. 2).

[b] The title, as Keune, " Custos," Pauly-Wissowa, iv, 1901,
p. 1903, indicates, is not to be taken literally, since the German bodyguard was not organized thus.

[c] *Cf.* § 87.

[d] Apparently L. Norbanus Balbus, consul in 19 (the gap
in years between 19 and 41 is not sufficient to support the
guess that our Norbanus was his son). In all probability,
according to Stein, " Norbanus," no. 8, Pauly-Wissowa,
xvii[1], 1936, p. 931, he was the grandson of Lucius Cornelius
Balbus the Younger, who had fought with Julius Caesar in

τοῖς τῶν πολιτῶν καὶ πολλοὺς αὐτοκράτορας παρ-
124 εχόμενος τῶν προπατόρων. καὶ μηδὲν αἰδουμένων
αὐτοῦ τὴν ἀξίωσιν ἰσχύι προὔχων ἀφαιρεῖται τὸ
ξίφος τῷ πρώτῳ τῶν ἐπιόντων συμπλακεὶς φανερός
τε ἦν οὐκ ἀπραγμόνως τεθνηξόμενος, μέχρι δὴ
περισχεθεὶς πολλοῖς τῶν ἐπιφερομένων ἔπεσεν ὑπὸ
125 πλήθους τραυμάτων. τρίτος δὲ Ἀντήιος τῶν ἐκ
τῆς βουλῆς σὺν ὀλίγοις, οὐ τυχαίως τοῖς Γερμανοῖς
καθάπερ οἱ πρότερον περιπεσών, ὑπὸ δὲ φιλοθεα-
μοσύνης καὶ ἡδονῆς[1] τοῦ αὐτόπτης γενόμενος[2] Γαΐου
κειμένου μῖσος εὐφρᾶναι τὸ πρὸς αὐτόν[3]· τὸν γὰρ
πατέρα τοῦ Ἀντηίου καὶ ὁμώνυμον φυγάδα ἐλάσας
καὶ μὴ ἀρκεσθεὶς κτείνει στρατιώτας ἀποπέμψας.
126 καὶ παρῆν μὲν διὰ τάδε εὐφρανούμενος θεωρίᾳ τοῦ
νεκροῦ, θορυβουμένης δὲ τῆς οἰκίας κρύπτειν αὐτὸν
ἐνθυμησάμενος οὐ διαφυγγάνει τῶν Γερμανῶν τό τε
εἰς τὴν ἔρευναν ἀκριβὲς κἀπὶ τοῖς φόνοις ὁμοίως
τῶν τε αἰτίων καὶ μὴ ἐξαγριωσάντων. καὶ οἵδε
μὲν ταύτῃ τεθνήκεσαν.
127 (16) Εἰς δὲ τὸ θέατρον ἐπεὶ ἀφίκετο ὁ λόγος περὶ
τῆς Γαΐου τελευτῆς, ἔκπληξίς τε καὶ ἀπιστία ἦν· οἱ
μὲν γὰρ καὶ πάνυ ἡδονῇ δεχόμενοι τὸν ὄλεθρον
αὐτοῦ κἂν πρὸ πολλοῦ ἡγησάμενοι σφίσιν ἀγαθὸν

---

[1] ἡδονῇ coni. Petersen.
[2] γενέσθαι E.
[3] μῖσος . . . αὐτόν] διὰ μίσους ἐφέρετο πρὸς αὐτὸν E.

---

the Civil War, and who in turn was a nephew of Lucius Cornelius Balbus the Elder, who had served under Caesar in
Spain and Gaul. Since Josephus says that he could boast of
many generals among his ancestors, he may also have been
a descendant of Gaius Norbanus, who had fought unsuccess-
fully against Sulla.
    [a] Otherwise unknown, though perhaps the brother of

of the noblest of the citizens, who could boast of many generals among his ancestors. When the Germans showed no respect for his rank, his superior strength enabled him, on grappling with the first of his assailants, to snatch away his sword. He let it be seen that he would not let them kill him at their ease, but at last he was enclosed in a circle of assailants and succumbed to their many blows. The third victim was Anteius,[a] one of the most distinguished senators. He did not, like his predecessors, fall foul of the Germans accidentally, but was attracted by the love of a spectacle and by the pleasure of seeing the prostrate Gaius with his own eyes in order to gratify his hatred for him. For Gaius had driven Anteius' father,[b] who bore the same name, into exile ; and, not content with that, he had sent a body of soldiers after him to put him to death. Such cause Anteius had to rejoice as he stood there looking on. But when the uproar began in the palace, and the need to conceal himself became urgent, he did not escape the vigilant search of the Germans nor the savage fury with which they slew both the guilty and the innocent alike. And so these three men died thus.

(16) When the news of the death of Gaius reached the theatre, there was consternation and incredulity. Some, who heartily welcomed his assassination and would have regarded it long since as a blessing to

*The theatre is stunned by news of Gaius' death.*

Publius Anteius, who was legate in Dalmatia in 51/52 and committed suicide in 66 (Tac. *Ann.* xvi. 14 ; *cf.* Rohden, " Anteius," no. 4, Pauly-Wissowa, i, 1894, p. 2349).

[b] Otherwise unknown, unless he is to be identified with the Anteius who was one of those whom Germanicus put in charge of constructing a fleet in 16 (Tac. *Ann.* ii. 6 ; *cf.* Rohden, " Anteius," no. 1, Pauly-Wissowa, i, 1894, p. 2349).

128 συνελθεῖν ὑπὸ δέους ἐν ἀπιστίᾳ ἦσαν. εἰσὶ δ' οἷς
καὶ πάνυ ἀπ' ἐλπίδων ἦν διὰ τὸ μὴ ἐθέλειν τι
τοιόνδε περὶ τῷ Γαΐῳ γεγονέναι μήτε ἀληθείᾳ προστίθεσθαι διὰ τὸ μὴ οἷόν τε ἀνθρώπῳ εἶναι τοιάδε
129 ἀρετῇ χρῆσθαι. γύναια δ' ἦν ταῦτα καὶ παῖδες
ὁπόσοι τε δοῦλοι καί τινες τοῦ στρατιωτικοῦ, οἱ
μὲν διὰ τὸ μισθοφορεῖν καὶ οὐδὲν ἀλλ' ἢ συντυραν-
νοῦντες καὶ διακονίᾳ τῆς κατ' ἐκεῖνον ὕβρεως ἐπανα-
σειόμενοι τοῖς κρατίστοις τῶν πολιτῶν τιμῆς τε
130 ἅμα καὶ ὠφελειῶν τυγχάνειν, ἡ δὲ αὖ γυναικωνῖτις
καὶ τὸ νεώτερον, ὅπερ ὄχλος φιλεῖ, θεωρίαις τε καὶ
μονομαχιῶν δόσεσιν καί τινων κρεανομιῶν ἡδοναῖς
ἀνειλημμένοι, ἃ ἐπράσσετο λόγῳ μὲν ἐπὶ θεραπείᾳ[1]
τῆς πληθύος,[2] τὸ δ' ἀληθὲς ἐκπιμπλάντα τῆς μανίας
131 Γαΐου τὴν ὠμότητα· οἱ δὲ δοῦλοι διὰ τὸ ἐν προσηγορίᾳ τε εἶναι καὶ καταφρονήματι τῶν δεσποτῶν,
ἀποστροφῆς τῷ ὑβρίζοντι αὐτοὺς[3] οὔσης τῆς κατ'
ἐκεῖνον ἐπικουρίας· ῥᾴδιον γὰρ ψευσαμένοις τε κατὰ
τῶν κυρίων πεπιστεῦσθαι καὶ τὰ χρήματα ἐνδεί-
ξασιν αὐτῶν ἅμα ἐλευθέροις τε εἶναι καὶ πλουσίοις
μισθῷ τῶν κατηγοριῶν διὰ τὸ ἆθλα αὐτοῖς προκεῖ-
132 σθαι τὰς ὀγδόας τῶν οὐσιῶν. τῶν δὲ εὐπατριδῶν
εἰ καί τισιν πιστὸς ὁ λόγος φανείη, τοῖς μὲν ἐκ τοῦ
προειδέναι τὴν ἐπιβουλήν, τοῖς δ' ὑπὸ τοῦ θέλειν
εὐκτὸν ἡγουμένοις, σιγῇ παρεδίδοτο οὐ μόνον ἡ ἐπὶ

---

[1] A : θεωρίᾳ MW et i. marg. A.
[2] ἃ ἐπράσσετο . . . πληθύος] quas in ludis agebat Gaius, ut
quasi populo voluptatem exhiberet Lat.
[3] ed. pr. : αὐτὴν codd. : αὐτῶν coni. Niese.

themselves, were incredulous from fear. There were others to whom the news was quite contrary to their hopes because they had no desire that any such thing should befall Gaius ; and they did not credit it, because it seemed to them impossible for any human being to have the courage to kill Gaius. Among them were silly women, children, all the slaves, and some of the army. The last named were of this mind because they were mercenaries, and no less than partners in his tyranny ; by playing the lackey to his insolence, they gained both honour and profit, for the noblest citizens were in terror of them. The women-folk and the youth, after the fashion of the mob, were captivated by his shows and by the gladiatorial combats that he presented, as well as by the enjoyment of portions of meat that he distributed. The reason given for such provision was to cater to the crowd, but the truth was that Gaius' own savage madness fed on such things. The slaves supported him because they were now on familiar terms with, and contemptuous of, their masters, and found in his intervention a refuge from their masters' rough treatment, for it was easy for them to gain credence when they informed falsely against their lords. They also found it easy, by giving information about their masters' possessions, to gain both freedom and wealth as a reward for such denunciations, since the informer's fee was one-eighth of the property.[a] As to the patricians, if there were any who credited the report, some from their foreknowledge of the plot and others because of wishful thinking, they not only consigned to silence their joy at the announcement

---

[a] Actually the informer's fee under Tiberius had been one-fourth (*Camb. Anc. Hist.* x, 1934, p. 627).

τοῖς ἠγγελμένοις χαρά, ἀλλὰ καὶ ἡ δόξα τῆς ἀκρο-
133 άσεως, οἱ μὲν δεδιότες μὴ καὶ ψευσθεῖσιν ἐλπίδος
τιμωρία συνέλθοιεν ὡς προεξορμήσασιν ἀποφήνα-
σθαι τὴν διάνοιαν ἑαυτῶν, οἱ δ᾽ ἐξεπιστάμενοι διὰ
τὸ τῆς ἐπιβουλῆς μετασχεῖν μειζόνως ἔκρυπτον
ἀλλήλων ἀγνοία καὶ δεδιότες, μὴ πρός τινα εἰπόντες,
οἷς ἡ τυραννὶς ἑστῶσα ὠφέλιμος ἦν, ζῶντος Γαΐου
134 κολασθεῖεν ἐνδείξεως γενομένης. ἐπεὶ καὶ ἕτερος
ἐπεφοιτήκει λόγος ὡμιληκέναι μὲν τραύμασιν,[1] οὐ
μὴν ἀποθανεῖν, ἀλλὰ ζῶντα ἐν θεραπείαις ὑπὸ τῶν
135 ἰατρῶν εἶναι. ἦν τε πιστὸς οὐθεὶς[2] οὐδενί, ᾧ κἂν
θαρσήσας γνώμην ἀποφαίνοιτο τὴν αὑτοῦ· ἢ γὰρ
φίλος ὢν ὕποπτος ἐγίνετο εὐνοίᾳ τῆς τυραννίδος ἢ
καὶ μίσει πρὸς ἐκεῖνον χρώμενος τῷ πρὸς αὐτὸν
οὐδαμόθεν εὐνοίᾳ χρωμένῳ διαφθείρειν τὴν ἐπὶ τοῖς
136 λεγομένοις πίστιν. ἐλέγετο δὲ ὑπό τινων, οἳ καὶ
μάλιστα τοῖς εὐπατρίδαις ἠφάνιζον τὸ εὐθυμοῦν τῆς
ἐλπίδος, ἐν ἀμελείᾳ κινδύνων γεγονότα καὶ ἄφροντιν
κομιδῇ τῶν τραυμάτων, ὥσπερ εἶχεν ἡματωμένον
ἐπὶ τῆς ἀγορᾶς διεκπεσεῖν κἂν δημηγορίαις εἶναι.
137 καὶ τάδε μὲν εἰκάζετο βουλήσει τῇ ἀλογίστῳ τῶν
θροεῖν προθεμένων καὶ ἐπ᾽ ἀμφότερα δόξῃ τῶν
ἀκουόντων λαμβανόμενα· οὐ μὴν τήν γ᾽ ἐνέδραν[3]
ἐξέλιπον δεδιότες τὴν ἐπενεχθησομένην προεξιοῦσιν
αἰτίαν· οὐ γὰρ ἐφ᾽ ἧς ἀξιοῖεν[4] διανοίας γενήσεσθαι

---

[1] ὡμιληκέναι . . . τραύμασιν] quia res quidem a coniuratis
fuisset temptata Lat.
[2] ex Lat.: αὖθις codd.: οὐδεὶς Bekker.
[3] ἐνέδραν] loca suae custodiae Lat.: ἕδραν Dindorf.
[4] ἐξίοιεν Hudson ex Lat.

but even pretended not to have heard of it. They were afraid lest, if they were disappointed in their expectation, they would be brought to punishment because they had started too soon to show what they thought. Those who had knowledge of the plot, because they were partners in it, were still more secretive, since they did not know who the others were in the plot and feared that if they spoke of it to anyone who stood to gain by the continuance of the tyranny, they would be denounced and punished if Gaius still lived. For another story had got about to the effect that though wounded, Gaius was not dead, but alive and being attended by physicians. There was no one who had sufficient confidence in anyone else to pluck up courage and tell him what he thought. For if the other were a friend of Gaius, he was suspected because of the goodwill that he bore to the tyranny, or else, if he hated Gaius, confidence was undermined in what he said by his unwillingness to tolerate anything favourable about Gaius from any source. It was reported by some— and it was they who most of all banished all optimism from the patricians' minds—that Gaius, in disregard of danger and quite unconcerned to get his wounds treated, had escaped, bloodstained as he was, to the Forum and was haranguing the people. Such were the pictures drawn by the unreasoning desire of those who took it upon themselves to wag their tongues ; the effect on the hearers depended on their attitude one way or the other. None, however, left their seats, because they feared the charge which might be brought against any who were the first to go out ; for they would be judged guilty or innocent not because of the intention with which they might claim

περὶ αὐτοῖς τὴν κρίσιν,[1] ἀλλ' ἀφ' ἧς εἰκάζειν[2] ἐθελήσειαν οἵ τε κατηγορήσοντες καὶ οἱ δικάζοντες.[3]

138 (17) Ἐπεὶ δὲ καὶ πλῆθος τῶν Γερμανῶν περιέσχε
τὸ θέατρον ἐσπασμένων τὰ ξίφη, πᾶσι τοῖς θεωροῖς
ἐλπὶς ἦν ἀπολεῖσθαι, καὶ πρὸς πᾶσαν οὕτινος εἴσοδον πτοία εἶχεν αὐτούς, ὡς αὐτίκα μάλα συγκοπή-
σοιντο, ἐν ἀμηχάνοις τε ἦσαν οὔτ' ἀπιέναι θάρσος
εἰσφερόμενοι οὔτε ἀκίνδυνον τὴν διατριβὴν τὴν ἐπὶ
139 τοῦ θεάτρου πεπιστευκότες. εἰσπιπτόντων τε ἤδη
βοὴ τοῦ θεάτρου ῥήγνυται καθ' ἱκετείαν τρεπομένου
τῶν στρατιωτῶν, ὡς πάντων ἀγνοίας αὐτοῖς[4] γενομένης καὶ τῶν βουλευθέντων τοῖς ἐπαναστᾶσιν, εἰ
δή τις καὶ γέγονεν ἐπανάστασις, καὶ τῶν γεγονό-
140 των. φείδεσθαι οὖν καὶ μὴ τόλμης ἀλλοτρίας παρὰ
τῶν οὐδ' ἐν αἰτίᾳ γενομένων ἀπολαμβάνειν τιμωρίαν, παρέντας ἐρεύνην[5] τῶν πεπραχότων ὅ τι καὶ
141 πεπραγμένον εἴη καταστῆναι. καὶ οἱ μὲν ταῦτά τε
καὶ περαιτέρω μετὰ δακρύων καὶ τύψεως προσ-
ώπων ἐπιθειάζοντες καὶ ποτνιώμενοι ὁπόσα ἀνεδίδασκεν αὐτοὺς ὁ κίνδυνος ἑστὼς πλησίον, καὶ ὡς
ἄν τις ἀγωνιζόμενος περὶ τῆς ψυχῆς εἴποι τι, ἔλεγον.
142 θραύεται δὲ τῶν στρατιωτῶν πρὸς ταῦτα ἡ ὀργὴ
καὶ μεταμελῆσαν αὐτοῖς τοῦ ἐπὶ τοῖς θεωροῖς βου-
λεύματος, ὠμόν τε γὰρ ἦν τοῦτο καὶ ἐκείνοις καίπερ
ἐξηγριωκόσιν ἐδόκει, τὰς κεφαλὰς τῶν περὶ τὸν
143 Ἀσπρῆναν ἐπὶ τὸν βωμὸν ἀπερεισαμένοις. πρὸς

---

[1] οὐ γὰρ . . . κρίσιν] quando non qua voluntate discederent
accusari poterant aut damnari Lat.

[2] A : ἐγκαθίζειν MW.

[3] οἵ τε κατηγορήσοντες καὶ οἱ δικάζοντες] Lowthius (κατηγορήσοντες coni.: κατηγορήσαντες Lowthius) : τούς τε κατηγορήσον-
τας καὶ τοὺς δικάζοντας codd.

to have acted but because of whatever construction
would-be prosecutors and jury might chose to put
upon the act.

(17) But when in fact a troop of Germans with
drawn swords surrounded the theatre, all the spectators expected a massacre ; they cringed when anyone entered, no matter who, convinced that they
would be cut to pieces that very instant. They were
thus at a loss what to do, for on the one hand they
were unable to pluck up courage to depart, and on
the other hand they had no confidence that it was
safe to stay in the theatre. When the troops now
streamed in, the people in the theatre burst into cries,
turning in supplication to the soldiers and pleading
that they had had no knowledge of anything, neither
of the designs of the rebels, supposing that a rebellion
had occurred, nor of actual events. They therefore entreated the soldiers to spare them and not to make innocent men pay the penalty for the rashness of others,
and to abandon the idea of instituting a search for
those who had done whatever it was that had actually
been done. Such were their words and more, as they
wept and beat their faces, conjuring them to listen
with agonized appeals such as the danger that hovered
near schooled them to repeat. Each man spoke as a
man must speak when life hangs on his eloquence.
The anger of the soldiers gave way under the impact
of these words, and they repented of their intended
attack on the spectators, which would have been
cruel and appeared so even to them, furious though
they were. But first they fixed the heads of Asprenas
and their other victims upon the altar. At this sight,

---

[4] coni. Niese : αὐτῇ codd. : αὐτῷ ed. pr.
[5] Niese : ἐρεύνη A : ἐν ἐρεύνη MW.

ἃς μειζόνως ἔπαθον οἱ θεωροὶ λογισμῷ τε ἀξιώσεως
τῶν ἀνδρῶν καὶ ἐλέῳ τοῦ πάθους, ὥστε παρ' ὀλίγον
καὶ αὐτοῖς οὐδὲν ἐλλιπεστέρως τὰ τῶν κινδύνων
ὁμιλήσαντα ἐπανασεσεῖσθαι, ὧν ἄδηλον εἶναι τὴν
συμφορὰν εἴπερ εἰς τέλος φευχθῆναι δύναιτ' ἄν.

144 ὥστε κἂν εἴ τινες τῶν προθύμως μισούντων καὶ
μετὰ δίκης τὸν Γάιον ἀφαιρεῖσθαι τῶν ἐπ' αὐτῷ
εὐφροσυνῶν τῆς χώρας,[1] διὰ τὸ ἐν ῥοπῇ μὲν τοῦ
συναπολουμένου[2] γεγονέναι,[3] τὸ δὲ πιστὸν τοῦ
περιεῖναι μηδέπω καὶ τότε ἐχέγγυον συνελθεῖν.

145 (18) *Ἦν δὲ Εὐάρεστος Ἀρούντιος[4] τῶν κηρυσ-
σόντων τὰ πωλούμενα καὶ δι' αὐτὸ φωνῆς τε μεγέθει χρώμενος καὶ χρήματα περιβεβλημένος[5] ὅμοια
τοῖς Ῥωμαίων πλουσιωτάτοις, δύναμίς τε αὐτῷ ἦν
ἐφ' οἷς ἐθελήσειε πράσσειν[6] κατὰ τὴν πόλιν ἔν

146 τε τῷ τότε κἂν τοῖς ὕστερον. οὗτος διαθεὶς αὐτὸν ὡς ἐνῆν πενθιμώτατον, καίτοι μίσει καὶ παρ'
ὁντινοῦν ἐχρῆτο πρὸς Γάιον, ἀλλὰ μὴν κρείσσων
ἡ διδασκαλία τοῦ φόβου καὶ στρατηγία περὶ τοῦ
κερδησομένου τὴν σωτηρίαν τῆς εἰς τὸ παρὸν ἡ-

147 δονῆς, πάντα κόσμον ἐπιτηδεύσας ὡς ἄν τις ἐπὶ
τοῖς τιμιωτάτοις παρεσκεύαστο ἀπολωλόσιν, ἀποσημαίνει τοῦ Γαΐου τὸν θάνατον ἐπὶ τὸ θέατρον
παρελθὼν καὶ ἔπαυσεν τοὺς ἀνθρώπους ἐπὶ πλέον

148 ἀγνοίᾳ συμπεριφέρεσθαι τοῦ γεγονότος. ἤδη δὲ
καταστείλας[7] Ἀρούντιος παρῆν[8] ἀνακαλῶν τοὺς

---

[1] τῆς χώρας] τῆς χάρας ed. pr. : καὶ τῆς χαρᾶς Hudson.
[2] ed. pr. : συναπολογουμένου codd.
[3] διὰ τὸ . . . γεγονέναι] cum ad tanta pericula pervenissent
Lat.   [4] A : Ἀρούντινος MW : Aruntius Lat.
[5] χρήματα περιβεβλημένος] indutus vestibus diversi coloris
Lat.   [6] agendi Lat. : πιπράσκειν Naber.
[7] καταστείλας] Post : καὶ Στήλας AW : καὶ σύλας, σ ex στ

the spectators were still more deeply moved both by consideration of the rank of the deceased men and by pity for their fate. As a result, they themselves were almost equally daunted by close contact with the threatened fate, since it was still uncertain whether in the end they would be able to make good their escape. And so even those who hated Gaius heartily and with justice were left with no chance to rejoice at his death, because they were on tenterhooks for fear of perishing with him and they had not yet even then had any trustworthy assurance that they would survive.

(18) Now Euarestus Arruntius was a professional auctioneer and therefore possessed of a powerful voice; he had accumulated money till he had as much as the wealthiest of the Romans, and was able both then and later to do just as he liked throughout the city. This man arrayed himself in the deepest possible mourning; for though he hated Gaius as much as anyone, yet the discipline of fear and the strategy required to secure his survival outweighed any pleasure of the moment. He therefore dressed himself with all the detail that would have been employed in mourning the most honoured dead, and passed into the theatre, where he announced the death of Gaius, thus putting an end to any further activity on the part of the people that was due to misinformation as to what had happened. By now Arruntius had got control[a] and accompanied the

An auctioneer announces the death of Gaius, and the Germans are quieted.

---

[a] Text emended. The best manuscript reads " Stelas [i.e. Stella] Aruntius [i.e. Arruntius] " for " Arruntius had got

corr., ύ in ras. A: καὶ στείλας M: καὶ στίλλας E: etiam statuas Lat.: Παῦλος Dindorf ex § 102.

[b] παρῆν] circumibat Lat.: περιῄει Dindorf ex Lat.

Γερμανοὺς καὶ οἱ χιλίαρχοι σὺν αὐτῷ κελεύοντες
κατατίθεσθαι τὸν σίδηρον καὶ διασαφοῦντες Γαΐου
149 τὴν τελευτήν. τοῦτο καὶ σαφέστατα ἔσωσεν τοὺς
ἐν τῷ θεάτρῳ συνειλεγμένους καὶ πάντας, οἳ καὶ
ὁπωσοῦν[1] τοῖς Γερμανοῖς περιτύχοιεν· ἐλπίδος γὰρ
αὐτοῖς παραγενομένης ἔμπνουν κεῖσθαι τὸν Γάιον
150 οὐκ ἔσθ᾽ οὗτινος κακῶν ἂν ἀπέσχοντο. τοσόνδε
ἐπερίσσευσεν αὐτοῖς εὐνοίας τῆς πρὸς αὐτόν, ὡς
κἂν μετὰ τοῦ καθ᾽ αὑτοὺς ἀπολουμένου τῆς ψυχῆς
κτήσασθαι τὸ ἀνεπιβούλευτον αὐτῷ καὶ τοσαύτῃ
151 δυστυχίᾳ μὴ συνεσόμενον.[2] παύονται δὲ τοῦ ὠργη-
κότος εἰς τὴν τιμωρίαν μαθήσεως σαφοῦς παραγενομένης αὐτοῖς ἐπὶ τῇ τελευτῇ, διά τε τὸ εἰς
ἀχρεῖον ἐπιδείξασθαι τὸ πρόθυμον τῆς εὐνοίας, ὃς
ἀμείψαιτο αὐτοὺς ἀπολωλότος, καὶ δέει, μὴ καὶ
περαιτέρω τῇ ὕβρει χρωμένων ἐπιστροφὴ γένοιτο
ὑπὸ τῆς βουλῆς, εἴπερ εἰς ἐκείνην περισταίη τὸ
152 κράτος, ἢ ὑπὸ τοῦ ἐπικαταστάντος ἄρχοντος. καὶ
Γερμανοὶ εἰ καὶ μόλις, ἀλλ᾽ οὖν ἐπαύσαντο λύσσης
τῆς ἐπὶ Γαΐῳ τῷ θανάτῳ καταλαμβανομένης αὐτούς.

153 (19) Χαιρέας δέ, σφόδρα γὰρ περὶ Βινουκιανῷ[3]
ἔδεισε, μὴ διαφθαρείη μανίᾳ τῶν Γερμανῶν περιπεσών, ἕκαστόν τε τῶν στρατιωτῶν μετῄει προμηθεῖσθαι τῆς σωτηρίας αὐτοῦ δεόμενος καὶ μὴ
154 ἀπολώλοι πολλὴν ἐξέτασιν ποιούμενος. καὶ Βινου-

[1] ὁπωσοῦν] ed. pr. : ὅπως ἂν codd.
[2] μὴ συνεσόμενον] Hudson : συνεσόμενον codd.
[3] coni. Niese (cf. § 18) : Μινουκιανῷ codd.

---

control.'' If so, this may be the Arruntius Stella who in 55
had charge of the games that were prepared by the emperor
(Tac. *Ann.* xiii. 22). But it seems unlikely that Josephus,

tribunes recalling the Germans, bidding them sheathe
their swords and giving a full account of the death of
Gaius. This was certainly the thing that saved those
who were assembled in the theatre and all who in any
way came in contact with the Germans ; for, had the
Germans been given any hope that Gaius still lay
breathing, there is no crime from which they would
have refrained. So great was their loyalty to him
that they would even have risked their own lives to
secure for him immunity from plots and avoidance [a]
of so great a disaster. But an end was put to their
furious quest for vengeance, once they had been
fully informed about the death of Gaius ; for it was
of no use to display their ardent devotion, now that
the one who would have rewarded them had perished.
They feared, moreover, that, if they proceeded further
in their lawless mood, they might attract attention
from the senate, supposing that it should succeed to
power, or from the imperial ruler who won control.
So the Germans did, at any rate, though it was a
narrow escape, desist from the frenzy that took possession of them at the death of Gaius.

(19) Chaerea was much alarmed for Vinicianus [b]
lest he should meet with and be killed by the frenzied
Germans. He went among the soldiers one by one,
begging them to take precautions for Vinicianus'
safety, and satisfying himself by much questioning
that he had not lost his life. Meanwhile, Vinicianus

immediately after mentioning and identifying Euarestus
Arruntius, should mention, without further identification,
another man named Arruntius who performed a similar
function of giving an account of Gaius' death.

[a] The mss. have "participation in," but the negative is
clearly intended from the context.

[b] mss. (here and in § 154) Minucianus ; *cf.* note on § 18.

κιανὸν¹ μὲν Κλήμης, ἀνάγεται γὰρ ἐπὶ τοῦτον, μεθίησιν πολλῶν μετ' ἄλλων συγκλητικῶν δικαιοσύνην τῇ πράξει συμμαρτυρῶν καὶ ἀρετὴν τοῖς ἐντεθυ-
155 μημένοις καὶ πράσσειν μὴ ἀποδεδειλιακόσι²· τυραννίδα γὰρ εἰς ὀλίγον μὲν ἐλθεῖν³ ἡδονῇ τοῦ ὑβρίζειν ἐπαρθεῖσαν, εὐτυχεῖς δὲ οὐκ ἄρα ποιεῖσθαι τὰς ἀπαλλαγὰς τοῦ βίου μίσει τῆς ἀρετῆς πρὸς αὐτὸν
156 χρωμένης, ἀλλὰ μετὰ τοιαύτης δυστυχίας, ὁποίᾳ δὴ Γάιον συνελθεῖν πρὸ τῶν ἐπαναστάντων καὶ συνθέντων⁴ τὴν ἐπίθεσιν αὐτὸν⁵ ἐπίβουλον αὐτῷ γενόμενον⁶ καὶ διδάξαντα οἷς ὑβρίζων ἀφόρητος ἦν ἀφανίζων τοῦ νόμου τὴν πρόνοιαν πολέμῳ πρὸς αὐτὸν χρῆσθαι τοὺς φιλτάτους, καὶ νῦν λόγῳ μὲν εἶναι τούτους οἳ ἀνηρήκασι Γάιον, ἔργῳ δὲ αὐτὸν ὑφ' ἑαυτοῦ κεῖσθαι διολωλότα.
157 (20) Ἤδη δὲ καὶ τὸ θέατρον ἐξανίστατο τῶν φυλακῶν αἱ τὸ κατ' ἀρχὰς⁷ πάνυ πικραὶ ἐγένοντο ὑπανεισῶν.⁸ αἰτία δ' ἦν τοῦ προθύμως καὶ⁹ διαφευξομένου τῶν θεωρῶν Ἀλκύων¹⁰ ὁ ἰατρός, συναρπασθεὶς μὲν ὡς ἐπὶ θεραπείᾳ τινῶν τραυματιῶν, ἐκπέμψας δὲ τοὺς συνόντας λόγῳ μὲν ὡς καὶ μετελευσομένους ὁπόσα εἰς τὴν ἴασιν τοῖς τραυμα-

¹ coni. Niese (cf. § 18): Μινουκιανὸν E Lat.: Μινουκιανὸς codd.
² καὶ Βινουκιανὸ . . . ἀποδεδειλιακόσι] et Minucianum quidem Clemens adduxit in medium. ad Chaeream vero conversus cum multis aliis senatoribus iustitiaeque et virtuti testabatur eius laudans cogitationem et actum sine formidatione completum Lat.
³ ἀνθεῖν Hudson.
⁴ Dindorf: συντεθέντων codd.
⁵ ed. pr.: αὐτὸν codd.
⁶ εὐτυχεῖς . . . γενόμενον] quippe cum non posset felix vita illi praeberi, qui virtuti probaretur odibilis, sed cum tali calamitate deficere quali Gaius, qui etiam ante coniuratorum

was brought up before Clemens, who released him ;
for Clemens, together with many others of senatorial
rank, bore witness to the justice of the deed and to
the valour of those who had made the plans and shown
no weakness in the execution of them. " For," he
said, " tyranny, which is motivated by lust for un-
restrained violence, lasts but a short time. As we
see, there is no happy ending for the life of a tyrant,
since the virtuous hate him. No, he is visited with
such disaster as has come to Gaius, who had plotted
against himself before there was any uprising or any
organization of the attack. It was by the lessons
that he gave to those who could not endure his violations, and by his abolition of legal protection, that he
taught his dearest friends to make war on him. And
now, though they are said to be the slayers of Gaius,
he has fallen, in fact, a victim to his own design."

(20) By now the occupants of the theatre were
rising from their seats, the guard which at first had
been so cruel being somewhat relaxed. The person
responsible for the spectators being allowed to depart
so readily was Alcyon the physician. He had been
seized and carried off in order that he might care
for some wounded men. He then dispatched those
present with him, as if they were to fetch some sup-
plies that he needed to treat the patients, but his

---

consensum proprium facinus sibi constituit inimicum Lat. ;
γενόμενον] ed. pr. : γενομένην AW : γενησομένην M.

[7] αἲ τὸ κατ᾽ ἀρχὰς] i. marg. A, quod etiam Lat. habuisse
vid. : καὶ ἀρχαὶ codd. : καὶ ταραχαὶ ed. pr.

[8] ὑπανεισῶν] coni. Niese : ὑπανίσως A : τοῦ πᾶν εἴσω MW :
τῶν εἴσω ed. pr. : ὑπανειεισῶν Herwerden : ἤδη . . . ὑπανεισῶν]
iam ergo surgebant de theatro custodiae, quae principio per-
niciosae fuerant, quando omnes velociter abscedere festina-
bant Lat.                                        [9] om. W.

[10] A (λ in ras.) : Ἀρκύων M : Ἀρκύων W : Alcyon Lat.

τίαις πρόσφορα, τὸ δ' ἀληθὲς ὡς ἀπέσοιντο[1] κινδύνου
158 τοῦ κατειληφότος. ἐν τούτῳ δὲ βουλῆς τε γίνεται
σύνοδος καὶ ὁ δῆμος ἧπερ καὶ εἰώθασιν ἐκκλη-
σιάζειν ἐπὶ τῆς ἀγορᾶς καταστὰς ἐν ζητήσει τῶν
σφαγέων τῶν Γαΐου ἦσαν, ὁ μὲν δῆμος καὶ πάνυ
159 ἐκθύμως, δοκεῖν δὲ καὶ ἡ βουλή. καὶ ἦν γὰρ
Ἀσιατικὸς Οὐαλέριος ὑπατικὸς ἀνήρ, οὗτος ἐπὶ
τὸν δῆμον καταστάς, θορυβούντων καὶ δεινὸν τιθεμένων τὸ ἔτι λανθάνον τῶν τὸν αὐτοκράτορα ἀπ-
εκτονότων, ἐπεὶ προθύμως πάντες αὐτὸν ἤροντο, τίς
160 ὁ πράξας τυγχάνει, " εἴθε γὰρ ἔγωγε," φησί. καὶ
προῦθεσαν δὲ καὶ οἱ ὕπατοι διάγραμμα Γαΐου μὲν
κατηγορίας ποιούμενοι, κελεύοντες δὲ τῷ τε[2] δήμῳ
καὶ τοῖς στρατιώταις ἐπὶ τὰ αὑτῶν ἀπιέναι, τῷ μὲν
δήμῳ πολλὴν ἀνέσεως ἐπαγγελλόμενοι ἐλπίδα, τῷ
στρατιωτικῷ δὲ τιμῶν, εἰ ἐν κόσμῳ μείνειαν τῷ
εἰωθότι μηδὲν ὑβρίζειν ἐξαγόμενοι· δέος γὰρ ἦν, μὴ
ἐξαγριωσάντων ἀπολαύσειεν τοῦ κακοῦ ἡ πόλις
καθ' ἁρπαγὰς αὑτῶν καὶ συλήσεις τῶν ἱερῶν τρε-
161 πομένων. ἐφθάκει δὲ ἤδη τῶν βουλευτῶν τὸ πᾶν
πλῆθος συνειλεγμένον καὶ μάλιστα οἱ εἰς[3] τοῦ Γαΐου
συνελθόντες[4] τὸν φόνον θράσει τε ἤδη χρώμενοι
κἂν καταφρονήματι[5] μεγάλῳ ὄντες ὡς εἰς αὑτοὺς
ἀνακειμένων δὴ τῶν πραγμάτων.
162 (ii. 1) Ἐν τούτῳ δὴ ὄντων τῶν πραγμάτων
αἰφνίδιον ἁρπάζεται Κλαύδιος ἐκ τῆς οἰκίας· οἱ γὰρ

---

[1] ed. pr. : πείσοιντο AM : πέσοιντο W : (pericula) decli-
narent Lat.
[2] δὲ τῷ τε] Ernesti : τε τῶ A : δὲ τῶ τότε MW : δὲ τῶ E.
[3] A : om. MWE.
[4] συνθέντες E.        [5] φρονήματι E.

---

[a] Cf. §§ 102 and 252.

real purpose was to remove them from the danger
that had overtaken them. Meanwhile, a meeting of
the senate was convened ; and the people also met
in the Forum, where they customarily hold their
assemblies. Both were engaged in an investigation
of the murderers of Gaius. The populace was in fact
quite zealous, but the senate merely made a show of
zeal. Now there was a certain Valerius Asiaticus,[a]
a man of consular rank, presiding over the popular
assembly,[b] who, when the people were in an uproar
and indignant that the emperor's murderers were
still undetected, and when everybody urgently demanded to be told who had done the deed, replied,
" Would that it had been I." The consuls also proposed a decree bringing charges against Gaius, and
bade both the people and the soldiers depart to their
quarters, giving the people every assurance that they
would receive some relief, while the soldiers were to
receive rewards, if they maintained the usual discipline and did not resort to violence. For the consuls
feared that if they ran amuck, the city would suffer
the consequences, once they turned to plunder the
citizens and violate the temples. By now all the
senators had assembled, and in particular those who
had plotted the assassination of Gaius. These latter
were now full of confidence and had great notions of
their own exalted position, thinking that the government was now in their hands.

(ii. 1) Such was the political scene when Claudius [c]
was suddenly kidnapped from his house. For the

*Marginal notes:* Meetings of the senate and popular assembly. The soldiers veto demo-cracy and

---

[b] In Dio lix. 30. 2 he addresses an assembly of the praetorian guard. His statement so alarms them that they stop
their outcry.

[c] There is a parallel, but much briefer, account of the
accession of Claudius in *B.J.* ii. 204-214.

στρατιῶται συνόδου γενομένης αὐτοῖς, ἀλλήλοις καὶ
αὐτοῖς λόγον δόντες περὶ τοῖς ποιητέοις ἑώρων δημοκρατίαν ἀδύνατόν τε ὂν ἐν κράτει τοσῶνδε ἂν
ποτε γενέσθαι πραγμάτων ἐξικομένην τε οὐκ ἐπ'
163 ἀγαθῷ τῷ αὐτῶν κτήσασθαι τὴν ἀρχήν, εἴ τέ τις
τῶν κατὰ ἕνα σχήσοι τὴν ἡγεμονίαν, εἰς πάντα λυ-
πηρὸν αὐτοῖς εἶναι μὴ οὐ συνεργοῖς τῆς ἀρχῆς κατα-
164 στᾶσιν.[1] καλῶς οὖν ἔχειν ἀκρίτων ἔτι ὄντων τῶν
πραγμάτων ἡγεμόνα αἱρεῖσθαι Κλαύδιον, πάτρωά
τε ὄντα τοῦ τεθνεῶτος καὶ τῶν εἰς τὴν βουλὴν
συλλεγομένων οὐδενὸς οὗτινος οὐκ ἀξιολογώτερον
προγόνων τε ἀρετῇ καὶ τῷ[2] κατ' αὐτὸν παιδείαν με-
165 μελετηκότι, καὶ σταθέντα αὐτοκράτορα τιμήσειν τε
τὰ εἰκότα καὶ ἀμείψεσθαι[3] δωρεαῖς. ταῦτα δια-
νοοῦνταί τε καὶ ἔπραξαν ἐκ τοῦ παραχρῆμα. ἥρ-
παστο μὲν δὴ Κλαύδιος ὑπὸ τοῦ στρατιωτικοῦ.
166 Ναῖος[4] δὲ Σέντιος[5] Σατορνῖνος[6] καίτοι πεπυσμένος
τὴν Κλαυδίου ἁρπαγήν, καὶ ὡς ἐπιδικάζοιτο τῆς
ἀρχῆς[7] ἄκων μὲν δοκεῖν, τὸ δὲ ἀληθὲς καὶ βουλήσει τῇ αὐτοῦ, καταστὰς ἐπὶ τῆς συγκλήτου καὶ
μηδὲν ἐκπλαγεὶς ἐλευθέροις τε καὶ γενναίοις ἀνδράσι πρεπόντως ποιεῖται παραίνεσιν τάδε λέγων.
167 (2) '' Εἰ καὶ ἄπιστον, ὦ Ῥωμαῖοι, διὰ τὸ χρόνῳ
πολλῷ ἥκειν ἀνέλπιστον οὖσαν ἡμῖν, ἀλλ' οὖν
ἔχομεν τοῦ ἐλευθέρου τὴν ἀξίωσιν, ἄδηλον μὲν

---

[1] ἐξικομένην . . . καταστᾶσιν] nec sibi utile siquis illorum,
qui operatores in nece Gai fuerant, ad imperium perveniret
Lat.          [2] Herwerden : τῶν codd.
[3] ed. pr. : ἀμείψασθαι codd. E.
[4] Niese : νέος codd. E : Γνέος ed. pr. : om. Lat. : Γναῖος
Hudson.
[5] Σέντιος] Σέρτιος ex Σέντιος corr. A : ἔτι ὢν E.
[6] AM : Σατορνῖλος W.          [7] MW : ἀρετῆς A.

soldiers had held a meeting and had taken counsel elect Claudius emperor. with each other to decide what should be done. They saw that it was out of the question for a democracy to control such a mighty realm. Even if it did succeed, it would not govern in their interest. On the other hand, if any single individual should gain supreme authority, it would be constantly harmful to them not to have taken a stand to help establish the government. It was therefore best, they thought, while matters were still undecided, to choose Claudius as emperor. He was an uncle of the deceased, and there was no one among those assembled in the senate whom he did not excel both by distinction of his ancestors and by his own studious devotion to learning.[a] And so, once established as emperor, he would reward them with the usual privileges and repay them with gifts. No sooner had they formed these plans than they put them into effect. Claudius was, therefore, kidnapped by the soldiers. Meanwhile, Gnaeus Sentius Saturninus,[b] although he had heard that Claudius was kidnapped and, despite an apparent unwillingness, had really agreed to accept and was a suitor for the throne, yet stood up in the senate, and, nothing daunted, gave them words of exhortation, such as free and noble men may fittingly speak, to this effect :

(2) " Incredible as it may appear, Romans, because Speech of Sentius Saturninus in the senate. it has come upon us unexpectedly after so long a time, nevertheless we enjoy the dignity of freedom.

[a] Or " by his own careful education." Cf. Suetonius, Claud. 3, who notes that Claudius had applied himself seriously to literature from childhood and had published some of his attainments.

[b] Cf.·B.J. ii. 205. Consul in 41, he was, in all probability, the son of the identically named consul of A.D. 4.

ἐφ' ὁπόσον παρατείνουσαν καὶ γνώμῃ θεῶν οἱ
ἐχαρίσαντο αὐτὴν κειμένην, εὐφραίνειν δὲ ἀρκοῦσαν
καὶ εἴπερ ἀφαιρεθείημεν αὐτῆς[1] εὐδαιμονίᾳ συν-
168 άγουσαν· ἱκανὴ γὰρ καὶ μία ὥρα τοῖς ἀρετῆς αἰσθα-
νομένοις καὶ μετ' αὐτοτελοῦς[2] τῆς διανοίας[3] ἐν
αὐτοδίκῳ τῇ πατρίδι καὶ μετὰ νόμων, οἷς ποτε ἤν-
169 θησε, διαιτωμένῃ βιωθεῖσα. ἐμοὶ δὲ τῆς μὲν πρότερον ἐλευθερίας ἀμνημονεῖν ἔστι διὰ τὸ κατόπιν
αὐτῆς γεγονέναι, τῆς δὲ νῦν ἀπλήστως πιμπλαμένῳ
μακαριστούς τε ἡγεῖσθαι τοὺς ἐγγενηθέντας καὶ ἐν-
τραφέντας[4] αὐτῇ καὶ τῶν θεῶν οὐδὲν μειόνως ἀξίους
τιμῆς τούσδε τοὺς ἄνδρας, οἳ ὀψὲ γοῦν κἂν τούτῳ
170 τῆς ἡλικίας ἡμᾶς γεύσαντας αὐτῆς. καὶ εἴη μὲν εἰς
πᾶν τοῦ αἰῶνος τὸ ἐπιὸν παραμεῖναι τὴν ἄδειαν
αὐτῆς, ἀρκοῦσα δ' ἂν γένοιτο καὶ ἥδε ἡ ἡμέρα τοῖς
τε νεωτέροις ἡμῶν καὶ ὅσοι γεγηράκαμεν αἰ-
ὼν ὑπείληπται, τοῖς πρεσβυτέροις δ' εἰ τῶν[5] ἀγαθῶν αὐτῆς ἐν ὁμιλίᾳ γεγονότες μεταστᾶιεν,[6] τοῖς
171 δὲ νεωτέροις παίδευμα ἀρετῆς καταστάσεως[7] ἀγαθὸν ὂν[8] ἀνδράσι τοῖσδε ἀφ' ὧν γεγόναμεν, νῦν δὲ
ἤδη καὶ ἡμῖν διὰ τὴν ἄρτι ὥραν οὐδὲν προυργιαί-
τερον εἴη τοῦ ζῆν μετὰ ἀρετῆς, ἢ μόνη ἐκφροντίζει

---

[1] εἴπερ . . . αὐτῆς] si eius felicitatem nequiverimus amit-
tere Lat.
[2] μετ' αὐτοτελοῦς] ed. pr. : μετὰ ταῦτα τέλους (τέλος M) codd.
[3] μετ' . . . διανοίας] cum secura voluntate Lat.
[4] ed. pr. : nutritos Lat. : ἐγγραφέντας codd.
[5] δ' εἰ τῶν] Warmington : δ' ἐὰν τῶν Petersen : ἐὰν τῶν
           ἐ
Hudson : δόντων A : δεόντων MW.
[6] μεταστᾶιεν] A : μέγα δὲ ἐν M : μέγα τε ἐν W : moriemur
(i.e. μεταστᾶιμεν) Lat.
[7] καταστησάσης Hudson.

We cannot tell how long it will last, a matter to be determined by the gods who bestowed the gift, yet what we have now suffices for rejoicing, and even if we should be robbed of it, to possess it is bliss. Indeed, for those who appreciate virtue, it is sufficient to live but for a single hour with freedom to think as we please, in a country that is subject to its own sense of right, and that regulates itself by the constitution under which it once became a flourishing state. For myself, though I cannot recall the former age of liberty because I was born after that era, yet, as I insatiably steep myself in our present liberty, I count those enviable who were born and brought up in it ; and I hold worthy of honour not less than the gods these men here who at this late date and at this stage of our lives, have treated us to one sip of liberty that we may know its taste. I pray that the security of our present liberty may remain for all time to come. But even this one day should be sufficient for those of us who are younger, while for those who are grown old, it counts as a lifetime : to the older men if only they may depart with some experience of its joys, while to the younger it counts as a lesson in the essence [a] of virtue, a lesson which was the glory of those men from whom we are sprung.[b] Now, therefore, for us too, because we have this present hour, nothing can be more advantageous than to live virtuously, for virtue alone ponders and finds the

[a] Or " establishment."

[b] Text emended. Prof. Post, adopting Hudson's emendation, καταστησάσης, suggests " a lesson in the virtue that established the good fortune of those men from whom we sprang."

---

[8] ὃν post ἀγαθὸν add. Petersen : aliquid ante ἀγαθὸν deesse putat Niese.

172 τῷ ἀνθρωπείῳ τὸ ἐλεύθερον[1]· ἐγὼ γὰρ τὰ παλαιὰ
οἶδα ἀκοῇ παραλαβών, οἷς δὲ ὄψει ὁμιλήσας ἠσθό-
μην, οἵων κακῶν τὰς πολιτείας ἀναπιμπλᾶσιν αἱ
τυραννίδες, κωλύουσαι μὲν πᾶσαν ἀρετὴν καὶ τοῦ
μεγαλόφρονος ἀφαιρούμεναι τὸ ἐλεύθερον, κολα-
κείας δὲ καὶ φόβου διδάσκαλοι καθιστάμεναι διὰ τὸ
μὴ ἐπὶ σοφίᾳ τῶν νόμων, ἀλλ' ἐπὶ τῇ ὀργῇ τῶν
173 ἐφεστηκότων καταλιπεῖν τὰ πράγματα. ἀφ' οὗ γὰρ
Ἰούλιος Καῖσαρ φρονήσας ἐπὶ καταλύσει τῆς δη-
μοκρατίας καὶ διαβιασάμενος τὸν κόσμον τῶν νόμων τὴν πολιτείαν συνετάραξεν,[2] κρείσσων μὲν τοῦ
δικαίου γενόμενος, ἥσσων δὲ τοῦ κατ' ἰδίαν ἡδονὴν αὐτῷ κομιοῦντος, οὐκ ἔστιν ὅ τι τῶν κακῶν οὐ
174 διέτριψεν[3] τὴν πόλιν, φιλοτιμηθέντων πρὸς ἀλλήλους ἁπάντων, οἳ ἐκείνῳ διάδοχοι τῆς ἀρχῆς κατέστησαν, ἐπ' ἀφανισμῷ τοῦ πατρίου καὶ ὡς ἂν
μάλιστα τῶν πολιτῶν ἐρημίαν τοῦ γενναίου κατα-
λείποιεν, διὰ τὸ οἴεσθαι πρὸς ἀσφαλείας εἶναι τῆς
αὑτῶν τὸ κιβδήλοις ἀνδράσιν ὁμιλεῖν καὶ τῶν ἀρετῇ
προὔχειν πεπιστευμένων οὐ μόνον ὑφαιρεῖν τι τοῦ
αὐχήματος, ἀλλ' εἰς τὸ πᾶν ἐπιψηφίζειν αὐτῶν[4]
175 τοῖς ὀλέθροις τῶν ἁπάντων.[5] ἀριθμῷ τε πολλῶν
ὄντων καὶ βαρύτητα ἀνύποιστον ἐπιδειξαμένων καθ'
ἃ ἕκαστος ἦρξεν[6] εἷς ὢν ὁ Γάιος ὁ σήμερον τεθνεὼς
πλέω τε τῶν πάντων δεινὰ ἀπεδείξατο οὐ μόνον εἰς
τοὺς συμπολίτας, ἀλλὰ καὶ εἰς τοὺς συγγενεῖς καὶ
φίλους ἀπαίδευτον τὴν ὀργὴν ἐπαφιείς, ὁμοίως τοῖς
ἅπασι καὶ μείζω κακὰ ἐντριβόμενος ἀδίκως τὴν

---

[1] τοῖς πρεσβυτέροις . . . ἐλεύθερον] senibus quidem quando
eius conspicientes libertatem cum dulcedine moriemur, iuniori-
bus autem eo quod sit eis doctrina virtutis, unde constat per
viros istos quorum labore consistimus propter haec quae nuper
gesta noscuntur, quia nihil quam cum virtute degere maius

path of liberty for mankind. Past history I know Tirade<br>against<br>tyrants. from tradition, but from the evidence of my own eyes I have learned with what evils tyranny infects a state. For it frustrates all the virtues, robs freedom of its lofty mood, and opens a school of fawning and terror, inasmuch as it leaves matters not to the wisdom of the laws, but to the angry whim of those who are in authority. For ever since Julius Caesar was minded to destroy the democracy and caused an upheaval of the state by doing violence to law and order, setting himself above justice but really a slave to what would bring him private gratification, there is not a single evil that has not afflicted the city. All who succeeded him in the government vied with one another in abolishing our heritage and in allowing no nobility to remain among our citizens. For they supposed that the society of human counterfeits contributed to their own security, and that it was best not merely to diminish somewhat the glory of those who were believed to excel in virtue but to decree their complete extinction. But many in numbers as were these tyrants and intolerable as was the oppression that was conspicuous in their acts, Gaius, who to-day lies dead, in his sole person assailed our eyes with more outrages than all the rest. He vented an untutored rage not only upon his fellow citizens but also upon his kinsmen and his friends. For upon all alike he has inflicted evils greater than those in-

---

est, de qua consuevit libertas humana solummodo cogitare Lat.   ² συνετάραξεν] AM : οὐ συνετάραξε W : διετάραξε E.

³ MW : διέστρεψε (ex διέτριψεν corr. A) AE : invasit Lat.

⁴ ἐπιψηφίζειν αὐτῶν] E : ἐπιφημίζειν αὐτῷ codd.

⁵ ἀπάντων] ἀπάντων, ὧν coni. Niese.

⁶ ἀριθμῷ . . . ἦρξεν] singuli namque regnantium quaeque sunt gravia commiserunt Lat.

τιμωρίαν εἰσπράσσεσθαι ὠργικότων, ὁμοίως εἴς τε
176 ἀνθρώπους ἐξαγριώσας καὶ τοὺς θεούς.[1] τυραννίδι
γὰρ οὐ κερδαίνεται τὸ ἡδὺ οὐδὲ μεθ' ὕβρεως ἀπο-
χρῆται, οὐκ εἰς τὰ χρήματα λελυπῆσθαι[2] καὶ γαμετάς,
ἀλλὰ τὸ πᾶν κέρδος ἐκ τοῦ πανοικεσίᾳ διοχλουμέ-
177 νου[3] τῶν ἐχθρῶν.[4] ἐχθρὸν δὲ τυραννίδι πᾶν τὸ ἐλεύθερον, εἰς εὔνοιάν τε ἐκκαλεῖσθαι αὐτὴν καὶ τοῖς ἐν
ὀλίγῳ τιθεμένοις ὁπόσα πεπόνθοιεν οὐκ ἔστιν. ἐξεπιστάμενοι γὰρ ὧν ἀναπλήσειαν κακῶν ἔστιν οὓς
κἂν ἐκεῖνοι[5] μεγαλοφρόνως καταφρονήματι χρῶνται[6] πρὸς τὴν τύχην, αὐτοὶ λανθάνειν αὐτοὺς ὧν
πράξειαν μὴ δυνάμενοι[7] μόνως πιστεύουσιν κτήσε-
σθαι τοῦ ὑπόπτου τὸ ἀδεές, εἰ παντελὲς ἄρασθαι[8]
178 δυνηθεῖεν αὐτούς. τοιούτων δὴ κακῶν ἀπογεγονό-
τες καὶ ὑποτελεῖς ἀλλήλοις καταστάντες, αἵπερ
πολιτειῶν ἐχεγγυώταται πρός τε τὸ παρὸν εὔνουν
καὶ τὸ αὖθις ἀνεπιβούλευτον καὶ τὸ δόξαν οἰκείαν[9]
τῷ ὀρθουμένῳ τῆς πόλεως[10] δίκαιοί τε[11] προνοῆσαι
διὰ[12] τὸ εἰς κοινὸν αὐτοῦ τὴν ὠφέλειαν ἀπαντᾶν καὶ

---

[1] ὁμοίως τοῖς . . . θεούς] iniuste poenas exigens et veluti
furiosus in homines atque deos ferus existens Lat.

[2] λελύσθαι Thackeray.

[3] Bekker : διοχλουμένων codd. : διολλυμένου coni. Richards
et Shutt : διολουμένου Post.

[4] τυραννίδι . . . ἐχθρῶν] nihil etenim tyrannus suavitatis
habere potest. nonne cum iniuria vobis abusus est ? nonne
in pecuniis vos et coniugibus contristavit ? nonne omne votum
vestrum praecibus agebatur insistentibus inimicis ? Lat.

[5] κἂν ἐκεῖνοι] Bekker : κἀκεῖνοι codd.

[6] καταφρονήματι χρῶνται] A (litt. ι χρῶνται i. ras. m. 2 A) :
καταφροηημάτων τε codd.

[7] ἐξεπιστάμενοι . . . δυνάμενοι] scientes namque tyranni
quibus malis insignes viros adfligant et eos videntes inpatienter

flicted by persons unjustly passionate to exact vengeance ; and he has raged like a savage against men and gods alike. For a tyranny is not satisfied with an accrual of pleasure even lawlessly procured, nor with the grief caused by assaults on property and wives ; no, it must complete the total by utterly harassing its enemies with all their households. To tyrants all show of freedom is an enemy ; and it is impossible to elicit any goodwill from them even towards those who take little account of all that they have suffered. For the tyrants know full well what a plague of evil they have brought on some, and though the afflicted should magnanimously dismiss their ill fortune as trivial, yet can the tyrants not be unaware of their own acts. Thus they have no confidence in any safety from suspected foes unless they are able to remove them utterly. Now that you have rid yourselves of such evils, and obtained a government in which you have no obligation but to one another— and of all forms of government this most guarantees both present loyalty and future immunity from hostile intrigue as well as a fame that belongs to the prosperous city that is well governed—your duty now is to make prudent proposals for the common benefit,[a] or

---

[a] Thackeray's emendation will give : " You ought now to provide for that which you decide to be proper to the restoration of the city. Indeed, to do so conduces to its common welfare."

---

talia sustinere nec tamen ignorare quod geritur, sed solatium expectare fortunae Lat.

[8] coni. Niese: αἱρεῖσθαι codd. (i. marg. γρ ἀρέσθαι A): amputare Lat.        [9] οἰκεῖον coni. Thackeray.

[10] τὸ δόξαν . . . πόλεως] restituta civilitate Lat.

[11] δίκαιοί τε] δίκαιοί τε ἐστὲ Hudson : iustum est ut vos Lat.

[12] ἰδίᾳ Hudson.

# JOSEPHUS

ἀνταποφήνασθαι γνώμην, οἷς μὴ ἀρέσκοιτο τὰ
179 προεισηγημένα, οὐδαμῶς εἰς κίνδυνον φέρον,¹ διὰ
τὸ μὴ δεσπότην εἶναι τὸν ἐφεστηκότα, ᾧ ἀνεύθυνόν
τε βλάπτοντι τὴν πόλιν καὶ αὐτοκράτορι μεταστή-
180 σασθαι τοὺς εἰρηκότας. καὶ τέτροφε τὴν τυραννίδα
οὐδὲν ἕτερον² πλὴν ἥ τε ἀργία καὶ τὸ πρὸς οὐδὲν
181 τῶν ἐκείνῃ θελομένων ἀντιλογίᾳ χρώμενον· τῆς γὰρ
εἰρήνης τοῦ τερπνοῦ ἡσσώμενοι καὶ μεμαθηκότες
ἀνδραπόδων ἐν τρόπῳ ζῆν³ ὁπόσοι τε ἐπαίομεν συμ-
φορὰς ἀνηκέστους κακοῖς τε τοῖς πέλας ἐπείδομεν
φόβῳ τοῦ μετ' ἀρετῆς τελευτᾶν μετὰ αἰσχύνης τῆς
182 ὑστάτης ὑπομένοντες⁴ τὰς τελευτάς. πρῶτον δὲ⁵
τοῖς ἀραμένοις τὸν τύραννον τιμὰς αἵτινες μέγισται
ταύτας εἰσενεγκεῖν, μάλιστα δὲ Χαιρέᾳ τῷ Κασσίῳ·
σὺν γὰρ τοῖς θεοῖς εἷς ἀνὴρ οὗτος ποριστὴς ἡμῖν καὶ
183 γνώμῃ καὶ χερσὶ τῆς ἐλευθερίας πέφηνεν. οὐ καλὸν
μὴ ἀμνημονεῖν, ἀλλ' ἐπὶ τῆς τυραννίδος ὑπὲρ ἐλευθερίας τῆς ἡμετέρας προβεβουλευκότος τε ἅμα καὶ
προκεκινδυνευκότος, ἐπὶ τῆς ἐλευθερίας ψηφίσασθαι
τὰς τιμὰς πρῶτόν τε ἀνεπιτάκτους τοῦτο ἂν ἀπο-
184 φήνασθαι. ἔργον δὲ κάλλιστον καὶ ἐλευθέροις ἀνδράσι πρέπον ἀμείβεσθαι τοὺς εὐεργέτας, οἷος δὴ
καὶ ἀνὴρ οὗτος περὶ ἡμᾶς πάντας γέγονεν οὐδὲν
παραπλησίως⁶ Κασσίῳ καὶ Βρούτῳ τοῖς Γάιον
Ἰούλιον ἀνῃρηκόσιν, ἐπεί γε οἱ μὲν στάσεως καὶ
πολέμων ἐμφυλίων ἀρχὰς ἐπανερρίπισαν τῇ πόλει,

¹ Dindorf: φέρειν ex φέρων ut vid. corr. A: φέρων MW:
φέρουσαν Hudson.
² Naber: νεώτερον codd.
³ post ζῆν lacunam indicat Dindorf.
⁴ ὑπομένομεν Bekker.

else to make counterproposals, if some measure already proposed is not to your liking. There is no danger in opposition, for there is no longer a despot at the head of the state who is not only unaccountable for any injury that he inflicts on the city but has sole power to do away with those who have spoken. This tyranny was fostered by nothing but indolence [a] and our failure to speak in opposition to any of its wishes. We have succumbed to the seduction of peace and have learned to live like conquered prisoners. Whether we have suffered incurable disasters ourselves or have only observed the calamities of our neighbours, it is because we are afraid to die like brave men that we must be patient when slain with the utmost degradation. But our first duty is to confer the very highest honours on those who have removed the tyrant, and in particular on Cassius Chaerea ; for, with the help of the gods, this man above all has both by his counsel and action shown himself our purveyor of liberty. It is right, now that we are free, that we should not be unmindful of him, but that for one who both laid the plans in time of tyranny on behalf of our liberty and was first to risk the deed, we should, in time of liberty, vote these honours and make this our first spontaneous act. It is a most noble deed, and such as becomes free men, to requite a benefactor, such as this man has now shown himself in relation to all of us. He is beyond comparison with Cassius and Brutus, the slayers of Julius Caesar ; for they only fanned into fresh life the fires of sedition and civil war in the state, while

---

[a] mss. " not by any revolution but by indolence."

[5] δέ] δὲ δεῖ Dindorf.
[6] similis Lat. : παραπλήσιος Niese.

οὗτος δὲ μετὰ τῆς τυραννοκτονίας καὶ τῶν ἐντεῦθεν δεινῶν ἀπήλλαξεν τὴν πόλιν.·

185  (3) Σέντιος μὲν τοιούτοις ἐχρῆτο τοῖς λόγοις καὶ τῶν βουλευτῶν ἡδονῇ δεχομένων καὶ ὁπόσοι τῶν ἱππέων παρῆσαν. ἀναπηδήσας δέ τις Τρεβέλλιος[1] Μάξιμος περιαιρεῖται τὸν δακτύλιον τοῦ Σεντίου, λίθος δὲ εἰκόνα Γαΐου ἐγγεγλυμμένος ἐδεσμεύετο αὐτῷ, καὶ σπουδῇ τῶν λεγομένων καὶ ὧν ἐπενόει πράξειν, ὅπερ ᾤετο, ἐν λήθῃ γεγονότι,[2] καὶ ἡ μὲν
186 γλυφὴ κατάγνυται.[3] προελήλύθει δὲ ἡ νὺξ ἐπὶ μέγα, καὶ Χαιρέας δὲ σημεῖον ᾔτει τοὺς ὑπάτους, οἱ δὲ ἐλευθερίαν ἔδοσαν. ἐν θαύματι δὲ ἦν αὐτοῖς
187 καὶ ὅμοια ἀπιστίᾳ τὰ δρώμενα· ἔτει γὰρ ἑκατοστῷ,[4] μεθ᾿ ὃ τὴν δημοκρατίαν τὸ πρῶτον ἀφηρέθησαν,[5] ἐπὶ τοὺς ὑπάτους σημείου ἡ παράδοσις·[6] οὗτοι γὰρ πρότερον ἢ τυραννηθῆναι τὴν πόλιν κύριοι τῶν[7]
188 στρατιωτικῶν ἦσαν. Χαιρέας δὲ τὸ σημεῖον λαβὼν παρεδίδου τῶν στρατιωτῶν τοῖς πρὸς τὴν σύγκλητον συνεστηκόσιν. ἦσαν δὲ εἰς σπείρας τέσσαρας, οἷς τὸ ἀβασίλευτον τιμιώτερον τῆς τυραννίδος
189 προὔκειτο. καὶ οἵδε μὲν ἀπῇσαν μετὰ τῶν χιλιάρχων, ἀνεχώρει δὲ ἤδη καὶ ὁ δῆμος περιχαρὴς καὶ

---

[1] Trebellius Lat.: Στρεβέλλιος codd.
[2] lacunam post γεγονότι indicat Niese.
[3] κατά . . . γνυται A: καταπήγνυται MW: est agnita Lat.
[4] ἔτει γὰρ ἑκατοστῷ] Thomas Terry: ἔτι γὰρ ἕκαστος τῷ (ῶ in ῷ corr. A) codd.
[5] ἀφηρέθησαν] ἀφαιρεθεῖσαν Terry: ἀφηρέθησαν ἐπέστρεψεν Hudson ex Lat.: ἀφηρέθησαν ἐπανῆλθε (vel simile) coni. Niese.
[6] ἔτει γὰρ . . . παράδοσις] quia reversa videretur ad consules haec potestas Lat.
[7] τῶν] τῶν <πολιτικῶν καὶ> coni. Richards et Shutt ex Lat.

this man has not only slain the tyrant but has also relieved the city of the horrors which originated with him."

(3) Such was the address of Sentius, which was heartily approved both by the senators and by all the equites who were present. At this point a certain Trebellius Maximus [a] leapt up and snatched off Sentius' ring, in which was set a stone graven with the image of Gaius. For, as Trebellius supposed, Sentius was too much interested in his speech and in his plans of action to notice its presence; and so the image was smashed. And now, with the night far advanced, Chaerea asked the consuls for the watchword, and they gave "Liberty." This ritual filled them with wonder, and they were almost unable to believe their ears, for it was the hundredth [b] year since they had first been robbed of the democracy to the time when the giving of the watchword reverted to the consuls. For before the city came under a tyranny, it was they who had commanded the armies. Chaerea, having received the watchword, passed it on to such of the soldiers as had joined the side of the senate; there were a total of four cohorts [c] who regarded freedom from imperial rule as more honourable than tyranny. These cohorts now left with their tribunes. By this time the people were also with-

*The consuls give the watchword "liberty."*

[a] Mentioned by Tacitus, *Ann.* xiv. 46, as having carried out, together with Quintus Volusius and Sextius Africanus (who despised him), an assessment of Gaul. He was consul suffectus in 56.

[b] From 59 B.C., the first consulship of Julius Caesar, to A.D. 41, the date of the assassination of Gaius.

[c] The parallel passage, *B.J.* ii. 205, says that there were three cohorts. Since the strength of a cohort at this time was between 500 and 600 men, this would amount to a force of between 2000 and 2400 men.

ἐλπίδος καὶ φρονήματος¹ ἐπὶ τῷ κτησαμένῳ τὴν
ἡγεμονίαν αὐτοῖς, οὐκέτι ἐπὶ τῷ ἐφεστηκότι. καὶ τὰ
πάντα ἦν ὁ Χαιρέας αὐτοῖς.

190 (4) Χαιρέας δὲ ἐν δεινῷ τιθέμενος περιεῖναι τὴν
θυγατέρα Γαΐου καὶ τὴν γυναῖκα, ἀλλὰ μὴ πανοικὶ
τὸν ὄλεθρον αὐτῷ συντυχεῖν, ἐπεὶ καὶ πᾶν ὅ τι
ὑπολείποιτο αὐτῶν ἐπ' ὀλέθρῳ τῆς πόλεως λειφθή-
σεσθαι καὶ τῶν νόμων, ἄλλως τε πρόθεσιν ἐσπουδακὼς τελειώσασθαι τὴν αὐτοῦ καὶ πάνυ εὐφρᾶναι
μῖσος τὸ πρὸς Γάιον, Ἰούλιον ἐκπέμπει Λοῦππον²
ἕνα τῶν χιλιάρχων κτενοῦντα τήν τε γυναῖκα
191 Γαΐου καὶ τὴν θυγατέρα. Κλήμεντος δ' ὄντι συγ-
γενεῖ τῷ Λοῦππῳ τὴν ἐπὶ τοιοῖσδε προὔθεσαν λει-
τουργίαν, ὅπως μετασχὼν κἂν ἐπὶ τοιούτοις τῆς
τυραννοκτονίας ἀγάλλοιτο ἀρετῇ πρὸς τῶν πολιτι-
κῶν, ὡς καὶ τοῦ παντὸς ἐπιβουλεύματος δόξειε
192 κοινωνεῖν τὸ πρῶτον συνθεμένων. ἐνίοις δὲ τῶν
συνωμοτῶν καὶ ὠμὸν ἐδόκει τὸ ἐπὶ τῇ γυναικὶ
θράσει χρησόμενον αὐτῷ διὰ τὸ³ Γάιον φύσει τῇ
αὐτοῦ χρώμενον ἢ συμβουλῇ τῇ ἐκείνης τὰ πάντα
πρᾶξαι, ἐξ ὧν ἥ τε πόλις ἀπηγορεύκει τοῖς κατει-
ληφόσι κακοῖς καὶ τῶν πολιτῶν ὅ τι καὶ ἄνθος ἦν
193 ἀπώλετο. οἱ δὲ καὶ τῶν μὲν ἐπὶ τοιούτοις ἐνεκά-
λουν αὐτῇ γνώμην τὸ δὲ πᾶν καὶ τῶν ὑπὸ Γαΐου
πεπραγμένων κακῶν ἐκείνη τὴν αἰτίαν ἐπέφερον
φάρμακον τῷ Γάιῳ δοῦσαν ἐννοιῶν δούλωσιν καὶ
ἐρώτων ἐπαγωγὰς αὐτῇ ψηφιούμενον, εἰς μανίαν
μεταστάντος τὰ πάντα αὐτὴν εἶναι τὴν νεναυπηγη-

---

¹ καὶ ἐλπίδος καὶ φρονήματος] hanc spem habentes atque
eogitationem Lat. : μετ' ἐλπίδος καὶ φρονήματος Ernesti : καὶ
ἐλπίδος καὶ φρονήματος μεστὸς Dindorf.
² Lupum Lat.
³ ed. pr. : τὸν codd.

drawing, overjoyed and full of hope and pride because they had acquired self-government and no longer were under a master. Chaerea was everything to them.

(4) Chaerea was alarmed that the daughter and wife of Gaius should survive, and that his whole household had not shared his ruin. For any remnant of them that was left alive would remain a menace to the city and the laws. In any case, he was determined to do the job completely and to indulge to the full his hatred for Gaius. Thus he dispatched one of the military tribunes, Julius Lupus,[a] to put the wife and daughter of Gaius to death. They proposed Lupus for this mission because he was a kinsman of Clemens, in order that by taking part in the tyrannicide even in such a way, he might be exalted in prowess in the eyes of the citizens, and might be thought to be a confederate of those who were first to organize the whole conspiracy. Some of the conspirators, however, thought that the proposal to strike at [b] Gaius' wife was too cruel, because Gaius was following his own bent and not her counsel in all that he did to bring the city to exhaustion under its burden of calamity and to destroy the finest flowers among the citizens. But others accused her of responsibility for the policy that produced such effects, and laid upon her the entire blame for the evil deeds of Gaius, saying that she had given him a drug calculated to enslave his thinking and to excite his passion for her, and that this drove him mad. Thus she, they charged, had fitted out the whole fleet of troubles

*Murder of Gaius' wife and daughter.*

---

[a] Suetonius, who does not mention his name, calls him (*Calig.* 59) a centurion of the praetorian guard, but this is incorrect, according to Stein, " Iulius," no. 327, Pauly-Wissowa, x¹, 1917, p. 663.

[b] Lit. " to use boldness against."

μένην ἐπὶ ταῖς Ῥωμαίων τύχαις καὶ τῆς ὑποτελού-
194 σης αὐτοῖς οἰκουμένης.[1] καὶ πέρας κυρωθὲν ὥστε
αὐτὴν τελευτᾶν, οὐδὲν γὰρ οἱ ἀποσπεύδοντες οἷοί
τε ὠφελεῖν ἦσαν, ἐστέλλετο ὁ Λοῦππος· ἐβραδύνετο
δὲ οὐδὲν μελλήσει τῇ κατ' αὐτόν, ὥστε μὴ οὐκ εἰς
καιρὸν δεδιακονῆσθαι τοῖς ἀπεσταλκόσιν, θέλων
ἐπ' οὐδαμοῖς μεμπτὸς εἶναι τῶν ἐπ' ὠφελείᾳ τοῦ
195 δήμου πεποιημένων. παρελθὼν δὲ ἐπὶ τοῦ βασιλείου λαμβάνει τὴν Καισωνίαν,[2] γυνὴ δ' ἦν τοῦ
Γαΐου, παρακατακειμένην τῷ σώματι τοῦ ἀνδρὸς
χαμαιπετεῖ καὶ πάντων ἐν ἀτυχίᾳ ὢν χαρίζοιτ' ἂν
ὁ νόμος τοῖς μεταστᾶσιν,[3] αἵματί τε ἀναπεφυρ-
μένην ἐκ τῶν τραυμάτων καὶ πολλὴν τὴν ταλαιπωρίαν[4] συμφερομένην[5] τῆς θυγατρὸς παρερριμμένης·
ἠκούετό τε ἐν τοῖς τοιοῖσδε οὐδὲν ἕτερον ἢ κατά-
μεμψις τοῦ Γαΐου, ὡς πιθανὴν οὐ σχόντος πολλάκις
196 προηγορευκυῖαν αὐτήν. ἐπ' ἀμφότερα δὲ οὗτος ὁ
λόγος καὶ τότε εἰκάζετο καὶ νῦν ἐφ' ὁμοίοις πρόκειται τῇ διανοίᾳ τῶν ἀκροατῶν πρὸς ὅ τι θελή-
σειαν ῥοπὰς τὰς αὑτοῦ προστιθέμενοι.[6] οἱ μὲν γὰρ
ἀποσημαίνειν ἔφασαν τὸν λόγον, ὡς συμβουλευο-
μένης ἀποστάντα μανιῶν καὶ τοῦ εἰς τοὺς πολίτας
ὠμοῦ μετρίως καὶ μετ' ἀρετῆς ἐξηγεῖσθαι τῶν
πραγμάτων, μὴ[7] παρ' αὐτὸν ἀπολέσθαι τρόπῳ τῷ

---

[1] οἱ δὲ . . . οἰκουμένης] et illi quidem his assertionibus eam
defendere nitebantur. omnium autem malorum quae a Gaio
gesta fuerant haec erat caput ; Gaio namque dederat pocu-
lum, ut eius mentem suo potuisset subiugare servitio et amoris
incantationibus ad vesaniam transformatum ita sibi devin-
xerat, quatenus fortunae omnium Romanorum et totius orbis,
cui praesidebat, et subditae viderentur nihilque defensores
eius valere potuerunt Lat.

[2] Hudson : Κεσωνίαν A[1]WE : Κεσσωνίαν M et ex corr. A
et Busb. : Cesoniam Lat.

against the fortunes of Rome and of the inhabited
world subject to that city. In the end it was decided
to put her to death, for those who opposed the proposal were unable, despite their zeal, to do her any
service ; and Lupus was dispatched. He, on his part,
did not prolong his mission or fail to execute it in
good time for the group whose emissary he was, since
he was eager to incur no censure for an act performed
in the public interest. On entering the palace he
found Caesonia, the wife of Gaius, stretched beside
the corpse of her husband that lay on the floor un-
provided with any of the tributes that custom gra-
ciously bestows on the departed. She was all dabbled
with blood from his wounds and in a state of deep
misery, while her daughter had thrown herself down
at her side. In such a scene no word was heard except
her reproach of Gaius because he had not believed
her oft-repeated prediction. As to the interpretation
of these words, opinions at the time were divided ;
and to this day the opinions of those who hear them
repeated are similarly balanced, each assigning such
weight to them as he chooses. Some said that her
words signified that she warned him to desist from
his madness and barbarity to the citizens, to ad-
minister the government with moderation and virtue
and not to bring about his own destruction at their

---

³ καὶ πάντων . . . μεταστᾶσιν] et omnes in luctu positos
sicut moris est mortuis exhiberi Lat.

⁴ πολλὴν τὴν ταλαιπωρίαν] πολλῇ τῇ ταλαιπωρίᾳ Dindorf.

⁵ circumdata Lat. : συμπεριφερομένην Richards et Shutt.

⁶ ἐπ' ἀμφότερα . . . προστιθέμενοι] haec enim ratio et tunc
et nunc similiter aestimatur et in hominum mente sita est
circa eos quibus compatiuntur (patiuntur cod. Ambros.) Lat.

⁷ ed. pr.; καὶ codd.

197 αὐτοῦ χρώμενον. οἱ δέ, ὡς λόγου τοῦ περὶ τῶν
συνωμοτῶν ἐπιφοιτήσαντος Γαΐῳ κελεύσειεν μηδὲν
εἰς ἀναβολὰς ἀλλ' ἐκ τοῦ ὀξέος πάντας μεταχειρισά-
μενον αὐτούς, κἂν εἰ μηδὲν ἀδικοῖεν, ἐν ἀδεεῖ κινδύνων καταστῆναι, καὶ τοῦτ' εἶναι τὸ ἐπονειδιζό-
μενον, ὡς προηγορευκυίας διαπράξασθαι μαλακῷ
198 γεγονότι. καὶ τὰ μὲν λεχθέντα ὑπὸ τῆς Καισωνίας
καὶ ὁποῖα οἱ ἄνθρωποι περὶ αὐτῆς ἐφρόνουν ταῦτα
ἦν. ἡ δὲ ἐπεὶ θεᾶται τὴν πρόσοδον τοῦ Λούππου
τό τε σῶμα τοῦ Γαΐου προυδείκνυεν καὶ ἆσσον ἰέναι
199 παρεκάλει μετ' ὀλοφυρμοῦ καὶ δακρύων. ἐπεὶ δὲ
τῇ διανοίᾳ συνεστηκότα[1] ἑώρα τὸν Λούππον, καὶ
μηδὲν[2] προσιόντα ὡς ἐπὶ τρᾶξιν οὐκ αὐτῷ κεχαρισ-
μένην,[3] γνωρίσασα ἐφ' ὅ τι[4] ἐχώρει τήν τε σφαγὴν
ἐγύμνου καὶ πάνυ προθύμως ποτνιωμένη ὁποῖα
εἰκὸς τοὺς οὕτω σαφῶς ἐν ἀπογνώσει τοῦ ζῆν γεγονότας καὶ κελεύουσα μὴ μέλλειν ἐπὶ τελειώσει τοῦ
200 δράματος οὗ ἐπ' αὐτοῖς[5] συνέθεσαν. καὶ ἥδε μὲν
εὐψύχως ταύτῃ τελευτᾷ ὑπὸ τοῦ Λούππου καὶ ἐπ'
αὐτῇ τὸ θυγάτριον. καὶ Λοῦππος ταῦτα προαπαγ-
γέλλων ἔσπευδεν τοῖς περὶ τὸν Χαιρέαν.

201 (5) Γάιος μὲν δὴ τέταρτον ἐνιαυτὸν ἡγεμονεύσας
Ῥωμαίων λείποντα τεσσάρων μηνῶν οὕτως τελευτᾷ, ἀνὴρ καὶ πρότερον ἢ τῇ ἀρχῇ συνῆλθεν σκαιός

[1] συνεστηκότα] attonitum Lat. : μὴ συνεστηκότα Hudson.
[2] om. Hudson.
[3] καὶ μηδὲν . . . κεχαρισμένην] et nulla compassione motum
Lat.
[4] ὅ τι] Niese : ὃν codd. : quod Lat. : ὃ ed. pr.
[5] αὐτῆς cod. Laur. : αὐτῇ Busb. E.

---

[a] Lit. " had composed for them," *i.e.* for Gaius, his wife,
and his daughter.
[b] Suetonius, *Calig.* 58, reports that at the same time that

hands by following his own bent. Others said that a rumour had reached her concerning the conspirators and that she had bidden Gaius to do away with them all forthwith and without an instant's delay, even if they were innocent, and so render himself secure from risk; and that this was the meaning of her reproach, namely, that he had been too soft to do a thorough job when she had predicted the result. Such were Caesonia's words and such the judgements that men passed on them. When she saw Lupus approaching she pointed to the body of Gaius, bidding him, with tears and lamentation, to come nearer. But when she saw that Lupus was firmly determined and came on showing no sign that the deed was not to his liking, she recognized the object of his coming and bared her throat most willingly, raising such cries of horror as may be expected of one whose hope of life is so plainly lost, and bidding him not put off the final act of the drama that they had composed for the downfall of the royal family.[a] Thus she courageously met her death at Lupus' hands and her young daughter after her.[b] And Lupus made haste to be the first to bring word of this to Chaerea and the others.

(5) Such was the end of Gaius after he had been emperor of the Romans for four years lacking four months.[c] Even before he succeeded to office he was

Gaius' character and achievements.

Gaius was murdered, his wife Caesonia was stabbed with a sword by a centurion and his daughter's brains were dashed against a wall. Dio lix. 29. 7 says merely that Gaius' wife and daughter were promptly slain.

[c] So also in the parallel passage, *B.J.* ii. 204. Suetonius, *Calig.* 59, gives the length of his reign as three years, ten months, and eight days. Dio lix. 30. 1 says that it lasted three years, nine months, and twenty-eight days.

τε καὶ κακοτροπίας[1] εἰς τὸ ἄκρον ἀφιγμένος, ἡδονῇ
τε ἡσσώμενος καὶ φίλος διαβολῇ,[2] καὶ τὰ μὲν φο-
βερὰ καταπεπληγμένος καὶ διὰ τοῦτο ἐφ᾽ οἷς θαρ-
σήσειε φονικώτατος,[3] τῆς τε ἐξουσίας ἐφ᾽ ἑνὶ μόνῳ
πιμπλάμενος τῷ ὑβρίζειν, εἰς οὓς ἥκιστα ἐχρῆν
ἀλόγῳ μεγαλοψυχίᾳ χρώμενος καὶ πορῐστὴς ἐκ τοῦ
202 κτείνειν καὶ παρανομεῖν. καὶ τοῦ μὲν θείου καὶ
νομίμου μείζων ἐσπουδακὼς εἶναί τε καὶ δοκεῖν,
ἡσσώμενος δὲ ἐπαίνων τῆς πληθύος καὶ πάντα,
ὁπόσα αἰσχρὰ κρίνας ὁ νόμος ἐπιτιμᾷ τιμωρίαν,
203 ἐνόμισεν ἀρετῆς. καὶ φιλίας ἀμνήμων, εἰ καὶ
πλείστη τε καὶ διὰ μεγίστων γένοιτο, οἷς τότε[4]
ὀργισθείη ἐκπλήξει κολάσεως καὶ ἐλαχίσταις,[5] πο-
λέμιον δὲ ἡγούμενος πᾶν τὸ ἀρετῇ συνερχόμενον,
ἀναντίλεκτον ἐπὶ πᾶσιν οἷς κελεύσειε τὴν ἐπιθυμίαν
204 λαμβάνων· ὅθεν καὶ ἀδελφῇ γνησίᾳ συνῆν, ἐξ οὗ καὶ
μάλιστα αὐτῷ φύεσθαι παρὰ τοῖς πολίταις ἤρξατο
σφοδρότερον τὸ μῖσος διὰ τὸ πολλοῦ χρόνου μὴ
ἱστορημένον εἴς τε ἀπιστίαν καὶ ἔχθραν τὴν πρὸς
205 τὸν πράξαντα παρακαλεῖν. ἔργον δὲ μέγα ἢ βασίλειον οὐδὲν αὐτῷ πεπραγμένον εἴποι ἄν τις ἢ ἐπ᾽
ὠφελείᾳ τῶν συνόντων καὶ αὖθις ἀνθρώπων ἐσομένων, πλήν γε τοῦ περὶ Ῥήγιον καὶ Σικελίαν

---

[1] A : κακοπραγίας MW Exc. Peiresc.
[2] ἡδονῇ . . . διαβολῇ] ἡδονῆς θ᾽ ἡττώμενος καὶ φίλων διαβολῆς
coni. Richards et Shutt.
[3] ἡδονῇ . . . φονικώτατος] om. E.
[4] ποτε Exc. (?) Hudson : τε coni. Niese.
[5] ἐλαχίσταις] ἐλαχίστης ed. pr. : ἐπ᾽ ἐλαχίστοις Hudson ; καὶ
ἐλαχίσταις] κἀπ᾽ ἐλαχίσταις ⟨αἰτίαις⟩ coni. Post ; πάντα . . .
ἐλαχίσταις] quaecumque leges tamquam turpia puniunt sua
credidit esse tormenta, virtutis et amicitiarum immemor,
quando contra haec cum inlatione supplicii frequenter exor-
sus est Lat.

a sinister character who had reached the peak of
perversity, a slave to pleasure, a lover of slander, a
man dismayed by danger and consequently most
bloodthirsty against those of whom he was not afraid.
He was greedy of power with one object only, to
treat abusively or to bestow senseless largess where
it least behooved him, one who obtained his revenue
by means of slaughter and injustice. It was his
object to be and to be thought stronger than religion
or the law, but he had no strength to resist the flat-
teries of the mob, and regarded as virtuous achievement everything that the law condemns as disgraceful and on which it imposes a penalty. He was
unmindful of friendship, however close it was and
however great the occasion for it, and he would inflict
punishment for the slightest matter on any at whom
he became enraged. Everything that went with
virtue he regarded as hostile ; if he took a fancy to
anything he tolerated no opposition to any command
that he gave. Hence he even had sexual intercourse
with his own sister [a] : this conduct was the source
from which the citizens' hatred of him grew fiercer
and fiercer. For such a deed, which for ages past
had not been recorded, drew them to incredulity and
hatred of the doer. No great work, not even a palace,
can be cited as constructed by him for the benefit
either of his contemporaries or of posterity, excepting
the harbour which he planned near Rhegium and

---

[a] Julia Drusilla. Named in 37 to succeed Gaius, she died
in 38. She was married successively to Cassius Longinus
(cf. Ant. xv. 406, xx. 1 and 7) and Aemilius Lepidus (§§ 20,
49). The scandal of Gaius' incest with her is not mentioned
by Philo, Seneca, or Tacitus, but it is related by Suetonius,
Calig. 24, and Dio lix. 3. 6, both of whom declare that he
committed incest with all three of his sisters.

ἐπινοηθέντος ἐν ὑποδοχῇ τῶν ἀπ᾽ Αἰγύπτου σιτη-
206 γῶν πλοίων· τοῦτο δὲ ὁμολογουμένως μέγιστόν τε
καὶ ὠφελιμώτατον τοῖς πλέουσιν· οὐ μὴν ἐπὶ τέλος
γε ἀφίκετο, ἀλλ᾽ ἡμίεργον ὑπὸ τοῦ ἀμβλυτέρως
207 αὐτῷ ἐπιπονεῖν κατελείφθη. αἴτιον δ᾽ ἦν ἡ περὶ
τὰ ἀχρεῖα σπουδὴ καὶ τὸ δαπανῶντα εἰς ἡδονάς, αἳ
καταμόνας ἔμελλον ὠφελεῖν, αὐτῷ ὑφαιρεῖν τῆς
ἐπὶ τοῖς κρείσσοσιν ἀνωμολογημένοις φιλοτιμίας.
208 ἄλλως δὲ ῥήτωρ τε ἄριστος καὶ γλώσσῃ τῇ Ἑλλάδι
καὶ τῇ Ῥωμαίοις πατρίῳ σφόδρα ἠσκημένος συνίει
τ᾽ ἐκ τοῦ παραχρῆμα καὶ τοῖς ὑφ᾽ ἑτέρων συντε-
θεῖσίν τε καὶ ἐκ πλείονος προσυγκειμένοις ἀντειπὼν
ἐκ τοῦ ὀξέος φανῆναι πιθανώτερος ἐν μεγίστῳ
πράγματι παρ᾽ ὁντινοῦν γενόμενος, εὐκολίᾳ τε εἰς
αὐτὸ τῆς φύσεως καὶ τῷ¹ εἰς ἰσχὺν αὐτῇ προσλα-
209 βεῖν μελέτην² τοῦ ἐπιπονεῖν. ἀδελφοῦ γὰρ παιδὸς
υἱεῖ γεγονότι Τιβερίου, οὗ καὶ διάδοχος γίνεται,
μέγα ἀνάγκασμα παιδείας ἀντέχεσθαι διὰ τὸ καὶ
αὐτὸς εἰς τὰ πρῶτα ἐν αὐτῇ κατορθῶν διαπρέπειν,
καὶ συνεφιλοκάλει Γάϊος συγγενοῦς τε ἀνδρὸς καὶ

---

¹ Ernesti : τοῦ codd. Exc.
² Ernesti : μελέτῃ codd. Exc.

---

ᵃ Pliny, *Hist. Nat.* iv. 4. 10-5. 13 (so also Suet. *Calig.* 21),
cites one project undertaken by Gaius that would have been
of great commercial benefit, namely, the building of a canal
across the Isthmus of Corinth. But the project was never
completed. Frontinus, *Aquaed.* i. 13, declares that Gaius
began two aqueducts in Rome since the seven then existing
seemed insufficient to meet both the public needs and the
luxurious private demands of the day. These also were left
incomplete at Gaius' death but were finished by Claudius.
Suetonius, *Calig.* 21, however, cites several projects that
Gaius did complete : the temple of Augustus, Pompey's
theatre, and the repair of the city walls and temples at Syra-
cuse. He also mentions his plans to restore the palace of

Sicily for the reception of the grain transports from Egypt.[a] This was, admittedly, a very great work, and of the greatest utility to seafarers. It was not finished, however, but was left half-completed owing to the laggard way in which he dealt with the task. This is explained by his great interest in useless objects, and by his squandering [b] money on pleasures that would benefit no one but himself; and thus he suffered the gradual loss of any ambition for achievements that would have been without question greater. He was, moreover, a first-rate orator,[c] deeply versed in the Greek and Latin languages. He knew how to reply impromptu to speeches which others had composed after long preparation, and to show himself instantly more persuasive on the subject than anyone else, even where the greatest matters were debated. All this resulted from a natural aptitude for such things and from his adding to that aptitude the practice of taking elaborate pains to strengthen it. For, being the grandson of the brother of Tiberius, whom he succeeded, he was under a great compulsion to apply himself to education, because Tiberius himself also had conspicuously succeeded in attaining the highest place in it. Gaius followed him in his attachment to such noble pursuits, yielding to the

Polycrates at Samos, to finish the temple of the Didymaean Apollo at Ephesus, to found a city high up in the Alps, and to build an amphitheatre near the Saepta.

[b] Dio lix. 4. 5 also says that Gaius spent money most unsparingly. Suetonius, *Calig.* 37, gives a catalogue of his extravagances. Thus, for example, he would drink expensive pearls dissolved in vinegar and would serve his guests bread and meat of gold. He thereby squandered in less than a year the 2,700,000,000 sesterces that Tiberius had amassed.

[c] *Cf.* Dio lix. 19. 3: " Gaius always claimed to surpass all the orators."

ἡγεμόνος εἴκων ἐπιστολαῖς[1] ἐπρώτευσέν τε τῶν
210 κατ᾽ αὐτὸν πολιτῶν. οὐ μὴν ἀντισχεῖν οἷά τε
ἐγένετο αὐτῷ τὰ ἐκ τῆς παιδείας συλλεγέντα ἀγαθὰ
πρὸς τὸν ἐπελθόντα ὄλεθρον αὐτῷ ὑπὸ τῆς ἐξουσίας·
οὕτως ἄρα δυσπόριστον ἡ ἀρετὴ τοῦ σωφρονεῖν, οἷς
211 ἀνυπεύθυνον τὸ πράσσειν ῥᾳστώνῃ πάρεστιν. φίλοις
μὲν κεχρῆσθαι καὶ πάντα ἀξιολόγοις ὑποσπουδα-
σθείς[2] τὸ κατ᾽ ἀρχὰς ὑπό τε παιδείας καὶ[3] δόξης
ζήλου τῶν κρειττόνων, μέχρι δὴ[4] τῷ περιόντι τοῦ
ὑβρίζειν ἀπαμφίασις[5] εὐνοίας[6] ᾗ[7] πρὸς αὐτὸν ἐχρήσαντο, μίσους ὑποφυέντος ὑπ᾽ αὐτῶν ἐπιβουλευθεὶς
τελευτᾷ.[8]

212 (iii. 1) Κλαύδιος δέ, καθάπερ ἀνώτερον ἔφην,
ἀπορρήξεως αὐτῷ τῶν Γαΐου ὁδῶν γενομένης καὶ
τοῦ οἴκου θορυβηθέντος πάθει τῆς Καίσαρος τελευτῆς,[9] ἐν ἀμηχάνοις ὢν περὶ τῆς σωτηρίας ἔν
τινι στενωπῷ κατειλημμένος ἔκρυπτεν ἑαυτὸν
οὐδεμίαν κινδύνων αἰτίαν πλὴν τῆς γενναιότητος[10]
213 ὑφορώμενος· μέτριον γὰρ ἰδιώτης ὢν ἦγεν αὐτὸν
καὶ τοῖς παροῦσιν[11] ἀρκῶν ἦν, παιδείᾳ τε συνιὼν[12]

---

[1] καὶ συνεφιλοκάλει . . . ἐπιστολαῖς] Gaius itaque puer cole-
bat haec quasi cognatus et imago principis Lat.

[2] ὑπερσπουδασθείς coni. ex Liddell-Scott-Jones.

[3] καὶ] A : κατὰ M : καὶ τὰ W Exc.

[4] ed. pr. : δὲ codd. Exc.

[5] A : ἀπαμφιάσεις MW Exc. : γρ ἀπαλειφείσης i. marg. A :
ἀπαμφιασθείσης Lowthius.

[6] A (σ ex ι corr.) : εὐνοίᾳ MW.          [7] ed. pr. : τῇ codd.

[8] μέχρι . . . τελευτᾷ] postea perductus ad iniuriarum onus
et odium, quod circa eum homines omissa priore devotione
gerebant, ad id usque descendit, ut ab eisdem insidias passus
extingueretur Lat.

[9] ἀπορρήξεως . . . τελευτῆς] interruptione facta viarum e-
grediebatur de theatro. qui Gaio mortuo et domo Caesaris
nece turbata Lat.

312

injunctions of a man who was both his kinsman and his commander-in-chief. Thus he came to stand highest among the citizens of his time. For all that, the advantages obtained from education could not withstand the corruption wrought upon him by his rise to power ; so hard to achieve, it seems, is the virtue of moderation for those who find it easy to take action for which they need account to no one. At the outset, owing to education and a reputation for a zeal for the higher pursuits, he took some pains to cultivate the friendship of men who were in every respect worthy of regard ; but in the end, because of his surpassing brutality, their former loyalty was discarded ; when hatred had grown in its place, they aimed at him the plot that cost him his life.

(iii. 1) Now Claudius, as I said above, had broken away from the route taken by Gaius, and since the palace was thrown into an uproar by the death of Caesar, he had no means to secure his own safety. He was in a narrow passage when cut off and concealed himself there, though he could see no cause, other than his noble rank, for alarm. For in private life he bore himself modestly and was satisfied with what he had. He pursued his studies,[a] especially in Greek,[b]

*Claudius is found hiding by the praetorian guard.*

---

[a] Suetonius, *Claud.* 3 and 41, and Dio lx. 2. 1 say that he had applied himself seriously to literature from childhood and had composed some historical works.

[b] After becoming emperor, Claudius indicated his preference for Greek by often answering Greek envoys in their own language, by quoting Homer from the tribunal, and by writing twenty books of Etruscan history and eight of Carthaginian history in Greek (Suet. *Claud.* 42).

---

[10] μετριότητος E.
[11] Terry : πᾶσιν codd.
[12] A : συνὼν MWE : compositus Lat.

καὶ μάλιστα τῇ Ἑλληνίδι καὶ παντὸς τοῦ εἰς θόρυ-
214 βον ἀνακειμένου παντοίως ἀπαλλάσσων αὐτόν. τότε
δὲ πτοίας κατειληφυίας τὸν ὄχλον καὶ τοῦ βασιλείου
παντὸς στρατιωτικῆς μανίας ἀνάπλεω γεγονότος
καὶ δειλίας καὶ ἀταξίας ἰδιωτῶν οἷον ἀπειληφότων
σωματοφυλάκων,[1] οἱ περὶ τὸ[2] στρατηγικὸν καλού-
μενον, ὅπερ ἐστὶ τῆς στρατιᾶς καθαρώτατον, ἐν
βουλῇ περὶ τοῖς πρακτέοις ἦσαν, ὅσοι δὲ καὶ
παρετύγχανον, τὴν μὲν Γαΐου τιμωρίαν ἐν ὀλίγῳ
τιθέμενοι διὰ τὸ κατὰ δίκην αὐτῷ τὰς τύχας συν-
215 ελθεῖν, τὰ δὲ περὶ αὐτοὺς ἀνεσκοποῦντο μᾶλλον ὃν
τρόπον σχήσοι καλῶς καὶ[3] τῶν Γερμανῶν τε ἐν
τιμωρίαις τῶν σφαγέων ὄντων ὠμότητος χάριτι τῆς
216 ἑαυτῶν μᾶλλον ἢ τοῦ συμφέροντος τοῖς πᾶσιν. ὑφ'
ὧν ἁπάντων ὁ Κλαύδιος ἐθορυβεῖτο δεδιὼς περὶ
τῆς σωτηρίας, ἄλλως τ' ἐπειδὴ καὶ τῶν περὶ τὸν
Ἀσπρήναν ἐτεθέατο τὰς κεφαλὰς παραφερομένας·
εἱστήκει δὲ κατά τι προσβατὸν ὀλίγαις βαθμῖσι
217 χωρίον ὑπεσταλκὼς τῷ κατ' αὐτὸ σκότῳ.[a] καὶ
Γρᾶτος τῶν περὶ τὸ βασίλειόν τις στρατιωτῶν θεασάμενος καὶ τοῦ μὲν ἀκριβωσομένου τὴν ὄψιν
ἀμαθὴς ὢν διὰ τὸν σκότον, τοῦ δὲ ἄνθρωπον εἶναι
τὸν ὑπολοχῶντα κριτὴς εἶναι μὴ ἀπηλλαγμένος,
προσῄει τε ἐγγύτερον καὶ ὑποχωρεῖν ἠξιωκότος[b]
ἐπέκειτο καὶ καταλαβὼν ἐπιγνωρίζει, " Γερμανικὸς
μὲν οὗτος," φησὶν πρὸς τοὺς ἑπομένους, " καὶ στη-

---

[1] καὶ δειλίας . . . σωματοφυλάκων] et terror atque indisci-
plinatio cunctos privatos adpraehendisset Lat.
[2] ed. pr.: τὸν codd.
[3] δειλίας . . . καλῶς καί] om. E.

---

[a] Or " tucked away in the dark."
[b] Or " sought leave to withdraw."  According to Sueto-

and abstained completely from the kind of action that could lead to any disturbance. But now the crowd was panic-stricken, and the soldiers raged throughout the palace in their fury, while the emperor's body-guards reverted to a timidity and lack of discipline worthy of civilians. These troops, called the prae-torian guard, being the cream of the army, were in session debating their next move. Such as were present were little concerned to avenge Gaius, reasoning that he had justly met his fate. They were rather investigating what course would redound to their advantage. Even the German troops were en-gaged in vengeance on the assassins more to gratify their own ferocity than to promote the general good of all. Claudius was disturbed by all this and alarmed for his own safety, especially as he had seen the spectacle when the heads of Asprenas and the others were carried past. There he stood in an alcove to which a few steps led, making himself as small as he could *a* in the gloom. Gratus, one of the palace guard, caught sight of him, but was unable to make out his features well enough to recognize him in the dim light. Still he was not so far afield as not to determine that the lurking creature was human. He approached nearer, and when Claudius asked him to withdraw,*b* he pounced upon him and caught him. On recognizing him, he cried to his followers : " Here is a Germanicus *c* : let us set him up as emperor and

nius, *Claud.* 10, Claudius fell to his feet in terror. Dio lx. 1. 2-4 also confirms Josephus' account of how Claudius was dragged forth and reluctantly made emperor.

*c* Suetonius, *Claud.* 1, explains that among the honours voted to Claudius' father Drusus because of his victories in Germany was that the surname Germanicus should be re-tained by himself and his descendants forever.

218 σώμεθα τοῦτον ἡγεμόνα φερόμενοι.'' Κλαύδιος δὲ
ἐφ' ἁρπαγῇ παρεσκευασμένους ὁρῶν καὶ δείσας, μὴ
κατὰ φονὴν[1] ἀποθάνοι τὴν Γαίου,[2] φειδὼ σχεῖν
ἠξίου τοῦ κατ' αὐτὸν ἀνεπαχθοῦς ἀνάμνησιν αὐτοῖς
ὑποτιθεὶς καὶ τοῦ ἀπρομηθοῦς[3] τῶν γεγονότων.
219 καὶ ὁ Γρᾶτος μειδιάσας ἐπισπᾶται τῆς δεξιᾶς, καί,
'' παῦσαι,'' φησίν, '' μικρολογούμενος περὶ τῆς σωτηρίας δέον σε μεγαλοφρονεῖσθαι περὶ τῆς ἡγεμονίας,
ἣν οἱ θεοὶ Γαίου ἀφῃρημένοι τῇ σῇ συνεχώρησαν
ἀρετῇ πρόνοιαν τῆς οἰκουμένης λαβόντες. ἀλλ' ἴθι
220 καὶ τῶν προγόνων ἀπολάμβανε τὸν θρόνον.'' ἀν-
εβάσταζέν τε αὐτὸν οὐ πάνυ τοῖς ποσὶ βαίνειν δυνάμενον ὑπό τε φόβου καὶ χάρματος τῶν εἰρημένων.

221 (2) Συνεστρέφοντο δὲ περὶ τὸν Γρᾶτον ἤδη καὶ
πλείους τῶν σωματοφυλάκων καὶ θεωροῦντες τὸν
Κλαύδιον ἀγόμενον ἐσκυθρώπαζον[4] δόξῃ τοῦ ἐπὶ
κόλασιν ἕλκεσθαι[5] τῶν ἐπὶ τοιοῖσδε ζημιῶν ὡς ἄνδρα
ἀπράγμονα διὰ βίου τοῦ παντὸς καὶ κινδύνοις οὔτι
μετρίως ἐπὶ τῆς Γαίου ἀρχῆς ὡμιληκότα, τινὲς δὲ
καὶ αὐτῶν τοῖς ὑπάτοις ἐπιτρέπειν[6] κρίσιν ἠξίουν
222 τὴν περὶ αὐτόν.[7] καὶ πλειόνων τοῦ στρατιωτικοῦ
συστρεφομένων φυγαί τε ἦσαν τοῦ ὁμίλου καὶ προόδων[8] ἀπορία τῷ Κλαυδίῳ δι' ἀσθένειαν τοῦ σώματος, ἐπεὶ καὶ οἱ τὸ φορεῖον αὐτοῦ φέροντες περὶ[9]
τὴν ἁρπαγὴν αὐτοῦ παραγενομένης φυγῆς ἔσωζον

---

[1] A (ο ex ω corr., i. marg. φονὴν εἶπε τὸν φόνον ποιητικῶς):
φωνήν M : φωνὴν W.
[2] κατὰ φονὴν . . . τὴν Γαίου] propter Gaium Lat.
[3] ἀνυπευθύνου coni. Richards et Shutt.
[4] ἀγόμενον ἐσκυθρώπαζον] E : ἀγόμενον codd.
[5] post ἕλκεσθαι lacunam indicat Niese.
[6] E et i. marg. A : ἐντρέπειν A : ἐμπρέπειν MW.
[7] τινες . . . περὶ αὐτόν] om. Lat.

move fast." Claudius saw that they were prepared
to carry him off; and fearing that he might be put
to death for the slaying of Gaius, he asked them to
spare him, reminding them that he had never given
them offence, and that he had had no part in planning
the course of events. Gratus broke into a smile,
tugged at his right arm, and said : " Stop this nig-
gling about saving your life, when you should be
making big plans to gain the empire. The gods have
taken it from Gaius and granted it to you for your
virtue because they wished to promote the welfare
of mankind. Do come and accept the throne of your
ancestors that is your due." So off he carried him, for
Claudius was utterly unable to walk, from both fear
and joy at what Gratus had said.

(2) By this time, more of the bodyguard were
collected around Gratus, and when they saw Claudius
being hurried along,[a] apparently being dragged off
to punishment, they greeted with black looks the
penalization of such a man. For he had all his life
avoided meddling in public affairs and had also experienced no small share of danger under Gaius'
rule ; and some of them urged that his case should
be put before the consuls. As more of the soldiers
gathered, the crowd began to take flight, but Claudius
had no means of proceeding onward owing to his
physical weakness ; for, when he was seized, even
his litter-bearers took to their heels to save them-

---

[a] Suetonius, *Claud.* 10, says that the people who saw him
pitied him as if he were an innocent man being hurried to
execution.

---

[8] E : προσόδων codd. : fugere Lat.

[9] φέροντες περὶ] φέροντες πύστεως περὶ, litt. τες . . . περὶ i.
ras. m. 2 A.

αὐτοὺς ἀπ᾿ ἐλπίδος θέμενοι τὴν σωτηρίαν τοῦ δε-
223 σπότου. ἐν εὐρυχωρίᾳ δὲ τοῦ Παλατίου γενομένοις,
πρῶτον δὲ οἰκηθῆναι τῆς Ῥωμαίων πόλεως τοῦτο
παραδίδωσιν ὁ περὶ αὐτῆς λόγος, καὶ ἤδη τοῦ δη-
μοσίου ἀντιλαμβανομένοις πολὺ πλείων ἡ ἐπιφοί-
τησις ἦν τῶν στρατιωτῶν χαρᾷ τὴν ὄψιν δεχομένοις
τοῦ Κλαυδίου, περὶ πλείστου τε ἦν αὐτοῖς αὐτοκράτορα στήσεσθαι[1] τὸν ἄνθρωπον εὐνοίᾳ τε τοῦ[2]
Γερμανικοῦ, ἀδελφὸς δὲ ἦν αὐτοῦ ἐπὶ μέγα πᾶσιν
τοῖς ὡμιληκόσιν καταλελοιπότος[3] κλέος τὸ αὐτοῦ.
224 ἀναλογισμός τε αὐτοὺς εἰσῄει τῆς τε πλεονεξίας
τῶν ἐν τῇ συγκλήτῳ δυναστευόντων καὶ ὁπόσα ἐπὶ
225 τῆς πρὶν ἀρχῆς ἡμάρτητο αὐτῇ. πρὸς δὲ καὶ τὸ
ἀμήχανον τοῦ πράγματος κατενόουν, καὶ πάλιν εἰς
ἑνὸς ἀρχὴν μεθισταμένων τῶν ὅλων κινδύνους αὐτοῖς φέρειν δι᾿ ἑνὸς[4] κτησαμένου τὴν ἀρχὴν[5] παρὸν[6]
ἐπιχωρῆσει καὶ εὐνοίᾳ τῇ αὐτῶν λαβόντα Κλαύδιον
μνημονεύσεις τε χάριτος αὐτοῖς ἀποδιδόντα τιμήν,
ἣ ἐπὶ τοιούτοις γένοιτ᾿ ἂν ἀρκοῦσα.[7]
226 (3) Ταῦτα πρός τε ἀλλήλους καὶ δι᾿ ἑαυτοὺς διεξῄεσαν καὶ τοῖς ἀεὶ προσπίπτουσιν διηγοῦντο.[8] οἱ
δὲ πυνθανόμενοι προθύμως ἐδέχοντο τὴν πρόκλη-
σιν, συμφράξαντές[9] τε καὶ περικλάσαντες[10] ἦγον
ἐπὶ τοῦ στρατοπέδου φοράδην ἀναβαστάσαντες, ὡς

---

[1] στήσασθαι Niese.    [2] τῇ E.    [3] καταλελοιπὼς E.
[4] δι᾿ ἑνὸς] A : διά τινος MW.
[5] ἀρχὴν] Hudson : ἀρχὴν μεθισταμένων τῶν ὅλων codd.
[6] παρὸν] W : παρ᾿ ὃν AM : παρὰ τὸν Post.
[7] δι᾿ ἑνὸς . . . ἀρκοῦσα] quando quodcumque solus vellet
efficeret, sed etiam quia Claudius cum imperium susciperet,
pro favore senatui gratiam repensaret sufficienter Lat.
[8] Cocceji : διῃροῦντο codd. E.
[9] A : συμπράξαντές MW.
[10] MW : περικλείσαντες (ει ex α corr.) A.

318

selves, despairing of their master's life. But when
they had come to the open area of the Palatine—
legend has it that this was the first site of the city of
Rome to receive a settlement [a]—and were just reaching the Treasury,[b] there was a far larger concourse
of soldiers, who were overjoyed at the sight of
Claudius and who were determined to proclaim him
emperor because of the popularity of his brother
Germanicus, who had left behind him an immense
reputation among all who had known him. They
reflected on the rapacity of the powerful members of
the senate, and what errors the senate had committed when it was in power before. Moreover, they
took into account the impracticability of having the
senate handle affairs,[c] and also considered that if the
government again passed into the hands of a single
ruler they would take a risk upon themselves since
one individual would have gained the throne for himself, whereas it was possible for Claudius to receive it
by their motion and support. And Claudius would
then show his appreciation by an honorarium ade-
quate to such a service.

(3) They expounded their views to one another,
pondered them in their own minds, and reported
them to each group as it came in. They, on hearing
the report, welcomed the summons to action. They
closed their ranks about Claudius, wheeled around
and proceeded towards the camp, taking his litter

The
soldiers
decide to
proclaim
Claudius
emperor.

---

[a] Cf. Varro, Ling. Lat. v. 164, Tac. Ann. xii. 24, Diony.
i. 87. 3, and Livy i. 7.

[b] Lit. " public building." In Ant. xiii. 265-266 and xvi.
164 it refers to the public treasury. Suetonius, Claud. 10,
says that he was ultimately taken to the praetorian camp,
where he spent the night.

[c] Lit. " the impracticability of the matter."

227 μὴ ἐμποδίζοιτο αὐτοῖς ἡ ἔπειξις.¹ διειστήκεσαν δὲ
αἱ γνῶμαι τοῦ δήμου καὶ τῶν ἐκ τῆς βουλῆς· οἱ μὲν
ἀξιώματός τε τοῦ² πρότερον ὀρεγόμενοι καὶ δουλείαν ἔπακτον αὐτοῖς ὕβρει τῶν τυράννων γενομένην
228 φιλοτιμούμενοι διαδιδράσκειν χρόνῳ παρασχόν,³ ὁ
δὲ δῆμος φθόνῳ τε πρὸς ἐκείνην καθιστάμενος καὶ
τῶν πλεονεξιῶν αὐτῆς ἐπιστόμισμα τοὺς αὐτοκράτορας εἰδὼς καὶ αὐτοῦ καταφυγὴν ἔχαιρεν Κλαυδίου τῇ ἁρπαγῇ στάσιν⁴ τε ἔμφυλον, ὁποία καὶ ἐπὶ
Πομπηίου γένοιτο, ἀπαλλάξειν αὐτῶν ὑπελάμβα-
229 νον τοῦτον αὐτοκράτορα καθιστάμενον.⁵ γνοῦσα δ᾽
ἡ βουλὴ τὸν Κλαύδιον ὑπὸ τῶν στρατιωτῶν ἀφ-
ιγμένον εἰς τὸ στρατόπεδον πέμπει πρὸς ἐκεῖνον
ἄνδρας ἀρετῇ τοὺς ἐξ αὐτῶν προὔχοντας,⁶ οἳ δι-
δάξειαν μὴ δεῖν⁷ ἐπὶ καθέξει τῆς ἀρχῆς βιάζεσθαι,
230 παραχωρεῖν δὲ τῇ συγκλήτῳ τοσῶνδε ἀνδρῶν ἕνα
ὄντα ἡσσώμενον⁸ καὶ τῷ νόμῳ παραχωροῦντα τοῦ
ἐπὶ τοῖς κοινοῖς κόσμου τὴν πρόνοιαν, μνημονεύ-
οντα ὧν οἱ πρότεροι τύραννοι κακώσειαν τὴν πόλιν καὶ ὧν ὑπὸ Γαΐου καὶ αὐτὸς κινδυνεύσειεν σὺν
αὐτοῖς, μηδὲ μισήσαντα⁹ τὴν βαρύτητα τῆς τυραννίδος ὑφ᾽ ἑτέρων πρασσομένης τῆς ὕβρεως αὐτὸν
ἐθελουσίως ἐπὶ παροινίᾳ θαρσεῖν τῆς πατρίδος.
231 καὶ πειθομένῳ μὲν τοῦ πρότερον ἀπράγμονος τὴν

¹ MW : ἐπίδειξις A.
² E Lat. : οὐ codd.
³ Hudson : παρέσχον codd. ; χρόνῳ παρασχόν] om. Busb.
⁴ ed. pr. Lat. : πᾶσι codd.
⁵ Hudson : καθισταμένου codd. ; στάσιν . . . καθισταμένου]
tunc itaque paene bellum iam civile quale sub Pompeio fla-
grabat, quod tamen imperatore constituto sedatum est Lat.
⁶ αὐτῶν προὔχοντας] E : αὐτῶν codd. ; ἄνδρας . . . προὔ-
χοντας] viros de suo coetu virtute claros Lat.

on their shoulders in order that there might be no
drag on their speed. The will of the people and that
of the senators were at variance. The latter were
eager to regain their former prestige and earnestly
aspired, since after long years they now had the
chance, to escape a slavery brought upon them by
the insolence of the tyrants. The people, on the
other hand, were jealous of the senate, recognizing
in the emperors a curb upon the senate's encroach-
ments and a refuge for themselves. They rejoiced
in the seizure of Claudius, and supposed that his
securing the throne would avert from them any civil
strife such as had occurred in Pompey's day.[a] The
senate, having learned that Claudius had been
brought into the camp by the soldiers, sent some of
their men of superior character to impress on him
that he must not take forcible action to put himself
on the throne.[b] On the contrary, they said, he should
yield to the senate, submitting, as a single individual,
to so large a number of men, and allowing the law
to provide for the organization of the commonwealth.
He should remember what injuries former tyrants
had inflicted on the state and what perils he, along
with themselves, had undergone at the hands of
Gaius. Since he detested the cruelty of tyranny
when insolently practised by others, he should not
voluntarily take rash action and indulge in a burst
of violence against his fatherland. If he complied
and showed that his former good conduct in avoiding

[a] 49–46 B.C.
[b] Similarly Dio lx. 1. 4.

⁷ μὴ δεῖν] μηδὲν E et i. marg. A et ut vid. Lat.
⁸ A : ἢ ἐσόμενον MW.
⁹ μιμησάμενον Richards et Shutt.

ἀρετὴν ἐπιδεικνυμένῳ βέβαιον τιμάς τε ὑπάρξειν,
αἳ ὑπὸ ἐλευθέρων ψηφισθεῖεν τῶν πολιτῶν, καὶ
ἐπιχωρήσει τοῦ νόμου τὸ μέρος ἄρχοντά τε καὶ
232 ἀρχόμενον κερδανεῖν¹ ἔπαινον ἀρετῆς. εἰ δὲ ἀπο-
νοοῖτο μηδὲν ἐκ τῆς Γαΐου τελευτῆς σωφρονιζόμε-
νος οὔτι γε αὐτοὶ ἐπιτρέψειν· τῆς τε γὰρ στρατιᾶς
πολὺ εἶναι τὸ συνεστηκὸς αὐτοῖς ὅπλων τε εὐπορίαν
233 καὶ πληθὺν οἰκετῶν, οἳ χρήσαιντο αὐτοῖς.² μέγα
δὲ μέρος τήν τε ἐλπίδα εἶναι καὶ τὴν τύχην, τούς τε
θεοὺς οὐκ ἄλλοις συμμαχεῖν, ἀλλὰ τοῖς μετ' ἀρετῆς
καὶ τοῦ καλοῦ τοὺς ἀγῶνας ποιουμένοις. εἶναι δὲ
τούτους, οἳ ἂν περὶ ἐλευθερίας μάχωνται τῆς πατρίδος.

234 (4) Καὶ οἱ μὲν πρεσβευταὶ Οὐηράνιός³ τε καὶ
Βρόγχος,⁴ δήμαρχοι δὲ ἦσαν ἀμφότεροι, τοῖσδε
ἐχρῶντο τοῖς λόγοις καὶ καθικέτευον τοῖς γόνασιν
αὐτοῦ προσπεσόντες μηδαμῶς πολέμοις καὶ κακοῖς
ἐμβαλεῖν τὴν πόλιν, θεωροῦντες⁵ στρατιᾶς πληθύι
τὸν Κλαύδιον πεφραγμένον καὶ τὸ μηδὲν τοὺς ὑπά-
235 τους ὄντας συγκρίσει τῇ πρὸς αὐτόν. εἴ τε τῆς
ἀρχῆς ὀρέγοιτο, παρὰ τῆς βουλῆς δέχεσθαι διδο-
μένην· αἰσιώτερον γὰρ καὶ εὐδαιμονέστερον χρῆ-

¹ Niese : κερδαίνειν codd. E.
² οἳ χρήσαιντο αὐτοῖς] quibus adversus cum fortiter uteren-
tur Lat. : οἷς χρήσαιντο Hudson ex Lat.
³ ed. pr. ex Lat. : Οὐϊράνιός A : Οὐηΐράνιος M : Οὐϊηράνιος
W : γρ ἐν ἄλλοις Οὐράνιός i. marg. A.
⁴ Hudson : Βρόγχος A : Βρούχος MW : Βρόσχος E : Βρό-
χος Busb. : Bracchus Lat. : Βροῦτος Casaubonus.
⁵ θεωροῦντες] θεωροῦντες δὲ E.

322

trouble could be trusted to continue, he would obtain honours, which would be voted him by free citizens; for if he did his part in yielding to the law, he would gain plaudits for virtuous conduct whether as subject or as ruler. If, however, he was reckless and had learnt no wisdom from the death of Gaius, they certainly would not permit him to act thus; for they were supported by a large part of the army and were well supplied with arms and had a host of slaves to use them. Hope and Fortune, they remarked, were a large asset; and the gods seconded the efforts of those alone who strove to win without sacrificing moral and spiritual values, namely, those who fought for the freedom of their country.

(4) This message was delivered by the envoys Veranius [a] and Brocchus,[b] both tribunes of the people, who fell on their knees and besought him on no account to involve the city in wars and calamities; for they saw that Claudius was under protection of a large army and that the consuls were as nothing in comparison with him. They went on to say that if he sought the throne, he should receive it as a gift from the senate, for he would exercise it more aus-

---

[a] Quintus Veranius, tribunus plebis in 41 (so also *Inscr. Gr. ad Res Rom. per.* iii. 703), governor of Lycia (or Lycia-Pamphylia), consul in 49, governor of Britain in 58, where he died that same year (Tac. *Agr.* 14 and *Ann.* xiv. 29). From a new inscription discussed at length by A. E. Gordon ("Quintus Veranius Consul A.D. 49," *Univ. of Calif. Publ. in Class. Archaeol.* ii. 5, 1952, pp. 231-341), it appears that the emperor Claudius was connected with Veranius' being named to the consulship, and that during that year he was named augur and raised to the rank of patrician.

[b] The spelling in the MSS. varies: Bronchus, Brouchos, Broschus, Brochus, Bracchus. He is otherwise unknown. Of the various spellings only Brocchus is actually found in an inscription.

σθαι τὸν μὴ μετὰ ὕβρεως ἀλλ᾽ εὐνοίᾳ τῶν διδόντων
παραλαμβάνοντα.

236 (iv. 1) Κλαύδιος δέ, ἠπίστατο γὰρ μεθ᾽ οἵας
αὐθαδείας ἀποσταλεῖεν, καὶ πρὸς τὸ παρὸν γνώμῃ
τῇ αὑτῶν ἐπὶ τὸ μετριώτερον τρεπόμενος, οὐ μὴν
ἀλλὰ καὶ τῷ περὶ αὑτοὺς φόβῳ διαναστὰς ἅμα μὲν
θάρσει τῶν στρατιωτῶν ἅμα δὲ ᾿Αγρίππου τοῦ βασιλέως κελεύοντος μὴ¹ προέσθαι τῶν χειρῶν τηλι-
237 καύτην ἀρχὴν ἤκουσαν αὐτόματον. πράξας μὲν
καὶ περὶ Γάιον οἷον εἰκὸς ἄνδρα ὑπ᾽ αὐτοῦ διὰ
τιμῆς ἠγμένον, καὶ γὰρ τὸν νεκρὸν περιέσπεν² τοῦ
Γάιου καὶ ἀναθέμενος ἐπὶ κλίνης καὶ περιστείλας
ἐκ τῶν ἐνδεχομένων εἰς τοὺς σωματοφύλακας ὑπ-
εχώρει, ζῆν μὲν τὸν Γάιον ἀπαγγέλλων κακοπα-
θοῦντι³ δὲ⁴ ὑπὸ⁵ τραυμάτων ἰατροὺς μετέσεσθαι⁶
238 λέγων⁷· πυθόμενος δὲ τοῦ Κλαυδίου τὴν ὑπὸ τῶν
στρατιωτῶν ἁρπαγὴν ὠθεῖτο πρὸς αὐτὸν καὶ καταλαβὼν τεταραγμένον καὶ οἷόν τε ἐκχωρεῖν τῇ συγκλήτῳ ἀνήγειρεν ἀντιλαμβάνεσθαι κελεύων τῆς
239 ἡγεμονίας. ταῦτα δὲ πρὸς τὸν Κλαύδιον εἰπὼν
προσεχώρει πρὸς αὐτόν,⁸ καὶ μετακαλούσης αὐτὸν
τῆς βουλῆς χρισάμενος μύροις τὴν κεφαλὴν ὡς ἀπὸ

¹ om. Lat.
² Bekker: περιέπεσε (-σεν A¹) codd. E : περιέπλεξε Hudson.
³ κακοπαθοῦντα E.
⁴ MWE : γε A.
⁵ E Busb. : ἀπὸ codd.
⁶ A : μετίεσθαι M et i. marg. A : μεθίεσθαι W : μετελθεῖν
E : μετείσεσθαι coni. Niese dubitans.
⁷ καὶ γὰρ . . . λέγων] et eius lectum lugubriter prosecutus
Lat.
⁸ Hudson : αὐτόν codd.

---

ᵃ Cf. the parallel passage, B.J. ii. 206, where Agrippa has
the passive rôle and Claudius the active rôle, since it is

piciously and more fortunately if he obtained it not by violence but by favour of the donors.

(iv. 1) [a] Claudius knew with what contumacy they had been sent, but was for the present moved by their views to greater moderation. Nevertheless, he had recovered from his fear of them both because of the bold action of the soldiers and because of the advice of King Agrippa [b] not to let slip through his hands such an office which had come unsought. Agrippa had done for Gaius what was to be expected of one who had been held in honour by him For he attended to the corpse of Gaius, laid it upon a bier, and after dressing it with such materials as were at hand retired to the bodyguard and announced that Gaius was alive, saying that physicians would be arriving to aid him inasmuch as he was suffering from serious wounds. On hearing of the kidnapping of Claudius by the soldiers, Agrippa forced his way to him ; and finding him perplexed and on the point of yielding to the senate, he stirred him up and bade him make a bid for the empire. After these words to Claudius Agrippa returned home. On being summoned by the senate, he anointed his head with unguents as if he had arrived from a banquet that

*Agrippa persuades Claudius to become emperor and offers to persuade the senate.*

the latter who takes the initiative to summon the former— the reverse of the situation here. *Cf.* V. M. Scramuzza, *The Emperor Claudius,* 1940, pp. 58-59, who is justified in his scepticism of the account in the *Antiquities,* since it seems strange that the senators should think that they could win by persuasion what they could not obtain by force, especially since the senatorial envoys Veranius and Brocchus had already indicated (§§ 230-231) that the senate was ready to accept a compromise, namely that Claudius should receive his imperial power from the senate.

[b] Agrippa's rôle in helping to make Claudius emperor is also mentioned briefly by Dio lx. 8. 2.

συνουσίας γινομένης ἀναλύσεως αὐτῇ[1] παρῆν καὶ
240 ἤρετο τοὺς βουλευτάς, τί πέπραχε Κλαύδιος. τῶν
δὲ τὰ ὄντα φαμένων καὶ προσανερομένων, ἥντινα
γνώμην ἔχοι περὶ τοῖς ὅλοις, τελευτᾶν μὲν ὑπὲρ τοῦ
κατ᾽ ἐκείνην εὐκλεοῦς ἕτοιμος ἦν τοῖς λόγοις, σκο-
πεῖν δὲ ἐκέλευε περὶ τῷ συμφέροντι πᾶν ὅ τι καὶ
241 εἰς ἡδονὴν φέροι ὑπεξελομένους· χρείαν γὰρ εἶναι
τοῖς ἀρχῆς μεταποιουμένοις καὶ ὅπλων καὶ στρατιωτῶν, οἳ φράξαιντο αὐτοῖς, μὴ καὶ ἀπαράσκευοι
242 καταστάντες εἰς τάδε σφαλεῖεν. ἀποκριναμένης δὲ
τῆς βουλῆς ὅπλων τε εὐπορίαν καὶ χρήματα εἰσοί-
σειν, καὶ στρατιᾶς τὸ μέν τι αὐτοῖς εἶναι συνεστη-
κός, τὸ δὲ συγκροτήσειν ἐλευθερώσεως δούλων γενομένης. "εἴη μέν, ὦ βουλή," φησὶν ὁ Ἀγρίππας
ὑποτυχών, "πράσσειν ὁπόσα θυμὸς ὑμῖν, λεκτέον
δὲ οὐδὲν ἐνδοιάσαντί μοι διὰ τὸ ἐπὶ σωτηρίᾳ φέρειν
243 τὸν λόγον. ἴστε μὴν στρατόν, ὃς ὑπὲρ Κλαυδίου μα-
χεῖται, πλήθει χρόνου ὁπλιτεύειν μεμελετηκότα, τὰ δ᾽
ἡμέτερα, συγκλύδων ἀνθρώπων πλῆθος δ᾽ ἔσται καὶ
τῶν παρὰ δόξαν τῆς δουλείας ἀπηλλαγμένων, δυσ-
κράτητα. πρὸς δὲ τεχνίτας μαχούμεθα προαγαγόν-
244 τες ἄνδρας μηδ᾽ ὅπως σπάσαι τὰ ξίφη εἰδότας. ὥστε
μοι δοκεῖ πέμπειν ὡς Κλαύδιον πείσοντας κατατίθεσθαι τὴν ἀρχήν, πρεσβεύειν τε ἕτοιμός .εἰμι."
245 (2) Καὶ ὁ μὲν ταῦτα εἶπεν, καὶ συγκαταθεμένων
πεμφθεὶς σὺν ἑτέροις τήν τε ταραχὴν τῆς βουλῆς
διηγεῖται καταμόνας πρὸς τὸν Κλαύδιον ἐδίδασκέν
τε ἡγεμονικώτερον ἀποκρίνασθαι καὶ τῷ ἀξιώματι
246 τῆς ἐξουσίας χρώμενον. ἔλεγεν οὖν Κλαύδιος, οὐ

---

[1] Hudson : αὐτῶι ex corr. A : αὐτῷ MW.

[a] Cf. the parallel passage, B.J. ii. 208.

had just broken up, appeared before them and asked the senators what Claudius had done. They told him the state of affairs and asked him in return what he thought of the whole situation. He declared that he was ready to die for the honour of the senate, but bade them consider what was expedient and to set aside all personal predilections. For, he noted, those who made a bid to rule the state needed arms and soldiers for their defence, lest on taking a stand unprepared they should find that this was their fatal mistake. The senate replied that they were well supplied with arms and would contribute money, that they had something of an army standing by them, and that they would whip more troops into shape by liberating slaves. " May you succeed, senators," said Agrippa in reply, " in doing what you desire, but I must speak without shilly-shallying because my speech has a bearing on your security. You know, of course, that the army that will fight for Claudius has been long trained to bear arms, while ours will be a motley rabble consisting of men who have unexpectedly been released from slavery and who are consequently hard to control. We shall fight against experts, having brought into play men who do not even know how to draw their swords. Therefore my judgement is to send a deputation to Claudius to persuade him to lay down his office ; and I am ready to act as ambassador."

(2) So he spoke, and on their agreeing to his proposal he was dispatched with others. He thereupon recounted to Claudius in private the confusion of the senate and advised him to reply rather imperiously, speaking with the dignity of one in authority. <sup>a</sup> Claudius accordingly replied that he did not wonder

θαυμάζειν τὴν βουλὴν ἡδονῇ μὴ φέρουσαν ἄρχεσθαι
διὰ τὸ ὠμότητι τετρῦσθαι τῶν πρότερον ἐπὶ τὸ
ἡγεμονεύειν καταστάντων, γεύσειν τε αὐτοὺς ἐπι-
εικείᾳ τῇ καθ' αὑτὸν μετρίων καιρῶν, ὀνόματι μὲν
μόνῳ τῆς ἀρχῆς ἐσομένης, ἔργῳ δὲ κοινῆς πᾶσι
προκεισομένης¹ εἰς μέσον. διὰ πολλῶν δὲ καὶ
ποικίλων ὠδευκότι² πραγμάτων ἐν ὄψει τῇ ἐκείνων
247 καλῶς ἔχειν μὴ ἀπιστεῖν. καὶ οἱ μὲν πρέσβεις
τοιούτων ἀκροάσει λόγων καθομιληθέντες ἐξεπέμποντο. Κλαύδιος δὲ τῷ στρατῷ συλλεχθέντι δι-
ελέγετο ὅρκους λαμβάνων ἦ μὴν ἐμμενεῖν³ πίστει
τῇ πρὸς αὐτόν, δωρεῖται τοὺς σωματοφύλακας πεν-
τακισχιλίαις δραχμαῖς κατὰ ἕκαστον ἄνδρα, τοῖς τε
ἡγεμόσιν αὐτῶν ἀνάλογον τοῦ ἀριθμοῦ καὶ τοῖς
ὅποι ποτὲ στρατοπέδοις ὑπισχνεῖτο τὰ ὅμοια.

248 (3) Συνεκάλουν δὲ οἱ ὕπατοι τὴν βουλὴν εἰς τὸ
ἱερὸν τοῦ νικηφόρου Διός· ἔτι δὲ νὺξ ἦν. τῶν δὲ οἱ
μὲν ἐν τῇ πόλει κλέπτοντες ἑαυτοὺς ἐνεδοίαζον
πρὸς τὴν ἀκρόασιν, τοῖς δὲ ἐπὶ τῶν ἰδίων ἀγρῶν

---

¹ ἔργῳ . . . προκεισομένης] A : om. MW.
² Hudson : ὡδευκότας codd. : ὡδευκότων τῶν E.
³ Dindorf : ἐμμένειν codd. E.

---

ᵃ Cf. the parallel passage, B.J. ii. 208, where Claudius
similarly informs the senate through his envoy Agrippa that
he will be content with the honour of the title of emperor and
adds that even if he were not naturally moderate the death of
Gaius would be a sufficient warning to him to act thus.

ᵇ Or perhaps " the army."

ᶜ Balsdon, op. cit., p. 188, notes the discrepancy between
this figure in Josephus (=20,000 sesterces) and the figure
cited in Suetonius, Claud. 10 (15,000 sesterces =3750 drachmas) and remarks that the payment of this sum to the prae-

that the senate was not pleased at the prospect of submitting to authority because they had been oppressed by the brutality of those who had previously held the imperial office. But he promised to behave with such propriety that they would taste for themselves the savour of an era of fair dealing ; that only nominally would the government be his, that in reality it would be thrown open to all in common. Seeing that he had passed through many vicissitudes of fortune before their eyes, they would do well not to distrust him.[a] The envoys, conciliated by the words that they heard, were ushered out. Claudius assembled and addressed the army, binding them by oath that they would remain loyal to him. He presented the praetorian guard [b] with five thousand drachmas [c] apiece and their officers with a proportionate sum and promised similar amounts to the armies wherever they were.

(3) The consuls then called together the senate in the Temple of Jupiter Victor [d] while it was still night. Some of the senators who were in hiding in the city hesitated when they heard the summons ; others had departed to their private estates, fore-

Meeting of the senate in the Temple of Jupiter.

torian guard alone would have amounted to 135,000,000 sesterces.

[d] Livy x. 29. 14 and 18 refers to a vow by Q. Fabius Maximus Rullianus to build a temple to Jupiter Victor ; and Ovid, *Fasti* iv. 621-622, declares that the temple was dedicated on the Ides of April. Dio Cassius refers (xlv. 17. 2, xlvii. 40. 2) to temples or shrines to Ζεὺς Νίκαιος. But there is considerable doubt whether these refer to the same temple and where that temple was located. The epithet " Invictus " in inscriptions is probably an alternate for Victor. *Cf.* S. B. Platner and T. Ashby, *A Topographical Dictionary of Ancient Rome*, 1929, pp. 306-307. In the parallel passage (*B.J.* ii. 205), in Suetonius, *Calig.* 60, and in Dio lx. 1. 1 it is in the Capitol that the senate meets after Gaius' death.

ἐγεγόνεισαν ἔξοδοι προορωμένοις ᾗ χωρήσει τὸ
πᾶν ἐν ἀπογνώσει τοῦ ἐλευθέρου γεγονότος,[1] καὶ
πολὺ κρεῖττον ἐν ἀκινδύνῳ τοῦ δουλεύειν ὑπειληφότες διαβιοῦν ἀργίᾳ τοῦ πονεῖν ἢ κτώμενοι τὸ
ἀξίωμα τῶν πατέρων περὶ τῆς σωτηρίας ἀμφίβολοι
249 καταστῆναι. συνελέγησαν δ' ὅμως ἑκατὸν οὐ
πλείους, καὶ διαβουλευομένων περὶ τῶν ἐν χερσὶν
αἰφνίδιον αἴρεται βοὴ τοῦ συνεστηκότος αὐτοῖς
στρατιωτικοῦ στρατηγὸν αὐτοκράτορα κελευόντων
τὴν βουλὴν ἑλέσθαι καὶ μὴ φθείρειν πολυαρχίᾳ τὴν
250 ἡγεμονίαν. καὶ τὸ μὲν καθ' ἑαυτοὺς ἀπεφαίνοντο
περὶ τοῦ μὴ πᾶσιν, ἀλλ' ἑνὶ τὴν ἀρχὴν ἐφέσιμον
εἶναι, ὁρᾶν[2] δὲ ἐκείνοις ἐπιτρέπειν, ὅστις τοσαύτης
προστασίας ἄξιος. ὥστε ἐν ἀνίᾳ[3] τὰ τῶν συγκλητικῶν ἦν πολὺ πλέον δι' ἁμαρτίαν μὲν τοῦ κατὰ
τὴν ἐλευθερίαν αὐχήματος, φόβῳ δὲ τοῦ Κλαυδίου.
251 οὐ μὴν ἀλλ' ἦσαν οἱ ἐφιέμενοι γένους τε ἀξιώματι
καὶ οἰκειότησιν γάμου· καὶ γὰρ Βινίκιος[4] Μάρκος[5]
καὶ τὸ καθ' αὑτὸν γενναιότητι ἀξιόλογον ὄντα[6] καὶ
δὴ ἀδελφὴν Γαΐου γεγαμηκότα Ἰουλίαν, πρόθυμός
τε ἦν ἀντιποιεῖσθαι τῶν πραγμάτων, κατεῖχον δὲ οἱ
252 ὕπατοι πρόφασιν ἐκ προφάσεως ἀναρτῶντες. Οὐα-

---

[1] προορωμένοις . . . γεγονότος] prospicientes quoniam si
res ad effectum veniret in libertatis desperatione consisterent
Lat.   [2] ἐᾶν Naber.
[3] ἐν ἀνίᾳ] Niese : ἐνανίαι A : ἐναντία MW : contraria Lat. :
ἐν ἀδημονίᾳ E : τῷ δήμῳ ἐναντία coni. Richards et Shutt.
[4] coni. : Βινίκιος Naber: Μινουκιανὸς codd. : Μινουκιανὸν E.
[5] M : Μάρκου AWE.
[6] καὶ γὰρ . . . ὄντα] Minucianus namque Marcum forti-
tudine dignum Lat.

---

[a] Or perhaps " leisure for work."
[b] The parallel account, B.J. ii. 209, has the senate rejecting
Claudius' offer to rule with moderation and asserting that they

seeing how it would all come out. These latter despaired of liberty and deemed it far better to live out
their lives free from the perils of servitude and with
leisure from toil [a] than to maintain the dignity of
their fathers and have no assurance of surviving.
Nevertheless, one hundred—no more—assembled;
and, as they were deliberating [b] about the matter in
hand, suddenly a shout arose from the soldiers who
had stood by them, bidding the senate choose an
emperor [c] and not to ruin the empire by entrusting
it to a multitude of rulers. The senate replied that
they agreed that the government must be in the
hands not of everyone but of a single man, but they
must see to it that they put it in charge of someone
who was worthy of such pre-eminence. Thus the
position of the senators was much more distressing
because they had not retained the liberty about
which they were so eloquent and because they were
afraid of Claudius. Nevertheless, there were some
who aspired to the throne by reason both of their
distinguished birth and of their marriage connexions.
For instance, Marcus Vinicius [d] had a good claim
both because of his own noble birth and by his
marriage to Gaius' sister Julia. He was eager to
compete for the highest office but was restrained by
the consuls, who brought up one pretext after another.

*Rival claimants to the empire.*

will not submit to voluntary slavery. When Claudius hears
this he again sends Agrippa as his envoy to the senate and
threatens them with open war. It is only then that one of
the soldiers who has sided with the senate shouts out on
behalf of Claudius and rushes from the senate with his fellow
soldiers. Then the senators, now devoid of military support,
hurry to Claudius and capitulate.

[c] Or " a commander-in-chief."

[d] mss. Minucianus; *cf.* note on § 102. Variant " Vinicius
proposed Marcus, whose courage made him worthy . . . "

λέριον δὲ ᾿Ασιατικὸν Βινουκιανὸς[1] ἐκ τῶν Γαΐου
σφαγέων ἀνεῖχε τοιούτων διανοιῶν. ἐγεγόνει δ᾽
ἂν φόνος οὔ τινος ἐλάσσων ἐπιχωρηθέντων τῶν ἐπι-
θυμούντων τῆς ἡγεμονίας, ὥστε ἀντιτάξασθαι
253 Κλαυδίῳ, ἄλλως τε καὶ οἱ μονομάχοι, πλῆθος δ᾽
ἦν αὐτῶν ἀξιόλογον, καὶ τῶν στρατιωτῶν οἱ νυκτο-
φυλακοῦντες ἐπὶ τῆς πόλεως ἐρέται[2] τε ὁπόσοι
συνέρρεον εἰς τὸ στρατόπεδον, ὥστε τῶν μετιόντων
τὴν ἀρχὴν οἱ μὲν φειδοῖ τῆς πόλεως, οἱ δὲ καὶ φόβῳ
τῷ ὑπὲρ αὐτῶν ἀπέστησαν.

254 (4) Ὑπὸ δὲ πρώτην ἀρχὴν τῆς ἡμέρας καὶ Χαιρέας καὶ οἱ σὺν αὐτῷ παρελθόντες ἐν ἐπιχειρήσει
λόγων ἦσαν πρὸς τοὺς στρατιώτας. τῶν δὲ τὸ
πλῆθος ὡς ὁρᾷ παύσαντας[3] αὐτοὺς ταῖς χερσὶ καὶ
τοῦ εἰπεῖν οἵους τε ἄρχεσθαι, ἀνεθορύβησεν μὴ ἐφι-
έναι ὥστε εἰπεῖν διὰ τὸ ὡρμῆσθαι πάντας ἐπὶ τῷ
μοναρχεῖσθαι, τὸν δὲ ἡγησόμενον ἐκάλουν ὡς οὐκ
255 ἀνεξόμενοι τὰς τριβάς. τῇ συγκλήτῳ δὲ ἀπορία
ἄρχειν τε καὶ ὃν ἀρχθεῖεν ἂν τρόπον οὔτε δεχομένων
αὐτοὺς[4] τῶν στρατιωτῶν καὶ τῶν Γαΐου σφαγέων
256 συγχωρεῖν τοῖς στρατιώταις οὐκ ἐφιέντων. ἐν τοιούτοις δὲ ὄντων Χαιρέας τὴν ὀργὴν οὐκ ἀνασχόμενος
πρὸς τὴν αἴτησιν τοῦ αὐτοκράτορος δώσειν ἐπηγγέλλετο στρατηγόν, εἴ τις αὐτῷ σημεῖον παρὰ
257 Εὐτύχου κομίσειεν. ἦν δὲ ὁ Εὔτυχος οὗτος ἡνίοχος
τοῦ καλουμένου πρασίνου περισπούδαστος Γαΐῳ,
καὶ περὶ τὰς οἰκοδομὰς τῶν στάσεων τοῦ περὶ

---

[1] coni. Niese (cf. § 18) : Μινουκιανὸς codd.
[2] ed. pr. : αἱρεταί ex corr. A : αἱρεταί A¹MW : om. Lat.
[3] A : παύσοντας MW : παύοντας Niese.
[4] δεχομένων αὐτούς] Hudson : δεχομένους αὐτῶν codd.

---

[a] Cf. 102.    [b] mss. Minucianus ; cf. note on § 18.

Valerius Asiaticus [a] was restrained by Vinicianus,[b] who was one of Gaius' assassins, from similar designs.[c] There would have been a massacre second to none had those who coveted the empire been allowed to range themselves against Claudius. Above all, there were gladiators—and their number was considerable—and the soldiers of the night watch in the city and all the rowers of the fleet who were streaming into the camp. And so, of those who were candidates for the office, some withdrew in order to spare the city, others out of fear for themselves.

(4) About the break of day Chaerea and his companions came forward and attempted to talk with the soldiers. The majority of the soldiers, when they saw these men raising their hands for attention and ready to begin addressing them, clamorously protested that they should not be allowed to speak, because all were bent on having a single ruler. They consequently demanded their future ruler, for they would brook no delay. The senate was unable either to govern or to decide how they should be governed, for, on the one hand, the troops rejected them and, on the other hand, the assassins of Gaius did not permit them to give way to the soldiers. In this contingency Chaerea, unable to restrain his indignation at the soldiers' petition for an emperor, promised to give them a leader if someone would bring him the password from Eutychus. This Eutychus was a charioteer of the so-called " green faction," a great favourite of Gaius [d]; and the soldiers wore them- The senate is helpless in the face of the soldiers.

---

[c] A third candidate proposed for the throne was Galba, the future emperor (Suet. *Galba* 7).

[d] There were four factions, named after their colours, *albata* (white), *prasina* (leek-green), *russata* (red), and *veneta* (blue). Suetonius, *Calig.* 55, also reports the ardour with

ἐκεῖνον ἱππικοῦ[1] τὸ στρατιωτικὸν ἐτρίβετο[2] ἀτί-
258 μοις ἐργασίαις ἐπικείμενον. εἰς ἅπερ ὁ Χαιρέας
ὠνείδιζεν αὐτοὺς καὶ ἕτερα πολλὰ τοιαῦτα, τήν τε
κεφαλὴν κομιεῖν τοῦ Κλαυδίου· δεινὸν γάρ, εἰ μετὰ
259 μανίαν παραφροσύνῃ δώσουσι τὴν ἡγεμονίαν. οὐ
μὴν διετράπησάν γε ὑπὸ τῶν λόγων, ἀλλὰ σπασά-
μενοι τὰς μαχαίρας καὶ τὰ σημεῖα ἀράμενοι ᾧχοντο
ὡς τὸν Κλαύδιον κοινωνήσοντες τοῖς ὁμνύουσιν
αὐτῷ. κατελείπετο δὲ ἥ τε σύγκλητος ἐπ' ἐρημίας
τῶν ἀμυνούντων καὶ οἱ ὕπατοι μηδὲν ἰδιωτῶν δια-
260 φέροντες. ἔκπληξίς τε καὶ κατήφεια ἦν, οὐδ' ὅτι
χρήσαιντο αὐτοῖς τῶν ἀνθρώπων εἰδότων διὰ τὸ
ἀνηρεθίσθαι τὸν Κλαύδιον ἐπ' αὐτοῖς, ἀλλήλοις τε
261 ἐλοιδοροῦντο, καὶ μετάμελος ἦν αὐτοῖς.[3] καὶ Σαβῖνος εἷς τῶν Γαΐου σφαγέων σφάζειν πρότερον
αὐτὸν ἠπείλει παρελθὼν εἰς μέσους ἢ Κλαύδιον
ἄρχοντα στήσεσθαι καὶ δουλοκρατίαν ἐπόψεσθαι
καταλαβοῦσαν, τόν τε Χαιρέαν εἰς φιλοψυχίαν ἐπέ-
πλησσεν, εἰ καταφρονήσας Γαΐου πρῶτος[4] ἀγαθὸν
ὑπολαμβάνοι τὸ ζῆν τῆς ἐλευθερίας οὐδ' οὕτως
262 ἀποδοθῆναι δυναμένης τῇ πατρίδι. Χαιρέας δὲ
περὶ μὲν τοῦ θνήσκειν ἐνδοίαστον οὐδὲν φρονεῖν
ἔλεγεν, βούλεσθαι μέντοι διακωδωνίζειν διάνοιαν
τὴν Κλαυδίου.
263 (5) Καὶ οἱ μὲν ἐν τοῖσδε ἦσαν. ἐπὶ δὲ τοῦ στρα-

---

[1] τοῦ περὶ ἐκεῖνον ἱππικοῦ] ed. pr.: τοὺς περὶ ἐκεῖνον (ἐκείνων W) ἱππικοὺς codd.
[2] ἡνίοχος . . . ἐτρίβετο] agitator prasini Gaio et militibus
circa sollemnitates circensium et seditiones Lat.
[3] αὐτοῖς] suspectum indicat Niese.
[4] πρῶτον coni. Thackeray.

---

which Gaius supported the green faction.  He adds that

selves out building stables for his horses, being
assigned to tasks that were beneath them. This and
many other things of the sort Chaerea cast in their
teeth, and bade them bring the head of Claudius ; for
it would be monstrous, he said, if after being ruled
by a madman they should hand over the empire to
an addlepate. [a] The soldiers, however, were not de-
terred by his words, but drawing their swords and
hoisting their standards, went off to Claudius to make
common cause with those who were swearing alle-
giance to him. The senate was left without supporters,
and the consuls had no more authority than private
individuals. There was consternation and dejection,
for the senate knew not what course to take inasmuch as Claudius was incensed with them ; and they
berated one another and were sorry for what they
had done. Then Sabinus,[b] one of Gaius' assassins,
stepped forward into their midst and threatened to
kill himself rather than to set up Claudius as ruler and
witness their country in the grip of a slave-govern-
ment. He reproached Chaerea with cowardice, if
after showing contempt for Gaius he was the first
to regard life as a blessing when liberty could not
even thus be restored to the fatherland. Chaerea
replied that he had no hesitation in his mind about
dying, but that he wished to sound out the intentions
of Claudius.

(5) Such was the situation in the senate. Mean-

Gaius would frequently dine and spend the night in their
stables and that he once gave the driver Eutychus 2,000,000
sesterces in gifts. He provided his favourite horse, Incitatus,
with a home, slaves, and furniture, and planned, according
to report, to make him a consul.

[a] Cf. the parallel passage, B.J. ii. 211.
[b] Cf. § 46.

τοπέδου πανταχόθεν ὠθεῖτο κατὰ θεραπείαν.[1] καὶ
τῶν ὑπάτων ὁ ἕτερος Κόιντος Πομπώνιος[2] δι'
αἰτίας ἦν τῷ στρατιωτικῷ μᾶλλον ὡς ἐπ' ἐλευθερίᾳ[3]
τὴν σύγκλητον παρακαλῶν, ὥρμησάν τε σπασά-
μενοι τὰ ξίφη, κἂν ἐπέπρακτο αὐτοῖς μὴ Κλαυδίου
264 διακεκωλυκότος. παρακαθίζεται δὲ αὐτῷ τὸν
ὕπατον ἐξαρπάσας τοῦ κινδύνου, τῶν δὲ συγκλητικῶν ὅσον[4] ἦν σὺν τῷ Κοΐντῳ οὔ[5] μεθ' ὁμοίας
ἐδέχετο τιμῆς· τινὲς δὲ καὶ πληγὰς ἔλαβον αὐτῶν
ἀνωθούμενοι τῆς πρὸς αὐτὸν ἐντεύξεως, Ἀπώνιος[6]
δὲ τραυματίας ἀνεχώρει, ἦν τε κίνδυνος περὶ πάν-
265 τας αὐτούς. καὶ Ἀγρίππας ὁ βασιλεὺς προσελθὼν
τῷ Κλαυδίῳ ἀξιοῖ τοῖς συγκλητικοῖς ἠπιώτερον
καταστῆναι· γενομένου γάρ τινος κακοῦ περὶ τὴν
266 βουλὴν οὐχ ἕξειν ὧν ἄρξειεν ἑτέρων. πείθεται δὲ
Κλαύδιος καὶ συγκαλεῖ τὴν βουλὴν ἐπὶ τοῦ Παλατίου διὰ τῆς πόλεως φερόμενος παραπέμποντος
αὐτὸν τοῦ στρατιωτικοῦ σὺν πολλῇ πάνυ κακώσει
267 τῆς πληθύος.[7] προεξῄεσαν δὲ τῶν Γαΐου σφαγέων
εἰς τὸ φανερώτερον Χαιρέας καὶ Σαβῖνος εἰργόμενοι
προόδων κατ' ἐπιστολὰς Πολλίωνος, ὃν μικρῷ
πρότερον Κλαύδιος στρατηγὸν ᾕρητο[8] τῶν σωματο-

---

[1] θεραπείαν] θεραπείαν Κλαυδίου A.
[2] Hudson : Πομπήϊος codd. E Lat. ; cf. B.J. ii. 205.
[3] Niese : ἐλευθερίας codd. : ἐλευθερίαν E.
[4] Niese : ὃς codd. E : ὁ ed. pr.
[5] A : ὃ M : ὁ W.  [6] Apolinus Lat.
[7] σὺν πολλῇ . . . πληθύος] cum multo nimis impetu atque
ridiculo Lat.
[8] Bekker : ᾑρεῖτο (εἷτο i. ras. pressius scriptum A) AE :
ᾕρετο MW.

---

[a] Variant " respects to Claudius."
[b] Q. Pomponius Secundus, consul suffectus in 41. He

while, from all quarters men came hurrying towards the camp to pay their respects.[a] One of the two consuls, Quintus Pomponius,[b] was especially guilty in the eyes of the troops for summoning the senate in the cause of liberty. Drawing swords they rushed at him and would have murdered him had not Claudius intervened. Having rescued the consul from peril, Claudius took his seat beside him, but he did not receive the rest of the senators who accompanied Quintus with like honour. Some of them even received blows from the soldiers, who repulsed their attempts to get an audience with him. Aponius [c] retired wounded, and they were all in danger. King Agrippa then approached Claudius, and besought him to take a kinder attitude to the senators; for if any harm came to the senate, he would have no other subjects over whom to rule. Claudius agreed and summoned the senate to the Palatine, whither he was borne through the city, escorted by the soldiers, who dealt very harshly with the crowd. Of the assassins of Gaius, Chaerea and Sabinus had now come forward more openly, but they were prevented from advancing by the instructions of Pollio,[d] whom Claudius had shortly before chosen as praetorian prefect.

*Agrippa urges Claudius to spare the senators.*

later joined in a rebellion against Claudius (Tac. *Ann.* xiii. 43).

[c] Perhaps to be identified with Aponius Saturninus, who once, having fallen asleep during an auction conducted under Gaius' auspices, kept nodding his head until he had bought thirteen gladiators for 9,000,000 sesterces (Suet. *Calig.* 38).

[d] Rufrius Pollio. He later accompanied Claudius on his British campaign and was honoured by receiving the right to sit in the senate (Dio lx. 23. 2). If, as seems likely (so Stein, in Pauly-Wissowa, 2. Reihe, i, 1920, p. 1202), he is identical with Rofius (Rufius) Pomfilius (Sen. *Apocol.* 13. 5), he was among those later put to death by Claudius.

268 φυλάκων. Κλαύδιος δέ, ἐπείπερ εἰς τὸ Παλάτιον
ἀφικνεῖται συναγαγὼν τοὺς ἑταίρους¹ ψῆφον ἀνεδί-
δου περὶ Χαιρέου. τοῖς δὲ τὸ μὲν ἔργον λαμπρὸν
ἐδόκει, ἀπιστίαν δ' ἐπεκάλουν τῷ πεπραχότι καὶ
αὐτῷ τιμωρίαν ἐπιβάλλειν δίκαιον ἡγοῦντο ἐπ'
269 ἀποτροπῇ τοῦ μέλλοντος χρόνου.² ἀπήγετο οὖν
τὴν ἐπὶ θανάτῳ καὶ σὺν αὐτῷ Λοῦππός³ τε καὶ
Ῥωμαίων πλείους. λέγεται δὲ Χαιρέας μεγαλοφρόνως ἐνεγκεῖν τὴν συμφορὰν οὐ μόνον τῷ κατ'
αὐτὸν ἀμεταπτώτῳ τοῦ σχήματος, ἀλλὰ καὶ οἷς
ὀνειδίσειεν Λοῦππον εἰς δάκρυα ἐκτετραμμένον.⁴
270 ἀποτιθεμένου γέ τοι τὴν στολὴν τοῦ Λοῦππου καὶ
τὸ ῥῖγος⁵ αἰτιωμένου φησίν, ὡς οὐκ ἂν ἐναντία τοῦ
λούππου ποιήσαιτο πώποτε ῥῖγος. πλήθους τε ἀνθρώπων ἑπομένου κατὰ θέαν, ὡς ἧκεν ἐπὶ τὸ
χωρίον, ἤρετο τὸν στρατιώτην, εἰ διὰ μελέτης αὐτῷ
γεγόνοιεν αἱ σφαγαὶ ἢ εἰ πρῶτον ἔχοι τὸ ξίφος⁶
ἐκέλευέ τε⁷ κομίζειν ᾧ Γάιον μεταχειρίσαιτο αὐτός·
θνήσκει δὲ εὐδαιμόνως μιᾶς πληγῆς αὐτῷ γενο-
271 μένης. Λοῦππος δὲ οὐ πάνυ δεξιῶς ὑπεξῆλθεν
ἀθυμίᾳ καὶ πληγῶν πλειόνων γενομένων διὰ τὸ
μαλακῶς τὸν τράχηλον παρασχεῖν.

¹ MW : ἑτέρους A : alios Lat.
² ἀπιστίαν . . . χρόνου] sed Pollioni praecipue causam
mortis applicabant, qui tantum opus fieri persuaserat et ut
ipse pariter pro merito futuri temporis deperiret iustum esse
clamabant Lat.
³ Λοῦπος E (sed Λοῦππος Busb.).
⁴ resolutum Lat. : ἐκκεχυμένον Richards et Shutt.
⁵ ἀποτιθεμένου . . . ῥῖγος] om. E Lat.
⁶ εἰ διὰ . . . ξίφος] si interficiendi meditationem haberet
Lat. ; lacunam vel ante vel post τὸ ξίφος indicat Niese.

When Claudius reached the Palatine, he assembled his companions and put the case of Chaerea to a vote.[a] Their verdict was that the deed had been a splendid one; but they accused its perpetrator of disloyalty and thought it right to inflict punishment upon him as a deterrent for the future. Chaerea was accordingly led off to be executed, and with him Lupus [b] and several other Romans. It is reported that Chaerea bore his fate with great dignity, as was evident not only by his own unchanged countenance, but also by his reproach of Lupus, who had given way to tears. Indeed, when Lupus took off his robe and complained of the cold,[c] Chaerea remarked that "cold could never harm a wolf."[d] A crowd of people followed to see the sight. When Chaerea reached the place of execution he asked the soldier whether he had had practice in executions or whether this was the first time that he had held a sword and bade him bring the sword [e] with which he himself had dispatched Gaius. He was fortunate to be slain by the first blow. Lupus, for want of courage, was not very skilful in making his exit ; he received several blows because he stuck his neck out so gingerly.

[a] Dio lx. 3. 4 says that though Claudius was pleased that Gaius had been assassinated, he was displeased that an emperor had been assassinated, and so he put Chaerea and some others to death since he sought to insure his own safety.

[b] The military tribune who had slain Gaius' wife and daughter (§§ 190-200).

[c] This occurred a few days after Gaius' assassination on 24 January.

[d] There is a play on *lupus*, the Latin word for wolf.

[e] There is perhaps a slight lacuna here in the text, in which the soldier replied to Chaerea's question.

---

[7] ἐκέλευέ τε] E : rogavitque Lat. : καὶ ἐκέλευε ed. pr.: ἐκέλευε codd.

272 (6) Ὀλίγαις δὲ ὕστερον ἡμέραις ἐναγισμῶν ἐνεστηκότων Ῥωμαίων τὸ πλῆθος τοῖς αὐτῶν[1] ἐπι-
φέροντες καὶ Χαιρέαν μοίραις ἐτίμησαν εἰς τὸ πῦρ
τιθεμέναις, ἵλεων καὶ ἄμηνιν εἶναι τῆς εἰς αὐτὸν
ἀχαριστίας παρακαλοῦντες. καὶ Χαιρέᾳ μὲν τοι-
273 αύτη τελευτὴ τοῦ βίου συνέτυχεν. Σαβῖνος δὲ
Κλαυδίου μὴ μόνον τῆς αἰτίας παραλύοντος αὐτὸν
ἀλλὰ καὶ τὴν ἀρχὴν ἣν εἶχεν ἐφιέντος, ἄδικον
ἡγεῖτο τὴν ἐκλειπίαν τῆς πρὸς τοὺς συνωμότας
πίστεως, σφάζει θ᾽[2] ἑαυτὸν περιπεσὼν τῷ ξίφει
μέχρι[3] δὴ καὶ τὴν κώπην τῷ τραύματι συνελθεῖν.
274 (v. 1) Κλαύδιος δὲ τοῦ στρατιωτικοῦ πᾶν ὅ τι
ἦν ὕποπτον ἐκ τοῦ ὀξέος ἀποσκευασάμενος διάγραμμα προὐτίθει τήν τε ἀρχὴν Ἀγρίππᾳ βεβαιῶν,
ἣν ὁ Γάιος παρέσχε, καὶ δι᾽ ἐγκωμίων ἄγων τὸν
βασιλέα. προσθήκην τε αὐτῷ ποιεῖται πᾶσαν τὴν
ὑπὸ Ἡρώδου βασιλευθεῖσαν, ὃς ἦν πάππος αὐτοῦ,
275 Ἰουδαίαν καὶ Σαμάρειαν. καὶ ταῦτα μὲν ὡς
ὀφειλόμενα τῇ οἰκειότητι τοῦ γένους ἀπεδίδου·
Ἄβιλαν[4] δὲ τὴν Λυσανίου καὶ ὁπόσα ἐν τῷ Λιβάνῳ
ὄρει ἐκ τῶν αὐτοῦ προσετίθει, ὅρκιά τε αὐτῷ τέμ-
νεται πρὸς τὸν Ἀγρίππαν ἐπὶ τῆς ἀγορᾶς μέσης ἐν

---

[1] αὐτῶν Richards et Shutt, qui ἀπαρχὰς post αὐτῶν add.
[2] σφάζει θ᾽] coni. Niese : σφάζει codd. : σφάζει τε E : καὶ
σφάζει Suidas.
[3] μέχρι] μέχρι τοῦ coni. Richards et Shutt.
[4] Α : Ἄβελλαν M : Ἄβελαν W : Ἀβηλαν E : Abelan Lat.

---

[a] Since Gaius was murdered on 24 January, the reference
would seem to be to the Parentalia, 13-21 February. *Cf.*
Ovid, *Fasti* ii. 533 ff., for a description of the ceremonies,
which were performed annually at the tombs of the deceased.
[b] Sabinus' suicide is also mentioned by Dio lx. 3. 5.

(6) A few days later,[a] when the sacrifices to the dead were offered, the Roman people brought offerings to their deceased relatives and honoured Chaerea also with portions that they cast into the flames, beseeching him to be gracious and not vengeful because of their ingratitude to him. Such was the end of Chaerea's life. As for Sabinus, he was not only released by Claudius from the charge but allowed to retain the office which he held. Nevertheless, deeming it wrong to fail in loyalty to his fellow conspirators, he slew himself, falling upon his sword till the hilt actually reached the wound.[b]

(v. 1) [c] Claudius speedily purged the army of all unreliable units. He then promulgated an edict whereby he both confirmed the rule of Agrippa, which Gaius had presented to him, and delivered a panegyric on the king.[d] He also added to Agrippa's dominions all the other lands that had been ruled by King Herod, his grandfather, namely, Judaea and Samaria.[e] He restored these lands to him as a debt due to his belonging to the family of Herod. But he also added Abila,[f] which had been ruled by Lysanias,[g] and all the land in the mountainous region of Lebanon as a gift out of his own territory, and he celebrated a treaty with Agrippa in the middle of the

*Claudius confirms Agrippa in his kingdom and adds to it.*

---

[c] §§ 274-275 are parallel with *B.J.* ii. 215-216.

[d] Dio lx. 8. 2 adds that Claudius bestowed the rank of consul on Agrippa and the rank of praetor on Agrippa's brother Herod ; he then permitted them to enter the senate and to express their thanks to him in Greek.

[e] Also, according to *B.J.* ii. 215, Trachonitis and Auranitis, which Augustus had presented to Herod.

[f] Or Abela, on the northern slope of Mount Hermon, north-west of Damascus. *Cf. Ant.* xx. 138.

[g] See note on *Ant.* xviii. 237. Lysanias the tetrarch of Abilene is also mentioned in Luke iii. 1.

276 τῇ ᾿Ρωμαίων πόλει. ᾿Αντίοχον δὲ ἦν εἶχεν βασιλείαν ἀφελόμενος Κιλικίας μέρει τινὶ καὶ Κομ-
μαγηνῇ δωρεῖται. λύει δὲ καὶ ᾿Αλέξανδρον¹ τὸν
ἀλαβάρχην φίλον ἀρχαῖον αὐτῷ γεγονότα καὶ
᾿Αντωνίαν αὐτοῦ ἐπιτροπεύσαντα τὴν μητέρα ὀργῇ
τῇ Γαΐου δεδεμένον, καὶ αὐτοῦ υἱὸς Βερενίκην τὴν
277 ᾿Αγρίππου γαμεῖ θυγατέρα. καὶ ταύτην μέν, τελευτᾷ γὰρ Μᾶρκος ὁ τοῦ ᾿Αλεξάνδρου υἱὸς παρ-
θένον λαβών, ἀδελφῷ τῷ αὐτοῦ ᾿Αγρίππας ῾Ηρώδῃ
δίδωσιν Χαλκίδος αὐτῷ τὴν βασιλείαν εἶναι αἰτη-
σάμενος παρὰ Κλαυδίου.

278 (2) Στασιάζεται δὲ κατ᾽ αὐτὸν τὸν χρόνον ᾿Ιου-
δαίων² τὰ πρὸς ῞Ελληνας ἐπὶ τῆς ᾿Αλεξανδρέων
πόλεως. τελευτήσαντος γὰρ τοῦ Γαΐου τὸ ᾿Ιου-
δαίων ἔθνος³ ἐπὶ ἀρχῆς τῆς ἐκείνου τεταπεινωμέ-

¹ ᾿Αλέξανδρον] A : ᾿Αλέξανδρον Λυσίμαχον MWE : γρ Λυσίμαχον i. marg. A : Lysimachum Lat.
² ᾿Ιουδαίοις E.
³ γένος E.

ᵃ An alliance of Agrippa with the senate and the Roman
people is depicted on a coin, for which see F. W. Madden,
*Coins of the Jews*, 1881, pp. 136-137.
ᵇ Gaius had named Antiochus IV king of Commagene in
northern Syria in 38 and added the Cilician coast to his
realm (Dio lix. 8. 2). His kingdom was taken from him
shortly thereafter by Gaius, but it was soon returned to him
by Claudius in 41 (Dio lx. 8. 1). He was deprived of his
kingdom in 72. *Cf. B.J.* v. 461 and vii. 219-243 ; and *Ant.*
xviii. 140, xix. 338 and 355, and xx. 139.
ᶜ For Claudius' maintenance of the Roman policy of
establishing protectorates on the fringe of the empire even at
the expense of incorporated territory see also *Ant.* xix. 351
and 362, xx. 104 and 138 ; *B.J.* ii. 215-217, 223, and 247, vii.
97 ; and Dio lx. 8. 1 (cited by J. G. C. Anderson, in *Camb.
Anc. Hist.* x, 1934, p. 752). The kingdom of which Antio-

Forum in the city of Rome.[a]  He deprived Antiochus [b]
of the kingdom that he held, and presented him with
a portion of Cilicia and with Commagene.[c]  He
further liberated Alexander [d] the alabarch,[e] an old
friend of his, who had acted as guardian for his mother
Antonia and had been imprisoned by Gaius in a fit
of anger.  The son [f] of Alexander married Berenice,
the daughter of Agrippa.  After the death of Marcus,
son of Alexander, who was her first husband, Agrippa
gave her to his own brother Herod,[g] after asking
Claudius to give him the kingdom of Chalcis.[h]

(2) About this time, there arose a feud between
Jews and Greeks in the city of Alexandria.  For upon
the death of Gaius, the Jews, who had been humili-

Strife of
Greeks and
Jews in
Alexandria.

chus was deprived may have been in southern Lycaonia
north of the Taurus, since numismatic evidence indicates
that he ruled this area at one time.  More likely it is Josephus
who is confused, since it appears that the kingdom of which
Antiochus was deprived was Commagene, and that it was
Gaius who deprived him of it (*cf.* Dio lx. 8. 1).  It was then
restored to Antiochus by Claudius, as we learn also in Dio
lx. 8. 1.  See D. Magie, *Roman Rule in Asia Minor*, ii, 1950,
pp. 1367-1368 n. 49.

[d] Some mss. add " Lysimachus," but this is a gloss, as
noted by J. Schwartz, " Note sur la famille de Philon d'Ale-
xandrie," *Ann. d. l'Inst. d. Philol. et d'hist. or. et sl. : univ.
libre d. Brux.* xiii, 1953 ( = Mélanges Isidore Lévi), p. 596.

[e] *Cf. Ant.* xviii. 159 ff.

[f] Marcus Julius Alexander.  His name occurs frequently
in the ostraca of Nicanor, one of whose leading customers he
was during the period from 37 to 43/44.  These ostraca indicate that Marcus had important business dealings with Arab
countries and with India.  See A. Fuks, " Notes on the
Archive of Nicanor," *Jour. of Juristic Papyr.* v, 1951, pp.
207-216, esp. 214-215.

[g] The marriage took place in 43 or 44, as indicated by
A. Fuks, " Marcus Julius Alexander " [in Hebrew], *Zion*
xiii-xiv, 1948-1949, pp. 15-17.

[h] In the Lebanon valley : *cf. B.J.* i. 185.

νον καὶ δεινῶς ὑπὸ τῶν Ἀλεξανδρέων ὑβρισμένον[1]
279 ἀνεθάρσησέ τε καὶ ἐν ὅπλοις εὐθέως ἦν. καὶ Κλαύδιος ἐπιστέλλει τῷ ἐπαρχοῦντι[2] κατὰ τὴν Αἴγυ-
πτον ὥστε τὴν στάσιν καταστεῖλαι, πέμπει δὲ καὶ
διάγραμμα παρακεκληκότων αὐτὸν Ἀγρίππου τε
καὶ Ἡρώδου τῶν βασιλέων εἴς τε τὴν Ἀλεξάνδρειαν καὶ Συρίαν γεγραμμένον τοῦτον τὸν τρό-
280 πον· " Τιβέριος Κλαύδιος Καῖσαρ Σεβαστὸς Γερ-
281 μανικὸς[3] δημαρχικῆς ἐξουσίας λέγει.[4] ἐπιγνοὺς
ἀνέκαθεν τοὺς ἐν Ἀλεξανδρείᾳ Ἰουδαίους Ἀλεξανδρεῖς λεγομένους συγκατοικισθέντας[5] τοῖς πρώ-

[1] A: βιαζόμενον MWE.
[2] Dindorf: ἱππαρχοῦντι codd.: praefecto Lat.: ὑπαρχοῦντι
coni. Niese.
[3] ἀρχιερεὺς μέγιστος post Γερμανικὸς add. Hudson.
[4] λέγει] ὕπατος λέγει E.
[5] Dindorf: συγκατωκισθέντας (-ησθ- W) codd.

---

[a] Probably C. Vitrasius Pollio, but perhaps it is his successor L. Aemilius Rectus.

[b] The edict which follows mentions the rights of the Alexandrian Jews only, but presumably a similar edict, *mutatis
mutandis*, reaffirmed the civic rights granted the Jews of
Syria by Seleucus Nicator (*Ant.* xii. 119).

[c] Hudson adds " pontifex maximus," to make this edict
parallel with the edict sent by Claudius to the rest of the
world (§ 287). In his letter to the Alexandrians later in the
year (London Papyrus 1912 : published by H. I. Bell, *Jews
and Christians in Egypt*, 1924, pp. 1-37), Claudius also
refers to himself as pontifex maximus.

[d] There has been considerable debate as to the meaning
of the term Ἀλεξανδρεῖς (" Alexandrians "). If it means
simply " inhabitants of Alexandria," the edict would be
redundant in speaking of the Jewish inhabitants of Alexandria who are called inhabitants of Alexandria ; moreover,
the Greek says " so-called Alexandrians," with the implication that this is a technical term meaning something different
from mere inhabitants of Alexandria. Perhaps the term

ated under his rule and grievously abused by the Alexandrians, took heart again and at once armed themselves. Claudius commanded the prefect *a* of Egypt to put down the factional war. In addition, on the petition of Kings Agrippa and Herod, he issued an edict to Alexandria and Syria *b* to the following effect : " Tiberius Claudius Caesar Augustus Germanicus,*c* of tribunician power, speaks. Having from the first known that the Jews in Alexandria called Alexandrians *d* were fellow colonizers

Claudius' edict to Alexandria and Syria on behalf of the Jews.

'Αλεξανδρεῖς refers to the entire Greek population of Alexandria, whether citizens or not ; the term " called Alexandrians " would then mean that the Jews, because of the degree to which they were Hellenized, were indistinguishable from the Greek inhabitants of Alexandria. But such a " popular " use is unlikely in a legal document. A clue to the meaning of " Alexandrians " in the edict is, it would appear, to be found in a papyrus dating from the reign of Augustus (*B.G.U.* 1140 = V. A. Tcherikover, *Corpus Papyrorum Judaicarum*, no. 151), in which a man calling himself an Alexandrian petitions the Roman governor Gaius Turannius. Someone—it is not clear who—has substituted " a Jew from Alexandria " for " Alexandrian " in the papyrus ; and the most likely assumption, as indicated by V. A. Tcherikover, *Hellenistic Civilization and the Jews*, 1959, p. 312, is that when the Jew presented the petition he asserted his claim to civic rights, but that he was unable to prove this and hence was forced to designate himself merely as an inhabitant of Alexandria. The term " Alexandrians," therefore, probably implies civic rights ; " called Alexandrians " means that the Jews are alleged to have civic rights (πολιτεία). Thus in *Contra Apionem* ii. 38, Josephus mentions Apion's astonishment at the idea of Jews being called Alexandrians ; this indicates that Apion saw no basis for the claim. V. A. Tcherikover, *Corpus Papyrorum Judaicarum*, i, 1957, p. 41 n. 102, who has made a careful study of the papyrological documents, concludes that the term 'Αλεξανδρεῖς was applied to the whole body of citizens of Alexandria. Since, however, the papyri seem to speak of ἀστοί as distinct from 'Αλεξανδρεῖς, perhaps, though there is no evidence to prove it, the ἀστοί

345

τοις εὐθὺ καιροῖς Ἀλεξανδρεῦσι καὶ ἴσης πολιτείας
παρὰ τῶν βασιλέων τετευχότας, καθὼς φανερὸν

were those citizens who were enrolled in tribes and demes,
while the Ἀλεξανδρεῖς were citizens who were not thus enrolled (so M. Radin, *The Jews among the Greeks and Romans*,
1915, pp. 110-111), since, as Tcherikover, *ibid.*, has noted,
such an enrolment was probably connected with certain
pagan religious practices which would be repugnant to Jews.

 *a* Cf. *B.J.* ii. 487 and *Ap.* ii. 42, which record that Alexander the Great, as a reward for Jewish support against the
Egyptians, granted the Jews permission to colonize Alexandria on terms of equality (ἐξ ἰσομοιρίας, var. ἐξ ἰσοτιμίας)
with the Greeks.

 *b* Or perhaps " citizenship." There is a huge literature
on the question as to whether or not the Jews were citizens of
Alexandria. W. W. Tarn, *Hellenistic Civilization*,[3] 1952, p.
221, asserts that it is inconceivable that the Jews were citizens
of Alexandria or of any other Greek city since full citizenship
entailed worship of the city gods, and this meant apostasy
to the Jews. Perhaps, though we have no evidence, the Jews
were granted an exemption from this worship by the Ptolemies, just as in later times they were granted exemption by
the Roman emperors from worship of the emperors as gods ;
and in any case, as I have indicated (" The Orthodoxy of the
Jews of Hellenistic Egypt," *Jewish Soc. Stud.* xxii, 1960), the
Jews of Alexandria were probably not as orthodox as was
formerly thought, and we know from the papyri that there
were some Jews at least who were citizens. Elsewhere (*Ant.*
xiv. 188) Josephus says explicitly that Julius Caesar set up a
bronze tablet for the Jews in Alexandria declaring that they
were citizens (πολῖται) of Alexandria. Moreover, Philo, *In
Flacc.* 47, speaks of Jewish citizens ; and in *In Flacc.* 78-80,
while not explicitly stating that the Jews were citizens, he
does say that the Jews were classed with the Alexandrians
when it came to the method whereby they might be beaten.
But the publication of London Papyrus 1912 has led most
scholars to conclude that the Jews were not citizens. In this
papyrus Claudius addresses the Alexandrians (Ἀλεξανδρεῖς
μέν, line 82) and the Jews (Ἰουδέοις δέ, line 88), with the contrast clearly marked by the μέν and δέ ; hence the Jews were
not legally " Alexandrians," citizens of Alexandria. A

346

from the very earliest times *a* jointly with the Alexandrians and received equal civic rights *b* from the

crucial phrase in the letter (line 95) speaks of the Jews as
living " in a city not their own " (ἐν ἀλλοτρίᾳ πόλει) ; and it is
unlikely that Claudius, who appears impartial in the rest of
the letter, would thus speak of the Jews if they were citizens
of Alexandria. Finally, the letter forbids the Jews to partici-
pate in the athletic contests presided over by the gymnasi-
archs and cosmetae, and it is probable (though admittedly
somewhat doubtful : see S. Davis, *Race Relations in Ancient
Egypt*, 1952, pp. 106-107) that participation in these games
was restricted to citizens. It is possible that Claudius composed the edict quoted by Josephus under the influence of
Agrippa and before he had really heard the arguments on
both sides, and that later in the same year (41), when he had
had an opportunity to review the evidence more thoroughly,
he revised his views as to the Jewish rights. But the letter
(lines 87-88) indicates that there had been an official hearing
before the issuance of the edict. It is also possible that the
situation in Alexandria, or Claudius' view of the situation,
had changed between the time that he had issued the edict
and the time that he sent the letter, and that perhaps, as indicated by Tcherikover, *Corpus*, i, pp. 72-73, he was particularly disgusted by new factors indicated in the letter, namely,
the sending of delegations by two separate factions of the
Jewish community (perhaps, though it is only a guess, those
who were citizens and those who were not : so A. Momigliano, *Claudius*, 1934, p. 97), and the influx of Jews into
Alexandria from the Egyptian countryside and from Palestine. It is more likely that Claudius, as Tcherikover, pp.
71-73, has indicated, was not hasty in issuing the edict, and
that the letter did not contradict the edict. T. Zieliński,
" L'Empereur Claude et l'idée de la domination mondiale
des Juifs," *Rev. de l'Univ. de Brux.* xxxii, 1926–1927, pp.
128-148, wrongly assuming the identity of the edict and
the letter, asserts that the former was completely forged.
T. Reinach, " L'Empereur Claudius et les Juifs," *Rev. d. Ét.
juives* lxxix, 1924, pp. 125-126, seeking to reconcile the two,
proposes the elimination from the edict of the sentence on
equality of rights. Tcherikover, pp. 70-71 n. 45, attempts
to reconcile the two by asserting that parts of the edict are a
forgery, namely, the reference to the Jews as Alexandrians,

347

ἐγένετο ἐκ τῶν γραμμάτων τῶν παρ' αὐτοῖς καὶ
282 τῶν διαταγμάτων, καὶ μετὰ τὸ τῇ ἡμετέρᾳ ἡγεμονίᾳ Ἀλεξάνδρειαν ὑπὸ τοῦ Σεβαστοῦ ὑποταχθῆναι
πεφυλάχθαι αὐτοῖς τὰ δίκαια ὑπὸ τῶν πεμφθέντων
ἐπάρχων κατὰ διαφόρους χρόνους μηδεμίαν τε
ἀμφισβήτησιν περὶ τούτων γενομένην τῶν δικαίων
283 αὐτοῖς, ἅμα καὶ καθ' ὃν καιρὸν Ἀκύλας ἦν ἐν
Ἀλεξανδρείᾳ τελευτήσαντος τοῦ τῶν Ἰουδαίων
ἐθνάρχου τὸν Σεβαστὸν μὴ κεκωλυκέναι ἐθνάρχας
γίγνεσθαι βουλόμενον ὑποτετάχθαι ἑκάστους ἐμμέ-
νοντας τοῖς ἰδίοις ἔθεσιν καὶ μὴ παραβαίνειν ἀναγ-
284 καζομένους τὴν πάτριον θρησκείαν,[1] Ἀλεξανδρεῖς
δὲ ἐπαρθῆναι κατὰ τῶν παρ' αὐτοῖς Ἰουδαίων[2] ἐπὶ
τῶν Γαΐου Καίσαρος χρόνων τοῦ διὰ τὴν πολλὴν
ἀπόνοιαν καὶ παραφροσύνην, ὅτι μὴ παραβῆναι

[1] ἐπιγνοὺς . . . θρησκείαν] om. E.
[2] ἴσης πολιτείας τοῖς ἄλλοις Ἀλεξανδρεῦσι τετυχηκότων post
Ἰουδαίων add. E.

the statement that the Jews lived in Alexandria from the
very earliest times, and the assertion that the Jews enjoyed
ἴση πολιτεία with the Alexandrians. He suggests that the
first passage in the edict ran perhaps as follows: ἐπιγνοὺς
ἀνέκαθεν τοὺς ἐν Ἀλεξανδρείᾳ Ἰουδαίους, συγκατοικισθέντας ἐκ
πολλῶν χρόνων Ἀλεξανδρεῦσι καὶ ἰδίας πολιτείας παρὰ τῶν βασιλέων τετυχότας, etc. But there is no necessary contradiction:
(1) The Jews *claim* that they are Alexandrians, whereas
Claudius does not commit himself on the question; (2) It is
not unduly biased for Claudius to assert that the Jews were
residents of Alexandria from the earliest times—in the letter
he says that they have been inhabitants from olden times (ἐκ
πολλῶν χρόνων)—since this does not mean that they are en-
titled to citizenship; (3) The term ἴση πολιτεία may mean not
" equal citizen status " but equal status as a community
(πολίτευμα : see Davis, *op. cit.* pp. 101-104); and we know
that the Jewish community of Alexandria was autonomous

kings.[a] as is manifest from the documents in their possession and from the edicts ; and that after Alexandria was made subject to our empire by Augustus their rights were preserved by the prefects sent from time to time, and that these rights of theirs have never been disputed ; moreover, that at the time when Aquila was at Alexandria, on the death of the ethnarch of the Jews, Augustus did not prevent the continued appointment of ethnarchs,[b] desiring that the several subject nations should abide by their own customs and not be compelled to violate the religion of their fathers ; and learning that the Alexandrians rose up in insurrection against the Jews in their midst in the time of Gaius Caesar, who through his great folly and madness humiliated the Jews because they re-

under its own ethnarchs, as is indicated by the edict, § 283. H. Stuart Jones, " Claudius and the Jewish Question in Alexandria," *Jour. of Rom. Stud.* xvi, 1926, p. 28, suggests that the members of a πολίτευμα no doubt called each other πολῖται and referred to the bestowal of their πολιτεία on entering members of the community. In any case, Philo and Josephus, particularly the latter, since he was removed from the scene, may well be guilty of wishful thinking in their apologetics ; and their legal and technical terminology is likely to be looser than that of the emperor Claudius, whose letter on papyrus is, after all, first-hand evidence of what the emperor actually said.

[a] The Ptolemies. So also *B.J.* ii. 488.

[b] Philo, *In Flacc.* 74, apparently contradicts Josephus when he says that a council of elders (γερουσία) was appointed by Augustus to manage Jewish affairs after the death of the genarch (who must be the same as the ethnarch : see H. Box, *Philonis Alexandrini In Flaccum*, 1939, p. 102). Reinach, *op. cit.* p. 124 n. 5, suggests that the text of Josephus has probably been altered and that ἄρχοντας should be read for ἐθνάρχας. Box, p. 103, however, suggests that the discrepancy may be resolved by supposing that Augustus established a γερουσία, over which the ethnarch was to preside.

ἠθέλησεν τὸ Ἰουδαίων ἔθνος τὴν πάτριον θρησκείαν
καὶ θεὸν προσαγορεύειν αὑτόν, ταπεινώσαντος
285 αὐτούς· βούλομαι μηδὲν διὰ τὴν Γαΐου παραφροσύνην τῶν δικαίων τῷ Ἰουδαίων ἔθνει παραπε-
πτωκέναι, φυλάσσεσθαι δ᾽ αὐτοῖς καὶ τὰ πρότερον
δικαιώματα ἐμμένουσι τοῖς ἰδίοις[1] ἔθεσιν, ἀμφο-
τέροις τε διακελεύομαι τοῖς μέρεσι πλείστην ποιήσασθαι πρόνοιαν, ὅπως μηδεμία ταραχὴ γένηται
μετὰ τὸ προτεθῆναί μου τὸ διάταγμα."[2]
286 (3) Τὸ μὲν οὖν εἰς Ἀλεξάνδρειαν ὑπὲρ τῶν Ἰουδαίων διάταγμα τοῦτον ἦν τὸν τρόπον γεγραμ-
μένον· τὸ δ᾽ εἰς τὴν ἄλλην οἰκουμένην εἶχεν οὕτως[3]·
287 " Τιβέριος Κλαύδιος Καῖσαρ Σεβαστὸς Γερμανικὸς
ἀρχιερεὺς μέγιστος δημαρχικῆς ἐξουσίας ὕπατος
288 χειροτονηθεὶς τὸ δεύτερον λέγει. αἰτησαμένων με
βασιλέως Ἀγρίππα καὶ Ἡρώδου τῶν φιλτάτων
μοι, ὅπως συγχωρήσαιμι τὰ αὐτὰ δίκαια καὶ τοῖς
ἐν πάσῃ τῇ ὑπὸ Ῥωμαίοις ἡγεμονίᾳ Ἰουδαίοις
φυλάσσεσθαι, καθὰ καὶ τοῖς ἐν Ἀλεξανδρείᾳ,
ἥδιστα συνεχώρησα οὐ μόνον τοῦτο τοῖς αἰτησα-
289 μένοις με χαριζόμενος, ἀλλὰ καὶ αὐτοὺς ὑπὲρ ὧν
παρεκλήθην ἀξίους κρίνας διὰ τὴν πρὸς Ῥωμαίους
πίστιν καὶ φιλίαν, μάλιστα δὲ δίκαιον κρίνων μηδεμίαν μηδὲ Ἑλληνίδα πόλιν τῶν δικαίων τούτων
ἀποτυγχάνειν, ἐπειδὴ καὶ ἐπὶ τοῦ θείου Σεβαστοῦ
290 αὐταῖς ἦν τετηρημένα. καλῶς οὖν ἔχειν[4] καὶ
Ἰουδαίους τοὺς ἐν παντὶ τῷ ὑφ᾽ ἡμᾶς κόσμῳ τὰ
πάτρια ἔθη ἀνεπικωλύτως φυλάσσειν, οἷς καὶ αὐτοῖς
ἤδη νῦν παραγγέλλω μου ταύτῃ τῇ φιλανθρωπίᾳ
ἐπιεικέστερον χρῆσθαι καὶ μὴ τὰς τῶν ἄλλων

fused to transgress the religion of their fathers by addressing him as a god ; I desire that none of their rights should be lost to the Jews on account of the madness of Gaius, but that their former privileges also be preserved to them, while they abide by their own customs ; and I enjoin upon both parties to take the greatest precaution to prevent any disturbance arising after the posting of my edict."

(3) Such was the tenor of the edict sent to Alex- Claudius' andria on behalf of the Jews. And that to the rest of edict to the the world ran as follows : " Tiberius Claudius Caesar world. Augustus Germanicus Pontifex Maximus, of tribunician power, elected consul for the second time, speaks : Kings Agrippa and Herod, my dearest friends, having petitioned me to permit the same privileges to be maintained for the Jews throughout the empire under the Romans as those in Alexandria enjoy, I very gladly consented, not merely in order to please those who petitioned me, but also because in my opinion the Jews deserve to obtain their request on account of their loyalty and friendship to the Romans. In particular, I did so because I hold it right that not even Greek cities should be deprived of these privileges, seeing that they were in fact guaranteed for them in the time of the divine Augustus. It is right, therefore, that the Jews throughout the whole world under our sway should also observe the customs of their fathers without let or hindrance. I enjoin upon them also by these presents to avail themselves of this kindness in a more reasonable spirit,

---

¹ A : 'Ιουδαίων MWE.
² A : διάγραμμα MWE : dicta Lat.
³ τὸ μὲν . . . οὕτως] καὶ εἰς τὴν ἄλλην οἰκουμένην ἔστειλε διάγραμμα ταῦτα φράζον E.
⁴ ἔχει coni. Niese.

ἐθνῶν δεισιδαιμονίας ἐξουθενίζειν, τοὺς ἰδίους δὲ
291 νόμους φυλάσσειν. τοῦτό μου τὸ διάταγμα τοὺς
ἄρχοντας τῶν πόλεων καὶ τῶν κολωνιῶν καὶ μουνι-
κιπίων τῶν ἐν τῇ Ἰταλίᾳ καὶ τῶν ἐκτός, βασιλεῖς
τε καὶ δυνάστας διὰ τῶν ἰδίων πρεσβευτῶν ἐγ-
γράψασθαι βούλομαι ἐκκείμενόν τε ἔχειν οὐκ ἔλατ-
τον ἡμερῶν τριάκοντα ὅθεν ἐξ ἐπιπέδου καλῶς
ἀναγνωσθῆναι δύναται."

292 (vi. 1) Τούτοις μὲν δὴ τοῖς διατάγμασιν εἰς
Ἀλεξάνδρειάν τε καὶ τὴν· οἰκουμένην πᾶσαν ἀπο-
σταλεῖσιν ἐδήλωσεν ἣν περὶ Ἰουδαίων ἔχοι γνώμην
Κλαύδιος Καῖσαρ· αὐτίκα δὲ Ἀγρίππαν κομιού-
μενον τὴν βασιλείαν ἐπὶ τιμαῖς λαμπροτέραις ἐξέ-
πεμψε τοῖς ἐπὶ τῶν ἐπαρχιῶν ἡγεμόσιν καὶ τοῖς
ἐπιτρόποις διὰ γραμμάτων ἐπιστείλας ἐράσμιον
293 ἄγειν αὐτόν. ὁ δ', ὡς εἰκὸς ἦν τὸν ἐπὶ κρείττοσιν
τύχαις ἀνερχόμενον, μετὰ τάχους ὑπέστρεψεν, εἰς
Ἱεροσόλυμα δ' ἐλθὼν χαριστηρίους ἐξεπλήρωσε
294 θυσίας οὐδὲν τῶν κατὰ νόμον παραλιπών. διὸ καὶ
Ναζιραίων ξυρᾶσθαι διέταξε μάλα συχνούς, τὴν δὲ
χρυσῆν ἅλυσιν τὴν δοθεῖσαν αὐτῷ ὑπὸ Γαΐου ἰσό-
σταθμον τῇ σιδηρᾷ, ᾗ τὰς ἡγεμονίδας χεῖρας ἐδέθη,

---

ᵃ The last clause is practically identical with the Latin
formula *ut de plano recte legi possi(n)t*, " so that it (they)
can plainly be read from the ground," found abbreviated
*u.d.p.r.l.p.* in a law concerning the nomination of municipal
candidates (H. Dessau, *Inscr. Lat. Sel.²*, ii. 1, no. 6089, li; *cf.*
lxiii).

ᵇ The joy that one of Agrippa's subjects felt at his safe
return is to be seen in W. Dittenberger, *Or. Gr. Inscr. Sel.* i,
1903, no. 418, pp. 629-630.

ᶜ Lit. " shaven." It is hardly likely, as Whiston and
Mathieu-Herrmann translate the phrase, that Agrippa, who
was scrupulously observant of the Jewish religion (§ 331),
should have ordered the Nazirites to violate their vow of not

and not to set at nought the beliefs about the gods held by other peoples but to keep their own laws. It is my will that the ruling bodies of the cities and colonies and municipia in Italy and outside Italy, and the kings and other authorities through their own ambassadors, shall cause this edict of mine to be inscribed, and keep it posted for not less than thirty days in a place where it can plainly be read from the ground."[a]

(vi. 1) By these edicts which were sent to Alexandria and to the world at large Claudius Caesar showed what he had decided about the Jews. He forthwith sent Agrippa to take over his kingdom with more splendid honours than before, giving written instructions to the governors of the provinces and to the procurators to treat him as a special favourite. Agrippa naturally, since he was to go back with improved fortunes, turned quickly homewards. On entering Jerusalem, he offered sacrifices of thanksgiving, omitting none of the ritual enjoined by our law.[b] Accordingly he also arranged for a very considerable number of Nazirites to be shorn.[c] Moreover, he hung up, within the sacred precincts, over the treasure-chamber,[d] the golden chain which had

*Agrippa returns to Palestine and dedicates a golden chain.*

cutting their hair (Num. vi. 5). And even if the reference here is to temporary Nazirites, there is no indication that the time limit of all these Nazirites had simultaneously expired. It seems best, therefore, to assume that Agrippa had shouldered the expenses for the offerings of poor Nazirites. The same expression, *le-galeah*, " to shave," is found several times in the Mishnah, *Nazir* ii. 5 and 6 in the sense of " to bring the offerings of a Nazirite." The phrase is similarly to be interpreted in Acts xxi. 24. For a discussion of the origin of the phrase and for other Talmudic references see J. N. Epstein, " On the Terms of Naziriteship " [in Hebrew], in *Magnes Anniversary Book*, 1938, pp. 15-16.

[d] There were thirteen horn-shaped money-chests in the

353

τῆς στυγνῆς εἶναι τύχης ὑπόμνημα καὶ τῆς ἐπὶ τὰ
κρείττω μαρτυρίαν μεταβολῆς τῶν ἱερῶν ἐντὸς
ἀνεκρέμασεν περιβόλων ὑπὲρ τὸ γαζοφυλάκιον, ἵν'
ᾖ δεῖγμα καὶ τοῦ τὰ μεγάλα δύνασθαί ποτε πεσεῖν
295 καὶ τοῦ τὸν θεὸν ἐγείρειν τὰ πεπτωκότα· πᾶσι γὰρ
τοῦτ' ἐνεφάνιζεν ἡ τῆς ἁλύσεως ἀνάθεσις, ὅτι βασιλεὺς Ἀγρίππας ἀπὸ μικρᾶς αἰτίας εἰς δεσμώτην
ἀπέδυ τὸ πρὶν ἀξίωμα καὶ μετ' ὀλίγον τῆς πέδης
ἐκβὰς εἰς βασιλέα τοῦ πάλαι λαμπρότερον ἠγέρθη.
296 διὰ τούτων[1] ἐννοεῖσθαι, ὅτι τῆς ἀνθρωπίνης φύσεως
καὶ πᾶσιν[2] ὀλισθάνειν τὰ μεγέθη καὶ τὰ κλιθέντα
δύναται περιφανὲς λαβεῖν πάλιν ὕψος.
297 (2) Ἐντελῶς δ' οὖν θρησκεύσας τὸν θεὸν Ἀγρίππας Θεόφιλον μὲν τὸν Ἀνάνου τῆς ἀρχιερωσύνης
μετέστησεν, τῷ δὲ Βοηθοῦ Σίμωνι, τούτῳ Κανθη-
ρᾶς ἐπίκλησις ἦν, τὴν ἐκείνου προσένειμε τιμήν.

---

[1] διὰ τούτων] propter haec ergo Lat. : διὰ τοῦτ' οὖν Niese.
[2] MW : πεσεῖν A : spurium aut corruptum putat Niese.

forecourt ('azarah) of the temple, six of which were for
various kinds of freewill offerings (Mishnah, *Shekalim* vi. 5).
It is presumably one of these six that Agrippa hung his
golden chain.   J. Derenbourg, *Essai sur l'histoire et la
géographie de la Palestine*, 1867, p. 209 n. 1, says that this
chain is to be identified with the golden chains mentioned in
Mishnah, *Middot* iii. 8 ; but this is unlikely since the chains
mentioned in the Mishnah served as a ladder by which the
young priests could ascend and view the ornaments set over
the windows of the sanctuary, and it is improbable that
Agrippa's chain was of such size.

[a] *Ant.* xviii. 237.
[b] Cf. *Ant.* xviii. 123.
[c] Cf. *Ant.* xv. 320-322, xvii. 78, xviii. 109 and 136.   He is
perhaps to be identified (so H. Lichtenstein, " Die Fasten-
rolle," *Hebrew Union Coll. Ann.* viii-ix, 1931-1932, p. 300)
with the Simon the Righteous who is reported in the Talmud
(*Soṭah* 33a) to have heard a voice from the Holy of Holies in

been presented to him by Gaius,[a] equal in weight to
the one of iron with which his royal hands had been
bound, as a reminder of his bitter fortune and as a
witness to his reversal for the better, in order that it
might serve as a proof both that greatness may some-
time crash and that God uplifts fallen fortunes. For
the dedication of the chain was a symbol to show all
men that King Agrippa had on trifling grounds been
thrown into prison and been stripped of his former
rank, and that, not long after, he had stepped out of
his chains, and had been uplifted to rule as king with
greater glory than before. These things may lead us
to reflect that it lies in the nature of man for all
grandeurs to glide away and for fallen fortunes to
rise again to a resplendent eminence.

(2) Having thus fully discharged his service to God, Simon
Agrippa removed Theophilus [b] son of Ananus from Cantheras
the high priesthood and bestowed his high office on is appointed
Simon [c] son of Boethus,[d] surnamed Cantheras. Simon high priest.

the temple proclaiming "Annulled is the decree which the
enemy intended to introduce into the temple." The reference
is clearly to Caligula's order to have his statue brought into
the temple, since the account continues : " Then was Gaius
Caligula [the name is corrupted in the text] slain and his
decrees were annulled." It appears from Josephus that Simon
Cantheras was not appointed high priest until shortly after
Gaius' death, but he was certainly active as a priest in the
temple before then ; or we may follow the suggestion of P.
Winter, " Simeon der Gerechte und Caius Caligula," *Zeitsch.
f. Rel.- u. Geistesgesch.* vi, 1954, p. 73 n. 6, that Agrippa was
already exercising the functions of his office while still in
Rome (so Philo, *Leg.* 35) and that he may have appointed
Simon before his departure for Palestine, though Josephus in
the present passage says that he appointed him after he had
returned to Palestine and had expressed his thanks to God.
    [d] An Alexandrian. *Cf. Ant.* xv. 320, xvii. 78 and 339,

δύο δ' ἦσαν ἀδελφοὶ τῷ Σίμωνι καὶ πατὴρ Βοηθός, οὗ τῇ θυγατρὶ βασιλεὺς συνῴκησεν Ἡρώδης, ὡς
298 ἀνωτέρω δεδήλωται. σὺν τοῖς ἀδελφοῖς οὖν[1] τὴν ἱερωσύνην ἔσχεν ὁ Σίμων καὶ σὺν τῷ πατρί, καθὰ καὶ πρότερον ἔσχον οἱ Σίμωνος τοῦ Ὀνία παῖδες τρεῖς ὄντες ἐπὶ τῆς τῶν Μακεδόνων ἀρχῆς, ὅπερ ἐν ταῖς προαγούσαις γραφαῖς παρέδομεν.

299 (3) Καταστησάμενος δὲ τὰ περὶ τοὺς ἀρχιερεῖς οὕτως ὁ βασιλεὺς τοὺς Ἱεροσολυμίτας ἠμείψατο τῆς εἰς αὐτὸν εὐνοίας· ἀνῆκε γοῦν αὐτοῖς τὰ ὑπὲρ ἑκάστης[2] οἰκίας, ἐν καλῷ τιθέμενος ἀντιδοῦναι τοῖς ἠγαπηκόσιν στοργήν.[3] ἔπαρχον[4] δὲ ἀπέδειξεν παντὸς τοῦ στρατεύματος Σίλαν ἄνδρα πολλῶν αὐτῷ
300 πόνων συμμετασχόντα. παντάπασιν δὲ ὀλίγου χρόνου διελθόντος Δωρῖται νεανίσκοι τῆς ὁσιότητος προτιθέμενοι τόλμαν καὶ πεφυκότες εἶναι παραβόλως θρασεῖς Καίσαρος ἀνδριάντα κομίσαντες εἰς
301 τὴν τῶν Ἰουδαίων συναγωγὴν ἀνέστησαν. σφόδρα τοῦτο Ἀγρίππαν παρώξυνεν· κατάλυσιν γὰρ τῶν πατρίων αὐτοῦ νόμων ἐδύνατο. ἀμελλητὶ δὲ πρὸς Πούπλιον Πετρώνιον, ἡγεμὼν δὲ τῆς Συρίας οὗτος

[1] A : οὗ A¹MW.
[2] εἰς αὐτὸν . . . ἑκάστης] A : om. MW.
[3] ἐν καλῷ . . . στοργήν] om. E.
[4] A : ἵππαρχον MWE et i. marg. A : praefectum Lat.

xviii. 3. Niese, in the index to his edition, *s.v.* Βοηθός, says that the father of the Simon here mentioned seems to be different from the Boethus, father of the high priests Simon, Joazar, and Eleazar. Presumably Niese's suspicion is based on the long lapse of time between the two Simons, the first

had two brothers [a] and his father Boethus. Simon's
daughter was married to King Herod, as I explained
earlier.[b] Simon accordingly, as did his brothers and
father, obtained the high priesthood, repeating the
record of the three sons of Simon son of Onias under
the Macedonian rule, as we reported in an earlier account.[c]

(3) Having in this way taken care of the high
priesthood, the king recompensed the inhabitants of
Jerusalem for their goodwill to him by remitting to
them the tax on every house,[d] holding it right to
repay the affection of his subjects with a corresponding fatherly love. He also appointed as commander
of the entire army Silas, a man who had shared many
hardships with him. A very short time after this, The men of
certain young men of Dora,[e] who set a higher value Dora are
on audacity than on holiness and were by nature rebuked for
placing the
recklessly bold, brought an image of Caesar into the emperor's
synagogue of the Jews and set it up. This provoked statue in a
Agrippa exceedingly, for it was tantamount to an synagogue.
overthrow of the laws of his fathers. Without delay
he went to see Publius Petronius,[f] the governor of

having been appointed high priest about 24 B.C., the second
in A.D. 41. But it is clear from Josephus' reference to his
previous account of the marriage of Simon's daughter to
King Herod that he regarded the two Simons as identical.

[a] Joazar (*Ant.* xvii. 339, xviii. 3 and 26) and Eleazar (*Ant.*
xvii. 339, 341).

[b] *Ant.* xv. 320-322.

[c] *Ant.* xii. 224-225, 237-238.

[d] *Cf.* Mishnah *Baba Batra* i. 5, which mentions the
apparently common practice whereby citizens of a town are
compelled to contribute to the building of its walls.

[e] A city in Phoenicia (Hebrew *Dor*), somewhat north of
the modern village of *Tantura*, near Mount Carmel. *Cf. Ap.*
ii. 116, *Vita* 31, etc.

[f] *Cf. Ant.* xviii. 261 ff.

302 ἦν, παραγίνεται καὶ καταλέγει τῶν Δωριτῶν. ὁ δ'
οὐχ ἧττον ἐπὶ τῷ πραχθέντι χαλεπήνας, καὶ γὰρ
αὐτὸς ἔκρινεν ἀσέβειαν τὴν τῶν ἐννόμων παράβασιν,[1] τοῖς ἐπιστᾶσι[2] τῶν Δωριτῶν σὺν ὀργῇ ταῦτ'
303 ἔγραψεν· " Πούπλιος Πετρώνιος πρεσβευτὴς Τιβερίου Κλαυδίου Καίσαρος Σεβαστοῦ Γερμανικοῦ Δω-
304 ριέων[3] τοῖς πρώτοις λέγει. ἐπειδὴ τοσαύτη τόλμη
ἀπονοίας τινὲς ἐχρήσαντο ἐξ ὑμῶν, ὥστε μηδὲ διὰ
τὸ προτεθῆναι διάταγμα Κλαυδίου Καίσαρος Σεβαστοῦ Γερμανικοῦ περὶ τοῦ ἐφίεσθαι Ἰουδαίους
305 φυλάσσειν τὰ πάτρια πεισθῆναι ὑμᾶς αὐτῷ, τἀναντία δὲ πάντα πρᾶξαι, συναγωγὴν Ἰουδαίων κω-
λύοντας εἶναι διὰ τὸ μεταθεῖναι ἐν αὐτῇ τὸν Καίσαρος ἀνδριάντα, παρανομοῦντας οὐκ εἰς μόνους
Ἰουδαίους, ἀλλὰ καὶ εἰς τὸν αὐτοκράτορα, οὗ ὁ
ἀνδριὰς βέλτιον ἐν τῷ ἰδίῳ ναῷ ἢ ἐν ἀλλοτρίῳ ἐτί-
θετο καὶ ταῦτα ἐν τῷ τῆς συναγωγῆς τόπῳ, τοῦ
φύσει δικαιοῦντος[4] ἕνα ἕκαστον τῶν ἰδίων τόπων
306 κυριεύειν κατὰ τὸ Καίσαρος ἐπίκριμα· τοῦ γὰρ
ἐμοῦ ἐπικρίματος μιμνήσκεσθαι γελοῖόν ἐστιν μετὰ
τὸ τοῦ αὐτοκράτορος διάταγμα τοῦ ἐπιτρέψαντος
Ἰουδαίοις τοῖς ἰδίοις ἔθεσι χρῆσθαι, ἔτι μέντοι γε
καὶ συμπολιτεύεσθαι τοῖς Ἕλλησιν κεκελευκότος·
307 τοὺς μὲν παρὰ τὸ διάταγμα τοῦ Σεβαστοῦ τοιαῦτα
τετολμηκότας,[5] ἐφ' ᾧ καὶ αὐτοὶ ἠγανάκτησαν οἱ
δοκοῦντες αὐτῶν ἐξέχειν[6] οὐ τῇ ἰδίᾳ προαιρέσει

---

[1] καὶ γὰρ . . . παράβασιν] om. E.
[2] coni. Post : ἀποστᾶσι codd. : indisciplinatis Lat. : προ-
εστῶσι coni. Niese.
[3] A : Δωριαίων MW : γρ Δωριτῶν i. marg. A.
[4] τοῦ φύσει δικαιοῦντος] τῇ φύσει δικαίου ὄντος Hudson.
[5] εἰς τὴν Ἰουδαίων συναγωγὴν μετατεθεικότας τὸν ἀνδριάντα
post τετολμηκότας add. E.

358

Syria, and denounced the people of Dora. Petronius was no less angry at the deed, for he too regarded the breach of law as sacrilege. He wrote in anger to the leaders [a] of Dora as follows : " Publius Petronius, legate of Tiberius Claudius Caesar Augustus Germanicus, to the leading men of Dora speaks : Inasmuch as certain of you have had such mad audacity, notwithstanding the issuance of an edict of Claudius Caesar Augustus Germanicus pertaining to the permission granted the Jews to observe the customs of their fathers, not to obey this edict, but to do the very reverse, in that you have prevented the Jews from having a synagogue by transferring to it an image of Caesar, you have thereby sinned not only against the law of the Jews, but also against the emperor, whose image was better placed in his own shrine than in that of another, especially in the synagogue ; for by natural law each must be lord over his own place, in accordance with Caesar's decree. For it is ridiculous for me to refer to my own decree after making mention of the edict of the emperor which permits Jews to follow their own customs, yet also, be it noted, bids them to live as fellow citizens with the Greeks. As for those who have, in defiance of the edict of Augustus, been so rash as to act thus— at which deed even those who are regarded as eminent among the transgressors are indignant and assert that it was done not because anyone deliberately and

[a] mss. " apostates." But it is clear from the address in § 303 and from § 307 that Petronius is speaking to the leaders and that he is making a distinction between these leaders and the irresponsible young men of Dora.

[6] E et i. marg. A : ἐξεκείνου A : ἐξελεῖν MW ; οἱ δοκοῦντες αὐτῶν ἐξέχειν] eorum iudices Lat.

γεγενῆσθαι λέγοντες ἀλλὰ τῇ τοῦ πλήθους ὁρμῇ,
ὑπὸ ἑκατοντάρχου Πρόκλου Οὐιτελλίου¹ ἐκέλευσα
ἐπ' ἐμὲ ἀναχθῆναι τῶν πεπραγμένων λόγον ἀπο-
308 δώσοντας,² τοῖς δὲ πρώτοις ἄρχουσι παραινῶ, εἰ
μὴ βούλονται δοκεῖν κατὰ τὴν αὐτῶν προαίρεσιν
γεγενῆσθαι τὸ ἀδίκημα, ἐπιδεῖξαι τοὺς αἰτίους τῷ
ἑκατοντάρχῃ μηδεμιᾶς στάσεως μηδὲ μάχης ἐῶντας
ἀφορμὴν γενέσθαι, ἥνπερ δοκοῦσίν μοι θηρεύεσθαι
309 διὰ τῶν τοιούτων ἔργων, κἀμοῦ καὶ τοῦ τιμιωτά-
του μοι βασιλέως Ἀγρίππου οὐδενὸς μᾶλλον³ προ-
νοουμένων, ἢ ἵνα μὴ ἀφορμῆς δραξάμενοι τὸ τῶν
Ἰουδαίων ἔθνος ὑπὸ τῆς ἀμύνης προφάσει⁴ συν-
310 αθροισθὲν εἰς ἀπόνοιαν χωρῇ. ἵνα δὲ γνωριμώτε-
ρον ᾖ, τί καὶ ὁ Σεβαστὸς περὶ ὅλου τοῦ πράγματος
ἐφρόνησε, τὰ ἐν Ἀλεξανδρείᾳ αὐτοῦ διατάγματα
προτεθέντα προσέθηκα,⁵ ἅπερ εἰ καὶ γνώριμα πᾶσιν
εἶναι δοκεῖ, τότε καὶ ἐπὶ τοῦ βήματος ἀνέγνω ὁ
τιμιώτατός μοι βασιλεὺς Ἀγρίππας δικαιολογη-
σάμενος περὶ τοῦ μὴ δεῖν αὐτοὺς ἀφαιρεθῆναι τῆς
311 τοῦ Σεβαστοῦ δωρεᾶς. εἴς τε οὖν τὸ λοιπὸν παραγγέλλω μηδεμίαν πρόφασιν στάσεως μηδὲ ταραχῆς
ζητεῖν, ἀλλ' ἑκάστους τὰ ἴδια ἔθη θρησκεύειν."
312 (4) Πετρώνιος μὲν οὖν οὕτω προυνόησε διορθώ-
σεως μὲν τὸ παρανομηθὲν ἤδη τυχεῖν, γενέσθαι δὲ
313 παραπλήσιον μηδὲν εἰς αὐτούς.⁶ Ἀγρίππας δὲ ὁ
βασιλεὺς ἀφείλετο μὲν τὴν ἀρχιερωσύνην τὸν Καν-

---

¹ M : Οὐιτελίου AW : Οὐϊτενίου E.

personally proposed it, but by an impulse of the mob
—I have given orders that they are to be brought
before me by Proclus Vitellius the centurion to give
an account of their actions. To the ranking magistrates I give this warning : that, unless they wish to
have it thought that the wrong was committed with
their consent and intent, they must point out the
guilty parties to the centurion, allowing no occasion
to occur that could lead to strife or battle. For this,
in my opinion, is precisely what they hope to achieve
by such actions. For both King Agrippa, my most
honoured friend, and I have no greater interest than
that the Jews should not seize any occasion, under
the pretext of self-defence, to gather in one place
and proceed to desperate measures. And, that you
may be better informed of His Imperial Majesty's
policy concerning the whole matter, I have appended
his edicts which were published at Alexandria. Although they seem to be universally known, my most
honoured friend King Agrippa read them before my
tribunal at the time when he pleaded that the Jews
ought not to be despoiled of the privileges granted
by Augustus. For the future, therefore, I charge
you to seek no pretext for sedition or disturbance,
but to practise severally each his own religion."

(4) Such were the precautions taken by Petronius
to rectify the breach of law that had already occurred
and to prevent any similar offence against the Jews.
King Agrippa deprived Simon Cantheras of the high Agrippa
proposes to
replace

---

2 παρανομοῦντας οὐκ εἰς μόνους Ἰουδαίους, ἀλλὰ καὶ εἰς τὸν
αὐτοκράτορα post ἀποδώσοντας add. E.    3 ἧττον E.

4 ὑπὸ τῆς ἀμύνης προφάσει] ὑπὲρ τῆς ἀμύνης προφάσει E :
ἀμύνης προφάσει Dindorf : ὑπὸ τῆς ἀμύνης προφάσεως ed. pr.

5 ed. pr. : προέθηκα codd. : praeposui Lat.

6 εἰς αὐτούς] εἰσαῦθις coni. Richards et Shutt.

JOSEPHUS

θηρᾶν¹ Σίμωνα, Ἰωνάθην δὲ πάλιν ἐπ' αὐτὴν ἦγεν
τὸν Ἀνάνου τοῦτον ἀξιώτερον τῆς τιμῆς ὁμολογῶν
εἶναι. τῷ δὲ οὐκ ἀσμενιστὸν ἐφάνη τὴν τοσαύτην
ἀπολαβεῖν τιμήν, παρῃτεῖτο δ' οὖν ταῦτα λέγων·
314 " σοὶ μέν, ὦ βασιλεῦ, τετιμημένος χαίρω διὰ
ψυχῆς ἔχων τοῦθ' ὅ μοι γέρας δίδωσιν ἡ σὴ βουλή,²
καὶ πρὸς οὐδέν με τῆς ἀρχιερωσύνης ἄξιον ἔκρινεν
ὁ θεός. ἅπαξ δ' ἐνδὺς στολισμὸν ἱερὸν ἀρκοῦμαι·
τότε γὰρ αὐτὸν ἡμφιασάμην ὁσιώτερον ἢ νῦν ἀπολή-
315 ψομαι. σὺ δ', εἰ βούλει τὸν ἀξιώτερον ἐμοῦ νῦν τὸ
γέρας λαβεῖν, διδάχθητι· πάσης καὶ πρὸς τὸν θεὸν
ἁμαρτίας καὶ πρὸς σέ, βασιλεῦ, καθαρὸς ἀδελφὸς
ἔστι μοι· πρέποντα τῇ τιμῇ τοῦτον συνίστημι."
316 τούτοις ὁ βασιλεὺς ἡσθεὶς τοῖς λόγοις τὸν Ἰωνάθην
μὲν ἠγάσατο τῆς γνώμης, τἀδελφῷ δὲ αὐτοῦ
Ματθίᾳ³ τὴν ἱερωσύνην ἔδωκεν.⁴ καὶ μετ' οὐ πολὺ
Πετρώνιον μὲν Μάρσος διεδέξατο καὶ διεῖπε Συρίαν.
317 (vii. 1) Σίλας δ' ὁ τοῦ βασιλέως ἔπαρχος⁵ ἐπεὶ

¹ Ε: Κανθηρᾶ Α: Καθηρα MW: Catharam Lat.: Καθηρᾶν
Zonaras (cod. A).
² δίδωσιν ἡ σὴ βουλή] Α: δίδωσι βουλήσει MW: σῇ δίδως
βουλήσει Ε: σῇ δίδοται βουλήσει Lowthius; σοὶ μέν . . .
βουλή] tu quidem o rex meo honori congaudens hanc mihi
restituis proprio consilio dignitatem Lat.
³ τὸν Ἰωνάθην . . . Ματθίᾳ] Ε: τῶι (ὡι ex corr.) Ἰωνάθηι
(ηι ex ην corr.) μὲν γνώμη τἀδελφοῦ αὐτοῦ Ματθία, i. marg. γρ
τὸν Ἰωνάθην ἠγάσατο τῆς γνώμης τῶ ἀδελφῶ δὲ αὐτοῦ Ματθίαι Α:
τὸν Ἰωνάθην μὲν ἠγήσατο γνώμης τοῦ ἀδελφοῦ αὐτοῦ Ματθία MW:
τὸν Ἰωνάθη μὲν ἔασε, γνώμῃ δὲ τοῦ ἀδελφοῦ αὐτοῦ Ματθίᾳ ed. pr.
⁴ τούτοις . . . ἔδωκεν] in his ergo sermonibus rex Agrippa
collaudans Ionae voluntatem praebuit Mathiae eius fratri
pontificatum Lat.
⁵ Dindorf: ἵππαρχος codd. Ε: praefectus Lat.

ᵃ Cf. Ant. xviii. 95, 123. According to Ant. xx. 162-164,
he was slain by brigands at the instigation of the procurator
362

priesthood, and proposed to restore it to Jonathan [a] the son of Ananus,[b] conceding that he was more worthy of the honour. Jonathan, however, regarded the resumption of such an honour as unwelcome and declined it in the following words : " I rejoice, O king, to be honoured by you, and heartily appreciate this high prize offered me by your will, although God has adjudged me in no way worthy of the high priesthood. But I am content to have put on the holy vestments once, for then I arrayed myself in them with more regard for sanctity than would be shown if I were to take them back. But if you desire that another, worthier than I, should receive the honour, be instructed by me. I have a brother, pure of all sin against God and against you, O king. Him I recommend as suitable for the honour." The king rejoiced at these words, respected Jonathan for his decision, and gave the high priesthood to his brother Matthias. Not long after this, Petronius was succeeded by Marsus [c] as governor of Syria.

(vii. 1) Now Silas, the king's general,[d] had been

Simon as high priest with Jonathan son of Ananus.

Silas, Agrippa's

Felix. Mathieu-Herrmann, in their note on this passage, assert that he is identical with Theophilus the son of Ananus (§ 297), since the names Jonathan in Hebrew and Theophilus in Greek have similar meanings. But the meanings are somewhat different, since Jonathan means " God gave " or " God's gift " and Theophilus means " loved by God." Moreover, in *Ant.* xviii. 123, we are told that Theophilus succeeded Jonathan ; and it is unlikely that Josephus, who was himself a priest, would err in such a matter.

[b] *Cf. Ant.* xviii. 26 and note.

[c] C. Vibius Marsus, consul suffectus in 17. In 19 he was *legatus pro praetore* in Antioch in Syria. He succeeded Petronius as governor of Syria in 42. *Cf.* also *Ant.* xix. 326, 340-342, 363 ; xx. 1.

[d] The mss. read " master of the horse," but it seems clear from § 299 that Silas was commander of the entire army.

363

διὰ πάσης αὐτῷ τύχης ἐγεγόνει πιστὸς οὐδένα κίν-
δυνόν ποτε κοινωνεῖν ἀνηνάμενος, ἀλλὰ καὶ τοὺς σφα-
λερωτάτους ὑποδὺς πολλάκις πόνους, πεποιθήσεως
ἦν ἀνάπλεως, προσήκειν ὑπολαμβάνων ἰσοτιμίαν
318 βεβαιότητι φιλίας. οὐδαμῇ τοίνυν ὑποκατεκλίνε-
το βασιλεῖ, παρρησίαν δὲ διὰ πάσης ὁμιλίας ἦγεν,
κἂν ταῖς φιλοφρονήσεσιν ἐγίνετο φορτικὸς[1] σε-
μνύνων ἑαυτὸν ἀμέτρως καὶ πολλάκις τῷ βασιλεῖ
τὰ στυγνὰ τῆς τύχης ἄγων εἰς ἀνάμνησιν, ἵνα τὴν
ἑαυτοῦ τότε σπουδὴν παραδεικνύῃ, συνεχῶς δ' ἦν,
319 ὡς ὑπὲρ αὐτοῦ κάμοι, πολλὰ διεξιών.[2] τούτων οὖν
τὸ πλεονάζον ὀνειδισμὸς ἐδόκει[3]· διὸ προσάντως ὁ
βασιλεὺς ἐδέχετο τὴν ἀταμίευτον παρρησίαν τἀν-
δρός· οὐχ ἡδεῖαι γὰρ αἱ τῶν ἀδόξων χρόνων ἀνα-
μνήσεις, εὐήθης δὲ ὁ διηνεκῶς ἅ ποτε ὠφέλησεν
320 προφέρων. τέλος γοῦν ἀνηρέθισε σφόδρα ὁ Σίλας
τοῦ βασιλέως τὸν θυμὸν κἀκεῖνος ὀργῇ πλέον ἢ
λογισμῷ διδοὺς οὐ τῆς ἐπαρχίας[4] μόνον μετέστησε
τὸν Σίλαν, ἀλλὰ καὶ παρέδωκεν δεθησόμενον εἰς
321 τὴν ἐκείνου πατρίδα πέμψας. χρόνῳ δὲ τὸν θυμὸν
ἠμβλύνθη καὶ λογισμοῖς εἰλικρινέσι τὴν περὶ τἀνδρὸς κρίσιν ἐφῆκεν ἐν νῷ λαμβάνων ὅσους ὑπὲρ
αὐτοῦ[5] πόνους ἐκεῖνος ἀνέτλη. ἡμέραν οὖν ἑορτά-
ζων αὐτοῦ γενέθλιον, ὅτε πᾶσιν ὧν ἦρχεν εὐφροσύνη

[1] παρρησίαν . . . φορτικὸς] ita ut maxima ab eo beneficia
postulando onerosus esse videretur Lat.

[2] συνεχῶς . . . διεξιών] om. E.

[3] τούτων . . . ἐδόκει] quod cum crebro faceret ut mihi videtur improperare beneficia noscebatur Lat.

[4] Dindorf : a praefectura Lat. : ἱππαρχίας codd. E.

loyal to him through every vicissitude of fortune,[a] and had never refused to share any danger, but had often undertaken the most hazardous tasks. He was full of self-confidence, for he assumed that there could be no solid friendship without equal standing. Accordingly, he never deferred to the king,[b] but spoke frankly in all his conversation. Moreover, in convivial gatherings, he proved himself a nuisance by singing his own praises inordinately and by frequently reminding the king of the frowns of fortune in the past, which gave him an opportunity to display his own devotion at the time. He would incessantly relate at length how he had laboured on the king's behalf. The abundance of such talk gave the impression of a reproach, which accounts for the king's resentment in the face of the fellow's unstinted frankness. For it is unpleasant to be reminded of inglorious episodes; and one who perpetually brings up his former services is a simpleton. In the end, at any rate, Silas stirred the king to very great wrath; and the latter, more in passion than by calculation, not only removed Silas from his command, but sent him to his own country and consigned him to captivity. But in time his anger lost its edge, and he submitted his judgement on the man to dispassionate reflection, taking into consideration all the hardships that the man had borne for his sake. In consequence, when he was celebrating his birthday and all his

---

[a] Cf. Ant. xviii. 204, which records that he was among those who brought food and clothing and performed other services for Agrippa while the latter was imprisoned in Rome.

[b] Or perhaps " he would not sit lower than the king at table " (Whiston).

---

[5] Herwerden : ἐκείνου codd.

ἦν καὶ[1] καθίσταντο θαλίαι,[2] τὸν Σίλαν ἀνεκάλει παρ-
322 αυτίκα συνέστιον αὐτῷ γενησόμενον. τῷ δέ, τρόπος
γὰρ ἐλευθέριος ἦν, ἐδόκει προσειληφέναι δικαίαν
αἰτίαν ὀργῆς, ἣν οὐκ ἀπεκρύπτετο πρὸς τοὺς
323 μετιόντας αὐτὸν[3] λέγων· " ἐπὶ ποίαν ὁ βασιλεὺς
τιμὴν ἀνακαλεῖ με τὴν μετὰ μικρὸν ἀπολουμένην;[4]
οὐδὲ γὰρ τὰ πρῶτά μοι γέρα τῆς εἰς αὐτὸν εὐνοίας
324 ἐτήρησεν, ἀπεσύλησεν δ᾽ ὑβρίσας. ἢ πεπαῦσθαι
νενόμικέ με τῆς παρρησίας, ἣν ἀπὸ ποίου συνειδότος
ἔχων βοήσομαι μᾶλλον,[5] ὅσων αὐτὸν ἐξελυσάμην
δεινῶν, ὅσους ἤνεγκα πόνους ἐκείνῳ ποριζόμενος[6]
σωτηρίαν τε καὶ τιμήν, ὧν γέρας ἠνεγκάμην δεσμὰ
325 καὶ σκότιον εἱρκτήν. οὐκ ἐγώ ποτε τούτων λή-
σομαι· τάχα μοι τὴν τῆς ἀριστείας συνεποίσεται
μνήμην καὶ μεταστᾶσα τῆς σαρκὸς ἡ ψυχή." ταῦτα
ἀνεβόα καὶ διετάττετο τῷ βασιλεῖ λέγειν. ὁ δ᾽ ὡς
ἀνιάτως ἑώρα διακείμενον, πάλιν εἴασεν ἐν φρουρᾷ.
326 (2) Τὰ δὲ τῶν Ἱεροσολύμων τείχη τὰ πρὸς τὴν
καινὴν νεύοντα πόλιν δημοσίαις ὠχύρου δαπάναις,
τῇ[7] μὲν εὐρύνων εἰς πλάτος τῇ[8] δὲ εἰς ὕψος ἐξαίρων,
κἂν ἐξειργάσατο ταῦτα πάσης ἀνθρωπίνης κρείτ-
τονα βίας, εἰ μὴ Μάρσος ὁ τῆς Συρίας ἡγεμὼν
Κλαυδίῳ Καίσαρι διὰ γραμμάτων ἐδήλωσε τὸ
327 πραττόμενον. καὶ νεωτερισμόν τινα Κλαύδιος ὑπ-

---

[1] εὐφροσύνη ἦν καὶ] Post: εὐφροσύνη ᾗ A (ᾗ, ι i. ras.): εὐ-
φροσύναι MW: εὐφροσύνη coni. Niese.
[2] ὅτε . . . θαλίαι] om. E.
[3] τῷ δέ . . . αὐτόν] ille vero modum libertatis quem iustum
esse credebat venientibus ad se non tacuit Lat.
[4] A: ἀπολλυμένην MW: ablaturus est Lat.
[5] ἢ . . . μᾶλλον] cum qua ergo fiducia aut qua conscientia
ad eum veniam Lat.
[6] A: χαριζόμενος MW.
[7] Hudson: τὴν codd. E.      [8] Hudson: τὴν codd. E.

subjects were participating in the joyous festivities,
he recalled Silas at a moment's notice to share his
table. The latter, however, for he had an independent spirit, thought that he had had just cause for
anger, and this he did not conceal from those who
came to fetch him. " What honour is this," he said,
" to which the king recalls me—an honour so soon to
perish ? He has not even let me keep my former
rewards for the loyalty which I showed him, but has
wantonly stripped me of them. Does he think that I
have given up my habit of speaking my mind ? No,
I keep it and I shall shout the louder what I know
in my heart, mentioning all the bad scrapes from
which I rescued him and all the hardships that I bore
in securing his safety and position—as a reward for
which I received chains and a gloomy dungeon. I
will never forget these things ; perhaps my soul,
even when severed from my body, will carry with it
the memory of my prowess." These words he shouted
out and commanded the messengers to repeat them
to the king. The king, however, when he saw that
his malady was beyond remedy, decided again to
leave him in prison.

(2) [a] Agrippa fortified the walls of Jerusalem on
the side of the New City [b] at the public expense,
increasing both their breadth and height, and he
would have made them too strong for any human
force had not Marsus, the governor of Syria, reported
by letter to Claudius Caesar what was being done.
Claudius, suspecting that a revolution was on foot,

*Agrippa is ordered to desist from restoring the walls of Jerusalem.*

---

[a] *Cf.* the parallel passage, *B.J.* ii. 218. The wall is also
mentioned in *B.J.* v. 152.

[b] *Cf. B.J.* v. 151, which notes that in the vernacular this
district, which is to the north of Jerusalem, was known as
Bezetha.

οπτεύσας ἐπέστειλεν Ἀγρίππᾳ μετὰ σπουδῆς παύσασθαι τῆς τῶν τειχῶν ἐξοικοδομήσεως· ὁ δ᾽
ἀπειθεῖν οὐκ ἔκρινεν.[1]

328 (3) Ἐπεφύκει δ᾽ ὁ βασιλεὺς οὗτος εὐεργετικὸς
εἶναι ἐν δωρεαῖς καὶ μεγαλοφρονῆσαι ἔθνη[2] φιλό-
τιμος καὶ πολλοῖς[3] ἀθρόως δαπανήμασιν ἀνιστὰς
αὐτὸν εἰς ἐπιφάνειαν ἡδόμενος τῷ χαρίζεσθαι καὶ
τῷ βιοῦν ἐν εὐφημίᾳ χαίρων,[4] κατ᾽ οὐδὲν Ἡρώδῃ
τῷ πρὸ ἑαυτοῦ βασιλεῖ τὸν τρόπον συμφερόμενος·
329 ἐκείνῳ γὰρ πονηρὸν ἦν ἦθος ἐπὶ τιμωρίαν ἀπότομον
καὶ κατὰ τῶν ἀπηχθημένων ἀταμίευτον, Ἕλλησι
πλέον ἢ Ἰουδαίοις οἰκείως ἔχειν ὁμολογούμενος·
ἀλλοφύλων γέ τοι πόλεις ἐσέμνυνεν δόσει χρημάτων
βαλανείων θεάτρων τε[5] ἄλλοτε κατασκευαῖς, ἔστιν
αἷς ναοὺς ἀνέστησε, στοὰς ἄλλαις, ἀλλὰ Ἰουδαίων
οὐδεμίαν πόλιν οὐδ᾽ ὀλίγης ἐπισκευῆς ἠξίωσεν οὐδὲ
330 δόσεως ἀξίας μνημονευθῆναι. πραῢς δ᾽ ὁ τρόπος
Ἀγρίππᾳ καὶ πρὸς πάντας τὸ εὐεργετικὸν ὅμοιον.
τοῖς ἀλλοεθνέσιν ἦν φιλάνθρωπος κἀκείνοις ἐνδεικ-
νύμενος τὸ φιλόδωρον τοῖς ὁμοφύλοις ἀναλόγως
331 χρηστὸς καὶ συμπαθὴς μᾶλλον. ἡδεῖα γοῦν αὐτῷ
δίαιτα καὶ συνεχὴς ἐν τοῖς Ἱεροσολύμοις ἦν καὶ τὰ
πάτρια καθαρῶς ἐτήρει. διὰ πάσης γοῦν αὐτὸν

---

[1] ὁ δ᾽ ἀπειθεῖν οὐκ ἔκρινεν] om. E.
[2] ἔθνη] <πρὸς τὰ> ἔθνη Richards et Shutt.
[3] ed. pr. : πόλεως codd. : civitatem Lat.
[4] καὶ πολλοῖς . . . χαίρων] om. E ; καὶ τῷ . . .·χαίρων] et
favorabiliter suae vitae iura disponeret Lat.
[5] ed. pr. : δὲ codd. : τε καὶ E.

---

[a] Lit. " nations," but probably used, as in the Septuagint

earnestly charged Agrippa in a letter to desist from
the building of the walls ; and Agrippa thought it
best not to disobey.

(3) Now King Agrippa was by nature generous in
his gifts and made it a point of honour to be high-
minded towards gentiles [a] ; and by expending massive
sums he raised himself to high fame. He took pleasure
in conferring favours and rejoiced in popularity, thus
being in no way similar in character to Herod, who
was king before him. The latter had an evil nature,
relentless in punishment and unsparing in action
against the objects of his hatred. It was generally
admitted that he was on more friendly terms with
Greeks than with Jews. For instance, he adorned
the cities of foreigners by giving them money, building baths and theatres, erecting temples in some and
porticoes in others, whereas there was not a single
city of the Jews on which he deigned to bestow even
minor restoration or any gift worth mentioning.[b]
Agrippa, on the contrary, had a gentle disposition
and he was a benefactor to all alike. He was benevo-
lent to those of other nations and exhibited his generosity to them also ; but to his compatriots he was
proportionately more generous and more compas-
sionate. He enjoyed residing in Jerusalem and did
so constantly ; and he scrupulously observed the
traditions of his people. He neglected no rite of

(*e.g.* Ps. ii. 1), as a translation of Hebrew *goyim*, in the sense
of non-Jews.

[b] Though it is true that Herod gave money for the erection
of monuments in Rhodes, Athens, Sparta, and many other
cities outside Palestine, it is not true that he neglected
buildings in Jewish cities completely, since, of course, his
most magnificent work was the restoration of the temple in
Jerusalem.

ἦγεν ἁγνείας οὐδ' ἡμέρα τις παρώδευεν αὐτῷ τὰ
νόμιμα χηρεύουσα θυσίας.

332 (4) Καὶ δή τις ἐν τοῖς Ἱεροσολύμοις ἀνὴρ ἐπι-
χώριος ἐξακριβάζειν δοκῶν τὰ νόμιμα, Σίμων ἦν
ὄνομα τούτῳ, πλῆθος εἰς ἐκκλησίαν ἁλίσας τηνικάδε
τοῦ βασιλέως εἰς Καισάρειαν ἐκδεδημηκότος ἐτόλμησεν αὐτοῦ κατειπεῖν, ὡς οὐχ ὅσιος εἴη, δικαίως
δ' ἂν εἴργοιτο τοῦ ναοῦ τῆς εἰσόδου¹ προσηκούσης
333 τοῖς εὐαγέσιν.² δηλοῦται μὲν δὴ διὰ γραμμάτων
ὑπὸ τοῦ στρατηγοῦ τῆς πόλεως τῷ βασιλεῖ δημη-
γορήσας Σίμων ταῦτα, μεταπέμπεται δὲ αὐτὸν ὁ
βασιλεὺς καί, καθέζετο γὰρ ἐν τῷ θεάτρῳ τότε,
καθεσθῆναι παρ' αὐτὸν ἐκέλευσεν. ἠρέμα τε καὶ
πράως, " εἰπέ μοι," φησίν, " τί τῶν ἐνθάδε γινομένων

¹ ὡς . . . εἰσόδῳ] quasi non sanctum et iustum suadens
uti rex prohiberetur a templi limine Lat.
² τοῖς εὐαγέσιν] coni. Niese: τοῖς εὐγενέσι (-σιν A¹) AM :
τοῖς ἐγγενέσιν W : τῆς εὐγενέσι E : dignis Lat.

ᵃ His identity is otherwise unknown. There is no evidence
supporting the guess of Z. Frankel, Darke ha-Mishnah, 1859,
pp. 58-59, that he was perhaps the son of Hillel and father of
Gamaliel I.
ᵇ Lit. " unholy." But it is clear from § 331 and from the
Talmudic sources (Mishnah, Bikkurim iii. 4, Bab. Pesahim
107 b, Ketubot 17 a, Leviticus Rabbah iii. 5) that Agrippa
was scrupulously observant, at least in Jerusalem, and that
he was praised for his piety by the rabbis. (It is not always
certain, however, whether Agrippa I or II is meant in these
rabbinic references.)
ᶜ I have adopted Niese's emendation. One of the mss.
reads ἐγγενέσιν, " those who were natives," i.e. of Jewish
stock. This reading has some appeal since Agrippa's an-
cestry was a source of embarrassment to him, as he was part
Edomite, while the Torah demands that a king be " from
among thy brethren " (Deut. xvii. 15). Indeed we hear
(Mishnah, Soṭah vii. 8 : the reference, in all probability, is to

purification, and no day passed for him without the prescribed sacrifice.

(4) Here is a supreme example of his character. A native of Jerusalem named Simon *a* with a reputation for religious scrupulousness assembled the people in a public meeting at a time when the king was absent in Caesarea, and had the audacity to denounce him as unclean.*b* He asserted that the king ought properly to be excluded from the temple, since the right of entrance was restricted to those who were ritually clean.*c* The commanding officer in the city reported to the king by letter that Simon had made this harangue. The king thereupon sent for him, and, since he was sitting in the theatre at the time, bade Simon sit down beside him. " Tell me," he then said quietly and gently, " what is contrary to the law

Agrippa I rather than Agrippa II) that when Agrippa reached this passage he burst into tears. But only a non-Jew (Mishnah, *Kelim* i. 8) was excluded from the temple ; Agrippa (Mishnah, *Bikkurim* iii. 4) did enter the temple, bringing the first-fruits as far as the altar. We read, furthermore (Mishnah, *Soṭah* vii. 8), that the rabbis approved of his standing rather than sitting in the temple while reading the selection from Deuteronomy pertaining to the institution of the king ; hence they did not regard him as a non-Jew. He could not have been excluded as an Edomite since he was more than three generations removed from the Edomite Antipas, grandfather of Herod the Great, who was Agrippa's grandfather ; and Edomites were prohibited to enter the house of Israel only until the third generation (Deut. xxiii. 8). Hence the only possible reason for claiming that Agrippa ought to have been excluded is that he was impure (Mishnah, *Kelim* i. 8). It is possible that Agrippa contacted such impurity at or on his way to or from the theatre and that this is the significance of Agrippa's summoning Simon to the theatre and asking him what he found contrary to the law there, the implication being that Agrippa had taken proper precautions to prevent contact with uncleanliness there.

334 ἐστὶ παράνομον;'' ὁ δὲ εἰπεῖν ἔχων οὐδὲν τυχεῖν
ἐδεῖτο συγγνώμης. ἀλλὰ ὁ βασιλεὺς θᾶττον[1] ἢ
προσεδόκησέν τις διηλλάττετο[2] τὴν πραότητα
κρίνων βασιλικωτέραν ὀργῆς καὶ πρέπειν εἰδὼς
τοῖς μεγέθεσι θυμοῦ πλέον ἐπιείκειαν. τὸν Σίμωνα
γοῦν καὶ δωρεᾶς τινος ἀξιώσας ἀπεπέμπετο.

335 (5) Πολλοῖς δὲ κατασκευάσας πολλὰ Βηρυτίους
ἐξαιρέτως ἐτίμησεν· θέατρον γὰρ αὐτοῖς κατε-
σκεύασε πολυτελείᾳ τε καὶ κάλλει πολλῶν διαφέρον
ἀμφιθέατρόν τε πολλῶν ἀναλωμάτων βαλανεῖα πρὸς
τούτοις καὶ στοάς, ἐν οὐδενὶ τῶν ἔργων στενότητι
δαπανημάτων ἢ τὸ κάλλος ἀδικήσας ἢ τὸ μέγεθος.

336 ἐπεδαψιλεύσατο δ' αὐτῶν τὴν καθιέρωσιν μεγαλο-
πρεπῶς, ἐν τῷ θεάτρῳ μὲν θεωρίας ἐπιτελῶν πάνθ'
ὅσα μουσικῆς ἔργα παράγων καὶ ποικίλης ποιητικὰ
τέρψεως, ἐν δὲ τῷ ἀμφιθεάτρῳ πλήθει μονομάχων

337 τὴν αὐτοῦ δεικνὺς μεγαλόνοιαν. ἔνθα καὶ τὴν κατὰ
πλῆθος ἀντίταξιν βουληθεὶς γενέσθαι τῶν θεωμένων
τέρψιν ἑπτακοσίους ἄνδρας ἑπτακοσίοις μαχησο-
μένους εἰσέπεμψεν κακούργους ὅσους εἶχεν ἀποτά-
ξας εἰς τήνδε τὴν πρᾶξιν, ἵν' οἱ μὲν κολασθῶσιν, τὸ
πολέμου δ' ἔργον γένηται τέρψις εἰρήνης. τούτους
μὲν οὖν πασσυδὶ διέφθειρεν.[3]

338 (viii. 1) Ἐν Βηρυτῷ δὲ τελέσας τὰ προειρημένα
μετῆλθεν εἰς Τιβεριάδα πόλιν τῆς Γαλιλαίας. ἦν
δὲ ἄρα τοῖς ἄλλοις βασιλεῦσιν περίβλεπτος. ἧκε
γοῦν παρ' αὐτὸν Κομμαγηνῆς μὲν βασιλεὺς Ἀντί-

---

[1] θᾶττον] Hudson : αὐτὸν codd. : αὐτῷ E.
[2] ἀλλὰ . . . διηλλάττετο] tunc rex in aliis circa eum placatus quam ab aliquo crederetur Lat.
[3] τούτους . . . διέφθειρεν] om. E.

---

[a] Modern *Beirut*.          [b] *Cf.* § 276 and note.

in what is going on here ? " Simon, having nothing
to say, begged pardon. Thereupon the king was
reconciled to him more quickly than one would have
expected, for he considered mildness a more royal
trait than passion, and was convinced that considerate
behaviour is more becoming in the great than wrath.
He therefore even presented a gift to Simon before
dismissing him.

(5) He erected many buildings in many other
places but he conferred special favours on the people
of Berytus.[a] He built them a theatre surpassing
many others in its costly beauty ; he also built an
amphitheatre at great expense, besides baths and
porticoes ; and in none of these works did he allow
either the beauty or the size to suffer by stinting on
the expenses. He was also magnificently lavish in
his provision at the dedication of them ; in the
theatre he exhibited spectacles, introducing every
kind of music and all that made for a varied entertainment, while in the amphitheatre he showed his
noble generosity by the number of gladiators provided. On the latter occasion also, wishing to gratify
the spectators by ranging a number of combatants
against each other, he sent in seven hundred men to
fight another seven hundred. All these men were
malefactors set aside for this purpose, so that while
they were receiving their punishment, the feats of war
might be a source of entertainment in peace-time.
In this way he brought about the utter annihilation
of these men.

(viii. 1) Having completed the aforesaid ceremonies at Berytus, he went next to Tiberias, a city in
Galilee. Now he was evidently admired by the other
kings. At any rate, he was visited by Antiochus [b]

*Agrippa's buildings at Berytus.*

*Agrippa entertains certain kings at Tiberias.*

373

οχος, Ἐμεσῶν¹ δὲ Σαμψιγέραμος καὶ Κότυς,² τῆς
μικρᾶς Ἀρμενίας οὗτος ἐβασίλευσεν, καὶ Πολέμων
τὴν Πόντου κεκτημένος δυναστείαν³ Ἡρώδης τε·
οὗτος ἀδελφὸς ἦν αὐτοῦ, ἦρχεν δὲ τῆς Χαλκίδος.
339 ὡμίλησε δὲ πᾶσιν κατά τε τὰς ὑποδοχὰς καὶ φιλο-
φρονήσεις ὡς μάλιστα διαδείξας φρονήσεως ὕψος
καὶ διὰ τοῦτό γε δοκεῖν δικαίως τῇ τοῦ βασιλέως⁴
340 παρουσίᾳ⁵ τετιμῆσθαι.⁶ ἀλλὰ γὰρ τούτων διατρι-
βόντων ἔτι παρ' αὐτῷ Μάρσος ὁ τῆς Συρίας ἡγεμὼν παρεγένετο. πρὸς Ῥωμαίους οὖν τιμητικὸν
τηρῶν ὑπαντησόμενος αὐτῷ τῆς πόλεως ἀπωτέρω
341 σταδίους ἑπτὰ προῆλθεν ὁ βασιλεύς. τοῦτο δὲ ἄρα
ἔμελλεν τῆς πρὸς Μάρσον ἀρχὴ γενήσεσθαι δια-
φορᾶς· συγκαθεζόμενος γὰρ ἐπὶ τῆς ἀπήνης ἐπήγετο
τοὺς ἄλλους βασιλέας,⁷ Μάρσῳ δ' ἡ τούτων ὁμόνοια
καὶ μέχρι τοσοῦδε φιλία πρὸς ἀλλήλους ὑπωπτεύθη
συμφέρειν οὐχ ὑπολαμβάνοντι Ῥωμαίοις δυναστῶν

¹ Hudson ex Ant. xviii. 135: Δαμάσων codd. E: Damaso-
rum Lat.
² AW: Κότης M.
³ καὶ Πολέμων . . . δυναστείαν] qui etiam in Ponto Pole-
miaco regnabat Lat.
⁴ τοῦ βασιλέως] τῆς βασιλείας E: τῶν βασιλέων Hudson ex
cod. Voss.
⁵ A: παρουσίᾳ MW: προσηγορίᾳ Cocceji: παρρησίᾳ coni.
Niese.
⁶ ὡμίλησε . . . τετιμῆσθαι] habuitque colloquium apud eos
susceptione et amicitiis valde dignissimum, ita ut ostenderet
suae sapientiae culmen et in praesenti eos videretur regaliter
honorare Lat.
⁷ συγκαθεζόμενος . . . βασιλέας] sedens enim in tribunali
Agrippa invitavit alios reges Lat.

ᵃ His daughter Jotape was married to Agrippa's brother
Aristobulus. *Cf. Ant.* xviii. 135.

king of Commagene, Sampsigeramus [a] king of Emesa,[b] and Cotys [c] king of Armenia Minor,[d] as well as by Polemo,[e] who held sway over Pontus, and Herod [f] his brother, who was ruler of Chalcis. His converse with all of them when he entertained and showed them courtesies was such as to demonstrate an elevation of sentiment that justified the honour done him by a visit of royalty. It so happened, however, that while he was still entertaining them, Marsus the governor of Syria arrived. The king therefore, to do honour to the Romans, advanced seven furlongs outside the city to meet him. Now this action, as events proved, was destined to be the beginning of a quarrel with Marsus ; for Agrippa brought the other kings along with him and sat with them in his carriage ; but Marsus was suspicious of such concord and intimate friendship among them. He took it for granted that a meeting of minds among so many chiefs of state was prejudicial to Roman interests.

Marsus, governor of Syria, orders the kings to depart.

[b] Modern *Homs* in Syria Apamene on the Orontes River, just north-east of the Lebanese border.

[c] Son of the identically named king of Thrace. Appointed by Gaius in 37 to be king of Armenia Minor (*cf.* Dio lix. 12. 2). Tacitus, *Ann.* xi. 9, reports that in 47 he was stopped by a dispatch from the emperor Claudius from opposing by force the return of Mithridates, who was under Roman sponsorship, as ruler of Armenia.

[d] A small district west of Armenia proper.

[e] Julius Polemo (see *Pap. Brit. Mus.* iii. 1178, line 22), brother of Cotys, king of Armenia Minor. He was king of Pontus from 37 to 63. Dio lx. 8. 2 confuses this Polemo with the Marcus Antonius Polemo who was king of Cilicia ; but Josephus, *Ant.* xx. 145, rightly mentions the latter separately, as indicated by D. Magie, *Roman Rule in Asia Minor*, ii, 1950, p. 1407 n. 26.

[f] Cf. *Ant.* xviii. 133 ff. His kingdom of Chalcis was at the foot of Mount Lebanon (*cf. Ant.* xiv. 40).

τοσούτων συμφρόνησιν. εὐθὺς οὖν ἑκάστῳ τῶν
ἐπιτηδείων τινὰς πέμπων ἐπέστελλεν ἐπὶ τὰ ἑαυτοῦ
342 δίχα μελλήσεως ἀπέρχεσθαι. ταῦτα Ἀγρίππας
ἀνιαρῶς ἐξεδέχετο· καὶ Μάρσῳ μὲν ἐκ τούτου δια-
φόρως ἔσχεν. τὴν ἀρχιερωσύνην δὲ Ματθίαν ἀφελόμενος ἀντ᾽ αὐτοῦ κατέστησεν ἀρχιερέα Ἐλιωναῖον
τὸν τοῦ Κανθηρᾶ[1] παῖδα.

343 (2) Τρίτον δὲ ἔτος αὐτῷ βασιλεύοντι τῆς ὅλης[2]
Ἰουδαίας πεπλήρωτο, καὶ παρῆν εἰς πόλιν Καισάρειαν, ἣ τὸ πρότερον Στράτωνος πύργος ἐκαλεῖτο.
συνετέλει δ᾽ ἐνταῦθα θεωρίας εἰς τὴν Καίσαρος
τιμὴν ὑπὲρ τῆς ἐκείνου σωτηρίας ἑορτήν τινα ταύτην ἐπιστάμενος,[3] καὶ παρ᾽ αὐτὴν ἤθροιστο τῶν
κατὰ τὴν ἐπαρχίαν ἐν τέλει καὶ προβεβηκότων εἰς
344 ἀξίαν πλῆθος. δευτέρᾳ δὴ τῶν θεωριῶν ἡμέρᾳ
στολὴν ἐνδὺς ἐξ ἀργύρου πεποιημένην πᾶσαν, ὡς
θαυμάσιον ὑφὴν εἶναι, παρῆλθεν εἰς τὸ θέατρον
ἀρχομένης ἡμέρας. ἔνθα ταῖς πρώταις τῶν ἡλιακῶν

---

[1] Ἐλιωναῖον τὸν τοῦ Κανθηρᾶ] Hudson : Ἐλιωναῖον τὸν τοῦ
Κιθαίρου A : Ἀλιωναῖον τὸν τοῦ Κιθαίου MW : γρ Δηλιωλαῖον
τὸν τοῦ Κανθαρᾶ i. marg. A : Helioneum Cantherae Lat.

[2] τῆς ὅλης] om. Lat.

[3] ἐπιστησάμενος Thackeray : ἐνιστάμενος Post.

---

[a] This reading is found in the Latin version and in the
margin of one of the mss. The mss. read Cithaerus, but in
*Ant.* xx. 16, when the next change in the high priesthood is
reported, we hear of the deposition of " the high priest surnamed Cantheras." The Mishnah *Parah* iii. 5 speaks of a
high priest named Eliehonai (or Elioenai) ben Hakkof (or
Hakkayaf); apparently Elionaeus is there regarded as the
son of Joseph Caiaphas.

He therefore at once sent some of his associates with an order to each of the kings bidding him set off without delay to his own territory. Agrippa felt very much hurt by this and henceforth was at odds with Marsus. He also deprived Matthias of the high priesthood and appointed Elionaeus the son of Cantheras *a* to be high priest in his stead.

(2) After the completion of the third year *b* of his reign over the whole of Judaea, Agrippa came to the city of Caesarea,*c* which had previously been called Strato's Tower.*d* Here he celebrated spectacles in honour of Caesar,*e* knowing that these had been instituted as a kind of festival on behalf of Caesar's well-being. For this occasion there were gathered a large number of men who held office or had advanced to some rank in the kingdom. On the second day of the spectacles, clad in a garment woven completely of silver so that its texture was indeed wondrous, he entered the theatre at daybreak. There the silver,

Agrippa is hailed as a god in the theatre at Caesarea.

*b* So also in the parallel account, *B.J.* ii. 219.

*c* Acts xii. 19-20 also places the scene which follows—Agrippa's death—in Caesarea ; but there is no mention in Josephus of Agrippa's meeting with the ambassadors of Tyre and Sidon as reported in the narrative of Acts.

*d* In Phoenicia between modern *Jaffa* and *Tantura*. Herod built a magnificent harbour there and renamed the city Caesarea in honour of Augustus. *Cf. Ant.* xv. 331-341 and *B.J.* i. 408-414. A. H. M. Jones, *The Cities of the Eastern Roman Provinces*, 1937, p. 231, speculates that the name may imply that it was founded by one of the Stratos who were kings of Sidon in the fourth century, or it may be a hellenization of *Migdol Astart*, lit. "Astarte's Tower," just as Strato itself represents *Abd Astart*.

*e* Thackeray's emendation, " which he [*i.e.* Agrippa] had instituted," is unlikely because these were presumably the quinquennial games (*B.J.* i. 415) which Herod had instituted and named after Caesar.

ἀκτίνων ἐπιβολαῖς ὁ ἄργυρος καταυγασθεὶς θαυ-
μασίως ἀπέστιλβε μαρμαίρων τι φοβερὸν καὶ τοῖς
345 εἰς αὐτὸν ἀτενίζουσι φρικῶδες. εὐθὺς δὲ οἱ κόλακες
τὰς οὐδὲ ἐκείνῳ πρὸς ἀγαθοῦ[1] ἄλλος ἄλλοθεν[2]
φωνὰς ἀνεβόων, θεὸν προσαγορεύοντες, " εὐμενής τε
εἴης," ἐπιλέγοντες, " εἰ καὶ μέχρι νῦν ὡς ἄνθρωπον
ἐφοβήθημεν, ἀλλὰ τοὐντεῦθεν κρείττονά σε θνητῆς
346 φύσεως ὁμολογοῦμεν." οὐκ ἐπέπληξεν τούτοις ὁ
βασιλεὺς οὐδὲ τὴν κολακείαν ἀσεβοῦσαν[3] ἀπετρί-
ψατο. ἀνακύψας δ' οὖν μετ' ὀλίγον τὸν βουβῶνα
τῆς ἑαυτοῦ κεφαλῆς ὑπερκαθιζόμενον εἶδεν ἐπὶ
σχοινίου τινός. ἄγγελον τοῦτον εὐθὺς ἐνόησεν
κακῶν εἶναι τὸν καί ποτε τῶν ἀγαθῶν γενόμενον,
καὶ διακάρδιον ἔσχεν ὀδύνην, ἄθρουν δ' αὐτῷ τῆς
κοιλίας προσέφυσεν[4] ἄλγημα μετὰ σφοδρότητος

[1] ἀγαθοῦ] MW : ἀγαθοῦ ταῖς ἀληθείαις A ; τὰς οὐδὲ . . .
ἀγαθοῦ] om. E : quae nec illi bonae pro veritate videbantur
Lat.

[2] τὰς οὐδὲ . . . ἄλλοθεν] i. ras. pressius scripta m. 2 A.

[3] ἀσεβοῦσαν] ἀσεβῆ οὖσαν vel. ⟨ὡς⟩ ἀσεβοῦσαν coni. Richards
et Shutt.

[4] codd.: γρ προσεφοίτησεν i. marg. A : προσέφυ L. Dindorf:
προσίθυσεν Busb.

[a] J. Morgenstern, " The Chanukkah Festival and the
Calendar of Ancient Israel," *Hebrew Union Coll. Ann.* xx,
1947, pp. 90-91, presents the extravagant suggestion that
Agrippa was playing the rôle of a sun-god and that the festival was actually an equinoctial or solstitial New Year's Day
festival. He compares the festival with that celebrated by
the Roman legions at Durostorum in Lower Moesia (*cf. Acta
Dasii*) in which there is a human victim clothed in royal
garments and playing the rôle of a divine king who is required
to sacrifice himself after thirty days.

[b] Acts xii. 21-22 similarly reports that after Herod
[Agrippa], arrayed in royal apparel, had sat upon his throne

illumined by the touch of the first rays of the sun,[a] was wondrously radiant and by its glitter inspired fear and awe in those who gazed intently upon it. Straightway his flatterers raised their voices from various directions—though hardly for his good—addressing him as a god.[b] " May you be propitious to us," they added, " and if we have hitherto feared you as a man, yet henceforth we agree that you are more than mortal in your being." The king did not rebuke them nor did he reject their flattery as impious. But shortly thereafter he looked up and saw an owl perched on a rope over his head. At once, recognizing this as a harbinger of woes just as it had once been of good tidings,[c] he felt a stab of pain in his heart. He was also gripped in his stomach by an ache that he felt everywhere at once and that was intense from the start.[d] Leaping

Agrippa sees an owl and is smitten with illness.

and made an oration, the people shouted : " The voice of a god, and not of man ! "

[c] In *Ant.* xviii. 195, Josephus mentions that an owl alighted on the tree against which Agrippa was leaning after he had been imprisoned by Tiberius. Another prisoner, a German, interprets this as a portent of Agrippa's speedy release from chains and of his advance to great power. Agrippa is told, however (*Ant.* xviii. 200), that when he sees the owl again, it will indicate that his death is to follow within five days.

[d] Acts xii. 23 does not mention the owl, but says that immediately after the people had called Agrippa a god, " an angel of the Lord smote him, because he did not give God the glory ; and he was eaten by worms and died." *Cf.* also Eusebius, *Hist. Eccl.* ii. 10, in whose account it is not an owl but an angel that Agrippa sees above his head. A physician, E. M. Merrins, " The Deaths of Antiochus IV, Herod the Great, and Herod Agrippa I," *Bibliotheca Sacra* lxi, 1904, pp. 561-562, says that the immediate cause of Agrippa's death was surely peritonitis, and that Agrippa was afflicted with appendicitis, which is the most frequent cause of such abdominal pain as is here described. He thinks,

347 ἀρξάμενον. ἀναθορὼν¹ οὖν πρὸς τοὺς φίλους, " ὁ
θεὸς ὑμῖν ἐγώ," φησίν, " ἤδη καταστρέφειν ἐπιτάτ-
τομαι τὸν βίον, παραχρῆμα τῆς εἱμαρμένης τὰς
ἄρτι μου² κατεψευσμένας φωνὰς ἐλεγχούσης³· ὁ
κληθεὶς ἀθάνατος ὑφ' ὑμῶν ἤδη θανεῖν ἀπάγομαι.
δεκτέον δὲ τὴν πεπρωμένην, ᾗ θεὸς βεβούληται·
καὶ γὰρ βεβιώκαμεν οὐδαμῇ φαύλως, ἀλλ' ἐπὶ τῆς
348 μακαριζομένης λαμπρότητος." ταῦθ' ἅμα λέγων
ἐπιτάσει τῆς ὀδύνης κατεπονεῖτο· μετὰ σπουδῆς
οὖν εἰς τὸ βασίλειον ἐκομίσθη καὶ διῇξε λόγος εἰς
πάντας, ὡς ἔχοι τοῦ τεθνάναι παντάπασι μετ' ὀλίγον.
349 ἡ πληθὺς δ' αὐτίκα σὺν γυναιξὶν καὶ παισὶν ἐπὶ
σάκκων καθεσθεῖσα τῷ πατρίῳ νόμῳ τὸν θεὸν
ἱκέτευεν ὑπὲρ τοῦ βασιλέως, οἰμωγῆς δὲ πάντ' ἦν
ἀνάπλεα καὶ θρήνων. ἐν ὑψηλῷ δ' ὁ βασιλεὺς
δωματίῳ κατακείμενος καὶ κάτω βλέπων αὐτοὺς
πρηνεῖς καταπίπτοντας ἄδακρυς οὐδ' αὐτὸς διέ-
350 μενεν. συνεχεῖς⁴ δ' ἐφ' ἡμέρας πέντε τῷ τῆς
γαστρὸς ἀλγήματι διεργασθεὶς τὸν βίον κατέστρεψεν, ἀπὸ γενέσεως ἄγων πεντηκοστὸν ἔτος καὶ
351 τέταρτον, τῆς βασιλείας δ' ἕβδομον. τέτταρας μὲν
οὖν ἐπὶ Γαΐου Καίσαρος ἐβασίλευσεν ἐνιαυτοὺς τῆς
Φιλίππου μὲν τετραρχίας εἰς τριετίαν ἄρξας, τῷ

¹ A: ἀναθεωρῶν MWE Eus. : respiciens Lat.
² ἄρτι μου] ΑW : ἀτίμους καὶ M.
³ παραχρῆμα . . . ἐλεγχούσης] repente namque increpitus
sum, cum mendaces ad me voces adclamarentur Lat.
⁴ συνεχῶς E Eus. et i. marg. A.

following the account in Acts, that roundworms, so common
in Eastern countries, may have hastened his death by becoming active in Agrippa's alimentary canal, since these
worms become notably more destructive when any part of

up [a] he said to his friends : " I, a god in your eyes, am now bidden to lay down my life, for fate brings immediate refutation of the lying words lately addressed to me. I, who was called immortal by you, am now under sentence of death. But I must accept my lot as God wills it. In fact I have lived in no ordinary fashion but in the grand style that is hailed as true bliss." Even as he was speaking these words, he was overcome by more intense pain. They hastened, therefore, to convey him to the palace ; and the word flashed about to everyone that he was on the very verge of death. Straightway the populace, including the women and children, sat in sackcloth in accordance with their ancestral custom and made entreaty to God on behalf of the king. The sound of wailing and lamentations prevailed everywhere. The king, as he lay in his lofty bedchamber and looked down on the people as they fell prostrate, was not dry-eyed himself. Exhausted after five straight days by the pain [b] in his abdomen, he departed this life in the fifty-fourth year of his life and the seventh of his reign. He had reigned for four years [c] under Gaius Caesar, ruling during three of them over the tetrarchy of Philip, and adding that

*Death of Agrippa.*

the body is diseased. J. Meyshan, " The Coinage of Agrippa the First," *Israel Explor. Jour.* iv, 1954, p. 187 n. 2, suggests that Agrippa was poisoned by arsenic, the standard poison of the era. A quantity of arsenic less than 0·1 gram is undetected in food and will bring about either sudden death or an agony extending over a few days and culminating in death.

   [a] Variant " looking up."

   [b] Variant " Exhausted after five days by the unremitting pain."

   [c] 37–41. *Cf.* the less precise statement in the parallel passage, *B.J.* ii. 219.

τετάρτῳ δὲ καὶ τὴν Ἡρώδου προσειληφώς, τρεῖς
δ' ἐπιλαβὼν τῆς Κλαυδίου Καίσαρος αὐτοκρατορίας,
ἐν οἷς τῶν τε προειρημένων ἐβασίλευσεν καὶ τὴν
Ἰουδαίαν προσέλαβεν Σαμάρειάν τε καὶ Καισά-
352 ρειαν. προσωδεύσατο δ' ὅτι πλείστας[1] αὐτῶν προσ-
φορὰς διακοσίας ἐπὶ χιλίαις μυριάδας,[2] πολλὰ μέντοι
προσεδανείσατο· τῷ γὰρ φιλόδωρος εἶναι δαψιλέστερα τῶν προσιόντων ἀνήλισκεν,[3] ἦν δὲ ἀφειδὲς
αὐτοῦ τὸ φιλότιμον.

353 (3) Ἀγνοουμένης γε μὴν τοῖς πλήθεσιν τῆς ἐκπνοῆς αὐτοῦ συμφρονήσαντες Ἡρώδης τε ὁ τῆς
Χαλκίδος δυναστεύων καὶ Ἑλκίας ὁ ἔπαρχος[4] καὶ
φίλος τοῦ βασιλέως Ἀρίστωνα ἔπεμψαν τῶν ὑπη-
ρετῶν τὸν ἐπιτήδειον[5] καὶ Σίλαν, ἐχθρὸς γὰρ ἦν
αὐτοῖς, ἀπέσφαξαν ὡς δὴ τοῦ βασιλέως κελεύσαντος.

354 (ix. 1) Ἀγρίππας μὲν οὖν ὁ βασιλεὺς τρόπῳ
τοιούτῳ κατέστρεψεν τὸν βίον, γένει[6] δὲ αὐτῷ
κατελέλειπτο υἱὸς μὲν Ἀγρίππας ἄγων ἔτος ἑπτα-
καιδέκατον, τρεῖς δὲ θυγατέρες, ὧν ἡ μὲν Ἡρώδῃ
τοῦ πατρὸς ἀδελφῷ γεγάμητο Βερενίκη τὸ ἐκκαι-

---

[1] ὅτι πλείστας] E: ὅτι πλείστους codd.: πλείστας coni. Post:
innumera Lat.    [2] διακοσίας . . . μυριάδας] om. Lat.
[3] δαψιλέστερα . . . ἀνήλισκεν] supplicantibus larga munera
conferebat Lat.    [4] ὕπαρχος Zonaras.
[5] codd. E: fidelissimum Lat.: ἐπιτηδειότατον Ernesti.
[6] γενεά Richards et Shutt.

---

[a] Herod Antipas, who had come to Rome to seek rights
equal to those accorded by Gaius to Agrippa, only to be
deprived of his tetrarchy and sent into exile (*Ant.* xviii. 252).
[b] 41–44.
[c] About £1,157,143 or $3,240,000. The word " drachmas "
is not in the text, but it appears to be understood. If one reads
πλείστας the meaning would be that the revenue that Agrippa

of Herod [a] during the fourth year. He reigned further for three years [b] under the emperor Claudius Caesar, during which time he ruled over the territory mentioned above and received in addition Judaea, Samaria, and Caesarea. He derived as much revenue as possible from these territories, amounting to twelve million drachmas,[c] but he borrowed much, for, owing to his generosity, his expenditures were extravagant beyond his income, and his ambition knew no bounds of expense.[d]

(3) While the populace was yet unaware that he had breathed his last, Herod [e] the ruler of Chalcis, conspiring together with Helcias [f] the prefect [g] and friend of the king, sent Ariston, the most suitable of their attendants, and slew Silas,[h] who was their enemy, pretending that they had had orders from the king.

(ix. 1) Such was the final scene of King Agrippa's life.[i] He left one son,[j] Agrippa, in his seventeenth year, and three daughters. Of these, one, Berenice, who was sixteen years old, was married to Herod,[k]

---

received from these territories amounted at the highest to twelve million drachmas.

[d] Or " his ambition never counted the cost." A. Momigliano, *Camb. Anc. Hist.* x, 1934, p. 851 n. 1, speculates that the bad financial administration of Agrippa was one of the factors that helped to bring about the reabsorption of Judaea into the empire.           [e] See above, § 338.

[f] See *Ant.* xviii. 273 and note.

[g] Presumably he held the position formerly filled by Silas, ἔπαρχος παντὸς τοῦ στρατεύματος, commander-in-chief of the entire army (so W. Otto, in Pauly-Wissowa, viii, 1913, p. 96).

[h] Agrippa's general who was now in prison. *Cf.* §§ 299 and 317-325.

[i] *Cf.* the parallel passage, *B.J.* ii. 220.

[j] Another son, Drusus, had died before reaching adolescence (*Ant.* xviii. 132).           [k] The ruler of Chalcis.

δέκατον ἔτος γεγονυῖα, παρθένοι δ᾽ ἦσαν αἱ δύο
Μαριάμμη τε καὶ Δρούσιλλα, δεκαετὴς μὲν ἡ ἑτέρα,
355 ἑξαετὴς δὲ Δρούσιλλα· καθωμολόγηντο δ᾽ ὑπὸ τοῦ
πατρὸς πρὸς γάμον Ἰουλίῳ¹ μὲν Ἀρχελάῳ τοῦ
Ἑλκίου² παιδὶ Μαριάμμη, Δρούσιλλα δὲ Ἐπιφανεῖ,
τοῦ δὲ τῆς Κομμαγηνῆς βασιλέως Ἀντιόχου³ υἱὸς
356 ἦν οὗτος. ἀλλὰ γὰρ ὅτε ἐγνώσθη τὸν βίον ἐκλιπὼν Ἀγρίππας, Καισαρεῖς καὶ Σεβαστηνοὶ τῶν εὐ-
ποιιῶν αὐτοῦ λαθόμενοι τὰ τῶν δυσμενεστάτων
357 ἐποίησαν· βλασφημίας τε γὰρ ἀπερρίπτουν εἰς τὸν
κατοιχόμενον ἀπρεπεῖς λέγεσθαι καὶ ὅσοι στρατευό-
μενοι τότε ἔτυχον, συχνοὶ δ᾽ ἦσαν, οἴκαδε ἀπῆλθον
καὶ τοὺς ἀνδριάντας τῶν τοῦ βασιλέως θυγατέρων
ἁρπάσαντες ὁμοθυμαδὸν ἐκόμισαν εἰς τὰ πορνεῖα
καὶ στήσαντες ἐπὶ τῶν τεγῶν ὡς δυνατὸν ἦν ἀφύ-
358 βριζον⁴ ἀσχημονέστερα διηγήσεως δρῶντες, ἐπί τε
τοῖς δημοσίοις κατακλινόμενοι τόποις πανδήμους
ἑστιάσεις ἐπετέλουν στεφανούμενοι καὶ μυριζό-
μενοι καὶ σπένδοντες τῷ Χάρωνι προπόσεις τῆς
τοῦ βασιλέως ἐκπνοῆς ἀλλήλοις ἀνταποδιδόντες.⁵
359 ἀμνήμονες δ᾽ ἦσαν οὐκ Ἀγρίππα μόνον χρησαμένου πολλαῖς εἰς αὐτοὺς φιλοτιμίαις, καὶ τοῦ πάπ-

---

¹ om. Lat.
² coni. (cf. Ant. xx. 140) : Χελκίου codd.
³ A : om. MW.
⁴ AM : ἀφύπνιζον W : ἐφύβριζον E.
⁵ καὶ σπένδοντες . . . ἀνταποδιδόντες] et orco sacrificia tur-
piter exhibentes prandiaque sibimet alterutri pro regia morte
reddentes Lat.

ᵃ Cf. Ant. xx. 140, 147. See also Ap. i. 51, where Josephus
names him as one of those to whom he sold a copy of his
Bellum Judaicum.

her father's brother, and two were unmarried,
namely Mariamme and Drusilla, aged respectively
ten and six years. They had been promised by their
father in marriage, Mariamme to Julius Archelaus,[a]
son of Helcias,[b] and Drusilla to Epiphanes,[c] the son
of Antiochus king of Commagene. But when it
became known that Agrippa had departed this life,
the people of Caesarea and of Sebaste,[d] forgetting
his benefactions, behaved in the most hostile fashion.
They hurled insults, too foul to be mentioned, at the
deceased ; and all who were then on military service
—and they were a considerable number—went off to
their homes, and seizing the images [e] of the king's
daughters carried them with one accord to the
brothels, where they set them up on the roofs and
offered them every possible sort of insult, doing
things too indecent to be reported. Moreover, they
reclined in the public places and celebrated feasts for
all the people, wearing garlands and using scented
unguents ; they poured libations to Charon,[f] and
exchanged toasts in celebration of the king's death.
In this they were unmindful not only of Agrippa,
who had treated them with much generosity, but

[b] mss. Chelcias, but in *Ant.* xx. 140 the name is given as
Helcias.

[c] The marriage never took place, since Epiphanes was
unwilling to convert to the Jewish religion, though he had
contracted with Agrippa to do this (*Ant.* xx. 139).

[d] Samaria.

[e] That one as pious as Agrippa (*cf.* § 331) should have
erected images of his daughters seems remarkable. But
Schürer, i, 1901, p. 161, well notes that on Agrippa's coins
also there is the same inconsistency, for those minted in Jerusalem have no image, while those from other cities often have
the image of Agrippa or of the emperor.

[f] The mythical ferryman of the dead over the river Styx
or Acheron in the Lower World.

που δὲ ῾Ηρώδου· τὰς πόλεις ἐκεῖνος αὐτοῖς ἔκτισεν
λιμένας τε καὶ ναοὺς κατεσκεύασεν λαμπροῖς δαπανήμασιν.

360 (2) ῾Ο δὲ τοῦ τεθνεῶτος υἱὸς ᾿Αγρίππας ἐπὶ
῾Ρώμης ἦν ἐν τῷ χρόνῳ τούτῳ τρεφόμενος παρὰ
361 Κλαυδίῳ Καίσαρι. πυθόμενός γε μὴν Καῖσαρ, ὅτι
τέθνηκεν ᾿Αγρίππας, Σεβαστηνοὶ δὲ καὶ Καισαρεῖς
ὑβρίκασιν εἰς αὐτόν, ἐπ᾿ ἐκείνῳ μὲν ἤλγησεν, ἐπὶ δὲ
362 τοὺς ἀχαριστήσαντας ὠργίσθη.[1]  πέμπειν οὖν εὐθέως ὥρμητο τὸν νεώτερον ᾿Αγρίππαν τὴν βασιλείαν διαδεξόμενον ἅμα βουλόμενος ἐμπεδοῦν τοὺς
ὀμωμοσμένους ὅρκους, ἀλλὰ τῶν ἐξελευθέρων καὶ
φίλων οἱ πολὺ παρ᾿ αὐτῷ δυνάμενοι ἀπέτρεψαν,
σφαλεε ῖρὸν ναι λέγοντες κομιδῇ νέῳ μηδὲ τοὺς
παιδὸς ἐκβεβηκότι χρόνους ἐπιτρέπειν βασιλείας
τηλικοῦτον μέγεθος, ᾧ μὴ δυνατὸν τὰς τῆς διοική-
σεως φροντίδας ἐνεγκεῖν, καὶ τελείῳ δ᾿ οὖν εἶναι
βαρὺ βάσταγμα βασιλείαν.[2]  ἔδοξεν οὖν αὐτοὺς
363 εἰκότα λέγειν ὁ Καῖσαρ. ἔπαρχον οὖν τῆς ᾿Ιου-
δαίας καὶ τῆς ἁπάσης βασιλείας ἀπέστειλεν Κού-
σπιον Φᾶδον τῷ κατοιχομένῳ διδοὺς τιμὴν τὸ μὴ
Μάρσον ἐπαγαγεῖν εἰς βασίλειον[3] αὐτῷ διάφορον.
364 ἐγνώκει δὲ πρὸ πάντων ἐπιστεῖλαι[4] τῷ Φάδῳ
Καισαρεῦσιν καὶ Σεβαστηνοῖς ἐπιπλῆξαι τῆς εἰς
τὸν κατοιχόμενον ὕβρεως καὶ παροινίας εἰς τὰς ἔτι

---

[1] ἐπ᾿ ἐκείνῳ . . . ὠργίσθη] gravi dolore perculsus est Lat.
[2] καὶ τελείῳ . . . βασιλείαν] om. E.
[3] codd. E : regnum Lat. : βασιλείαν Hudson.
[4] εἰς βασίλειον . . . ἐπιστεῖλαι] εἰς τὸ βασίλειον αὐτῷ ἐπεὶ διάφορον τοῦτον ἐγνώκει. πρὸ πάντων δ᾿ ἐπέστειλε Ε.

[a] Cf. Ant. xv. 296-298.
[b] A reference to the solemn treaty that Claudius had made
with Agrippa in the Roman Forum (§ 275).

also of his grandfather Herod, who had built their cities and had erected harbours and temples at lavish expense.[a]

(2) Agrippa, the son of the deceased, was at Rome at this time, where he was being brought up at the court of Claudius Caesar. Caesar, on hearing of the death of Agrippa, and of the insults heaped upon him by the people of Sebaste and Caesarea, was grieved for him and angry at his ungrateful subjects. He had accordingly resolved to send the younger Agrippa at once to take over the kingdom, wishing at the same time to maintain the sworn treaty[b] with him. He was, however, dissuaded by those of his freedmen and friends who had great influence with him, who said that it was hazardous to entrust so important a kingdom to one who was quite young and had not even passed out of boyhood[c] and who would find it impossible to sustain the cares of administration ; even to a grown man, said they, a kingdom was a heavy responsibility. Caesar accordingly decided that their arguments were plausible. He therefore dispatched Cuspius Fadus[d] as procurator of Judaea and of the whole kingdom, so far honouring the deceased as not to bring Marsus, who, he knew, had a quarrel with Agrippa, into his royal capital.[e] Above all, he had resolved to instruct Fadus to rebuke the people of Caesarea and Sebaste for their insults to the deceased, and for their intemper-

Cuspius Fadus is appointed procurator of Judaea, since Agrippa II is still a minor.

---

[c] The term used in Greek, παῖς, is hardly appropriate for one who was sixteen. He was now actually a μειράκιον, "a stripling."

[d] A.D. 44.

[e] According to Hudson's emendation, "into his kingdom" ; i.e. Claudius honoured Agrippa's memory by not choosing Marsus to succeed him.

365 ζώσας, τὴν ἴλην δὲ τῶν Καισαρέων καὶ τῶν Σε-
βαστηνῶν καὶ τὰς πέντε σπείρας εἰς Πόντον μετα-
γαγεῖν, ἵν᾿ ἐκεῖ στρατεύοιντο, τῶν δ᾿ ἐν Συρίᾳ
Ῥωμαϊκῶν ταγμάτων ἐπιλέξαι στρατιώτας κατ᾿
366 ἀριθμοὺς καὶ τὸν ἐκείνων ἀναπληρῶσαι τόπον. οὐ
μὴν οἱ κελευσθέντες μετέστησαν· πρεσβευσάμενοι
γὰρ Κλαύδιον ἀπεμειλίξαντο καὶ μένειν ἐπὶ τῆς
Ἰουδαίας ἐπέτυχον, οἳ καὶ τοῖς ἐπιοῦσι χρόνοις τῶν
μεγίστων Ἰουδαίοις ἐγένοντο συμφορῶν ἀρχὴ τοῦ
κατὰ Φλῶρον πολέμου σπέρματα βαλόντες.[1] ὅθεν
Οὐεσπασιανὸς κρατήσας, ὡς μετ᾿ ὀλίγον ἐροῦμεν,
ἐξήγαγεν[2] αὐτοὺς τῆς ἐπαρχίας.[3]

---

[1] Hudson: λαβόντος codd.: λαβόντες E.
[2] ἐξέβαλεν E.
[3] A: ἀρχῆς MW: regione Lat.

---

[a] Latin *ala*, numbering either 500 or 1000 men. These squadrons often bore titles, as here, indicating the country from which they had been enrolled.

[b] The Sebastenian troops are frequently mentioned in Josephus (*cf. B.J.* ii. 52 and note, and *Ant.* xx. 122) and in inscriptions (listed by Schürer, i, p. 461 n. 51). They and the Caesareans made up one corps and were stationed together at Caesarea.

ate attack on his still living daughters, to transfer to
Pontus the squadron [a] of cavalry composed of men
from Caesarea and Sebaste;[b] together with the five
cohorts,[c] in order to do their service there, and to
enrol a proportionate number of soldiers from the
Roman legions in Syria to fill their place. The troops
were not, however, transferred as they had been
ordered, for they sent a deputation which appeased
Claudius and obtained leave to remain in Judaea.
These men, in the period that followed, proved to be
a source of the greatest disasters to the Jews by
sowing the seed of the war in Florus' time.[d] For
this reason Vespasian, on coming to the throne, as
we shall shortly relate,[e] deported them from the
province.

[c] Since a cohort had a strength of 500 to 600 men, this
would amount to 2500 to 3000 men.

[d] Procurator 64/65. *Cf. Ant.* xviii. 25, xx. 252-258, *B.J.*
ii. 277 ff..

[e] This account of the expulsion of the Sebasteni is not
extant in any of the existing works of Josephus. H. Petersen, " Real and Alleged Literary Projects of Josephus,"
*Am. Jour. of Philol.* lxxix, 1958, pp. 273-274, has effectively
pointed out that Josephus could easily have fulfilled this and
his other promised treatments in his autobiography. That
he did not do so indicates that he probably changed his plans.

## ADDITIONAL NOTE ON *ANT.* XVIII. 343, PAGE 195

The reading ἀνὴρ . . . κτιλίων, as Professor Abraham
Schalit in a forthcoming article notes, reflects a common
Aramaic phrase, *gavra ktila* (" slain man "), found several
times in the Talmud (*Pesaḥim* 110 b, *Sanhedrin* 71 b, 81 a,
and 85 a). According to it the brothers Anilaeus and Asinaeus
declared the Parthian general a " dead man," *i.e.* one to be
slain with impunity by anyone. Josephus' source for the
episode of the Babylonian brothers may well have been in
Aramaic, the language of the Jews of Babylonia.

# APPENDIX A

## AN ANCIENT TABLE OF CONTENTS

### ΒΙΒΛΙΟΝ ΙΗ

α΄.[1] Ὡς Κυρίνιος[2] ὑπὸ Καίσαρος ἐπέμφθη τιμητὴς Συρίας καὶ Ἰουδαίας καὶ ἀποδωσόμενος τὴν Ἀρχελάου οὐσίαν.[3]

β΄. Ὡς Κωπώνιος ἐκ τοῦ ἱππικοῦ τάγματος ἐπέμφθη ἔπαρχος Ἰουδαίας.

γ΄. Ὡς Ἰούδας ὁ Γαλιλαῖος ἔπεισεν[4] τὸ πλῆθος μὴ ἀπογράψασθαι τὰς οὐσίας,[5] μέχρις Ἰώζαρος[6] ὁ ἀρχιερεὺς ἔπεισεν αὐτοὺς μᾶλλον ὑπακοῦσαι Ῥωμαίοις.[7]

δ΄. Τίνες αἱρέσεις καὶ ὁπόσαι παρὰ Ἰουδαίοις φιλοσόφων καὶ τίνες οἱ νόμοι.

ε΄. Ὡς Ἡρώδης καὶ Φίλιππος οἱ τετράρχαι πόλεις ἔκτισαν εἰς τιμὴν Καίσαρος.

---

[1] numeros hab. (α΄-κβ΄ W, I-XXI Lat.) W Lat.

[2] P: Κυρήνιος AMW.

[3] + μεταπεσούσης τῆς Ἰουδαίας ἐκ βασιλείας εἰς ἐπαρχίαν AMW Lat.

[4] ἔπεισεν] P: καί τινες ἕτεροι ἔπεισαν AMW Lat.

[5] + καὶ πολλοὶ ἠκολούθησαν αὐτῶν ταῖς γνώμαις AMW Lat. (in Lat. numeratur hoc cap. IIII).

[6] P: Ἰωάζαρος AMW: Iozarus Lat.

[7] + καὶ ἀποτιμήσασθαι τοὺς βίους AMW Lat.

# APPENDIX A

## AN ANCIENT TABLE OF CONTENTS

### BOOK XVIII

*a* Some MSS. add " after Judaea had changed from a kingdom to a procuratorship."

*b* Some MSS. add " and certain others."

*c* Some MSS. add " and many followed their advice."

*d* Some MSS. add " and to give an evaluation of their properties."　　　　*e* Augustus.

ϛ'. Ὡς Σαμαρεῖς ὀστᾶ νεκρῶν διαρρίψαντες εἰς τὸ ἱερὸν[1] τὸν λαὸν ἑπτὰ ἡμέρας ἐμίαναν.

ζ'. Ὡς Σαλώμη ἡ ἀδελφὴ Ἡρώδου τελευτήσασα τὰ αὑτῆς[2] κατέλιπεν Ἰουλίᾳ τῇ τοῦ Καίσαρος γαμετῇ.

η'. Ὡς Πόντιος Πιλᾶτος ἠθέλησε κρύφα εἰς Ἱεροσόλυμα εἰσενέγκαι προτομὰς Καίσαρος, ὁ δὲ λαὸς οὐ κατεδέξατο στασιάσας.[3]

θ'. Τὰ συμβάντα Ἰουδαίοις ἐν Ῥώμῃ κατὰ τοῦτον τὸν καιρὸν ὑπὸ τῶν Σαμαρέων.[4]

ι'. Κατηγορία ὑπὸ Σαμαρέων Πιλάτου ἐπὶ Οὐιτελλίου καὶ[5] ὡς Οὐιτέλλιος ἠνάγκασεν αὐτὸν ἀναβῆναι εἰς Ῥώμην λόγον τῶν πεπραγμένων ἀποδώσοντα.[6]

---

[1] + ἑορτῆς ἐνεστηκυίας AMW Lat.

[2] τὰ αὑτῆς] P : Ἰάμνειαν (ει i. ras. A, Ἰαμνίαν W) καὶ τὴν τοπαρχίαν αὐτῆς καὶ Φασαηλίδα (Faselidam Lat.) καὶ Ἀρχελαΐδα AMW Lat.

[3] ὁ δὲ . . . στασιάσας] P : γνοὺς δὲ ὁ λαὸς ἐστασίασε πρὸς αὐτὸν ἄχρι ἐξεκόμισεν αὐτὰς ἀπὸ Ἱεροσυλύμων εἰς Καισάρειαν AMW Lat.

[4] ὑπὸ τῶν Σαμαρέων] P : παρὰ τῆς ἐν Σαμαρείᾳ καταφθορᾶς τοῦ πλήθους καὶ ὡς πολλοὺς ἀπώλεσε Πιλᾶτος AMW Lat.

[5] καί] P : om. AMW Lat. novum caput incipientes.

[6] λόγον . . . ἀποδώσοντα] P : πρὸς Καίσαρα καὶ ἀποδοῦναι λόγον περὶ τῶν πεπραγμένων. Οὐϊτελλίου (οὐ ιουτελλίου W) ἀνάβασις εἰς Ἱεροσόλυμα καὶ τιμὴ ὑπὸ τοῦ λαοῦ καὶ ὡς ἐπὶ τούτοις παρεχώρησεν αὐτοῖς τὴν ἱερὰν στολὴν ἐν τῇ Ἀντωνίᾳ κειμένην ὑπὸ τῇ Ῥωμαίων ἐξουσίᾳ ὑφ' αὑτοῖς (ἑαυτοῖς MW) ἔχειν AMW Lat.

---

[a] Some mss. add " during a festival."

[b] For " her estate " some mss have " Jamnia and its territory, together with Phasaëlis and Archelaïs."

# ANCIENT TABLE OF CONTENTS

[c] The table omits special mention of the dynastic struggles n Parthia (§§ 39-52).

[d] For " how the people rose up against him and refused to permit it " some mss. have " how the people, having learnt of it, rose up against him until he withdrew them from Jerusalem to Caesarea." The table omits special mention of Jesus and of Paulina (§§ 63-80).

[e] Some mss. have, in place of " at the instigation of the Samaritans," " arising from the destruction in Samaria, and how Pilate slew many." Regardless of the reading, there is some confusion, since the troubles of the Jews in Rome arose not from the Samaritans but from certain unscrupulous Jews living in Rome who misled Fulvia, a Roman lady (§§ 81-84).

[f] Some mss. add " The ascent of Vitellius to Jerusalem and the honour accorded him by the people, and how he thereupon permitted them to keep under their own control the sacred robe that lay in Antonia in custody of the Romans" (§§ 90-95).

ια'. Πόλεμος Ἡρώδου τοῦ τετράρχου πρὸς
Ἀρέταν τὸν Ἀράβων βασιλέα καὶ ἧττα.[1]

ιβ'. Ὡς Τιβέριος Καῖσαρ ἔγραψεν Οὐιτελλίῳ
Ἀρταβάνην μὲν τὸν Πάρθον πεῖσαι ὁμήρους αὐτῷ
πέμψαι, πρὸς Ἀρέταν δὲ πολεμεῖν.

ιγ'. Τελευτὴ Φιλίππου καὶ ὡς ἡ τετραρχία αὐτοῦ
ἐπαρχία ἐγένετο.[2]

ιδ'. Ἀπόπλους Ἀγρίππα εἰς Ῥώμην καὶ ὡς
κατηγορηθεὶς ὑπὸ τοῦ ἰδίου ἀπελευθέρου ἐδέθη.

ιε'. Ὃν τρόπον ἐλύθη ὑπὸ Γαΐου μετὰ τὴν Τιβερίου τελευτὴν καὶ ἐγένετο βασιλεὺς τῆς Φιλίππου
τετραρχίας.[4]

ις'. Ὡς Ἡρώδης ἀναβὰς εἰς Ῥώμην[5] ἐξωρίσθη
καὶ ὡς τὴν τετραρχίαν αὐτοῦ ἐδωρήσατο Γάιος
Ἀγρίππᾳ.

ιζ'. Στάσις τῶν ἐν Ἀλεξανδρείᾳ Ἰουδαίων καὶ
Ἑλλήνων καὶ πρεσβεία ἀφ' ἑκατέρων πρὸς Γάιον.

ιη'. Κατηγορία Ἰουδαίων ὑπὸ Ἀπίωνος καὶ τῶν
συμπρέσβεων ἐπὶ τῷ μὴ ἔχειν Καίσαρος ἀνδριάντα.

ιθ'. Ὡς ἀγανακτήσας Γάιος πέμπει Πετρώνιον

---

[1] πόλεμος . . . ἧττα] post ἐγένετο (ιγ') tr. MW, in Lat.
antecedentibus continuo adiuncta sunt.
[2] + de baptista Iohanne Lat. (numero non adiecto).
[3] + πρὸς Τιβέριον Καίσαρα AMW Lat.
[4] ὃν τρόπον . . . τετραρχίας] om. Lat.
[5] + κατηγορηθεὶς ὑπὸ Ἀγρίππα AMW Lat.

---

[a] The table omits special mention of the listing of Herod
the Great's descendants (§§ 130-142) and of Agrippa's up-
bringing in Rome, his voyage to Judaea, and his proposed
suicide (§§ 143-150).
[b] This section and section xiii belong before section xi.
[c] Artabanus in the text of this book (§§ 48 ff.).
[d] The Latin version adds " Concerning John the Baptist"
(§§ 116-119).

# ANCIENT TABLE OF CONTENTS

[e] Some MSS. add " to Tiberius Caesar."
[f] The table omits special mention of the thwarting of Tiberius' scheme to bestow the succession to the empire upon his grandson Gemellus (§§ 205-223).
[g] Some MSS. add " and after being accused by Agrippa."

ἡγεμόνα εἰς Συρίαν¹ πολεμῆσαι Ἰουδαίους, ἐὰν μὴ θελήσωσιν εἰσδέξασθαι αὐτοῦ τὸν ἀνδριάντα.

κ'. Τὴν συμβᾶσαν φθορὰν τοῖς ἐν Βαβυλῶνι Ἰουδαίοις δι' Ἀσιναῖον καὶ Ἀνιλαῖον τοὺς ἀδελφούς.

Περιέχει ἡ βίβλος χρόνον ἐτῶν λβ'.

¹ + δοὺς ἐντολὰς συναγαγόντα δύναμιν AMW Lat.

---

ᵃ Some mss. add : " giving him orders to collect a force and . . . "

ᵇ The table omits special mention of Agrippa's successful

# ANCIENT TABLE OF CONTENTS

This book covers a period of thirty-two years.

plea with Gaius to give up the proposal of setting up the statue in the temple (§§ 289-301). It also omits Petronius' escape, through the intervention of Gaius' death, from the death penalty for insubordination.

## ΒΙΒΛΙΟΝ ΙΘ

α΄.[1] Ὡς Γάιος Καῖσαρ ἐπιβουλευθεὶς ὑπὸ Κασσίου Χαιρέου ἀνῃρέθη καὶ ὡς[2] Κλαύδιος ὁ θεῖος αὐτοῦ βιασθεὶς ὑπὸ τῶν στρατιωτῶν τὴν ἀρχὴν παρέλαβεν.

β΄. Στάσις τῆς βουλῆς καὶ τοῦ δήμου πρὸς αὐτὸν καὶ τὰ σὺν αὐτῷ στρατεύματα.[3]

γ΄. Πρεσβεία τοῦ βασιλέως Ἀγρίππα πρὸς τὴν βουλήν, καὶ ὡς συνθέμενοι οἱ στρατιῶται οἱ μετὰ τῆς βουλῆς ἀπεχώρησαν πρὸς Κλαύδιον καὶ κύριον αὐτὸν κατέστησαν τῶν πραγμάτων, ἡ δὲ βουλὴ μονωθεῖσα παρεκάλει Κλαύδιον αὐτῇ διαλλαγῆναι.

δ΄. Ὡς Κλαύδιος Καῖσαρ ἀποδίδωσιν Ἀγρίππᾳ τὴν πατρῴαν αὐτοῦ βασιλείαν ἅπασαν προσθεὶς αὐτῷ καὶ τὴν Λυσανίου τετραρχίαν.

ε΄. Προγράμματα Κλαυδίου Καίσαρος ἐν Ἀλεξ- ανδρείᾳ ὑπὲρ τῶν ἐκεῖ Ἰουδαίων καὶ ἐν πάσῃ αὐτοῦ ἀρχῇ.[4]

ϛ΄. Ἀπόπλους Ἀγρίππα τοῦ βασιλέως εἰς Ἰου- δαίαν.

[1] numeros hab. (α΄-ι΄ W, I-VIII Lat.) W Lat.

[2] καὶ ὡς] AW : ὡς M : qualiterque Lat. (capitulum indi- cant MW Lat.).

[3] στάσις . . . στρατεύματα] antecedenti capiti adiungit Lat.

[4] προγράμματα . . . ἀρχῇ] priori capiti adiungit Lat.

# BOOK XIX

ζ'. Ἐπιστολὴ Πουπλίου Πετρωνίου τοῦ Συρίας ἡγεμόνος πρὸς Δωρίτας ὑπὲρ Ἰουδαίων.

η'. Ὡς βασιλεὺς Ἀγρίππας τὰ Ἱεροσολύμων τείχη πολυτελῶς κατασκευάζων ἀτελῆ τὴν σπουδὴν ἔσχεν μεταξὺ τελευτήσας.

θ'. Ὅσα ἔπραξεν ἐν τρισὶν ἔτεσιν ἄχρι τῆς τελευτῆς αὐτοῦ καὶ ὃν τρόπον τὸν βίον κατέστρεψεν.

Περιέχει ἡ βίβλος χρόνον ἐτῶν γ' μηνῶν ϛ'.

---

ᵃ The table omits special mention of Silas' removal by Agrippa from his command of Agrippa's army (§§ 317-325).

# ANCIENT TABLE OF CONTENTS

This book covers a period of three years and six months.

# APPENDIX B[a]

SELECTED LITERATURE ON QUIRINIUS' ASSESSMENT
(*Ant.* xviii. 1)

Bleckmann, F., " Die erste syrische Statthalterschaft des P. Sulpicius Quirinius," *Klio* 17 (1921), 104-110.

Corbishley, T., " Quirinius and the Census : A Restudy of the Evidence," *Klio* 29 [=Neue Folge, 11] (1936), 81-93.

Heichelheim, F. M., in T. Frank, *An Economic Survey of Ancient Rome* iv, 1938, 160-162 (with full bibliography).

Krenkel, M., *Josephus und Lucas ; der schriftstellerische Einfluss des jüdischen Geschichtschreibers auf den christlichen,* esp. pp. 64-75. 1894.

Lecoultre, H., *De censu Quiriniano et anno nativitatis Christi secundum Lucam evangelistam.* 1883.

**Lodder, W., *Die Schätzung des Quirinius bei Flavius Josephus.* 1930.

Mommsen, T., " De P. Sulpicii Quirinii Titulo Tiburtino," in *Res Gestae*[2], pp. 161-178. 1883.

a In the following bibliographies a single asterisk indicates a work presenting an especially good introductory survey : a double asterisk indicates a work indispensable for specialists. This system has been adopted from R. Marcus, " Selected Bibliography (1920-1945) of the Jews in the Hellenistic-Roman Period," *Proc. of the Am. Acad. for Jew. Res.* 16 (1946-7), 87-181.

# APPENDIX B

Ramsay, W. M., *The Bearing of Recent Discovery on the Trustworthiness of the New Testament*[4], pp. 275-300. 1920.

Ramsay, W. M., " The Census of Quirinius," *Expositor* 1 (1897), 274-286, 425-435.

Ramsay, W. M., *Was Christ Born at Bethlehem : A Study on the Credibility of St. Luke*, pp. 229-280. 1898.

**Schürer, E., *Geschichte des jüdischen Volkes im Zeitalter Jesu Christi* i[4], 1901, Anhang 1 : " Die Schätzung des Quirinius, Luc. 2, 1-5," 508-543 (with full bibliography).

Syme, R., " Galatia and Pamphylia under Augustus : the Governorships of Piso, Quirinius and Silvanus," *Klio* 27 (1934), 122-148, esp. 131-138.

Taylor, L. R., " Quirinius and the Census of Judaea," *Am. Jour. of Philol.* 54 (1953), 120-133.

Weber, M., " Der Census des Quirinius nach Josephus," *Zeitsch. f. d. neutest. Wiss.* 10 (1909), 307-319.

# APPENDIX C

SELECTED LITERATURE ON THE PHARISEES AND
THE SADDUCEES (*Ant.* xviii. 12-17)

Abrahams, I., *Studies in Pharisaism and the Gospels*, 2 vols. 1917, 1924.

Allon, G., " The Attitude of the Pharisees toward Roman Rule and the Herodian Dynasty " [in Hebrew], *Zion* 3 (1935), 300-322.

Aptowitzer, V., *Parteipolitik der Hasmonäerzeit im rabbinischen und pseudoepigraphischen Schrifttum*. 1927.

Baeck, L., " The Pharisees," in *The Pharisees and Other Essays*, pp. 3-50. 1947.

Baron, S. W., *A Social and Religious History of the Jews* ii, 1952, 35-54, 342-350.

Bevan, E. R., " Jewish Parties and the Law," *Camb. Anc. Hist.* ix, 1932, 406-416.

Brüne, B., " Der Pharisäismus bei ·Josephus," in *Flavius Josephus und seine Schriften in ihrem Verhältnis zum Judentume, zur griechischen römischen Welt und zum Christentume*, pp. 150-157. 1913.

Cohen, J., *Les Pharisiens*, 2 vols. 1877.

Derenbourg, J., *Essai sur l'histoire et la géographie de la Palestine d'après les Thalmuds et les autres sources rabbiniques*, Part 1, pp. 76-82, 119-144, 452-456. 1867.

# APPENDIX C

Elbogen, I., *Die Religionsanschauungen der Pharisäer mit besonderer Berücksichtigung der Begriffe Gott und Mensch.* 1904.

**Finkelstein, L., *The Pharisees : The Sociological Background of Their Faith,* 2 vols.[2] 1939.

Geiger, A., " Sadducäer und Pharisäer," *Jüdische Zeitschrift f. Wiss. u. Leben* 2 (1863), 11-54.

*Ginzberg, L., " The Religion of the Pharisees," in *Students, Scholars, and Saints,* pp. 88-108. 1928.

Guttmann, H., *Die Darstellung der jüdischen Religion bei Flavius Josephus.* 1928.

*Herford, R. T., *The Pharisees.* 1924.

Hölscher, G., *Der Sadduzäismus, eine kritische Untersuchung zur späteren jüdischen Religionsgeschichte,* esp. pp. 2-12. 1906.

Kohler, K., " Pharisees," in *Jewish Encyclopedia,* ix, 1905, 661-666 ; and " Sadducees," x, 1905, 630-633.

Lafay, J., *Les Sadducéens.* 1904.

*Lauterbach, J. Z., " The Pharisees and Their Teachings," *Heb. Union Coll. Ann.* 6 (1929), 69-139.

Lauterbach, J. Z., " The Sadducees and Pharisees : A Study of Their Respective Attitudes towards the Law," in *Studies in Jewish Literature issued in honor of Prof. Kaufmann Kohler,* pp. 176-198. 1913.

**Leszynsky, R., *Die Sadduzäer,* esp. pp. 15-35. 1912.

Leszynsky, R., *Pharisäer und Sadduzäer (Volksschriften über die jüdische Religion,* I. Jahrgang, II. Heft). 1912.

Lightley, J. W., *Jewish Sects and Parties in the Time of Jesus,* pp. 11-178. 1925.

Marcus, R., " The Pharisees in the Light of Modern Scholarship," *Jour. of Religion* 32 (1952), 153-164.

**Moore, G. F., " Fate and Free Will in the Jewish Philosophers according to Josephus," *Harv. Theol. Rev.* 22 (1929), 371-389.

**Moore, G. F., *Judaism in the First Centuries of the Christian Era*, 3 vols. 1927-30, esp. vol. 1, pp. 56 ff.

Poznanski, A., *Über die religionsphilosophischen Anschauungen des Flavius Josephus.* 1887.

Rasp, H., " Flavius Josephus und die jüdischen Religionsparteien," *Zeitsch. f. d. neutest. Wiss.*, 23 (1924), 27-47.

Schlatter, A., *Die Theologie des Judentums nach dem Bericht des Josefus* ( = *Beitr. z. Förder. Christl. Theol.* II. Reihe, 26 [1932]), 195-213.

**Schürer, E., *Geschichte* ii⁴, 1907, 447-489.

*Smith, M., " Palestinian Judaism in the First Century," in M. Davis, ed., *Israel : Its Role in Civilization*, pp. 67-81. 1956.

Thackeray, H. St. J., " On Josephus' Statement of the Pharisees' Doctrine of Fate," *Harv. Theol. Rev.* 25 (1932), 93.

Wellhausen, J., *Die Pharisäer und die Sadducäer : eine Untersuchung zur inneren jüdischen Geschichte*². 1924.

*Zeitlin, S., " The Pharisees : A Historical Study," *Jew. Quart. Rev.* 52 (1961-2), 97-129.

*Zeitlin, S., *The Sadducees and the Pharisees.* 1937.

# APPENDIX D

SELECTED LITERATURE ON THE ESSENES
(*Ant.* xviii. 18-22)

Bauer, W., " Essener," *RE* Suppl. iv, 1924, 386-430, esp. 398-407.

Baumgarten, J. M., " Sacrifice and Worship among the Jewish Sectarians of the Dead Sea (Qumràn) Scrolls," *Harv. Theol. Rev.* 46 (1953), 141-159.

Black, M., " The Account of the Essenes in Hippolytus and Josephus," in W. D. Davies and D. Daube, edd., *The Background of the New Testament and Its Eschatology : Studies in Honor of C. H. Dodd*, pp. 172-175. 1956.

Carmignac, J., " Conjecture sur un passage de Flavius Josèphe relatif aux Esséniens," *Vet. Test.* 7 (1957), 318-319.

Cumont, F., " Esséniens et Pythagoriciens, d'après un passage de Josèphe," *Comptes Rendus de l'Académie des inscriptions et belles-lettres* (1930), 99-112.

Del Medico, H. E., *L'Énigme des manuscrits de la mer Morte.* 1957.

Del Medico, H. E., *Le Mythe des Esséniens des origines à la fin du moyen âge.* 1958.

Del Medico, H. E., " Les Esséniens dans l'œuvre de Flavius Josèphe," *Byzantinoslavica* 13 (1952–3), 1-45, 189-226, esp. 215-222.

Derenbourg, J., pp. 166-175.

Dupont-Sommer, A., " On a Passage of Josephus Relating to the Essenes (*Antiq.* xviii. 22)," *Jour. of Sem. St.* 1 (1956), 361-366.

Dupont-Sommer, A., *The Jewish Sect of Qumran and the Essenes.* 1954.

Frankel, Z., " Die Essäer : eine Skizze," *Zeitschr. f. d. rel. Interessen d. Judenthums* 3 (1846), esp. 441-461.

Frankel, Z., " Die Essäer nach talmudischen Quellen," *Monatsschr. f. Gesch. u. Wiss. d. Jud.* 2 (1853), 30-40, 61-73.

Friedländler, M., " Die essenische Bewegung," in *Die religiösen Bewegungen innerhalb des Judentums im Zeitalter Jesu,* pp. 114-168.  1905.

Ginsburg, C. D., *The Essenes : Their History and Doctrines ; The Kabbalah : Its Doctrines, Development and Literature.*  1863-4.

Goosens, R., " La Secte de la Nouvelle Alliance et les Esséniens," *Le Flambeau* (1952), 145-154.

Kohler, K., " Essenes," in *Jewish Ency.* v, 1903, 224-232.

Kruse, H., " Noch einmal zur Josephus-Stelle Antiq. 18, 1, 5," *Vet. Test.* 9 (1959), 31-39.

Lieberman, S., " The Discipline in the So-called Dead Sea Manual of Discipline," *Jour. of Bibl. Lit.* 71 (1952), 199-206.

Lightley, J. W., *Jewish Sects and Parties in the Time of Jesus,* pp. 268-322.

Marcus, R., " Pharisees, Essenes, and Gnostics," *Jour. of Bibl. Lit.* 73 (1954), 157-161.

Marcus, R., " Philo, Josephus, and the Dead Sea Yaḥad," *Jour. of Bibl. Lit.* 71 (1952), 207-209.

Meyer, E., *Ursprung und Anfänge des Christentums* ii, . 1925, 393-402.

Moehring, H. R., " Josephus and the Marriage Cus-

# APPENDIX D

toms of the Essenes : Jewish War II. 119-166 and Antiquities XVIII. 11-25," in Wikgren, A., ed., *Early Christian Origins*, pp. 120-127. 1961.

van der Ploeg, J., " The Belief in Immortality in the Writings of Qumran," *Biblioth. Or.* 18 (1961), 118-124.

Roberts, B. J., " The Qumran Scrolls and the Essenes," *New Test. St.* 3 (1956-7), 58-65.

Roth, C., " Were the Qumran Sectaries Essenes ? A Re-examination of Some Evidence," *Jour. of Theol. St.* 10 (1959), 87-93.

**Schürer, E., *Geschichte* ii⁴, 1907, 651-680.

Smith, M., " The Description of the Essenes in Josephus and the Philosophumena," *Heb. Union Coll. Ann.* 29 (1958), 273-313.

**Strugnell, J., " Flavius Josephus and the Essenes : Antiquities XVIII. 18-22," *Jour. of Bibl. Lit.* 87 (1958), 106-115.

Sutcliffe, E. F., *The Monks of Qumran as Depicted in the Dead Sea Scrolls*, pp. 125-127, 229-237. 1960.

Teicher, J. L., " The Essenes," *Studia Patristica* 1 (1957) (= *Texte u. Untersuch. z. Gesch. d. altchr. Lit.*, 63), 540-545.

**Wagner, S., *Die Essener in der wissenschaftlichen Diskussion vom Ausgang des 18. bis zum Beginn des 20. Jahrhunderts ; eine wissenschaftsgeschichtliche Studie* (=*Beihefte z. Zeitsch. f. d. alttest. Wiss.* 79). 1960.

Wallace, D. H., " The Essenes and Temple Sacrifice," *Theol. Zeitsch.* 13 (1957), 335-338.

Zeitlin, S., " The Essenes and Messianic Expectations : A Historical Study of the Sects and Ideas during the Second Jewish Commonwealth," *Jew. Quart. Rev.* 45 (1954), 83-119.

# APPENDIX E

SELECTED LITERATURE ON THE FOURTH PHILOSOPHY
(*Ant.* xviii. 23-25)

Aptowitzer, V., *Parteipolitik der Hasmonäerzeit im rabbinischen und pseudoepigraphischen Schrifttum.* 1927.

**Farmer, W. R., *Maccabees, Zealots, and Josephus : An Inquiry into Jewish Nationalism in the Greco-Roman Period.* 1956.

**Hengel, M., *Die Zeloten : Untersuchungen zur jüdischen Freiheitsbewegung in der Zeit von Herodes I bis 70 n. Chr.* (= *Arbeiten zur Geschichte des Spätjudentums und Urchristentums,* i). 1961.

Herford, R. T., *The Pharisees,* pp. 176-197. 1924.

Kennard, J. S., Jr., " Judas of Galilee and His Clan," *Jew. Quart. Rev.* 36 (1945-6), 281-286.

*Kohler, K., " Zealots," in *Jew. Ency.* xii. 639-643.

Lightley, J. W., *Jewish Sects,* 324-395.

Roth, C., *The Historical Background of the Dead Sea Scrolls.* 1958.

Roth, C., " The Zealots—A Jewish Religious Sect," *Judaism* 8 (1959), 33-40.

Roth, C., " The Zealots and Qumran : The Basic Issue," *Rev. d. Qum.* 2 (1959-60), 81-84.

Schlatter, A., *Die Theologie des Judentums nach dem Bericht des Josefus,* pp. 214-224. 1932.

# APPENDIX F

SELECTED LITERATURE ON THE SAMARITANS
(*Ant.* xviii. 29-30, 85-87, etc.)

*Cowley, A., " Samaritans," in *Jew. Ency.* x, 1905, 669-681.

Cowley, A., " Some Remarks on Samaritan Literature and Religion," *Jew. Quart. Rev.* O.S. 8 (1895-6), 562-575.

Cowley, A., " The Samaritan Doctrine of the Messiah," *Expositor* (March, 1895), 161-174.

Gaster, M., *The Samaritan Oral Law and Ancient Traditions.* 1. *Samaritan Eschatology.* 1932.

Gaster, M., *The Samaritans : Their History, Doctrines, and Literature.* 1925.

Hilgenfeld, A., " Der Taheb der Samaritaner nach einer neu aufgefundenen Urkunde," *Zeitschr. f. Wiss. Theol.* 37 (1894), 233-244.

Kautzsch, E., " Samaritaner ", in Herzog-Hauck, *Real-Ency. f. Prot. Theol. u. Kirche* xvii³, 1906, 428-445.

Lightley, J. W., *Jewish Sects*, pp. 180-265.

**Montgomery, J. A., *The Samaritans, The Earliest Jewish Sect : Their History, Theology, and Literature*, esp. pp. 75-88, 239-251 (with very full bibliography). 1907.

Thomson, J. E. H., *The Samaritans : Their Testimony to the Religion of Israel.* 1919.

# APPENDIX G

SELECTED LITERATURE ON THE ROMAN PROCURATORS (EXCEPT PÓNTIUS PILATE) (*Ant.* xviii. 31-35, etc.)

Derenbourg, J., *Essai*, 197-198, 230-236.

Ginsburg, M. S., *Rome et la Judée*, pp. 107-134. 1928.

Kellner, H., " Die römischen Statthalter von Syrien und Judäa zur Zeit Christi und der Apostel, 2 : Die Kaiserlichen Procuratoren von Judäa," *Zeitschr. f. kathol. Theol.* 12 (1888), 630-655.

Klausner, J., *History of the Second Temple*[2] [in Hebrew], iv, 1950, 196-206.

**Momigliano, A., " Ricerche sull' organizzazione della Giudea sotto il dominio romano 63 A.C.–70 D.C.," *Annale della scuola normale superiore di Pisa 3* (1934), 183-221, 347-396.

Ricciotti, G., *Storia d' Israele*, ii : *Dall' Esilio al 135 dopo Christo*[2], pp. 431-469. 1935.

Schalit, A., *Roman Administration in Palestine* [in Hebrew], pp. 82-89. 1937.

**Schürer, E., *Geschichte*, i[4], 1901, 449-507, 564-585.

# APPENDIX H

### Selected Literature on Parthian Affairs
(*Ant.* xviii. 39-52, etc.)

**Debevoise, N. C., *A Political History of Parthia.* 1938.

Dobias, J., " Les Premiers Rapports des Romains avec les Parthes et l'occupation de Syrie," *Archiv Orientalni* 3 (1931), 215-256.

Gutschmid, A. von, *Geschichte Irans und seiner Nachbarländer.* 1888.

Gutschmid, A. von, " Gotarzes," in *Kleine Schriften*, iii, esp. 43-124. 1892.

**Kahrstedt, U., *Artabanos III und seine Erben.* 1950.

Magie, D., " Roman Policy in Armenia and Transcaucasia," *Ann. Report of the Am. Hist. Assoc. for 1919*, 1 (1923), 297 ff.

Markwart, J., " Iberer und Hyrkanier," *Caucasica* 8 (1931), 78-113.

Momigliano, A., " Corbulone e la politica romana verso i Parti," *Atti del II° Congresso Nazionale di Studi Romani*, pp. 368 ff. 1931.

Rawlinson, G., *The Sixth Great Oriental Monarchy ; or, The Geography, History, and Antiquities of Parthia, Collected and Illustrated from Ancient and Modern Sources.* 1872.

Schneiderwirth, J. H., *Die Parther ; oder, Das neupersische Reich unter den Arsaciden nach griechischrömischen Quellen*, esp. pp. 78-145. 1874.

413

Schur, W., " Die Orientalpolitik des Kaisers Nero,"
*Klio*, Beiheft 15 (1923), 70-76.

Simonetta, B., " Note di numismatica partica. Vo-
none II, Vologese I e Vardane II," *Riv. Ital.
d. Num.* 60 (1958), 3-10.

**Täubler, E., *Die Parthernachrichten bei Josephus.* 1904.

Täubler, E., " Zur Geschichte der Alanen," *Klio* 9
(1909), 14-28.

Willrich, H., " Caligula," *Klio* 3 (1903), 297-304.

# APPENDIX I

SELECTED LITERATURE ON THE INCIDENT OF THE
EMPEROR'S STANDARDS (*Ant.* xviii. 55-59)

*Bevan, E., *Holy Images*, pp. 48-63.  1940.
Domaszewski, A. von, " Die Fahnen im römischen
    Heere," *Abh. d. arch.-epig. Sem. d. Univ. Wien* 5
    (1885).
Domaszewski, A. von, " Die Religion des römischen
    Heeres," *Westdeut. Zeitsch. f. Gesch. u. Kunst* 14
    (1895), 1-124.
Frey, J. B., " La Question des images chez les Juifs
    à la lumière des récentes découvertes," *Biblica*
    15 (1934), 265-300, esp. 273-282.
*Goodenough, E. R., *Jewish Symbols in the Greco-Roman
    Period*, viii : *Pagan Symbols in Judaism*, pp. 121-
    142.  1958.  (Also earlier vols., esp. vol. iv.)
Gutmann, J., " The ' Second Commandment ' and
    the Image in Judaism," *Heb. Union Coll. Ann.* 32
    (1961), 161-174.
**Kraeling, C. H., " The Episode of the Roman Stan-
    dards at Jerusalem," *Harv. Theol. Rev.* 35 (1942),
    263-289.
Kubitschek, W., " Signa," in *RE*, II. Reihe, ii. 2,
    1923, 2325-2345.
Nock, A. D., " The Roman Army and the Roman Re-
    ligious Year," *Harv. Theol. Rev.* 45 (1952), 187-
    252, esp. 236-240.

# JEWISH ANTIQUITIES

Parker, H. M. D., *The Roman Legions*, esp. pp. 36-42. 1958.

Reinach, A. J., " Signa Militaria," in Daremberg-Saglio, *Dictionnaire des Antiquités*, iv. 2, 1909, 1307-1325.

Rostovtzeff, M., " Vexillum and Victory," *Jour. of Roman St.* 32 (1942), 92-106.

# APPENDIX J

SELECTED LITERATURE ON PONTIUS PILATE, ESPECIALLY
HIS DISMISSAL FROM THE PROCURATORSHIP
(*Ant.* xviii. 60-62, 85-89)

Corbishley, T., " Pontius Pilate," *Clergy Rev.* 12
(1936), 368-381.
De Laet, S. J., " Le Successeur de Ponce-Pilate,"
*L'Antiquité Classique* 8 (1939), 413-419.
Doyle, A. D., " Pilate's Career and the Date of the
Crucifixion," *Jour. of Theol. St.* 42 (1941), 190-
193.
Garofalo, S., " Ponzio Pilato, procuratore della
Giudea," *Quaderni ACI* 9 (1952), 55-70.
Hedley, P. L., " Pilate's Arrival in Judaea," *Jour. of
Theol. St.* 35 (1934), 56-57.
Holzmeister, U., " Wann war Pilatus Prokurator von
Judaea ?", *Biblica* 13 (1932), 228-232.
Mueller, G. A., *Pontius Pilatus, der fünfte Prokurator
von Judäa und Richter Jesu von Nazareth. Mit
einem Anhang " Die Sagen über Pilatus " und einem
Verzeichnis der Pilatus-Literatur.* 1888.
**Peter, H., " Pontius Pilatus, der Römische Land-
pfleger in Judäa," *Neue Jahrb. f. d. klass. Alt.* 19
(1907), 1-40.
*Ross, A. H., *And Pilate Said—A New Study of the
Roman Procurator,* by F. Morrison (pseud.). 1940.
**Schürer, E., *Geschichte,* i⁴, 487-493.

# JEWISH ANTIQUITIES

Smallwood, E. M., " The Date of the Dismissal of Pontius Pilate from Judaea," *Jour. of Jew. St.* 5 (1954), 12-21.

Stauffer, E., " Zur Münzprägung und Judenpolitik des Pontius Pilatus," *Nouvelle Clio* 1-2 (1950), 495-514.

418

# APPENDIX K

SELECTED LITERATURE ON THE *TESTIMONIUM
FLAVIANUM* (*Ant.* xviii. 63-64)

Barnes, W. E., *The Testimony of Josephus to Jesus
  Christ.* 1920.
**Bienert, W., *Der älteste nichtchristliche Jesusbericht,
  Josephus über Jesus, unter besonderer Berücksichti-
  gung des altrussischen " Josephus."* 1936.
Bloch, J., " Josephus and Christian Origins," *Jour. of
  the Soc. of Or. Res.* 13 (1929), 130-154.
*Burkitt, F. C., " Josephus and Christ," *Theologisch
  Tijdschrift* 47 (1913), 135-144.
Corssen, P., " Die Zeugnisse des Tacitus und Pseudo-
  Josephus über Christus," *Zeitsch. f. d. neutest.
  Wiss.* 15 (1914), 114-140.
**Creed, J. M., " The Slavonic Version of Josephus'
  History of the Jewish War," *Harv. Theol. Rev.* 25
  (1932), 277-319.
Dornseiff, F., " Zum Testimonium Flavianum, "
  *Zeitsch. f. d. neutest. Wiss.* 46 (1955), 245-250.
**Eisler, R., " Flavius Josephus on Jesus Called the
  Christ," *Jew. Quart. Rev.* 21 (1930), 1-60, esp.
  21-30.
Eisler, R., *Flavius Josephus-Studien, I : Das Testi-
  monium Flavianum : eine Antwort an Dr. Walter
  Bienert.* 1938.

**Eisler, R., *Iêsous Basileus ou Basileusas.* 1929.

Gerlach, E., *Die Weissagungen des Alten Testamentes in den Schriften des Flavius Josephus und das angebliche Zeugniss von Christo.* 1863.

Goetz, K. G., " Die ursprüngliche Fassung der Stelle Josephus Antiq. xviii, 3, 3 und ihre Verhältnis zu Tacitus Annal. xv, 44," *Zeitsch. f. d. neutest. Wiss.* 14 (1913), 286-297.

Harnack, A., " Der jüdische Geschichtsschreiber Josephus und Jesus Christus," *Internat. Monatsschr. f. Wiss. Kunst u. Technik* 7 (1913), 1037-1068.

Höhne, E., *Über das angebliche Zeugniss von Chritos bei Josephus, Antiquitatum lib. XVIII, 3, 3.* 1871.

Jackson, F. J. F., *Josephus and the Jews : The Religion and History of the Jews as Explained by Flavius Josephus.* 1931.

Kars, H. W., " Der älteste nichtchristliche Jesusbericht," *Theolog. Studien* 108 (1937), 40-64.

Kneller, C. A., "Flavius Josephus über Jesus Christus," *Stimmen aus Maria-Laach. Kath. Blätter* 53 (1897), 1-19, 161-174.

van Liempt, L., " De testimonio Flaviano," *Mnemosyne* 55 (1927), 109-116.

Linck, K., *De antiquissimis veterum quae ad Iesum Nazarenum spectant testimoniis* (=*Religionsgesch. Versuche u. Vorarbeiten.* Bd. 14, Heft 1), esp. pp. 3-31. 1913.

**Martin, C. " Le ' testimonium flavianum ' : vers une solution définitive ? ", *Rev. Belge de Philol. et d'Hist.* 20 (1941), 409-465.

Müller, G. A., *Christus bei Josephus Flavius*². 1895.

Niese, B., *De testimonio Christiano quod est apud Josephum Antiq. Jud. XVIII 63 sq. disputatio.* 1893-4.

# APPENDIX K

Norden, E., " Josephus und Tacitus über Jesus Christus und eine messianische Prophetie," *Neue Jahrb. f. d. klass. Altertum* 31 (1913), 637-666.

Pharr, C., " The Testimony of Josephus to Christianity," *Am. Jour. of Philol.* 48 (1927), 137-147.

Reinach, S., " Jean-Baptiste et Jésus suivant Josèphe," *Rev. d. Ét. juives* 87 (1929), 113-136.

Reinach, T., " Josèphe sur Jésus," *Rev. d. Ét. juives* 35 (1897), 1-18.

Scheidweiler, F., " Das Testimonium Flavianum," *Zeitsch. f. d. neutest. Wiss.* 45 (1954), 230-243.

Schoedel, F. H., *Flavius Iosephus de Iesu Christo testatus : vindiciae Flavianae.* 1840 (gives a full bibliography up to 1840).

Schürer, E., *Geschichte* i[4], 1901, 544-549 (includes good bibliography).

Thackeray, H. St. J., *Josephus the Man and the Historian,* esp. pp. 125-153. 1929.

Ussani, V., " Quaestiones Flavianae, i : il *Testimonium Christi* e la magìa di Gesù," *Riv. d. Fil. e d. Istruz. Class.* 38 (1910), 1-12.

Wertheimer, M., *Das echte und unechte Josephus Flavius-Zeugnis über Jesus aus Nazareth.* 1929.

Wieseler, K., " Des Josephus Zeugnisse über Christus und Jakobus, den Bruder des Herrn," *Jahrb. f. deut. Theol.* 23 (1878), 86-109.

Zeitlin, S., *Josephus on Jesus ; with particular reference to the Slavonic Josephus and the Hebrew Josippon.* 1931.

# APPENDIX L

Selected Literature on the Expulsion of the
Jews by Tiberius (*Ant.* xviii. 65-84)

Heidel, W. A., " Why Were the Jews Banished from
Italy in 19 A.D. ? ", *Am. Jour. of Philol.* 41 (1920),
38-47.

Merrill, E. T., " The Expulsion of the Jews from Rome
under Tiberius," *Class. Philol.* 14 (1919), 365-372.

Moehring, H. R., " The Persecution of the Jews and
the Adherents of the Isis Cult at Rome, A.D.
19," *Novum Test.* 3 (1959), 293-304.

Radin, M., *The Jews among the Greeks and Romans*,
esp. pp. 306-313. 1915.

Schürer, E., *Geschichte* iii⁴, 1909, 150-188.

**Smallwood, E. M., " Some Notes on the Jews under
Tiberius," *Latomus* 15 (1956), 314-329.

Volkmar, G., " Die Religionsverfolgung unter Kaiser
Tiberius und die Chronologie des Fl. Josephus
in der Pilatus-Periode," *Jahrb. f. Prot. Theol.* 11
(1885), 136-143.

## APPENDIX M

SELECTED LITERATURE ON THE DEATH OF JOHN
THE BAPTIST (*Ant.* xviii. 116-119)

Abrahams, I., *Studies in Pharisaism and the Gospels*, 1st
 Series, pp. 30-35. 1917.
Belser, D., " Über Johannes den Täufer," *Theol.
 Quartalschr.* 72 (1890), 355-399.
Creed, J. M., " Josephus on John the Baptist," *Jour.
 of Theol. St.* 23 (1922), 59-60.
Dibelius, M., " Die urchristliche Überlieferung von
 Johannes dem Täufer," *Forsch. z. Rel. u. Lit. d.
 Alten u. Neuen Test.* (1911).
**Eisler, R., *The Messiah Jesus and John the Baptist*, pp.
 221-311. 1931.
Kampmeier, A., " Did John the Baptist Exist ? ",
 *Open Court* 27 (1913), 433-437.
Klöpper, A., " Ein paar Bemerkungen zu dem Ur-
 theil des Josephus über Johannes den Täufer,"
 *Zeitschr. f. wissensch. Theol.* 28 (1885), 1-20.
Kraeling, C. H., *John the Baptist*. 1951.
Loman, A. D., " Het bericht van Flavius Josephus
 aangaande de oorzaak en het datum der executie
 van Johannes den dooper, vergleken met de
 verhalen der synoptici," *Theol. Tijdschr.* 25
 (1891), 293-315.
Reinach, S., " Jean-Baptiste et Jésus suivant Jo-
 sèphe," *Rev. d. Ét. juives* 87 (1929), 113-136.
Schürer, E., *Geschichte* i⁴, 1901, 436-445.

# APPENDIX N

## Selected Literature on Agrippa I
### (*Ant.* xviii. 143 ff.)

Abel, F. M., *Histoire de la Palestine depuis la conquête d'Alexandre jusqu'à l'invasion arabe* i, 1952, 443-455.

*Charlesworth, M. P., "The Native Ruler (Agrippa I)," in *Five Men : Character Studies from the Roman Empire* (Martin Classical Lectures, vi), pp. 1-30. 1936.

De Saulcy, F., " Étude chronologique de la vie et des monnaies des rois juifs Agrippa I$^{er}$ et Agrippa II," *Mém. de la Soc. franç. de Num. et d'Arch.* (Section d'histoire et d'ethnographie), pp. 26-56. 1869.

Derenbourg, J., *Essai*, 205-219.

*Grätz, H., *Geschichte der Juden* iii. 1$^5$, 1905, 317-360.

Jones, A. H. M., *The Herods of Judaea*, pp. 184-216. 1938.

Klausner, J., *History of the Second Temple*[2] iv, 1950, 287-305 [in Hebrew].

Meyshan (Mestschanski), J., " The Coinage of Agrippa the First," *Isr. Expl. Jour.* 4 (1954), 186-200.

*Perowne, S., *The Later Herods*, pp. 58-83. 1958.

Reifenberg, A., " A Memorial Coin of Herod Agrippa I," *Bull. of the Jew. Pal. Expl. Soc.* 5 (1937-8), 117-118 [in Hebrew].

# APPENDIX N

Reifenberg, A., *Ancient Jewish Coins*[2], pp. 20-23, 46-47.  1947.

**Schürer, E., *Geschichte* i[4], 1901, 549-564.

Willrich, H., *Das Haus des Herodes zwischen Jerusalem und Rom*, pp. 147-156.  1929.

# APPENDIX O

## Selected Literature on the Emperor Gaius' Dealings with the Jews (*Ant.* xviii. 257 ff.)

Balsdon, J. P. V. D., "The Chronology of Gaius' Dealings with the Jews," *Jour. of Rom. St.* 24 (1934), 13-24.

Balsdon, J. P. V. D., *The Emperor Gaius (Caligula)*. 1934.

Bell, H. I., "Antisemitism in Alexandria," *Jour. of Rom. St.* 31 (1941), 1-18.

Bell, H. I., *Juden und Griechen im römischen Alexandreia* (Beihefte zum "Alten Orient," 9), esp. pp. 16-24. 1926.

Bludau, A., *Juden und Judenverfolgungen im alten Alexandria*, pp. 66-88. 1906.

Fuchs, L., *Die Juden Aegyptens in ptolemäischer und römischer Zeit*. 1924.

Gelzer, M., "Iulius (Caligula)," in *RE*, x, 1919, 381-423.

Grätz, H., "Präcisirung der Zeit für die, die Judäer betreffenden Vorgänge unter den Kaiser Caligula," *Monatsschr. f. d. Gesch. u. Wiss. d. Jud.* 26 (1877), 97-107, 145-156.

Juster, J., *Les Juifs dans l'empire romain* i, 1914, esp. pp. 339-354.

Klausner, J., *History of the Second Temple*² iv, 1950, 267-286 [in Hebrew].

# APPENDIX O

Momigliano, A., *Claudius: the Emperor and His Achievement.* 1934.

von Premerstein, A., *Alexandrinische Geronten vor Kaiser Gaius (Mitth. a. d. Papyrussamm. d. Giessener Univ. 5).* 1939.

Radin, M., *The Jews among the Greeks and Romans,* esp. pp. 257-286. 1915.

Schürer, E., *Geschichte* i⁴, 1901, 500-507.

**Smallwood, E. M., ed., *Philonis Alexandrini Legatio ad Gaium.* 1961.

**Wilcken, U., " Zum Alexandrinischen Antisemitismus," *Abh. d. Königl. Säch. Gesell. d. Wiss.* 57 (1909), 783-839.

# APPENDIX P

## Selected Literature on the Sources of Book XIX

Bloch, H., *Die Quellen des Flavius Josephus in seiner Archäologie.* 1879.

Feldman, L. H., " The Sources of Josephus' *Antiquities,* Book 19," *Latomus* 21 (1962), 320-333.

Hoelscher, G., *Die Quellen des Josephus für die Zeit vom Exil bis zum Jüdischen Kriege,* pp. 66-69. 1904.

Mommsen, T., " Cornelius Tacitus und Cluvius Rufus," *Hermes* 4 (1870), 320-322.

Schemann, F. A. C., *Die Quellen des Flavius Josephus in der jüdischen Archaeologie Buch xviii-xx=Polemos ii, chap. vii-xiv, 3.* 1887.

Timpe, D., " Römische Geschichte bei Flavius Josephus," *Historia* 9 (1960), 474-502.

# APPENDIX Q

SELECTED LITERATURE ON THE CITIZENSHIP OF THE
ALEXANDRIAN JEWS AND ON CLAUDIUS' EDICT
(*Ant.* xix. 280-285)

Bell, H. I., " Antisemitism at Alexandria," *Jour. of Rom. St.* 31 (1941), 1-18.

**Bell, H. I., *Jews and Christians in Egypt : The Jewish Troubles in Alexandria and the Athanasian Controversy*, pp. 1-37. 1924.

Bell, H. I., *Juden und Griechen im römischen Alexandreia : eine historische Skizze des alexandrinischen Antisemitismus*, esp. pp. 24-30. 1926.

Bickermann, E., " À propos des 'Αστοί dans l'Égypte gréco-romaine," *Rev. d. philol.* 53 (1927), 362-368.

Davis, S., " The Question of Jewish Citizenship at Alexandria," in *Race-Relations in Ancient Egypt*, pp. 93-112. 1952.

**De Sanctis, G., " Claudio e i Giudei d' Alessandria," *Riv. d. Fil. Class.* 52 (1924), 473-513.

Engers, M., " Der Brief des Kaisers Claudius an die Alexandriner," *Klio* 20 (1925), 168-178.

Engers, M., " Die staatsrechtliche Stellung der alexandrinischen Juden," *Klio* 18 (1923), 79-90.

Engers, M., " Politeuma," *Mnemosyne* 54 (1926), 154-161.

Fuchs, L., *Die Juden Aegyptens in ptolemäischer und römischer Zeit*, pp. 79-105. 1924.

# JEWISH ANTIQUITIES

Jones, H. S., " Claudius and the Jewish Question at Alexandria," *Jour. of Rom. St.* 16 (1926), 17-35.

Juster, J., *Les Juifs dans l'empire romain* ii, 1914, 1-18.

Lagrange, M. J., " La Lettre de Claude aux Alexandrins," *Rev. Bib.* 40 (1931), 270-276.

Laqueur, R., " Der Brief des Kaisers Claudius an die Alexandriner," *Klio* 20 (1925), 89-106.

Loesch, S., *Epistula Claudiana : der neuentdeckte Brief des Kaisers Claudius vom Jahre 41 n. Chr. und das Urchristentum ; eine exegetisch-historische Untersuchung.* 1930.

Marchiano, G., *Lo storico giudaico Giuseppe Flavio e i suoi giudizi sugl' imperatori di casa Giulia Claudia.* 1934. (Not seen by present editor.)

Momigliano, A., *Claudius the Emperor and His Achievement,* esp. pp. 96-98, n. 25. 1934.

Radin, M., *The Jews among the Greeks and Romans,* pp. 108-111. 1915.

Reinach, T., " L'Empereur Claude et les Juifs d'apres un nouveau document," *Rev. d. Ét. juiv.* 79 (1924), 113-144.

Ruppel, W., " Politeuma : Bedeutungsgeschichte eines staatsrechtlichen Terminus," *Philologus* 82 (1927), 268-312, 433-454.

Schürer, E., *Geschichte* iii, 1909, 121-134.

Scramuzza, V. M., *The Emperor Claudius,* pp. 64-79. 1940.

Segré, A., " Note sullo *Status Civitatis* degli Ebrei nell' Egitto tolemaico e imperiale," *Bull. de la Soc. roy. d'Arch. d'Alex.* 28 (1933), 143-182.

Segré, A., " The Status of the Jews in Ptolemaic and Roman Egypt : New Light from the Papyri," *Jew. Soc. St.* 6 (1944), 375-400.

## APPENDIX Q

**Tcherikover, V., *Hellenistic Civilization and the Jews*,
    pp. 309-328, 409-415. 1959.
**Tcherikover, V. A., and Fuks, A., *Corpus Papyrorum
    Judaicarum* i, 1957, 39-41, 56-57, 62, 69-74 ; ii,
    1960, 25-107.
Wolfson, H. A., " Philo on Jewish Citizenship in
    Alexandria," *Jour. of Bibl. Lit.* 63 (1944), 165-168.
Zielinski, T., " L'Empereur Claude et l'idée de la
    domination mondiale des Juifs," *Rev. de l'Univ.
    de Bruxelles* 32 (1926-7), 128-148.